# CENTURY 21® 10e
## Digital Information Management

**Lessons 1–145**

### Jack P. Hoggatt, Ed. D.

*Assistant Dean and Director of Center for Advising, Development, and Enrichment*
University of Wisconsin - Eau Claire
Eau Claire, Wisconsin

### Jon A. Shank, Ed. D.

*Professor of Education, Emeritus*
Robert Morris University
Moon Township, Pennsylvania

### James R. Smith, Jr., Ed. D.

*Assistant Teaching Professor*
North Carolina State University
Raleigh, North Carolina

## SOUTH-WESTERN
CENGAGE Learning·

Australia • Brazil • Japan • Korea • Mexico • Singapore • Spain • United Kingdom • United States

## SOUTH-WESTERN
CENGAGE Learning®

**Century 21® Digital Information Management, Tenth Edition**
**Jack P. Hoggatt, Jon A. Shank, James R. Smith, Jr.**

SVP Global Product Management, Research, School & Professional: Frank Menchaca

General Manager, K-12 School Group: CarolAnn Shindelar

Publishing Director: Eve Lewis

Sr. Developmental Editor: Dave Lafferty

Development Consulting Editor: Jean Findley, LEAP Publishing Services Inc.

Marketing Manager: Kelsey Hagan

Sr. Content Project Manager: Martha Conway

Sr. Media Editor: Mike Jackson

Sr. Website Project Manager: Ed Stubenrauch

Manufacturing Planner: Kevin Kluck

Production Service: Lumina Datamatics, Inc.

Copyeditor: Gary Morris

Sr. Art Director: Michelle Kunkler

Internal and Cover Designer: Grannan Design LTD.

Cover Images: Fancy Photography/Veer/ © italianestro/ Shutterstock.com; © Yuri Arcurs/ Shutterstock.com

Fancy Photography/Veer; © italianestro/ Shutterstock.com

Key reach images: © Cengage Learning, Cengage Learning/Bill Smith Group/Sam Kolich

Teamwork photo: © Chad Baker/Ryan McVay/Getty Images, Inc.

Design feature images: telephone, Photodisc/ Getty Images; clock/phone collage, Greg Kuchik/Photodisc/Getty Images; handshake, Keith Brofsky/Photodisc / Getty Images; CD technology, Paul Cooklin/Stockbyte/Getty Images; Digital landscape, Paul Cooklin/Stockbyte/Getty Images; four teens, Chad Baker/Ryan McVay/Photodisc/Getty Images

Intellectual Property Analyst: Kyle Cooper

Intellectual Property Project Manager: Lisa Brown

Photo Researcher: Lumina Datamatics, Inc.

For product information and technology assistance, contact us at
**Cengage Learning Customer & Sales Support, 1-800-354-9706**
For permission to use material from this text or product,
submit all requests online at **www.cengage.com/permissions**
Further permissions questions can be emailed to
**permissionrequest@cengage.com**

States' Career Clusters Initiative, 2007,
**www.careerclusters.org**

**The Career Clusters icons are being used with permission of the:**

ISBN: 978-1-111-57740-5

**Cengage Learning**
20 Channel Center Street
Boston, MA 02210
USA

Cengage Learning is a leading provider of customized learning solutions with office locations around the globe, including Singapore, the United Kingdom, Australia, Mexico, Brazil, and Japan. Locate your local office at:
**www.cengage.com/global**

Cengage Learning products are represented in Canada by Nelson Education, Ltd.

For your course and learning solutions, visit **www.cengage.com/school**
Visit our company website at **www.cengage.com**

Printed in the United States of America
Print Number: 01    Print Year: 2014

# Century 21
## Digital Information Management, 10e

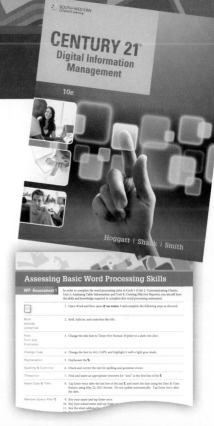

Provide your students with the best in computing education from the proven business education leader—now stronger than ever! *Century 21 Digital Information Management* propels students into the realm of computing education with innovative solutions updated to reflect today's business challenges. Trust the leader who has taught more than 90 million people to type—bringing 100 years of publishing experience and a century of innovations together in a complete line of computing solutions.

## No Need to Repeat the Basics—Focus on the Skills You Want Students to Master!

▶ An *intermediate* **approach** to computer applications to reflect changing trends in computer applications instruction and to optimize learning time.

▶ **More units** of instructions—two cycles for a full year—Essentials and Intermediate

▶ **Pre-assessments** help place students within the lessons. **Assessments** cover new topics covered in each Part.

▶ **21st century skills approach** organizes business documents and computer topics

## Contents—Emphasis on Intermediate Computer and Business Skills

# An Instructional Design to Learn, Apply, Reinforce, and Assess

**Cycles** cover **units** of instruction, which are comprised of **lessons** and rotate computer topics.
**Reference Guides** present concepts before the lessons.

Cycle 1

LESSONS 1–80

Intermediate Personal, Academic, and Business Information Management Skills

Unit 1 Managing Digital Information
Unit 2 Communicating Clearly
Unit 3 Analyzing Table Information

In this cycle, you will strengthen your personal and interpersonal skills to help you transition successfully to the workforce and postsecondary

**Learning outcomes** are mapped to lesson activities. **Business Documents** are listed per lesson.

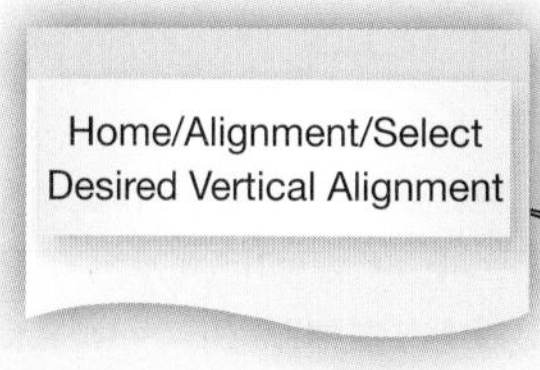

**LESSON 20** — **Format Cells and Columns**

OUTCOMES
- Merge cells.
- Align text vertically.
- Wrap text.
- Shrink text to fit in a cell.
- Indent text in a cell.

**Business Documents**
- Enrollment Report
- Recycling Materials
- Shareholder Distribution
- Common Stock Fund Report

Home/Alignment/Select Desired Vertical Alignment

Emphasis on **Ribbon path** (Tab/Group/Command) enables students to quickly navigate the software.

## Intermediate Approach for Computer Applications

| Chapter Topics | Sample from Chapter Quick Check or Lesson Documents |
|---|---|
| **Managing Digital Information** is a review of basic computer concepts and introduces hardware, software, the Internet, operating systems, the Cloud, and security issues. | QUICK ✔ 1. What factors do you need to consider when building a team for a project that might use online applications and shared files? 2. Who do you think should decide which team members get access to which documents online? 3. What disadvantages do you see to sharing information online with coworkers or project team members? |
| **Word Processing** skill is further enforced by following the model documents for letters, tables, reports, mail merge, and special documents such as agendas, minutes, itineraries, newsletters, purchase orders, invoices, and other business documents. | QUICK ✔ Your completed two-page letter should look like this: 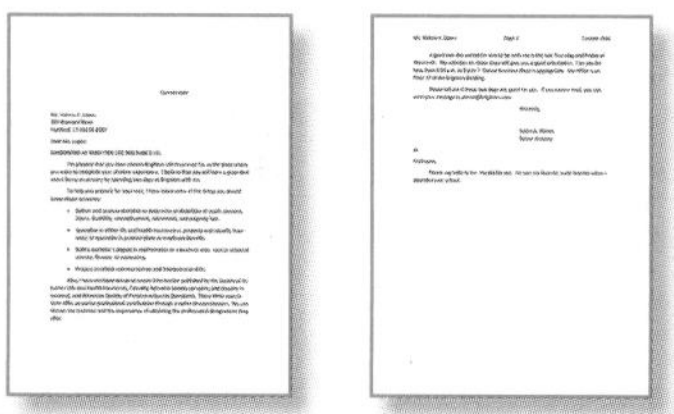 |

# Integrated Approach Continued

| Chapter Topics | Sample from Chapter Quick Check or Lesson Documents |
|---|---|
| **Presentations** coverage includes creating presentations for businesses using graphics, animations, transitions, SmartArt, sound, and delivering an effective presentation. | |
| **Spreadsheet** activities include formatting, views, charting, advanced functions, and other intermediate tasks for various financial and sales reports, planning, and data analysis. Integrating documents with Word is also covered. | |
| **Database** coverage includes data mining and analyzing records for use with queries, computed fields, and mail merge for letters, envelopes, and labels. | |
| **Personal Information Management Skills** include managing contacts, e-mail, meetings, and other calendar features. | |
| **Websites** cover creating web pages in Word and Excel, using graphics, hyperlinks, bookmarks and Web construction. | |

# Integrated Approach Continued

| Chapter Topics | Sample from Chapter Quick Check or Lesson Documents |
|---|---|
| **Digital Citizenship** has projects for digital etiquette, communications, law, security, and online commerce. | 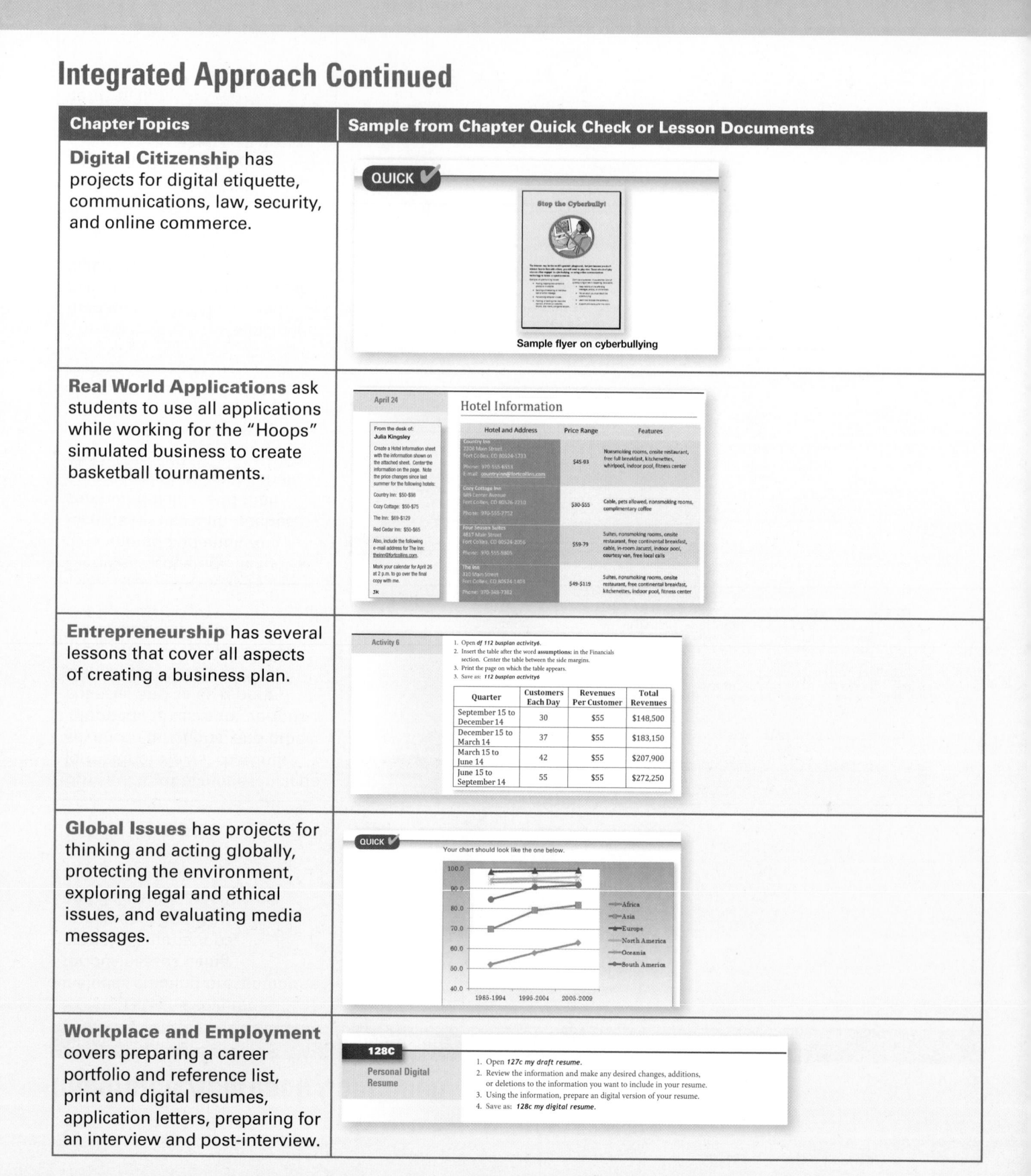 Sample flyer on cyberbullying |
| **Real World Applications** ask students to use all applications while working for the "Hoops" simulated business to create basketball tournaments. | |
| **Entrepreneurship** has several lessons that cover all aspects of creating a business plan. | |
| **Global Issues** has projects for thinking and acting globally, protecting the environment, exploring legal and ethical issues, and evaluating media messages. | |
| **Workplace and Employment** covers preparing a career portfolio and reference list, print and digital resumes, application letters, preparing for an interview and post-interview. | |

# Special Features

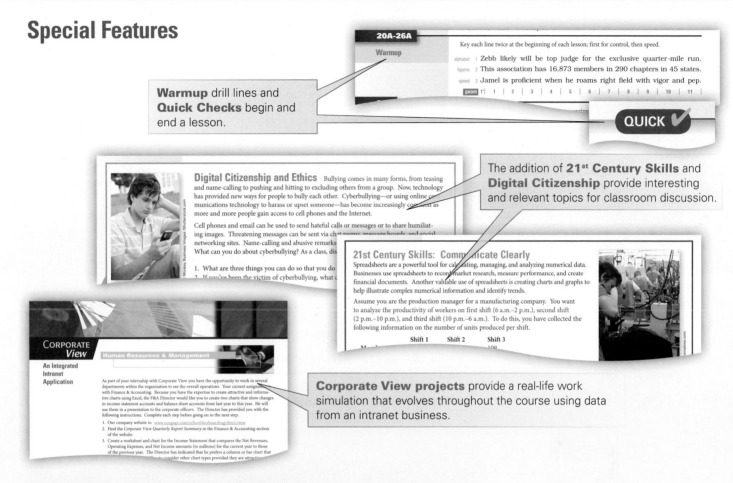

**20A–26A**

**Warmup**

Key each line twice at the beginning of each lesson; first for control, then speed.

alphabet 1 Zebb likely will be top judge for the exclusive quarter-mile run.
figures 2 This association has 16,873 members in 290 chapters in 45 states.
speed 3 Jamel is proficient when he roams right field with vigor and pep.

gwam 1' | 1 | 2 | 3 | 4 | 5 | 6 | 7 | 8 | 9 | 10 | 11 |

QUICK ✓

**Warmup** drill lines and **Quick Checks** begin and end a lesson.

**Digital Citizenship and Ethics** Bullying comes in many forms, from teasing and name-calling to pushing and hitting to excluding others from a group. Now, technology has provided new ways for people to bully each other. Cyberbullying—or using online communications technology to harass or upset someone—has become increasingly common as more and more people gain access to cell phones and the Internet.

Cell phones and email can be used to send hateful calls or messages or to share humiliating images. Threatening messages can be sent via chat rooms, message boards, and social networking sites. Name-calling and abusive remarks
What can you do about cyberbullying? As a class, dis

1. What are three things you can do so that you do
2. If you've been the victim of cyberbullying, what c

The addition of **21st Century Skills** and **Digital Citizenship** provide interesting and relevant topics for classroom discussion.

**21st Century Skills: Communicate Clearly**
Spreadsheets are a powerful tool for calculating, managing, and analyzing numerical data. Businesses use spreadsheets to record market research, measure performance, and create financial documents. Another valuable use of spreadsheets is creating charts and graphs to help illustrate complex numerical information and identify trends.

Assume you are the production manager for a manufacturing company. You want to analyze the productivity of workers on first shift (6 a.m.–2 p.m.), second shift (2 p.m.–10 p.m.), and third shift (10 p.m.–6 a.m.). To do this, you have collected the following information on the number of units produced per shift.

|  | Shift 1 | Shift 2 | Shift 3 |
| --- | --- | --- | --- |

**CORPORATE VIEW**
**Human Resources & Management**

**An Integrated Intranet Application**

As part of your internship with Corporate View you have the opportunity to work in several departments within the organization to see the overall operations. Your current assignment is with Finance & Accounting. Because you have the expertise to create attractive and informative charts using Excel, the F&A Director would like you to create two charts that show changes in income statement accounts and balance sheet accounts from last year to this year. He will use them in a presentation to the corporate officers. The Director has provided you with the following instructions. Complete each step before going on to the next step.

1. Our company website is: www.cengage.com/school/keyboarding/dim/cview
2. Find the *Corporate View Quarterly Report Summary* in the Finance & Accounting section of the website.
3. Create a worksheet and chart for the Income Statement that compares the Net Revenues, Operating Expenses, and Net Income amounts (in millions) for the current year to those of the previous year. The Director has indicated that he prefers a column or bar chart that
   to consider other chart types provided they are attractive.

**Corporate View projects** provide a real-life work simulation that evolves throughout the course using data from an intranet business.

# New End-of-Unit Academic/Career Connections

**New end-of-unit projects for Academic and Career Preparation** provide the connection to *Common Core* integration. The coverage of **Career Cluster** and the NEW **School and Community** Activities emphasize critical thinking.

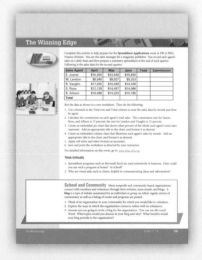

End-of-unit projects also include Timed Writings, Grammar/Writing, Communications, Science, Social Studies, and Math.
**Winning Edge** provides activities for practice for competitive events such as with BPA and FBLA.

# Digital Solutions Take You Beyond the Book!

As **Digital Information Management** is for more intermediate courses, **MicroType™ 6 with CheckPro** is used for document checking. In addition, keyboarding practice for skillbuilding and review are also available with this program.

**MicroType 6 with CheckPro** checks keystrokes and formatting in Microsoft Word and Excel, providing the most comprehensive teaching and learning tool.

An **Interactive eBook** provides students with an interactive, online-only version of the printed textbook to be used at school or at home with indexing, highlighting, and quick navigation.

## Visit Us Online!

For more information on this innovative textbook—as well as a wealth of teaching and learning resources—visit www.cengage.com/school/keyboarding/c21dim today!

- ▶ Data Files
- ▶ Web Links
- ▶ Assessments/Tests
- ▶ Flashcards
- ▶ Solution Files
- ▶ Lesson Plans
- ▶ PowerPoint Presentations
- ▶ And much more!

The tenth edition of *Century 21*® has a new intermediate course: *Digital Information Management*. This new course helps students prepare for a lifetime of computer success with innovative solutions updated to reflect today's business challenges. Students tap into the latest technology, learn to master computer applications using Microsoft® Office, and increase communication skills with relevant activities throughout. Experience with a prior keyboarding course is assumed. Basic computer skills are also pre-assessed for placement in these intermediate lessons.

*Digital Information Management* infuses 21st Century Skills into the activities and work products contained in each unit. Integrated simulations are interspersed throughout the units that provide students with opportunities to use the computer skills and applications they have learned while enhancing independent decision-making skills as they complete real world tasks. In every unit, students are presented opportunities to collaborate with classmates to complete certain tasks. The text's Special Features provide focused attention on topics important to students for school, work and life.

The 10th Edition uses two cycles for a year-long course and presents choices in intermediate computer concepts, word processing, database, spreadsheet, and presentation software features—but with a lesson structure that promotes their use in business. Word processing becomes more about communications; spreadsheet more about making economic choices and financial analysis; database becomes more about data mining and analysis; presentations become more about being effective with communications. Additionally, other topics include managing communications and schedules, creating web sites, becoming a successful digital citizen, entrepreneurship, understanding our world, and preparing for the workplace and becoming an effective employee. Real-world application projects integrate all skills learned. In short, this text is about applying intermediate computer applications to needed life skills.

New special features highlight specific 21st Century Skills and themes for Digital Citizenship. New end of unit activities include Academic and Career Connections, language arts, math, Career Clusters, School and Community, and The Winning Edge for preparation for student organizations' competitive events.

For this edition, South-Western/Cengage Learning surveyed business teachers, employed content reviewers, and met with focus groups to determine the needs of today's keyboarding students and instructors. The features of *Century 21 Digital Information Management, 10th Edition*, address those needs.

The *Century 21* family includes a full range of high-quality supplementary items to enhance your courses, including a Web site at www.cengage.com/school/keyboarding/c21key. Thank you for choosing *Century 21*. Whether you are a new instructor, new to *Century 21*, or simply updating your *C21* materials, we know that you will find this edition an exciting solution for your classes.

# How to Use this Book

There are a number of ways that the many available digital and print resources can be used in a classroom/lab.

## Student Edition

The **student text** (ISBN 9781111571405) contains a number of features designed to meet your instructional needs. Each unit opens with a listing of lessons. Within each unit there are a series of lessons broken up by activities. A **Reference Guide** starts the unit with a discussion of concepts and introduces learning and shows miniature models of the documents presented in the unit. Some guides have activities for reinforcement. Each lesson has a listing of outcomes and documents used, along with instructions for documents to create. **Pre-assessment activities** provide a means of lesson placement. **Corporate View projects** provide a real-life work simulation that evolves throughout the course using data from an intranet business.

There are also these special features within a unit: **QuickCheck** for discussion and checking progress with lesson activities, **21st Century Skills**, and **Digital Citizenship**. The latter two features contain questions for critical thinking and discussion. Lessons contain activities for warmup drills, computer applications used for learning and applying skills, documents to format, tips in the margins provide helpful hints, data files assist with the completion of longer activities. Certain activities are identified as suitable for **teamwork** projects.

Most units end with an Application and Assessment lesson. The end-of-unit materials include **Academic and Career Connections (for Common Core)**, grammar and language activities; math activities, **Career Cluster** projects; **School and Community** projects, and **Winning Edge** competitive events practice. Keyboarding reinforcement is provided through skill building and timed writings at the end of most units.

## Resources

In addition to the textbook, the complete instructional program includes a **wrap-around instructor's Edition** (ISBN 9781111571740), an **Instructor's Resource CD-ROM** (ISBN 9781111579456) containing an **Instructor's manual** in PDF format with solutions and teaching tips, a **Spanish Language supplement** in PDF format, **Style Manual** in PDF format, lesson plans, PowerPoint presentations, teaching suggestions, printable rubrics, end-of-unit answers, and tests.

Also available is **Cognero online testing** (ISBN 9781285978505) and a **PC Keyboard Wall Chart** (ISBN 9781115811305).

**MicroType 6™ with CheckPro™** is the software that reinforces keyboarding skills and checks documents in Word and Excel 2013. This is available as a network version. See the companion website www.cengage.com/school/keyboarding/21 key for more information.

There are also available **e-Book versions** of the text; call for more information on these (800-354-9706).

## About the Authors

**Dr. Jon A. Shank** is a Professor Emeritus of Education at Robert Morris University in Moon Township, Pennsylvania. For more than 20 years, he served as Dean of the School of Applied Sciences and Education at Robert Morris. Most recently, Dr. Shank taught keyboarding and software methods courses to undergraduate and graduate students who were studying to become business education teachers. Dr. Shank holds memberships in regional, state, and national business education organizations. He has received many honors during his career, including Outstanding Post-Secondary Business Educator in Pennsylvania.

**Dr. Jack P. Hoggatt** is Assistant Dean of Student Affairs and CADE Director for the University of Wisconsin-Eau Claire. He has taught courses in Business Writing, Advanced Business Communications, and the communication component of the university's Masters in Business Administration (MBA) program. Dr. Hoggatt has held offices in several professional organizations, including president of the Wisconsin Business Education Association. He has served as an advisor to local and state business organizations and been named the Outstanding Post-Secondary Business Educator for Wisconsin.

**Dr. James R. Smith, Jr.** is a Teaching Assistant Professor in the Department of Curriculum, Instruction and Counselor Education. He had been a secondary business and marketing teacher, a North Carolina State Consultant for Business and Information Technology, and a local school system Career and Technical Education Administrator. Currently, he is the undergraduate and graduate program coordinator for the Business and Marketing Education teacher education program at NC State University. Dr. Smith has held offices in professional organizations and has received the Outstanding Leadership Award from the National Association of Supervisors of Business Education and the Outstanding Career and Technical Educator from the North Carolina Career and Technical Education Association—Business Education Division.

## Note from the Authors

This text will serve as a solid foundation upon which you can build your course to meet the varying needs of your students. It contains an appropriate balance between keyboarding reinforcement, and applying frequently used documents for different business and personal uses using features from various software application packages. Each software application is presented in the breadth and depth needed for students to be able to use their software competencies to enhance their productivity as they continue their education, carry out their personal affairs, and enter the workplace. The unit activities, including the variety of end-of-unit activities, provide teachers with many opportunities to connect computer skills and applications to other curricular goals valued by administrators, other teachers, and the community.

## Reviewers

Sandra Almanza
Deming High School
Deming, NM

Teresa Alexander
Enterprise High School
Redding, CA

Margaret Blue
Biloxi High School
Biloxi, MS

Dr. Catherine Bertelson
Central Washington University
Ellensburg, WA

Katie Cortez
Muskego High School
Muskego, WI

Carrie Davis
Yoncalla High School
Yoncalla, OR

Diane Harrington
Sault Area High School and Career Center
Sault Ste. Marie, MI

Sally Irons
Southside School
Niles, MI

Barbara Luna
Gainesville High School
Gainesville, MO

Jerre L. McManama, Jr
Roncalli High School
Indianapolis, IN

Billie Miller
Cosumnes River College
Sacramento, CA

Beverly Nix
Spartanburg High School Freshman Academy
Spartanburg, SC

Kitty Olson
Blue Ridge High School
Greer, SC

Laurel Stevenson
Holly Hill School
Holly Hill, FL

# CONTENTS

## Cycle 2
### ADVANCED PERSONAL, ACADEMIC, AND BUSINESS INFORMATION MANAGEMENT SKILLS

# FEATURES

# Cycle 1

## Intermediate Personal, Academic, and Business Information Management Skills

© iStockphoto.com/Vetta Collection/Henk Badenhorst

In this cycle, you will strengthen your personal and interpersonal skills to help you transition successfully to the workforce and postsecondary education.

You will apply technical skills to use emerging technologies, create word-processing documents, develop spreadsheets, formulate a database, and make an electronic presentation. In addition, you will work with Personal Information Management (PIM) software, create web pages, and learn how to become a better digital citizen.

You will apply these skills in real-world scenarios that give you hands-on experience selecting and using software as a tool to clearly communicate your ideas.

directly in front of the chair. The front edge should be even with the edge of the table or desk.

Place the monitor for easy viewing. Some experts maintain that the top of the screen should be at or slightly below eye level. Others recommend placing the monitor even lower. Set it a comfortable distance from your eyes—at least an arm's length away.

Position the monitor to avoid glare (an antiglare filter can help). Close blinds or pull shades as needed. Adjust the brightness and contrast controls, if necessary, for readability. Keep the screen clean with a soft, lint-free cloth and (unless your instructor tells you otherwise) a nonalcohol, nonabrasive cleaning solution or glass cleaner.

If you cannot adjust your equipment and the desk or table is too high, try adjusting your chair. If that does not work, you can sit on a cushion, a coat, or even a stack of books.

Use a straight-backed chair that will not yield when you lean back. The chair should support your lower back (try putting a rolled-up towel or sweater behind you if it does not). The back of your knees should not be pressed against the chair. Use a seat that allows you to keep your feet flat on the floor, or use a footrest. Even a box or a backpack will do.

Position the mouse next to and at the same height as the keyboard and as close to the body as possible. Research has not shown conclusively that one type of pointing device (mouse, trackball, touch pad, stylus, joystick, etc.) is better than another. Whatever you use, make sure your arms, hands, and fingers are relaxed. If you change to a new device, evaluate it carefully first and work up gradually to using it all the time.

Arrange your work material so you can see it easily and maintain good posture. Some experts recommend positioning whatever you look at most often (the monitor or paper material) directly in front of you so you do not have to turn your head to the side while keying.

### Exercise And Take Breaks

Exercise your neck, shoulders, arms, wrists, and fingers before beginning to key each day and often during the workday. Neck, shoulder, wrist, and other exercises appear at the Cornell University ergonomics website listed below.

Take a short break at least once an hour. Rest your eyes from time to time as you work by focusing on an object at least 20 feet away. Blink frequently.

### Use Good Posture And Proper Techniques

Sit erect and as far back in the seat as possible. Your forearms should be parallel to the slant of the keyboard, your wrists and forearms low, but not touching or resting on any surface. Your arms should be near the side of your body in a relaxed position. Your shoulders should not be raised, but should be in a natural posture.

Keep your fingers curved and upright over the home keys. Strike each key lightly using the finger*tip*. Grasp the mouse loosely. Make a conscious effort to relax your hands and shoulders while keying.

For more information on mouse and keyboard use and CTS/RSI, visit the following Internet sites:

- http://kidshealth.org/kid/ (search for *ergonomics*)
- http://www.tifaq.org
- http://ergonomics.ucla.edu/
- http://www.office-ergo.com
- http://ergo.human.cornell.edu/

### Ergonomic Keyboards

Ergonomic keyboards (see illustration at left) are designed to improve hand posture and make keying more comfortable. Generally they have a split design with left and right banks of keys and the ability to tilt or rotate the keyboard for comfort. More research is needed to determine just how effective ergonomic keyboards are in preventing RSI injuries and carpal tunnel syndrome.

# Assessing Basic Computer Skills

## Computer Concepts: Assessment 1

Match the term in the left column with the definition in the right column.

**Term**

1. cursor
2. operating system
3. computer virus
4. active window
5. Shift
6. Ctrl
7. motherboard
8. keyword search
9. ergonomics
10. netiquette

**Definition**

a. key to hold down when copying files by dragging
b. window in which you can work
c. another name for the CPU
d. proper positioning to avoid physical stress while keyboarding
e. rules of common courtesy when working online
f. computer code or a program designed to harm or gain access to your computer
g. a flashing line that indicates the position where you begin keying
h. used to store and organize data files
i. keying a word or phrase in a search tool to find information on the Internet
j. key to hold down when selecting more than one file

## Computer Concepts: Assessment 2

Match the term in the left column with the definition in the right column.

**Term**

1. ROM
2. browser
3. Charm bar
4. pointer
5. bit
6. title bar
7. online apps
8. GNU/Linux
9. cloud computing
10. WAN

**Definition**

a. viewed from within a Web browser
b. a system in which your software and files are stored on remote computers, and you access them through the Internet
c. the most basic unit of data stored or processed by a computer
d. displays at the top of a document or above the ribbon
e. an example of open-source software
f. a network of computers across a city
g. offers quick access to various aspects of Windows 8
h. used to store programs that run when the computer starts
i. allows your computer to see online documents and websites
j. the arrow that represents the mouse's position

**Repetitive stress injury (RSI)** is a result of repeated movement of a particular part of the body. It is also known as repetitive motion injury, musculoskeletal disorder, cumulative trauma disorder, and by a host of other names. A familiar example of RSI is "tennis elbow." RSI is the number-one occupational illness, costing employers more than $80 billion a year in health-care fees and lost wages.

Of concern to keyboard and mouse users is the form of RSI called **carpal tunnel syndrome** (CTS). CTS is an inflammatory disease that develops gradually and affects the wrists, hands, and forearms. Blood vessels, tendons, and nerves pass into the hand through the carpal tunnel (see illustration below). If any of these structures enlarge, or the walls of the tunnel narrow, the median nerve is pinched and CTS symptoms may result.

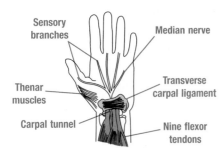

Sensory branches
Median nerve
Thenar muscles
Transverse carpal ligament
Carpal tunnel
Nine flexor tendons

Palm view of left hand

### Symptoms Of RSI/CTS

CTS symptoms include numbness in the hand; tingling or burning in the hand, wrist, or elbow; severe pain in the forearm, elbow, or shoulder; and difficulty in gripping objects. Symptoms usually appear during sleeping hours, probably because many people sleep with their wrists flexed.

If not properly treated, the pressure on the median nerve, which controls the thumb, forefinger, middle finger, and half the ring finger, causes severe pain. The pain can radiate into the forearm, elbow, or shoulder. There are many kinds of treatment, ranging from simply resting to surgery. Left untreated, CTS can result in permanent damage or paralysis.

The good news is that 99 percent of people with carpal tunnel syndrome recover completely. Computer users can avoid reinjuring themselves by taking the precautions discussed later in this article.

### Causes Of RSI/CTS

RSI/CTS often develops in workers whose physical routine is unvaried. Common occupational factors include (1) using awkward posture, (2) using poor techniques, (3) performing tasks with wrists bent (see below), (4) using improper equipment, (5) working at a rapid pace, (6) not taking rest breaks, and (7) not doing exercises that promote graceful motion and good techniques.

RSI/CTS is not limited to workers or adults. Keying school assignments, playing computer or video games, and surfing the Internet are increasing the incidence of RSI/CTS in younger people.

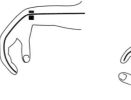

Improper wrist positions for keystroking

CTS is frequently a health concern for people who use a computer keyboard or mouse. The risk of developing CTS is less for those who use proper furniture or equipment, keyboarding techniques, posture, and/or muscle-stretching exercises than for those who do not.

### Reducing The Risk Of RSI/CTS

By taking the following precautions, keyboard and mouse users can reduce the risk of developing RSI/CTS and can keep it from recurring. Experts stress that good computer habits like these are very important in avoiding RSI/CTS. They can also help you avoid back, neck, and shoulder pain, and eyestrain.

### Arrange The Work Area

Arrange your equipment in a way that is natural and comfortable for you. Position the keyboard at elbow height and

## Computer Concepts: Assessment 3

Fill in the blank with the correct word or phrase.

1. The keyboard is an example of a(n) _____ device.

2. A(n) _____ is typically composed of 8 bits.

3. A(n) _____ is a piece of hardware that works with the CPU.

4. DVDs and thumb drives are examples of _____ devices.

5. _____ is a set of step-by-step instructions to tell the computer what to do with data.

6. *Microsoft Word* is an example of _____ software.

7. The first consideration when purchasing hardware or software is generally your _____.

8. The _____ displays different portions of the document in the document window.

9. _____ consist(s) of icons or buttons that represent commands.

10. The Office _____ interface organizes related commands on tabs.

11. After you maximize a window, the _____ button replaces the Maximize button.

12. *File Explorer* shows files in a(n) _____ or tree view.

13. In the filename *lesson01.docx*, the *.docx* portion is called the _____.

14. When you delete a file, the file goes to the _____.

15. The _____ is a global network of computers comprised of servers and their links.

16. When two or more computers are connected either by a cable or wireless connection, the computers are part of a(n) _____.

17. The *.com* portion of a URL address is known as the _____.

18. Unsolicited or unwanted online messages are referred to as _____.

19. You must seek _____ from the owner or author of Web content such as text and pictures before reusing them for your personal website.

20. Installing and using _____ software on your machine is the best way to protect your system from attack.

## Computer Concepts: Assessment 4

Open *File Explorer*
Select a drive
Create a folder

1. Open *File Explorer.*
2. Click the C drive if necessary to display its folders.
3. Create a new folder named **Security.**
4. Create a second new folder on the C: drive named **Routine Maintenance.**

Start *Word*

5. Open *Word* and then open *df cc assess 4a.*
6. In the first blank ¶, key the title **Set Up a Maintenance Schedule.**

The numbered parts are found on most computers. The location of some parts will vary.

1. **CPU (Central Processing Unit):** Internal operating unit or "brain" of computer.
2. **CD-ROM drive:** Reads data from and writes data to a CD.
3. **Monitor:** Displays text and graphics on a screen.
4. **Mouse:** Used to input commands.
5. **Keyboard:** An arrangement of letter, figure, symbol, control, function, and editing keys and a numeric keypad.

© Dmitry Melnikov/Shutterstock.com

## KEYBOARD ARRANGEMENT

© PixAchi/Shutterstock.com

1. **Alphanumeric keys:** Letters, numbers, and symbols.
2. **Numeric keypad:** Keys at the right side of the keyboard used to enter numeric copy and perform calculations.
3. **Function (F) keys:** Used to execute commands, sometimes with other keys. Commands vary with software.
4. **Arrow keys:** Move insertion point up, down, left, or right.

5. ESC **(Escape):** Closes a software menu or dialog box.
6. TAB: Moves the insertion point to a preset position.
7. CAPS LOCK: Used to make all capital letters.
8. SHIFT: Makes capital letters and symbols shown at tops of number keys.
9. CTRL **(Control):** With other key(s), executes commands. Commands may vary with software.

10. ALT **(Alternate):** With other key(s), executes commands. Commands may vary with software.
11. **Space Bar:** Inserts a space in text.
12. ENTER **(**RETURN**):** Moves insertion point to margin and down to next line. Also used to execute commands.
13. DELETE: Removes text to the right of insertion point.

14. NUM LOCK: Activates/deactivates numeric keypad.
15. INSERT: Activates insert or typeover.
16. BACKSPACE: Deletes text to the left of insertion point.

| | |
|---|---|
| Apply boldface | 7. Select the title text and make it boldface by clicking the Bold icon in the Font group of the Home tab on the Ribbon (or use the keyboard shortcut, Ctrl+ B)<br>8. Tap Enter, turn off boldface, and key the following text:<br>Experts suggest that you schedule tasks on a daily, weekly, or monthly basis according to how important the tasks are for your system's operational well-being. |
| Save a document | 9. Save the document in the Security folder you created in step 3 as *cc assess 4a*. |
| Print a document | 10. Print the document and then close it and exit *Word*. |
| Copy a file | 11. In *File Explorer*, navigate to the location of your data files. Select *df cc assess 4b* and copy the file to the Security folder. |
| Rename a file | 12. Rename the *df cc assess 4b* file as *cc assess 4b*. |
| Move a file | 13. Move the *cc assess 4a* file to the Routine Maintenance folder.<br>14. Create a new folder on the desktop name **Computer Concepts Assessment.** |
| Move folders | 15. Move the Routine Maintenance and Security folders into the Computer Concepts Assessment folder.<br>16. Close *File Explorer*. |

## Computer Concepts: Assessment 5

| | |
|---|---|
| | 1. Start *Word* and save the new, blank document as *cc assess 5*.<br>2. Key the title **Computer Concepts: Application 5,** and tap Enter to move to a new line. |
| Key and format text | 3. Select the title text and make it boldface. |
| Start a browser<br>Open a search tool | 4. Start your browser and then open your favorite search tool. |
| Perform keyword searches | 5. Search for the answers to the following questions, and record the answers in the *cc assess 5* document. Number the answers as 5a, 5b, and so on.<br>  a. What is the name of the horse that won the Triple Crown in 1978, and what jockey rode him in all three races?<br>  b. What is a capsulotomy of the eye, and when would you need one?<br>  c. What is the highest point in your state? What is the elevation, and in what county can you find the high point?<br>6. Search for information on the Cape Hatteras lighthouse, and then answer these questions:<br>  a. How many lighthouses have existed in the Buxton location on the Outer Banks?<br>  b. What happened to the current lighthouse in 1999?<br>  c. How tall is the lighthouse?<br>7. Save the file, print, and close the file.<br>8. Exit your browser and *Word*. |

## Electronic Resume (Resume 1)

Douglas H. Ruckert
8503 Kirby Drive
Houston TX 77054-8220
(713) 555-0121
dougr@suresend.com

SUMMARY

Strong communication and telephone skills; excellent keyboarding, computer, and Internet skills; and good organizational and interpersonal skills.

EDUCATION

Will graduate from Eisenhower Technical High School in June 2014 with a high school diploma and information technology emphasis. Grade point average is 3.75.

RELEVANT SKILLS AND COURSES

Proficient with most recent versions of Windows and Office, including Word, Excel, Access, PowerPoint, and Publisher.

Excelled in the following courses: Computer Applications, Business Communications, and Information Technology.

MAJOR ACCOMPLISHMENTS

Future Business Leaders of America: Member for four years, vice president for one year. Won second place in Public Speaking at District Competition; competed (same event) at state level.

Varsity soccer: Lettered three years and served as captain during senior year.

Recognition: Named one of Eisenhower's Top Ten Community Service Providers at end of junior year.

WORK EXPERIENCE

Hinton's Family Restaurant, Server (2012-present): Served customers in culturally diverse area, oriented new part-time employees, and resolved routine customer service issues.

Tuma's Landscape and Garden Center, Sales (2010-2012): Assisted customers with plant selection and responsible for stocking and arranging display areas.

COMMUNITY SERVICE

First Methodist Church Vacation Bible School teacher assistant (2012-2013).

Race for the Cure publicity committee (2013).

ETHS Senior Citizens Breakfast server (2011-2014).

United Youth Camp student helper (2013).

REFERENCES

Will be furnished upon request.

**Electronic Resume (Resume 1)**

## Print Resume (Resume 2)

Douglas H. Ruckert

8503 Kirby Drive
Houston TX 77054-8220
(713) 555-0121
dougr@suresend.com

Objective: To use my computer, Internet, communication, and interpersonal skills in a challenging customer service position.

Education: Will graduate from Eisenhower Technical High School in June 2014 with a high school diploma and business technology emphasis. Grade point average is 3.75.

**Relevant Skills and Courses:**

❏ Proficient with most recent versions of Windows and Office, including Word, Excel, Access, PowerPoint, and FrontPage.

❏ Excelled in the following courses: Keyboarding, Computer Applications, Business Communications, and Information Technology.

**Major Accomplishments:**

❏ Future Business Leaders of America: Member for four years, vice president for one year. Won second place in Public Speaking at the District Competition; competed (same event) at state level.

❏ Varsity soccer: Lettered three years and served as captain during senior year.

❏ Recognition: Named one of Eisenhower's Top Ten Community Service Providers at end of junior year.

Work Experience: Hinton's Family Restaurant, Server (2012-present): Served customers in culturally diverse area, oriented new part-time employees, and resolved routine customer service issues.

Tuma's Landscape and Garden Center, Sales (2010-2011): Assisted customers with plant selection and responsible for stocking and arranging display areas.

References: Will be furnished upon request.

**Print Resume (Resume 2)**

## Employment Application Form

| Application for Employment | | An Equal Opportunity Employer |
|---|---|---|

Regency Insurance Company

### PERSONAL INFORMATION

| NAME (LAST FIRST): Ruckert, Douglas H. | SOCIAL SECURITY NO. 368-56-2890 | CURRENT DATE 5/22/2014 | PHONE NUMBER (713) 555-0121 |
|---|---|---|---|

| ADDRESS (NUMBER, STREET, CITY, STATE, ZIP CODE) 8503 Kirby Dr., Houston, TX 77054-8220 | | US CITIZEN ☒ YES ☐ NO | DATE YOU CAN START 6/10/2012 |
|---|---|---|---|

| ARE YOU EMPLOYED NOW? ☒ YES ☐ NO | IF YES, MAY WE INQUIRE OF YOUR PRESENT EMPLOYER? ☒ YES ☐ NO | IF YES, GIVE NAME AND NUMBER OF PERSON TO CALL. James Veloski, Manager (713) 555-0169 |
|---|---|---|

| POSITION DESIRED Customer Service | SALARY DESIRED Open | STATE HOW YOU LEARNED OF POSITION From Ms. Anne D. Salgado Eisenhower Information Technology Instructor |
|---|---|---|

HAVE YOU EVER BEEN CONVICTED OF A FELONY?
☐ YES ☒ NO    IF YES, EXPLAIN.

### EDUCATION

| | NAME AND LOCATION OF SCHOOL | YEARS ATTENDED | DID YOU GRADUATE? | SUBJECTS STUDIED |
|---|---|---|---|---|
| COLLEGE | | | | |
| HIGH SCHOOL | Eisenhower Technical High School Houston, TX | 2010 to 2014 | Will graduate 06/2014 | Information Technology |
| GRADE SCHOOL | | | | |
| OTHER | | | | |

SUBJECTS OF SPECIAL STUDY/RESEARCH WORK OR SPECIAL TRAINING/SKILLS DIRECTLY RELATED TO POSITION DESIRED

Windows and Office Suite, including Word, Excel, Access, PowerPoint, and Publisher

Office Procedures course with telephone training and interpersonal skills role playing

### FORMER EMPLOYERS (LIST LAST POSITION FIRST)

| FROM - TO (MTH & YEAR) | NAME AND ADDRESS | SALARY | POSITION | REASON FOR LEAVING |
|---|---|---|---|---|
| 9/2012 to present | Hinton's Family Restaurant, 1204 S. Wayside Avenue, Houston, TX 77021-8841 | Minimum wage plus tips | Server | Want full-time position in my field |
| 6/2010 to 9/2014 | Tuma's Landscape and Garden Center, 10155 East Freeway, Houston, TX 77029-4419 | Minimum wage | Sales | Employed at Hinton's |

### REFERENCES (LIST THREE PERSONS NOT RELATED TO YOU, WHOM YOU HAVE KNOWN AT LEAST ONE YEAR)

| NAME | BUSINESS ADDRESS | PHONE NUMBER | TITLE | YEARS KNOWN |
|---|---|---|---|---|
| Ms. Anne D. Salgado | Eisenhower Technical High School, 100 W. Cavalcade, Houston, TX 77009-2451 | (713) 555-0134 | Information Technology Instructor | Four |
| Mr. James R. Veloski | Hinton's Family Restaurant, 1204 S. Wayside Avenue, Houston, TX 77021-8841 | (713) 555-0169 | Manager | Two |
| Mrs. Helen T. Landis | Tuma's Landscape and Garden Center, 10155 East Freeway, Houston, TX 77029-4419 | (713) 555-0182 | Owner | Three |

I UNDERSTAND THAT I SHALL NOT BECOME AN EMPLOYEE UNTIL I HAVE SIGNED AN EMPLOYMENT AGREEMENT WITH THE FINAL APPROVAL OF THE EMPLOYER AND THAT SUCH EMPLOYMENT WILL BE SUBJECT TO VERIFICATION OF PREVIOUS EMPLOYMENT DATA PROVIDED IN THIS APPLICATION, ANY RELATED DOCUMENTS, OR DATA SHEET. I KNOW THAT A REPORT MAY BE MADE THAT WILL INCLUDE INFORMATION CONCERNING ANY FACTOR THE EMPLOYER MIGHT FIND

RELEVANT TO THE POSITION FOR WHICH I AM APPLYING, AND THAT I CAN MAKE A WRITTEN REQUEST FOR ADDITIONAL INFORMATION AS TO THE NATURE AND SCOPE OF THE REPORT IF ONE IS MADE.

Douglas H. Ruckert
SIGNATURE OF APPLICANT

**Employment Application Form**

## Employment Application Letter

8503 Kirby Drive
Houston, TX 77054-8220
May 10, 2014

Ms. Jenna St. John
Personnel Director
Regency Insurance Company
219 West Greene Road
Houston, TX 77067-4219

Dear Ms. St. John:

Ms. Anne D. Salgado, my business technology instructor, informed me of the customer service position with your company that will be available June 15. She speaks very highly of your organization. After learning more about the position, I am confident that I am qualified and would like to be considered for the position.

As indicated on the enclosed resume, I am currently completing my senior year at Eisenhower Technical High School. All of my elective courses have been computer and business-related courses. I have completed the advanced computer application class where we integrated word processing, spreadsheet, database, presentation, and Web page documents by using the latest suite software. I have also taken an office technology course that included practice in using the telephone and applying interpersonal skills.

My work experience and school activities have given me the opportunity to work with people to achieve group goals. Participating in FBLA has given me an appreciation of the business world.

An opportunity to interview with you for this position will be greatly appreciated. You can call me at (713) 555-0121 or e-mail me at dougr@suresend.com to arrange an interview.

Sincerely,

Douglas H. Ruckert

Enclosure

**Employment Application Letter**

# UNIT 1 Managing Digital Information

Lesson 1 Computers in the 21st Century
Lesson 2 Exploring Your Computer
Lesson 3 Maintaining a System
Lesson 4 Keeping Resources Secure
Lesson 5 Improving Internet Skills
Lesson 6 Working in the Cloud

## LESSON 1 Computers in the 21st Century

**OUTCOMES**

- Analyze the importance of computers.
- Explain how computers process information.
- Describe hardware and software.
- Explain information systems, information communication technology, and information technology.
- Evaluate technology for specific needs.

### 1A

**Computers Past, Present, and Future**

A computer is a machine that processes data and performs tasks according to a set of instructions. Even if you do not have a computer of your own, you come in contact with computers many times each day.

Figure 1-1 The ENIAC digital computer had to be programmed by hand for every task

Computers have a longer history than you might imagine. Mechanical calculators invented during the 1600s are considered to be a first step toward the automated calculation that is one of the chief functions of modern computers. Machines such as Jacquard's loom, invented early in the nineteenth century, allowed tasks to be programmed (to a limited extent) and carried out automatically.

Early digital computers, such as the ENIAC shown in Figure 1-1, could not store the programs used to run them. The first stored-program computers were developed in the late 1940s. The first personal computers began to gain attention in the 1970s, only 30 years or so later. By the end of the century, most people in the world knew what a computer was and interacted with computers in some form on a daily basis.

Early personal computers were developed by and for hobbyists, but within a very few years, computers began to make their way into the mainstream. Once advances in computer technology made them small enough to fit on a desktop, relatively inexpensive, and easy to use, computers revolutionized the way people worked, learned, communicated, and played.

- Beginning in 1969, when the first ATM opened for business, people could withdraw cash and perform other bank transactions any time of the day or night.
- In 2001, with the introduction of the iPod, people could take their music with them anywhere they went. The iTunes music store enabled customers to buy single songs at a minimal charge, changing the way everyone purchased music.
- When Twitter was introduced in 2006, people had a new way to communicate with each other instantly, another step in the social networking phenomenon that began with the viral popularity of Facebook.

## Agenda

**[Company/Department Name]**

**Agenda**

[Date]

[Time]

Type of Meeting:  [Description of meeting]

Meeting Facilitator:  [Name of meeting facilitator]

Invitees:  [List of invitees]

I.   Call to order

II.   Roll call

III.   Approval of minutes from last meeting

IV.   Open issues

    a)   [Description of open issue]

    b)   [Description of open issue]

    c)   [Description of open issue]

V.   New business

    a)   [Description of new business]

    b)   [Description of new business]

    c)   [Description of new business]

VI.   Adjournment

VII.

**Agenda**

---

## Itinerary

| | | TRAVEL ITINERARY FOR LISA PEROTTA | |
| --- | --- | --- | --- |
| | | 222 Pine View Drive | |
| | | Coraopolis, PA 15108 | |
| | | (412) 555-1320 | |
| | | perotta@fastnet.com | |
| | | Pittsburgh, PA to Santa Ana, CA—April 18-22, 20-- | |
| **Date** | **Time** | **Activity** | **Comments** |
| Tuesday April 18 | 3:30 p.m. (ET) | Depart **Pittsburgh International Airport** (PIT) for Santa Ana, CA Airport (SNA) on **USEast Flight 146**. *Arrival time is 5:01 p.m.(PT)*. | The flight is non-stop on an Airbus A319, and you are assigned seat 22E. |
| | 5:30 p.m. (PT) | Reservation with **Star Car Rental** (714-555-0190).  Return by 12 noon (PT) on April 22. | Confirmation No.: 33-345. Telephone:  714-555-1030. |
| | 6:00 p.m. (PT) | Reservations at the Hannah Hotel, 421 Race Avenue, Santa Ana for April 18 to April 22 for a single, non-smoking room at $145 plus tax.  Telephone:  714-555-0200. | Confirmation No.: 632A-04/18. Check-in after 6 p.m. is guaranteed. Check out by 11 a.m. |
| Saturday April 22 | 1:25 p.m. (PT) | Depart **Santa Ana Airport** (SNA) for Pittsburgh International Airport (PIT) on **USEast Flight 148**. *Arrival time is 8:52 p.m. (ET)*. | The flight is non-stop on an Airbus A319, and you are assigned seat 16A. |
| Travel Agency Contact Information—Agent is Mary Grecco; 444 Grant Street, Pittsburgh, PA 15219; Telephone: 412-555-0087; Fax:  412-555-0088; E-Mail:  greccom@netway.com | | | |

**Itinerary**

---

## Meeting Minutes

**[Company/Department Name]**

**Meeting Minutes**

[Date]

I.   **Call to order**

    [Name of Meeting Facilitator] called to order the regular meeting of the [Organization/Committee Name] at [time of meeting] on [date of meeting] in [Location of Meeting].

II.   **Roll call**

    [Name of Organization Secretary] conducted a roll call. The following persons were present: [List of Attendees]

III.   **Approval of minutes from last meeting**

    [Name of Organization Secretary] read the minutes from the last meeting. The minutes were approved as read.

IV.   **Open issues**

    a)   [Open issue/summary of discussion]

    b)   [Open issue/summary of discussion]

    c)   [Open issue/summary of discussion]

V.   **New business**

    a)   [New business/summary of discussion]

    b)   [New business/summary of discussion]

    c)   [New business/summary of discussion]

VI.   **Adjournment**

    [Name of Meeting Facilitator] adjourned the meeting at [time meeting ended].

Minutes submitted by:  [Name]

**Meeting Minutes**

---

## News Release

# News Release

For Release:  Immediate

Contact:  Heidi Zemack

CLEVELAND, OH, May 25, 20--.  Science teachers from school districts in six counties are eligible for this year's Teacher Excellence awards funded by The Society for Environmental Engineers.

Nominations can be submitted through Friday, July 31, by students, parents, residents, and other educators.  Nomination forms are available from the participating school districts or on the Society's website at http://www.tsee.webhost.com.

An anonymous committee reviews the nominations and selects ten finalists.  From that group, seven "teachers of distinction" and three award winners are selected.  The top award winner receives $5,000, the second receives $2,500, and the third receives $1,500.  Each teacher of distinction receives $500.  The teachers of distinction and the award winners will be announced on September 5 at a dinner at the Cleveland Inn.

School districts participating in the program include those in these counties:  Cuyahoga, Lorain, Medina, Summit, Lake, and Geauga.

###

**News Release**

The importance of computers in everyday life suggests that designers will always be searching for ways to improve them. As the twenty-first century progresses, we can assume that computers will become smarter, faster, and more sophisticated. Instead of using electronic components, they might use light-sensitive organic compounds to speed computer operations or DNA to store information and perform calculations. It may be only a matter of years before our computers are communicating with us in ways that were formerly the stuff of science fiction.

QUICK ✔

Consider one task you did yesterday that used a computer. How would that task have been done before computers were readily available? How might it be done 20 years from now?

## 1B

## How Computers Process Information

To work with data, all computers have five basic functions: input, processing, output, distribution, and storage. See Figure 1-2 for an illustration of this process.

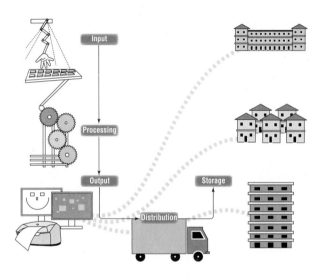

**Figure 1-2** The five steps of information processing.

**Input** is the raw data you enter into the computer. Input data can include any kind of information that can be represented digitally, such as letters and numbers entered on a keyboard, music converted to MP3 files, photographs converted to digital format by a scanner, or videos captured with a digital camera.

The computer converts input data into a program language that enables the computer to process it. To be used by the computer, the data is converted into bits and bytes, which are coded combinations of just two digits—0s and 1s. For this reason, computers and other electronic devices are often called digital devices.

A **bit** is the most basic unit of data stored or processed by a computer. A bit is either a 1 or a 0. The 1 corresponds to an on state in the computer's electronic circuits, indicating that electrical current is flowing. The 0 signifies the off state, indicating no current. A byte is typically composed of a group of 8 bits. A megabyte is approximately one million bytes, and a gigabyte is a little over a billion bytes.

Every piece of information you use in a computer is merely a coded group of 0s and 1s—for example, the coded format for the letter A in bits is 01000001.

Once data is converted into **bytes**, **processing** occurs, which means the computer is doing something to manipulate the data. The instructions that tell the computer what to do with the data are called **software**.

## Report Documentation

Good report writing includes proof that the reported statements are sound. The process is called **documenting.**

Most school reports are documented in the body and in a list. A reference in the body shows the source of a quotation or paraphrase. A list shows all references alphabetically.

In the report body, references may be noted (1) in parentheses in the copy (textual citations or parenthetical documentation); (2) by a superscript in the copy, listed on a separate page (endnotes); or (3) by a superscript in the copy, listed at the bottom of the text page (footnotes). A list may contain only the sources noted in the body (REFERENCES or Works Cited) or include related materials (BIBLIOGRAPHY).

Two popular documenting styles are shown: *Century 21* and MLA (Modern Language Association).

### Century 21
**Examples are listed in this order: (1) textual citation, (2) endnote/footnote, and (3) References/Bibliography page.**

*Book, One Author*
(Schaeffer, 1997, 1)

[1]Robert K. Schaeffer, *Understanding Globalization*, (Lanham, MD: Rowman & Littlefield Publishers, Inc., 1997), p. 1.

Schaeffer, Robert K. *Understanding Globalization* (Lanham, MD: Rowman & Littlefield Publishers, Inc., 1997).

*Book, Two or Three Authors*
(Prince and Jackson, 1997, 35)

[2]Nancy Prince and Jeanie Jackson, *Exploring Theater* (Minneapolis/St. Paul: West Publishing Company, 1997), p. 35.

Prince, Nancy, and Jeanie Jackson. *Exploring Theater*. Minneapolis/St. Paul: West Publishing Company, 1997.

*Book, Four or More Authors*
(Gwartney, et al., 2014, 9)

[3]James D. Gwartney, et al., *Economics: Private and Public Choice* (Cincinnati: South-Western, Cengage Learning, 2014), p. 9.

Gwartney, James D., et al. *Economics: Private and Public Choice*. Cincinnati: South-Western, Cengage Learning, 2014.

*Encyclopedia or Reference Book*
(*Encyclopedia Americana*, 2008, Vol. 25, p. 637)

[4]*Encyclopedia Americana*, Vol. 25 (Danbury, CT: Grolier Incorporated, 2008), p. 637.

*Encyclopedia Americana*, Vol. 25. "Statue of Liberty." Danbury, CT: Grolier Incorporated, 2008.

*Journal or Magazine Article*
(Harris, 1993, 755)

[5]Richard G. Harris, "Globalization, Trade, and Income," *Canadian Journal of Economics*, November 1993, p. 755.

Harris, Richard G. "Globalization, Trade, and Income." *Canadian Journal of Economics*, November 1993, 755–776.

*Website*
(Railton, 2014)

[6]Stephen Railton, "Your Mark Twain," http://www.etext.lib.virginia.edu/railton/sc_as_mt/yourmt13.html (September 24, 2014).

Railton, Stephen. "Your Mark Twain." http://www.etext.lib.virginia.edu/railton/sc_as_mt/yourmt13.html (24 September 2014).

### Modern Language Association
**Examples include reference (1) in parenthetical documentation and (2) on Works Cited page.**

*Book, One Author*
(Schaeffer 1)

Schaeffer, Robert K. *Understanding Globalization*. Lanham, MD: Rowman & Littlefield, 1997.

*Book, Two or Three Authors*
(Prince and Jackson 35)

Prince, Nancy, and Jeanie Jackson. *Exploring Theater*. Minneapolis/St. Paul: West Publishing, 1997.

*Book, Four or More Authors or Editors*
(Gwartney et al. 9)

Gwartney, James D., et al. *Economics: Private and Public Choice*. Cincinnati: South-Western, Cengage Learning, 2014.

*Encyclopedia or Reference Book*
(*Encyclopedia Americana* 637)

*Encyclopedia Americana*. "Statue of Liberty." Danbury, CT: Grolier, 2008.

*Journal or Magazine Article*
(Harris 755)

Harris, Richard G. "Globalization, Trade, and Income," *Canadian Journal of Economics*. Nov. 1993: 755–776.

*Website*
(Railton)

Railton, Stephen. *Your Mark Twain Page*. (24 Sept. 2014) http://www.etext.lib.virginia.edu/railton/sc_as_mt/yourmt13.html.

After the computer processes the data, it displays the completed work as **output**. The output may be displayed on a screen, printed on a report, played over speakers as sound, or sent via a network link to another computer.

Next, **distribution** enables the computer to share information with computers and other users, typically across a network. Networks enable you to distribute data in ways such as sending email, texting, or posting a picture to a website.

Finally, you can save the data the computer has processed on a **storage device**. This enables you to keep the data for use at a later time. You will learn more about storage devices in the next section.

## Computer Hardware

Hardware refers to the parts of a computer that you can touch. Hardware provides the mechanisms to carry out software instructions.

For a personal computer or laptop, hardware includes the **central processing unit (CPU)** as well as the monitor, keyboard, and mouse or touch pad (Figure 1-3). Other devices that attach to the computer, called **peripherals**, are also considered to be hardware. Common peripherals include speakers, printers, removable drives, scanners, and microphones.

Monitor

Speakers

Keyboard

Disk drive

CPU (inside case)

Mouse

© iStockphoto.com/gabyjalbert

**Figure 1-3** Common Components of a desktop PC

© windu/Shutterstock.com

**Figure 1-4** The CPU is the brains of the computer

Many of the computer's key components are located inside the laptop or the casing of the PC. These components include the CPU, the primary storage device, and what is commonly referred to as the motherboard, which is where the CPU and other internal components are attached.

The CPU (Figure 1-4) processes the instructions of the computer's various programs. You may have heard a CPU referred to simply as a processor or microprocessor. The CPU is a small square device that plugs directly into the motherboard. The speed of the CPU is the most important factor in how fast a computer runs. The higher the speed, the more operations the CPU can handle every second.

CPU speed, usually called **clock speed**, is measured in megahertz (MHz) or gigahertz (GHz). One megahertz is equal to one million cycles per second. One gigahertz is equal to 1,000 MHz. Today's CPUs typically have clock speeds in the gigahertz range.

The primary storage device is commonly referred to as a computer's **memory**. There are two basic types of computer memory for storing data. **RAM**, which stands for random-access memory, is used for temporary storage while the computer is processing data. All data stored in RAM is lost once the computer is shut off.

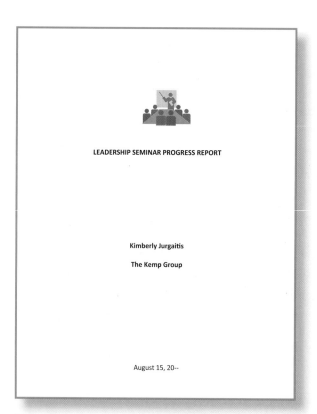

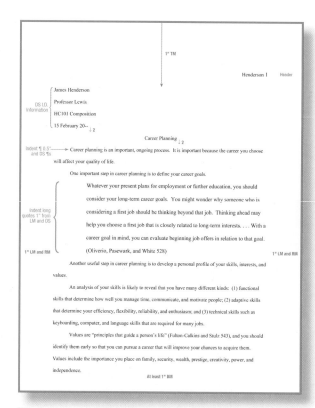

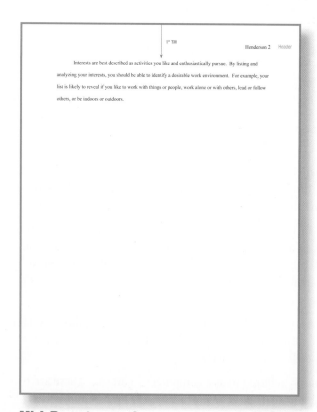

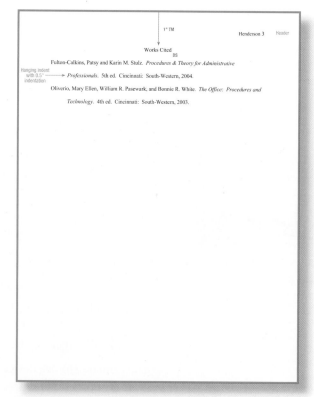

**Title Page**

**MLA Report, page 1**

**MLA Report, page 2**

**Works Cited Page for MLA Report**

RAM is measured in megabytes or gigabytes; the more RAM a system has, the more storage it offers running programs and the faster they will run. The integrated circuits that provide RAM memory plug into the motherboard in the form of cards such as the one shown in Figure 1-5.

The second type of memory is ROM, which stands for read-only memory. ROM is typically used for data that does not change, such as the programming that starts a computer. In contrast to RAM, where more is usually better, most computers need only a small amount of ROM.

Early personal computers included very little storage for programs and files, but today's computers typically offer much more storage to accommodate sophisticated programs and the large files that can be generated by pictures and videos. Storage devices may be internal or external.

All computers include one or more hard drives inside the computer case. A hard drive consists of platters that rotate on a spindle with a head to read and write data (see Figure 1-6). Data is recorded magnetically on the platters.

Storage devices external to the computer case can include CDs or DVDs that are accessed through CD or DVD drives, external hard drives that are connected to the computer by cable, and USB drives that plug into USB ports.

Computer hardware also includes the input devices for getting information into the CPU and output devices for displaying or playing information. For a PC, the mouse and keyboard are the most common input devices. On laptop computers, pointing devices such as touch pads or rubber nubs are used instead of a mouse. Many computers and handheld devices allow you to select icons or text by touching the computer screen, as shown in Figure 1-7.

Other common input devices include microphones for speaking or recording voice data, tablets for recording written notes or drawing, game controllers for playing games, digital cameras, and scanners for scanning photos and documents into the computer.

The most common output device is the monitor or screen. Other peripheral output devices include printers, speakers, projectors, and other types of whiteboards or flat screens.

## Computer Software

The step-by-step instructions used to tell the computer what to do with data are called software. Software is the part of the system you cannot touch, in contrast with hardware. Software is written by computer programmers in a programming language such as Java, Visual Basic, or C.

Software can be generally divided into three types: system software, application software, and programming software. This section concentrates on system software and application software.

System software includes programs such as device drivers that control peripherals, operating systems that provide the user interface between you and the computer, and utilities that help you configure and maintain the computer.

Of these types of system software, the operating system is the most important. Your computer's operating system provides the instructions that control how you interact with the computer. The operating system also manages the computer's devices and controls how other software interacts with the computer hardware, allocating space in RAM for each program to operate.

**Figure 1-5** RAM mounted in a PC

**Figure 1-6** A hard drive outside a computer

**Figure 1-7** A tablet computer lets you input directly from the screen

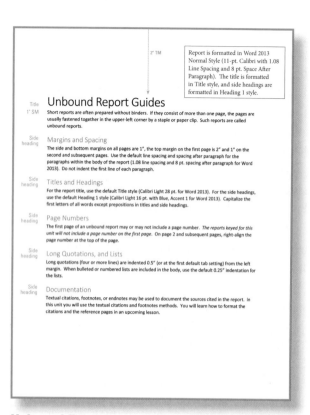

Report is formatted in Word 2013 Normal Style (11-pt. Calibri with 1.08 Line Spacing and 8 pt. Space After Paragraph). The title is formatted in Title style, and side headings are formatted in Heading 1 style.

2" TM

Title
1" SM **Unbound Report Guides**

Short reports are often prepared without binders. If they consist of more than one page, the pages are usually fastened together in the upper-left corner by a staple or paper clip. Such reports are called unbound reports.

Side heading
Margins and Spacing

The side and bottom margins on all pages are 1", the top margin on the first page is 2" and 1" on the second and subsequent pages. Use the default line spacing and spacing after paragraph for the paragraphs within the body of the report (1.08 line spacing and 8 pt. spacing after paragraph for Word 2013). Do not indent the first line of each paragraph.

Side heading
Titles and Headings

For the report title, use the default Title style (Calibri Light 28 pt. for Word 2013). For the side headings, use the default Heading 1 style (Calibri Light 16 pt. with Blue, Accent 1 for Word 2013). Capitalize the first letters of all words except prepositions in titles and side headings.

Side heading
Page Numbers

The first page of an unbound report may or may not include a page number. *The reports keyed for this unit will not include a page number on the first page.* On page 2 and subsequent pages, right-align the page number at the top of the page.

Side heading
Long Quotations, and Lists

Long quotations (four or more lines) are indented 0.5" (or at the first default tab setting) from the left margin. When bulleted or numbered lists are included in the body, use the default 0.25" indentation for the lists.

Side heading
Documentation

Textual citations, footnotes, or endnotes may be used to document the sources cited in the report. In this unit you will use the textual citations and footnotes methods. You will learn how to format the citations and the reference pages in an upcoming lesson.

**Unbound Report**

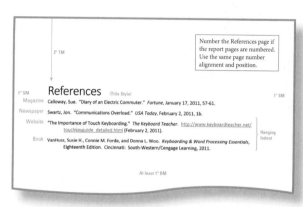

2" TM

Number the References page if the report pages are numbered. Use the same page number alignment and position.

1" SM **References**   (Title Style)                                    1" SM

Magazine   Calloway, Sue. "Diary of an Electric Commuter." *Fortune*, January 17, 2011, 57-61.

Newspaper   Swartz, Jon. "Communications Overload." *USA Today*, February 2, 2011, 1b.

Website   "The Importance of Touch Keyboarding." *The Keyboard Teacher*. http://www.keyboardteacher.net/ touchkeyguide_detailed.html (February 2, 2011).

Book   VanHuss, Susie H., Connie M. Forde, and Donna L. Woo. *Keyboarding & Word Processing Essentials*, Eighteenth Edition. Cincinnati: South-Western/Cengage Learning, 2011.

Hanging Indent

At least 1" BM

**References Page**

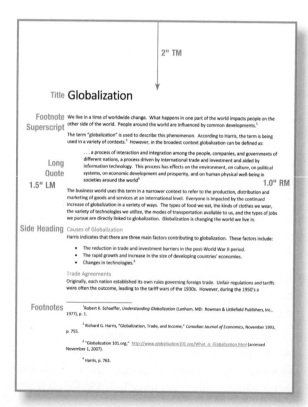

2" TM

Title **Globalization**

Footnote Superscript   We live in a time of worldwide change. What happens in one part of the world impacts people on the other side of the world. People around the world are influenced by common developments.[1]

The term "globalization" is used to describe this phenomenon. According to Harris, the term is being used in a variety of contexts.[2] However, in the broadest context globalization can be defined as:

Long Quote
1.5" LM
. . . a process of interaction and integration among the people, companies, and governments of different nations, a process driven by international trade and investment and aided by information technology. This process has effects on the environment, on culture, on political systems, on economic development and prosperity, and on human physical well-being in societies around the world[3]
1.0" RM

The business world uses this term in a narrower context to refer to the production, distribution and marketing of goods and services at an international level. Everyone is impacted by the continued increase of globalization in a variety of ways. The types of food we eat, the kinds of clothes we wear, the variety of technologies we utilize, the modes of transportation available to us, and the types of jobs we pursue are directly linked to globalization. Globalization is changing the world we live in.

Side Heading   Causes of Globalization

Harris indicates that there are three main factors contributing to globalization. These factors include:

- The reduction in trade and investment barriers in the post-World War II period.
- The rapid growth and increase in the size of developing countries' economies.
- Changes in technologies.[4]

Trade Agreements

Originally, each nation established its own rules governing foreign trade. Unfair regulations and tariffs were often the outcome, leading to the tariff wars of the 1930s. However, during the 1950's a

Footnotes
[1] Robert K. Schaeffer, *Understanding Globalization* (Lanham, MD: Rowman & Littlefield Publishers, Inc., 1977), p. 1.

[2] Richard G. Harris, "Globalization, Trade, and Income," *Canadian Journal of Economics*, November 1993, p. 755.

[3] "Globalization 101.org," http://www.globalization101.org/What_is_Globalization.html (accessed November 1, 2007).

[4] Harris, p. 763.

**Bound Report with Long Quotation and Footnotes**

Contents

**Table of Contents**

Popular operating systems include *Microsoft Windows 7*, *Macintosh OS X*, and *GNU/Linux*. *Google Chrome OS* is designed for users who spend most of their time on the Internet, and *Windows 8* is an interface radically different from previous versions of Windows. Users can manipulate programs and files from the tiles on the opening screen (Figure 1-8) using touch technology or more traditional mouse or keyboard input.

**Figure 1-8** *Windows 8* is a radical redesign of the Windows user interface

Most operating systems are single-user systems that allow only one person to be working with the operating system at a time. Single-user systems may offer user accounts that allow a number of users to personalize the operating system interface and maintain a level of security for their files. An administrator account is required to make some changes to the system, such as installing new software or running certain programs.

Application software provides instructions for accomplishing a specific type of task, such as creating a word processing document, sending email, or finding information on the Web. Application software can be a stand-alone program dedicated to one specific task, such as editing photos or videos, or it may contain several different applications, such as an office applications suite. Office suites such as *Microsoft Office* are some of the most commonly used commercial software products in business. Accordingly, most of the hands-on applications in this book will use the *Microsoft Office* suite.

Software can be proprietary or open source. Proprietary software is owned by the software publisher, and a user must agree with licensing restrictions to use the software. Typical restrictions include how many times the software may be installed and on how many computers. Open-source software can be downloaded and installed without the user having to agree to any restrictions.

Application software may be stored on your system, or you may use online applications that are available when working on the Internet. Online applications (or online apps) provide another way to accomplish specific tasks such as finding directions, browsing multimedia content, sending email, or creating office documents such as presentations and spreadsheets. You will explore more about using online apps in Lesson 6 of this Unit.

## Envelope Guides

### Return Address

Use block style, SS, and Initial Caps or ALL CAPS. If not using the Envelopes feature, begin as near to the top and left edge of the envelope as possible—TM and LM about 0.25".

### Receiver's Delivery Address

Use block style, SS, and Initial Caps. If desired, use ALL CAPS instead of initial caps and omit the punctuation. Place city name, two-letter state abbreviation, and ZIP Code +4 on last address line. One space precedes the ZIP Code.

If not using the Envelopes feature, tab over 2.5" for the small envelope and 4" for the large envelope. Insert hard returns to place the first line about 2" from the top.

### Mailing Notations

Key mailing and addressee notations in ALL CAPS.

Key mailing notations, such as SPECIAL DELIVERY and REGISTERED, below the stamp and at least three lines above the envelope address.

Key addressee notations, such as HOLD FOR ARRIVAL or PERSONAL, a DS below the return address and about three spaces from the left edge of the envelope.

If an attention line is used, key it as the first line of the envelope address.

### Standard Abbreviations

Use USPS standard abbreviations for states (see list below) and street suffix names, such as AVE and BLVD. Never abbreviate the name of a city or country.

### International Addresses

Omit postal (ZIP) codes from the last line of addresses outside the U.S. Show only the name of the country on the last line. Examples:

```
Mr. Hiram Sanders
2121 Clearwater St.
Ottawa, Onkia   OB1
CANADA
```

```
Ms. Inge D. Fischer
Hartmannstrasse 7
4209 Bonn 5
FEDERAL REPUBLIC OF GERMANY
```

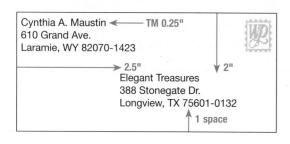

## Folding Procedures

### Small Envelopes (Nos. 6¾, 6¼)

1. With page face up, fold bottom up to 0.5" from top.
2. Fold right third to left.
3. Fold left third to 0.5" from last crease.
4. Insert last creased edge first.

### Large Envelopes (Nos. 10, 9, 7¾)

1. With page face up, fold slightly less than one-third of sheet up toward top.
2. Fold down top of sheet to within 0.5" of bottom fold.
3. Insert last creased edge first.

### Window Envelopes (Letter)

1. With page face down, top toward you, fold upper third down.
2. Fold lower third up so address is showing.
3. Insert sheet into envelope with last crease at bottom.
4. Check that address shows through window.

## State and Territory Abbreviations

| | | | | | | | |
|---|---|---|---|---|---|---|---|
| Alabama | AL | Illinois | IL | Nebraska | NE | South Carolina | SC |
| Alaska | AK | Indiana | IN | Nevada | NV | South Dakota | SD |
| Arizona | AZ | Iowa | IA | New Hampshire | NH | Tennessee | TN |
| Arkansas | AR | Kansas | KS | New Jersey | NJ | Texas | TX |
| California | CA | Kentucky | KY | New Mexico | NM | Utah | UT |
| Colorado | CO | Louisiana | LA | New York | NY | Vermont | VT |
| Connecticut | CT | Maine | ME | North Carolina | NC | Virgin Islands | VI |
| Delaware | DE | Maryland | MD | North Dakota | ND | Virginia | VA |
| District of Columbia | DC | Massachusetts | MA | Ohio | OH | Washington | WA |
| Florida | FL | Michigan | MI | Oklahoma | OK | West Virginia | WV |
| Georgia | GA | Minnesota | MN | Oregon | OR | Wisconsin | WI |
| Guam | GU | Mississippi | MS | Pennsylvania | PA | Wyoming | WY |
| Hawaii | HI | Missouri | MO | Puerto Rico | PR | | |
| Idaho | ID | Montana | MT | Rhode Island | RI | | |

System and application software may be installed on new computers or may be purchased for installation by individuals. When business organizations buy software, they may choose to buy licenses rather than multiple copies of the program. Buying a license to install a program, (say, ten times) can be less expensive than buying ten copies of the boxed software.

Most types of software are updated on a regular basis by the publisher. Updates may fix problems in the software, address security issues, or improve functionality. To make sure you are always using the most up-to-date version of a program, turn on automatic updates to allow your system to download and install updates as they become available.

Software may also be upgraded periodically as new features are developed. When a new version of a program becomes available, you usually have the option to upgrade to the new version, either for free or for a reduced upgrade price.

## QUICK ✔

Match the term in the left column with the definition in the right column.

1. operating system
2. hard drive
3. peripherals
4. CPU
5. application software
6. monitor
7. input
8. megabyte
9. RAM
10. distribution

a. platters that rotate on a spindle with a head to read and write data
b. the most common output device
c. enables the computer to share information with other computers and users
d. one million bytes
e. used for temporary storage while the computer is processing data
f. processes the instructions of the computer's programs
g. provides the instructions that control how you interact with the computer
h. the raw data entered into the computer
i. provides instructions for accomplishing a specific type of task
j. other hardware devices that attach to the computer

## 1D

### Understanding Information Systems

Information is the lifeblood of twenty-first-century businesses. Even the smallest small business, such as a baker who makes cookies at home, needs a fair amount of information to be successful. For example, how much should the baker charge for each cookie to cover expenses and earn a profit? Where is the best location to sell the cookies? What kind of packaging will maintain freshness and minimize breakage? What kind of advertising will attract buyers?

Information can come from a wide variety of sources and exist in a number of formats, as shown in Figure 1-9. Information on sales may be stored in a spreadsheet. Information on employees may be stored in a database. Information on competitors may be included in reports. Information on what consumers want may be found in marketing surveys. Information on new trends and new technologies may be available in up-to-the-minute Internet communications such as blog posts. Information on office policies may be delivered by email.

**Information management** is an important part of every business, from the home baker to global organizations. Concepts such as information systems, information communication technology, and information technology have developed to address how information is controlled in the digital age.

*Information systems* are systems that businesses employ to gather and analyze digital information. Information systems can include people, procedures, data, software, and hardware.

**Figure 1-9** Information can exist in a variety of formats

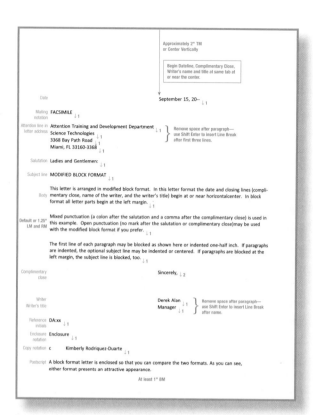

**Letter in Modified Block Format with Postscript**

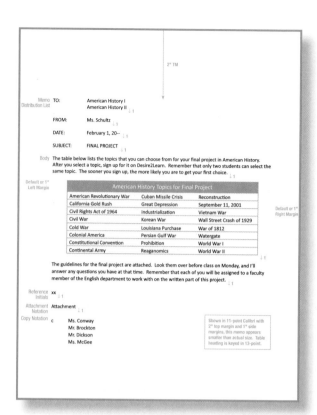

**Memo with Special Features**

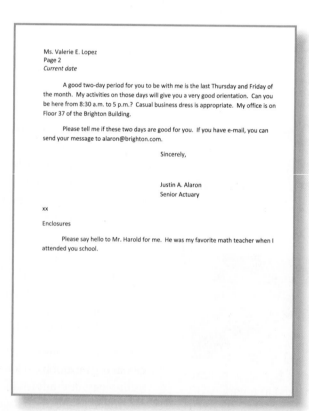

**Letter in Modified Block Format with Paragraph Indentations and List**

**Letter (p. 2) Showing Second-Page Heading**

*Information communications technology* refers to the digital technology that makes it possible to control information by storing it, retrieving it, manipulating it, sending it, or receiving it. Such communications technology can include computers and the application software they run, networks, voice communication devices, and PDAs or smartphones that can be used to store a wide variety of information.

Businesses offer careers in *information technology* (IT) to help them manage information. IT personnel may be responsible for tasks such as:

- Repairing, updating, and networking computers of various types.
- Creating and maintaining communications networks, websites, intranets, and services such as email, instant messaging, and video conferencing.
- Programming computers and other digital devices.

**Figure 1-10** Digitizing paper records like these is an example of information systems at work

Because the goal of information systems is to make a business more effective and more efficient, information systems play a strategic role in businesses and organizations. The necessity of having up-to-date communications technology is also clear. It is therefore important for businesses to include information systems in their strategic planning and to analyze how information systems and communications technology can help them achieve their goals and objectives.

Integrating information systems planning with strategic planning can smooth operations. Suppose, for example, a business has paper records (Figure 1-10) that frequently need to be searched for information. Digitizing these records will make operations more efficient. Considering the contribution that information communications technology can make to this task allows the organization to allocate money wisely for scanning technology to convert the records to digital format, for storage media to hold the digital files, for a database program to store the digital records in easily searchable fields, for an IT team to create the necessary queries in the database, and so on.

The rewards of incorporating information systems in planning can be obvious, but sound business practices dictate that possible drawbacks also be considered and evaluated. Will it be cost-effective to implement sophisticated information management technologies to achieve a goal? Will it be safe to store sensitive records on a company intranet where an unauthorized person may gain access to them?

 **QUICK** ✔

Consider a small business in your neighborhood. Make a list of the kinds of information that business needs to control in order to continue operating successfully.

## 1E

### Choosing the Right Technology

**Figure 1-11** Multimedia projector

Evaluating and selecting appropriate technology is a part of the information systems approach to working efficiently. The ability to choose technology for a given task is equally important for the individual computer user.

For example, you might be asked to create a multimedia presentation for an upcoming meeting with the staff in your business or organization. The first decisions you must make involve evaluating both the hardware and software you use for these needs.

Should you use a digital camera or your smartphone to capture pictures for the presentation— or would you be better served to purchase images you find from an online search? Should you create the presentation using a word processing application or presentation software? Do you need to use a separate multimedia application to edit the photos, videos, and music? Do you need a projector such as the one shown in Figure 1-11 to deliver the presentation?

**Interoffice Memo**

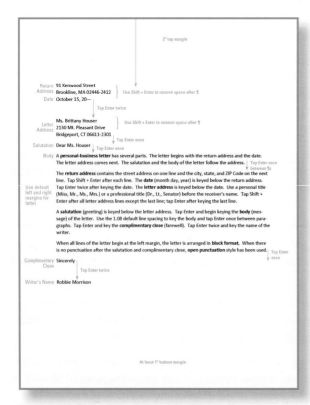

**Personal-Business Letter in Block Format
with Open Punctuation**

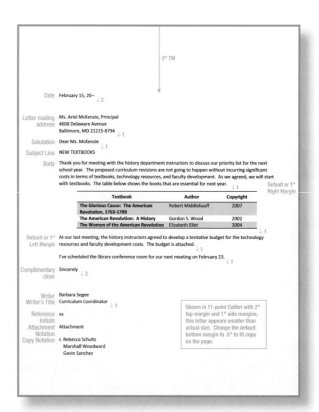

**Business Letter in Block Format
with Special Features**

Evaluating and choosing the right technology is also important when you're making purchase decisions for your own needs. When buying computer hardware and other digital devices, you have to consider several factors, including:

- Your budget.
- What applications you will use with the hardware.
- System requirements for the applications you want to use. If your applications require a considerable amount of memory, for instance, you want to make sure your system has plenty of RAM.

When purchasing software applications, the same basic considerations apply:

- Your budget.
- What you will do with the software.
- System requirements for the software and how well they match the hardware you have.

For example, many types of software are available that can be used for writing. Some are very basic, allowing you simply to key and save your words, such as the *Notepad* application shown in Figure 1-12. Others provide extensive options for formatting and output. If you just want to take notes in class, you might choose a simple accessory or freeware program. But, if you need to produce a fancy color brochure or newsletter, you may need to buy a more expensive software package.

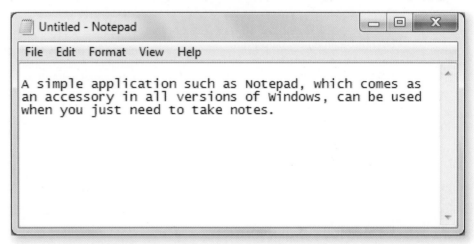

**Figure 1-12** Notepad is a simple writing program that comes with *Windows*

If you choose to use shareware, freeware, or open source software, be sure to download the software from a reliable source to avoid harming your computer system. Also, be sure not to download pirated software that has been copied or distributed illegally. Downloading or distributing pirated software is ethically wrong and is also a violation of copyright law.

You and a friend have a lawn care business that you would like to expand to add landscape design, planting, and maintenance. The new company will have an office and plenty of space for vehicles and nursery stock. Another friend has agreed to join the business to handle communications and office work.

1. List the types of information this new business might need to manage.
2. List the types of hardware and software the business will need to start operations, as well as other types of equipment and supplies needed for the office.
3. Describe the key considerations you should make when selecting the hardware and software. How does the type of business influence the choices of technology?

Proofreaders' marks are used to mark corrections in keyed or printed text that contains problems and/or errors. As a keyboard user, you should be able to read these marks accurately when revising or editing a rough draft. You also should be able to write these symbols to correct the rough drafts that you and others key. The most-used proofreaders' marks are shown below.

|  |  |
|------|---------|
| ‖ | Align copy; also, make these items parallel |
| ¶ | Begin a new paragraph |
| Cap ≡ | Capitalize |
| ⌒ | Close up |
| ℓ | Delete |
| <# | Delete space |
| No ¶ | Do not begin a new paragraph |
| ∧ | Insert |
| ⌄ | Insert comma |
| ⊙ | Insert period |
| ⌄⌄ | Insert quotation marks |
| #> | Insert space |
| ⌄ | Insert apostrophe |
| stet | Let it stand; ignore correction |
| lc | Lowercase |
| ⎣⎦ | Move down; lower |
| ⊏ | Move left |
| ⊐ | Move right |
| ⎡⎤ | Move up; raise |
| O sp | Spell out |
| ∼ tr | Transpose |
| ——— | Underline or italic |

## Email Format And Software Features

Email format varies slightly, depending on the software used to create and send it.

### Email Heading

Most email software includes these features:

**Attachment:** line for attaching files to an email message

**Bcc:** line for sending copy of a message to someone without the receiver knowing

**Cc:** line for sending copy of a message to additional receivers

**Date:** month, day, and year message is sent; often includes precise time of transmittal; usually is inserted automatically

**From:** name and/or email address of sender; usually is inserted automatically

**Subject:** line for very brief description of message content

**To:** line for name and/or email address of receiver

### Email Body

The message box on the email screen may contain these elements or only the message paragraphs (SS with DS between paragraphs).
- Informal salutation and/or receiver's name (a DS above the message)
- Informal closing (e.g., "Regards," "Thanks") and/or the sender's name (a DS below the message). Additional identification (e.g., telephone number) may be included.

### Special Email Features

Several email features make communicating through email fast and efficient.

**Address list/book:** collection of names and email addresses of correspondents from which an address can be entered on the To: line by selecting it, instead of keying it.

**Distribution list:** series of names and/or email addresses, separated by commas, on the To: line.

**Forward:** feature that allows an email user to send a copy of a received email message to others.

**Recipient list (Group):** feature that allows an email user to send mail to a group of recipients by selecting the name of the group (e.g., All Teachers).

**Reply:** feature used to respond to an incoming message.

**Reply all:** feature used to respond to all copy recipients as well as the sender of an incoming message.

**Signature:** feature for storing and inserting the closing lines of messages (e.g., informal closing, sender's name, telephone number, address, fax number).

## LESSON 2 — Exploring Your Computer

**OUTCOMES**
- View computer resources.
- Work with *File Explorer* to manage and manipulate files.

**2A**

**Viewing Computer Resources**

All operating systems provide a way for you to view the system's drives, storage devices, and other resources. Knowing the current status of file storage is one important aspect of information management.

To view your computer's resources, key This PC in the Search charm. Click This PC and a window opens similar to the one shown in Figure 1-13.

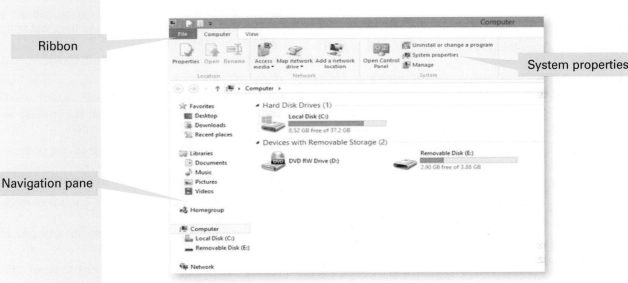

Figure 1-13 Computer tab

The left pane of this window is the *navigation pane*. You use this pane to open libraries and view the contents of folders. This pane is always in view when computer resources are displayed.

The right pane displays the contents of the object selected in the navigation pane. When Computer is selected, as shown in the figure, the right pane shows the computer's resources. In Figure 1-13, you can see that the computer has one disk drive (C), one DVD/RW Drive (D), and a removable USB drive.

1. Start your computer.
2. Key **This PC** in the Search Charm and display the Computer window.
3. Compare your Computer window to the one shown in Figure 1-13.

You can see a graphic representation of how much space on each drive is free or in use and also tells you the amount of storage that is still free. You can also right-click the drive and select Properties to see a pie chart showing disk usage (Figure 1-14).

Figure 1-14 Disk usage shown as a pie chart

Click System properties on the ribbon to review additional information about the computer, including what kind of processor it has, the amount of installed memory, and the computer's name. Additional links in the left pane of the System window allow you to view a list of all devices in current use and adjust settings for automatic updates, among other options.

## Confusing Words

**accept** (vb) to receive; to approve; to take
**except** (prep/vb) with the exclusion of; leave out

**affect** (vb) to produce a change in or have an effect on
**effect** (n) result; something produced by an agent or a cause

**buy** (n/vb) to purchase; to acquire; a bargain
**by** (prep/adv) close to; via; according to; close at hand

**choose** (vb) to select; to decide
**chose** (vb) past tense of "choose"

**cite** (vb) use as support; commend; summon
**sight** (n/vb) ability to see; something seen; a device to improve aim
**site** (n) location

**complement** (n) something that fills, completes, or makes perfect
**compliment** (n/vb) a formal expression of respect or admiration; to pay respect or admiration

**do** (vb) to bring about; to carry out
**due** (adj) owed or owing as a debt; having reached the date for payment

**farther** (adv) greater distance
**further** (adv) additional; in greater depth; to greater extent

**for** (prep/conj) indicates purpose on behalf of; because of
**four** (n) two plus two in number

**hear** (vb) to gain knowledge of by the ear
**here** (adv) in or at this place; at or on this point; in this case

**hole** (n) opening in or through something
**whole** (adj/n) having all its proper parts; a complete amount

**hour** (n) the 24th part of a day; a particular time
**our** (adj) possessive form of "we"; of or relating to us

**knew** (vb) past tense of "know"; understood; recognized truth or nature of
**new** (adj) novel; fresh; existing for a short time

**know** (vb) to be aware of the truth or nature of; to have an understanding of
**no** (adv/adj/n) not in any respect or degree; not so; indicates denial or refusal

**lessen** (vb) to cause to decrease; to make less
**lesson** (n) something to be learned; period of instruction; a class period

**lie** (n/vb) an untrue or inaccurate statement; to tell an untrue story; to rest or recline
**lye** (n) a strong alkaline substance or solution

**one** (adj/pron) a single unit or thing
**won** (vb) past tense of win; gained a victory as in a game or contest; got by effort or work

**passed** (vb) past tense of "pass"; already occurred; moved by; gave an item to someone
**past** (adv/adj/prep/n) gone or elapsed; time gone by

**personal** (adj) of, relating to, or affecting a person; done in person
**personnel** (n) a staff or persons making up a workforce in an organization

**plain** (adj/n) with little decoration; a large flat area of land
**plane** (n) an airplane or hydroplane

**pole** (n) a long, slender, rounded piece of wood or other material
**poll** (n) a survey of people to analyze public opinion

**principal** (n/adj) a chief or leader; capital (money) amount placed at interest; of or relating to the most important thing or matter or persons
**principle** (n) a central rule, law, or doctrine

**right** (adj) factual; true; correct
**rite** (n) customary form of ceremony; ritual
**write** (v) to form letters or symbols; to compose and set down in words, numbers, or symbols

**some** (n/adv) unknown or unspecified unit or thing; to a degree or extent
**sum** (n/vb) total; to find a total; to summarize

**stationary** (adj) fixed in a position, course, or mode; unchanging in condition
**stationery** (n) paper and envelopes used for processing personal and business documents

**than** (conj/prep) used in comparisons to show differences between items
**then** (n/adv) that time; at that time; next

**to** (prep/adj) indicates action, relation, distance, direction
**too** (adv) besides; also; to excessive degree
**two** (n/adj) one plus one

**vary** (vb) change; make different; diverge
**very** (adv/adj) real; mere; truly; to high degree

**waist** (n) narrowed part of the body between chest and hips; middle of something
**waste** (n/vb/adj) useless things; rubbish; spend or use carelessly; nonproductive

**weak** (adj) lacking strength, skill, or proficiency
**week** (n) a series of seven days; Monday through Sunday

**wear** (vb/n) to bear or have on the person; diminish by use; clothing
**where** (adv/conj/n) at, in, or to what degree; what place, source, or cause

**your** (adj) of or relating to you as possessor
**you're** (contraction) you are

The ribbon at the top of Windows 8 (Figure 1-15) lets you to move back and forth among windows or go to a specific window such as the Computer window. The ribbon's tabs and buttons allows you to navigate your computer's resources and perform various functions related to the computer's operation.

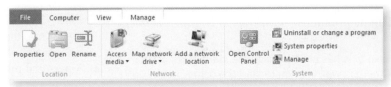

**Figure 1-15** The This PC ribbon

You can use the navigation pane in the This PC window to access any drive, folder, or file in the same way you use a program such as *File Explorer,* which you will work with later in this lesson. Double-click the appropriate drive, and then continue to double-click on folders until you reach the file you want to use.

This window also allows you to create new folders in the file list. Click in the drive or folder where you want the new folder to appear, click the New folder command in the toolbar, and then key the folder name.

1. In the navigation pane look to see how much free space you currently have on your computer's C drive.
2. View the properties for your system, and write down the type of processor the system has, as well as how much RAM is currently installed.
3. Return to the This PC window.
4. Double-click the C drive to display the folders on this drive.
5. Click the New folder command in the toolbar. Key **Century21** as the folder name and tap Enter.

**2B**

**Using File Explorer**

The Computer window gives you one way to view the folders and files on your system. Another option for working with files is to start *File Explorer*. Instead of seeing the drives and other resources in the right pane when you start the program, you see the system's libraries.

Libraries are collections of folders in the categories of documents, music, pictures, and videos (Figure 1-16). You can specify that any folder on your system, or even on an external drive or another computer, be shown in a library. The folder does not move from its original location, so you can still find it using the *File Explorer* navigation options. But because programs such as *Microsoft Word 2013* open the Documents library by default, adding a folder that you intend to use often to that library can make it faster and easier for you to locate your files.

## Basic Grammar Guides

### Use a singular verb

1. With a singular subject.

   Dr. Cho was to give the lecture, but he is ill.

2. With indefinite pronouns (*each, every, any, either, neither, one,* etc.)

   Each of these girls has an important role in the class play.
   Neither of them is well enough to start the game.

3. With singular subjects linked by *or* or *nor*; but if one subject is singular and the other is plural, the verb agrees with the nearer subject.

   Neither Ms. Moss nor Mr. Katz was invited to speak.
   Either the manager or his assistants are to participate.

4. With a collective noun (*class, committee, family, team,* etc.) if the collective noun acts as a unit.

   The committee has completed its study and filed a report.
   The jury has returned to the courtroom to give its verdict.

5. With the pronouns *all* and *some* (as well as fractions and percentages) when used as subjects if their modifiers are singular. Use a plural verb if their modifiers are plural.

   Some of the new paint is already cracking and peeling.
   All of the workers are to be paid for the special holiday.
   Historically, about 40 percent has voted.

6. When *number* is used as the subject and is preceded by *the*; use a plural verb if *number* is the subject and is preceded by *a*.

   The number of voters has increased again this year.
   A number of workers are on vacation this week.

### Use a plural verb

1. With a plural subject.

   The players were all here, and they were getting restless.

2. With a compound subject joined by *and*.

   Mrs. Samoa and her son are to be on a local talk show.

### Negative forms of verbs

1. Use the plural verb *do not* or *don't* with pronoun subjects *I, we, you,* and *they* as well as with plural nouns.

   I do not find this report believable; you don't either.

2. Use the singular verb *does not* or *doesn't* with pronouns *he, she,* and *it* as well as with singular nouns.

   Though she doesn't accept the board's offer, the board doesn't have to offer more.

### Pronoun agreement with antecedents

1. A personal pronoun (*I, we, you, he, she, it, their,* etc.) agrees in person (first, second, or third) with the noun or other pronoun it represents.

   We can win the game if we all give each play our best effort.
   You may play softball after you finish your homework.
   Andrea said that she will drive her car to the shopping mall.

2. A personal pronoun agrees in gender (feminine, masculine, or neuter) with the noun or other pronoun it represents.

   Each winner will get a corsage as she receives her award.
   Mr. Kimoto will give his talk after the announcements.
   The small boat lost its way in the dense fog.

3. A personal pronoun agrees in number (singular or plural) with the noun or other pronoun it represents.

   Celine drove her new car to Del Rio, Texas, last week.
   The club officers made careful plans for their next meeting.

4. A personal pronoun that represents a collective noun (*team, committee, family,* etc.) may be singular or plural, depending on the meaning of the collective noun.

   Our women's soccer team played its fifth game today.
   The vice squad took their positions in the square.

### Commonly confused pronouns

it's (contraction): it is; it has
its (pronoun): possessive form of *it*

It's good to get your email; it's been a long time.
The puppy wagged its tail in welcome.

their (pronoun): possessive form of *they*
there (adverb/pronoun): at or in that place; sometimes used to introduce a sentence
they're (contraction): they are

The hikers all wore their parkas.
Will they be there during our presentation?
They're likely to be late because of rush-hour traffic.

who's (contraction): who is; who has
whose (pronoun): possessive form of *who*

Who's seen the movie? Who's going now?
I chose the one whose skills are best.

 You may find that libraries temporarily disappear after you work with them. To redisplay all libraries, right-click on Libraries in the navigation pane and click Restore default libraries. The original libraries and any libraries you added will be listed.

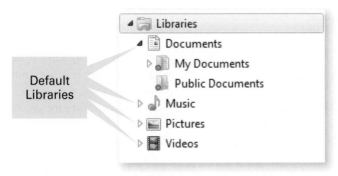

**Figure 1-16** Libraries collect folders from anywhere on your computer or network

When you add a folder to a library, you will be asked if you want to share the folder. If you are not using an administrator account, you will need to obtain permission from the administrator to share a folder. You can choose not to share the folder, which does not require permission.

You can create new libraries to collect folders for a particular use. You can delete any library, but you should not delete any of the four default libraries.

1. Key **File Explorer** in the Search charm to open the *File Explorer* See Figure 1-16.
2. Click on the C drive under Computer to expand the list of folders.
3. Locate the Century21 folder you created earlier in this lesson.
4. Click the folder once to select it. Then right-click the file to open a drop-down menu. Select Include in library to display a list of libraries.
5. Click Documents. If prompted, click No, don't share this folder.
6. Note that the Century21 (C:) folder is now displayed below the Documents library in the navigation pane.

### File Management

The *File Explorer* Home tab allows you to manage and manipulate files and folders in a number of ways. You can create a new folder, copy and paste or move files and folders to new locations, rename files and folders, and delete files and folders you no longer need. See Figure 1-17.

**Figure 1-17** File Explorer Home tab

### Create Folders

1. Open *File Explorer*. Tap or click This PC.
2. Select the location of the new folder in the Navigation Pane.
3. Create a new folder by selecting New Folder from the Home tab.
4. Where you see *New Folder*, key the name for the new folder.
5. Tap ENTER or click outside the folder to have the computer accept the folder name you keyed in step 4.

### Delete Files or Folders

1. Select the file or folder you would like to delete.
2. Click the Delete button on the Home tab.

 If you copy or move a file to a location that contains a file with the same name as the one you are moving or copying, Windows will ask if you want to replace the existing file.

## Punctuation Guides  (continued)

### Use an exclamation point

1. After emphatic interjections.

   Wow!      Hey there!      What a day!

2. After sentences that are clearly exclamatory.

   "I won't go!" she said with determination.
   How good it was to see you in New Orleans last week!

### Use a hyphen

1. To join parts of compound words expressing the numbers twenty-one through ninety-nine.

   Thirty-five delegates attended the national convention.

2. To join compound adjectives preceding a noun they modify as a unit.

   End-of-term grades will be posted on the classroom door.

3. After each word or figure in a series of words or figures that modify the same noun (suspended hyphenation).

   Meeting planners made first-, second-, and third-class reservations.

4. To spell out a word.

   The sign read, "For your c-o-n-v-i-e-n-c-e."  Of course, the correct word is c-o-n-v-e-n-i-e-n-c-e.

5. To form certain compound nouns.

   WGAL-TV    spin-off    teacher-counselor    AFL-CIO

### Use italic

To indicate titles of books, plays, movies, magazines, and newspapers.  (Titles may be keyed in ALL CAPS or underlined.)

   A review of *Runaway Jury* appeared in *The New York Times*.

### Use parentheses

1. To enclose parenthetical or explanatory matter and added information.

   Amendments to the bylaws (Exhibit A) are enclosed.

2. To enclose identifying letters or figures in a series.

   Check these factors: (1) period of time, (2) rate of pay, and (3) nature of duties.

3. To enclose figures that follow spelled-out amounts to give added clarity or emphasis.

   The total award is fifteen hundred dollars ($1,500).

### Use a question mark

At the end of a sentence that is a direct question.  But use a period after requests in the form of a question (whenever the expected answer is action, not words).

   What has been the impact of the Information Superhighway?
   Will you complete the enclosed form and return it to me.

### Use quotation marks

1. To enclose direct quotations.

   Professor Dye asked, "Are you spending the summer in Europe?"
   Was it Emerson who said, "To have a friend is to be one"?

2. To enclose titles of articles, poems, songs, television programs, and unpublished works, such as theses and dissertations.

   "Talk of the Town" in the *New Yorker*     "Fog" by Sandburg
   "Survivor" in prime time                          "Memory" from *Cats*

3. To enclose special words or phrases or coined words (words not in dictionary usage).

   The words "phony" and "braggart" describe him, according to coworkers.
   The presenter annoyed the audience with phrases like "uh" and "you know."

### Use a semicolon

1. To separate two or more independent clauses in a compound sentence when the conjunction is omitted.

   Being critical is easy; being constructive is not so easy.

2. To separate independent clauses when they are joined by a conjunctive adverb, such as *consequently* or *therefore*.

   I work mornings; therefore, I prefer an afternoon interview.

3. To separate a series of phrases or clauses (especially if they contain commas) that are introduced by a colon.

   Al spoke in these cities: Denver, CO; Erie, PA; and Troy, NY.

4. To precede an abbreviation or word that introduces an explanatory statement.

   She organized her work; for example, naming folders and files to indicate degrees or urgency.

### Use an underline

To call attention to words or phrases (or use quotation marks or italic).

   Take the presenter's advice: <u>Stand</u> up, <u>speak</u> up, and then <u>sit</u> down.
   Students often confuse <u>its</u> and <u>it's</u>.

3. You can also right-click the file or folder.  Choose Delete from the pop-up menu.
4. Answer Yes when asked whether you want to send the file to the Recycle Bin folder.

### Rename a File or Folder

1. Select the file or folder you would like to rename.
2. Click the Rename button on the Home tab.
3. Key the new name of the file or folder and tap **ENTER**.
4. You can also right-click the file or folder.  Choose Rename from the pop-up menu.
5. Key a new name for the file or folder.  Click a blank area of the right pane to accept the new name.

### Copy and Paste a File or Folder

1. Select the file or folder you would like to copy.
2. Click the Copy button on the Home tab.
3. Open the new location for the file or folder and click Paste.  The file or folder will exist in both locations.

### Move/Cut and Paste a File or Folder

1. Select the file or folder you would like to move.
2. Click Cut.
3. Open the new location for the file or folder and click Paste.  The file or folder will exist only in the new location.

1. Open *File Explorer* and click the triangle to the left of the Pictures library in the Navigation Pane to expand the list of folders for this library.
2. Expand the Public Pictures folder and click the Sample Pictures folder to display the sample pictures included with *Windows*.
3. Copy and paste the first four pictures to the Century 21 folder in the Documents library.
4. Expand the Videos library, expand the Public Videos folder, and click the Sample Videos folder.
5. Move the sample video to the Century 21 folder by using cut and paste.
6. Open the Century 21 folder to display the files in the file list.  Rename the pictures as **Picture 1, Picture 2, Picture 3,** and **Picture 4**.
7. Delete the sample video file.
8. Close *File Explorer*.

### Working with Files in the File List

*Windows* may or may not show file extensions for known file types such as the JPEG and WMV files you worked with in the previous activity.  Although each file type has its own unique icon, displaying extensions allows you to easily identify each file type in a file list.  You can change a folder view option to display file extensions.  Using one of your Folders, select the View tab in *File Explorer*.  In the Show/Hide group, check File name extensions to show the type of files in your folder.  Use the selections in the Layout group to see how the files in your folder are displayed as well as the information shown.

To locate a file, use the search box in the upper-right corner of the *File Explorer* window.  As you key the search term, Windows begins searching in the current location and then displays all instances that match the search term.

**TIP** Note that as long as the file or folder remains in the Recycle Bin, it has not been completely removed from the computer.  From the Recycle Bin, you can restore the file if you need it.

**TIP** Because *Windows* begins searching in the current folder, make sure to select the folder or drive where you think the file might be located before you start the search.

## Punctuation Guides

### Use an apostrophe

1. As a symbol for *feet* in charts, forms, and tables or as a symbol for *minutes*. (The quotation mark may be used as a symbol for *seconds* and *inches*.)

   12' x 16'    3' 54"    8' 6" x 10' 8"

2. As a symbol to indicate the omission of letters or figures (as in contractions).

   can't    do's and don'ts    Class of '14

3. To form the plural of most figures, letters, and words used as words rather than for their meaning: Add the apostrophe and *s*. In market quotations and decades, form the plural of figures by the addition of *s* only.

   7's    ten's    ABC's    Century 4s    1960s

4. To show possession: Add the apostrophe and *s* to (a) a singular noun and (b) a plural noun that does not end in *s*.

   a woman's watch    men's shoes    girl's bicycle

   Add the apostrophe and *s* to a proper name of one syllable that ends in *s*.

   Bess's Cafeteria    James's hat    Jones's bill

   Add the apostrophe only after (a) plural nouns ending in *s* and (b) a proper name of more than one syllable that ends in *s* or *z*.

   girls' camp    Adams' home    Martinez' report

   Add the apostrophe (and *s*) after the last noun in a series to indicate joint or common possession by two or more persons; however, add the possessive to each of the nouns to show separate possession by two or more persons.

   Lewis and Clark's expedition
   the secretary's and the treasurer's reports

### Use a colon

1. To introduce a listing.

   These poets are my favorites:  Shelley, Keats, and Frost.

2. To introduce a question or a long direct quotation.

   The question is this:  Did you study for the test?

3. Between hours and minutes expressed in figures.

   10:15 a.m.    4:30 p.m.    12:00 midnight

### Use a comma (or commas)

1. After (a) introductory phrases or clauses and (b) words in a series.

   When you finish keying the report, please give it to Mr. Kent.
   We will play the Mets, Expos, and Cubs in our next home stand.

2. To set off short direct quotations.

   Mrs. Ramirez replied, "No, the report is not finished."

3. Before and after (a) appositives—words that come together and refer to the same person, thing, or idea—and (b) words of direct address.

   Colette, the assistant manager, will chair the next meeting.
   Please call me, Erika, if I can be of further assistance.

4. To set off nonrestrictive clauses (not necessary to meaning of sentence), but not restrictive clauses (necessary to meaning).

   Your report, which deals with that issue, raised many questions.
   The man who organized the conference is my teacher.

5. To separate the day from the year in dates and the city from the state in addresses.

   July 4, 2005    St. Joseph, Missouri    Moose Point, AK

6. To separate two or more parallel adjectives (adjectives that modify the noun separately and that could be separated by the word *and* instead of the comma).

   The big, loud bully was ejected after he pushed the coach.
   The big, powerful car zoomed past the cheering crowd.
   Cynthia played a black lacquered grand piano at her concert.

   A small red fox squeezed through the fence to avoid the hounds.

7. To separate (a) unrelated groups of figures that occur together and (b) whole numbers into groups of three digits each. (Omit commas from years and page, policy, room, serial, and telephone numbers.)

   By the year 2015, 1,200 more local students will be enrolled.
   The supplies listed on Invoice #274068 are for Room 1953.

### Use a dash

Create a dash by keying two hyphens or one em-dash.

1. For emphasis.

   The skater—in a clown costume—dazzled with fancy footwork.

2. To indicate a change of thought.

   We may tour the Orient—but I'm getting ahead of my story.

3. To emphasize the name of an author when it follows a direct quotation.

   "All the world's a stage. . . ."—Shakespeare

4. To set off expressions that break off or interrupt speech.

   "Jay, don't get too close to the—."  I spoke too late.
   "Today—er—uh," the anxious presenter began.

You can change the layout of the file list to see files represented by icons of various sizes, in a list, or with details, as shown in Figure 1-18. Changing the layout can make it easier to identify files, especially picture files, and can give you important information such as when a file was modified.

Figure 1-18  The View tab of *File Explorer*

To get additional information about a file, you can right-click on it in the file list and view the properties in a pop-up window. These properties can tell you the type of file, the author's name, the file size, and when the file was created, modified, and last saved. You can add properties to a file directly from this pane.

If you have a number of files that you want to send to someone else, you can compress them to make the file transfer faster. Select the files, right-click, point to Send to, and then click Compressed (zipped) folder.

1. With the contents of the Century 21 folder visible in the file list, click the View tab of File Explorer. In the Show/hide group, check the Filename extensions box. You can now see the file extensions for the files in the folder.
2. Click the C drive under Computer in the navigation pane. In the search box, key **Jellyfish.** Windows begins searching at once and should display several instances of the jellyfish image, including the original file you copied in the Sample Pictures folder.
3. When the search is complete, click the Century 21 folder in the Documents library.
4. Click the View tab and select Files from the Layout group. Then select Large Icons. Finally, change the layout to Details.
5. Open *Microsoft Word* to create a new document. Key the following text:

   The accompanying files show the high quality of samples available in Windows.

6. Save the file as **2b activity 1** in the Century 21 folder, and then close the file.
7. Switch back to *File Explorer* and display the contents of the Century 21 folder. Click the **2b activity 1** file and view the contents in the far right pane.
8. Click the Picture1.jpg file, hold down Shift, and click Picture4.jpg. Right-click on the selected files, point to Send to, and then click Compressed (zipped) folder.
9. Rename the compressed file as **2b sample files**.
10. Close *File Explorer*.

## Leadership

Consider these attributes of a successful leader, and write your responses to the following questions in the form of a ¶.

- A successful leader accepts responsibility and accountability for results.
- A successful leader has self-discipline, good character, and is committed to personal development.
- A successful leader is a great communicator.
- A successful leader has great people skills.

# Reference Guide

## Language and Writing References

### Capitalization Guides

**Capitalize**

1. The first word of every sentence and complete quotation. Do not capitalize (a) fragments of quotations or (b) a quotation resumed within a sentence.

   Crazy Horse said, "I will return to you in stone."
   Gandhi's teaching inspired "nonviolent revolutions."
   "It is . . . fitting and proper," Lincoln said, "that we . . . do this."

2. The first word after a colon if that word begins a complete sentence.

   Remember:  Keep the action in your fingers.
   These sizes were in stock:  small, medium, and extra large.

3. First, last, and all other words in titles except articles, conjunctions, or prepositions of four or fewer letters.

   *The Beak of the Finch*          *Raleigh News and Observer*
   "The Phantom of the Opera"

4. An official title when it precedes a name or when used elsewhere if it is a title of distinction.

   In what year did Juan Carlos become King of Spain?
   Masami Chou, our class president, met Senator Thurmond.

5. Personal titles and names of people and places.

   Did you see Mrs. Watts and Gloria while in Miami?

6. All proper nouns and their derivatives.

   Mexico     Mexican border     Uganda     Ugandan economy

7. Days of the week, months of the year, holidays, periods of history, and historic events.

   | | | |
   |---|---|---|
   | Friday | July | Labor Day |
   | Middle Ages | Vietnam War | Woodstock |

8. Geographic regions, localities, and names.

   | | |
   |---|---|
   | the East Coast | Upper Peninsula Michigan |
   | Ohio River | the Deep South |

9. Street, avenue, company, etc., when used with a proper noun.

   Fifth Avenue     Wall Street     Monsanto Company

10. Names of organizations, clubs, and buildings.

    | | |
    |---|---|
    | National Hockey League | Four-H Club |
    | Biltmore House | Omni Hotel |

11. A noun preceding a figure except for common nouns, such as line, page, and sentence.

    Review Rules 1 to 18 in Chapter 5, page 149.

12. Seasons of the year only when they are personified.

    the soft kiss of Spring     the icy fingers of Winter

### Number Expression Guides

**Use words for**

1. Numbers from one to ten except when used with numbers above ten, which are keyed as figures.  Common business practice is to use figures for all numbers except those that begin a sentence.

   Did you visit all eight websites, or only four?
   Buy 15 textbooks and 8 workbooks.

2. A number beginning a sentence.

   Twelve of the new shrubs have died; 48 are doing well.

3. The shorter of two numbers used together.

   fifty 45-cent stamps      150 twenty-cent stamps

4. Isolated fractions or indefinite numbers in a sentence.

   Nearly seventy members voted, which is almost one-fourth.

5. Names of small-numbered streets and avenues (ten and under).

   The theater is at the corner of Third Avenue and 54th Street.

**Use figures for**

1. Dates and times except in very formal writing.

   The flight will arrive at 9:48 a.m. on March 14.
   The ceremony took place the fifth of June at eleven o'clock.

2. A series of fractions and/or mixed numbers.

   Key 1/4, 1/2, 5/6, and 7 3/4.

3. Numbers following nouns.

   Case 1849 is reviewed in Volume 5, page 9.

4. Measures, weights, and dimensions.

   6 feet 9 inches          7 pounds 4 ounces
   8.5 inches by 11 inches

5. Definite numbers used with percent (%), but use words for indefinite percentages.

   The late fee is 15 percent of the overdue payment.
   The brothers put in nearly fifty percent of the start-up capital.

6. House numbers except house number *One*.

   My home is at 8 Rose Lane; my office is at One Rose Plaza.

7. Amounts of money except when spelled for emphasis (as in legal documents).  Even amounts are keyed without the decimal.  Large amounts (a million or more) are keyed as shown.

   | | | | |
   |---|---|---|---|
   | $17.75 | 75 cents | $775 | seven hundred dollars ($700) |
   | $7,500 | $7 million | $7.2 million | $7 billion |

**Think Critically**

1. What attributes of a successful leader apply to ethical and appropriate computer use?
2. Describe ways in which you have demonstrated leadership abilities when using the computer, the Internet, or a mobile device such as a cell phone.
3. Write your responses in ¶ form, and give the page to your instructor.

## LESSON 3   Maintaining a System

OUTCOMES
- Discuss the importance of regular maintenance.
- Learn software maintenance tasks.
- Learn hardware maintenance tasks.
- Set up a maintenance schedule.

### 3A

**Understanding the Importance of Routine Maintenance**

Maintaining your system can prevent catastrophes

Maintaining a computer system is not merely a good idea; it is essential to safeguarding your investment in hardware and software. If you intend to continue to work efficiently, you need to schedule maintenance on a routine basis. Regular maintenance is an important responsibility not only for an organization's IT department but also for the individual user.

A number of problems can occur if a system's hardware and software are not maintained. For instance:

- Your computer may start slowly or take an unusual amount of time to perform routine tasks.
- Applications may stop working temporarily, or the entire system may lock up.
- Your Internet connection may be slow.

You can eliminate some common problems that affect computer performance by performing regular maintenance on your software and hardware. *Windows* provides system tools specifically designed to help you keep your system in tune. Even if you are not a computer expert, you can also do some physical maintenance on your system that will help to prevent hardware problems. Setting up and following a checklist of regular maintenance procedures is the best way to ensure that you and your system can work at optimum efficiency.

The following sections discuss maintenance tasks that any computer user can perform. More advanced maintenance tasks should be undertaken only by professionals. Tasks that should be performed only by a computer specialist include any chore requiring a computer's case to be opened, such as cleaning inside the case, upgrading RAM, or replacing a hard drive.

### 3B

**Performing Software Maintenance**

A slow computer that freezes up or fails to process data efficiently is likely to have some or all of the following problems:

- Unnecessary files such as temporary files or files that download when you view some web pages
- Too many programs or processes running at the same time, particularly at start-up
- Fragmented files
- Computer viruses or spyware
- Inadequate hardware for the programs running

The issue of inadequate hardware—not enough RAM, or a processor that is not fast enough for the programs you want to run—is one that should be addressed when you are buying the system or software, and thus it is not really part of a routine maintenance program.

The issue of what programs start with the computer is one that should be handled by an expert. Other issues on this list can, however, be handled by regular use of standard maintenance utilities and a reasonable approach to what you install on your system.

Key 2 5' writings on all ¶s combined; find *gwam* and errors.

 **all letters used**

| | gwam 3' | 5' |
|---|---|---|

Small businesses are the majority of United States businesses.  They | 5 | 3
are a vital part of the economy.  As we analyze the data, they provide jobs | 10 | 6
for more than half of the workers in our country.  Each year, most of the | 14 | 9
new jobs created come from small businesses.  They generate more than | 19 | 11
half of our nation's income.  Small businesses have been and will always | 24 | 14
be a powerful force in the economy. | 26 | 16

Small businesses often create more innovations than do larger | 30 | 18
corporations.  Small companies often attract competent and talented | 35 | 21
people who develop new products or new ways to use current products. | 39 | 24
These small business owners have gone on to gain immense fame and | 44 | 26
fortune.  Some of the founders of these great empires have gained a place | 48 | 29
in our own history.  Others have changed the way business is done today. | 53 | 32
At the end of the day, we quote their great wisdom and we try to duplicate | 58 | 35
their successes in hopes that one day our ideas will become a success. | 63 | 38

Small businesses benefit us in other ways and offer us the products | 67 | 40
and services we have grown to expect. Their impact is felt at home and | 72 | 43
around the globe. They provide revenue and are the engines that drive our | 77 | 46
local, state, and national economies. Small businesses provide growth and | 82 | 49
innovation to the areas in which they were founded. | 85 | 51

gwam 3' | 1 | 2 | 3 | 4
5' | 1 | 2 | 3

## Checking for Viruses and Spyware

A problem that very frequently causes your system to run slowly is an undetected collection of spyware programs. A problem that can prevent your computer from running at all is infection by one or more of the many hundreds of viruses that are constantly circulating around the Internet.

Computer viruses can lead to serious system problems

Every system needs a program for detecting malware, and every user needs a plan for running that program on a regular basis. Malware such as viruses and spyware are all too easy to pick up during Web browsing sessions and from plausible-seeming email messages. It is essential to detect dangerous programs before they can infect your system. You can configure detection programs to scan on a regular schedule to locate potential threats.

You may have separate programs for detecting viruses and controlling spyware, or you may use one program that detects all kinds of malware. Many malware detection programs are available for free download, although you may not receive automatic updates to them unless you pay for the programs.

More than any other program, antivirus and spyware programs must be kept up to date because new threats are always arising. Antivirus and spyware programs generally configure themselves to search for updates automatically every day so you do not have to remember to do so, but it is your responsibility to make sure the automatic updates are turned on and working correctly. If you do not have automatic updates on, you need to schedule updates on a frequent basis.

It is also important to view settings to see what the program is checking during regular scans. You should confirm that it is checking all files on all drives in your system, as well as email and instant messaging attachments. You usually also have some control over checking of other threats, such as tracking cookies and unwanted scripts.

1. Open your antivirus program by keying its name in the Search charm. Ask your teacher for the name of the program your lab or school is using.
2. Check the current schedule for scanning your system. How often is the scan scheduled, and when does the scan begin?
3. Check the update schedule to make sure automatic updates are on.
4. View settings to see what kinds of files the program is checking and what other kinds of threats the program is looking for.
5. Close the antivirus program without making any changes.

 **TIP** Antivirus software should always be configured to start with the operating system. This is especially important if the computer has a live Internet connection when it is running.

 **TIP** If you are not using an administrator account, the settings will be grayed out, but you will still be able to see them.

2. Apply the following animations:

## Animation

| Slide No. | Animation | Effect Option | Effect Option: Sequence | Duration |
|---|---|---|---|---|
| Slide 2 | ★ Wheel | ◪ 3 Spokes | ⬡ As One Object | 01.00 |
| Slide 3 | ★ Wheel | ✳ 8 Spokes | One by One | 01.00 |
| Slide 4 | ☆ Fly In | ↗ From Bottom-Left | All at Once | 00.50 |
| Slides 6 & 8 | ☆ Zoom | ★ Object Center | | 00.50 |
| Slides 10 & 12 | ☆ Shape | ⤢ In | All at Once | 01.00 |

3. **Save as:** *145c presentation.*

**TRY IT!**
If permitted on classroom equipment, you can work with Windows Update settings in Appendix B, My Personal-Use Folder.

### Keeping Other Programs Updated

As with antivirus and spyware programs, a user should make sure that programs such as the operating system, browser, and other important applications are configured to receive and install regular updates. Keeping software up to date is part of any good maintenance program. Updates address issues such as security problems and operational improvements; by updating regularly, you ensure that your programs are working as efficiently as they can.

**QUICK** ✔

You dislike seeing prompts to update your operating system, and you especially dislike the way your operating system installs them after you turn off your computer. You decide to turn off automatic updates and instead make a note to yourself to update your operating system once a month. Will your decision help you work more efficiently?

## 3C

### Performing Hardware Maintenance

**TIP** Never spray any kind of liquid near any computer component. Always spray on the cleaning cloth.

**TIP** Keyboards that are shared by a number of individuals can spread infectious diseases such as colds and the flu. Keep your keyboard clean!

Avoid computer problems by taking safety precautions

Most serious inside-the-case hardware maintenance should be done by IT professionals, but you can perform a number of chores outside the box that will improve system performance and help you avoid having to call in the pros. Turn off the computer before doing these tasks.

- Wipe the monitor with a soft, damp cloth to remove dust, fingerprints, and other spots that interfere with your view of the screen. The dampening agent depends on the type of monitor; check maintenance information from the monitor's manufacturer to determine the best cleaning agent for your monitor.
- Vacuum around the computer case to remove dust and hair. Dust that has been sucked into a computer case by the system fan can collect on hardware inside the case and ultimately cause it to fail.
- An amazing amount of dust and dirt can collect around the keys of the keyboard, causing keys to stick. On a laptop, material that sifts in around the keys may end up inside the computer, where it can affect the motherboard and other sensitive components. Use a can of compressed air to blow away dirt. Then dampen a cloth with alcohol or a disinfectant to wipe each key.
- Wipe the mouse and each of its buttons or wheels with a damp cloth to clean. You can also improve mouse operations by cleaning the mouse pad with a damp cloth (or just replace the mouse pad periodically).

In addition to performing these types of routine maintenance, you can head off trouble by adhering to some common computer safety rules.

- Keep air vents unobstructed to prevent the computer from overheating.
- Keep food and liquids away from your computer. Spilled liquids may damage your keyboard or, in a laptop, may ultimately corrode the motherboard.
- Keep wiring under control to prevent people from tripping over cords and knocking computer components to the ground.
- Avoid electrical discharge anywhere near the inside of your computer. Electrical vacuum cleaners, which are prone to static electricity, are usually not used when cleaning the inside of a computer for this reason.
- Keep your computer in a room-temperature environment; avoid locations with excessive heat or cold.

Slide 8

Slide 10

Slide 12

## 145C

### Apply Transitions and Animations

1. Continue working with the presentation you started in 145B. Apply the following transitions:

**Transitions**

| Slide No. | Transition | Effect Option | Duration |
|---|---|---|---|
| Slide 3 | Vortex | From Left | 01.25 |
| Slides 5, 7, 9, & 11 | Glitter | Diamonds from Left | 02.00 |
| Slides 6, & 8 | Rotate | From Right | 01.50 |
| Slides 10 & 12 | Conveyor | From Right | 01.60 |
| Slide 13 | Doors | Vertical | 01.40 |

Knowing what you can do to maintain your computer system is half the battle; your next step is to set up a schedule for performing those tasks. If you work in a company, it is likely that your IT department has such a schedule in place already. If you are an individual user, you are responsible for creating and following your own schedule.

Experts suggest that you schedule tasks on a daily, weekly, or monthly basis according to how important the tasks are for your system's operational well-being. The following table shows suggested frequency of maintenance tasks. You may want to perform some, such as backups, more often. Some tasks are already automated for this schedule.

| Daily | Check for antivirus updates |
|---|---|
| | Check for spyware updates |
| **Weekly** | Update Windows and other applications |
| | Delete temporary files |
| | Do a full backup of important files |
| | Run a complete virus/spyware scan |
| **Monthly or as needed** | Defragment the hard drive (if this is not automatic) |
| | Uninstall programs not being used regularly |
| | Clean computer components |

**Table 1-1** Suggested maintenance schedule

**QUICK ✔**

1. Following the guidelines on maintenance you have read about in this lesson, create a table or chart for the next month and assign regular maintenance tasks by day, week, or month.

2. Create a checklist to post beside your computer that shows maintenance tasks so you can check them off as you complete them.

# LESSON 4    Keeping Resources Secure

**OUTCOMES**

- Safeguard files.
- Maintain system security.
- Recover from disasters.
- Explore online and workplace safety issues.

**4A**

**Safeguarding Files**

Some strategies you learned in Lesson 3 for maintaining your computer can also be used to safeguard its resources. When you back up files to an external drive, for example, you have the option of copying files away from your system to a safe storage location. Any disaster that might affect your computer, such as fire, flood, tornado, or the like, will not completely wipe out your files if you have backups stored elsewhere.

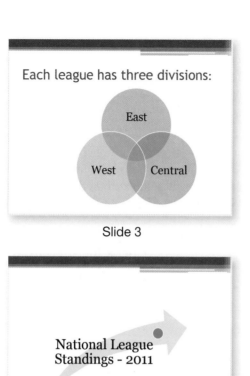

Slide 3

Slide 5

Slide 7

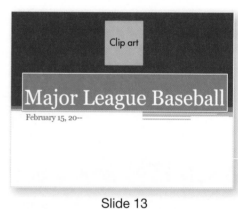

Slide 9

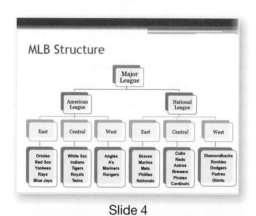

Slide 11

Slide 13

## MLB Structure

Slide 4

## American League Standings

| East | | Central | | West | |
|------|------|---------|------|------|------|
| TEAM | G.B. | TEAM | G.B. | TEAM | G.B. |
| Yankees | | Detroit | | Texas | |
| Rays | 6.0 | Cleveland | 15.0 | Los Angeles | 10.0 |
| Boston | 7.0 | White Sox | 16.0 | Oakland | 22.0 |
| Toronto | 16.0 | Royals | 24.0 | Seattle | 29.0 |
| Baltimore | 28.0 | Twins | 32.0 | | |

Slide 6

Use a password to protect files or other resources

You have some other options for safeguarding individual files to protect them from unauthorized access or to prevent users from changing content without permission. Password protection, editing restrictions, and permissions can be applied from within an application. You can also apply a digital signature as a way to authenticate the author of the document and indicate to other readers that any changes made to the document after the signature was applied may be unauthorized.

## Password Protecting a File

You are no doubt familiar with the value of using a password to prove your identity when you log on to your computer or the Internet. You may also need to use a password when you set up online accounts that allow you to make secure transactions online.

You can apply a password to files you create in application programs to protect them from unauthorized access. Password protection can prevent someone from opening the file without providing the correct password. In an application such as *Microsoft Word 2013*, you can apply password protection from Backstage view. To display the Backstage view, which is where you manage information about your Microsoft documents, click File.

1. Start *Microsoft Word*. In the new, blank document, key the following text:

   Protecting your files is a way of protecting scarce resources such as the time required to research, write, and edit a report.

2. Click File, click Info, and then click Protect Document.
3. Click Encrypt with Password to open the Encrypt Document dialog box (Figure 1-19).

**Figure 1-19** Key a password in the Password box

4. Key your name as the password in the following format: First_Last. Click OK.
5. Rekey the password to confirm, and click OK.
6. Save the file in your Century21 folder in the Documents Library as *4a activity1*.
7. Click File and then click Close.
8. Click File. In the Recent list, click *4a activity1*. When the Password dialog box appears, key your password and click OK to open the file.
9. Close the file but leave *Word* open.

10. Which mentor's group had the lowest average GPA for this semester?
11. Which mentor's group had the highest average GPA for this semester?
12. Which mentor's group had the +-biggest increase in GPA?
13. Which mentor's group had the smallest increase in GPA?
14. Should we continue the Academic Focus Groups? Please explain your answer.
15. **Save as:** *144e answer sheet.*

## 144F

**Report**

1. Open *df 144f report* and format it as a report.
2. Key **Jones Memorial Hospital Update** as the first line of the report. Format it in Title style.
3. Format the side headings in Heading 1 style.
4. Insert a page number at the bottom center of the pages, but hide it on page 1.
5. Insert a table of contents before page 1. It should contain page numbers, dot leaders, and hyperlinks.
6. Key **Page** above the first page number.
7. Key **Table of Contents** in Title Style as the first line on the page.
8. Key **Return to Top** below the last line of the report.
9. Bookmark the title of the report.
10. Hyperlink the text *Return to Top* to the bookmark.
11. **Save as:** *144f report.*

## LESSON 145   Presentation and Input Skills

**OUTCOMES**
- Assess presentation skills.
- Assess input speed and accuracy skills.

**Business Document**
- Create a Presentation

## 145B

**Presentation**

1. Open *df 145b pp* and create the slides shown.
2. Order the slide by the slide number beneath the slide.

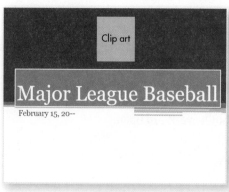

Slide 1

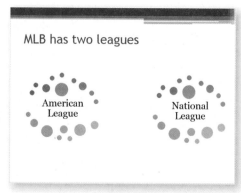

Slide 2

## Maintaining System Security

Safeguarding your system is as important as maintaining it

Keeping your system secure is every bit as important as the routine maintenance you learned about in Lesson 3. Recovery from a determined cyber attack is almost always expensive in one way or another. If the only way to eliminate the virus is to reformat your system, you may lose all your files.

As an individual computer user or in your role as a responsible corporate user, you have an obligation to keep your system safe and secure. You have already read about ways to keep your system secure, in this lesson and in Lesson 3. The following sections cover the most important steps you can take to prevent or minimize the damage from a security breach.

### Critical Defensive Measures

The best defense against security attacks is a good offense, in the form of good-quality antivirus and spyware applications. These applications are designed to scan your system continuously as you work, to check emails for problems, and even to recommend against opening some websites that may threaten your system.

Even the best security program, however, can fail to prevent access if it is not kept current with regular updates. Make sure that your antivirus program is always on and always up to date, and run a full system scan at least once a week.

It is equally important to keep other programs updated, especially browsers and your operating system. Many of the patches and fixes that are installed with updates to these programs address security issues, such as programming issues that can allow unauthorized access to your system.

Another important defensive application is a firewall. While antivirus and spyware programs can detect malware that has been downloaded to your computer, a firewall can prevent such malware from getting into your computer at all. A firewall works by checking incoming data against specific rules and then either allows the data to pass or blocks it. Because many computers today maintain a constant connection to the Internet whenever they are on, having a firewall in place to control the data stream is essential.

In a large organization, the IT department determines what kinds of data can pass through the firewall and monitors firewalls constantly for evidence of cyber attack. Home users rely on the firewalls that accompany their antivirus software or on the Windows Firewall. Figure 1-20 shows the Windows Firewall is connected and is protecting access to the PC and network.

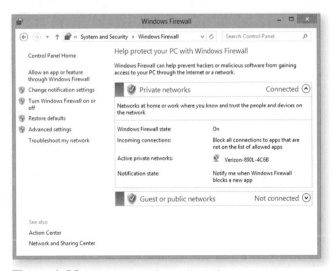

**Figure 1-20** *Windows 8* firewall settings

4. Save the query as **144c increased gpa> 1 Females**.

5. Run a query to show all students who increased their GPA by more than 2 points. Include the same information as in No. 1.

6. Save the query as **144c increased gpa> 2**.

## 144D

**Complete Query Worksheet**

Each focus group is supervised by a peer mentor who has already completed the course with an A grade. The coordinator would like to know which mentors were most successful in increasing the GPAs of the students in their group.

Create queries to provide the information needed to complete the following table. Open **df 144d worksheet** and record your answers in the table provided. **Save as: 144d worksheet**.

| Mentor | Average GPA for Last Semester | Average GPA for Current Semester | Increase/Decrease in GPA |
|---|---|---|---|
| Barton | | | |
| Buhl | | | |
| Comstock | | | |
| Davidson | | | |
| Hofacker | | | |
| Jackson | | | |
| Larson | | | |
| Layton | | | |
| Martins | | | |
| Monday | | | |
| Poquette | | | |
| Rose | | | |
| Rubio | | | |
| Sanchez | | | |
| Smyth | | | |

## 144E

**Analyze Information from Queries**

Open **df 144e answer sheet**. Use the queries created in 145 B, C, and D to answer the questions.

1. What was the average GPA for last semester?

2. What was the average GPA for this semester?

3. How much did the average GPA increase or decrease from last semester to this semester?

4. How many students increased their GPA this semester by at least 1 point over last semester?

5. How many of those students increasing their GPA by 1 point were female?

6. How many of those students increasing their GPA by 1 point were males?

7. How many students increased their GPA this semester by at least 2 points over last semester?

8. Which mentor's group started with the lowest average GPA from last semester?

9. Which mentor's group started with the highest average GPA from last semester?

## Permissions and Passwords

Whenever possible, limit access to your system or its files by restricting permissions and requiring passwords. You can control who has permission to make changes to your system by creating only one administrator account and making sure it is used only to perform routine system maintenance tasks.

You learned in the first part of this lesson about the importance of using a standard user account rather than an administrator account for ordinary computer work. You may be surprised to know that some routine tasks, such as browsing the Internet, can be more dangerous if you are using an administrator account. If you pick up a virus or a Trojan horse, your systems are at far greater risk when you are logged on as an administrator. This is the reason Microsoft suggests that you use a standard account for everyday tasks and use your administrator account only to adjust system settings.

When creating new user accounts, make a practice of creating standard accounts. The fewer people have permission to change system settings, the more secure your computer will be.

Get the most out of your password protection by using unique, strong passwords for every instance when you need a password. Using the same password over and over may make it easy for you to remember, but it will also make it easy for anyone who gains unauthorized access to your computer to get into sensitive files and important accounts. Likewise, make a practice of not sharing your password with anyone.

A strong password is at least 14 characters long, with a mixture of capital and lowercase letters, numbers, and symbols. Try to avoid obvious options such as your birthday, your address, or the names of friends or family members. Microsoft offers a simple method for converting a meaningful sentence into a strong password.

1. Start with a sentence:
   Wait and see what I bought for you
2. Remove spaces from the sentence:
   WaitandseewhatIboughtforyou
3. Replace words with numbers, symbols, or shorthand:
   W8&CwatIbot4U
4. Add length to the string with numbers that mean something to you:
   W8&CwatIbot4U91

If you doubt that you can remember your strong passwords, you can write them down and keep them in a safe place. Do not store your passwords on your computer or near your computer.

## Commonsense Security Practices

Use common sense to avoid putting your computer and its resources at risk:

- Access only safe websites, and be careful what you download from the Internet.
- Don't run programs if you are not sure where they came from or that they are safe.
- Don't open attachments to email if you don't know the sender, and even then use caution. Some malware can use the email contact lists from legitimate users to send dangerous attachments. If you are not certain about an attachment, save it to your hard drive, and then use your antivirus software to scan the file.
- Turn off your computer when you are not using it. If you share a computer and cannot turn it off, log out of your account to protect your files.
- Keep your computer physically safe by making sure it cannot be reached from an open window. You can also attach a lock to secure your computer to an immovable object.

 **TIP** If you have a number of passwords to organize for access to sensitive information such as bank accounts, you may want to invest in a password manager, which allows you to store your account names and passwords in an encrypted database.

## LESSON 144 | Database and Report Formatting Skills

**OUTCOME**
- Assess database and report formatting skills.

### Business Documents
- Create Queries with Computed Fields
- Create Queries with Criteria
- Complete Query Worksheet
- Analyze Information from Queries
- Business Report

---

**144B**

**Create Query with Computed Fields**

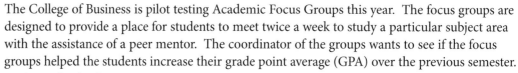

The College of Business is pilot testing Academic Focus Groups this year. The focus groups are designed to provide a place for students to meet twice a week to study a particular subject area with the assistance of a peer mentor. The coordinator of the groups wants to see if the focus groups helped the students increase their grade point average (GPA) over the previous semester.

1. Open the database *df 144b academic focus groups*.
2. Open the AFG Groups table in the *Academic Focus Groups* database.
3. Create a query that includes the following information:
   a. Last Name
   b. First Name
   c. Gender
   d. Peer Mentor Last Name
   e. Last Semester GPA
   f. Current Semester GPA
   g. GPA Increase or Decrease
4. You will need to use the Expression Builder to calculate the information for this field.
   **GPA Increase or Decrease: [Current Semester GPA]-[Last Semester GPA]**
5. Use the Totals feature to calculate the averages for the following fields:
   Last Semester GPA
   Current Semester GPA
   GPA Increase or Decrease
6. Save the query as *144b gpa increase or decrease*.

---

**144C**

**Create Queries with Criteria**

The coordinator would also like to know how many students increased their GPA by more than 1 point, how many of those who increased their GPA by more than 1 point were females, and how many increased their GPA by more than 2 points.

1. Using the *GPA Increase or Decrease* query created for 144b, create a query to show all students who increased their GPA by more than 1 point. Include the following fields in the query:
   a. Last Name
   b. First Name
   c. Gender
   d. GPA Increase or Decrease
2. Save the query as *144c increased gpa> 1*.
3. Run a query to show all female students who increased their GPA by more than 1 point. Include the same fields as in No. 1.

---

1. Review security procedures that you currently follow for your computer. For example, what kind of user account do you have? How often do you run a virus scan? What kind of firewall do you use?
2. Make a list of your current security procedures. Add to your list any procedures you are not doing that you should be doing.
3. Make a list of the passwords you currently use for various programs and accounts. Do you use some passwords more than once?
4. Review your passwords for strength. How could you modify some of your passwords to make them stronger?

## 4C

### Recovering from Disaster

© Monkey Business Images/ Shutterstock.com

An IT technician can help you recover from a virus attack

All computer users should have a plan of action in case a virus scan reveals an active "infection." If you work for a company, you may be able to appeal to an IT department for aid, but if you are working in a small company or on your own, you should know the basic steps that will help you eliminate the threat.

Experts suggest you take the following steps when you discover your system has been infected with a virus or other malware.

1. First, disconnect the computer from any network it may be connected to, to avoid spreading the virus to other systems on the network. You may also need to disconnect the computer from the Internet, especially if you suspect your computer is being used to attack other systems.
2. Clean your system using your antivirus software. You may need to use special software tools to eliminate the virus infecting your computer. Your antivirus program's manufacturer can often offer free or pay-per-incident help to clean up your computer.
3. Reinstall any programs that have been damaged by the virus. This can mean reinstalling applications as well as your operating system. Make sure you have your original software (along with registration or serial numbers) available to reinstall programs.
4. Scan your restored system to make sure all traces of the virus have been removed, making sure to use the most recent updates of your antivirus program.
5. Restore any files that have been lost or damaged, using your most recent uninfected backup.
6. Change all your passwords immediately. Some malware can capture your passwords, which can then be cracked to gain access to your programs and accounts.
7. Review your current security procedures to make sure you are doing everything you can to prevent another attack, and change procedures if you think they may have contributed to the attack.

Safeguarding your resources by following regular maintenance and standard security procedures can take time and effort. But the time, the effort, and the cost of repairing a system that has been damaged by outside attack can be far greater.

Create a chart that lists and illustrates the steps given in the previous section for recovering from a virus attack. Post the chart near your personal computer or over the desk where you usually work on your laptop.

1. Design a flyer to present the information below. Use SmartArt or WordArt, shapes or text boxes, and clip art or pictures in your flyer. You decide other formatting features.
2. Save as: *143h flyer*.

| | |
|---|---|
| Event: | Lifestyle Program for Young Adults |
| Description: | A one-hour presentation about a new program that will make it easier for you to lead a healthier life and offers financial incentives for your efforts! |
| When: | Friday, January 11 |
| Time: | 8:30 p.m. |
| Where: | Redbank High School Auditorium |
| Instructor: | Dr. Jerome T. Noseck, Certified Personal Trainer |
| Main Feature: | Participants will learn that the way we live has a real impact on how we feel. When we take care of ourselves, we have more drive and energy and better attitudes. |

1. Open *df 143i newsletter*.
2. Key the following information at the top of the newsletter:

Healthscape

Published by Jones Memorial Hospital                    February 20--

3. Format as a two-column newsletter, but have the heading information you inserted span the width of both columns.
4. Use WordArt to format the newsletter name (*Healthscape*).
5. Use 1.0 line spacing, 10-point spacing after ¶, justification, and hyphenation for the report body.
6. Format the side headings in Heading 1 style.
7. Insert a vertical line between the columns.
8. Insert the text below in a shaded text box between the first and second articles on page 1.

**Tip of the Week**

Skiers may injure their thumbs when falling if they're using ski poles with molded plastic grips, which are not flexible. The American Physical Therapy Association recommends using ski poles with soft webbing or leather straps.

9. You decide all other formatting.
10. Save as: *143i newsletter*.

## Exploring Online and Workplace Safety Issues

Proper computer posture is one aspect of workplace safety

### Online Safety

You have a responsibility to keep yourself safe when working or playing online. Careless behavior online can put not only your system but your own personal safety at risk.

- Beware of emails that seem to come from reputable sources but ask for sensitive information such as your account numbers.
- Never give your full name, personal address, phone number, school address, or other private information to individuals you do not know personally, and never agree to a face-to-face meeting alone with a person you have met online.
- If you are using a social network, follow their safety procedures to keep your account safe and control who sees your information.

### Workplace Safety

Setting up your computer and workspace correctly to avoid stress and strain on muscles, tendons, and bones is one aspect of workplace safety. To ensure that you are working comfortably and efficiently, follow these guidelines:

- Arrange your desk to minimize glare from overhead lights, desk lamps, and windows to avoid eyestrain.
- Keep hands, wrists, and forearms straight, in line, and parallel to the floor.
- Your head should be level or bent slightly forward; you should not have to look up at your monitor.
- Your shoulders and upper arms should be relaxed, and your elbows should be close to your body, bent between 90 and 120 degrees.
- Your feet should be fully supported on the floor or a footrest.
- Your back should be fully supported by your chair, and you should be sitting up straight or leaning back slightly.
- Your thighs and hips should be parallel to the floor, with knees about the same height as the hips and feet slightly forward.

To further reduce stress, change your working position frequently by stretching fingers, hands, and arms and by standing up and walking around occasionally.

Maintaining a safe office environment is another important aspect of workplace safety. Some of the responsibility for office safety falls on your employer, who should ensure that the workplace has well-marked emergency exits, proper ventilation, no hazardous materials, adequate lighting, and secure doors and windows. You are responsible for reporting any problems such as light outages or locks that don't work properly. You are also responsible for using the office resources properly—don't, for example, overload outlets with multiple plugs that could result in electrical outages or fires, and don't operate office equipment in ways that might damage it.

Your employer should also have a safety policy in place that explains what to do in the event of a fire, explosion, natural disaster, or other catastrophe. Fire extinguishers and first-aid kits should be provided at convenient locations, and training should be provided in how to use extinguishers. You can contribute to your safety by keeping emergency supplies such as a flashlight, water bottle, and nonperishable food in your desk.

## 143C

**Worksheet with Calculations and Conditional Formatting**

1. Open *df 143c worksheet*.
2. Calculate the hours worked by each employee in column G.
3. Write an IF function for calculations in column H so that all hours worked up to and including 40 are paid at the hourly rate in cell D17.
4. Write an IF function for column I to calculate overtime pay that is paid at two times the hourly rate in D17 for all hours worked over 40.
5. In column J, calculate each employee's gross pay and apply conditional formatting to highlight those who earned more than $475.
6. Calculate totals for cells G11–J11.
7. Calculate the average pay in cell D14, the minimum pay in D15, and the maximum pay in D16.
8. Use two decimal places for currency.
9. Use data bars in column I (cell I4:I10) to show different levels of overtime pay.
10. **Save as:** *143c worksheet*.

## 143D

**What If**

1. If needed, open *143c worksheet* and answer this question: What is the total payroll if the hourly rate is increased to $12.00?
2. Clear the conditional formatting in column J and then reapply to highlight those who would earn more than $525 at the $12.00 pay rate.
3. **Save as:** *143d worksheet*.

## 143E

**Letter with Linked Worksheet**

1. Open *df 143e source* (*Excel* file) and save as *143e source* but do not close it.
2. Open *df 143e destination* (*Word* file) and copy/paste the worksheet, with a link, into the letter between the first and second ¶s. Center the table horizontally in the letter and adjust the space before and after the table as needed.
3. Save the *Word* file as *143e destination* and close both files.

## 143F

**Update Letter with Link**

1. Open worksheet *143e source* and decrease the amounts in the 19+ quantity column by 5 cents. Save as *143e source* and close the file.
2. Open *Word* file *143e destination*, which will update the letter with the new amounts. Use today's date and address it to:

   Dr. Dorothy Latham

   1246 Helena Drive

   Denver, CO 80221-7463

3. **Save as:** *143f destination*.

## 143G

**Financial Functions**

1. Open a new worksheet. In cell A1, use the future value function to determine what Jamie's current $15,000 investment in stocks that she expects will earn 5 percent interest will be worth in three years if she buys no additional shares.
2. In cell A3, use the present value function to determine what amount needs to be invested today at 6 percent interest to have $20,000 for college in four years.
3. In cell A5, use the payment function to determine how much the monthly payments will need to be to pay off a five-year $4,000 student loan at 6 percent interest. The payments are made at the beginning of the month.
4. **Save as:** *143g functions*.

Assume you are working in a small business whose office is on the second floor of a building. The office space consists of three rooms, a kitchen, and a bathroom. Access to the office space is via a stairway from the first floor. The landlord has not yet replaced a decrepit fire escape, but it is only a six-foot drop from the kitchen window to the roof of the building next door.

Create an emergency plan that explains what employees should do in the event of fire or tornado. Include in your plan a list of emergency supplies that should be stored in the office or in each employee's desk.

## LESSON 5   Improving Internet Skills

**OUTCOMES**
- Use a browser more efficiently.
- Explore advanced search strategies.
- Evaluate search results.

### 5A

**Using a Browser More Efficiently**

People in all walks of life now use the Internet as their primary research option. The adage, "You can find anything on the Internet" reflects the shift toward Internet searching as the quickest way to find information on any subject, from the lyrics of a song to symptoms of medical conditions to pictures of the Martian surface.

This lesson reviews basic skills and introduces more advanced ways to work with Internet resources. Improving your Internet skills can make you a more efficient and productive worker.

#### Navigating in a Browser

The chief navigation options in a browser are located in the upper-left corner of the browser window, as shown in Figure 1-21. Use the address bar to key the address of the website you want to visit. If you have visited the site before, you may see a drop-down list of sites that begin with the same letters you are keying. You can click a site from this autocomplete list to save keying time.

Use the Back and Forward buttons to move backward and forward through pages you have previously viewed. To return to a previous web page, for example, click the Back button. Once you have clicked the Back button, you can return to the page you were viewing by clicking the Forward button.

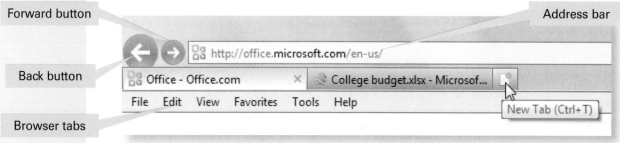

Forward button    Address bar

http://office.microsoft.com/en-us/

Back button

Office - Office.com    College budget.xlsx - Microsof...

File    Edit    View    Favorites    Tools    Help

New Tab (Ctrl+T)

Browser tabs

**Figure 1-21** Browser navigation options in *Internet Explorer 9*

## 142E

**Mail Merge Letters**

1. Create a main document in block letter format with mixed punctuation to merge with *142d data*. Save the main document file as *142e main*.
2. Perform the mail merge and print the last two letters in the merged file.
3. Save merged letters as *142e letters*.

February 15, 20--

<<AddressBlock>>

<<GreetingLine>>

This letter is to inform you that your company has been selected to participate in an experimental recycling program for various businesses in Ohio. The program will begin March 1 and is scheduled to end August 31.

<<Title>><<Last Name>>, this recycling program requires you to separate paper products into four categories for recycling purposes. The categories are white paper, newspapers, cardboard boxes, and mixed paper. The enclosed pamphlet describes in detail the kinds of paper that are to go into each of these categories.

Early in September, we will send you a survey to complete. The survey results will provide us with much of the information we need to determine if the paper recycling program will be continued and expanded to other business in the state.

Your cooperation and compliance throughout this six-month period is expected and appreciated. If you have any questions that are not answered by the information in the pamphlet, give me a call at 214-555-0119.

Sincerely, | OHIO RECYCLING AUTHORITY | Jeremy Morales | Executive Director | xx | Enclosure |

## 142F

**Mail Merge Address Labels**

1. Prepare a standard address label for each record in the data source *142d data*. Include the company name in the address. Save the main document file as *142f main*.
2. Print the address labels.
3. Save merged files as *142f labels*.

# LESSON 143

## Spreadsheet Skills and Column Document Formatting Skills

**OUTCOMES**
- Assess spreadsheet skills.
- Assess column document formatting skills.

**Business Documents**
- Sales Report Table, Worksheet, and Chart
- Payroll Journal
- Business Letter Linked with Worksheet
- Flyer
- Newsletter

## 143B

**Integrate Word and Excel and Charting**

1. Open *df 143b wptable*.
2. Open a new worksheet file and copy the table into a blank worksheet; make formatting adjustments as desired.
3. Create a column chart with chart title, axis titles, legend, and other features you choose.
4. Move the chart to a chart sheet.
5. Save the worksheet as *143bss table* and close both files.

Most browsers support tabbed browsing, which allows you to collect a number of web pages in the browser at the same time so you can easily compare information from one page to that on another page. Tabs may display beneath the address bar or to the right of it. To move from one page to another, simply click its tab. To open a new tab, click New Tab and then key or select a website to display on the tab. To close a tab, click its close button.

## Working with Favorites and History

As you identify websites that may be useful for work or personal information, you will want to save those addresses to make it easy to find the information again. To store a website address, use a bookmark or add the site to a favorites list.

To add a website to a favorites list in a program such as *Internet Explorer 9*, display the Favorites list, and click the Add to favorites button or command. In the Add a Favorite dialog box, modify the name, if desired, and then choose the folder in which the bookmark should be stored, or create a new folder. Then click Add. Accessing that website is now as easy as clicking the bookmark on the Favorites list.

If you have not identified a site as a favorite but want to return to it, you can often find it in the history list. Display favorites and click the History tab, shown in Figure 1-22.

Click on a date option, such as Last Week or Today, to see a list of websites you visited during that time span. Click the site name to see the pages you visited at that site, as shown for the *Microsoft Office* website.

To adjust the number of days pages stay in the history list, click the Tools icon or menu in *Internet Explorer*, click Internet Options, and click the Settings button in the Browsing history section.

You can control how many days your browser will maintain history files. By default, for example, *Internet Explorer 9* will save 20 days of history files.

## Browser Safety Options

The most recent versions of popular browsers have security measures built in that can help safeguard your system as well as prevent others from readily tracing your Web surfing activities. You can delete your browsing history each time you shut down the computer, for example, or use a feature such as InPrivate Browsing (in *Internet Explorer 9*) to prevent the browser from storing information about your browsing, including cookies, temporary Internet files, and history files.

**Figure 1-22** A history list shows where you have been

1. Open your browser and key www.microsoft.com in the address bar. Tap Enter.
2. Click the Products tab in the menu bar to display a drop-down list, and then click All Office products.
3. Click the images button in the menu bar to display the clip art and media web page.
4. Click the Back button to return to the Office page.
5. Click the Back button again to return to the Microsoft page.
6. Click the Forward button to return to the Office page.
7. Click the Templates tab and click one of the free templates shown.
   The online application opens as a new tab or a new window in the browser.

1. Create a data source file for the following eight records.
2. Sort in ascending order by postal code and then alphabetically by last name and then first name.
3. **Save as:** *142c data.* Keep the file open.

| | |
|---|---|
| Doris Adams<br>2405 Grandview Avenue<br>Cincinnati, OH 45206-2220 | Roger Harris<br>4381 Antioch Drive<br>Enon, OH 45323-6492 |
| Albert Aitken<br>440 Long Pointe Drive<br>Avon Lake, OH 44012-2463 | Larry McClintock<br>6821 Burgundy Drive<br>Canton, OH 44720-4592 |
| Barbara Aitken<br>440 Long Pointe Drive<br>Avon Lake, OH 44012-2463 | Mary Springer<br>81 Mayflower Drive<br>Youngstown, OH 44512-6204 |
| Bruce Gioia<br>Route 3, Box 416<br>Marietta, OH 45750-9057 | William Eiber<br>387 Cranberry Run<br>Youngstown, OH 44512-2504 |

1. Open *142c data*, if needed.
2. Add a Title field, add the four records below, and delete the Eiber record.
3. Add the titles and company names for the other records as given.
4. Sort by postal code in descending order and then alphabetically by last name and then first name.
5. **Save as:** *142d data.*

| | |
|---|---|
| Mr. Gerald Bruni<br>Bruni Auto Parts<br>11184 Greenhaven Drive<br>Navarre, OH 44662-9650 | Mrs. Mary Phillip<br>Union Cleaning Co.<br>123 Marrett Farms<br>Union, OH 45322-3412 |
| Ms. Ruth O'Hara<br>Warren Florists<br>426 Forest Street<br>Warren, OH 44483-3825 | Mr. Henry Lewis<br>Lewis Printing<br>3140 Beaumont Street<br>Massilon, OH 44647-3140 |

| Last Name | Title | Company |
|---|---|---|
| Adams | Mrs. | Adams Medical Association |
| Aitken, Albert | Mr. | Compilers Plus |
| Aitken, Barbara | Mrs. | Database & More |
| Gioia | Mr. | Four Springs Golf Course |
| Harris | Mr. | Brite House Electricians |
| McClintock | Mr. | Banquets Unlimited |
| Springer | Mrs. | County Motors |

8. Click the New Tab button to open a new tab in the browser. In the address bar, key www.msnbc.com and tap Enter to see current headlines and news.
9. Click the Office – Office.com tab to make that page active.
10. Click the icon or menu that displays favorites or bookmarks, and then click the button or command that adds the current site to the favorites list.
11. Click the tab that displays the Web app template, and click the close button.
12. Close the MSNBC tab, and then click the Home icon to go to your home page.
13. Display the favorites list, and click the Office.com favorite.
14. Click the History button on the favorites list, and expand the list for today.
15. Click the office.microsoft folder to show the Office pages you visited today, and then click the Images – Clip Art, Photos, Sounds entry to open that page.
16. Click the Home icon to return to your home page. Close all other tabs.

## 5B
## Using Advanced Internet Search Strategies

If you have done any amount of searching on the Internet, you know that you often end up with lots of material to wade through to find exactly what you want. In this section, you learn some advanced search strategies that can help you select an appropriate search tool, limit search results, and evaluate the results you do get.

### Choosing a Search Tool

Google has been on the top of the heap of search engines for so long that the company name has become a verb in standard use: "I Googled him to find out more about him." However, Google is not the only search tool on the Internet. Other search tools that display results in different ways or use different methods for obtaining results can provide you with a different view of the information available on the Internet. Other popular search tools include bing, Ask, Yahoo, and DuckDuckGo.

It often takes time to identify the search tool you like best. As you work with each search tool, analyze the features and decide which are most helpful. You may appreciate the suggestions that come up as you key search terms in Google and the helpful related searches options in bing and Ask. DuckDuckGo has a clean, simple interface with few ads that you may find less cluttered than some other search tools. Figure 1-23 shows how differently two popular search tools display results.

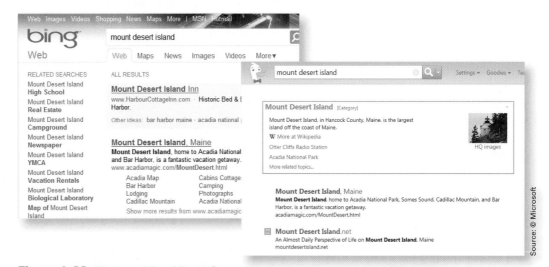

**Figure 1-23** Bing and DuckDuckGo present search results very differently

**Timed Writings**

Key 2 5' writings on all ¶s combined; find *gwam* and errors.

 **all letters used**

gwam | 3' | 5'

You are nearing the end of your keyboarding classes.  The | 4 | 2 | 53

skill level you have attained is much better than that with which | 8 | 5 | 55

you started when you were given keyboarding instruction for the | 13 | 8 | 58

very first time.  During the early phase of your training, you were | 17 | 10 | 61

taught to key the letters of the alphabet and the figures by touch. | 22 | 13 | 64

During the initial period of learning, the primary emphasis was | 26 | 16 | 66

placed on your keying technique. | 28 | 17 | 67

After learning to key the alphabet and figures, your next | 32 | 19 | 70

job was to learn to format documents.  The various types of | 36 | 22 | 72

documents formatted included letters, tables, and manuscripts. | 40 | 24 | 75

During this time of training, an emphasis also was placed on | 44 | 27 | 77

increasing the rate at which you were able to key.  Parts of the | 49 | 29 | 80

lessons keyed at this time also were used to help you recognize the | 53 | 32 | 82

value of and to improve language skills. | 56 | 34 | 84

The final phase of your training dealt with increasing your | 60 | 36 | 86

skill at producing documents of high quality at a rapid rate. | 64 | 38 | 89

Directions were provided for keying special documents; drills | 68 | 41 | 91

were given to build skill; and problems were provided to assess | 72 | 43 | 94

your progress.  You were also given a number of simulations to | 77 | 46 | 96

allow you to apply what you had learned.  Now you have a skill | 81 | 49 | 99

that you will be able to use throughout your life. | 84 | 51 | 101

gwam | 3' | 1 | 2 | 3 | 4
| 5' | 1 | 2 | 3

A good way to determine the relative merits and drawbacks of different search tools is to perform the same search in several of them to see how the results vary.

1. In your browser, key www.google.com in the address bar and tap Enter.
2. In the search box, key the words **mount desert island**. As you key, Google may display search terms in a drop-down list that match what you are keying.
3. Click the New Tab button to open a new browser tab, and key www.bing.com in the address bar. Tap Enter. Repeat the keyword search from step 2. Like Google, bing supplies suggested terms as you key.
4. Click the New Tab button to open a new browser tab, and key www.ask.com in the address bar. Repeat the keyword search for mount desert island.
5. Click the New Tab button, and key www.duckduckgo.com in the address bar. Repeat the keyword search for *mount desert island*. You now have four browser tabs open with results of searches for *Mount Desert Island, Maine*.
6. View the results on each tab, and then answer the following questions:
   a. Which website is identified at the top or near the top of the search results on all four tabs?
   b. Which search tool includes a map of the island?
   c. Which set of results includes the most ads?
   d. Which tab includes the most useful related searches, in your opinion?
   e. Which tab seems the most "cluttered"?
   f. Which tab seems the simplest to navigate?
7. Leave your browser open for the next activity.

## Limiting Search Results

A search such as the one you did in the last activity can result in literally millions of results. Learning how to limit the search results to those that match most closely what you want to know is an important aspect of improving your Internet skills. The fewer links you have to check in search of your desired information, the more efficiently you can work.

Most search engines build in quick ways to limit search results. When Google suggests phrases that match your search term, for example, it often supplies additional words or phrases in a drop-down list that match common searches, as shown in Figure 1-24. Selecting any of these options in the drop-down list narrows the search.

| mount desert is**land** |
| mount desert is**land** |
| mount desert is**land marathon** |
| mount desert is**land real estate** |
| mount desert is**land hospital** |

**Figure 1-24** Narrow a search by picking a more exact search phrase

Choosing related search options supplied on the results page is another way to narrow a search to sites that relate to a particular aspect of the topic. Related search suggestions may display in the form of links to the left or right of the main search results. In DuckDuckGo, you can choose one of the search ideas that display with a plus sign, such as *+acadia national park*. Clicking one of these search ideas adds the text to the original keyword search term, limiting search results to sites that contain all of those keywords.

For today's search tools, the more keywords you supply, the more you limit search results. You can simply key as many keywords as you think necessary to define the topic you are researching, or you can key a real-language question such as "how do you remove mold from vinyl siding."

# UNIT 26

## Assessing Advanced Information Management Skills

Lesson 142 Input and Mail Merge Skills
Lesson 143 Spreadsheet Skills and Column Document Formatting Skills

Lesson 144 Database and Report Formatting Skills
Lesson 145 Presentation and Input Skills

---

## LESSON 142 — Input and Mail Merge Skills

**OUTCOMES**
- Assess Input speed and accuracy skills.
- Assess mail merge skills.

### Business Documents
- Data Source File
- Main Document File
- Modified Block Business Letters Using Mail Merge
- Address Labels Using Mail Merge

---

### 142A–145A

**Warmup**

Key each line twice at the beginning of each lesson; first for control, then speed.

alphabet 1 Zev and Che saw pilots quickly taxi many big jets from the gates.

figures 2 She sold 105 shirts, 28 belts, 94 skirts, 36 suits, and 47 coats.

speed 3 Jen sat by the right aisle for the sorority ritual at the chapel.

gwam 1' | 1 | 2 | 3 | 4 | 5 | 6 | 7 | 8 | 9 | 10 | 11 | 12 | 13 |

Some search tools, such as Google, allow you to work with an advanced search form similar to the one shown in Figure 1-25. By adding words or phrases you want to appear in the search results and subtracting words or phrases you do not want to see, you can limit results substantially.

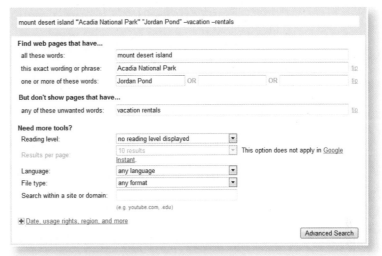

**Figure 1-25** Google's advanced search form

Note how the search box displays the words and phrases you add and subtract. Additional keywords can be added without having to use AND or a plus sign. Surround phrases with quotation marks to find the words in that phrase in that exact order. Use minus signs to exclude words or phrases from the search results. You can use these guidelines in any search tool to limit results.

Another way to limit search results is to choose what kind of results you want to see. Most search tools initially display all results from the Web, but also supply a list of options such as Images, News, Video, and so on. Clicking one of these options filters the search results to show only sites that match that type of content.

1. On the DuckDuckGo tab, click the *+bar harbor* search idea at the right side of the screen. Note that the phrase *bar harbor* is added to the phrase in the search box. Review the search results to see the boldface words that match the search phrase.

2. Click the Ask.com tab. In the search box, key **–Hotels** following the current search term, and tap Enter. Note how the search results change to eliminate sites relating to hotels on the island.

3. Click the bing tab, and note the number of results for the previous search near the top of the page. Then click one of the related search terms to the left of the main search results, such as *Mount Desert Island Newspaper*. How many search results display for this related search?

4. Click the Google tab, and then click the Advanced search link below the magnifying glass button. In the "this exact wording or phrase" box, key **Acadia National Park**. In the "one or more of these words" box, key **Jordan Pond**. Click Advanced Search.

5. Note that you have far fewer results with this more limited search. Click Images at the left side of the screen to see images of Jordan Pond. Then click Videos. How many results do you have now?

6. Close all tabs except the Google tab.

## Timed Writings

Key two 3' or 5' writings on the three ¶s; determine *gwam*; count errors.

 **all letters used**

|  | gwam | 3' | 5' |

Speaking before a group of people can cause a great deal of · · · · · · 4 | 2 | 60

anxiety for an individual.  This anxiety is so extensive that it · · · · 8 | 5 | 63

was ranked as the greatest fear among adults in a recent survey. · · · 13 | 8 | 66

Such fear suggests that many people would rather perish than go · · · · 17 | 10 | 68

before the public to give a talk.  Much of this fear actually · · · · · 21 | 13 | 71

comes from a lack of experience and training in giving public · · · · · 25 | 15 | 73

speeches.  People who excel in the area of public speaking have · · · · 30 | 18 | 76

developed this unique skill through hard work. · · · · · · · · · · · · · 33 | 20 | 78

Planning is a key part to giving a good talk.  The speech · · · · · · · 36 | 22 | 80

should be organized into three basic parts.  These parts are the · · · 41 | 24 | 83

introduction, the body, and the conclusion.  The introduction is · · · 45 | 27 | 85

used to get the attention of the audience, to present the topic of · · 50 | 30 | 88

the talk, and to establish the credibility of the speaker.  The · · · · 54 | 32 | 90

body of the speech is an organized presentation of the material · · · · 58 | 35 | 93

the speaker is conveying.  The conclusion is used to summarize · · · · · 62 | 37 | 95

the main points of the talk. · · · · · · · · · · · · · · · · · · · · · · 64 | 39 | 97

Several things can be done to lower the level of anxiety · · · · · · · · 68 | 41 | 99

during a talk.  Learning as much as possible about the audience · · · · 72 | 43 | 101

prior to the talk can reduce uncertainty.  Advance planning and · · · · 77 | 46 | 104

preparing are essential; the lack of either is a major cause of · · · · 81 | 49 | 107

anxiety.  Having the main points written on note cards to refer · · · · 85 | 51 | 109

to when needed is also helpful.  Using visual aids can also lessen · · · 90 | 54 | 112

the exposure a person feels.  These are but a few ideas that may · · · · 94 | 56 | 114

be used to develop better speaking skills. · · · · · · · · · · · · · · · 97 | 58 | 116

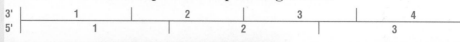

| gwam | 3' | 1 | 2 | 3 | 4 |
| 5' | 1 | 2 | 3 |

One important aspect of improving your Internet searching skills is learning how to evaluate the results you receive from a search. It is never wise to believe everything you read on the Internet. Outdated or downright wrong information is as easy to find as up-to-date reputable sources.

The criteria in Table 1-2 are often used to evaluate any kind of information source, including those you may identify with an Internet search.

> **★TIP** You can often get a good idea about the quality of a website's information from the URL of the site. URLs from educational (.edu) or government (.gov) sites may be more trustworthy than those from organizations (.org) or commercial (.com) sites.

| | |
|---|---|
| **Accuracy** | Are there typographical errors or obvious factual errors that lead you to question the accuracy of the information? Are there links to other sites that provide additional information that supports the information on the main site? Is there a bibliography that gives sources for the website's information? |
| **Authority** | Who created the website or wrote the specific article you are reviewing? If an article has an author, what are his or her credentials? Does he or she have the relevant education or experience to write with authority on the topic? |
| **Objectivity** | Websites created by some organizations may have a slant or a bias toward the opinions of that organization and consequently may not supply objective information. What can you determine about the agenda, hidden or obvious, of the organization behind the website? |
| **Currency** | When was the site created, and how recently has it been updated? Do links from the site work correctly? If not, the site may not be regularly maintained. |
| **Coverage** | Is the website appropriate for your search? If you are conducting research for a scholarly article, for example, you need to identify sites with an academic approach. Does the content include citations that indicate reputable sources? |

**Table 1-2** Criteria for evaluating search results

Remember as you are evaluating your search results that the first website listed may not be the best or most reliable source—it may just be the site visited most often. Popular websites such as Wikipedia may often show up at the top of the list, and you may indeed find plenty of good information in its pages. But keep in mind that wikis can be modified at any time by users anywhere in the world. Make sure you verify information you find in a source such as Wikipedia.

1. With the Google website open in your browser, key the search phrase **oil and gas drilling in national parks**. Select Everything in the list at left of the search results.
2. In the search results that display, locate:
   a. An article that is obviously not current. What is the URL, what is the title, and what year was the article published?
   b. An article that comes from an obviously biased source. What organization authored the website, and what is its point of view?
   c. An article that attempts to give both sides of the story on drilling in national parks. What is the URL, and what is the title of the article?
3. Click the News link to the left of the search results to see news stories about oil and gas drilling. What is the most recent news story filed on this subject? What are the URL, the title, and the point of view of the article?
4. Close your browser.

1. Key three 1' timings on each ¶; determine *gwam* and count errors on each timing. If errors are two or fewer on any timing, goal is to increase speed by one or two *gwam* on the next timing. If errors on any timing are more than two, goal is control on the next timing.

2. Key two 3' timings on ¶s 1–3 combined. Your goal is to maintain your highest 1' speed on a 1' timing with two or fewer errors. Also, strive to make six or fewer errors on the 3' timing. Determine *gwam* and count errors to see if you met your goals.

3. Key a 5' timing on ¶s 1–3 combined. Your goal is to maintain your 3' speed with not more than 10 errors (two errors per minute). Determine *gwam* and count errors to see if you met your goal.

  all letters used

| | gwam | 3' | 5' |
|---|---|---|---|

|  | 3' | 5' |
|---|---|---|
| Attempts to maximize the standard of living for humans | 4 | 2 |
| through the control of nature and the development of new products | 8 | 5 |
| have also resulted in the pollution of the environment. In some | 13 | 8 |
| parts of the world, the water, air, and soil are so polluted that | 17 | 10 |
| it is unsafe for people to live there because of the heightened | 21 | 13 |
| risk from disease. | 23 | 14 |
| Pollution of the air, land, and water has existed since | 27 | 16 |
| people began to live in cities. People living in these early | 31 | 19 |
| cities took their garbage to dumps outside the main part of | 35 | 21 |
| the city or just put it into the streets or canals. Both of these | 40 | 24 |
| disposal methods helped create the pollution process. | 44 | 26 |
| Pollution is one of the most serious problems facing | 47 | 28 |
| people today. Clean air, water, and land are needed by all living | 52 | 31 |
| things. Bad air, water, and soil cause illness and even death | 56 | 34 |
| to people and other living things. Bad water quickly kills fish | 61 | 36 |
| and ruins drinking water; bad soil reduces the amount of land | 65 | 39 |
| that is available for growing food. | 67 | 40 |

gwam 3' | 1 | 2 | 3 | 4 |
5' | 1 | 2 | 3 |

You have been asked to write an article about the decrease of small mammal populations in the Everglades, a problem that, you have been told, results from the growth in populations of species not native to Florida.

1. What would you use as an initial search string to begin exploring this issue?
2. After reviewing your search results, how could you refine your search string to get more detailed information?
3. Once again review your search results to determine what type of predator is feeding on native Everglades animals. Where do these predators come from?
4. Find a news article about the subject. Print the article and then review it using the criteria in Table 1-2 to determine if the source is credible.

## Digital Citizenship and Ethics

lifescapes/Alamy

A computer is a very powerful tool that has many uses. Unfortunately, not everyone uses the computer for good and moral purposes. In other words, computer usage has ethical dimensions that should concern all of us. Use a search engine to research computer ethics, and then write a ¶ describing what you have learned about computer ethics. Print at least one page from a website that is a good resource for this activity.

### Think Critically

1. Evaluate the sources of the information you found—is the information reliable?
2. Describe how easy access to information on the Internet can lead you into ethical dilemmas.
3. Describe ways that you can avoid unethical behavior in order to be a good digital citizen.

## LESSON 6 — Working in the Cloud

**OUTCOMES**

- Describe cloud computing.
- Understand how to use online applications.
- Discuss the importance of sharing documents online.

### 6A

#### Understanding Cloud Computing

Cloud computing is applications and services that are delivered to clients over the Internet. Some of these services are free, such as the Web email services available from providers like Yahoo and Google. Other services are provided by producers who want to deliver a specific product to customers who will pay for the right to use the product, as shown in Figure 1-26.

# SKILL BUILDER 4

**OUTCOMES**

- Improve keying techniques.
- Improve keying speed and accuracy.

## Warmup

Key each line twice, first for control and then for speed.

alphabet 1 Vicki expects to query a dozen boys and girls for the major show.

fig/sym 2 Ramon Jones & Company's fax number was changed to (835) 109-2647.

speed 3 If the tug slams the dock, it may make a big problem for the men.

gwam 1' | 1 | 2 | 3 | 4 | 5 | 6 | 7 | 8 | 9 | 10 | 11 | 12 | 13 |

## Technique: Keystroking Patterns

Key each line twice.

**Adjacent key**

1 ore her has sag ion oil wet new art join drop sage hope grew
2 err gas rent ever past same void week view weave short pound
3 more maker lease salsa radio prior opera trial choice import

**Technique Cue**
Key at a continuous pace; eliminate pauses.

**One hand**

4 as bag car dad ear fad gas him ill gave hymn kilo noon onion
5 oil pop red see tar ump vat yoyo zest ages best caves zebras
6 beef crews defer fears graft holly milky puppy excess pompom

**Balanced hand**

7 it ant bow cod doe elf fit got ivy jake keys naps odor prowl
8 rod sow torn vial worn yams zori auto buck clams forks giant
9 hair idle kept lapel proxy quake theory turkey naught mentor

gwam 1' | 1 | 2 | 3 | 4 | 5 | 6 | 7 | 8 | 9 | 10 | 11 | 12 |

## Technique: Number Keys/Tab

Key each line twice (key number, tap TAB, key next number).  Concentrate on figure location; quick tab spacing; eyes on copy.

| 95 | 107 | 403 | 496 | 572 | 824 | 590 | 576 | 871 |
| 82 | 458 | 314 | 307 | 891 | 103 | 721 | 980 | 645 |
| 73 | 669 | 225 | 218 | 600 | 206 | 843 | 109 | 312 |
| 64 | 320 | 678 | 592 | 438 | 579 | 684 | 432 | 908 |

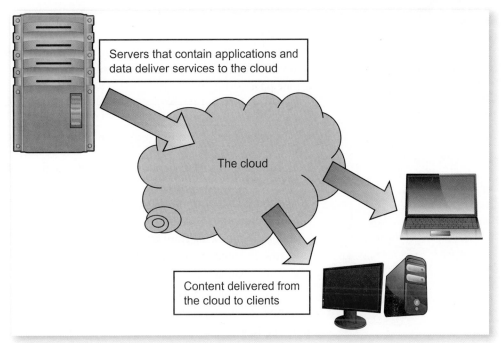

**Figure 1-26** Producers make services available through the cloud to clients

Suppose, for example, a software designer has developed a new database program aimed specifically at managing and manipulating health records. The designer could distribute the program using physical means—copying to DVDs that are packaged in boxes and then shipped to various retail outlets—or the designer could save time and money by making the program available via the cloud to clients who want to use the program in their own companies. Clearly, there are advantages to distributing the service by Internet.

Cloud computing is sometimes discussed in terms of **private clouds** and the **public cloud.** Services offered to everyone over the Internet are said to use the public cloud. If the services are offered only within one large company or organization, using the company network and behind the company firewall, they are in a private cloud.

Cloud computing has advantages for both producers and clients.

- Costs are often reduced for the producer. The producer needs a server to connect to the cloud and storage to contain the data generated by the program, electricity to keep everything running, and premises for the hardware. This can be far more cost-effective than running a software replicating and distribution business.
- Programs can be easily updated. The producer updates on the server, and every client is automatically updated at the same time.
- Costs can also be reduced for clients. Rather than having to buy or license numerous copies of an application, clients often pay a subscription fee to use the cloud application, or even pay according to how much time they spend using it. Companies may also save because they do not have to develop specialized software themselves; they can instead purchase it from a service that bears all the costs of development.
- Cloud computing can be far more flexible than traditional approaches to providing hardware and software to employees. If a business upturn leads to hiring of new employees who need applications immediately, providing applications through the cloud can be faster than having to buy new copies of software and then get that software installed.

I need you to use the 2nd worksheet in 135 job19 to record the transactions within each of the revenue and expense accounts appearing on the Revenue Statement. Rename the 2nd worksheet Transactions and follow the directions on the To Do List so the transactions entered on the Transaction worksheet will be included in the calculations on the Revenue worksheet. When you're done, print out both worksheets for me to review. Save the file as 135 job20 revenue.

*mh*

### To Do List

1. In the columns in row 1 in the Transactions worksheet, key from left to right the following text. Wrap the text as needed and scale the worksheet so it does not exceed the width of one page.

| Date | Contributions | Loan Payments | Transfers In | New Loans |
|------|---------------|---------------|--------------|-----------|
| Transfers Out | Meeting | Printing | Office | |

2. In row 20 in the Transactions worksheet, use the SUM function to calculate column totals for the 8 account names listed in columns B through I in row 1. Have the SUM function add the values in rows 2 through 19. Format all cells in columns B through I as dollars and cents.

3. Enter the following transactions as indicated.
   - row 2: January 5, enter $15.45 under Printing
   - row 3: January 6, enter $33.89 under Office
   - row 4: January 6, enter $200 under contributions
   - row 5: January 7, enter $1,345.67 under Loan Payments

4. In the Revenue worksheet, enter 3-D cell references so the totals in row 20 in the Transactions worksheet will automatically appear in the appropriate cells.

5. Make needed adjustments to the Revenue worksheet so all calculations are correctly displayed.

- Companies that are using cloud computing no longer have to have space for their own servers. Instead, storage is provided off-site on the servers of the provider that is offering the specific application.
- Employees of client companies can have access to their applications even if they are not on company premises, a great convenience for employees who travel or telecommute.
- Organizations may no longer need the same amount of IT support they require when they have all their network and storage onsite.

In an organization that follows the principles of information systems, covered in Lesson 1, cloud computing can be an important way to control costs while keeping communications technology at a high level.

Cloud computing can have some drawbacks, however.

- When a program is in the public cloud, data is stored by the service provider, and the client has no control over the storage. Clients may not even know where the data is being stored. The client may risk losing data if something happens to the service provider's hardware. For this reason, a public cloud service provider often builds in a number of **redundant** systems, so that all client data can be copied to one or more backup systems.
- Clients that are using cloud services may find that their operations are tied to the health of the service provider. If that company has financial woes or fails, what happens to the client data being stored? It is sometimes not easy to move data from one cloud service provider to another.
- Clients have no way to oversee the policies of the service provider, such as how often data is backed up and what disaster recovery procedures are in place.
- Depending on the type of Internet connection, applications may run more slowly than they do on a local computer. And if the Internet connection is lost, users have no access to online resources.
- Security can also be an issue, especially for companies that generate sensitive information. Many companies will not want to use services that result in their data being stored somewhere else.
- Another aspect to the security issue is the possibility of an unauthorized user gaining access to secure data, which may be especially easy because users can log in from anywhere. As you have already learned in this unit, there are ways to control access using passwords and other forms of authentication, and these methods need to be rigorously enforced to keep resources secure.

A savvy computer user will consider both the risks and rewards of working in the cloud before choosing this kind of information technology.

Cloud computing services store client data in multiple redundant servers

© twobee/Shutterstock.com

QUICK ✔

1. What do you think is the chief advantage of working with cloud services?
2. If you were a cloud service provider, why would it be critical to have redundant data storage systems?

## 6B

## Working with Online Applications

Online applications (or online apps) provide a way to accomplish specific tasks on the Web, such as finding directions, browsing multimedia content, and sending email. Online versions of office applications allow you to create office documents such as presentations and spreadsheets and handle tasks and appointments.

**Newspaper Ad**

*I need to send ad copy over to the advisor of the CVHS newspaper. Here's the information I want in the ad, but please arrange it attractively. If you can, arrange it on 11" × 14" paper so it is the size of the newspaper page. If not, the advisor said the student editors can adjust it. Use some text boxes and/or tables to display some of the information. You should use color, since there is likelihood that this issue of the newspaper will be printed in color. Save the file as 135 job18 ad.*

*mh*

Scholarships
### *administered by the*
Central Valley Education Foundation

| Insert clip art related to your school logo, mascot, etc. |
| --- |

*Supporting the youth of our community*

If you plan to continue your education beyond CVHS, you should apply for one or more of the 22 scholarships that are available to members of the CVHS Class of 2015. The scholarships range from $1,000 to $3,000.

There are scholarships for those who
- attend any college and major in any field of study
- attend a technical school or community college
- major in business; computer or information science; education; engineering, math, or science; or a health-related field

There are scholarships for those who have been successful in
- academic, special, or vocational education
- visual and/or performing arts
- service to the church
- athletics
- overcoming a personal or family hardship

Information on each scholarship and scholarship applications is available at www.cvef.org.

*I need to create a workbook to record the financial transactions that will appear on the 2015 CVEF loan program revenue statement. Using the information on the To Do List, create a worksheet with all the necessary formulas needed to do the calculations. We won't enter any numbers at this time. Format it appropriately and use cell borders to show columns where additions and subtractions are made. If needed, you can review last year's statement in df 135 job13 insert. Rename the worksheet tab Revenue. Save the file as 135 job19 revenue.*

*mh*

**To Do List**

2015 CVEF Loan Program Revenue Statement

Revenue

   Contributions

   Loan Repayments Including Interest

   Transfers In from Savings

          Total Income

Expenditures and Transfers Out

   Loans Granted

   Transfers Out to Savings

   Operational Expenses

     Annual Meeting

     Printing

     Office Expenses

       Total Expenditures and Transfers Out

        Revenue Over Expenditures

Online apps are viewed from within your Web browser. The software for the application is stored on the host server rather than on your local computer, and the data you input to the online app is also sent to the server for processing and storage.

Some online apps are available free of charge, such as the *Microsoft Office* applications available in the Windows Live SkyDrive. Other online apps, such as Google Apps, are designed to be installed on a corporate domain, allowing all company employees to access apps such as Google Docs, Google Calendar, and other communications apps.

**TRY IT!**
You can work with the Windows Web Apps in Appendix B, My Personal-Use Folder.

Windows Live SkyDrive, shown in Figure 1-27, gives easy access to the Web Apps versions of *Word, Excel, PowerPoint,* and *OneNote*. You organize and manipulate files as you would in *File Explorer*: Use the default My Documents folder, or create your own folders. You see folders and files in a file list; double-click a folder to open it, and click a file to view it in the browser. Use the navigation list at the left to display all documents, photos you have uploaded to share with others, recent documents, or documents that others are sharing with you. You can search your documents or the Web using the search box.

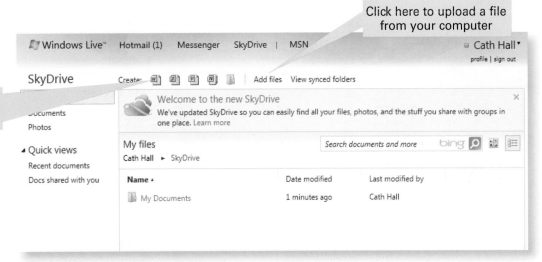

**Figure 1-27** Windows Live SkyDrive

The Web Apps versions of *Word, Excel, PowerPoint,* and *OneNote* resemble their *Office 2013* versions, with the familiar Ribbon interface, as shown in Figure 1-28. Each Web App has only a few tabs, in comparison with the *Office 2013* version, but the commands available on these tabs allow users to perform tasks such as formatting and styling text, inserting pictures and clip art (and SmartArt, in *PowerPoint*), performing calculations and creating charts in Excel, and changing views in all applications.

You have the option to open the Web Apps document on your local computer in the *Office 2013* version of the application. Opening an online file in your local *Office* application allows you to work on it at times you do not have an Internet connection, such as when you are traveling. Changes that you save update the online version so that it is always the most recent version.

## Job 13

### Appendix

Open 135 job12 report and insert Appendix A as a title on a new sheet at the end of the report. Then insert the worksheet in df 135 job13 insert, centered horizontally. You may need to adjust the top margin so the worksheet will fit on the page. Insert bookmarks and hyperlinks so the reader can move quickly to the appendix and back to page 1. Save the file as 135 job13 report.

*mh*

## Job 14

### Annual Report

We now need to prepare a final draft of the annual report. Open 135 job13 report. We need to
- Hyphenate the report
- Verify the report is formatted in an appropriate style
- Add a table of contents with page numbers and hyperlinks to each of the side headings
- Number the pages correctly
- Keep tables from splitting over two pages
- Verify page endings and beginnings are correct

When you are satisfied that it is a final draft, print or email me a copy so I can see it. Save the file as 135 job14 report.

*mh*

## Job 15

### Cover Page

Create a cover page for the report. You may use one from the gallery or design one yourself. Include the foundation's name, the title of the report, and indicate that the report was prepared by me (include my title). Save the file as 135 job15 cover page.

*mh*

## Job 16

### Presentation

Most of the slide presentation that I will be using for parents and students at CVHS is in df 135 job16 presentation. I didn't get it all done so you need to add the information on the To Do List before the last slide. I think you'll need two slides. Also, select an appropriate design and transitions and include some clip art where you think it will complement the slide content. Save the file as 135 job16 presentation.

*mh*

**To Do List**

Scholarships Based on Intended College Major
- Business
  - Marilyn Kessler Scholarship
- Computer or Information Sciences
  - Friends of CVHS Scholarship
- Education
  - Children First Education Scholarship
- Engineering, Math, or Science
  - Donald Graham Memorial Scholarship
- Health-Related Field
  - Sally M. Merriman Scholarship

## Job 17

### News Release

I want to send the news release on the To Do List to the local papers. Use the template that is in df 135 job17 news release. Use January 21, 2014 as the date and Elizabeth for the city. List my name, 412-555-0337 as the phone number, and hardy.m@cvef.org as the email for the contact information. Save the file as 135 job17 news release.

*mh*

**To Do List**

**Elizabeth—January 21, 2014 —** The Central Valley Education Foundation will be awarding 22 scholarships to Central Valley High School graduates at the end of this school year. The total value of the scholarships is $30,300 and they range in value from $1,000 to $3,000. Both the number and value of this year's scholarships is an increase over those awarded in June 2014.

To learn more about the scholarships available, the criteria applicants have to meet, and the application procedure and deadline, visit www.cvef.org/scholarship or call CVEF at 412-555-0337. Applications are available on the website or at the CVHS Guidance Office.

If you would like to establish a scholarship to assist a deserving graduate, complete the donor form at www.cvef.org/scholarship.

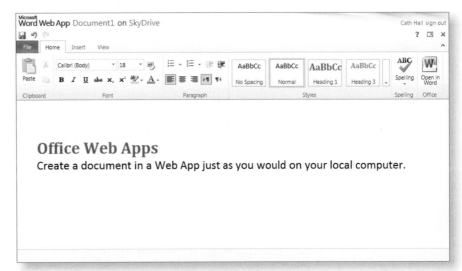

**Figure 1-28** Web Apps version of *Microsoft Word*

If you do not want to create a document in the SkyDrive but want an existing document to be stored in the SkyDrive, you can click the Add files link and navigate to a file stored on your computer. Once you upload the file, you can view it and work with it in the SkyDrive, just as if you were editing it on your local computer.

As for working in the cloud in general, working with online applications has both advantages and disadvantages. On the plus side:

- You can access your files from anywhere, on any computer, at any time. All you require is a computer with an Internet connection.
- Applications such as the *Office* suite no longer have to be bought and stored on every computer, a savings in software costs.
- Updates are handled by the service provider, so users can be assured they are always working with the most up-to-date version.

On the minus side:

- Experienced users are more likely to prefer the desktop versions of familiar applications, which have far more features and options.
- Online applications require an Internet connection. Using online apps may be a problem in regions where online access is not available or not dependable.
- Even when a good Internet connection is available, applications may run more slowly over the Internet than they do on a local desktop.
- Users cannot be completely certain that their data, stored by the online application service, is completely secure.

**QUICK**

1. When you create and save a document in an online application, where is that document stored?
2. Why do you think a sales representative might choose to use online applications rather than desktop applications?
3. What do you think is the most important drawback to using online applications exclusively, rather than desktop applications?

*Here's the first part of the annual report I'm preparing. Format it as a report using a style of your choice. Correct any errors you find. Save the file as 135 job9 report.*

*mh*

### 2014 CVEF Student Loan Program Annual Report
### January 1, 2014, through December 31, 2014
### Prepared by Marilyn Hardy, CVEF Assistant Director

Central Valley Education Foundation has fulfilled its mission during the past year by lending money to deserving residents of the Central Valley High School who are pursuing undergraduate studies as full-time students and collecting funds from the borrowers who have completed their undergraduate studies. The latter has presented more challenges this year than usual. This report will highlight the successes and the challenges CVEF has had during this past year and concerns and recommendations for the upcoming year.

Financial Condition

The financial condition of the CVEF loan program is strong. Revenues slightly exceeded expenses during 2014; therefore, no transfers from savings or investments was needed to fund the $24,500 in loans that was awarded and no transfers to savings were made. The loan program has $113,764.41 in cash and investments, which permits CVEF to make available up to $28,000 in loans in 2015. Refer to Appendix A to revue the 2014 financial statements.

Individuals Paying Off Loans

Table 1 contains information about the three borrowers who repaid their loans during 2014. All three loans were repaid prior to the maturity date. Danielle Dennard repaid her entire loan prior to the date the first payment was dew, Jordan Korenoski repaid his loan within the first four months, and Alexi Kenny repaid her loan six months early.

#### Table 1: Individuals Paying Off Loans in 2014

| First | Last | Principal | Date Paid Off |
|---------|-----------|-----------|---------------|
| Danielle | Dennard | $2,500 | Jul-14 |
| Jordan | Korenoski | $1,500 | Oct-14 |
| Alexi | Kenny | $14,000 | Jan-14 |

*I need you to proofread the rest of the text for the annual report. It is in df 135 job10 report. Use track changes and/or comments to mark errors or suggest revisions and then save the file so I can check it once more as well. I'm verifying the information in the tables now; we'll insert them later. Save the file as 135 job10 report.*

*mh*

*I checked your corrections in 135 job10 report and then proofed it again. I saved the latest version as df135 job11 report. Insert this file at the end of 135 job9 report while I finish the tables. Save the file as 135 job11 report.*

*mh*

*The tables are now ready to be inserted into the 135 job11 report. Insert df 135 job12 table2, df 135 job12 table3, and df 135 job12 table5 below the appropriate table title in the text. Adjust the space above and below the tables as needed. Center each table horizontally. Save the file as 135 job12 report.*

*mh*

## Sharing Information Online

Sharing information online allows team members to work anywhere

One of the most important reasons to work with a platform such as the Windows Live SkyDrive is the ease with which you can share files with others. Today, it is not unusual for members of a team to be working in different offices, different cities, or even different countries. Online applications allow team members to access documents anytime and anywhere.

Team members can create documents online or easily upload existing files for others to review. When all team members have access to a shared folder accessed by browser, the process of working together on a project can be fast and efficient.

Other advantages to sharing information online include the following:

- Multiple users can work on a single document at the same time, and as changes are made to the document, everyone's version of it updates.
- Working with the most up-to-date version of a document allows team members to identify and correct mistakes in a timely fashion. Mistakes often cost money, and minimizing them can help to keep a project not only on schedule but on budget.
- Sharing information online can be a green alternative. Rather than printing multiple drafts of a report for all team members to view and edit, the document can be edited online, with the input of all team members resolved to create the final report.

Sharing a document online usually requires the user to change the permission status for a file or folder. You may have the option of sharing with selected persons or with everyone to make the file or folder public. A good example of a folder you might want to make public in this way would be a photo album you want to share widely. If you are sharing a folder that may contain sensitive information, you would limit access to the fewest number of people possible. You may also have the option of specifying whether a sharer can simply view a file or can edit files and add or delete files from a folder.

Once you have selected the people to share files or folders, you can, if desired, send them a notification to let them know they have access to the folder. Once you have designated users to share your folder, they can see documents you are sharing with them and are able to open those documents and view or edit them.

**QUICK** ✔

1. What factors do you need to consider when building a team for a project that might use online applications and shared files?
2. Who do you think should decide which team members get access to which documents online?
3. What disadvantages do you see to sharing information online with coworkers or project team members?

www.cengage.com/school/
keyboarding/c21key

*Here are the minutes I took at the Scholarship Committee meeting. Please prepare them in an appropriate format for me to review. If you want, you can use a template (df 135 job8 minutes). Save the file as 135 job8 minutes.*

*mh*

I. Call to order

Pauline Cooper called to order the quarterly meeting of the Scholarship Committee at 4:30 p.m. on January 15 in the Board Room.

II. Roll call

The following committee members were present: Pauline Cooper, Chair; Meryl Pogue; and Katherine Ralston

III. Approval of minutes from last meeting

Marilyn Hardy read the minutes from the last meeting. The minutes were approved as read.

IV. Open issues

1. 2014 Program Review: Seventeen scholarships totaling $17,750 were awarded to CVEF seniors in June 2014. This was an increase of four scholarships for $4,500 when compared to June 2013. More than 125 applications were received from 35 graduating seniors. Each recipient received ½ of the scholarship amount at the Senior Awards evening prior to commencement and the remaining ½ will be dispersed during this January. This method of payment has caused some administration problems, and a proposal to change it will be discussed under new business.

2. 2015 Program Preview: It is expected that there will be 22 scholarships totaling slightly more than $30,000 available for the June 2015 graduates. The significant increase in the number of scholarships can be attributed mostly to a mailing to alumni who were inducted into the CVHS Hall of Fame during the past three years as well as having a greater presence at the Hall of Fame banquet. Also of importance is the fact that all of last year's scholarship sponsors continued their scholarships for this year—some offering higher award amounts.

V. New business

1. A proposal to limit the number of scholarships a senior can be awarded to two. After a lengthy discussion, the committee voted to limit the amount any one senior can receive to a maximum of $2,500. Therefore, a senior can receive more than one scholarship provided the combined amount does not exceed $2,500.

2. CVEF will continue its practice of inviting the sponsor of the scholarship to present the scholarship to the recipient at the Senior Awards evening. If the sponsor cannot attend, he/she can designate the person to present the scholarship or choose to have CVEF select a presenter.

3. A proposal to pay the entire scholarship amount to the recipient at the Senior Awards evening was approved, provided the scholarship donor does not specify another method of payment.

VI. Adjournment; Pauline Cooper adjourned the meeting at 5:35 p.m.

Minutes submitted by: Marilyn Hardy

# Academic and Career Connections

Complete the following exercises that introduce various topics that involve academic themes and careers.

## Grammar/Writing

### Capitalization

**MicroType 6**

- References/Communication Skills/Capitalization
- CheckPro/Communication Skills 1
- CheckPro/Word Choice 1

1. Go to *MicroType 6* and use this feature path for review: References/Communication Skills/ Capitalization.
2. Click Rules and review the rules of using capitalization.
3. Then, under Capitalization, click Posttest.
4. Follow the instructions to complete the posttest.

*Optional Activities*

1. Go to this path: CheckPro/Communication Skills 1.
2. Complete the activities as directed.
3. Go to this path: CheckPro/Word Choice 1.
4. Complete the activities as directed.

## Communications

### Composition

1. Read the following article about lost email messages and data security.

How would you feel if you logged on to your email account only to find that all of your messages and your contacts had disappeared? That's exactly what happened to thousands of users of Google's Gmail service. All of their saved messages and contact information simply disappeared.

Of course, Google apologized for the disruption in service and quickly found an answer for what went wrong. The emails were lost because of a problem with a software update Google was installing on all of its computer servers.

How was Google able to find and restore those millions of lost messages? Google, like many other online businesses, stores all of its data in huge warehouses filled with computers in sites around the world. These data centers house more than one backup copy of every message ever sent on Gmail.

But how was Google able to retrieve all the emails and contacts successfully? Google still relies on what many may consider to be outdated technology—Google stores all of its backup data on tape.

The blog Data Center Knowledge confirms that tape is still a safe way to back up data, even if it may seem strange to save "virtual" messages on a hard copy tape:

"Even today, tape has two significant advantages over other media: cost and portability. These two advantages outweigh the more significant (logically speaking) disadvantages of tape media: fragility, replacement rate, failure rate, vulnerability to theft, and unencrypted data storage."

2. Write a two-¶ response to this article, describing your concerns as well as ideas for how you might protect the safety of your email messages and other data.
3. If requested, give the response you have written to your instructor.

## Job 6

### Worksheet

I need a scholarship worksheet using what I have outlined on the To Do List. Basically, I need a row for each applicant to record the scholarship(s) for which he/she has applied. Temporarily, key numbers 1–50 in the name column. In the next 20+ columns, enter an identifying name for the scholarships. You can get the names from 135 job4 data. To save space, use vertical text feature for all columns except column 1. In the last column and last row, enter formulas to calculate totals for each applicant and each scholarship. Use Landscape orientation and repeat the columns headings on the 2nd page. Save the file as 135 job6 scholarship.

mh

**To Do List**

| Name | Allen | Alumni | → | Wilson | Totals |
|------|-------|--------|---|--------|--------|
| 1 | | | | | |
| 2 | | | | | |
| 50 | | | | | |
| Totals | | | | | |

## Job 7

### Worksheet

I just received the first batch of applicants for our scholarships from the guidance counselor. Please enter them in 135 job6 scholarship, beginning in row 2—just replace the number with the name (last name, first name format) and then key a 1 in the appropriate scholarship column(s). Sort the applicants alphabetically by last name. Verify that the totals are correct. Shrink worksheet as needed to fit on 1 page horizontally and 2 pages vertically. Save the file as 135 job7 scholarship.

mh

**To Do List**

| Name | | Scholarship(s) | | | | | |
|------|-------|----------------|----------|--------|--------|--------|--------|
| Jim | Greene | Byrnes | Thornton | Felton | Allen | | |
| Maria | Lopez | Booster | Bennett | | | | |
| Raul | Piesa | Alumni | Bennett | Connors | CVCC | | |
| Janet | Veriman | Felmer | Allen | Johnson | | | |
| Kerri | Malinchak | Wilson | Bennett | Felton | Redman | Byrnes | Graham |
| Mark | Morrison | Kessler | Alumni | Dellante | | | |

1. Katherine has saved $750 to buy a new computer and office applications software for her school work. If she has any money left over from the computer purchase, she would also like to buy a new cell phone. She has shopped online and at local electronics stores and found that the best options are the following:
   a. Basic laptop computer: $539
   b. Desktop computer: $700
   c. Slim tablet computer (must be docked to a desktop computer for full functionality): $499
   d. Office applications software suite: $150
   e. Fully loaded smartphone with games, text messaging, Internet, and music: $250
   f. Normal cell phone with basic phone service and text messaging: $100

2. Which combination of computer, software, and phone will best fit Katherine's needs and still remain within her budget? Is it possible for her to buy all three items for $750?

3. Katherine's friend Emilio tells her that he has heard of an electronics store that is offering a special limited-time $50 discount for purchasing a basic laptop and a normal cell phone with basic phone service. Will this enable Katherine to purchase everything she needs?

# Introducing Career Clusters

There are many different career opportunities available to you once you graduate from high school. Some careers require no additional education, while others require many years of additional education.

The career exploration activities in this text will help you understand the requirements for some of the careers in which you may have an interest. Begin your exploration by completing the following steps.

1. Access www.careertech.org.
2. Complete the Career Clusters Interest Survey. Your instructor will provide you with a copy of the survey and the Sixteen Career Clusters pages that follow the Interest Survey.
3. Obtain a folder for your Career Exploration Portfolio from your instructor, write your name and class period on it, place your completed Interest Survey and descriptions of the career clusters in the folder, and file the folder as instructed.

Source: © careertech.org

## Job 4

### Mail Merge

*We need to send a letter to the contact person for each of the scholarships that has been established. Before doing that we need to update df 135 job4 data. See the To Do List for specifics.*

*mh*

**To Do List**

1. Add Mrs. Pauline Cooper, 298 Mohawk Drive, McKeesport, PA 15135-5035 to the data source file for the Bennett scholarship. Change fields in Redman record to Mrs. and last name to Newton. Sort it alphabetically by Scholarship. Save it as *135 job4 data*.

2. Open *df 135 job4 letter* and proof it carefully for errors since I proofed it quickly. I wasn't certain of the exact field names, so you may have to delete these field names and insert the ones from the data source file. You'll also have to format the letter.

3. Prepare a letter for each contact person in *135 job4 data* using the Mail Merge feature. Print the last letter in the merged file. Save the letters as *135 job4 letters*.

4. Prepare an address label for each person. Save the labels as *135 job 4 labels*.

## Job 5

### Reservation Form

*The administrative assistant who supports the CVHS alumni association and committees organizing class reunions is on sick leave and will not return for a week. Her supervisor, Greta Hamilton, asked me if you could format a newsletter that has to be sent in a few days. I said you could do it. She said most of the directions are in df 135 job5 newsletter as comments. She wants the form added to the bottom of the newsletter so it spans the width of the paper like the newsletter title and date. You may have to arrange the info on the form differently. Save the file as 135 job5 newsletter.*

*mh*

><×><×><×><×><×><×><×><×><×><×><×><×><×><×><×><×><×><×

Classmate Information and Banquet Reservation Form

Please complete and return this form before May 1, 2015. Please complete and return it even if you are unable to attend so we have current information on you. Send it to:

CVHS Class of '65

Larry Gray

3305 Oakland Drive

McKeesport, PA 15132-7913

Please reserve ❑ one banquet meal at $60; ❑ two banquet meals at $120.

My check for ❑ $60; ❑ $120 payable to CVHS Class of 65 is enclosed.

❑ Please accept my regrets. I will not be attending the Class Reunion.

❑ Please email a copy of the Program Booklet.

Name _____ Maiden name, if applicable _____

Street _____

City/State _____ ZIP _____ Telephone _____

Email*_____ Telephone _____

❑ Guest or ❑ Spouse's Name _____

If spouse is a CVHS alum, provide year of graduation _____ and maiden name, if applicable _____

Additional Information for the Program Booklet:

Occupation _____

Retired: ❑ Yes ❑ No

Occupation of Spouse, if member of Class of '65 _____

Retired: ❑ Yes ❑ No

Names of Children _____

Names of Grandchildren_____

Names of Great Grandchildren _____

*May we print your email address in the Program Booklet:

❑ Yes ❑ No, use for contact purposes only

# The Winning Edge

A Career Technical Student Organization (CTSO), such as Business Professionals of America and Future Business Leaders of America-Phi Beta Lambda, offer a variety of individual and group programs and activities that help you prepare for life after high school. Members of a student organization:

- meet students from other schools around the country who have similar interests and goals.
- are part of a motivated and positive group that encourages them to explore new ways of thinking and strengthens teamwork skills.
- participate in events that build confidence and communication skills.
- apply classroom knowledge and skills to real-world experiences.
- identify career interests and goals and have the chance to win scholarships.

### Business Professionals of America (BPA)

BPA is a national organization for students interested in careers in business management, office administration, information technology, and other related careers. It offers the Workplace Skills Assessment Program (WSAP), a series of conferences in which students showcase their workplace skills through participation in various competitive events. Go to www.bpa.org for more information.

### Future Business Leaders of America-Phi Beta Lambda (FBLA-PBL)

FBLA-PBL is a nationwide business education association for students preparing for a career in business. Its membership also consists of educators, administrators, and business professionals. Through its National Awards Program, students demonstrate their business knowledge in a variety of competitive events. Go to www.fbla-pbl.org for more information.

### Think Critically

1. How can joining a CTSO help you identify a career that interests you?
2. Why would an employer want to hire a worker who is or was a member of a CTSO?
3. How could being a member of a CTSO help you in your academic pursuits?

## School and Community
Volunteering in your school and your community is an important part of developing your leadership and professional skills. Volunteer work can be anything as simple as helping to clean up your neighborhood streets, to working in a political campaign on election day. Often, volunteering your time and talents to a worthy cause is more important than any financial contribution you can make.

1. Get started with volunteer work by researching volunteer opportunities at your school or in your community. Find at least one opportunity at school and in the community. Which opportunities appeal to you?
2. State three ways the opportunities you have selected will help other people.
3. Write a brief statement describing how these opportunities might help improve your career skills or contribute to your resume and help improve your chances for success when applying for a job. If requested, give the statement to your instructor.

OUTCOMES

- Integrate your digital information management skills.
- Use creative thinking and analysis skills to solve problems, obtain information, and make correct decisions.

## Business Documents

- Agenda
- Worksheet with *Word* Document
- Data Source Files
- Modified Block Business Letter
- Address Labels
- Newsletter
- Multiple-Page Worksheets

- Meeting Minutes
- Annual Report with Appendix, Table of Contents, and Cover Page
- Financial Statements
- Presentation Slides
- News Release
- Newspaper Advertisement

---

### Job 1

**Agenda**

*The CVEF Scholarship Committee will meet on January 15 at 4:30 p.m. in the CVEF Board Room. I listed the open issues and new business that will be discussed. Please prepare an agenda for the committee members: Pauline Cooper, Chair; Meryl Pogue; and Katherine Ralston. Ms. Cooper will serve as the facilitator. If you want, you can use our agenda template (df135 job1 agenda). Save the file as 135 job1 agenda.*

*mh*

**To Do List**

**Scholarship Committee Agenda**

Open issues

   a)  Review 2013–2014 Scholarship Program Highlights

   b)  Preview 2014–2015 Scholarship Program

New business

   a)  Selecting Recipients

   b)  Presenting Scholarships

   c)  Paying Scholarships

Adjournment

---

### Job 2

**Worksheet**

*I was reviewing the account statements in df 135 job2 loans and found that we need to take Step 1 action for Larry Parry, who has missed his last three payments. How about opening his account record and inserting this information as a Word file beneath the entry. Save the file as 135 job2 loans.*

*mh*

**To Do List**

This is a reminder that you have missed your last three payments. It is important that you make regular payments. If you need to discuss the reason why you have not made your payments, call me at 412-555-0337.

Marilyn Hardy

January 2015

---

### Job 3

**Address Labels**

*I need address labels for alums that have loans but are still in college. I'll be sending them an update form in the near future. Do not prepare one for Cole Wehner, as he was graduated last month. We'll take care of updating his record later. I believe you can find the addresses in df 135 job3 data. We are using Avery 5160 Easy Peel labels. Save the file as 135 job3 labels.*

*mh*

# Assessing Basic Word Processing Skills

<table>
<tr><td>**WP: Assessment 1**</td><td>In order to complete the word processing units in Cycle 1 (Unit 2, Communicating Clearly; Unit 3, Analyzing Table Information; and Unit 8, Creating Effective Reports), you should have the skills and knowledge required to complete this word processing assessment.</td></tr>
</table>

1. Open *Word* and then open ***df wp assess 1*** and complete the following steps as directed.

**Bold**
**Italicize**
**Underline**

2. Bold, italicize, and underline the title.

**Font**
**Font size**
**Font color**

3. Change the title font to Times New Roman 16 point in a dark red color.

**Change Case**

4. Change the font to ALL CAPS, and highlight it with a light gray shade.

**Hyphenation**

5. Hyphenate the ¶s.

**Spelling & Grammar**

6. Check and correct the text for spelling and grammar errors.

**Thesaurus**

7. Find and insert an appropriate synonym for "unit" in the first line of the ¶.

**Insert Date & Time**

8. Tap Enter twice after the last line of the last ¶, and insert the date using the Date & Time feature, using May 22, 2011 format. Do not update automatically. Tap Enter twice after the date.

**Remove Space After ¶**

9. Key your name and tap Enter once.
10. Key your school name and tap Enter once.
11. Key the street address for your school, and tap Enter once.
12. Key the city, state, and ZIP Code for your school. Tap Enter once.
13. Remove the space after the first three lines you keyed.

**Bullets and Numbering**

14. Key the following four items as a bulleted list below the last line of your school address:
    **Paper      Pencil      Notebook      Data files**
15. Tap Enter three times and key the following team names as a numbered list below your bulleted list:
    **Pirates      Reds      Indians      Orioles**
16. Tap Enter twice.

# UNIT 25 Real-World Application IV

## Work Assignment at Central Valley Education Foundation

This unit is designed to extend experiences you likely would have working in an administrative assistant position. Assume you are completing the second half of the Central Valley High School (CVHS) service-learning requirement that you started in Unit 19.

You are continuing your assignment at the Central Valley Education Foundation (CVEF) that strives to support the Central Valley School District in a variety of ways.

You will continue working with Marilyn Hardy, Assistant Director, and will assist her with the scholarship program and the student loan program as well as other activities that are assigned to you. As you may recall, Ms. Hardy, a graduate of CVHS, has been with CVEA since its inception in 2005 and has been directing the scholarship program since it was started in 2010 and the student loan program since it was transferred from the Central Valley Student Aid Fund, a separate association, to CVEA in 2007.

For the purposes of this simulation, assume you are completing your service learning during the beginning weeks of 2015. This assumption is necessary because many of the documents and transactions are date specific.

## General

The guidelines you followed for the first half of your assignment with CVEF will continue to apply. They are:

1. You are to follow all directions that are given.
2. If a formatting guide or direction is not given, use what you have learned in your digital information management course at CVHS to prepare the documents.
3. Always be alert to and correct errors in punctuation, capitalization, spelling, and word usage.

## Correspondence

Prepare all letters in modified block format with mixed punctuation and no ¶ indentations. Supply an appropriate salutation and complimentary close and use your reference initials and other letter parts as needed.

## Reports

Use the unbound report format with footnotes to prepare reports. Unless directed otherwise, apply an appropriate style set. Number all pages except page 1.

## Tables and Charts

Unless directed otherwise, you can decide whether spreadsheet or word processing software should be used to prepare tables. Be sure to format and identify the various parts of these documents so the reader can easily read or interpret the data you present. Print the loan worksheets on one sheet of paper unless directed otherwise.

## Data Source Files

Ms. Hardy will determine the fields that are to be included in the data source file.

You should apply what you have learned and your creativity to prepare other documents if specific instructions are not provided.

## Filenames

Since Ms. Hardy will need to access the files you create, she will suggest filenames for you to use; however, you should add your initials at the end of each filename. The filenames (including worksheet and workbook names) will be referenced in her notes to you.

| | | |
|---|---|---|
| Left Tab | 17. | Set a left tab at 1", a right tab at 2.75", and decimal tabs at 3.75" and 5". |
| Right Tab | 18. | Key the following two lines beginning at the Left tab. Use the Tab key to move from one |
| Decimal Tab | | column to another. Remove the space between the two lines of text: |

**Jim Ball**     6,750     88.395     0.25
**Kay Kent**     30          367.31     32.0678

| | | |
|---|---|---|
| Show/Hide ¶ | 19. | Below the last line of text, key a description of the symbols that are used to denote hidden formatting marks for spaces between words, the use of the Tab key, and the end of a ¶. |
| | 20. | **Save as:** *wp assess 1*. Print and close the file. |

| | | |
|---|---|---|
| Envelopes | 21. | Open a new word processing document. |
| | 22. | Prepare a large envelope that is to be sent to your teacher. Use your name and home address as the return address. |
| | 23. | Print and close the file. |

## WP: Assessment 2

In order to complete the word processing units in Cycle 1 (Unit 2, Communicating Clearly; Unit 3, Analyzing Table Information; and Unit 8, Creating Effective Reports), you should have the skills and knowledge required to complete this word processing assessment.

| | | |
|---|---|---|
| Insert Table | 1. | Open a new word processing document, and create a table that is three columns and four rows. |
| | 2. | Key the following information in the cells. |

| Player | Class | Position |
|--------|-------|----------|
| Jim | Junior | Third Base |
| Ned | Senior | Outfielder |
| Mark | Sophomore | Pitcher |

| | | |
|---|---|---|
| Select and Format Cell Content | 3. | Center-align the text in columns 2 and 3. |

| | | |
|---|---|---|
| Insert/Delete Rows and Columns | 4. | Insert two rows at the bottom, and key the following text into them: |

| Jerry | Senior | Catcher |
|-------|--------|---------|
| Luiz | Junior | Infielder |

5. Insert one column at the right, and key the following text in the column:

| Average |
|---------|
| .345 |
| .298 |
| .262 |
| .301 |
| .295 |

## Assembling a Career Portfolio

As you learned in Unit 23, a career portfolio contains information about you and samples of items that show how your previous activities and achievements relate to your career pursuits. The contents of the career portfolio can include such things as:

- Certificates, letters, newspaper articles, programs, brochures, and so on, that document your accomplishments.
- Samples of your writing and projects you have completed.
- Course grades and results from standardized tests such as the SAT and/or ACT tests that are important for the job you are seeking.
- Your personal resume and list of references.
- Letters of recommendation from your references.
- Standard cover letter to accompany your resume.
- Standard thank-you letter to send as a follow-up to an interview.
- Career plan.

Throughout this course, you have prepared a variety of personal job search documents and other files that would be suitable for your portfolio. In this activity, you will gather those items to assemble the printed version of your portfolio. You should also consider compiling an electronic version of your portfolio so that interviewers can refer to it as they make their hiring decision.

1. Review the Career Plan you prepared in the *Careers* activity in Unit 22. Check spelling and grammar and make any modifications you feel are necessary. Note that you might want to apply similar formatting to all your job search documents to give your materials a consistent look. Print the Career Plan.
2. Review the print resume you prepared in Unit 23. Finalize the document and print.
3. Review the list of references you prepared in Unit 23. Update contact information and formatting as necessary. Print the list.
4. Review the cover letter you prepared in the *Careers* activity in Unit 23. Check spelling and grammar and make modifications as necessary. Print the letter.
5. Review the interview follow-up letter you created in Activity 133C of Unit 23. You can customize this letter as necessary. Print the letter.
6. Make a copy of your most recent report card and/or create a list of relevant courses and the grades you received.
7. Obtain letters of recommendation from your references.
8. Gather certificates, letters, newspaper articles, and so on, that document your accomplishments.
9. Gather samples of your writing (including creative pieces, research reports, presentation handouts, etc.), artwork (take photos of large, 3-dimensional, or fragile pieces), and other printable files that illustrate your skills.

| | |
|---|---|
| Format Painter | 6. If needed, use the Format Painter to format the text just keyed. |
| Split Cells | 7. Split cells in column 1 into two columns. Beginning in cell A2, key the following names into the new column: |

| Wilson |
|---|
| Menzies |
| Greene |
| Pasco |
| Gomez |

| | |
|---|---|
| Select and Format Cell Content | 8. Select and merge cells A1 and A2. |
| Adjusting Column Width and Row Height | 9. Specify the height of row 1 to be 0.5". <br> 10. Change the font size of row 1 to 14 point. <br> 11. Adjust column widths so they are as wide as the longest item within each column. |
| Table Styles | 12. Apply the List Table 4 – Accent 1 style from the Table Styles group. <br> 13. Change the Table Style from Banded Rows to Banded Columns. |
| Vertical Alignment | 14. Align the column headings in row 1 so they are aligned at the bottom left. <br> 15. Insert a row at the bottom, merge the cells, and key the following text, right-aligned: |

| Injured Players for the Jefferson Game |
|---|

| | |
|---|---|
| Shading and Borders | 16. Place a 3-point blue border around the table. <br> 17. Shade the last row using Orange, Accent 2, Lighter 40 from the Table Styles group. |
| Portrait/Landscape Orientation | 18. Change the orientation to Landscape. |
| Centering Tables | 19. Center the table on the page. |
| Sort | 20. Sort the table by Average in descending order. <br> 21. **Save as:** *wp assess 2*. Print and close the file. |

# Academic and Career Connections

Complete the following exercises that introduce various topics that involve academic themes and careers.

## Communications: Composition

Businesses demonstrate their social responsibility in many ways: They provide opportunities for employees to grow and succeed in both their personal and professional lives; they recognize their role in protecting and preserving the environment; and they actively participate in programs to benefit and improve their community.

1. Select a business in your community or region. It can be any type of business, large or small, public or privately owned.
2. Gather information on what the company does to promote social responsibility. For example, does it sponsor charitable community events, offer programs to benefit employee health and wellness, or take a stand on environmental issues? You might find this information on the company's website or by interviewing the owner or another member of management.
3. Prepare a one-page report on how the company demonstrates social responsibility. Format the report as desired. As directed by your instructor, share your report with the class.

## Art

To maintain a productive workforce and manage health care costs, many companies offer programs to promote employee health and wellness. These address issues such as eating a balanced diet, getting proper exercise, avoiding risky behaviors, and maintaining a healthy lifestyle.

1. Research the issues noted above and other health and wellness topics. Create a list of at least five things you can do to promote your own health and wellness.
2. Design a poster that is based on your research and list. You can create the poster by hand or on the computer. (Note that poster templates are available at Office.com.)
3. As you design the poster, check for attention-getting devices, such as vivid descriptions, action verbs, and engaging graphics.
4. Share your poster with the class.

---

### School and Community
Through a community or school-sponsored rummage sale, people can sell things they don't want anymore and at the same time raise money for a good cause.

1. Identify a charity you would like to support or a cause to which you would like to donate money. You will organize a rummage sale to benefit the charity or cause.
2. Determine the location for the sale. An indoor facility is ideal, but outdoors in a parking lot or other public venue will work. Make sure to secure necessary permissions.
3. Contact potential participants, such as classmates, neighbors, and local businesses. You can allow them to set up individual tables or drop off items in a designated location.
4. Collect bags and newspapers for wrapping purchases.
5. Advertise the sale. You can post free ads on websites such as Craigslist and Facebook. You should also post ads on telephone poles; in supermarkets, libraries, and neighborhood churches; and on community bulletin boards.

---

In order to complete the word processing units in Cycle 1 (Unit 2, Communicating Clearly; Unit 3, Analyzing Table Information; and Unit 8, Creating Effective Reports), you should have the skills and knowledge required to complete this word processing assessment.

1. Open *df wp assess 3* and complete the following steps as directed.

**Text From File**

2. Position your cursor on the line below the end of the ¶ before REFERENCE.
3. Insert the text from *df wp assess insert*.

**Line and ¶ Spacing**

4. Change the line spacing to 2.0 line spacing.
5. Change the spacing before and after ¶s to 0 points.

**Page Break**

6. Insert a hard page break so the reference appears on a separate page.

**Line and Page Breaks**

7. Use Keep with Next and Widow Orphan as needed to have the pages begin and end correctly.

**Page Numbers**

8. Number the pages with a page number at the bottom center of the page, but hide the number on page 1.

**Indentations**

9. Format the reference on the last page with a hanging ¶ indent.
10. Format page 1 so it has a top margin of approximately 2". Do the same for the page on which the reference appears.

**Styles**

11. Format the report title on page 1 and REFERENCE on page 4 using Title style.
12. Format the side headings with Heading 1 style.

**Insert Footnote**

13. Insert the following footnote at the end of the last line of the report on page 3:
Jack P. Hoggatt and Jon A. Shank, *Century 21 Computer Applications and Keyboarding*, 9th edition (Mason, Ohio: South-Western, Cengage Learning, 2010), p. 86.

**Line and Page Breaks**

14. Correct page endings and beginnings as needed.
15. **Save as:** *wp assess 3*. Print and close the file.

Key 2 5' writings on all ¶s combined; find *gwam* and errors.

 all letters used                                    `gwam`  3' | 5'

Stress qualifies as either good or bad depending on the          4 | 2
circumstances and ability of people to cope.  It is good when it        8 | 5
has resulted from a pleasant event, such as a promotion.  In          12 | 7
addition, it may increase job performance if the pressure is not        16 | 10
too great.  On the other hand, stress is bad when caused by an        21 | 12
unpleasant event, such as being passed over for a prized promo-        25 | 15
tion.  Furthermore, it may interfere with the performance of a        29 | 17
task when the pressure is excessive.        31 | 19

The major point to recognize is that stress is quite normal        35 | 21
and will be experienced at times by all.  Avoiding stress is not        40 | 24
an issue, but learning to handle day-to-day stress in a proper        44 | 26
manner is.  A few methods that work are taking the time for        48 | 29
regular exercise, getting enough sleep, and eating well-balanced        52 | 31
meals.  These specific methods relate to personal habits.  In        56 | 34
addition, using some stress reducers that more directly relate to        61 | 36
the job also will be helpful.        63 | 38

A good way to reduce stress in the office is to use tech-        66 | 40
niques known to improve time management.  These include analyzing        71 | 43
the tasks performed to see if all are necessary, judging which        75 | 45
ones are most important so that priorities can be set, and using        79 | 48
most of the time to do the jobs that are most important.  Office        84 | 50
workers who do not use these procedures may expend considerable        88 | 53
energy on less valuable tasks and feel stressed when more impor-        92 | 55
tant ones go unfinished.        94 | 56

`gwam` 3' |___1___|___2___|___3___|___4___|
       5' |____1____|____2____|____3____|

## Reference Guide

### Memos

**TIP** In many organizations, email messages have replaced memos. However, many organizations still prepare a document in memo format for interoffice communication when a higher degree of formality is preferred. The memo is usually sent as an email attachment rather than through interoffice mail.

Memos (interoffice memorandums) are written messages used by employees within an organization to communicate with one another. For example, a supervisor could send a memo to his staff about a new procedure that everyone should follow. Memos are usually created from "scratch" in a new word processing document (Figure 2-1) or from a memo template—a sample memo with standard text and formatting that is likely to remain the same in all memos and space for text that differs from memo to memo. They may be printed on plain or letterhead paper or sent as an email message. A standard format (arrangement) for memos follows, and it is illustrated on page 60.

### Margins and Line Spacing

**Top margin:** At least 2" on page 1 (tap Enter 3 times); 1" on subsequent pages
**Bottom margin:** At least 1"
**Side margins:** Default or 1"
**Line spacing:** Default line spacing (1.08 with 8-pt. spacing after ¶) unless otherwise specified

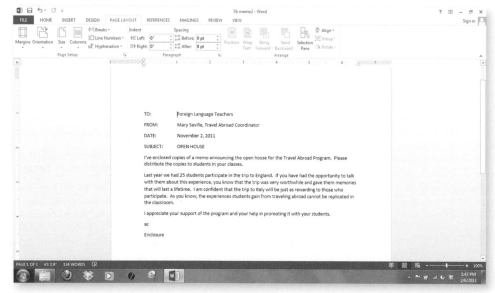

**Figure 2-1** Memo in *Microsoft Word* window

- Complete a program of studies that will lead to an undergraduate or graduate degree. For example, you may have a bachelor's degree in engineering but want to complete a master's degree program in business to enhance your opportunities to move into a position where you might supervise engineering or engineering functions of the business. Or, if you completed an undergraduate major in business and wish to become a registered nurse, you could complete a nursing program of study that leads to licensure or one that leads to licensure and a two- or four-year nursing-related degree.

**Professional, Trade, and Service Associations**—Another avenue for increasing your job performance or advancing your career is to become a member of professional, trade, and service associations that are important in your career field.

These associations often operate at the local, state, regional, national, and/or international level. As a member, you will have continuous access to valuable information that will keep you informed about issues, trends, conditions, and new developments within the industry, profession, or community served by the association. You can keep informed by accessing the association's website, reading the association's research and publications, and attending association meetings, conferences, and conventions.

The associations may also provide you with many opportunities to develop and refine your organizational and leadership skills by serving on or chairing committees or serving as an officer. Some of the professional associations sponsor student organizations that provide high school and college students the opportunity to develop and practice important career skills while they are in school.

**Networking**—Networking is the practice of establishing and maintaining associations with persons to support mutually beneficial relationships. Networking is an excellent means to find jobs because those who make the actual hiring decisions would much rather consider hiring someone who has been recommended by someone they know and trust. Not only does the recommendation serve as a reference check, it saves the employer the time and effort he would spend sorting through the resumes a position advertisement is likely to generate.

Networking is done through interactions with people in a wide variety of venues. You are networking when you develop meaningful connections with people at school, professional meetings, conferences, seminars, sporting events, church, and so on. A meaningful connection is usually developed when the person knows your name, remembers positive things about you, and is likely to refer you to others at appropriate times.

Your neighbors, teachers, classmates, relatives, and friends with whom you have a meaningful connection are also in your network. In other words, your network can be as large as the number of people you interact with in meaningful ways and the number of people with whom they have meaningful interactions. However, it is important to remember that an effective network is built upon a relationship that will benefit the other person as well as yourself. You should always think of ways you can help those in your network as well as how they can help you.

In addition to networking face-to-face with people, you can use Web 2.0 tools to network online. For example, you can use discussion boards to carry on conversations with those who have similar interests and social networking sites to develop professional linkages.

2. Open *134e report* and in the appropriate place in the 134f section:
   - Identify at least five individuals from your school (teachers, coaches, counselors, principals, classmates, etc.) you would include in your professional network and briefly state why.
   - Identify the position you aspire to hold within 10 years from now and describe the education that you need for the position and a career path that will enable you to attain the desired position.

3. Save as: *134f report*.

## Memo Features

*Memo heading.* The memo heading includes who the memo is being sent to (TO), who the memo is from (FROM), the date the memo is being sent (DATE), and what the memo is about (SUBJECT). Use ALL CAPS for the headings beginning at the left margin, and tap Enter as directed to achieve proper vertical line spacing. Use initial caps for the text in the subject line; however, it is also acceptable to use ALL CAPS for the text. When the memo message is sent as an email, you insert the TO and SUBJECT information and the email software inserts the FROM and DATE when the message is sent. See Figure 2-2.

TO:       Tap Tab twice and then key name. (Tap Enter once.)

FROM:    Tap Tab twice and then key name. (Tap Enter once.)

DATE:    Tap Tab twice and then key date. (Tap Enter once.)

SUBJECT: Tap Tab once and then key subject. (Tap Enter once.)

*Memo body.* The ¶s of the memo body begin at the left margin. (Tap Enter once at the end of each ¶.)

*Reference initials.* If someone other than the originator of the memo keys it, his/her initials are keyed in lowercase letters at the left margin. (Tap Enter once after keying the initials)

*Distribution list.* When a memo is sent to several individuals, a distribution list is used in the To: line. Format the distribution list as shown:

TO: (Tab twice) Tim Belows (Press Shift + Enter)
(Tab twice) Carla Dunlap (Press Shift + Enter)
(Tab twice) Ramon Garcia (Press Shift + Enter)
(Tab twice) Gwen Littleton (Press Shift + Enter)

**★TIP** You may need to Undo Automatic Capitalization to key the first letter in the reference initials in lowercase if AutoCorrect options are not changed.

Interoffice Memo

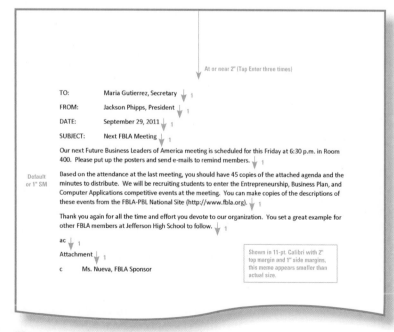

At or near 2" (Tap Enter three times)

| | |
|---|---|
| TO: | Maria Gutierrez, Secretary ↓ 1 |
| FROM: | Jackson Phipps, President ↓ 1 |
| DATE: | September 29, 2011 ↓ 1 |
| SUBJECT: | Next FBLA Meeting ↓ 1 |

Our next Future Business Leaders of America meeting is scheduled for this Friday at 6:30 p.m. in Room 400. Please put up the posters and send e-mails to remind members. ↓ 1

Default or 1" SM

Based on the attendance at the last meeting, you should have 45 copies of the attached agenda and the minutes to distribute. We will be recruiting students to enter the Entrepreneurship, Business Plan, and Computer Applications competitive events at the meeting. You can make copies of the descriptions of these events from the FBLA-PBL National Site (http://www.fbla.org). ↓ 1

Thank you again for all the time and effort you devote to our organization. You set a great example for other FBLA members at Jefferson High School to follow. ↓ 1

ac ↓ 1

Attachment ↓ 1

c     Ms. Nueva, FBLA Sponsor

Shown in 11-pt. Calibri with 2" top margin and 1" side margins, this memo appears smaller than actual size.

Tetra Images/Jupiter Images

**Figure 2-2** Memo

- Show initiative and don't be afraid to volunteer to do something that may be new or different or will help you expand the scope of your position.
- Follow through to completion the duties and responsibilities of your position.
- Always try to create a favorable impression with all people you meet and work with as you cannot predict who may affect your career opportunities.

2. Open *134d report* and in the 134e section, describe at least five situations in which you demonstrated one or more of the above actions that help project a professional image. You may include activities related to school, community, church, work, or home.

3. **Save as:** *134e report.*

## 134F

### Advancing Your Career

1. Read the suggestions below relating to advancing your career.

If you are like most working individuals, you will strive to advance to higher-level positions. This is especially true during the early years when you aspire to advance beyond entry-level positions to ones that have expanded duties and responsibilities. Advancements usually result in higher earnings and greater recognition from your peers, family, friends, and acquaintances. Unfortunately, each advancement may not bring with it job satisfaction. If job dissatisfaction becomes a concern in your career, you should consider taking a different path in your career to regain the level of job satisfaction you desire. There are many paths that individuals can follow to advance their career. Among them are:

- Working for the same employer while seeking promotions or transfers that will advance your career.
- Changing employers to obtain promotions or transfers that will advance your career.
- Seeking a position that will enable you to remain employed while pursuing concurrent self-employment opportunities.
- Becoming self-employed on a full-time basis.

Other avenues you can use to advance your career include such things as continuing your educations, getting involved in professional and trade associations, and networking.

**Education**—Once you have achieved the level of education that is needed for entry into your chosen career field, it is good to plan to complete additional education that will help you be more effective and advance your career or is required to maintain a professional license, certification, or designation. Trade schools, colleges and universities, professional and trade associations, and government agencies usually offer educational opportunities in a variety of formats, including distance learning, to meet the educational needs of workers. Some employers will pay part or all of the tuition if the additional education is of value to their business. The desired education can usually be completed as a part-time student allowing you to continue your employment. The educational objectives of workers are varied and may include learning in one of the following formats:

- Complete one or a series of courses that will provide the content you want. For example, if you are working in information technology and want to learn a new programming language, you could complete that programming course at a trade school, community college, or college or university.
- Complete the course requirements to earn or maintain a license or certification. For example, if you are an English teacher and want to be able to also teach social studies, you could complete the required courses at a college or university that certifies social studies teachers. Or, if you are a certified financial planner and need to complete continuing education to maintain your certification, you could complete approved course work offered by the professional association that awards the certification.

A letter written by an individual to deal with business of a personal nature is called a **personal-business letter.** A personal-business letter is typically printed on personal stationery that does not have a preprinted return address as shown in Figure 2-3a. A **business letter** is written by an individual who is fulfilling a responsibility related to his/her employment. Business letters are typically printed on letterhead stationery (stationery that has a preprinted return address and other information about the business) as shown in Figure 2-3b.

**Figure 2-3a** Personal-business letter

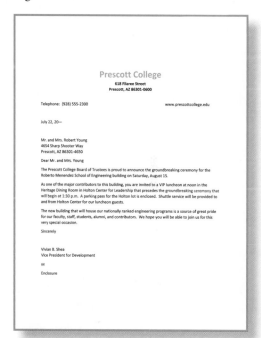

**Figure 2-3b** Business letter

### Margins and Line Spacing

**Top margin:** At or near 2" on page 1 (tap Enter 3 times); 1" on subsequent pages. If the letterhead extends near or below the 2" line, begin the date about 0.5" below the last line of the letterhead.

**Bottom margin:** At least 1"

**Side margins:** Default or 1"

**Line spacing:** Default line spacing (1.08 with 8-pt. spacing after ¶) unless otherwise specified.

### Basic Letter Features

The basic parts of a letter are described in order of placement on the paper. Differences between the parts of a personal-business letter and a business letter are identified.

- **Return address.** The return address on a personal-business letter (start at or near the 2" line) consists of a line for the street address and one for the city, state, and ZIP Code. Press Shift + Enter once after each line of the return address.

    The return address on a business letter need not be keyed because the street, city, state, and ZIP Code are preprinted on letterhead stationery. In addition, the company name, phone numbers, and/or website are usually part of the letterhead.

- **Date.** When keying a personal-business letter, key the month, day, and year on the line below the city, state, and ZIP Code. Tap Enter twice to begin the letter address.

    When keying a business letter, begin the date at or near the 2" line or 0.5" below the last line of the letterhead, whichever is lower. Tap Enter twice to begin the letter mailing address.

2. Open **134b report** and preview the information requested in the 134c section and then key the information described below in the appropriate space.
   - Identify your priorities for today and describe your plan for accomplishing them.
   - Identify special projects, tasks, and/or activities you need to accomplish within the next four weeks and describe your plan for accomplishing them.
   - Identify what major priorities you want to accomplish this summer and describe your plan for accomplishing them.
3. **Save as:** **134c report**.

## 134D

### Selecting a Mentor

1. Read about establishing a mentoring relationship with someone.

A mentor is someone who is willing to share experiences and knowledge that you can consider when making a decision or solving a problem relating to your present job or career opportunities.

A mentor may be someone who works for the same or a different employer, a family member, a teacher, a coach, and so on. An effective mentor will be available as needed to provide you with information, make positive suggestions, point out possible consequences of different actions, and provide the guidance needed so you can make a decision or solve a problem. As your career advances and your responsibilities change, you may need to establish a relationship with a different mentor who has the experience and knowledge appropriate for your present circumstances.

Mentors usually know your abilities, strengths and weaknesses, interests, and career goals and will oftentimes spread the "good word" about you to their colleagues when they know of opportunities for career advancement that could benefit you.

2. Open **134c report** and preview the information requested in the 134d section.
3. In the space provided, name one person you would want to serve as your mentor when you are graduated from high school and begin to pursue your career via pursuing further education, entering the workforce, or serving in the military. Identify your relationship with this person and the experience and knowledge she has that you believe will be helpful to you as you embark on your career or preparation for your career.
4. **Save as:** **133d report**.

## 134E

### Professionalism

1. Read the following about professionalism.

One important aspect of being an effective employee and enjoying a rewarding career is to act professionally at all times. You should strive to earn a reputation for being dependable, believable, honest, cooperative, and eager to learn. While professionalism has many dimensions, the following are practical actions that project a professional image.
   - Always be on time, respect the time of others, and don't be known for rushing to leave at the end of the workday.
   - Dress professionally, neatly, and appropriately for the situation.
   - Display a positive attitude, especially during difficult situations when others may be negative.
   - Don't whine, make excuses, or blame others when things don't go your way.
   - Ask questions when you are not sure what to do or how to do something.
   - Be flexible, take chances to grow, and try to make things work.

- **Letter address.** Key the first line of the letter (delivery) address below the date. A personal title (Miss, Mr., Mrs., Ms.) or a professional title (Dr., Lt., Senator) is keyed before the receiver's name. Press Shift + Enter to move from line to line within the mailing address. Tap Enter once after keying the last line of the mailing address to begin the salutation.
- **Salutation.** Key the salutation (greeting). Include a courtesy title with the person's name, e.g., Dear Ms. Jones. Tap Enter once after keying the salutation.
- **Body.** Key the letter body (message) using the default line spacing (1.08). Tap Enter once after each ¶ and after the last line of the last ¶ in the body to begin the complimentary close.
- **Complimentary close.** Key the complimentary close (farewell). Capitalize only the first word in the complimentary close. Tap Enter twice. Key the name of the writer.
- **Name of the writer.** Key the name of the writer. The name may be preceded by a personal title (Miss, Mrs., Ms.) to indicate how a female prefers to be addressed in a response. If a male has a name that does not clearly indicate his gender (Kim, Leslie, Pat), the title Mr. may precede his name.
- **Position title.** In many letters, a position title (Manager, President, Salesperson, etc.) is used with the name of the writer. The position title may be keyed on the same line as the name of the writer (separated with a comma) or on the next line. If placed on the next line, press Shift + Enter and then key the position title. Tap Enter once to begin the next letter part, if any.
- **Reference initials.** If someone other than the originator of the letter keys it, his/her initials are keyed in lowercase letters at the left margin below the writer's name and/or title. Tap Enter once to begin the next letter part.

© kRie/Shutterstock.com

# 21st Century Skills: Digital Citizenship and Ethics

More everyday activities such as finding directions, making purchases, and transferring data are happening over the Web, and social networking sites such as Facebook, Twitter, and FourSquare enable users to connect with friends and family by sharing photos, videos, music, status updates, and even their current locations.

In addition, online services enable you to store and retrieve data such as music, photos, and videos on the Web so the files are accessible anywhere, any time. This is sometimes known as **cloud computing.**

One downside to storing and transferring all this personal data online is the possibility of identity theft. Because people consider PCs, laptops, tablets, and cell phones to be personal devices, they may be unaware that nearly anything they send online can be accessed by others if it is not sent or posted in a secure manner.

Identity theft can occur when malicious users gain access to personal data such as credit card information, bank account data, social security numbers, personal photographs, phone numbers, or addresses.

## Think Critically

1. What do you think might happen to a victim of identity theft?
2. Describe some things you can do to help yourself avoid identity theft.
3. Do you think identity theft will become more or less prevalent as more businesses and services store data online with cloud computing? State the reasons for your answer.

# LESSON 134    Being Effective and Advancing Your Career

**OUTCOMES**
- Learn the importance of continuous improvement.
- Set priorities and develop plans for the present, near future, and long term.
- Identify a mentor.
- Learn how to project professionalism.
- Learn important ways to advance a career.

## Business Document

### 134B

**Continuous Improvement**

- Report in Table Format

1. Read about the need to improve continuously to enhance the likelihood that you will be effective in the jobs you hold during your career and enjoy a rewarding career.

As you learned in Lesson 132, it is important that you be able to demonstrate that you possess the competencies, skills, and personal qualities that are expected of all employees. In this lesson, the focus is on continuously developing your competencies, skills, and personal qualities to higher levels and expanding them as new knowledge and technology impact your workplace. Through continuous improvement, you will increase your effectiveness in your present position and the likelihood that you will have opportunities to advance to higher-level positions during your career. Continuous improvement is also important for those who own their own business because the higher-level and expanded skills and knowledge will increase the chances that the owner will be able to sustain or grow the business.

2. Open *df 134b report*. Review the information requested in the 134b section of the form.
3. Working with one or more classmates, identify at least five new products or product enhancements that have become available during the past five years and briefly describe how each has affected the way people work.
4. Record your findings in the space provided in *df 134b report*.
5. **Save as:** *134b report*.

### 134C

**Planning**

1. Read about the importance of planning and prioritizing.

Effective employees begin every endeavor with an end in mind; that is, they plan and set priorities.
- They plan and set priorities for the day—What do I need to accomplish during this workday and how will I get it done?
- They plan and set priorities for the near future—What do I need to do to increase my chances for a promotion this year?
- They plan and set priorities for the long-term future—What do I need to do within the next five years to obtain the position I aspire to?

Planning and prioritizing take on more importance in today's world since most people no longer stay with one employer or in one career during their working years. Technology advances and the need to compete in a global environment have caused changes in the workplace that have both positively and negatively affected employees. In today's environment, many employers expect their employees to plan and pursue their own professional development so they will be able to take advantage of employment opportunities that arise with the present employer, with a different employer, or as an entrepreneur.

## Additional Memo and Letter Features

The following parts are frequently included in memos and letters. Unless otherwise noted, tap Enter once at the end of the line that preceded the part you are including. If more than one part is to be included, key them in the order listed.

*Attachment/Enclosure notation.* If used, the notation follows the Reference Initials. If another document is attached to a letter, the word *Attachment* is keyed at the left margin. If the additional document is not attached, the word *Enclosure* is used. If more than one document is attached or enclosed, make the notation plural.

*Copy notation.* A copy notation indicates that a copy of the letter is being sent to someone other than the addressee. The person(s) receiving the copy have an interest in the information but aren't expected to take any action. Key *c* and then tab to .05 to key the name(s) of the person(s) to receive a copy. If there is more than one name, list names vertically as shown below (press Shift + Enter to remove space between the names; tap Enter once after keying the last name in the list).

c　　Hector Ramirez
　　　Ursula O'Donohue

*Postscript.* A postscript is an optional message added to a letter or memo as the last item on the page. A postscript may be used to emphasize information in the body or to add a personal message to a business letter. Block or indent the first line of the postscript to match the ¶ indentations in the letter or memo. Do not use the postscript abbreviation (P.S.).

*Blind copy notation.* When a copy of a memo or letter is to be sent to someone without disclosing to the person receiving the memo or letter, a blind copy (bc) notation is used. When used, bc and the name of the person receiving the blind copy are keyed at the left margin one line below the last memo or letter part on all copies of the memo or letter *except* the original. Format the bc the same way as copy notations.

*Second-page header.* If a letter or memo is more than one page, a header is placed on all pages except the first using the Header feature. The header consists of three lines blocked at the left margin. Line 1 contains the addressee's name, line 2 contains the word *Page* and the page number, and line 3 contains the date. Alternatively, the header may also be formatted across one line with the addressee's name at the left margin, the page number centered, and the date aligned at the right margin.

> **Note:** Document formats in the textbook may vary slightly from the guidelines presented in the FBLA/PBL *Chapter Management Handbook*. The FBLA format guidelines are available on the IRCD or can be accessed at www.fbla-pbl.org.

Performance reviews are usually based on criteria stated on a form provided by the employer. The criteria describe the components of the position that will be evaluated and a rating scale that describes various levels of performance. Employees typically have access to the performance review form so they know the criteria against which their performance is being judged. Also, the same form is typically used to evaluate all employees within similar job classifications to increase the likelihood that employees are assessed similarly.

In this activity you will complete a self-appraisal form for recently hired employees. Your supervisor would consider your self-appraisal when completing her review of your performance in your new job.

2. Assume that this class is your new job and that you are to complete the requirements of this class to the best of your ability. Your teacher is your supervisor and is required to assess your performance in this class. As part of the performance review process for a new employee, you are required to complete a self-appraisal of your performance every three months. Your supervisor will consider your self-appraisal when assessing your performance. Your supervisor's assessment will determine if you will continue in a probationary status, must reach specific goals during the next review period to retain your employment, or will be reclassified as a regular employee.

3. Open *df 133e self-appraisal*. *Note:* As you key text into the document in the following steps, you should adjust the vertical spacing as needed to make the form attractive and easy to read and understand. If needed, the form can be more than one page.

4. Complete the first part of the form using your name, *Student* as the position, the date you began the class as the start date, the last three months as the review period, and your teacher's name as your supervisor.

5. Read the description for each Performance Rating and identify the points assigned to each rating.

6. Complete the six items in the Performance Component section. Include the number of the rating you believe you deserve in the Rating column. Key statements and/or identify evidence that supports your rating. For example, you could cite specific assignments that serve as evidence of the quality of your work. Or you could state that you have missed no classes to support your work habits rating.

7. Print the completed form, sign and date it.

8. **Save as:** *133e self-appraisal*.

The following parts are frequently included in letters. Unless otherwise noted, tap Enter once at the end of the line that preceded the part you are including. If more than one part is to be included, key them in the order listed.

*Mailing and addressee notations.* Mailing notations (such as REGISTERED, CERTIFIED, or FACSIMILE) and addressee notations (such as CONFIDENTIAL) may be included on a letter as well as on the envelope. Tap Enter once after keying the notation, and then key the letter address. On the envelope, key a mailing notation below the stamp, about 0.5" above the envelope address. Tap Enter once to key an addressee notation at the left margin below the return address.

*Attention line.* An attention line should only be used when the writer does not know the name of the person who should receive the letter. For example, if a writer wants a letter to go to the director of special collections of a library but doesn't know the name of that person, *Attention Special Collections Director* could be used. When an attention line is used in a letter, key it as the first line of the letter and envelope address. Within the letter, the correct salutation is *Ladies and Gentlemen* when an attention line has been used.

*Subject line.* The subject line specifies the topic discussed in the letter. Key the subject line in ALL CAPS or initial caps and lowercase between the salutation and the body of the letter.

## Letter Formats

View/Show/Ruler

*Block letter format* (as shown in Figure 2-4 and on page 60). All parts of a letter arranged in block format begin at the left margin. The ¶s are not indented.

*Modified block letter format* (as shown in Figure 2-5 and on page 67). Return address (if keyed), date, complimentary close, and name and position of writer begin at the center of the line of writing (set a left tab at 3.25 on the Ruler Bar when 1" side margins are used). The first line of each ¶ may be indented 0.5". All other letter parts begin at the left margin.

**Figure 2-4** Block letter format

**Figure 2-5** Modified block letter format

## Letter Punctuation Styles

*Mixed punctuation.* When mixed punctuation is used, place a colon after the salutation and a comma after the complimentary close.

*Open punctuation.* When open punctuation is used, do not key any punctuation after the salutation and complimentary close.

1. Open *df 133d form w-4*, an interactive PDF document.
2. Save it as *133d form w-4* but do not close it.
3. Read the instructions at the top of p. 1 of the document.
4. Open *df 133d questions* and key the answers to the questions in the space provided.
5. **Save as:** *133d questions*.
6. Using *133d form w-4*, complete the Personal Allowances Worksheet on p. 1 and the Two-Earners/Multiple Jobs Worksheet on p. 2 based on the following information:
   - You cannot be claimed as a dependent by anyone else.
   - You are married with a working spouse and two young children you will claim as dependents on your tax return.
   - You and your spouse file tax returns using the Married Filing Jointly category.
   - You earn $50,000 and your spouse earns $34,000.
   - You claim all allowances on your W-4.
   - You have child care expenses that exceed $1,900.
   - The names on your social security cards are correct.
   - You do not want any additional amount withheld from your paychecks.
7. **Save as:** *133d form w-4* but do not close the file.
8. Using your name, address, and 123-45-6789 as the social security number, complete Parts 1-7 of the Form W-4 at the bottom of p. 1.
9. Print p. 1 of the form.
10. Save completed form as *133d form w-4*.

**Figure 24-2** Form W-4

## 133E

Performance Reviews

1. Read the information below about employee performance reviews.

Most employees have their job performance reviewed annually by their supervisors. Some employees are evaluated more frequently, including those employees who have been recently hired. Newly hired employees may be assigned a conditional, provisional, or probationary status that may last until the performance review results warrant reclassification either to a regular status or dismissal from the position.

The performance review process often requires an employee to complete a self-appraisal that the supervisor will consider when completing her appraisal of the employee's performance (see Figure 24-3). Additionally, the review process may require the employee to achieve specific goals during the next performance review period. The results of an employee's job performance review may be used to determine such matters as:
- If an employee's employment will be continued or terminated.
- If an employee is ready to accept additional duties and responsibilities within his present position.
- If an employee deserves a raise in pay and/or a bonus and the size of the raise or bonus.
- If an employee will be promoted to a more responsible position.
- Professional development activities for the employee.

**Figure 24-3** Performance review form

## Memos

**OUTCOME**

- Format and key memos.

**Business Documents**

- Memo—Announcement and Request for Action
- Memo—Announcement
- Memo—Request for Guidance
- Memo—Information and Request for Action

**7A–14A**

**Warmup**

Key each line twice at the beginning of each lesson; first for control, then speed.

alphabet 1 Quin, zip that jacket and fix your muffler to brave raging winds.

fig/sym 2 My policy (#312-40-X) paid $26.97 interest and a $47.58 dividend.

speed 3 Pa's neighbor may fish off the dock at the lake by the cornfield.

**gwam** 1' | 1 | 2 | 3 | 4 | 5 | 6 | 7 | 8 | 9 | 10 | 11 |

Interoffice Memo

At or near 2" (Tap Enter three times)

TO:            Maria Gutierrez, Secretary ↓ 1

FROM:        Jackson Phipps, President ↓ 1

DATE:        Current Date ↓ 1

SUBJECT:    Next FBLA Meeting ↓ 1

Our next Future Business Leaders of America meeting is scheduled for this Friday at 6:30 p.m. in Room 400.  Please put up the posters and send e-mails to remind members. ↓ 1

**Default or 1" SM**

Based on the attendance at the last meeting, you should have 45 copies of the attached agenda and the minutes to distribute.  We will be recruiting students to enter the Entrepreneurship, Business Plan, and Computer Applications competitive events at the meeting.  You can make copies of the descriptions of these events from the FBLA-PBL National Site (www.fbla.org). ↓ 1

Thank you again for all the time and effort you devote to our organization.  You set a great example for other FBLA members at Jefferson High School to follow. ↓ 1

xx ↓ 1

Attachment ↓ 1

c    Ms. Nueva, FBLA Sponsor

> Shown in 11-pt. Calibri with 2" top margin and 1" side margins, this memo appears smaller than actual size.

persons to be covered by the plan. Once a plan is selected, it generally cannot be changed until the following year. State and federal laws allow employees a range of choices in terms of their medical benefits and who provides them services.

**Life Insurance**—If an employer provides life insurance as a benefit, employees will need to designate a primary and a secondary beneficiary. If living, the primary beneficiary would receive the life insurance proceeds if the employee dies during the time the policy is in effect. If the primary beneficiary is deceased at the time of the employee's death, the proceeds would go to the secondary beneficiary. Beneficiary designations may be changed when the employee has a need to make a change. For example, the birth or adoption of an additional child may require a change in the beneficiary designations.

**Local Income Taxes**—Many municipalities and school districts levy an income tax on earnings of workers. If you reside within the school district or municipality where the employer is located, the tax is likely to be deducted from your pay. If you do not live within the school district or municipality where you work, you may need to pay these taxes directly to the taxing agency where you reside. In that case, you may need to verify that you pay the income tax to your taxing agencies to avoid having it deducted from your pay.

**Direct Deposit**—Employees who have the option to have their paychecks deposited directly into their bank accounts will need to provide employers their account numbers and bank account routing numbers that are printed at the bottom of their bank checks.

3. Open **df 133b questions** and key the answers to the questions in the space provided.
4. **Save as: 133b questions.**

## 133C

**Form I-9**

1. Open **df 133c form i-9**, an interactive PDF document.
2. Save it as **133c form i-9** but do not close it.
3. Read the instructions on pp. 1–6 of the document, referring to pp. 7 and 8 as needed.
4. Open **df 133c questions** and key the answers to the questions in the space provided.
5. **Save as: 133c questions.**
6. Using **133c form i-9**, read the information above Section 1.
7. Using your name, address, and date of birth; 123-45-6789 as the social security number; and your email address and telephone number, complete Section 1 of the form.
8. Print the pages with Section 1 and sign the Form I-9.
9. Save the completed Form I-9 as **133c form 1-9**.

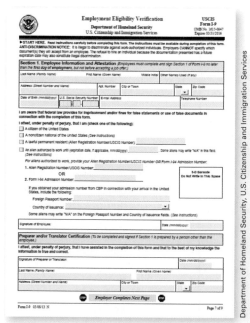

**Figure 24-1** Form I-9, page 1

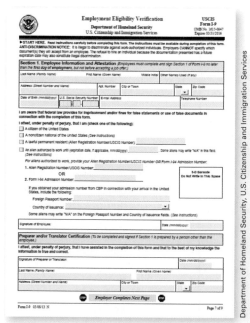Department of Homeland Security, U.S. Citizenship and Immigration Services

## Learn: Interoffice Memos

 Replace the reference initials xx with your initials in this and other documents where xx is used.

 Each time the year is indicated with 20—, replace it with the current year.

### Memo 1

1. Using the *Reference Guide* on page 46, read and study the *Memos* section on page 46, the Additional Memo and Letter Features section on page 50, and the model copy on page 47 to learn to format memos. Note the vertical and horizontal placement of the memo parts.
2. Format and key the model memo on page 52.
3. Proofread your copy; correct all keying and formatting errors.
4. **Save as:** *7b memo1*.

### Memo 2

1. Format and key the following information as a memo.
2. Proofread your copy; correct all errors.
3. **Save as:** *7b memo2*.

TO:          Foreign Language Teachers

FROM:       Mary Seville, Travel Abroad Coordinator

DATE:       November 2, 20--

SUBJECT:  OPEN HOUSE

I've enclosed copies of a memo announcing the open house for the Travel Abroad Program. Please distribute the copies to students in your classes.

Last year we had 25 students participate in the trip to England. If you have had the opportunity to talk with them about this experience, you know that the trip was very worthwhile and gave them memories that will last a lifetime. I am confident that the trip to Italy will be just as rewarding to those who participate. As you know, the experiences students gain from traveling abroad cannot be replicated in the classroom.

I appreciate your support of the program and your help in promoting it with your students.


xx

Enclosure

*Self-Management*—assesses own knowledge, skills, and abilities accurately; sets well-defined and realistic personal goals; monitors progress toward goal attainment and motivates self through goal achievement; exhibits self-control and responds to feedback unemotionally and non defensively; is a "self-starter."

*Integrity/Honesty*—can be trusted. Recognizes when faced with making a decision or exhibiting behavior that may break with commonly held personal or societal values; understands the impact of violating these beliefs and codes on an organization, self, and others; and chooses an ethical course of action.

2. Open ***df 132g qualities***. Assume you are the employee and your teacher is your employer. Indicate how your teacher would rate you on each of the SCANS personal qualities as directed in the appraisal form.
3. **Save as:** ***132g qualities***.

# LESSON 133 — Establishing Yourself in a New Job

**OUTCOMES**

- Learn about employment documentation needed when beginning to work for a new employer.
- Complete a Form I-9.
- Complete a Form W-4.
- Complete a new employee self-appraisal form.

## Business Documents

- U.S. CIS Form I-9
- U.S. IRS Form W-4
- New Employee Self-Appraisal Form

### 133B

**Employment Documentation**

1. Read the following information about two employment forms you will be required to complete each time you begin working for a new employer.

**Form W-4**—This form is required by the U.S. Internal Revenue Service (IRS) and is used to determine the amount of federal income tax your employer will deduct from your gross pay each pay period.

**Form I-9**—This record is required by the U.S. Citizenship and Immigration Services and is used to document that a new employee is authorized to work in the United States.

2. Read about documentation you may need to provide when you change employers, your pay changes, or your benefits change. The number and types of forms you may need to complete will depend to a great extent on the kinds of benefits offered by your employer.

Paul Doyle/Alamy

**Retirement Plans**—Employees may be able to invest part of their earnings in several retirement savings options, one of which is the 401K program. If your employer offers a retirement plan, you will need to document your selection of a desired savings plan and the amount you want deducted from your pay as your contribution. Oftentimes, employers will match your contribution up to a specified amount. With 401Ks, employees do not pay taxes on the money that is set aside or on the interest earned from stock, bonds, or other savings instruments used to increase the fund until after they retire.

**Medical Insurance**—Many employers offer employees medical insurance to help pay for hospital costs, doctor bills, drug costs, and/or dental services. Oftentimes, employees will need to document their selection of a specific plan from those offered by the employer and indicate the

**Memo 3**

1. Format and key the following text in memo format. If needed, review how to format a distribution list on page 56.
2. Proofread your copy and correct all errors.
3. Save as: *7b memo3*.

TO:  Dr. Harriet Houston, Principal
    Mr. Kenneth Gassner, FBLA Cosponsor
    Ms. Marianne Southmore, FBLA Cosponsor

FROM: Kara Newsome, FBLA President

DATE: November 2, 20--

SUBJECT: REQUEST FOR GUIDANCE

At the October 26 meeting of the FBLA Club, the members decided to seek approval to sponsor a business career fair this coming spring. This event would be open to all high school students. The only requirement is that each student brings an up-to-date resume to the career fair so the employer will be able to relate the student's abilities, interests, and activities to opportunities within their business.

It is our intention to invite employers located within our school district to share their expertise and discuss the skills, knowledge, and educational requirement to be successful within their career field. We would invite employers from manufacturing and service industries as well as representatives from private and nonprofit organizations.

Before proceeding further, we think it is necessary to seek your guidance before taking on this activity. Our desire is to hold the career fair in the cafeteria on a school day in March where the employers could staff an exhibit table.

Our next meeting is scheduled for November 16, and we invite you to attend to give us direction for this project.

xx

## Thinking Skills Required in the Workplace

**Thinking Skills**

- Creative Thinking
- Decision Making
- Problem Solving
- Seeing Things in the Mind's Eye
- Knowing How to Learn
- Reasoning

1. Read the following to learn about the thinking skills that are included in the three-part foundation of SCANS skills and personal qualities.

**Thinking Skills**

*Creative Thinking*—uses imagination freely, combines ideas or information in new ways, makes connections between seemingly unrelated ideas, and reshapes goals in ways that reveal new possibilities.

*Decision Making*—specifies goals and constraints, generates alternatives, considers risks, and evaluates and chooses best alternatives.

*Problem Solving*—recognizes that a problem exits (i.e., there is a discrepancy between what is and what should or could be), identifies possible reasons for the discrepancy, and devises and implements a plan of action to resolve it. Evaluates and monitors progress, and revises plan as indicated by findings.

*Seeing Things in the Mind's Eye*—organizes and processes symbols, pictures, graphs, objects or other information; for example, sees a building from a blueprint, a system's operation from schematics, the flow of work activities from narrative descriptions, or the taste of food from reading a recipe.

*Knowing How to Learn*—recognizes and can use learning techniques to apply and adapt new knowledge and skills in both familiar and changing situations. Involves being aware of learning tools such as personal learning styles (visual, aural, etc.), formal learning strategies (note-taking or clustering items that share some characteristics), and informal learning strategies (awareness of unidentified false assumptions that may lead to faulty conclusions).

*Reasoning*—discovers a rule or principle underlying the relationship between two or more objects and applies it in solving a problem. For example, uses logic to draw conclusions from available information, extracts rules or principles from a set of objects or written text, applies rules and principles to a new situation, or determines which conclusions are correct when given a set of facts and a set of conclusions.

2. Open *df 132f thinking skills* and rate your competence on each of the SCANS basic and thinking skills as directed in the appraisal form.

3. Save as: *132f thinking skills*.

## Personal Qualities Required in the Workplace

**Personal Qualities**

- Responsibility
- Self-Esteem
- Sociability
- Self-Management
- Integrity/Honesty

1. Read the following to learn about the personal qualities that are included in the three-part foundation of SCANS skills and personal qualities.

**Personal Qualities**

*Responsibility*—exerts a high level of effort and perseverance toward goals attainment. Works hard to become excellent at doing tasks by setting high standards, paying attention to details, working well, and displaying a high level of concentration even when assigned an unpleasant task. Displays high standards of attendance, punctuality, enthusiasm, vitality, and optimism in approaching and completing tasks.

*Self-Esteem*—believes in own self-worth and maintains a positive view of self, demonstrates knowledge of own skills and abilities, is aware of impact on others, and knows own emotional capacity and needs and how to address them.

*Sociability*—demonstrates understanding, friendliness, adaptability, empathy, and politeness in new and ongoing group settings. Asserts self in familiar and unfamiliar social situations, relates well to others, responds appropriately as the situation requires, and takes an interest in what others say and do.

## Memo 4

1. Format and key the following information as a memo.
2. The memo goes to the Foreign Language Department Students and is from Travel Abroad Coordinator Mary Seville.  Date the memo November 2, 20—; supply an appropriate subject line.
3. Use the spelling checker; proofread and correct all errors, and then compare your format to that shown in the following Quick Check.
4. **Save as:** *7b memo4.*

*Are you ready for a summer you will never forget?  Then you will want to sign up for this year's Travel Abroad Program.  You will travel to the country that famous writers like Virgil, Horace, and Dante called home. The music of Vivaldi, Verdi, and Puccini will come to life.  You will visit art museums exhibiting the art of native sons such as Michelangelo Buonarotti and Giovanni Bellini.*

*By now you have probably guessed that we will be taking a trip to Italy this summer.  Touring* **Rome, Florence, Venice,** *and* **Naples** *gives you the opportunity to experience firsthand the people, the culture, the history, and the cuisine of Italy.*

*If you are interested in learning more about traveling to Italy this summer, attend our open house on* <u>*November 15*</u> *at* <u>*3:30*</u> *in Room 314.*

Your completed memo should look like this:

TO:        Foreign Language Department Students

FROM:     Mary Seville, Travel Abroad Coordinator

DATE:      November 2, 20–

SUBJECT:   TRAVEL ABORAD PROGRAM OPEN HOUSE

Are you ready for a summer you will never forget?  Then you will want to sign up for this year's Travel Abroad Program.  You will travel to the country that famous writers like Virgil, Horace, and Dante called home.  The music of Vivaldi, Verdi, and Puccini will come to life.  You will visit art museums exhibiting the art of native sons such as Michelangelo Buonarotti and Giovanni Bellini.

By now you have probably guessed that we will be taking a trip to Italy this summer.  Touring **Rome, Florence, Venice,** and **Naples** gives you the opportunity to experience firsthand the people, the culture, the history, and the cuisine of Italy.

If you are interested in learning more about traveling to Italy this summer, attend our open house on <u>November 15</u> at <u>3:30</u> in Room 314.

xx

## Basic Skills Required in the Workplace

**Basic Skills**
- Reading
- Writing
- Arithmetic
- Mathematics
- Listening
- Speaking

1. Read the following to learn about the basic skills that are included in the three-part foundation of SCANS skills and personal qualities.

### Basic Skills

*Reading*—locates, understands, and interprets written information in prose and documents (including manuals, graphs, and schedules) to perform tasks; learns from text by determining the main idea or essential message; identifies relevant details, facts, and specifications; infers or locates the meaning of unknown or technical vocabulary; and judges the accuracy, appropriateness, style, and plausibility of reports, proposals, or theories of other writers.

*Writing*—communicates thoughts, ideas, information, and messages in writing; records information completely and accurately; composes and creates documents such as letters, directions, manuals, reports, proposals, graphs, flow charts; uses language, style, organization, and format appropriate to the subject matter, purpose, and audience. Includes supporting documentation and attends to level of detail; checks, edits, and revises for correct information, appropriate emphasis, form, grammar, spelling, and punctuation.

*Arithmetic*—performs basic computations; uses basic numerical concepts such as whole numbers and percentages in practical situations; makes reasonable estimates of arithmetic results without a calculator; and uses tables, graphs, diagrams, and charts to obtain or convey quantitative information.

*Mathematics*—approaches practical problems by choosing appropriately from a variety of mathematical techniques; uses quantitative data to construct logical explanations for real-world situations; expresses mathematical ideas and concepts orally and in writing; and understands the role of chance in the occurrence and prediction of events.

*Listening*—receives, attends to, interprets, and responds to verbal messages and other cues such as body language in ways that are appropriate to the purpose; for example, to comprehend; to learn; to critically evaluate; to appreciate; or to support the speaker.

*Speaking*—organizes ideas and communicates oral messages appropriate to listeners and situations; participates in conversation, discussion, and group presentations; selects an appropriate medium for conveying a message; uses verbal language and other cues such as body language appropriate in style, tone, and level of complexity to the audience and the occasion; speaks clearly and communicates a message; understands and responds to listener feedback; and asks questions when needed.

2. Open **df 132e basic skills** and rate your competence on each of the SCANS basic skills as directed in the appraisal form.
3. Save as: **132e basic skills**.

# LESSON 8

## Tracking Changes

- Use Comments and Track Changes features.
- Format, key, and edit memos.

---

## Business Document

### 8B

- Informational Memo with Table

**Learn: Comments**

Review/Comments/
New Comment

Review/Comments/
Delete Comment, Previous
Comment, and Next
Comment

1. Read the following information to learn about using comments and complete the activity.

   Comments enable you or someone who is reviewing your writing to insert suggestions or notes that may improve the content or format without changing the written text. The comments can be inserted in a document with the **New Comment** feature by selecting the text where the comment is to be inserted, selecting New Comment, and then keying the comment in the area that opens up near the right of the document. When comments are keyed, they are linked to the text to which they refer. Once closed, a Comment icon appears to the right of the document. To view the comment, click the Comment icon. The Show Comments feature can be used to display the comments to the right of the document rather than the icons.

   Comments can be edited the same way as other text is edited, and they can be deleted individually or all at one time by using the **Delete Comment** feature. You can move from one comment to another by using the **Previous Comment** or **Next Comment** features.

   View the comments in Figure 2-6. Note that the reviewer is identified automatically by the word processing software. If someone else reviews your document and makes comments, they will be identified as well.

**Figure 2-6a** Comment balloons

2. Open *df 8b comments*. If needed, show the comments.
3. Make the changes to the text that are indicated in the comments, and then delete the comments.

**Workplace Competencies**

1. Read the following information to learn about the final two competencies identified and defined in the SCANS Report.

### Systems

*Understands Systems*—knows how social, organizational, and technological systems work and operates effectively within them.

*Monitors and Corrects Performance*—distinguishes trends, predicts impact of actions on system operations, diagnoses deviations in the function of a system/organization, and takes necessary action to correct performance.

*Improves and Designs Systems*—makes suggestions to modify existing systems to improve products or services, and develops new or alternative systems.

### Technology

*Selects Technology*—judges which set of procedures, tools, or machines, including computers and their programs, will produce the desired results.

*Applies Technology to Task*—understands the overall intent and the proper procedures for setting up and operating machines, including computers and their programming systems.

*Maintains and Troubleshoots Technology*—prevents, identifies, or solves problems in machines, computers, and other technologies.

2. If needed, open *132c competencies*.
3. Complete your report by selecting at least one of the descriptors within each of the two competencies above and describing at least one situation in which you successfully demonstrated that you possess the competency.
4. Save as: *132d competencies*.

---

## 21st Century Skills: Flexibility and Adaptability

Conflict can be defined as a disagreement between two or more people. Often, it is caused by differences in values and standards, or by misunderstanding and miscommunication, or simple differences in personalities. Being able to manage and resolve conflict is one of the most important and valued skills you can bring to your job.

You can demonstrate your conflict management skills by showing respect and understanding for others, offering alternatives, and avoiding stereotyping and offensive or condescending language. Other conflict management strategies include:

- Intervention, in which an objective third party provides a setting for discussing and resolving the conflict.
- Confrontation, in which the two parties approach each other directly and work together toward a solution.
- Compromise, in which both parties give up something in return for a workable solution.

### Think Critically

1. How would you handle a conflict between yourself and a classmate? Between you and a teacher or other administrator?
2. Why do you think conflict management skills could make you a stronger leader?

**Figure 2-6b** Displayed comments

4. Key **Insert text about keying and editing text** as a comment after the word *icon* in ¶ 2, line 2.
5. Key **Insert text about just clicking it to make it active** as a comment after the word *group* in ¶ 2, line 5.
6. Save as: *8b comments*.

---

## 8C

**Learn: Track Changes and Display for Review**

Review/Tracking/
Track Changes

1. Read the following information to learn about tracking changes and complete the activity.

When the **Track Changes** feature is active (see Figure 2-7), each insertion, deletion, or formatting change made while editing a document is tracked. A markup is inserted in the document where changes are made. By default, in *Word 2013* the Display for Review option is **Simple Markup,** where the location of the changes is shown by a line near the left margin. If you want to see the changes, click the line or select **All Markup** from the Display for Review drop down list. With All Markup (or **Final: Show Markup,** the default in earlier versions of *Word*) activated, insertions are shown underlined in a colored text in the document, and deletions and formatting changes are shown in the right margin (see Figure 2-8).

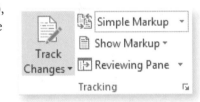

**Figure 2-7** Tracking features

### Track Changes

This document shows the <u>three</u> kinds of editing changes that are tracked when the Track Changes feature is activated. The first change reveals a formatting change—the title has been changed to a 14-point, bold font. The word "three" in the first line that is underlined, indicates that "three" was inserted into the document. The second change at the right indicates a deletion. More specifically, the words "that appears" were deleted. The next change is in the second paragraph where made is underlined to indicate it is an insertion. The final item in the right margin is a comment. Please read it carefully and do what it suggests.

Jon
**Formatted:** Font: 14 pt

Jon
**Deleted:** that appears

Jon
Read the last two paragraphs carefully to learn about two other Display for Review options.

**Figure 2-8** Track Changes and Comment balloons

## Workplace Competencies

**All American high school students must develop a new set of competencies and foundation skills if they are to enjoy a productive, full, and satisfying life.** Whether they go next to work, apprenticeship, the armed services, or college, all young Americans should leave high school with the know-how they need to make their way in the world. In this document, know-how has two parts: competence and a foundation of skills and personal qualities.

—An excerpt from a letter to parents, employers, and educators from the Secretary of Labor and the Secretary's Commission on Achieving Necessary Skills contained in the SCANS Report.

### Five Competencies
- Resources
- Interpersonal
- Information
- Systems
- Technology

1. Read the excerpt at the left from the SCANS Report and the following information to learn about three of the five SCANS competencies that employers expect every employee to possess.

### Resources

*Time*—selects relevant, goal-related activities; ranks them in order of importance; and understands, prepares, and follows schedules.

*Money*—uses or prepares budgets, including making cost and revenue forecasts; keeps detailed records to track budget performance; and makes appropriate adjustments.

*Material and Facility Resources*—acquires, stores, and distributes materials; supplies, parts, equipment, or final products in order to make best use of them.

*Human Resources*—assesses knowledge and skills and distributes work accordingly, evaluates performance, and provides feedback.

### Interpersonal

*Participates as a Member of a Team*—works cooperatively with others and contributes to group with ideas, suggestions, and effort.

*Teaches Others*—helps others learn.

*Serves Clients/Customers*—works and communicates with clients and customers to satisfy their expectations.

*Exercises Leadership*—communicates thoughts, feelings, and ideas to justify a position; encourages, persuades, convinces, or otherwise motivates an individual or groups, including responsibly challenging existing procedures, policies, or authority.

*Negotiates*—works toward an agreement that may involve exchanging specific resources or resolving divergent interests.

*Works with Cultural Diversity*—works well with men and women and with a variety of ethnic, social, or educational backgrounds.

### Information

*Acquires and Evaluates Information*—identifies need for data, obtains it from existing sources or creates it, and evaluates its relevance and accuracy.

*Organizes and Maintains Information*—organizes, processes, and maintains written or computerized records and other forms of information.

*Interprets and Communicates Information*—selects and analyzes information and communicates the results to others using oral, written, graphic, pictorial, or multimedia methods.

*Uses Computers to Process Information*—employs computers to acquire, organize, analyze, and communicate information.

2. Open a new *Word* document.
3. Select one of the descriptors within each of the three competencies and write a report that describes at least one situation in which you successfully demonstrated that you possess the competency. Include an appropriate title and side headings to make your report attractive and easy to understand.
4. Save as: *132c competencies*.

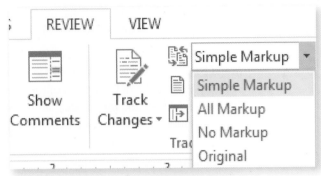

**Figure 2-9** Display for Review options

See Figure 2-9 for the other options in the Display for Review feature. **No Markup** (**Final** in earlier versions of *Word*) hides all the changes or prints the document with all suggested changes included. **Original** displays and prints the document as it was before any changes were made.

2. Open *df 8c changes* and display the tracked changes and comment.
3. Change the Display for Review option to **Original**. Verify that the editing changes and comments are hidden and the text does not include any of the suggested changes.
4. Change the Display for Review option to **No Markup** (**Final** for earlier versions of *Word*). Verify that the editing changes and comments are hidden and the suggested changes are included in the text. Print the file. Close the file without saving changes.

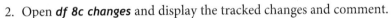
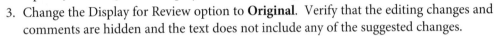

## 8D

### Learn: Track Changes

Review/Tracking/
Track Changes

1. Read the following information to learn about tracking changes and complete the activity.

When the Track Changes feature is activated, you can make changes to your document without losing the original text. If desired, the Track Changes feature can remain deactivated while editing a document if the changes do not have to be tracked.

2. Open *df 8d reviews,* activate Track Changes, and make the following changes with the changes and comments displayed.
   a. Insert **WITH *WORD 2013*** at the end of the title; format *WORD 2013* in italics.
   b. Make the revisions suggested in the comments.
   c. Insert **to revise** at the end of the 1st sentence in ¶ 1.
   d. Delete **you want** from the 1st sentence in ¶ 2.
   e. Replace "will make" in line 2, ¶ 2 with "insert."
   f. Insert a comma after "display" in line 1, ¶ 3.
3. **Save as:** *8d reviews.*

and foundation skills and personal qualities that workers needed regardless of the jobs they held or careers they pursued as the early years of the 21st century grew nearer.

Workers who developed the necessary competencies and foundation skills and personal qualities would be more likely to be successful workers and enjoy fulfilling careers. While the SCANS Report preceded the development of the Framework for 21st Century Skills, they retain a high degree of relevancy for workplace readiness for today's students. Many of the SCANS components are embedded in the 21st Century Skills that are addressed in this textbook.

As you complete the activities in this lesson, try to make connections between the SCANS competencies, foundations skills, and personal qualities with the 21st Century Skills activities in this textbook and what is expected of you in order to be successful in your studies and school activities.

2. Open a new *Word* document.
3. Compose a ¶ that states why employers try to hire employees who are adequately prepared for the workplace and why it is in your best interest to demonstrate that you are prepared to enter the workplace.
4. **Save as:** *132b effective employees.*

Blaise Hayward/Photodisc/Getty Images

## Digital Citizenship and Ethics
Employers often attribute higher productivity and stronger sales to the increased use of digital technologies in the workplace. But using digital technology at work requires that you adhere to certain rules of etiquette and acceptable use.

- Do not conduct personal business, such as texting friends, shopping online, blogging, pleasure reading, and social networking, on company time or on company equipment.
- Do not post, send, or forward jokes, personal photos, or any other material that could be offensive to others.
- Do not post confidential or sensitive information about your employer on a social networking page or in other public forums.
- Do not download software or email attachments to company computers.
- Set strong passwords and do not share your passwords.
- Do not share software or install software on machines for which it is not licensed, and make sure you understand intellectual property rights.

As a class, discuss the following:
1. How might the improper use of digital technologies negatively impact worker productivity?
2. Every worker at some point needs to make or take a personal call during normal business hours. What is the best way to handle this?

**Apply: Memo with Track Changes and Comments**

1. Open *df 8e memo1.*
2. Activate the Track Changes feature.
3. Make the changes suggested in the comments.
4. Delete the comments.
5. Proofread carefully and use Track Changes to record the changes to be made.
6. **Save as:** *8e memo1.*

### Optional Steps

1. Exchange *8e memo1* file with a classmate via email, thumb drive, or other means.
2. Open your classmate's file.
3. Review the changes recorded, and use Track Changes to add others to be made.
4. Save as *8e memo2* and return it to your classmate so he/she can see the changes you suggested.

© Semjonow Juri/Shutterstock.com

## 21st Century Skills: Initiative and Self-Direction

Initiative and self-direction are important skills and attributes to attain as you develop as a student and as a person. These skills and attributes will help you succeed in any task you set out to do.

Taking initiative means making the decision to do something—a job, a project, a specific task—without needing to be prompted by someone else. You see what needs to be done, and you do it. Self-direction means you are able to guide yourself and motivate yourself through the various steps of a job, project, or task. You make good decisions about what needs to be done next, and if necessary, you push yourself to do it. As with any other skill, learning to keyboard properly requires a certain amount of initiative and self-direction.

### Think Critically

1. What prompted you to want to learn computer applications?
2. Now that you have worked through the first lessons of this book, how do you think you can demonstrate initiative and self-direction as you learn these skills?
3. Describe some ways in which you have demonstrated initiative and self-direction at home, at school, or on a job.

# UNIT 24    Being an Effective Employee

Lesson 132 Understanding Employer Expectations

Lesson 133 Establishing Yourself in a New Job

Lesson 134 Being Effective and Advancing Your Career

## LESSON 132    Understanding Employer Expectations

**OUTCOMES**

- Learn what employers expect of employees.
- Learn the SCANS competencies.
- Learn the SCANS basic skills.
- Learn the SCANS thinking skills.
- Learn the SCANS personal qualities.

### Business Documents

- Report
- Self-Appraisals
- Employer Appraisal

### 132A–134A

**Warmup**

Key each line twice at the beginning of each lesson; first for control, then speed.

alphabet   1   Wixie plans to study my notes just before taking the civics quiz.

figures   2   Our soccer league had 4,129 boys and 3,687 girls playing in 2005.

speed   3   The busy fieldhand kept the fox in a big pen to keep it in sight.

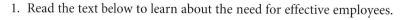

| gwam 1' | 1 | 2 | 3 | 4 | 5 | 6 | 7 | 8 | 9 | 10 | 11 | 12 | 13 |

### 132B

**Need for Effective Employees**

© aastock/Shutterstock.com

1. Read the text below to learn about the need for effective employees.

Employers attempt to hire employees who can demonstrate that they are prepared to be productive workers within their workforce. Productive employees are needed so employers can compete at the highest level within the market they serve. If an employee who is not adequately prepared is hired, the employer's orientation, training, and retraining costs are likely to be greater, which increases the employer's expenses, lowers the employer's profits that are needed to sustain or expand a business entity, and lessens the chances that the employee will be successful.

Businesses, government agencies, and educational institutions have conducted many studies, independently and collectively, to identify specific skills and knowledge that employers expect of workers, regardless of the job held or the career path being pursued. The results of these studies help schools design appropriate curriculum and activities, assist individuals in improving the likelihood of securing and being successful in a job and career they desire, and aid employers in identifying prospective candidates who have the needed skills and knowledge.

One such study conducted by the U.S. Labor Department Secretary's Commission on Achieving Necessary Skills was published in a report titled *What Work Requires of Schools*. This report has become known as the SCANS Report. It identified competencies

# LESSON 9 · Block Format Letters

**OUTCOMES**
- Accept/Reject tracked changes.
- Use block letter format and open and mixed punctuation styles.

## Business Documents

**9B**

- Personal-Business Letter of Request
- Business Letter of Request
- Business Letter of Invitation

### Learn: Reviewing Changes

1. Read the following information to learn about reviewing tracked changes and complete the activity.

   Revisions that have been marked by the Track Changes feature can be accepted or rejected in a variety of ways. One way is to review each change in sequence and accept or reject changes one at a time. Another way is to accept or reject all changes at one time. Rejecting all tracked changes at once will not delete comments. Comments need to be deleted in a separate step.

   Use the buttons and drop-down lists in the Changes group (see Figure 2-10) to accept or reject individual or all tracked changes and to move to the previous or next comment or tracked change.

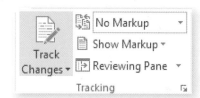

**Figure 2-10** Changes group

   If you are going to share an electronic copy of your document with another person and don't want any tracked changes or comments to display, you can use the Reviewing Pane in the Tracking group to verify that all changes have been accepted or rejected and that all comments have been deleted (see Figure 2-11).

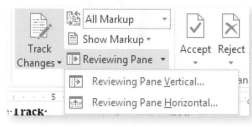

**Figure 2-11** Reviewing Pane with options

   The Reviewing Pane can be displayed vertically or horizontally. Once all markups have been accepted/rejected or deleted, they will not appear within the document.

2. Open *df 9b changes* and read the document.
3. Accept or reject changes as directed:

   ### Review/Changes/ Accept or Reject

   a. Make the formatting change suggested in the first comment, and then delete the comment.
   b. Accept all changes related to text in ¶ 1.
   c. Accept all changes in ¶ 2.
   d. Accept each change in ¶ 3.
   e. Reject the change in ¶ 4.
   f. Accept the changes in ¶ 5, and delete the comment.

   ### Review/Tracking/ Reviewing Pane

   g. Use the Reviewing Pane to ensure no tracked changes or comments remain in the document.
   h. Deactivate the Track Changes feature.

4. **Save as:** *9b changes*.

## Writing a Cover Letter

As you learned in this unit, a cover letter typically accompanies any resume you send to a prospective employer. The cover letter is meant to summarize the skills and abilities you can bring to a job and highlight your individuality and personality. In other words, it is your first chance to make a good impression! Refer to Lesson 129.

1. Create a cover letter to accompany the resume you created for yourself in Lesson 127 of this unit. You can create the letter from scratch or use a *Word* template (see the cover letter templates within the Letters group of templates). You may refer to your resume as well as the Career Plan document you created in Unit 22 to help you write the content. The letter should be in personal-business format and should be no more than one page long. Include the following information:
   a. Return address and date.
   b. Contact name, company name, and mailing address of employers. You may use actual employer information or insert placeholder text.
   c. Salutation.
   d. Body of the letter, which should address three topics, each in its own ¶: 1) position for which you are applying, how you learned of the opening, and something positive about the company; 2) evidence that you qualify for the position and how your qualifications relate to the job; and 3) a request for an interview with precise information for contacting you to arrange it.
   e. Complimentary close and your name.
2. As you write, keep in mind that what you write and how you write it can influence the employer's preconceptions about you. Pay attention to spelling and grammar, word choice, and sentence structure.
3. Format the cover letter appropriately. You may want to use formatting that is similar or complimentary to the formatting applied to your resume.
4. **Save as:** *u23 [your name] cover letter.*
5. Exchange letters with a classmate and make edits and suggestions for improving the content and appearance of the letter.
6. Review the edits to your letter and make revisions as necessary. With your instructor's permission, print the letter.

## School and Community

Habitat for Humanity International is a nonprofit organization that was founded to build simple and affordable homes for those in need of decent housing. Through volunteer labor and donations of money and materials, Habitat works with homeowner families to build and rehab simple and affordable homes. Local residents in each community are responsible for selecting Habitat families, securing volunteers and donations, and constructing and rehabbing houses.

1. Contact your local Habitat for Humanity affiliate and gather information on opportunities for volunteers in your age group.
2. Use a *Word* template to prepare a flyer on volunteer opportunities. With your instructor's permission, post in your school.

**Learn:
Personal-Business
Letter—Block
Format with Open
Punctuation**

1. Read and study the Margins and Line Spacing, Basic Letter Features, Additional Memo and Letter Features, Letter Formats, and Letter Punctuation Styles in the *Reference Guide* on pp. 46–50. Pay particular attention to the guides that refer to personal-business letters and open punctuation.
2. Study the personal-business letter model copy below.
3. Open a new document, and format and key the model letter below.
4. Proofread and correct any formatting or keying errors.
5. **Save as:** *9c letter*.

Personal-Business Letter in Block Format with Open Punctuation

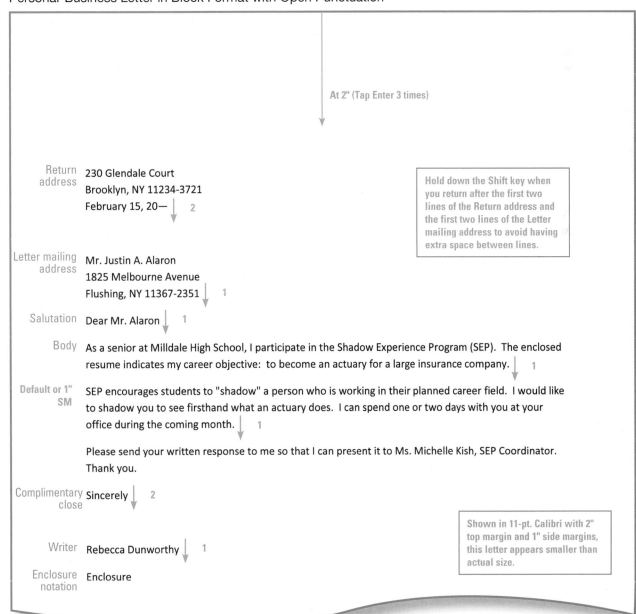

At 2" (Tap Enter 3 times)

Return address — 230 Glendale Court
Brooklyn, NY 11234-3721
February 15, 20—  2

Hold down the Shift key when you return after the first two lines of the Return address and the first two lines of the Letter mailing address to avoid having extra space between lines.

Letter mailing address — Mr. Justin A. Alaron
1825 Melbourne Avenue
Flushing, NY 11367-2351  1

Salutation — Dear Mr. Alaron  1

Body — As a senior at Milldale High School, I participate in the Shadow Experience Program (SEP). The enclosed resume indicates my career objective: to become an actuary for a large insurance company.  1

Default or 1" SM — SEP encourages students to "shadow" a person who is working in their planned career field. I would like to shadow you to see firsthand what an actuary does. I can spend one or two days with you at your office during the coming month.  1

Please send your written response to me so that I can present it to Ms. Michelle Kish, SEP Coordinator. Thank you.

Complimentary close — Sincerely  2

Shown in 11-pt. Calibri with 2" top margin and 1" side margins, this letter appears smaller than actual size.

Writer — Rebecca Dunworthy  1

Enclosure notation — Enclosure

# Academic and Career Connections

Complete the following exercises that introduce various topics that involve academic themes and careers.

## Communications: Speaking

You are going to give a presentation to your class on credit bureaus and what they do.

1. Open the data file **df u23 communications**. The document contains a summary of the typical activities of a credit bureau.
2. Create a new PowerPoint presentation from the summary and save it as **u23 communications**. The presentation should have a minimum of 10 slides, including a title slide. You may copy and paste the information from the document into individual slides as desired or add more of your own. Incorporate visuals such as SmartArt, pictures, animations, and transitions to enhance the presentation as desired.
3. Add speaker notes to each slide. With your instructor's permission, print the notes.
4. Rehearse the presentation with a classmate. Pay attention to your tone of voice, facial expressions, posture, and body language. Your goal is to deliver the presentation without having to read directly from your printed notes.
5. As directed by your instructor, deliver your presentation to the class.

## History

A business cycle is the movement of a country's economy from one condition to another and back again. The cycle is driven by the state of the gross domestic product (GDP). GDP is the market value of all final goods and services produced and purchased within a country during a given time period. Business cycles have the following four phases:

**Prosperity:** High point of the cycle in which the demand for goods and services is high, unemployment is low, wages are good, and the rate of GDP growth increases.

**Recession:** Period in which demand begins to decrease, businesses lower production, unemployment beings to rise, and GDP growth slows.

**Depression:** Phase marked by a prolonged period of high unemployment, weak consumer sales, and rapidly falling GDP.

**Recovery:** Period in which unemployment begins to decrease, demand for goods and services increases, and GDP begins to rise again.

1. Open the data file **df u23 history**. The worksheet contains historic data on the U.S. GDP. In a new *Word* document, write a ¶ that summarizes the business cycle between the years 1929 and 1935.
2. Write a second ¶ that summarizes the business cycle between 2007 and 2010. Save the document as **u23 history**.

**Apply: Business Letter—Block Format with Mixed Punctuation**

1. Review as needed the information in the Margins and Line Spacing, Basic Letter Features, Additional Memo and Letter Features, Letter Formats, and Letter Punctuation Styles on page 50 in the *Reference Guide*. Pay particular attention to the guides that refer to business letters, mixed punctuation, and copy notations.
2. Study the business letter model copy on the following page.
3. Open a new document, and format and key the model letter on the following page.
4. Proofread and correct any formatting or keying errors.
5. Save as: *9d letter*.

**9E**

**Apply: Business Letter—Block Format with Open Punctuation**

1. Open a new document, and format and key the following letter in block format with open punctuation.
2. Proofread and correct any errors. Compare results to the following Quick Check.
3. Save as: *9e letter*.

July 22, 20-- | Mr. and Mrs. Robert Young | 4654 Sharp Shooter Way | Prescott, AZ 86301-4650 |Dear Mr. and Mrs. Young

The Prescott College Board of Trustees is proud to announce the groundbreaking ceremony for the Roberto Menendez School of Engineering building on Saturday, August 15.

As one of the major contributors to this building, you are invited to a VIP luncheon at noon in the Heritage Dining Room in Holton Center for Leadership that precedes the groundbreaking ceremony that will begin at 1:30 p.m. A parking pass for the Holton lot is enclosed. Shuttle service will be provided to and from Holton Center for our luncheon guests.

The new building that will house our nationally ranked engineering programs is a source of great pride for our faculty, staff, students, alumni, and contributors. We hope you will be able to join us for this very special occasion.

Sincerely | Vivian B. Shea | Vice President for Development

**QUICK** ✔

Your completed letter should look like this:

# CORPORATE *View*

## An Integrated Intranet Application

As you approach the end of your internship assignment with Corporate View, you decide that you would like to pursue a full-time position at the company upon graduation. While most of the positions at Corporate View require an associate's or a bachelor's degree, your current supervisor has told you that applications are being accepted for the administrative assistant position that reports to the North American sales administrator. The position is located in Boulder, Colorado, does not require a college degree, and will be available in the middle of June. Furthermore, your supervisor indicated that she will be happy to serve as one of your references.

Since you have an interest in this position, you decide to do the following:

1. Review the position requirements at Corporate View website by using this link as the starting point: www.cengage.com/school/keyboarding/dim/cview
2. Click Human Resources and Management, then Current Job Openings @ Teleview, then Marketing, Sales, & Support. Select the position you are interested in from the list.
3. Review the position posting and then copy and paste it to a new *Word* document so you will have a printed copy of it to reference when you complete the online application and prepare for other aspects of the employment process as they develop. Save the printed copy as *u23 corp view position.*
4. Navigate Corporate View's website until you find the link to the Corporate View Application Form. Click on it and then follow the directions to complete, print, and submit your application. You may want to have a copy of your digital resume available to assist you. Print your application information before you submit it. If you need to return to the Submit option, use your browser's Back button.

### Think Critically

1. Once you're done submitting your application for this position, you decide to find other positions within Corporate View for which you are qualified and then discuss them with your supervisor, who has indicated her willingness to help you in your job search.
2. Using the Corporate View website, review all the available positions. When you identify a position for which you qualify, cut and paste enough information about it in a new *Word* document so you will be able to discuss each position with your supervisor before you submit an application.
3. Save as: *u23 corp view possibles.*

Business Letter in Block Format with Mixed Punctuation Style

2" TM (Tap Enter 3 times)

Date  February 15, 20—  2

Press Shift + Enter when you return after the first three lines of the Letter address, after the writer's name, and after the first two lines of the names receiving a copy to avoid having extra space between lines.

Letter mailing address
Dr. Diana Patsiga
Apartment 256
320 Fort Duquesne Road
Pittsburgh, PA 15222-0320  1

Salutation  Dear Dr. Patsiga:  1

Body  After discussions with members of the Presidential Planning Council, I believe that Sundy Junior College should carefully review the curriculum for developing mathematical reasoning skills.  1

Default or 1" Left Margin
To do so, I am establishing a task force composed of faculty from various disciplines and my planning council.  Dean Carolyn Pucevich will chair the task force.  The primary charge to the task force is to determine what mathematical content is to be learned and applied in required general education courses, including required math courses.  1

If you are interested in serving on this task force, please attend an informational meeting on June 2 at 2:30 p.m. in Carter Hall, Board Room C.  A tentative agenda for the meeting is attached.  1

Complimentary close  Sincerely,  2

Writer  Mary B. Trunno
Writer's Title  President  1

Shown in 11-pt. Calibri with 2" top margin and 1" side margins, this letter appears smaller than actual size.

Reference Initials  xx  1
Attachment Notation  Attachment  1
Copy Notation  c
        Rebecca Schultz
        Marshall Woodward
        Gavin Sanchez

Key 2 5' writings on all ¶s combined; find *gwam* and errors.

 **all letters used**                                    gwam  3' | 5'

| | 3' | 5' |
|---|---|---|
| Many obvious steps should be taken when you search for a | 4 | 2 |
| job.  One step that is not so obvious and often is overlooked by | 8 | 5 |
| applicants is reviewing the interview session.  By taking the time | 13 | 8 |
| and effort needed to accomplish this, you might give yourself the | 17 | 10 |
| slight advantage you need to convince an employer that you are the | 21 | 13 |
| person who should be hired.  This critical step involves reviewing | 26 | 16 |
| and analyzing all aspects of the interview to determine what went | 30 | 18 |
| well and what did not.  Your review should be completed as soon as | 35 | 21 |
| the interview is over, and it should give you the information you | 39 | 24 |
| need when you call or write the interviewer for the follow-up step. | 44 | 26 |
| Begin the survey by listing all the questions you were asked | 48 | 29 |
| during the interview session and then examine your answers.  Were | 52 | 31 |
| they clear, complete, accurate, and to the point?  Next, list your | 57 | 34 |
| best qualities for the job, and relate them to what you studied. | 61 | 37 |
| Did you stress your assets for the position?  Last, try to figure | 65 | 39 |
| how you could have presented yourself in a better way.  Did you | 70 | 42 |
| project interest and energy, use proper body language, and respond | 74 | 44 |
| to every question properly?  Jot down notes you acquired from the | 79 | 47 |
| session that may help you if you are interviewed again for this | 83 | 50 |
| job or contact another company. | 85 | 51 |

gwam  3' | 1 | 2 | 3 | 4 | 5 |
      5' | 1 | | 2 | | 3 |

# Communicating Clearly with Letters

**OUTCOMES**
- Communicate clearly.
- Compose a letter of request.

## Business Document
### 10B

Learn:
Communicating
Clearly

- Draft of a Personal-Business Letter of Request

Daniel Laflor/Jupiter Images

1. Read and study the following information and complete the activity.

*Importance of communicating clearly.* Employers highly value employees who can communicate clearly. Employees who have this ability are more likely to have their messages understood and acted upon as desired than those who cannot express their thoughts adequately. To communicate clearly, you must identify the purpose of your message and the medium through which you should communicate. The purpose may be to inform, persuade, congratulate, request, show respect, thank, etc. The medium you select may be oral or written communications.

*Choosing the appropriate medium.* The media for written communications include email and text messages, social media postings, memorandums, letters, notes, reports, charts, tables, etc. The writer must decide the appropriate medium for the message being communicated. For example, let's assume your principal has decided to acknowledge one of your recent exemplary accomplishments and to let you know how much it is appreciated. Should she give you this message orally in the hallway? Should she send you an email message? Should she send you an email message with a copy to your teachers? Should she write you a letter on school stationery? Should she write you a letter on school stationery with copies to your teachers? Most would say the latter is the most appropriate manner to acknowledge an accomplishment that goes above and beyond the ordinary.

*Tips for writing clearly.* You do not have to wait until you are employed to benefit from writing clearly. You may benefit by being able to express your thoughts clearly when writing a response to an exam question; applying for a scholarship; providing a writing sample to the college, university, or technical school you wish to attend; or writing a proposal to your teacher or school administrators to achieve a goal that is important to you and other students. It takes time and effort to be an effective writer, and you should consider the following things when completing your writing tasks.

- **Identify the audience.** This will help you determine the appropriate vocabulary and tone to use. Your vocabulary and tone should be formal when writing for academic- or business-related purposes. It may be informal when writing to a friend for a social purpose. For example, you may use emoticons and abbreviations like *LOL* when emailing or texting a friend in a social situation, but you should not use these informal devices when emailing or texting a businessperson about a business matter.
- **When writing for a business-related purpose, show respect for the recipient.** Use a correct personal title (Mr., Ms., Mrs., Dr., etc.); spell his/her name correctly; use an appropriate salutation (Dear Mr. Thomas); use an appropriate complimentary closing (Sincerely or Sincerely yours).
- **Do not try to write "final draft" on "first attempt."** Writing is a process that takes time and effort. Your written message is likely to be improved if you write a draft, set it aside while you reflect on what you wrote, and then revise the draft based on your reflections. The more times you can repeat these steps, the better your final draft is apt to be.

**Interview Follow-up
Letter**

1. Read the following information to learn about interview follow-up letters.

An **interview follow-up letter** is sent to the person(s) interviewing you to thank them for the time given and courtesies extended to you during the job interview. This personal-business letter lets each interviewer know that you are still interested in the job, and it reminds him/her of your application and qualifications. This letter should be mailed within 24 hours after the interview to increase the likelihood that it is received before an applicant is selected for the job. Since many people do not send the follow-up letter, doing so may give you a competitive advantage when you are one of the top finalists for a position.

If you have reliable information that the employer is likely to select the person for the position before your letter would be delivered, you may consider sending an email message to those who interviewed you. The message should be the same that you would have written in your letter.

2. Key the follow-up letter as a personal-business letter in block style with mixed punctuation.

3. Save as: *131c letter*.

Figure 23-6 Interview Follow-Up Letter

150 Preston Court | Meriden, CT 06450-0403 | May 25, 20-- | Ms. Jenna St. John | Personnel Director | Harper Insurance Company | 3 Colony Street | Meriden, CT 06450-4127 | Dear Ms. St. John

Thank you for discussing the customer service opening at Regency Insurance Company. I have a much better understanding of the position after meeting with you and Mr. Meade.

Mr. Meade was extremely helpful in explaining the specific job responsibilities. My previous jobs and my business technology classes required me to complete many of the tasks that he mentioned. With minimal training, I believe I could be an asset to your company.

Even though I realize it will be a real challenge to replace a person like Mr. Meade, it is a challenge that I will welcome. If there is further information that would be helpful as you consider my application, please let me know.

Sincerely, | Jennifer H. Greenawald

**Compose Interview
Follow-up Letter**

1. Assume you have been interviewed for the Meriden College customer support position (see page 540, 129c).

2. Compose a follow-up letter.

3. Save as: *131d letter*.

Therefore, leave ample time to complete each writing task. For example, if you have a term paper due in school in two weeks, start it now so you have time to write, reflect, and revise several times before printing the final draft you will turn in for a grade.

- **Be concise in your language.** Try to state your message completely with as few words as possible. For example, don't write "My personal opinion is" when "My opinion is" conveys the same message. Another example is don't write "Enclosed please find a copy" when you can say the same thing more concisely by writing "Enclosed is a copy."

- **Make your writing public.** Unless you are completing a writing assignment that is to be done only by you, share your writing with others to get their feedback. In business, it is not uncommon for a person to have his/her writing reviewed by colleagues. The writing is frequently shared when the writer believes she is near a final draft of an email message, memo, letter, chart, table, report, etc. Remember, many of your colleagues are willing to help you "polish" your writing, but very few are willing to assume most of the writing task for you.

- **Proofread your writing several times.** Yes, you can use the spelling and grammar check feature of your software, but that cannot be the end of your proofreading. You must read the final draft for content and correctness. Read the writing out loud to see if the thoughts are expressed as you intended. Read the final draft several more times focusing on one or two of the following on each reading: correct word usage, punctuation, spelling, pronoun/antecedent agreement, subject/verb agreement, etc.

- **Be professional.** An ability to write clearly will reflect positively on the personal and professional image your colleagues will have of you.

2. **Scenario:** Think of an email or a text message you sent recently to an adult, and then key answers to the following questions:
   a. Who was the audience?
   b. What was the purpose of the message?
   c. Was the email or text message an appropriate medium for communicating the message? If no, why not? If yes, why was it appropriate?

3. **Scenario:** You need to communicate with a financial aid counselor at a technical school or college to which you have been admitted to determine if there are any academic scholarships available to you and to give them a resume that lists your accomplishments and educational and career goals. Key answers to the following questions:
   a. Who is the audience for your communication? Do you know his/her name and title? If not, how can you find out the name and title?
   b. What is the purpose of the message?
   c. What is an appropriate medium to communicate your request and accomplishments?
   d. When will you prepare a first draft of the message if you want to send it one week from today?
   e. Who can you ask to read your message and provide feedback before you have a final draft?

## Employment Application

Your application will be considered active for 30 days—to be considered for a job after that you must reapply.

### PERSONAL INFORMATION

| Name (Last, First) | | Social Security Number | Current Date __/__/__ | Home Phone: |
|---|---|---|---|---|
| Address (Number, Street, City, State, Zip Code) | | | Date of Birth: __/__/__ | Cell Phone: |

| Are you a citizen of the U.S. or do you have a legal right to work in the U.S.?  ☐ Yes ☐ No | Have you ever been convicted of a felony?  ☐ Yes ☐ No   If yes, explain |
|---|---|

| Are You Employed Now?  ☐ Yes ☐ No | If yes, may we inquire of your present employer?   ☐ Yes ☐ No | If yes, give name and number of person to call |
|---|---|---|

| Position Desired | ☐ Full-Time ☐ Part-Time ☐ Summer ☐ Temporary ☐ Anytime | Available start date: __/__/__ Total hours available each week: ____  Hours available each day: ___M ___T ___W ___R ___F ___S ___S |
|---|---|---|

### Education

| | Name and Location of Schools Attended | Years | Program | GPA | Graduated? |
|---|---|---|---|---|---|
| College | | | | | ☐ Yes ☐ No |
| High School | | | | | ☐ Yes ☐ No |
| Other | | | | | ☐ Yes ☐ No |

### Subjects/research, special training, activities, honors, &/or skills directly related to position desired

### Employment History (list last position first & you may include volunteer work)

| From - To (Mo. & Yr.) | Name and Address | Position | Rate of Pay |
|---|---|---|---|
| | | | |
| | | | |
| | | | |

### References (list three persons not related to you, whom you have known at least one year)

| Name | Address | Phone Number |
|---|---|---|
| | | |
| | | |
| | | |

I certify that the information given in this application is true and complete o the best of my knowledge.  I understand that I shall not become an employee until I have signed an employment agreement with the final approval of the employer and that such employment will be subject to verification of previous employment data provided in this application, any related documents, or data sheet. I know that a report may be made that will include information concerning any factor the employer might find relevant to the position for which I am applying, and that I can make a written request for additional information as to the nature and scope of the report if one is made.

Applicant's Signature _____     Date _____

**Online Application Form**

**Apply: Writing a First Draft**

**Scenario:** Assume you want to attend a ten-day leadership program at a nearby college campus this summer to experience firsthand what it would be like to be employed in a career in which you are interested. In addition, the conference will help develop your leadership potential that would be beneficial as you progress through school and college as well as the career you ultimately pursue. Another advantage of the conference is that you will experience coursework that has the rigor of a college-level course. If you successfully complete the coursework, you will have the option to earn college credit that may be used to fulfill course and credit requirements when you enroll in college.

The tuition and fees for the program are approximately $2,500 and include room and board in a dormitory for the ten-day period. In addition, you will need about $100 spending money for incidentals during your attendance.

Unfortunately, you have only about $250 in your savings account that you can use for the program. You have discussed your desire to attend a leadership program with your parents, and they believe that they can provide you with about half of the tuition and fees. Your parents suggested that you try to raise the remaining $1,100 by saving as much as you can before the program begins and by raising funds from your relatives, friends, and others who may be willing to support you. You agree that you will take the initiative to raise at least $1,100 from your relatives and friends.

Your task:

1. Identify your audience by keying a list of the names of the people from whom you will solicit funds. Beside their names, identify their relationship to you (grandparent, aunt, uncle, cousin, family friend, friend, teacher, coach, employer, etc.).

2. Draft the body of a letter that you believe will convince each recipient that he or she should contribute money to you so you can benefit from this program. While your letter should reflect your personality and situation, you may want to include the following:
   a. Provide a reason for the letter.
   b. Provide the name, location, and dates of the leadership program you want to attend. Perhaps it is a program related to one of the following career fields: Architecture, Actuarial Science, Business and Finance, Culinary Arts, Education, Engineering, Entrepreneurship, Forensic Science, Journalism, Law, Medicine and Health Care, Policy and Politics, Sports and Entertainment, etc. If you are not interested in one of these, substitute one that interests you.
   c. Explain why the program is important to you and what you expect to gain from the experience.
   d. Describe the cost of the program and how you plan to pay for it.
   e. Make your request for financial support, and provide a date by which you would like a response.
   f. Include a thank-you.

3. Save your first draft as *10c my letter1*. You will edit the letter during the next few lessons, striving to improve it each time you edit it.

# LESSON 131

## Preparing Application Forms and Post-interview Documents

**OUTCOMES**

- Prepare an employment application form.
- Prepare an interview follow-up letter.

---

## Business Documents

### 131B

**Employment Application Forms**

- Employment Application Form
- Interview Follow-up Letter

---

1. Read the following information to learn about employment application forms.

   Many companies require an applicant to complete an **application form** even though a resume and application letter have been received. Applicants often fill in forms at the company, using a pen to write on a printed form (see application form model on page 544) or keying information into an **online employment application form**. You should strive to provide information that is accurate, complete, legible, and neat.

   Much of the information required for the application form is likely to be on your resume and reference list; therefore, you should have copies of both available when you complete the employment application form. However, you should be prepared to provide information such as social security number, name and telephone number of your present supervisor, grade point averages, pay rates, etc. that is not on your resume or reference list.

   Sometimes applicants may take an application form home, complete it, and return it by mail or in person. In this case, the information should be printed in blue or black ink on the form. To lessen the chance of error on a printed application, make a copy of the blank form to complete as a rough draft.

2. Study the sample employment application form on page 544, paying particular attention to the information you would need to complete the form.

3. Open *df 131b form*. Print one copy of the form.

4. Assume you have been interviewed for the customer service position at Meriden College (see job posting on page 540, 129c) and have been asked to fill out an employment application form after the interview. You may use your reference list and resume to complete the form.

**Figure 23-5** Employment Application Form

5. If you could not provide applicable requested information, make a list of the needed information and describe how you will make sure that information is available if needed in the future. Save your list as *131b list*.

6. Submit your completed employment application form and list to your instructor.

---

# LESSON 11

## Modified Block Format Letters with Additional Letter Features

**OUTCOMES**

- Format and key letters using the modified block format.
- Format and key mailing notations, attention and subject lines, and postscripts.
- Revise a letter.

### Business Documents

- Business Informational Letters in Modified Block Format
- Business Thank-You Letters in Modified Block Format
- Draft of Personal-Business Letter of Request

## 11B

**Learn: Business Letter—Modified Block with Mixed Punctuation**

### Letter 1

1. Read and study the information about postscripts, mailing and addressee notations, attention lines, subject lines, and modified block letter format in the *Reference Guide* on pages 50 and 51.
2. Study the model copy of the modified block business letter on the following page.
3. Open a new document, and format and key the model letter on the bottom of the following page.
4. Proofread and correct any formatting or keying errors.
5. **Save as:** *11b letter1.*

### Letter 2

1. Open *11b letter1* and make these changes:
   a. Delete the subject line and mailing notation.
   b. Change the letter address to:

   Attention Office Manager
   Family Practice Associates
   875 Kenilworth Avenue
   Indianapolis, IN 46246-0087

   c. Use open punctuation. Indent first line of ¶s 0.5".
   d. Change wording of ¶s 2 and 3 to reflect changes in punctuation style and ¶ indentations.
   e. Use Times New Roman, 11-pt. font.
2. **Save as:** *11b letter2.*

## 11C

**Apply: Business Letter**

1. Open *df 11c letter.*
2. Format as a modified block letter with mixed punctuation by accepting/rejecting tracked changes, following directions in the comments, and making any other changes necessary.
3. Proofread and correct unmarked errors, and then compare the format of your letter to that shown in the following Quick Check on the next page.
4. Prepare a large envelope.
5. **Save as:** *11c letter.*

Mailings/Create/Envelopes

a job offer has been made. Here is a sample of questions that would be appropriate for the internship position:

- What personal qualities do you want the intern to possess?
- Tell me about the people I will be working with.
- How will you assess my performance and will I have an opportunity to learn from the assessment?
- Why do you like working for this employer?
- Will I need training or an orientation period for this position?

2. Open a new *Word* document.

3. Access the Internet and identify and research a few resources you can use to develop questions you would ask interviewer(s). If desired, use ***interviewee questions*** as the search terms. Copy and paste into the *Word* document at least two resources that you found most helpful.

4. **Save as:** *130e resources*.

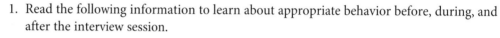

## 130F

**Creating a Favorable Impression at the Interview**

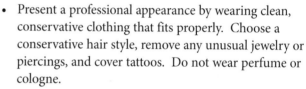
© AntonioDiaz/Shutterstock.com

1. Read the following information to learn about appropriate behavior before, during, and after the interview session.

It is important that you create a favorable impression with everyone you meet on the day of the interview. By doing the following, you are more likely to accomplish that goal:

- Present a professional appearance by wearing clean, conservative clothing that fits properly. Choose a conservative hair style, remove any unusual jewelry or piercings, and cover tattoos. Do not wear perfume or cologne.
- Take your career portfolio, including multiple copies of your resume and reference list, to the interview.
- Plan your travel carefully so you arrive at least 10 minutes early at the specified meeting location.
- Greet all people with a smile, shake hands firmly, and make eye contact during your conversations. Show respect by using personal titles and last names if they are known.
- Listen intently and speak professionally at all times. Use a pleasant tone of voice and exhibit self-confidence when you speak or answer questions.
- Answer questions with concrete examples, show examples of your work, and use your knowledge of the company at appropriate times when answering interviewer questions.
- At the close of the interview, state your interest in the position and confidence that you can do the job. Ask the interviewer if there is anything else you should do and when they expect to notify you about the hiring decision.

2. Open a new *Word* document and develop, in a few ¶s, a plan that you can implement to enhance the probability of success whenever a new interview has been scheduled.

3. **Save as:** *130f interview*.

Your completed letter for 11c
should look like this:

Business Letter in Modified Block Format
with Mixed Punctuation

Approximately 2" TM or Center Vertically

> Begin dateline, complimentary close, writer's name, and title at a left tab at the center (3.25" when side margins are 1").

**Date**             September 15, 20— ↓ 1

**Mailing notation**   FACSIMILE ↓ 1

**Attention line in letter address**
Attention Training and Development Department ↓ 1
Science Technologies ↓ 1
3368 Bay Path Road ↓ 1
Miami, FL 33160-3368 ↓ 1

> Remove space after ¶—use Shift Enter to insert line break after first three lines.

**Salutation**   Ladies and Gentlemen: ↓ 1

**Subject line**   MODIFIED BLOCK FORMAT ↓ 1

**Body** This letter is arranged in modified block format.  In this letter format, the date and closing lines (complimentary close, name of the writer, and the writer's title) begin at or near horizontal center.  In block format, all letter parts begin at the left margin. ↓ 1

**Default or 1" LM and RM** Mixed punctuation (a colon after the salutation and a comma after the complimentary close) is used in this example.  Open punctuation (no mark after the salutation or complimentary close) may be used with the modified block format if you prefer. ↓ 1

The first line of each paragraph may be blocked as shown here or indented one-half inch.  If paragraphs are indented, the optional subject line may be indented or centered.  If paragraphs are blocked at the left margin, the subject line is blocked too. ↓ 1

**Complimentary close**             Sincerely, ↓ 2

**Writer's name Writer's title**          Derek Alan ↓ 1
                         Manager ↓ 1

> Remove space after ¶—use Shift Enter to insert line break after name.

**Reference Initials**   xx ↓ 1

**Enclosure notation**   Enclosure ↓ 1

**Copy notation**   c      Kimberly Rodriquez-Duarte

**Postscript** A block format letter is enclosed so that you can compare the two formats. As you can see, either format presents an attractive appearance.

**At least 1" BM**

You will likely approach the interview with some nervousness, but your nervousness can be tempered by knowing that the employer has selected you as one of the candidates they want to learn more about. If they were not interested in pursuing you, you would not get to the interview stage. You can also temper your nervousness by being very well prepared for the interview. In this lesson, you will focus on preparing yourself by researching the employer, preparing responses to anticipated interview questions, preparing questions that you want to ask the interviewer(s), and displaying appropriate conduct on the day of the interview.

## 130C

### Researching Employers

1. Read the following information to learn about researching the employer.

   Prior to your scheduled interview, you should research the employer to learn about such things as the mission of the organization, the products and/or services it provides, the number of locations it has, how the area in which the position you are applying for fits within the organization, and the personnel within the area. Learning about the employer will help you provide appropriate responses and will demonstrate to the interviewers that you have initiative and a willingness to learn. If the employer has a website, use it as a resource. If you know someone who works for the employer, contact them to get the desired information.

2. Identify a business or organization in which you would like to complete a summer internship, and assume you have a personal interview scheduled. Use the Internet or another resource to gather information about its mission, primary products or services, and other information you believe will help you in your interview.

3. Open a new *Word* document and compose a ¶ or two that describes what you have learned about the employer.

4. **Save as: *130c research*.**

## 130D

### Developing Responses to Interview Questions

1. Read the following information to learn about interviewer questions.

   While it is not possible to know in advance the specific questions you will be asked during the interview, it is still beneficial to develop responses to questions in areas that are typically pursued in an interview. Here is a sample of typical questions you may be asked in the interview for the internship position:

   - How would your favorite teacher describe you?
   - How will this internship position help you achieve your educational and/or career goals?
   - Describe a recent conflict you had with another student and what you did to resolve it.
   - What obstacle have you had to overcome in your life and what did you do to overcome it?
   - What achievement are you most proud of and why?

2. Open a new *Word* document.

3. Identify a position you would like to have now or when you are graduated from high school or college and then compose your response to at least two of the above questions that would prepare you for an interview for the position.

4. **Save as: *130d responses*.**

## 130E

### Asking Questions at the Interview

1. Read the following information about questions you may want to ask an interviewer.

   During the interview, it is likely that you will be given an opportunity to ask questions. Take advantage of these opportunities so you will be better able to decide if you want to accept the job if it is offered to you. Try to ask questions that relate to the requirements of the job, the people you will be working with, how performance is measured, information about working for the employer, etc. Do not ask questions about wages and benefits until

**Apply: Editing**

1. Open *10c my letter1*.
2. Edit the letter using the Track Changes and New Comment features.
3. Display the letter in Final mode and proofread it. Use Track Changes to make any additional edits. When done, switch back to Final: Show Markup mode, and notice that any additional changes you made while in Final mode are included in the markups.
4. Print the letter in Final: Show Markup mode.
5. **Save as:** *11d my letter2*.

# LESSON 12

## Additional Letter and Memo Features

**OUTCOMES**

- Format and key letters and memos with addressee notations and blind copy notations.
- Use Find and Replace features.
- Revise a letter.

## Business Documents

- Business Congratulatory Letter in Modified Block Format
- Business Letter of Confirmation in Modified Block Format
- Draft of Personal-Business Letter of Request

**12B**

**Learn: Find and Replace**

Home/Editing/Replace

1. Read and study the following information about the Find and Replace feature and complete the activity.

   The Find and Replace feature (see Figure 2-12) is used to find a specified keystroke, word, or phrase in a document and replace it with the desired keystroke, word, or phrase. All occurrences of the specified text can be replaced at one time, or replacements can be made individually (selectively). You can refine this feature by using the More button to display various search and find and replace options. To access the Find and Replace feature, choose Replace from the Editing group (see Figure 2-13).

**Figure 2-12** Find and Replace dialog box

**Figure 2-13** Find and Replace

2. Open a new document, and key the following text.

   An individual has to pay a number of assessments. FICA assessments are the assessments that support the social security system and are subtracted from your pay each month. Federal income assessments are also subtracted from your check each month. Assessments that are not subtracted from your check each month include property assessments and sales assessments.

3. Find and replace all occurrences of these words: *assessments* with **taxes,** *subtracted* with **deducted,** *month* with **pay period.**
4. **Save as:** *12b replace*.

## 129C

**Application Letters**

1. Open *129b letter*.
2. Revise the letter as necessary to apply for each position advertised.
3. **Save as:** *129c letter1*, *129c letter2*, and *129c letter3*.

| CUSTOMER SERVICE | CUSTOMER SERVICE REPRESENTATIVE | CUSTOMER SERVICE OPPORTUNITY |
|---|---|---|
| Meriden College is seeking both full-time and part-time motivated individuals to provide customer service to the college community.  Good analytical, mathematical, personal computer skills are required.  Excellent communications and interpersonal skills are essential.  We will provide training for our network-based systems.  ***Meriden College is an affirmative action, equal opportunity employer.***  Please respond with letter and resume to:  J. W. Salazar  Meriden College  13 Broad Street  Meriden, CT 06450-0100  or email:  resume@exchange.hr.mc.edu | IHM, an international direct marketing company, is currently seeking candidates to work in our customer service center.  IHM has openings for full- and part-time positions to handle customer inquiries for the U.S. and Canada.  **We have openings for Spanish-speaking reps.**  To qualify, you must have excellent telephone and communication skills, strong keyboarding and PC skills, the ability to work in a structured environment, and a desire to learn.  Please mail or fax resume and letter to:  Human Resources Department, IHM  1264 Main Street  Meriden, CT 06450-1000  Fax: (203) 555-0153 | **PTI** is seeking an outstanding individual for our expanding Customer Service team.  Qualified candidates will demonstrate strong organizational skills, creativity, powerful problem-solving ability and a passion for delighting customers.  Strong computer skills including knowledge of suite software is essential.  If you are interested in an exceptional opportunity to be a part of a growing organization where you can have a real impact, submit your employment documents to:  hr@pti.com  Precision Therapeutics, Inc.  Suite 30  637 Colony Street  Meriden, CT 06450-5000 |

## 129D

**Personal Print Resume**

1. Open *127c my draft resume* or *128c my digital resume,* whichever you prefer, to use to prepare a final draft of your personal print resume.
2. Review the information and make any desired changes, additions, or deletions to the information you want to include in your print resume.  Also decide how your print resume will be formatted.
3. Using the information and desired format, prepare a print version of your resume.
4. **Save as:** *129d my print resume*.

## LESSON 130 — Preparing for the Personal Interview

**OUTCOME**

- Be prepared for a personal employment interview.

**Business Documents**

- Company Information
- Interviewer Questions
- Answers to Interview Questions
- Internet Resources for Interviewee Questions
- Successful Interview Plan

## 130B

**Understanding the Personal Interview Process**

1. Read the following information to learn about the personal interview.

The **personal interview** is a very important part of the employment process.  While the interview may be conducted in a variety of ways and may involve one or more persons over one or more days, most interviews have common purposes.  First, the interview provides the employer an opportunity to assess your personal attributes, demeanor, job qualifications, etc. in a formal setting to assist them in selecting the best person for the position.  Second, the interview provides you with an opportunity to demonstrate that you are the best candidate and to gather information that will help you decide if you want the position.

## 12C

**Apply: Business Letter with Blind Copy Notation**

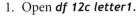

1. Open *df 12c letter1*.
2. Follow the directions in the comments, and then delete the comments.
3. Accept/reject the changes marked.
4. Replace all occurrences of *Duncan* with **Duncan College** and *January* with **September.**
5. If needed, review how to format and key a blind copy notation in the *Reference Guide* on page 597. Insert a bc notation for **Dr. Walter Milligan, Chair, Presidential Scholarship Committee** on the copy you will send to Dr. Milligan.
6. Proofread the letter and correct any errors.
7. Prepare a large envelope, and print the copy with the bc notation.
8. Save as: *12c letter1*.

## 12D

**Apply: Memos**

### Memo 1

1. Format the following text as a memo, supplying reference initials and enclosure notation.

TO: Mary Guerra, Science Department Chair | FROM: Jose L. Domingo, Principal | DATE: April 15, 20-- | SUBJECT: PHYSICS LABORATORY EQUIPMENT DONATION

Antech Laboratories has up-to-date physics laboratory furniture and equipment that it can donate to our high school. They are confident that our physics teacher and students will derive great benefits from what they are offering.

A list of the major items Antech can donate is enclosed. All items will be available before the end of July so they can be delivered and installed before school starts in late August.

Please let me know if you can attend a meeting with me at Antech next Tuesday at 3:15 p.m. The purpose of the meeting is to see the laboratory equipment. Antech will need a decision within ten days after the meeting.

2. Proofread and correct errors.
3. Save as: *12d memo1*.

### Memo 2

1. Open *12d memo1*; change all occurrences of *Antech* to **AnTech** by using the Find and Replace feature.
2. Save as: *12d memo2*.

## 12E

**Apply: Editing**

1. Open *11d my letter2*.
2. Proofread the letter carefully using Track Changes to record editing changes.
3. Save as: *12e my letter3*.

# Preparing Employment Application Letters

**OUTCOMES**
- Compose an employment application letter.
- Prepare a personal print resume.

## Business Documents
### 129B

**Employment Application Letters**
- Employment Application Letters
- Personal Print Resume

1. Read the following information to learn about employment application letters.

   An **employment application letter** should always accompany a resume, whether print or digital. This personal-business letter should be limited to one page. The application letter should include three topics—generally in three to five ¶s. The first topic should specify the position you are applying for and may state how you learned of the opening and something positive about the company.

   The second topic (one to three ¶s) should include evidence that you qualify for the position. This is the place to interpret information presented in your resume and to show how your qualifications relate to the job you are applying for to create a favorable impression. The last ¶ should request an interview and give precise information for contacting you to arrange it.

2. Open a new *Word* document.
3. Key the employment application letter below as a personal-business letter in block format with mixed punctuation.
4. Check the content of this application letter against the guidelines above.
5. **Save as:** *129b letter*.

**Figure 23-4** Employment application letter

150 Preston Court | Meriden, CT 06450-0403 | May 10, 20-- | Ms. Jenna St. John | Personnel Director | Harper Insurance Company | 3 Colony Street | Meriden, CT 06450-4219 | Dear Ms. St. John

Ms. Anne D. Salgado, my business and information technology instructor, informed me of the customer service position within your company that will be available June 15. She speaks very highly of your organization. After learning more about the position, I am confident that I am qualified and would like to be considered for the position.

Currently I am completing my senior year at Meriden High School. All of my elective courses have been computer and business-related courses. I have completed the advanced digital information and management course where we integrated advanced word processing, spreadsheet, database, and presentation software features to prepare business documents. I have also taken the business communications course that enhanced my oral and written communication skills.

My work experience and school activities have given me the opportunity to work with people to achieve group goals. Participating in FBLA has given me an appreciation of the business world and the opportunity to develop my leadership and public speaking skills.

The opportunity to interview with you for this position will be greatly appreciated. You can call me at (203) 555-0121 or email me at Greenawald.j@fastsend.com to arrange an interview.

Sincerely | Jennifer H. Greenawald | Enclosure

# LESSON 13 | Multiple-Page Letters and Memos

**OUTCOMES**
- Insert a second- and subsequent-page heading in a header.
- Format and key multiple-page letters and memos.
- Get feedback on draft of letter from classmate.

## Business Documents

- Informational Multiple-Page Memo
- Informational Multiple-Page Business Letter in Block Format
- Draft of Personal-Business Letter of Request

### 13B

**Learn: Header and Footer**

1. Read the following information to learn about using headers and footers and complete the activity.

Insert/Header & Footer/Header or Footer

A header is text (such as a title, name, page number, date, etc.) printed in the top margin of a page (see two built-in options in Figure 2-14). Letters, memos, and reports that are longer than one page often contain a header.

A footer is similar to a header, except the information is placed at the bottom of the page.

**Figure 2-14** Insert Header options

Like the Page Number feature, headers and footers are often omitted on page 1 of a document.

2. Open **df 13b header**.
3. On page 2, insert the three-line header (blocked at the left margin) using the Built-In Blank style.

> Gwen Johnson
> Page 2
> April 12, 20—

**★TIP** You may need to press Shift + Enter to remove the space between the lines. Also, use the Page Number feature to insert the page number.

4. Hide the header on page 1 by selecting the Different First page feature.
5. Insert a one-line footer using the Built-In Blank (Three Column) style. Use the same information as you used for the header.
6. View the pages to see the header and footer.
7. **Save as: 13b header**.

### 13C

**Learn: Second-Page Headers**

### Document 1 (Two-Page Memo)

1. Review the format guide for second-page headers in the *Reference Guide* on page 50.
2. Key the following text in memo format using 1.25" side margins and a 12-pt. font.
3. Insert the file **df 13c insert** below the text you keyed. Read the inserted text to reinforce your knowledge of second-page headers.
4. Format the text as needed and include any missing memo parts.
5. Proofread the memo and make any necessary changes.
6. Insert a three-line second-page header blocked at the left margin on page 2.
7. **Save as: 13c memo**.

Adam Tyrell
15550 Burnt Store Road
Punta Gorda, FL 33955-1500
941-555-6367
tyrell.adam@speedconnect.net

SUMMARY

Strong communication and telephone skills, excellent keyboarding, computer, and Internet skills, and good organizational and personal skills.

EDUCATION

Will be graduated from Garrison High School in June 2014 with a strong background in academic and business information technology.  Grade point average of 3.64.

RELEVANT COURSES

AP English (11-12), Computer Skills and Applications I and II (10), Digital Communications Information (11), Computer Assisted Design (11), Sport Management (12).

MAJOR AWARDS AND RECOGNITION

National Principal's Leadership Award (2014), 1st Place in Regional Computer Fair (2013), Punta Gorda Rotary Club Student of the Month (2013), National Honor Society (2013-14).

EXTRA-CURRICULAR ACTIVITIES

PGHS Golf Team (9-12), PGHS Interact Club (member 10-12; Historian 12), PGHS Class Treasurer (12), PGHS Musicals (9-12), PGHS Future Business Leaders of America (10-12),

COMMUNITY SERVICE

Punta Gorda Methodist Church Vacation Bible School teacher assistant (2010-2013), Race for the Cure publicity committee (2012), Fallen Timber Animal Shelter student helper (2011),  PGHS Senior Citizens Breakfast server (2011-2014), United Youth Camp student helper (2013).

WORK EXPERIENCE

DeCesare Brothers Restaurant (2013 to present):  Take and serve customer orders, balance receipts for restaurant, ensure customer satisfaction, assisted in redesign of menu distributed to customers.

Certified soccer official (2010 to present):  Officiate boys and girls (ages 8 to 18) indoor soccer matches at Family Sports Complex.

REFERENCES

Will be furnished upon request.

**Digital Resume Model**

TO: All Employees | FROM: Melanie J. Kohl | DATE: May 12, 20-- | SUBJECT: SECOND-PAGE HEADINGS

This memo provides information about controlling line breaks when paragraphs are split between two pages and when side headings appear as the last line on a page. It also reviews how to format and insert headings in letters and memos that are longer than one page.

**Controlling Line Breaks in a Paragraph**

It is important to verify that a paragraph that continues from the bottom of one page to the top of the next page is divided appropriately. Paragraphs should always be divided so that at least two lines of the paragraph appear at the bottom of a page and at least two lines appear at the top of the next page. This means that a three-line paragraph should not be divided. If you have the Widow/Orphan control activated to control paragraph splits, the word processor will divide the paragraph correctly. If you do not have the Widow/Orphan control activated, you will need to insert manual page breaks as needed to format paragraph splits correctly.

To activate the "Widow/Orphan control," check the "Widow/Orphan control" box accessed by Page Layout/Paragraph group dialog box launcher/Line and Page Breaks tab.

**Keeping Side Headings with Text**

If your letter or memo contains a side heading and the word processor displays it at the bottom of a page by itself or with only one line of text following it, you need to move the heading (and single line, if applicable) to the next page. The "Keep with next" feature can be activated to control this type of line break. To activate "Keep with next," check the "Keep with next" box accessed by Page Layout/Paragraph group dialog box launcher/Line and Page Breaks tab.

*(insert file df 13c insert here)*

## Document 2 (Two-Page Letter)

1. Open *df 13c letter*.
2. Format the letter in modified block style with indented ¶s and mixed punctuation.
3. Add this postscript to the letter:

   "Please say hello to Mr. Harold for me. He was my favorite math teacher when I attended your school."

4. Change the font size to 12 pt. and the side margins to 1.25".
5. Proofread carefully and then insert a second-page header formatted across one line.
6. Compare your two-page letter to that shown in the following Quick Check.
   Save as: *13c letter*.

# LESSON 128    Preparing Digital Resumes

**OUTCOME**

- Prepare a digital resume.

## Business Document

### 128B

**Digital Resumes**

- Digital Resumes

1. Read the following information to learn about **digital resumes**.

   Many companies convert the information on a resume into a database file that is stored on a computer, and then software is used to search the files for specific information to select applicants for further consideration. They may search for education level, work experience, or keywords that are closely related to the position being filled.

   Use a digital version of your resume when you are requested to submit a resume that will be scanned, send your resume as an email message or attachment, or submit your resume as part of an online application process. If you are asked to send your resume as an email attachment but not told which version to send, consider sending the print and digital versions. That way, the employer will have a copy that is likely to be accurately converted to a database file and a more attractive version that can be printed and distributed to those involved in the hiring decision. See Figure 23-3.

   Your digital resume should use a standard font and size such as 11-point Calibri or 12-point Times New Roman. Do not use word processing features such as indentations, columns, borders, and shading; and text enhancements, such as bold, bullets, text effects, underlines, etc. These features can cause errors or disappear entirely or partially when a resume is processed for storage in a computer database.

   To increase the likelihood that your resume will be selected in a database search, consider replacing the Objective section with a Summary section (see digital resume on the next page). The summary contains keywords describing your education, positions held, and skills that relate to the position being sought.

2. Study the digital resume model on page 538.
3. Open a new *Word* document.
4. Using the defaults margins and font settings, key the digital resume.
5. **Save as:** *128b resume*.

**Figure 23-3** Digital resume

### 128C

**Personal Digital Resume**

1. Open *127c my draft resume*.
2. Review the information and make any desired changes, additions, or deletions to the information you want to include in your resume.
3. Using the information above, prepare a digital version of your resume.
4. **Save as:** *128c my digital resume*.

Your completed two-page letter should look like this:

## 13D

**Apply: Making Writing Public**

1. Open *12e my letter3*.
2. Proofread the letter carefully using Track Changes to record editing changes.
3. Accept/reject all changes, and delete all comments.
4. Share your letter with a classmate by giving him/her a copy of *12e my letter3* file and having him/her use Track Changes and New Comment to suggest changes to your letter. Have your classmate save his or her suggestions as *13d my letter 4*. If you cannot share a copy of the file, print a copy of *12e my letter3* and have your classmate use proofreaders' marks to suggest changes to the letter.
5. When your letter is returned, accept/reject the suggested changes.
6. **Save as:** *13d my letter5*.

## LESSON 14 — Memo and Letter Applications

**OUTCOMES**
- Format memos and letters.
- Use Track Changes and Find and Replace.
- Prepare final draft of letter.

## Business Documents

- Memo of Announcement
- Informational Memo
- Business Letter of Confirmation in Modified Block Format
- Informational Business Letter in Block Format
- Final Draft of Personal-Business Letter in Block Format

## 14B

**Apply: Memos and Letters**

### Memo 1

1. Format the following text as a memo, supplying reference initials and enclosure notation.
2. **Save as:** *14b memo1*.

TO: All Intermediate and Senior High School Science Teachers | FROM: Mudi Mutubu, Department Head | DATE: April 15, 20-- | SUBJECT: LABORATORY RENOVATIONS

1. Read the following information to learn about guidelines to use when creating your print resume.

   - Do use a simple design. Default top, bottom, and side margins are acceptable but may vary slightly depending on the amount of information presented. Use an appropriate amount of white space between lines and between resume sections.

   - Do key your name at the top of the page on a line by itself. Key your address below your name, and list each telephone number on a separate line. Include a business-appropriate email address below the last line. If needed, obtain and use an email address that does not use nicknames or "cute" names that convey a message that you are not mature.

   - Do arrange the resume parts attractively on the page. The arrangement may vary with personal preference and the purpose of the resume.

   - Use boldface and plain bullets to attract attention; avoid using italic and ALL CAPS because they are more difficult to read, especially when used with large blocks of text.

   - Do use a basic font, such as 11-point Calibri or 12-point Times New Roman.

   - Do use white, ivory, or light-colored (gray or tan) paper, standard size (8.5" x 11") for a print resume.

   - Don't insert your photograph in the resume.

2. Open a new *Word* document.

3. Prepare a first draft of your print resume. Be concerned primarily with keying the major sections and the information you want to include in your resume. You will format and edit your resume in a later lesson.

4. **Save as:** *127c my draft resume.*

© littleny/Shutterstock.Com

## 21st Century Skills: Environmental Awareness

The world's population has surpassed 7 billion and is projected to grow to 9 billion by the year 2045. Experts say that the world's food production will need to double in order to feed that many people. But while farmers and ranchers are working to meet the demand, another problem is affecting our food supply. As our population grows, the variety and diversity of our food supply is dwindling. The trend is known as "food variety extinction." It is being driven largely by the need to mass-produce foods that have high yields and that are bred to ship well and have a uniform appearance.

It is estimated that 90 percent of the fruit and vegetable varieties that have grown in the United States are gone. For example, in the 1800s, there were more than 7,000 apple varieties and now there are fewer than 100. Of the 8,000 breeds of livestock known in the world, about 20 percent are extinct or endangered.

To address this food supply issue, seed banks are being established around the world with the sole purpose of storing and preserving heirloom seeds that have been around for hundreds of years. The foods produced from these unique and sometimes exotic seeds are popping up more and more in farmers markets and small groceries where consumers are showing an increased interest in buying locally grown foods.

### Think Critically

1. Why is food supply variety important to the world's overpopulation problem?
2. What can an individual consumer do to limit food variety extinction?

I've met several times with our school district architects and the science facility consultants they employed to plan the renovations needed for our biology, chemistry, and physics laboratories at the intermediate and senior high schools.

The architect is prepared to have us review and discuss the enclosed preliminary drawings that show the proposed changes to the facilities, including the preparatory rooms and laboratory furniture. I've scheduled a meeting for Wednesday, April 22, at 2:30 p.m. in the conference room near the Principal's Office.

Please arrange your schedules so you can attend this important meeting. The meeting should not last more than one hour, and we will then have ten days to make recommendations so the architect can prepare the second set of drawings.

### Letter 1

1. Format the following business letter in modified block format with mixed punctuation and indented ¶s.
2. Prepare a large envelope.
3. **Save as:** *14b letter1.*

April 17, 20— | Ms. Kelly Zelasco | Public Relations | AnTech Laboratories | 8201 E. Skelly Drive | Tulsa, OK 74107-8201 | Dear Ms. Zelasco

SUBJECT: PHYSICS LABORATORY EQUIPMENT DONATION

This letter confirms East Tulsa High School's interest in the physics laboratory furniture and equipment that AnTech Laboratories is able to donate.

Ms. Mary Guerra, Science Department Head, and I would like to meet with you on April 24 at AnTech's offices at 3:15 p.m. There is a possibility that one or two of the physics teachers will join us. Please let me know if this date and time are good for you.

Support such as this from business and industry is needed for today's schools to prepare students for the changing world of work. Your generosity is greatly appreciated.

Sincerely | Jose L. Domingo, Ph.D. | Principal | JLD:xx | c Dr. Randy DuPont, Superintendent | Mrs. Guerra is familiar with many AnTech laboratory employees since she worked in several of your labs as part of our Teachers in the Workplace program.

### Memo 2 (Track Changes)

1. Open *df 14b memo2.*
2. Activate Track Changes feature, if needed.
3. Follow the directions in the comments, and then delete the comments.
4. Use the Track Changes feature to edit (correct errors).
5. Print the memo so it looks as if the changes were made.
6. **Save as:** *14b memo2.*

**Jennifer H. Greenawald**

**150 Preston Court**
**Meriden, CT 06450-0403**
**(203) 555-0121**
Greenawald.j@fastsend.com

**Objective:**    To use my computer, Internet, communication, and interpersonal skills in a challenging customer service position.

**Education:**    Will be graduated from Meriden High School in June 2014, with a business information technology emphasis.  Grade point average is 3.87.

**Relevant Skills and Courses:**

- ❑    Proficient with most recent versions of Windows and Office, including Word, Excel, Access, PowerPoint, and Publisher.

- ❑    Excelled in the following courses:  Keyboarding, Computer Skills and Applications, Digital Information and Management, and Business Communications.

**Major Accomplishments and Recognition:**

- ❑    Future Business Leaders of America:  Vice President (junior year) and President (senior year).  Won first place in Public Speaking at the district competition and third place at the state level.

- ❑    Varsity field hockey:  Lettered three years and served as captain during senior year.

- ❑    Received Meriden Tribune Outstanding Young Citizen award (2014).

- ❑    Received National Principal's Leadership Award (2013).

- ❑    Inducted into National Honor Society (2013).

**Work Experience:**    Hinton's Family Restaurant, Server (2011-present):  Served customers in culturally diverse area, oriented new part-time employees, and resolved routine customer service issues.

Volunteer, Meriden Animal Safe Haven (2009-2010):  Assisted administrative staff in processing digital records for animals arriving and departing the facility; assisted with caring for the animals.

**References:**    Will be furnished upon request.

**Print Resume Model**

### Letter 2 (Find and Replace)

1. Open *df 14b letter2*.
2. Format the letter in modified block format without ¶ indentions using open punctuation.
3. Set side margins at 1.25", and use a 12-pt. Calibri font.
4. Use *Sincerely* as the complimentary close.
5. Add **Gold** before *Instant Access* in ¶ 1. Change all instances of *automatic teller* to **ATM.**
6. Proofread the document; identify and correct the 12 embedded errors in the letter body.
7. Save as: *14b letter2*.

### Letter 3 (Blind Copy)

1. Open *14b letter2* and prepare it as a blind copy for **Mr. Kerry Johnson.**
2. Save as: *14b letter3*.

**14C**

**Apply: Writing
Final Draft**

1. Open *13d my letter5*.
2. Proofread the letter carefully, making any corrections needed.
3. If needed, accept/reject all changes and delete all comments.
4. Arrange your letter as a personal-business letter in block format. Address it to one or two of the people you will send it to. Include your name as the writer.
5. If it is a multiple-page letter, include a second-page heading and verify that page endings and beginnings are correct.
6. Print the letter. Sign the letter.
7. Save as: *14c my final*.

**14D**

**Timed Writing**

Two 3' writings on two ¶s; determine *gwam;* count errors.

 **all letters used**

Whether you are an intense lover of music or simply enjoy hearing good music, you are more than likely aware of the work completed by Beethoven, the German composer. He is generally recognized as one of the greatest composers to ever live. Much of his early work was influenced by those who wrote music in Austria, Haydn and Mozart.

It can be argued whether Beethoven was a classical or romantic composer. This depends upon which period of time in his life the music was written. His exquisite music has elements of both. It has been said that his early works brought to a conclusion the classical age. It has also been stated that Beethoven's later work started the romantic age of music.

www.cengage.com/school/
keyboarding/c21key

# Preparing Print Resumes

**OUTCOMES**

- Format a print resume.
- Draft your print resume.

**Business Document**

**127B**

**Print Resumes**

- Print Resumes

**Figure 23-2** Print resume

1. Read the following information to learn about print resumes.

   A **resume** is an honest summary of your experiences and qualifications for the position you are seeking. For most job seekers, the resume (print or digital) is one of the first employment documents that can demonstrate your suitability for the position you are seeking. Prospective employers typically scan each resume very quickly to determine which applicants deserve a personal interview. If your resume does not clearly show how your abilities and activities relate to the position you are seeking or if your resume contains language skill errors or keyboarding errors, you will not likely be given further consideration.

   **Print resumes** are those printed on paper. They are usually mailed to a prospective employer as an enclosure with your letter of application, included in your print portfolio, and distributed to those interviewing you. In most cases, a print resume for a recent high school graduate should be limited to one page. The information presented usually covers six major areas:

   - *personal information* (your name, home address, email address, and telephone number[s]);
   - *position objective* (clear definition of position desired);
   - *education* (courses and/or program taken, skills acquired, grade point average [and grades earned in courses directly related to job competence], and graduation date);
   - *school and/or community activities or accomplishments* (organizations, leadership positions, and honors and awards);
   - *work experience* (position name, name and location of employer, and brief description of responsibilities);
   - *references* (names of people familiar with your character, personality, and work habits) that will be provided upon request.

   In general, the most important information is presented first, which means that most people who have recently graduated from high school will list educational background before work experience, unless their work experience is directly related to the desired position. The information in each section is listed in chronological order with the most recent first. The reference section is usually last on the page.

2. Study the printed resume model on page 535.
3. Open a new *Word* document.
4. Using the table feature, insert a 2 by 5 table. Set width of column 1 at 1.5" and column 2 at 5". Merge the cells in row 1 and key the name and contact information as shown in the resume model.
5. Key the remaining text in the four rows, formatting it as shown in the model resume.
6. Remove all table borders. If desired, make adjustments to the white space between ¶s to enhance appearance.
7. **Save as:** *127b resume.*

# Academic and Career Connections

Complete the following exercises that introduce various topics that involve academic themes and careers.

## Grammar and Writing

### Terminal Punctuation

**MicroType 6**

- References/Communication Skills/Terminal Punctuation
- CheckPro/Communication Skills 2
- CheckPro/Word Choice 2

1. Go to *MicroType 6* and use this feature path for review: References/Communication Skills/Terminal Punctuation.
2. Click *Rules* and review the rules of using terminal punctuation.
3. Then, under *Terminal Punctuation*, click *Posttest.*
4. Follow the instructions to complete the posttest.

*Optional Activities:*
1. Go to this path: CheckPro/Communication Skills 2.
2. Complete the activities as directed.
3. Go to this path: CheckPro/Word Choice 2.
4. Complete the activities as directed.

## Communications

### Listening

1. Listen carefully to the sounds around you for three minutes.
2. As you listen, key a list of every different sound you hear.
3. If requested, give the document you have keyed to your instructor.

## Math Skills

1. Julian and Maria have started a new business after school and on weekends selling artwork they and their classmates have made in an online store. They have decided to price each item as follows:
   a. Art photographs: $10 each
   b. Paintings and drawings: $15 each
   c. Sculptures: $20 each
   d. Jewelry: $15 each
   e. Clothing: $15 each
2. How much money will Julian and Maria collect in the first month of operations if they sell the following items: seven photos, three paintings, two sculptures, six pieces of jewelry, and three T-shirts?
3. Julian and Maria have determined that they need to sell at least $175 per month to cover the operating costs of the business, including website design and hosting fees, marketing expenses (creating ads and posting them on other sites), and the cost of their time. What will their gross profit be for the first month? This is the amount they sold minus monthly operating expenses (and doesn't include paying any taxes).
4. How much money will Julian and Maria each make if they divide the gross profits among themselves and the three other classmates who contributed items to the business? (*Hint:* Divide the gross profit by five.)
5. What is the average selling price of each item in the first month? (*Hint:* Divide the total amount sold by the number of items sold.)

An alternate design could use a 2" top margin and default side margins. A title, such as *References for*, could be centered in a slightly larger font size. Center your name and contact information as shown above with the space removed between the lines within this section. Key each reference as a blocked ¶ using default vertical spacing.

2. Open a new *Word* document and key the information on the previous page as a reference list. You decide all formatting features.

3. **Save as:** *126c references*.

1. Identify at least three people you want to serve as your references during your job search.

2. Open a new *Word* document and insert a 3-column table with at least 3 rows.

   - In column 1, key the names of the persons you have identified.
   - In column 2, briefly describe why you have chosen each person.
   - In column 3, identify the information you need to get from each person to complete your reference list.
   - Insert an appropriate title and column headings for your table and format it so it is attractive and easy to read.

3. **Save as:** *126d references*.

© StockLite/Shutterstock.com

## Digital Citizenship and Ethics
Through texting and instant messaging, users of digital technologies have developed their own form of shorthand or texting slang; for example, most of us are familiar with HRU for "how are you?" and the popular LOL for "laugh out loud." This type of exchange is acceptable between friends and in casual, nonbusiness communications. But more and more, it is finding its way into the professional world.

According to a recent survey of human resource managers, strong written communication skills are essential not only for getting hired, but also to advance in a career. Employers expect workers at every level to be able to string together clear, coherent thoughts in all forms of written communication. In a competitive job environment, successful digital citizens must be able to distinguish between appropriate writing for personal and professional purposes. They must pay close attention to the quality of their writing and how to use it effectively to reflect their best selves.

As a class, discuss the following:

1. How might the use of texting slang and shorthand in a business situation reflect negatively on an individual's communication skills?
2. What measures can you take now in your daily digital activities to strengthen your written communication skills?

**Business Management & Administration**

## Planning a Career in Business Management and Administration

Every type of business needs people to help manage it and run it. Whether the business is a multibillion-dollar international corporation or a neighborhood shop run by a single owner, the same basic principles apply in developing the business—from creating a product or service, marketing and selling the product or service, to administering all the financial and staffing needs of the company.

The business management and administration services industry is one of the highest-paying career pathways, with a wide variety of opportunities for workers in both large and small business settings. Workers in entrepreneurial or small business settings often must apply many different kinds of skills in the course of running their businesses.

### What's It Like?

When you see a new store opening in your community or hear about an international corporation providing a new product or service, the skills of workers in business management have made it happen. Entrepreneurs can take an idea for a new product and develop it into a business that will earn thousands or millions of dollars for themselves and for the people who work and invest in the company.

One example is the story of Bert and John Jacobs, two brothers who worked for five years selling their T-shirts at street fairs and college dorms. One day, the inspiration for the Life Is Good character hit, and they sold out all 48 shirts they printed for a local street fair. Sales took off from there, and Life Is Good is now a multimillion-dollar corporation (Figure 2-15).

Most workers in this field work in offices, and most jobs require at least a bachelor's degree from a four-year college or university. Entrepreneurial jobs and positions with small businesses can provide a more varied workday in a store, home, or small office setting.

Eric Fowke/Alamy

**Figure 2-15** Entrepreneur Bert Jacobs Selling Life Is Good T-shirts

### Employment Outlook

Employment is expected to grow faster than average for most business management and administration careers, especially business information management and human resources management, with predicted growth of up to 17 percent.

### What About You?

This career cluster is covered in box 4 of the Interest Survey Activity you completed in Unit 1 of this text. If this box had one of the three highest scores on your survey, you should further explore the cluster's pathways and related occupations.

1. Why do you think a career in business management and administration could be a good choice? Can you picture yourself doing this type of job?
2. Why are these jobs important to our economy?

- Samples of your writing and projects you have completed.
- Course grades and results from standardized tests such as the SAT and/or ACT tests that are important for the job you are seeking.
- Your personal resume and list of references.
- Letters of reference.

2. Open a new *Word* document and briefly describe the career you are presently planning to pursue upon graduation from high school or college.
3. Key a list that identifies the items you would include in your career portfolio and indicate why you would include them.
4. **Save as:** *126b portfolio.*

## 126C

### Reference Lists

**Figure 23-1** Reference list

1. Read the following information to learn about reference lists.

You should choose your references carefully, as employers use them to confirm what they have learned about you from your employment documents and the personal interview and to learn more about the kind of employee you are likely to be. Teachers, clergy, and current or previous employers usually make good references.

Choose references who can speak positively about your accomplishments and abilities to work effectively and efficiently to accomplish team and personal goals as well as your personal attributes. After you have selected your references, you must ask them if they are willing to serve as your reference. If they agree, confirm that you have correct information to include on your reference list. Verify that you have the correct spelling of their names; company name and position title, if applicable; and mailing address, email address, and telephone number(s).

It is a good practice to keep your references informed about your progress in searching for a job. You can do this by telephoning or emailing them as needed. When you accept a position, write a note to each reference thanking her and letting her know what position you have accepted.

Reference lists (as shown in Figure 23-1) should contain your name and contact information centered at the top of the page and the contact information for each reference. Format the information attractively on a page. The reference list shown below was arranged in table format, started 2" from the top of the page, centered horizontally, and printed without gridlines.

### References for

Gretchen Klettner
151 Meeting Street
Charleston, SC 29401
843-555-6450
gretchenk.66@mxn.com

### References

| Mrs. Paulette Wylie | Mr. James D. Ekaitis | Rev. David Donnelly |
|---|---|---|
| 143 Tradd Street | Internship Coordinator | Associate Pastor |
| Charleston, SC 29401 | Williams & Beatty, Inc. | Victory Church |
| 843-555-1792 | 210 Wentworth Street | 66 Dunneman Street |
| wyliep143e@quiktime.net | Charleston, SC 29401 | Charleston, SC 29403 |
| | 843-555-7813 | 843-555-3342 |
| | jekaitis@wb.com | pastor.david@victory.org |

# The Winning Edge

Fuse/Jupiter Images

Complete this activity to help prepare for the Computer Literacy Open event in BPA's Administrative Support division. Participants in this event are tested on their understanding of computer terminology related to operating systems, hardware components, and software applications. You learned in Unit 1 that a computer has five basic functions. In a new word processing document, write a descriptive ¶ about each of these functions:

- **Input:** Data you enter by keyboard, photos you scan, music you download, and video you record. Describe the ways you input data and the hardware and peripheral devices you use.
- **Processing:** Software that tells the computer what to do and in some way manipulates the data you input. Describe the different operating systems in use today and the types of software applications you use to complete common tasks.
- **Output:** Display of the processed data. Describe the ways you output data and the hardware and peripheral devices you use.
- **Distribution:** Enables the computer to share information with other computers, typically across a network. Describe the ways you distribute data to or share data with others.
- **Storage:** Enables you to keep data for use at a later time. Describe the two basic types of computer storage and the hardware and media you use to store data.

You may use electronic and hard-copy references to assist in preparing the ¶s (e.g., help screens, spell-check, thesaurus, user's manual, and dictionary). When you are done writing, be sure to proofread and revise the document as necessary. Apply formatting and text enhancements (bold, italics, and underline) as appropriate. Save and print the document as directed by your instructor.

## Think Critically

1. How can a strong understanding of the computer's basic functions help you in your career pursuits?
2. Why do you think basic computer skills are important to an employer?
3. What activities can you participate in now that will strengthen your computer skills and knowledge?

## School and Community
The arts appeal to many of us in one way or another. One way to express your interest in the arts is to volunteer at a local museum or theater. These are often not-for-profit organizations that are eager to have volunteers.

1. Get started with volunteer work in the arts by researching volunteer opportunities in your community. What kinds of arts organizations can use your help?
2. Identify your two favorite types of artistic expression, and describe how you might apply these interests to volunteer work in your school or community.
3. Write a brief summary of the importance of art in your school and community. Describe how art has contributed to your own personal development and how you can use this experience to develop your resume or work portfolio. If requested, give the statement to your instructor.

# UNIT 23 — Preparing for the Workplace

## Reference Guide

**Employment Documents**

When searching for a job, employment documents provide job applicants with opportunities to present their best qualities to prospective employers. These qualities are represented by the content of the documents as well as by their accuracy, format, and neatness. It is essential that you learn how to prepare the employment documents presented in this unit to create favorable impressions throughout the various stages of the employment process.

In this unit you will plan a career portfolio and reference list, prepare print and digital resumes, compose a letter of application, complete an application form, prepare for a personal interview, and compose a post-interview letter.

## LESSON 126 — Preparing a Career Portfolio and Reference List

**OUTCOMES**

• Identify appropriate contents for a career portfolio.
• Prepare a reference list.

## Business Documents

• Portfolio Content List
• Reference List

### 126A–131A

**Warmup**

Key each line twice at the beginning of each lesson; first for control; then for speed.

alphabet 1 We realize expert judges may check the value of the unique books.

figures 2 A teacher will have 75 test items from pages 289-306 for Unit 41.

speed 3 The dorm officials may name six sorority girls to go to a social.

**gwam** 1' | 1 | 2 | 3 | 4 | 5 | 6 | 7 | 8 | 9 | 10 | 11 | 12 | 13 |

### 126B

**Career Portfolio**

1. Read the following information to learn about career portfolios.

Early in your job search, you should build a **career portfolio** that contains information about you and samples of items that show how your previous activities and achievements relate to the job you are pursuing. You should consider compiling a printed version and a digital version of your portfolio. A printed version should be taken to the personal interview so its contents can be conveniently and quickly shared with the interviewers at appropriate times. A copy of your digital version can be given to the interviewers for them to refer to as they make their decisions as to which applicant will be hired for the position. The contents of the career portfolio can include such things as:

• Certificates, letters, newspaper articles, programs, brochures, etc. that document your accomplishments.

Lesson **15** Table Tabs, Indentations, and Lists
Lesson **16** Tables to Text and Text to Tables
Lesson **17** Tables with Repeated Headings
Lesson **18** Table Calculations
Lesson **19** Table Applications and Analysis

## Reference Guide

### Tables

Table with nine columns and seven rows

A **table** is an arrangement of data (words and/or numbers) in rows and columns. Columns are labeled alphabetically from left to right; rows are labeled numerically from top to bottom. Tables range in complexity from those with only two columns and a main heading to those with several columns, a secondary heading, multiple-level column headings, column/row totals and averages, decimal tabs, bullets and numbering, source notes, etc.

Tables are frequently used in business to convey information in an attractive, easy-to-read format. The table may be a separate document or part of another document such as a letter, memo, report, newsletter, etc. Tables organize information and make it easier to compare data. For example, tables typically provide information about where an aspect of business has been, is, or is going.

In this unit, you will process many tables that are routinely used in business. They include tables that report information relating to sales, inventories, distributors, customers, budgets, payroll matters, work schedules, forms of business ownership, and other information needed to carry out business-related functions.

### Formatting Table Parts

**★ TIP** If spacing has already been added by using this feature, the option will be Remove Space After Paragraph.

Tables have some or all of the following parts and are formatted as indicated unless directed to do otherwise:

- **Main heading.** Usually formatted in bold, ALL CAPS or Mixed Case, centered in first row or placed above the gridlines of the table.
- **Secondary heading.** Usually formatted in bold, capital and lowercase letters, centered in second row or one line below the main title above the gridlines.
- **Column headings.** Usually formatted in bold with center alignment.
- **Body** (data entries). The vertical and horizontal alignment of data within cells may vary. Within columns, words may be left-aligned or center-aligned. Whole numbers are right-aligned if a column total is shown; decimal numbers are decimal-aligned; other figures may be center-aligned. Within rows, data may be vertically aligned at the top, center, or bottom. Heading rows most often use center alignment. Data rows usually are aligned at the center or bottom.
- **Source note.** Placed in the bottom left in last row or beneath the gridlines of the table. If placed beneath the gridlines, use the Add Space After Paragraph feature to place space between the gridlines and the source note (Home/Paragraph/Line and Paragraph Spacing/ Add Space After Paragraph), and set a tab to place the source note at the table's left edge.
- **Gridlines.** Usually printed but may be hidden.

# Career Clusters

### Creating a Career Plan

You have learned about the 16 career clusters in previous units. In this activity, you will focus on a career in a selected cluster and develop a career plan document.

1. Refer to the Interest Survey you completed in Unit 1 of this text. At the bottom of the survey, you identified the top three Career Clusters you were interested in. Select the one that interests you the most. If your interests have changed, consult with your instructor.

2. Identify a pathway and job within the cluster that interests you. Go to the Career Technical Education website at www.careertech.org. Click the Career Clusters link and then click Career Clusters and Pathways. Review your selected cluster and its pathways. Then, on the right side of the page, click the Resources for Career Clusters link. Click the Career Cluster Career Frames link. Find your career cluster on the page and then select the format in which you want to open the Career Frames page. This page organizes the cluster by its pathways and the types of jobs that fall within each pathway.

3. Prepare a career plan. You can create this in a *Word* document or write on paper first and then key into a document.

    a. Write a statement that summarizes your career goal; for example, *I will live in Texas and have a job as a landscape architect by the time I am 24 years old.*

    b. Write a statement that summarizes the postsecondary education you will need to achieve your goal; for example, *I will need a 4-year degree in the design or pre-construction field from an accredited college or university.*

    c. List the skills you will need to achieve your goal; for example, organizing and allocating resources, working with others, using technology, etc.

    d. List the school classes that will help you achieve your goal. Be sure to include the date or grade level when you will take (or took) the class and the skills acquired.

    e. List the school activities that will help you achieve your goal. Again, include participation dates and skills acquired.

    f. List the out-of-school and volunteer activities that will help you achieve your goal. Include participation dates and skills acquired.

    g. List work experiences that will help you in your career. Include dates worked and skills acquired.

    h. List awards and achievements related to your career goal.

    i. List the personal skills, talents, interests, and work ethics that will help you achieve your career goal.

    j. List any skills you feel need to be improved in order for you to meet your career goal. Write a statement on how you will strengthen each skill.

4. Format the document as desired. Be aware that a career plan is a suitable document to go in your career portfolio, so it should look professional and be easy to read.

5. **Save as:** *u22 career plan.*

## Additional Table Formatting Guidelines

Page Layout/Page Setup/
Orientation/Portrait
or Landscape

**★TIP** The Table Tools tab is displayed when a table is selected.

Table Tools Layout/
AutoFit/AutoFit Contents

Table Tools Layout/Merge

Table Tools Design/Table
Styles

Follow these guidelines to make your tables easy to read and attractive when you are not given specific directions to do otherwise.

- **Vertical placement.** Center tables vertically between the top and bottom margins or begin 2" from top of page. If a table is inserted into the text of a letter, memo, report, etc., leave at least 6 pts. of space before and after the table.
- **Horizontal placement.** Center tables horizontally between the side margins.
- **Page orientation.** Use portrait orientation (vertical—8½" × 11"). If the number of columns is too wide to fit on the page, use landscape orientation (horizontal—11" × 8½").
- **Font size.** Format table heading in a font size that is larger than the column heading font size; use a column heading font size that is larger than the size used for the data entries.
- **Row height.** Use the default row height.
- **Column width.** Use the **AutoFit Contents** feature to automatically resize the column widths to the size of the longest entry in the column.
- **Merge/Split cells.** To make a table attractive and easy to read, merge (join) two or more cells into one cell for the main title, source note, and other data as needed. Any existing cell can be split (divided) into two or more smaller cells if necessary.
- **Table Styles design.** The Table Styles feature of the software provides a quick way to enhance the appearance of a table. Table Styles can be selected and applied at any time after a table has been created or inserted into a document. Once the Table Style has been applied, changes to the format for the selected style can be made such as bolding or removing preset bolding, changing font size, changing alignment, etc., to further enhance the appearance of the table.

© Yuri Arcurs/Shutterstock.com

# Academic and Career Connections

Complete the following exercises that introduce various topics that involve academic themes and careers.

## Communications: Reading

Open the **df u22 communications** file. Carefully read the article on e-commerce. When you have finished reading, close the file. Open a new word processing document and key your answers in complete sentences to the following questions.

1. What is the definition of e-commerce?
2. Provide a definition and an example for each of the four e-commerce models:
   - Business-to-Consumer (B2C)
   - Business-to-Business (B2B)
   - Consumer-to-Business (C2B)
   - Consumer-to-Consumer (C2C)
3. How do you think having an online presence can contribute to the success of a business?
4. **Save as: u22 communications**.

## Geography

The U.S. Bureau of Labor Statistics (BLS) publishes reports on wages and compensation in the nine regions of the country as established by the U.S. Census Bureau.

1. Open the *Excel* workbook **df u22 geography**. The worksheet lists each of the nine regions and the mean (average) hourly earnings for civilian, private industry, and government workers at various levels.
2. Go to the BLS website at www.bls.gov/bls/blswage.htm. Locate the section on wage data by region and click the link for the census divisions. Click the links for each division or use the national map to determine the states in each region.
3. In the worksheet, insert rows under each region to list the states that fall within that region. Apply indents or other formatting to enhance the appearance of the data.
4. In column E, enter a formula to average the hourly wages for workers in the three categories. Format as necessary.
5. **Save as: u22 geography**. Close the workbook.

**School and Community**  Recent statistics indicate that more than 14 percent of U.S. households (or one in seven) are "food insecure," meaning that one or more household members were hungry at some time during the year. Research a hunger relief organization and develop a plan for how you can get involved in the fight against hunger. Prepare a report or presentation that you can share with the class. Three organizations you might consider:
- Feeding America provides hunger relief through a nationwide network of member food banks.
- Heifer International provides families with a food source that helps them achieve self-reliance and sustainability.
- The Great American Bake Sale, organized by Share Our Strength, is a national campaign that seeks to end hunger by having local bake sales across the country.

# LESSON 15    Table Tabs, Indentations, and Lists

**OUTCOMES**
- Create tables to report information.
- Use decimal tabs and hanging indentations within cells.
- Use bulleted lists, and numbered lists within cells.

## Business Documents
**15A–19A**

- Inventory List
- Distributors List
- List of Business Documents

**Warmup**

Key each line twice at the beginning of each lesson; first for control, second for speed.

alphabet  1  Jaxie amazed the partial crowd by kicking five quick field goals.

figures  2  Call 555.375.4698 by May 27 to set the 10 a.m. meeting with Sara.

speed  3  Their visit may end the problems and make the firm a tidy profit.

## 15B

**Review: Table**

1. Open a new word processing document, and key the following table, using the alignments shown.

| INVENTORY OF DISCONTINUED APPLIANCES | | | |
|---|---|---|---|
| **Appliance** | **Model Number** | **Inventory Remaining** | |
| | | **Last Month** | **This Month** |
| Microwave Oven | M-010-B | 135 | 101 |
| Dishwasher | D-320-A | 25 | 20 |
| Refrigerator | R-279-C | 47 | 29 |
| Garbage Disposal | G-345-G | 74 | 68 |

2. Format the table to make it attractive and easy to read by applying an appropriate Table Style.
3. Center the table on the page.
4. **Save as:** *15b table*.

## 15C

**Learn: Table with Decimal Tabs and Hanging Indentation.**

1. Read the following information about tabs and hanging indentation.

Decimal tabs and hanging indentation can be used to position numbers and text in columns to make the information in the cells easy to read. The Horizontal Ruler can be used to set the tabs and indentation (see Figures 3-1 and 3-2). Select all the cells in the column in which the tab or indentation is to be used before setting the tab or indentation. Otherwise the change will only apply in the cell where the insertion point is positioned.

**Figure 3-1** Decimal tab at 1" in column 1

**Figure 3-2** Hanging indentation at 1 3/4" in column 2

Your flyer should look similar to the one below; photo may vary.

### Analyzing Media Messages

The process of analyzing a media message can be challenging, because most media messages are constructed by experts who want to garner a particular reaction from you. That reaction might be to back a cause, to donate money, to take better care of your health, to volunteer your services, or even to go to your local SPCA and adopt an abandoned cat. Before you commit your beliefs, money, or time, learn to step back and understand some key points about any media message.

**The Author**
All media messages are constructed by people, with "constructed" being the operative word. When you see a video in a news report, you may think you are seeing pure reality, but in fact you are actually seeing precisely what some writer or producer wants you to see. The people who create media messages choose wording, images, and in some case sounds that support their purpose. It is possible for these constructions to become a sort of reality, because we tend to accept what we see as truth—"seeing is believing."

**The Presentation**
Authors of media messages use various tools and techniques to draw your attention to a message. You may pay particular attention to a message on television, for example, because of a song used in the message. A particularly striking picture in a magazine layout may attract your eye. Pay attention to the first thing you notice about a message—you can be sure the author of the message carefully selected that element to make an impact. Each medium has its own techniques of persuasion. Print media rely on word choice, for example, while visual media rely on techniques such as close-ups, camera angle, and lighting to control emotional response.

**The Audience**
Each member of the message's audience may interpret the message in a different way. What you see in a message may depend on what has happened to you that day, whether you are male or female, how old you are, your race, or your cultural background. When you view a media message, consider how someone from a background different from your own might understand it.

**The Content**
The content of a media message can give you a number of clues about the point of view of the person or persons who constructed the message. What does the author choose to show in the message? What, equally important, is *not* shown? The content of a media message can communicate subtle—or not so subtle, sometimes—statements about values and attitudes. Typically, these values reflect those of the prevailing culture. Content can thus reinforce stereotypes—think of a commercial, for example, that represents an athlete as a dumb jock—but it can also be a means of challenging stereotypes. The content of media messages can also have important social and political implications. A series of hard-hitting news stories on a political candidate can influence an election.

**The Purpose**
All media messages are aimed at a specific payoff. It is up to us to look beyond the visual or audio "distractions" to understand the purpose behind the message. That purpose may be as simple as desiring you to buy a product. Or the message may want to convince you to adopt a particular point of view about a situation or person. Even a public service announcement has a purpose that a canny viewer should learn to detect.

*Insert clip art photo*

© ollyy/Shutterstock.com

## Digital Citizenship and Ethics

Sam is a high school student who just got his own laptop computer. He uses it for schoolwork and also to chat with friends, watch videos, play games, and surf the Web. He often takes it to school or to the library and works on it in different rooms of his home. After a few months, Sam notices a dull ache in his hands and wrists and has also begun to experience headaches more frequently. In addition, his mother has noticed redness in his eyes. At a visit to the family doctor, Sam learns that his health problems are caused by his extended use of the new laptop.

As we use digital technologies, it is important to recognize the dangers they pose to our physical health. Some of the most common dangers include the following:

- Carpal tunnel syndrome, which is a condition of pain and weakness in the hand or wrist caused by repetitive motions, such as keyboarding and using a mouse.
- Eyestrain, also called computer vision syndrome, which results from staring at a digital screen for hours at a time without a break.
- Poor posture, as a result of using digital technologies on inappropriate surfaces, such as a bed or the floor.

As a class, discuss the following:

1. In addition to the physical dangers discussed above, what other risks are involved with extended use of digital technologies?
2. What measures can you take to minimize or eliminate the physical risks associated with digital technologies?

2. Open a new word processing document. Using a top margin of 2", create a 2 × 4 table with column widths of 2".

3. Set a hanging indent at 1/4" in column 1 and a decimal tab at 2 3/4" in column 2 to make it easier to compare and understand the numbers.

4. Key the following information in the table.

| Hanging Indent at ¼" | Decimal Tab at 2 ¾" |
|---|---|
| As I key this text, it wraps to the next line with a hanging indent. | 1.2345<br>12.345<br>123.45 |
| The hanging indent can make text easier to read in cells. | 0.98765<br>9876.5 |
| As I key the numbers in column 2, they will line up at the decimal point | 456.789<br>45.67<br>4.5 |

5. **Save as:** *15c table*.

**15D**

**Learn: Table with Bulleted and Numbered Lists**

Home/Paragraph/Bullets or Numbering

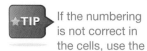

**TIP** If the numbering is not correct in the cells, use the Auto Correct pop-up icon to change to the desired numbering—either Restart Numbering or continue Numbering

1. Read the following information about tabs and hanging indentation.

The **Bullets** and **Numbering** features can be used in tables as they are used in ¶s. In some instances, you may want to use the **Horizontal Ruler** bar to decrease the indent on the bulleted or numbered items to make the list more attractive.

2. Open a new word processing document. Using a top margin of 2", create a 2 × 3 table.

3. Key the following information as shown. Decrease the bullet indent to about 1/8" in column 1. Use the default indent for the items in column 2.

| Bulleted List with Decreased Indent | Numbered List with Default Indent |
|---|---|
| • Monday<br>• Tuesday<br>• Wednesday | 1. Monday<br>2. Tuesday<br>3. Wednesday |
| • Thursday<br>• Friday<br>• Saturday<br>• Sunday | 1. Thursday<br>2. Friday<br>3. Saturday<br>4. Sunday |

4. **Save as:** *15d table*.

## Analyzing Media Messages on World Issues

All media messages are constructed to get a particular point across. The point may be to acquaint you with the impacts on a Japanese village of a tsunami, or to convince you that a particular presidential candidate has an excellent economic plan. Media messages use various tools to persuade you—carefully selected images, text containing just the right language, sounds or music, even concepts that all people readily understand.

Even messages that seem to be unbiased, such as print or television news stories, have a point of view that you can detect if you pay attention to the images chosen to accompany the story, analyze the story's text, and consider where the story is placed in the broadcast or newspaper.

**Figure 22-17** What is the point of view of an author who includes an image like this one in a report?

Knowing how to analyze media messages helps you to understand the point of view behind the message (Figure 22-17). The following questions can help you identify key points about the message. (You will read more about these key points in the next activity.)

- Who (or what organization) is the author of this message?
- How does the presentation of the message draw your attention?
- How will the many different types of people who make up the audience of a message understand and interpret the message?
- How does the content of a message reflect the author's point of view?
- What is the real purpose of the message?

Media messages are tremendously important to global awareness, because most of what you know about other countries or even your own country comes to you through the media. Charitable institutions that want you to donate money to help children in developing countries may employ images of children in distress to appeal to your emotions. Organizations that are working to increase literacy may film happy children and adults smiling as they concentrate on their books. It is up to you to use your critical thinking skills to analyze these messages and then come to your own conclusions about what they are really saying to you.

## Media Literacy Concepts Flyer

Home/Font/Text Effects

Picture Tools Format/ Picture Styles/Picture Effects/Shadow

1. Start your word processing program and open *df 125d media messages*.
2. Apply the Retrospect theme, or a similar theme.
3. Change the font size of the title to 26. Center the title and then apply the Orange, Accent 1 Shadow text effect.
4. Click Text Effects again, click Outline, and select No Outline.
5. Change the page margins to Narrow.
6. Select all text below the title and apply two-column formatting.
7. Apply the Heading 2 style to the five headings.
8. Apply a drop cap to the first ¶ of text.
9. Insert a clip art photo that relates to television news.
10. Use the Position command to position the photo in Middle Center with Square Text Wrapping.
11. Apply a page border to the page using the Box setting and a color of White background 1, Darker 50%.
12. Check your flyer against the Quick Check below.
13. Save as: *125d media messages*.
14. Print the flyer, close the document, and exit your word processing program.

**Table 1**

1. Open a new word processing document. Create a 3 × 7 table with column widths of 1.5".
2. Key the following information as shown using Center Left alignment and hanging indentation in column 2 and a decimal tab at or near 3.5" in column 3.

| Current Distributor By Product Number | | |
|---|---|---|
| **Item** | **Distributor** | **Product Number** |
| Desktop Computer | Wells and Greene, Greenville, PA | 1356.7946 |
| LCD Monitor | Derkson Brothers, Newton Falls, OH | 13.90569 |
| Wireless Mouse | Wells and Greene, Greenville, PA | 985.45 |
| Wireless Keyboard | Malone Supplies Indian Land, SC | 1035.0793 |
| Wireless Printer | James Coleman, Inc., Chicago, IL | 564.68 |

3. Format the table to make it attractive and easy to read. Center it on the page.
4. **Save as:** *15e table1*.

**Table 2**

1. Open a new word processing document. Create a 3 × 5 table.
2. Key the following information as shown using a bulleted list and numbered list, each with decreased indentation.

| BUSINESS DOCUMENTS | | |
|---|---|---|
| **Category** | **Document Type** | **Word Processing Features Frequently Used** |
| Correspondence | • Memorandums<br>• Personal-Business Letter<br>• Business Letters | 1. Margins<br>2. Vertical Line spacing<br>3. Font Attributes |
| Reports | • Unbound Report<br>• Unbound Report with Footnotes<br>• Reference Page<br>• Cover Page | 1. Styles<br>2. Insert Footnote<br>3. Hard Page Break<br>4. Cover Page |
| Tables | • Basic Table using AutoFit<br>• Table with Merged Cells<br>• Table with Table Styles<br>• Table with Reference | 1. Insert Table/AutoFit to Contents<br>2. Merge Cells<br>3. Table Styles<br>4. Add Space After Table |

3. Format the table appropriately. Center it on the page.
4. Compare the format of your table to that shown in the following Quick Check.
   **Save as:** *15e table2*.

9. On slide 7, create a SmartArt diagram using the same layout as on slide 6 and key the following entries in the diagram:

   1  Bakersfield – Delano, CA
   2  Visalia – Porterville, CA
   3  Phoenix – Mesa – Glendale, AZ
   4  Los Angeles – Long Beach – Riverside, CA
   5  Hanford – Corcoran, CA

10. Apply a SmartArt style of your choice to both diagrams. Change the colors of the diagram on slide 6 to Colored Fill – Accent 1. Change the colors of the diagram on slide 7 to Color Fill – Accent 3.

11. Animate the charts to Fly In From Bottom with the One by One Sequence.

12. Run the presentation to read all text and check animations.

13. **Save as:** *124f air quality.* Close the presentation, and exit all open programs.

---

## LESSON 125    Evaluating Media Messages

**OUTCOMES**
- Understand the importance of media messages.
- Analyze media messages on world issues.
- Create an informational flyer in a word processing program.

**Business Document**

**125B**

- Informational Flyer

**Understanding the Importance of Media Messages**

Much of what you know about global issues you will have learned through the media: from video and news stories on television, through photos and articles in print media, and even through movies. What you read and see may be in the form of unbiased and objective journalism, or it may have a particular slant designed to prompt you to think about an issue in a certain way. What is your reaction, for example, to the following media messages?

Fred Watkins/Disney ABC Television Group/Getty Images

**Figure 22-16** Bill and Melinda Gates donate millions to help developing countries

- A public service announcement about children at risk whom you can support with only a few dollars per week.
- A news story about the Bill & Melinda Gates Foundation's programs to fight polio and malaria in developing countries (Figure 22-16).
- Coverage of a city heavily damaged by an earthquake and obviously in need of support from the global community.
- Footage of waterfowl covered with black sludge following an oil spill.

You have learned about several kinds of literacy in this unit. Media literacy is another type of literacy that everyone should master in order to understand fully the messages we receive on a daily basis from many sources. True global awareness means getting the real picture, so to speak, and learning to analyze media messages can help you to see global issues more clearly.

QUICK ✔

1. Name one movie you have seen that has given you an insight into living conditions in a developing country. What kind of impact did the movie make on you?
2. Describe a public service announcement that has affected you strongly.

Your completed table should look like this:

| BUSINESS DOCUMENTS | | |
|---|---|---|
| **Category** | **Document Type** | **Word Processing  Features Frequently Used** |
| Correspondence | • Memorandums<br>• Personal-Business Letter<br>• Business Letters | 1. Margins<br>2. Vertical Line spacing<br>3. Font Attributes |
| Reports | • Unbound Report<br>• Unbound Report with Footnotes<br>• Reference Page<br>• Cover Page | 1. Styles<br>2. Insert Footnote<br>3. Hard Page Break<br>4. Cover Page |
| Tables | • Basic Table using AutoFit<br>• Table with Merged Cells<br>• Table with Table Styles<br>• Table with Reference | 1. Insert Table/AutoFit to Contents<br>2. Merge Cells<br>3. Table Styles<br>4. Add Space After Table |

## 15F

**Apply:  Presenting Information**

1.  Read the following information:

The Eastern Region Sales for the first quarter of the current year are:  Jim Colson sold 175 units in January, 215 in February, 195 in March.  Libby Reed sold 193 in January, 217 in February and 155 in March.  Gwen Gassner sold 145 in January, 231 in February, and 203 in March.

2.  Using the information, key a 5 × 5 table.  In row 1, merge the cells and key **First Quarter Eastern Region Sales**.

3.  In row 2, starting in column A, key the following as column headings:  **Sales Rep, January, February, March, Quarter.**

4.  In rows 3–5, key the information for each sales rep, and then compute the quarterly sales for each rep in column E and the total for each month in row 6.

5.  Format the table to make it easy to read and understand.

6.  Using the information in your table or the ¶ in step 1, answer the following questions.  Key your answers at the left margin below the table.
    a.  Who had the highest quarterly sales?
    b.  Who had the highest January sales?
    c.  Who had the highest February sales
    d.  Who had the highest March sales?

7.  Did you use the table to answer the questions since it organizes the information so it is easier to read and understand?

8.  Save as:  *15f table*.

*© iStockphoto.com/starfotograf*

Proponents of the legislation point to the impact on business of complying with increasingly tougher environmental regulations. In a slow economy, every job is important—especially so when many jobs have moved out of the country to nations where environmental regulation is not as important as it is in the United States.

This issue will continue to be hotly contested. Choosing whether clean air is worth extra costs, decreased production, and jobs is not as easy a decision as it would appear.

## 124F

**Air Quality Presentation**

1. Start your presentation program and open *df 124f air quality*. On slide 1, replace *Your Name* with your name.
2. Start your word processing program and open *df 124f air quality levels*. Select the entire table and click Copy. Close the document.
3. In the presentation, display slide 5. Click Paste.
4. Resize the table to 4.4" high and 8.5" wide. Position the table so that its left edge aligns with the slide title and the entire table is above the tan horizon line.
5. Format the table as follows:
   a. Use the No Style No Grid command on the Table Styles gallery to remove all fills and borders.
   b. Change font size to 14 and adjust column widths and row heights as necessary to fit the table above the horizon line.
   c. Center the headings; change vertical alignment of *Meaning* to Align Bottom.
   d. Center the numbers in the *Numerical Value* column.
6. Apply shading to the table rows as follows:
   a. Apply White, Text 1, Darker 25% to the first row.
   b. Apply the Light Green standard color to the second row.
   c. Apply the Yellow standard color to the third row.
   d. Apply the Orange standard color to the fourth row.
   e. Apply the Red standard color to the fifth row.
   f. For the sixth row, click More Fill Colors and click the hexagon at the far right of the bottom row of the color palette.
   g. For the bottom row, click More Fill Colors and click the hexagon at the far right of the third row from the bottom of the color palette.

7. Select the first four rows and change font color to black. Your table should look similar to Figure 22-15.
8. Display slide 6. Create a SmartArt diagram using the Vertical Chevron List layout and key the following entries in the diagram, with the numbers in the chevrons:
   5  Honolulu, HI
   4  Dothan – Enterprise – Ozark, AL
   3  Savannah – Hinesville – Fort Stewart, GA
   2  Santa Fe – Espanola, NM
   1  Duluth, MN – WI

| Levels of Health Concern | Numerical Value | Meaning |
| --- | --- | --- |
| Good | 0 to 50 | Air quality is considered satisfactory, and air pollution poses little or no risk |
| Moderate | 51 to 100 | Air quality is acceptable; however, for some pollutants there may be a moderate health concern for a very small number of people who are unusually sensitive to air pollution |
| Unhealthy for Sensitive Groups | 101 to 150 | Members of sensitive groups may experience health effects; the general public is not likely to be affected |
| Unhealthy | 151 to 200 | Everyone may begin to experience health effects; members of sensitive groups may experience more serious health effects |
| Very Unhealthy | 201 to 300 | Health alert: everyone may experience more serious health effects |
| Hazardous | 301 to 500 | Health warnings of emergency conditions; the entire population is more likely to be affected |

© Adapted from airnow.gov

**Figure 22-15** Air Quality Index Table

# LESSON 16    Tables to Text and Text to Tables

**OUTCOMES**
- Change the direction of text in tables.
- Convert tables to text and text to tables.

## Business Documents

- List of Scores
- Top Salesperson Report
- Weekly Work Schedule
- U.S. Constitution Provisions
- New Patrons List
- Sales Report

## 16B

### Learn: Change Text Direction

Table Tools Layout/
Alignment/Text Direction

1. Read the following information to learn about changing the direction of text in a table.

By default, text is arranged horizontally in tables. In some instances where the table has a number of narrow columns, the readability and appearance of the table may be improved if the column headings are displayed vertically with center alignment. To display the text vertically, use the **Text Direction** feature shown at the right.

**Figure 3-3**
Text Direction

2. Open *df 16b table*.
3. Display the text in row 2 vertically, using bottom center align. Adjust row 2 so its height is high enough to fit the highest entry.
4. Adjust column widths to fit contents.
5. Center the table on the page.
6. **Save as:** *16b table*.

## 16C

### Learn: Convert Table to Text

Table Tools Layout/Data/
Convert to Text

1. Read the following information to learn about converting a table into text.

There may be instances when you arrange your word processing document one way but later decide it may be better to arrange it another way. For example, in this activity you will learn how to convert a document that was prepared as a table into regular ¶ text. The information converted to text may be used by other software that can't use tables to prepare documents like mailing lists. In the next activity, you will learn to change a regular text document into a table if the table arrangement better serves your needs.

**Figure 3-4** Convert to Text

To convert a table into a regular ¶ text document use the Convert Table to Text feature (Figure 3-4). You must select a delimiter that will be used to separate the text in a meaningful way. In most instances, you will select Tab as the delimiter when converting a table to text (Figure 3-5).

**Figure 3-5**
Convert Table to Text Separators

2. Open *df 16b table* again.
3. Place your insertion point inside the table and select the Convert to Text feature with Tabs as the separator.
4. **Save as:** *16c table*.

6. In a text box at the bottom of the slide, add the following source line: U.S. FDIC http://www. fdic.gov/news/news/speeches/archives/2007/chairman/spapr1707.html

7. Run the presentation to read the text and test animations.

8. **Save as:** *124d mortgage*.

Check your diagram against the one shown below.

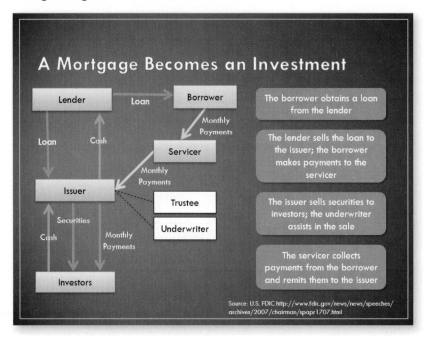

## 124E

**Recognizing Legal Issues That Affect Your World**

The dawning of the "green" movement arrived when the Environmental Protection Agency began operations in 1970. Since that time, the EPA has been instrumental in reversing damage to the environment from industry and maintaining standards of quality for air and water. In recent years, however, federal lawmakers have begun questioning long-standing air and quality regulations and have proposed that no further regulations be passed. The reasons behind this lack of support for an agency whose mandate is to improve the health of the nation's environment as well as of its citizens makes an interesting legal—as well as ethical—study.

No one would question the importance of clean air and water. However, complying with the regulations for air and water quality can be expensive. Businesses may need to undergo a lengthy permit process, or replace existing equipment at considerable cost, or change manufacturing processes. In some cases, businesses have found it impossible to afford the changes required by new regulations and have chosen to stop operating. Other businesses, such as many of the nation's coal-fueled power plants, maintain that compliance costs will raise energy rates, decrease production, and cost jobs.

Lawmakers have responded by proposing legislation that would require the EPA to consider not only the usual reasons for air quality regulations, but also the financial impact on businesses of complying with those regulations.

Opponents of the legislation consider this view short-sighted. They suggest that if polluters are allowed to continue polluting because it will cost them too much to clean up their air emissions, the nation's health might suffer.

## Learn: Convert Text to Table

Insert/Tables/Convert Text to Table

1. Read the following information to learn about converting text to a table.

If desired, regular text can be converted to a table. Use the Convert Text to Table feature, and specify the number of columns or rows, the desired AutoFit behavior, and the desired separation point in the Convert Text to Table dialog box. For example, if you are converting three columns of text that are separated by tabs and you want the table columns to be as wide as the longest entry, you would specify 3 columns, AutoFit to contents, and Tabs in the Convert Text to Table dialog box (Figure 3-6).

**Figure 3-6** Convert Text to Table

2. Open *df 16d text*.
3. Use Show/Hide to display the formatting symbols. Notice that the columns are separated by tabs.
4. Select the text.
5. Convert the text to a 4-column table that uses AutoFit to contents.
6. **Save as:** *16d table*.

## Apply: Tables

Table Tools Design/Table Styles and Table Style Options

### Table 1

1. Open a new word processing document, and key the following table, using Table Styles and Table Styles Options to format the table as shown.

| Work Schedule for Coming Week | | | | | | | |
|---|---|---|---|---|---|---|---|
| **Day** | Employee | | | | | | |
| | Melanie Delmar | Derek Evans | Kyle Landers | Brett Acheson | Melanie Dansick | Catherine Lash | Sandy Hixson |
| **Monday** | 9-5 | Off | 9-5 | Off | 9-5 | 1-9 | 1-9 |
| **Tuesday** | 9-5 | Off | 1-9 | 1-9 | Off | 9-5 | 9-5 |
| **Wednesday** | Off | 9-5 | 1-9 | 9-5 | Off | 9-5 | 1-9 |
| **Thursday** | Off | 9-5 | 9-5 | 1-9 | 1-9 | Off | 9-5 |
| **Friday** | 1-9 | 1-9 | Off | 9-5 | 9-5 | Off | 9-5 |
| **Saturday** | 1-9 | 1-9 | Off | 9-5 | 9-5 | 9-5 | Off |
| **Sunday** | 9-5 | 9-5 | 9-5 | Off | 1-9 | 1-9 | Off |

2. Center the table at the top of the page.
3. **Save as:** *16e table1*.

Figure 22-14 The dream of home ownership became the basis of an economic crisis

As early as the 1980s, the federal government began enacting legislation that would deregulate the banking industry, with the eventual result that banks were given a great deal of leeway in how they could lend money for mortgages. One act made possible the adjustable-rate mortgages that would cause considerable grief in the 2000s.

During the early 2000s, a great deal of money was coming into the country from foreign investors, so financial institutions had plenty of money to lend. Interest rates were also low. Many banks were thus more willing to lend money to people for mortgages (Figure 22-14). Some institutions required very little in the way of proof that a borrower could repay the mortgage, often waiving down payments entirely. In this climate of easy approval, some people purchased houses they were barely able to afford, using **adjustable-rate** or **subprime mortgages**.

Rather than holding the mortgages themselves, as was common in the last century, lenders sold mortgages to other investors. Selling mortgages reduced their own risk, in the event that a borrower would be unable to repay the mortgage, and also made a profit for the lender, which then allowed them to lend even more money.

Both borrowers and lenders assumed that they would be safe in these practices because the housing market had been strong for many years and, they guessed, would remain strong. And because lawmakers and financial experts believed in the importance of allowing financial markets to regulate themselves, they were slow to recognize that lack of regulation was creating a dangerous economic situation.

Then interest rates rose, and housing prices reached a peak and began to fall. People who had adjustable-rate mortgages found their mortgage payments rising, and as it became increasingly hard to sell houses, many found their loans were costing them more than their houses were worth. The only recourse for some borrowers was to default on their loans, causing lenders to lose income from the loans.

Many financial institutions had by this time built up considerable assets that were based on bundled home mortgages, so-called mortgage-backed securities. When homeowners found themselves unable to pay their mortgages, institutions that held mortgage-backed securities suffered catastrophic losses. The failure of U.S. financial institutions led to similar failures around the world in institutions that had also invested in U.S. mortgage-backed securities. In the global economy that has developed in this century, economic problems in one country almost always affect many others as well.

The breadth and depth of the economic crisis that stunned the world following 2007 underlines the importance of ethical actions. Borrowers, lenders, and the federal government all engaged in risky behavior, and recovery from these ethical lapses will take a long time.

### 124D

**Diagram on a Presentation Slide**

1. Start your presentation program and open *df 124d mortgage*. Replace *Your Name* on slide 1 with your name.
2. Duplicate slide 3 and move the duplicate to follow slide 5. Change the title to **A Mortgage Becomes an Investment.**
3. Using the Quick Check on the next page as a guide, modify existing shapes and add new shapes and arrows to show the process by which a mortgage is sold to investors.
4. Group shapes as necessary and apply shape styles and formatting as desired.
5. Animate the rounded rectangles to appear one after the other, adjusting duration and delay to make them easy to read in sequence.

**Table 2**

1. Open a new word processing document, and key the following table as shown.

| WHAT THE UNITED STATES CONSTITUTION PROVIDES | | |
|---|---|---|
| **The Executive Branch** | **The Legislative Branch** | **The Judicial Branch** |
| • President administers and enforces federal laws<br>• President chosen by electors who have been chosen by the states | • A bicameral or two-house legislature<br>• Each state has equal number of representatives in the Senate<br>• Representation in the House determined by state population<br>• Simple majority required to enact legislation | • National court system directed by the Supreme Court<br>• Courts to hear cases related to national laws, treaties, the Constitution; cases between states, between citizens of different states, or between a state and citizens of another state |

2. Set row 1 and 2 height at 0.5".
3. Format the table appropriately using Table Style and Table Style Options.
4. Center the table on the page.
5. Save as: *16e table2.*

**Table 3**

1. Open *df 16e text.*
2. Convert the text to a table, adjusting column widths to fit the contents.
3. Insert two rows at the top of the table, and key the following information as the title and column headings.

| New Patrons | | | |
|---|---|---|---|
| **Patron** | **Street** | **City** | **State** |

4. Format the table appropriately using Table Style and Table Style Options.
5. Center the table at the top of the page.
6. Save as: *16e table3.*

**Table 4**

1. Open *df 16e table4.*
2. Convert the table to text.
3. Compare the format of your text to that shown in the following Quick Check.
   Save as: *16e text.*

# LESSON 124 Exploring Today's Legal and Ethical Issues

OUTCOMES
- Explore the difficulty of making the right decision when faced with ethical and legal issues.
- Understand how unethical decisions have contributed to economic crises.
- Create a graphic that shows how mortgages were sold from lenders to investors.
- Explore some of the legal issues that may affect the world environment.
- Create a presentation that explains air quality measurement.

## Business Documents

- Presentation Containing a Diagram Created from Shapes
- Presentation with Table and SmartArt Diagrams

### 124B

**Making the Right Decisions**

Figure 22-13 Houses became very hard to sell in the wake of the housing collapse

Charting a path through the complex issues we face in the 21st century can require careful study of the ethics and legalities involved. Decisions made to improve the lives of many have sometimes resulted in hardships for many more. It is often difficult to know what the right decision is. Now more than ever, global citizens must be able to use critical-thinking skills to weigh the pros and cons of issues that affect them.

The economic downturn in the first decade of this century provides an ethical case in point. Decisions on the part of the U.S. government and many investment organizations led to thousands of home foreclosures and the failure of many well-entrenched financial institutions when the housing market collapsed. Many people faced considerable hardships when they could not sell their houses (Figure 22-13).

Some legal issues that relate to environmental regulation may affect all citizens of this country. Regulations on water and air quality are designed to improve the health of citizens, yet these regulations can be costly to implement. Many lawmakers are wondering if these regulations actually stand in the way of corporate progress. With so much U.S. manufacturing moving offshore to developing countries, many Americans are also wondering if U.S. laws are too restrictive.

In the following sections, you learn more about ethical and legal dilemmas that people in this country and throughout the world have faced and will continue to face. Making the right decisions on these issues may require a great deal of thoughtful consideration.

1. Can you think of a situation in which actions that were supposed to do good in a community instead caused problems? Was the negative impact a result of a poor ethical choice?
2. Do you live in an area that experiences a lot of air pollution? Do you think regulations to control air pollution are too strict or not strict enough?

### 124C

**Understanding Ethical Issues Behind Global Economic Problems**

Some of the economic troubles that affected countries around the world toward the end of the first decade of this century were fueled by the collapse of the housing market in the United States during that period and the subsequent failure of many financial institutions that had been investing in mortgages as a way to increase profits.

The housing collapse is a very complex issue with a number of causes, some extremely technical. But analysts agree that one of the first contributors to the problem was the praiseworthy goal that more people should be given the opportunity to buy a home. Home ownership is part of the "American dream," but in the past, this dream was out of reach for many citizens. Purchasing a home often meant saving up for years to afford a down payment as well as having a good job with the steady income needed for monthly mortgage payments.

Your completed table should look like this:

**SALES REPORT**

| Sales Rep. | Territory | Jan. | Feb. | March |
|------------|-----------|------|------|-------|
| Shawn Hewitt | Oregon | 15,680 | *17,305* | 7,950 |
| Jason Graham | Oregon | 15,900 | 16,730 | 9,290 |
| Juan Ramirez | Washington | 12,325 | 13,870 | 12,005 |
| Carolyn Plummer | Idaho | *20,370* | 13,558 | 12,654 |
| Maria Hernandez | Idaho | 9,480 | 16,780 | 14,600 |
| Tanya Goodman | Washington | 19,230 | 11,230 | 15,780 |
| Scott Bowe | Idaho | 15,750 | 14,560 | 16,218 |
| Cheryl Updike | Washington | 10,054 | 8,500 | 17,085 |
| Laura Chen | Washington | 17,320 | 9,108 | 18,730 |
| Brandon Olson | Oregon | 14,371 | 11,073 | *19,301* |

# LESSON 17    Tables with Repeated Headings

**OUTCOMES**

- Repeat header row in a long table.
- Change cell margins.
- Insert space after a table located between lines of text.

## Business Documents

### 17B

- Score Report
- Monthly Budget
- Sales Report

**Learn: Repeat Table Headers**

Table Tools Layout/Data/
Repeat Header Rows

1. Read the following information to learn about repeating header rows.

When a table is longer than one page, you can use Repeat Header Rows (Figure 3-7) to repeat header lines on second and subsequent pages to make the additional pages easier to understand.

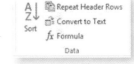

2. Open a new word processing document.
3. Create a 3 × 25 table using AutoFit Window.
4. Select all rows and change height to 0.5".
5. Key the following text in row 1:

**Figure 3-7** Repeat Header Rows

| Column Heading 1 | Column Heading 2 | Column Heading 3 |
|------------------|------------------|------------------|

6. Position cursor in row 1 and select the Repeat Header Rows feature.
7. Verify that the column headings appear in the first row on page 2.
8. **Save as:** *17b table1*.
9. Repeat steps 2–4.
10. Key the following text, and merge cells in Row 1 and Row 2 as shown.

| Merged Cells (A1 and A2) | Merged Cells (B1 and C1) | |
|--------------------------|------------------|------------------|
|  | Column Heading 1 | Column Heading 2 |

11. Position cursor in row 1, and select Repeat Header Rows feature.
12. Verify that the column headings in rows 1 and 2 appear in the first two rows on page 2.
13. **Save as:** *17b table2*.

10. Click in each table, click the Table Styles More button on the Table Tools Design tab, and click Clear to remove all table formatting. Then apply the List Table 4 Light Accent 3 table style to both tables.

11. Make the following format changes to both tables:
   a. Adjust the left border of the second table so it is as wide as the first table.
   b. Select all text in both tables *except* the main headings *You Can Recycle* and *You Cannot Recycle* and change the Paragraph space after to 6 points.
   c. Change the height of the two main heading rows to 0.4" and change the font color to white. Change alignment of the headings to Align Center.
   d. Remove duplicate items in the first column of each table.

12. Below each Material entry in the first table, find and insert a clip art photo that represents one of the items in that category. Size each photo with a width of 0.9" to fit in the first column. For vertical photos, merge cells in the first column as necessary to fit the photo.

**★TIP** You can also crop photos as necessary to fit.

13. Change left and right page margins to 0.75". Adjust column widths and picture size to keep both tables on one page. Adjust column widths of the second table to match those of the first table.

14. Save the document as *123f recycle flyer*. Print the flyer, close the document, and exit all open programs.

QUICK ✔

Your first table should look similar to the one below; the images may vary.

| You Can Recycle | | |
|---|---|---|
| **Material** | **Item** | **Examples** |
| **Glass**  Insert clip art photo | Jars, bottles | Beverage and food containers. Both clear and colored glass can be accepted. |
| **Metal** Insert clip art photo | Aluminum | Cans, foil, and pans. |
| | Steel or tin cans | Food cans, pet food cans. |
| **Paper** Insert clip art photo | Brown paper bags | Grocery bags and other brown or kraft paper bags. |
| | Cardboard | Corrugated cardboard boxes such as shipping boxes. |
| | Colored paper | Canary, goldenrod, blue, and other colored office paper, as well as construction paper in various colors. |
| | Magazines and catalogs | Slick paper trade magazines and catalogs, as well as advertising circulars. |
| | Newspaper | Daily newspaper, without slick four-color inserts. |
| | Paperboard containers | Cereal boxes, boxed food packaging, containers for canned beverages, detergent boxes. |
| | Telephone books | Both white and yellow pages. |
| | White office paper | Correspondence, reports, computer paper printouts. |
| **Plastic** Insert clip art photo | Bottles and jugs | Milk, soda, water, salad dressing, sports drinks, juice. Colored shampoo, detergent, and bleach bottles are also accepted. |
| | Plastic bags | Many stores that use plastic bags will also accept them for recycling. |
| | Six-pack rings | Plastic rings around soda or other beverage cans or bottles. |

## Learn: Cell Margins

Table Tools Layout/
Alignment/Cell Margins

1. Read the following information to learn about cell margins.

The Cell Margins (Figure 3-8) feature enables you to control how close text within a cell comes to the cell borders by changing the Top, Bottom, Left, and Right Margins in the Table Options dialog box (Figure 3-9). You can also change the amount of space between cells in the Table Options dialog box. This feature can be used to enhance the appearance and readability of a table.

Cell Margins

**Figure 3-8**
Cell Margins

**Figure 3-9** Table Options dialog box

2. Open **df 17c table**.
3. Access the Table Options dialog box, and change the Top and Bottom margins to .05, the Left and Right margins to .12, and set spacing between cells to be .03. Select the Automatically resize to fit contents option.
4. Center the table at the top of the page.
5. **Save as:** *17c table*.

## Learn: Insert Space After Table

Home/Paragraph/Line
and Paragraph Spacing/
Add Space Before
Paragraph

1. Read the following information to learn about inserting space after a table.

When you key a table in a document, the amount of space above and below the table should be the same. When the table is inserted into a *Word* document that uses the 1.08 default line spacing with 8 pt. of space after ¶s, space should be added above the ¶ following the table, if needed. The space can be added by clicking on the ¶ below the table, clicking the Line and Paragraph Spacing drop-down list, and selecting Add Space Before Paragraph.

**Figure 3-10** Add Space Before Paragraph

2. Open a new word processing document.
3. Key the following line of text, and then tap Enter.
    The table will be keyed after this paragraph.
4. Insert a 4 × 5 table grid.
5. Position your insertion point on the line below the table.
6. Use the Add Space Before Paragraph command.
7. Key this line of text on the line below the table, and then tap Enter.
    Space has been added above this paragraph.
8. Verify that the space above and below the table appears to be the same.
9. **Save as:** *17d table*.

**Figure 22-12** Thrift and consignment shops allow you to "buy recycled"

Making a commitment to buying recycled items is another step in the process of supporting the recycling effort. Many products such as various kinds of paper and aluminum foil are available in recycled versions. Manufacturers understand that there is now a market for such goods.

Reusing items is another green approach that can reduce the need to manufacture new items as well as reduce waste. Many items no longer needed in a household can be donated for reuse to charitable organizations, including clothing, furniture, household goods, and toys. These organizations provide jobs in the community and offer a way for people on a budget to buy good used merchandise (Figure 22-12).

Consignment shops will often pay for used clothing and accessories. Shopping at a consignment shop can be a way to find good-quality and even designer items at a fraction of their original price and support the concept of reusing at the same time.

Recycling and reusing electronic products deserve a special mention. Many digital devices contain materials that are not safe for landfills. You can minimize impacts on the environment by donating devices such as computers to schools, community centers, or members of your community who are not able to buy new. When a digital device no longer works, you should take it to a special recycling center that can remove any dangerous materials and recover any useful components.

 **TIP** Yard sales and garage sales are also good ways to sell items that are no longer wanted but still useful.

## 123F

### Word Table with Pictures

The Village of Montgomery is frequently asked what items can be recycled at its recycling centers. This information is stored in a database. In this activity, you will work with the database records and then copy the information to paste as a *Word* table to create an attractive handout for community residents.

1. Start your database program and open df *123f recycling*. Save the database as *123f recycling*.
2. Create a new query that uses all fields in the *What to Recycle* table except the *ID* field. Specify a criteria of Yes in the *Recyclable* field, and do not show this field in the query results. Sort ascending by Material and Item.
3. Run the query, and adjust the columns to show all data. Save the query as **You Can Recycle.**
4. Select all records in the query results and copy.
5. Start your word processing program and paste the copied data in the new blank document. Click the Paste Options button and choose to Keep Source Formatting. Tap Enter below the table to insert another blank ¶.
6. Return to the database program, close the query, and then create a duplicate of it named **You Cannot Recycle.** Change the criteria for the *Recyclable* field to No.
7. Run the query, copy the displayed records, and paste them in the second blank ¶ below the previously pasted records in the word processing document. You should have two tables separated by a blank line.
8. Close the query, the database, and the database program.
9. In the word processing document, change the theme to Basis or a similar theme.

**Table 1**

1. Open a new word processing document.
2. Key the following table, formatting it as shown.

| MONTHLY BUDGET | | | | | | |
|---|---|---|---|---|---|---|
| Utility | January | February | March | April | May | June |
| Telephone | | $73 | $45 | $45 | $45 | $45 |
| Sewage | $75 | | | $75 | | |
| Cable | $50 | $50 | $50 | $57 | $57 | $57 |
| Electricity | $111 | $109 | $66 | $79 | $113 | $102 |
| Natural Gas | $295 | $300 | $321 | $214 | $68 | $63 |
| Water | $45 | $48 | $45 | $49 | $45 | $51 |
| Garbage | | $57 | | | $57 | |
| Internet | $60 | $60 | $60 | $60 | $51 | $51 |

3. Improve the appearance of the table by changing the cell margins. Change the top and bottom margins to .05, the side margins to .15, and insert .02 space between cells.
4. Position it attractively on the page.
5. Save as: **17e table1.**

**Table 2**

Table Tools Layout/Data/
Sort

1. Open a new word processing document, and key the following memo. Be sure the space before and after the table appears to be equal.
2. Format the table so it is attractive and easy to read.
3. Sort the appropriate rows so the Sales column figures are arranged highest to lowest.
4. Save as: **17e table2.**

TO: All Marketing Managers | FROM: Harry Delaney, Vice President for Marketing |DATE: April 14, 20-- | SUBJECT: March Sales Report

Here are the preliminary sales results that I have compiled from the weekly reports you submitted during March.

| Sales Manager | State | Sales |
|---|---|---|
| Diane Aldredge | Connecticut | $304,568 |
| Marcia Kelly | Maine | $235,206 |
| Rubio Perez | Massachusetts | $248,981 |
| Orlando Alvarez | New York | $272,985 |
| Jonathan Akervik | New Hampshire | $212,674 |
| Rodger McMurray | Vermont | $214,623 |
| Total Sales | | $1,489,037 |

As soon as I have the final results from our accounting department, I will send you a comparison of this year's March sales compared to last year's.

xxx

11. In cell E11, sum the total expense in the *Expense* column above. Key the label **Total Expenses** in cell C11. Boldface cells C11 and E11.

12. Select the range A3:E11 and change the font size to 18. Adjust column widths to show all data.

13. Select the same range again and click Copy. Then save the workbook as *123d supply expenses and close it*.

14. Switch to the presentation, display slide 6, click the content placeholder to select it, and click Paste. Click the Paste Options button and choose the Picture paste option.

15. Change the width of the picture to 8" and center the picture vertically and horizontally on the slide.

16. Select the Rectangle shape and draw a rectangle around the cell that contains the total of $24,600. Remove the rectangle fill and change the shape outline color to Orange in the Standard colors. Change the outline weight to 3 point.

17. Apply animations as follows:

    a. On slide 6, select the orange rectangle and apply the *Wipe* animation to the rectangle, From Left.

    b. On slide 8, select the chart and apply the *Wipe* animation, From Bottom, By Category, After Previous.

    c. Animate the monthly total boxes to appear after the chart animates, using the *Fade* animation and a start of After Previous.

    d. Animate the Total Revenue box to Fly In From Right, After Previous. Animate the $25,303 box to Float In, After Previous.

18. View the presentation from the beginning to check your animations. Then save changes and close the presentation and all other open programs.

## 123E

### Recycling

The second two Rs in the three Rs approach stand for reusing and recycling. Reusing and recycling are additional ways to reduce the amount of new resources used in manufacturing as well as reduce waste. The many good reasons to recycle include:

- Recycling saves energy, because it generally takes less energy to make products from recycled resources.
- Recycling preserves natural resources. Making paper from recycled paper means fewer trees need to be cut down and pulped (see Figure 22-11).
- Recycling is generally a cleaner process, in terms of air and water pollution, than manufacturing from raw resources.
- Recycling keeps waste paper, plastic, glass, cardboard, and metal cans out of landfills.
- Recycling creates jobs. Workers are required to separate recyclable items at recycle centers, and firms that use recycled materials also need workers in their manufacturing processes.

**Figure 22-11** Recycling just one-tenth of U.S. newsprint would save 25 million trees a year

With environmental awareness on the rise, it is becoming easier to recycle waste products. Many cities and towns offer curbside recycling programs that allow citizens to put out a bin of recyclable materials for collection. Processing these materials not only reduces the municipal waste going into landfills, but also raises money when the municipality sells the separated waste to manufacturers. Schools and other community centers often offer bins that residents can use for their recyclable items. Regional recycling centers are usually available to collect items in the absence of other programs.

**Table 3**

1. Open *df 17e table3*.
2. Sort the table to arrange column 1 in Ascending Order
3. Align all cells center left
4. Repeat the header rows on the second page.
5. Save as: *17e table3*.

---

## LESSON 18   Table Calculations

**OUTCOMES**

- Perform basic mathematical calculations in tables by using the SUM, AVERAGE, MINIMUM, MAXIMUM, and COUNT functions.
- Write formulas to perform basic mathematical calculations in tables.
- Update calculations in tables.

---

**Business Document**

**18B**

**Learn: SUM Function in a Formula**

Table Tools Layout/Data/ Formula

Mileage Log

1. Read the following information to learn about the SUM function.

The Formula feature in most word processing software can be used to calculate answers to basic math problems, such as addition (+), subtraction (−), multiplication (*), and division (/) when numbers are keyed in a table. Word processing software can also recalculate answers when numbers are changed in a table.

**Figure 3-11** Formula

The built-in SUM function is the default formula that appears in the Formula box if you choose the Formula feature when the insertion point is below a column of numbers (see the default formula =SUM(ABOVE) in Figure 3-12) or in the cell to the right of a row of numbers (see the default formula =SUM(LEFT) in Figure 3-13).

**Figure 3-12** =SUM(ABOVE) formula

**Figure 3-13** =SUM(LEFT) formula

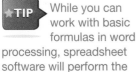

★**TIP** While you can work with basic formulas in word processing, spreadsheet software will perform the basic and more complex calculations in a more efficient manner.

Energy conservation is another way of controlling waste that can bring considerable rewards in the form of lower energy bills and decreased use of natural resources.

- Turn off lights and other electrical devices when they are not in use. If you can, replace older appliances with more energy-efficient ones, and replace incandescent light bulbs with more efficient compact fluorescent bulbs (Figure 22-10).
- Beware of "vampire" energy users, such as printers that stay on all the time; you can often turn off these devices to save energy.
- Use public transportation when possible, or carpool. If feasible, walk to your destination or ride a bike.

Many communities are taking the initiative to go green with community-wide programs that encourage citizens to compost and control use of resources. In the next activity, you will work on a presentation for a community that is exploring ways to reduce waste.

**Figure 22-10** Compact fluorescent light bulbs use less energy and last longer than incandescent bulbs

## 123D

### Community Action Presentation

The Village of Montgomery has recently completed a pilot study to introduce the community to ways they can conserve resources by composting, capturing stormwater runoff in rain barrels, and installing solar lights. The Village has made some of these products available to residents at a nominal charge and wants you to prepare a presentation that shows the results of the sales.

1. Start your presentation program and open *df 123d reducing waste*. Save the presentation as *123d reducing waste*.
2. Customize the presentation by changing the color scheme to Office, the fonts to Calibri, and the effects to Frosted Glass (or use similar themes).
3. Start your database program and open the *df 123d product database file*. Save the database as *123d product database*.
4. Open the *Products* table and add the following records:
   Solar Light      Modern      80      $ 40.00
   Rain Barrel      Flat Back      30      $150.00
5. Create a query that uses all fields except the *ID* field and sorts the data first by Category and then by Item.
6. Run the query and then save it as **Supply Expenses.**
7. Select all data in the query and click Copy. Then close the query and the database.
8. Start your spreadsheet program, open a blank workbook, and paste the copied data starting in cell A2. Click the Paste Options button and select Match Destination Formatting.
9. Adjust the formatting of the pasted data as follows:
   a. Change the color scheme to Marquee and the font scheme to Arial or to the themes you applied in step 2.
   b. Move the *Supply Expenses* heading to cell A1 and apply the Title cell style.
   c. Apply the Accent2 cell style to the column headings in row 3.
   d. Center the data in the *Ordered* column and center the range B3:E3.
10. In cell E3, key the column heading **Expense.** In cell E4, create a formula that multiplies the cost times the quantity ordered and fill the formula down the range E5 to E10. Reduce the number of decimal places to 0 for the range D4:E10.

2. Open a new word processing document, and key the following 4 × 4 table as shown.

| 10 | 20 | 30 | |
|---|---|---|---|
| 400 | 500 | 600 | |
| 7,000 | 8,000 | 9,000 | |
| | | | |

3. In cell D1, calculate the sum of the numbers in cells A1:C1.
4. In cell D2, calculate the sum of the numbers in cells A2:C2.
5. In cell D3, calculate the sum of the numbers in cells A3:C3.
6. In cell A4, calculate the sum of the numbers in cells A1:A3.
7. In cell B4, calculate the sum of the numbers in cells B1:B3.
8. In cell C4, calculate the sum of the numbers in cells C1:C3.
9. In cell D4, calculate the sum of the numbers in cells A1:C3.
10. **Save as:** *18b sum.*

## 18C

**Learn: AVERAGE, MAXIMUM, MINIMUM, and COUNT Functions**

Table Tools Layout/Data/ Formula

1. Read the following information to learn about several basic formulas.

By using built-in functions from the Paste function drop-down list, mathematical functions other than SUM can be used. In this activity you will use the AVERAGE function to compute the average of a series of numbers, the MAX function to identify the largest number in a series of numbers, the MIN function to identify the smallest number in a series of numbers, and the COUNT function to count the number of numeric values in a series of numbers.

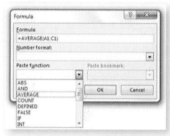

**Figure 3-14** AVERAGE function

To change from the SUM function to another, click in the cell where the answer is to appear, display the Formula dialog box, delete the existing formula but not the = sign, choose the desired function from the Paste function drop-down list, and key the desired direction (LEFT, RIGHT, ABOVE) or cell references (such as A3:C3) between the parentheses (see Figure 3-13).

2. Open a new word processing document, and key the following 4 × 5 table.

| 110 | 220 | 330 | |
|---|---|---|---|
| 2000 | 2100 | 2500 | |
| 3400 | 2400 | 1200 | |
| 5500 | 3590 | 2900 | |
| | | | |

3. In cell D1, calculate the average of the numbers in cells A1:C1.
4. In cell A5, calculate the average of the numbers in cells A1:A4. Change the number format to #,##0.
5. In cell D2, identify the maximum number in cells A2:C2.

Green issues of current importance include:

- Recycling and resource conservation. Many cities and towns have recycling programs in place to recover waste products, reducing the amount of waste while also generating income when the recycled materials are sold.
- Energy conservation. Movements toward renewable energy sources such as solar and wind power (Figure 22-9) are designed to conserve oil and gas reserves, and use of energy-efficient products is increasing.
- Habitat conservation. People have begun to understand the importance of conserving natural habitats as a means of preserving species of plants and animals that would otherwise be threatened with extinction.
- Clean air and water. In an increasingly industrial world, making sure people have clean water and air has assumed critical importance. Efforts to clean up polluted waterways and eliminate air pollution have succeeded in developed countries and are improving in developing countries.

The constantly rising global population imposes considerable impacts on the environment. Resources are being used up at a faster rate, and the byproducts of manufacturing put air and water quality at risk. The amount of waste that must be disposed of increases every year. We need to be aware of these trends and do our part to protect not only the local environment but the global environment.

**Figure 22-9** Wind is an infinitely renewable source of energy

Green organizations stress the concept of the three Rs: reduce, reuse, and recycle. You will learn more about reducing, reusing, and recycling in this lesson.

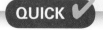
QUICK ✔

1. Would you buy an electric car? Why or why not?
2. What is one energy-efficient product you use in your daily life?

## 123C

**Controlling Waste**

One way that everyone in the world can protect the environment is to reduce the amount of waste that goes into the trash and then to landfills or other dumping sites on land and at sea. In developing countries, especially, increasing amounts of solid waste have become a consequence of what is often called a "throwaway" lifestyle. Many consumer products—including cell phones, televisions, and other electronics—have a limited life span, and once they can no longer be used, they are often simply thrown away. Convenience products such as bottled water and fast food generate a great deal of waste that can find its way even into the depths of the oceans.

Anyone can participate in the process of reducing waste, and it requires only commitment and a small amount of time. Here are a few ways you can control the amount of waste you and your household produce:

- Use mugs and reusable water bottles rather than disposable cups and throwaway plastic bottles.
- Use kitchen towels rather than paper towels.
- Compost kitchen and yard waste.
- Pick up trash and separate it if possible into bins for recyclable and non-recyclable waste.
- Take your own bags to the market or grocery to cut down on the use of plastic bags.

6. In cell B5, identify the maximum number in cells B1:B4.
7. In cell D3, identify the minimum number in cells A3:C3.
8. In cell C5, report how many numbers are in D1:D4.
9. In cell D5, report the average of the numbers in cells A1:C4.  Change the number format to #,##0.
10. **Save as:** *18c functions*.

## 18D

### Learn: Writing Formulas

Table Tools Layout/
Formula

1. Read the following information to learn about writing basic formulas.

In addition to using the built-in functions such as SUM and AVERAGE, formulas can be written in the Formula dialog box to add (+), subtract (−), multiply (*), and divide (/) numbers using the symbols shown in the parentheses.

To enter a formula, click in the cell where the answer is to appear, display the Formula dialog box, delete the existing formula but not the = sign, and write (key) the formula you desire—do not space between the parts of the formula.

2. Open a new word processing document, and key the following 4 × 4 table as shown.

| 11 | 22 | 33 | |
|----|----|----|--|
| 44 | 55 | 66 | |
| 77 | 88 | 99 | |
| | | | |

3. In cell D1, write a formula that adds cell A2 to B1 and then subtracts cell C2.
4. In cell D2, write a formula that divides cell B3 by cell B1 and then subtracts 4.  Change the number format to 0.
5. In cell D3, write a formula that adds cells A3 and C3 and divides that total by cell B1.
6. In cell A4, write a formula that calculates the difference between cell C1 and B1 and divides that result by B1.
7. In cell B4, write a formula that calculates the percent that cell B1 is of B3.
8. In cell C4, write a formula that adds 1,000 to cell C2 and B2 and then multiplies that result by 2.
9. **Save as:** *18d formulas*.

## 18E

### Learn: Recalculate Formulas

1. Read the following information to learn about recalculating a formula.

Unlike spreadsheet software, word processing software does not update an answer immediately when a change is made to a number that was used in the calculation.  However, the answer will be updated automatically when the document is reopened.  If an immediate update is desired, select the answer (field) to be updated, and then right-click and select Update Field from the list.  Alternatively, you can select the answer to be updated and tap F9.

2. Open *18b sum.*
3. Change cell C1 to 130.
4. Update the answer in cell D1.
5. Update the answer in cell C4.
6. Update the answer in cell D4.
7. **Save as:** *18e change*.

6. Adjust column widths as shown in the Quick Check below.
7. Apply the Heading 1 style to the October–November heading, and change space before the heading to 0 point.
8. Apply Grid Table 5 Dark – Accent 5 table style.
9. Apply Droplet or a similar theme.
10. Adjust the height of the first row and each merged row to 0.3". Change alignment of the first row to Align Center and the merged rows to Align Center Left.
11. **Save as:** *122f community calendar*. Print the document and close it. Exit the word processing program.

Your table should look similar to the one shown below.

**October–November**

| Category | Event | Description | Date | Time |
|---|---|---|---|---|
| **Literacy Programs** | | | | |
| | GED Practice Test | Find out if you are ready to take the official test | 11/5 | 9:00 a.m. |
| | Adult New Readers | Ongoing class for adults 17+ concentrating on reading for work and pleasure | T, Th | 6:30 p.m. |
| | BOOST tutoring | One-on-one reading support for children 6 – 12 | M, T, Th | 3:00 p.m. |
| **Computers & Technology** | | | | |
| | Adaptive Technology | Learn about screen reading options for the visually impaired | 10/29 | 10:00 a.m. |
| | Computers for Beginners | Fundamental skills such as how to navigate the desktop, how to use a mouse and keyboard, the difference between hardware and software, etc. | 10/12 | 10:00 a.m. |
| | Internet for Beginners | Basics of browsers, search engines, and online safety | 10/19 | 10:00 a.m. |
| | Word Processing Basics | Learn key skills such as working with fonts, changing margins and indention, copying and pasting, and basic keyboarding | 10/26 | 10:00 a.m. |
| **Job Searching & Support** | | | | |
| | Resume Writing | Learn how to create an attention-getting resume by using and modifying templates | 11/3 | 10:00 a.m. |
| | Career Transitions | Learn how to use reference resources to research career options | 11/12 | 2:00 p.m. |
| **Language Studies** | | | | |
| | Bilingual Story Time | Stories and games for children in English and Spanish | 11/19 | 11:30 a.m. |
| | ESL Conversation | Informal opportunity to practice English conversation for those for whom English is a second language | 11/17 | 1:00 p.m. |
| **Cultural Events** | | | | |
| | Understanding Día de Muertos | Learn more about the Mexican celebration of the Day of the Dead, and enjoy a sugar skeleton! | 10/29 | 2:00 p.m. |
| | Native American Harvest Celebration | Join Native American musicians and interpreters for songs and stories about harvest festivals, including our own Thanksgiving | 11/19 | 2:00 p.m. |
| **Community Events** | | | | |
| | Fall Community Cleanup Committee | Meet with the Committee in charge of picking up trash, planting spring bulbs, and maintaining the community's green spaces | 10/15 | 2:00 p.m. |
| | College of Pharmacy Health Fair | Students from Madison University's College of Pharmacy are offering blood glucose screenings and blood pressure checks to all community members. | 11/15 | 5:00 p.m |

# LESSON 123
## Protecting Your Environment

**OUTCOMES**

- Learn the importance of environmental conservation.
- Explore ways of controlling waste.
- Complete a community action presentation.
- Explore ways to recycle.
- Create a word processing table with inserted images.

## Business Documents
### 123B

- Presentation Containing Spreadsheet Data
- Word Processing Table Created from Database Data

**Going Green**

Issues that relate to responsible care of the environment, popularly called "green" issues, have become increasingly important in the first decade of the 21st century. People all over the world are becoming more aware of the necessity for conservation of natural resources, including habitats and ecosystems and the species of fish, birds, and animals that live in those habitats.

**Apply: Formulas**

1. Open *df 18f table*.
2. Calculate the Total Cycling miles in column F for rows 4:10 and the Total Jogging miles in column G for the same rows.
3. In row 11, calculate the averages for each column B:E.
4. In row 12, identify the maximum number in each row 4:10 for each column B:E.
5. Right-align all numbers.
6. Format the table appropriately.
7. Shade cells F12 and G12 to indicate they have no calculations.
8. Compare the format of your table to that shown in the following Quick Check.
   Save as: *18f table*.

**QUICK** ✔

Your completed table should look like this:

| HARRY LUKAS EXERCISE LOG | | | | | |
|---|---|---|---|---|---|
| Day | Week 1 | | Week 2 | | Total Cycling | Total Jogging |
| | Cycling | Jogging | Cycling | Jogging | | |
| Monday | 10 | 0 | 15 | 2 | 25 | 2 |
| Tuesday | 15 | 0 | 18 | 4 | 33 | 4 |
| Wedensday | 0 | 6 | 0 | 8 | 0 | 14 |
| Thursday | 20 | 3 | 12 | 4 | 32 | 7 |
| Friday | 10 | 5 | 6 | 6 | 16 | 11 |
| Saturday | 0 | 8 | 10 | 3 | 10 | 11 |
| Sunday | 24 | 0 | 22 | 0 | 46 | 0 |
| **Average** | 11.29 | 3.14 | 11.86 | 3.86 | 20.25 | 6.13 |
| **Maximum** | 24 | 8 | 22 | 8 | | |

# 21st Century Skills: Access and Evaluate Information

The Internet and World Wide Web have given computer users quick and easy access to information on virtually any topic. But how do you know that the information is accurate, timely, and written by a reliable and knowledgeable source? Following are some tips:

- Verify any information by checking another source.
- Identify the author or organization that publishes or sponsors the site, and identify the date the content was created or last updated.
- On the home page, look for a statement of purpose for the site.
- Examine the language of the site. Does it provide facts, opinions, or both? A reliable site should present information in a balanced and objective manner and should be free of spelling and grammatical errors.

### Think Critically

Open a new word processing document, and compose your answers to the questions below.

1. Why is it important to evaluate information you read on the Web?
2. Do you think the Internet is as reliable a source of information as your school or local library?
3. Describe ways in which you evaluate information you obtain in various formats, including the Internet, television, print publications, and in person.
4. Save as: *u03 21century*.

## Supporting Your Community

Many communities offer help to citizens who do not have adequate housing, or whose houses need repairs. Programs such as Habitat for Humanity (Figure 22-8) give a family the opportunity to build a new house, supported by volunteers from businesses and community and religious groups. Your community may also offer programs in which volunteers restore and paint houses of citizens such as seniors on fixed incomes who cannot afford these repairs.

You can support your community's seniors in other ways as well. Many seniors who no longer drive need transportation to groceries, markets, pharmacies, and other shops, as well as transportation to polling places on election days. Mowing grass, raking leaves, and shoveling snow are other ways you can help seniors in your neighborhood to keep their properties neat and safe.

Young people in your community may also be in need of support. You can make a difference to them by becoming a Big Brother or Big Sister, by coaching a youth team, or by volunteering in schools.

**Figure 22-8** You can work with your community to help your neighbors

You learned in Lesson 121 the importance of literacy as a global issue. Literacy can also be an important local issue. You can support literacy in your neighborhood by volunteering to tutor children who are learning to read or by working with adults from this country or other countries who are improving their literacy skills. You may also be able to help teach digital literacy to those unfamiliar with computers.

**★TIP** A good way to support literacy efforts in your community is to organize a book drive to collect used books for donation to shelters or to neighbors who would not otherwise be able to buy books for themselves or their children.

Providing support in your community doesn't have to be all work and no play. Be alert to opportunities to interact with community members from different countries, religions, or cultures. Members of your community may be invited to watch Buddhist monks creating a sand painting mandala, to participate in an *iftar* dinner marking the end of a day of fasting during the Muslim holy month of Ramadan, or to experience the Hindu "festival of lights," Diwali.

Your community may also celebrate feast days and events from the many cultures and nationalities. Attending such events in your community will give you an appreciation of customs and traditions from around the world and take you another step along the path of global awareness.

## Word Processing Table

You work for the Village of Montgomery's Community Center. Your supervisor has developed a listing of the events, classes, and programs available at the Center and wants you to create an attractive table that can be posted to the Center's website.

1. Start your word processing program and open *df 122f community calendar.*
2. Beginning with the Literacy Programs ¶, select the remaining ¶s in the document, then convert the text to a table, using Tabs as the separator.
3. Change the page orientation to Landscape and change margins to Narrow.
4. Insert a new column to the left of the first column. Merge all cells in the rows that contain category headings.
5. Insert a new row above the first row and split cell into five columns. Key the following column headings, from left to right: **Category, Event, Description, Date,** and **Time.**

Insert/Table/Convert Text to Table

# LESSON 19    Table Applications and Analysis

OUTCOMES
- Apply previously learned table features.
- Analyze the contents of a table.

## Business Documents

- Forms of Business Ownership
- Enrollment Report
- Monthly Pay Schedules
- Monthly Budget

### 19B

**Apply: Tables**

**Table 1**

1. Open a new word processing document, and key the following table. Set column 1 width to 1.25" and columns B:D widths to 1.75"; use bullets as shown, but you decide all other formatting features.

| FORMS OF BUSINESS OWNERSHIP | | | |
|---|---|---|---|
| **Form** | **Definition** | **Major Advantages** | **Major Disadvantages** |
| Proprietorship | A business that is owned and run by one individual | • Easy to start and end<br>• Owner has sole control over all business operations<br>• Owner receives all profits from the business | • Owner is liable for all debts<br>• Liability for debts include business and personal assets |
| Partnership | A business that is owned and run by two or more individuals who have entered into an agreement | • Easy to start<br>• Owners have control over all business operations<br>• Owners share profits according to terms of the agreement | • Each partner is liable for all of the debts<br>• Liability for debts include each partner's business and personal assets |
| Corporation | A business that is owned by one or more shareholders and managed by a board of directors. A corporation is treated as a separate legal entity and must be registered within a state. | • Limited liability—each owner's liability is limited to the amount invested in the corporation and does not extend to personal assets | • More difficult to form and must meet more legal requirements<br>• All owners do not have direct involvement in business operations<br>• Profits not shared among owners without board of directors' approval |

Source: Dlabay, Les R., James L. Burrow, and Brad Kleindl. *Intro to Business*, 7th edition. Mason, OH: South-Western Cengage Learning, 2009.

**Customizing a Presentation**

Home/New Slide down arrow/Reuse Slides

1. Start your presentation program and open *df 122d feeding your community*.
2. On slide 1, replace *Student Name* with your name. Then change the presentation design to Retrospect or another similar design.
3. On slide 7, right-click the bulleted text in the content area, click Convert to SmartArt, and then click More SmartArt Graphics on the pop-out gallery.
4. Click the List layout category and then choose the Vertical Box List layout (Figure 22-7). Change the SmartArt Style to Glossy Effect and the SmartArt colors to Gradient Range – Accent Colors 2.
5. Choose to reuse slides from another presentation. In the Reuse Slides pane, click the Browse button, click Browse File, and open *df 122d ways to help*. Insert slides 2, 3, 4, and 5 at the end of the *122d feeding your community* presentation.
6. On slide 8, insert a clip art photograph that relates in some way to volunteering. (Try keywords such as *soup kitchen*.) Size the image appropriately and position it in the top center of the slide.
7. On slide 11, select the phrase *Meals on Wheels* and insert a hyperlink to your local Meals on Wheels program, or one in a nearby town or city.
8. Apply the *Wipe* transition to all slides.
9. Apply animations as follows:
   a. On slide 4, animate each chart using the *Wipe* animation, From Top, By Series. Start each animation After Previous. Animate the text box at the bottom of the slide to *Fly In* from Bottom, After Previous.
   b. On slide 7, animate the SmartArt diagram using the *Fly In* animation, From Bottom, One by One. Keep the On Click start option, so you can display each statement and then click to show the answer.
10. Play the slide show to check your animations and view all content.
11. **Save as:** *122d feeding your community*. Close the presentation and presentation program.

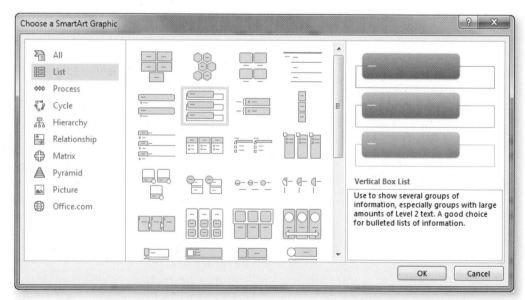

**Figure 22-7** Select Vertical Box List Layout

2. Save as: *19b table1*.

**Table 2**

1. Open *df 19b letter*.
2. Insert the table in file *df 19b insert* between the two ¶s in the body of the letter. Center it horizontally.
3. Calculate the sum of columns B:E in the Totals row.
4. Adjust the top and bottom cell margins in the table to .02.
5. If needed, adjust the space after the table to make it appear equal to the space before the table.
6. Save as: *19b letter*.

**Table 3**

1. Open *df 19b text*.
2. Convert it to a table.
3. Insert two rows at the top and key this text in them.

| APRIL PAY SCHEDULE | | | |
|---|---|---|---|
| Salesperson | Sales | Commission | Salary |

4. Insert two columns at the right. Merge the cells in the title row as needed. Key **Bonus** in cell E2 and **Total** in cell F2.
5. Key **$125** in cells E3:E7.
6. Calculate the row totals in column F. Change the number format for the totals to #,##0.
7. Insert a row at the bottom. In cell A8, key **Average** and then calculate the average for each column B:F. Change the number format for the averages to #,##0.
8. Format the table appropriately; position it at the top center of the page.
9. Save as: *19b table3*.

**TEAMWORK**

## Digital Citizenship and Ethics
The widespread use of the Internet for shopping and conducting financial transactions has led to scams in which online thieves trick users into supplying credit card and bank account numbers as well as other personal information. One such scam is known as **phishing**. In this scam, you get an official-looking email that appears to be from your bank or other financial institution. The email tells you there is a problem with your account and asks you to confirm your account number, social security number, or some other personal information. But the message is a fake.

As a class, discuss the following.

1. What are ways you can verify that an email message comes from a legitimate source?
2. If you suspect that you received a phishing email from a party posing as your bank, what course of action would you take?

Causes of hunger in this country will sound familiar, after what you learned in the previous lesson. In the United States, as elsewhere in the world, the leading cause of hunger is poverty. The United States produces enough to feed all of its citizens and still provide food for other countries, but some Americans simply cannot afford to buy it.

Some citizens may be unemployed, or may not earn enough to buy adequate food. Some may be on fixed incomes that do not allow them to spend as much on food as they need to. Citizens with disabilities that prevent them from working may have very few resources for feeding themselves and their families. Rising food costs over the past decade also play an important part in preventing people from buying food and other necessities. "Food deserts" in some cities mean citizens have no grocery store nearby.

You may think that poverty and hunger are limited to some areas of large cities, but they can occur anywhere, in suburbs as well as rural areas. Anywhere that people do not have good employment opportunities and access to fresh, wholesome food, hunger can become a problem.

When it comes to making sure that the people in your community have enough to eat, you have a number of options, as you will learn in the next activity. Relieving poverty and hunger in this country is a key goal for many local and national organizations. You will not have to look far to find a way to help hungry people in your community.

© juniart/Shutterstock.com

## 21st Century Skills: Global Awareness

Have you ever heard our country referred to as a "salad bowl"? The term is a metaphor for the integration of many different cultures in a single region—like the many different ingredients of a salad combined in a single bowl. Think of how the salad bowl concept applies to your school, your neighborhood, and your community. As you progress through your education and embark on a career, you will come in contact with all kinds of people from many different cultural backgrounds. In order to develop and strengthen relationships in a multicultural environment, you should keep the following in mind:

- Take the time to learn about the language, customs, and traditions of different cultures so that you are comfortable with the people around you.
- Do not stereotype people according to their ethnic or cultural heritage.
- Focus on similarities between you and others from different cultures. Most people have the same basic needs and wants.
- Consider the differences between you and others as a tool for learning more about our global society and understanding different perspectives.

### Think Critically

1. All of us belong to the American culture, but we also belong to subcultures based on things such as our religion, where we live, and our age. Create a presentation or report about a subculture to which you belong. Describe the characteristics (language, dress, traditions, etc.) of the culture; use images to illustrate.
2. Save the report or presentation as instructed and share it with the class.

1. Key the following table, formatting as shown.

| Monthly Budget | | |
|---|---|---|
| **Income** | **Typical Teenager** | **Mine** |
| • Wages/Paycheck | $185 | |
| • Allowance | 40 | |
| • Interest from Savings | 5 | |
| • Gifts | 20 | |
| • Other | 0 | |
| **Total Monthly Income** | | |
| **Expenses** | | |
| • Cell Phone | 25 | |
| • Clothes | 70 | |
| • Donations to Charity | 10 | |
| • Eating Out/Snacks/Fun | 60 | |
| • Gas for Family Car | 35 | |
| • Gifts | 15 | |
| • Savings Account | 15 | |
| • School Expenses | 20 | |
| • Other | 0 | |
| **Total Monthly Expenses** | | |

2. Compute the monthly income in cell B8 and the Total Monthly Expenses in cell B19.
3. Analysis:
   a. Do the income and expenses balance?
   b. In cell C10, record the percent of the teennager's income that she spends for her cell phone.
   c. If the teenager suddenly finds that her income from her job is going to be $30 lower each month due to a reduction in the hours she works, what expense item(s) would you recommend she immediately reduce to retain a balanced budget? Shade the cell of the expense item(s) in column 2 that you would reduce.

4. In column C, key your estimate of your monthly income and expenses. For example, if you receive approximately $300 each year from others for gifts, divide the $300 by 12 to get a monthly figure.

# LESSON 122    Acting Locally

**OUTCOMES**
- Understand local implications of global issues.
- Explore ways to feed local citizens.
- Customize a presentation.
- Explore ways to support a local community.
- Create a complex word processing table.

## Business Documents
### 122B

- Presentation
- Word Processing Document with a Table

**Understanding Local Implications of Global Issues**

Global awareness is important, but concentrating on what is happening in other countries should not blind you to the fact that your own city, town, or neighborhood is also a part of the world. Some of the issues that concern us globally are also to be found closer to home. Acting locally can contribute to an improvement in the lives of your neighbors, as well as help you to become a better citizen of the world.

Figure 22-6 Hunger is an issue in many communities

Jim West/Alamy

You can find many ways to act locally to help solve problems and support your community (Figure 22-6). Even in a nation as rich in resources as the United States, people do not have enough food and may lack other necessities as well, such as clothing, shelter, and medications.

Another aspect of acting locally is to open yourself to any chance to learn about people in your community who come from backgrounds different from your own. Such learning may take the form of mastering a foreign language, always an important first step in learning about the culture of a different country. Or it may take the form of volunteering to help a newcomer to learn your language, or participating in events that are special to other cultures.

In our increasingly mobile society, you may interact on a daily basis with people from different cultures, religions, and lifestyles. As a citizen of the world, you are called to treat everyone in your community with respect and tolerance. Giving of your time and energy can make your local community a better place for all of its citizens and can be the first step in a commitment to global awareness.

**QUICK ✔**

1  What could you do to collect money or resources for a food pantry in your community?
2. Do you know anyone who has recently come to the United States from another country? What country did he or she come from, and why?

5. Analysis:

   a. Do your income and expenses balance?  If not, make the appropriate adjustments to get a balanced budget.

   b. Add a column to the right of the last column.  Use Percent as the column heading and merge row 1 cells as needed.

   c. In the cell to the right of your highest expense item, calculate what percent it is of your total income.

   d. If your monthly income is likely to be reduced by 10 percent for the next six months, identify the expense(s) you would reduce to maintain a balanced budget.  Shade the cell of the expense item(s) in column 3 that you could reduce.

   e. If you are certain that your income would increase by 10 percent during the next six months, identify the expense(s) you would increase to maintain a balanced budget.  Bold and italicize the font of the text in the cells in column 3 that would be increased.

6. **Save as:** *19c analysis*.

## 19D

### Timed Writings

Two 3' writings on two ¶s; determine *gwam*; count errors.

 **A**   all letters used     gwam   3'

|  |  |
|---|---|
| The Arlington House is a place filled with the very | 4 |
| interesting history of our country.  The exquisite house | 8 |
| built for the grandson of Martha Washington, George | 11 |
| Custis, in time became the home of General Lee.  The | 15 |
| house was built in an amazing location which today looks | 18 |
| out over the capital city of our nation. | 21 |
| The home and land are also linked to other famous | 25 |
| people of United States history.  Soon after the Civil War | 29 |
| started, the home became the headquarters of the Union | 32 |
| army with much of the land to ultimately be used for what | 36 |
| is today known as Arlington National Cemetery.  President | 40 |
| Kennedy and President Taft are just a few of the notables | 44 |
| buried on the former estate of General Lee. | 47 |

gwam   3'     1     2     3     4

9. On the *regional literacy* worksheet, select the range A4:D10 and create a line chart using the Line with Markers option.
10. Modify the chart as follows:
    a. Switch row and column data so that the dates are on the horizontal axis.
    b. Select the vertical axis and then choose to format the selection.
    c. Select Fixed for the Minimum option and key **40.0.** Select Fixed for the Maximum option and key **100.0.** Select Fixed for the Major unit and key **10.0.** Click Close.
    d. Click the outside edge of the chart to select the Chart Area, and then choose to format the selection.
    e. Choose to apply a gradient fill to the chart area by selecting the Linear Up gradient. Your chart should look like the one shown in the Quick Check below.
    f. Save changes to the workbook.
11. On the *world literacy* worksheet, click the chart to select it and then click the Copy command.
12. Switch to the report in the word processing program, and click at the beginning of the ¶ that contains the source line beneath the Figure 1 caption.
13. Paste the chart and then tap Enter to move the source ¶ to a new line. If necessary, make adjustments to the chart size to fit on page.
14. Switch back to the workbook, click the *regional literacy* tab, select the chart, and click the Copy command.
15. Switch back to the report, click at the beginning of the last ¶ of text, and paste the chart. Tap Enter to move the text ¶ to a new line. If necessary, make adjustments to the chart size to fit on page.
16. **Save as:** *121f global literacy.*
17. Print the report, close the report, and then exit your word processing program and spreadsheet program.

**QUICK** ✔

Your chart should look like the one below.

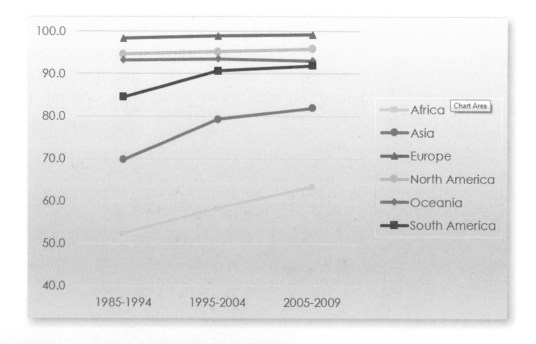

# Academic and Career Connections

Complete the following exercises that introduce various topics that involve academic themes and careers.

## Grammar and Writing

### Commas

**MicroType 6**

- References/Communication Skills/Commas
- CheckPro/Communication Skills 3
- CheckPro/Word Choice 3

1. Go to *MicroType 6* and use this feature path for review:  References/Communication Skills/Commas.
2. Click *Rules* and review the rules of using commas.
3. Then, under *Commas*, click *Posttest*.
4. Follow the instructions to complete the posttest.

*Optional Activities*

1. Go to this path:  CheckPro/Communication Skills 3.
2. Complete the activities as directed.
3. Go to this path:  CheckPro/Word Choice 3.
4. Complete the activities as directed.

## Communications

### Reading

1. Open *df u03 communications*.
2. Read the document carefully, and then close the file.
3. In a new document, key your answers to the following questions.
   a. Pearl Buck was the first American woman to win what award?
   b. What award did Pearl Buck win in 1932 for her novel *The Good Earth*?
   c. What country is the setting for *The Good Earth*?
   d. Which award discussed in the document is an international award given to writers from many different countries and cultures?
   e. Which award discussed in the document recognizes American authors?
   f. What is the main topic of the first ¶ in the document?
4. **Save as:** *u03 communications*.

## Math Skills

1. Ben uses his word processing software's built-in Help system to access the software manufacturer's website.  He sees that there are a number of software updates that he can download for free.  He selects a security update and sees that the application is 7.25 MB.  He begins the download process.  At one point, a message box opens that says the download is 40 percent complete.  How much of the application has been downloaded?
2. If 1 megabyte (MB) equals 1,048,576 bytes, how many bytes is the security update?  (*Hint:* When multiplying by a decimal, count the total number of decimal places in both factors, and then insert a decimal point in the answer so that it has the same total number of decimal places as the factors.)
3. After downloading the update, Ben wants to find out how much hard disk space he has left on his computer.  The size of his hard disk is 148 GB, and 3/4 of the space is being used.  How many gigabytes are still free?
4. Ben reviews the contents and properties of his main working folder on his hard disk.  The folder contains a total of 256 files.  Of the total, roughly 1/3 are word processing documents; 1/4 are presentation files; 1/6 are picture files; 1/8 are spreadsheet files; and the remaining 1/8 are various other formats.  How many of each type of file are in the folder?  (Round to the nearest whole number.)

Literacy is one of the most important steps an individual can take to avoid poverty. Encouraging literacy programs is one of the most important steps a country can take toward improving conditions for all citizens (Figure 22-4). A literate population is capable of handling more challenging and higher-paying jobs, which ultimately benefits the country in the form of increased revenue and consumer spending. Countries that are not expending a large portion of their resources in relieving hunger and poverty can invest in other improvements such as infrastructure and technology. And countries that are able to care for all their citizens do not need relief funds and supplies from the rest of the world.

No one in this century would deny the importance of literacy for adults and children, but many countries still have significant populations of illiterate individuals. Even in developed countries, literacy is by no means universal. Many adults in the United States cannot read or write well enough to read a help-wanted ad or fill out a job application.

Tracking global literacy can be a challenge, as countries have different definitions of what literacy means and different methods of collecting data on literacy. As you will see in the next activity, however, literacy is improving in almost every region of the world.

## 121F

**Insert a Spreadsheet Chart in a Word Processing Report**

1. Start your word processing program and open *df 121f global literacy*.
2. Apply Savon or a similar theme to the report and then apply styles as follows:
   a. Apply the Title style to the title on the first page of the report.
   b. Apply Heading 1 style to the four headings in the body of the report.
   c. Apply the Subtle Emphasis style to the two figure captions and to the source line below the Figure 1 caption. Change the font size of the source line to 8 point.
3. On the second page, at the end of the first ¶ below the heading *What Constitutes Literacy*, insert the following footnote: **Ibid., p. 18.**
4. Position the insertion point in the first blank ¶ on the first page and insert the Sideline cover page. Key the title **Global Literacy in the 21st Century.** Delete the Company and Subtitle content holders, key your name as the author, and pick the current date. Your cover page should look like the one shown in Figure 22-5.
5. Modify page numbers in the report as follows:
   a. With the insertion point in the first blank ¶ on the first page of the body of the report, insert a Continuous section break.
   b. With the insertion point in the First Page Header of Section 2, at the top of the first page of the report, click the Link to Previous button to break the link between this section and the previous one.
   c. Click the page number in the header on the third page of the report (it should have the number 1 when you click it) and open the Page Number Format dialog box. Change the *Start at* number to 1 and click OK. The third page of the report should now have the number 2.
6. Save the report and leave it open.
7. Start your spreadsheet program and open *df 121f literacy charts*. Save the spreadsheet as *121f literacy charts*.
8. Apply Savon or the same theme you used in step 2.

Global Literacy in the 21st Century

Student Name
2-10-2014

**Figure 22-5** Cover page for report

© iStockphoto.com/ryasick

### Planning a Career in Information Technology

Almost every type of business uses some form of information technology in its day-to-day activities. For example, a multinational corporation might maintain a wireless network connecting thousands of employees around the world; or an entrepreneur might launch a new website to market his services; or a doctor's office might supply medical personnel with handheld computers to access patient information at the touch of a button. Information technology, or IT, refers to the design, development, support, and management of hardware, software, multimedia, and systems integration services.

Individuals who work in the IT industry help build links between people and technology, whether that's developing an application for smart phones or providing Internet access to a classroom of students. Workers in this industry might focus on network systems, information support and services, Web and digital communications, and programming and software development.

### What's It Like?

Those who work in the IT field are charged with setting up, managing, and maintaining an organization's computer systems. For example:

- They coordinate the installation of new hardware, such as individual workstations, printers and other peripherals, and company-wide networks.
- They develop programs to meet the specific needs of the organization, such as an application that helps the business monitor its inventory needs.
- They develop Internet and intranet sites that enable both those within the organization (employees) and external customers to access information.
- They are increasingly involved with the upkeep, maintenance, and security of systems and networks.

IT professionals typically work in offices. They are employed by large and small businesses, nonprofit organizations, and public institutions such as schools and government offices. Jobs in this field can often be high pressure and require long hours, especially in those organizations where timely access to information and data is critical.

### Employment Outlook

Faster than average employment growth is forecasted for the IT industry, and job prospects are strong. According to the Bureau of Labor Statistics, employment is expected to grow 17 percent over the 2008–2018 decade, which is faster than the average for all occupations. Most employers require that IT workers have a bachelor's degree in a computer-related field, although many prefer a graduate degree, such as an MBA.

### What About You?

The Information Technology career cluster is covered in box 11 of the Interest Survey Activity you completed in Unit 1 of this text. If this box had one of the three highest scores on your survey, you should further explore the cluster's pathways and related occupations.

1. Why do you think a career in information technology could be a good choice?
2. Can you picture yourself doing this type of job?
3. Why are these jobs important to our economy?

1. Start your database program and open the *df 121d global hunger index* database. Save the database as *121d global hunger index*.

2. Open the *Global Hunger Index* table. Sort the datasheet view by number in descending order in the *2011* field. Answer these questions:
   a. What country has the highest GHI in 2011?
   b. Has this value gone up or down since 2001?

3. Close the table without saving changes to the layout.

4. Create a form based on the *Global Hunger Index* table, accepting the default name of *Global Hunger Index*. Apply Ion Boardroom or a similar theme to the form.

5. In Form view, filter the data to show the records where the region is Africa, and then sort by Country.

6. Find the record for Comores and edit the country name to **Comoros**.

7. Toggle the filter off, remove the sort, and close the form.

8. Create a query named *High GHI* that finds countries with an index number greater than or equal to 20 in the *2011* field. Include Region, Country, and 2011 in the query. Sort the query by Region and then by Country.

9. Create a report from the *High GHI* query using the Report Wizard.
   a. Add all fields to the report.
   b. Group the report by Region and sort by Country in ascending alphabetical order. Use the Stepped layout and Portrait orientation.
   c. Title the report **Countries with High GHI Scores**.

10. In Layout view, adjust the column widths and column layout so all data displays in the width of the page.

11. Save changes to the report, print it, and close it.

12. Close the database and exit your database program.

Literacy is generally defined as an ability to read and write. In the 21st century, definitions of literacy also include the ability to think critically, to understand basic mathematics, and to use technology. To become a productive member of a modern society, a person needs not only to be able to deal with written materials but also to interact with computers and other forms of technology.

Literacy is important on many levels, not only to individuals but to countries and ultimately the world.

- Mothers who are literate are more likely to send their children to school, which can begin a cycle of education that may lead to good jobs with income that can result in a higher standard of living.
- Educated people are more able to understand how to keep themselves and their families healthy; reducing illness in communities benefits not only their citizens but their countries.
- Math literacy, sometimes called *numeracy*, enables people to manage their money more carefully.
- Literate people tend to take a more active role in their community and government, because they are able to read information about issues and use critical-thinking skills to form opinions.

Liba Taylor/Alamy

**Figure 22-4** Literacy is an important step to avoiding poverty

© iStockphoto.com/Kali Nine LLC

Complete this activity to help prepare for the **Word Processing I** event in FBLA-PBL's Business Management and Administration division. Participants in this event demonstrate their basic word processing skills.

1. In a new word processing document, use the information you learned in this unit to write a business letter. Use the following guidelines to write your letter.

   - **Date:** Insert the current date.
   - **Letter Address:** Address the letter to **Mr. Ryan Wilcrest | Youth Arts Community Foundation | 705 W. Fourth Street | Cincinnati, OH 45202.**
   - **Body:** We are delighted to hear that the Youth Arts Community Foundation will sponsor a five-day summer camp for students in the Central City School District. Our staff and students are excited to be a part of this enrichment program. ¶At your convenience, please forward the necessary registration materials and information packets. We will distribute these to students who are eligible to participate in the program. ¶Thank you for choosing our school district as one of your summer camp sites. We look forward to working with you.
   - **Complimentary Close:** Use your name and the title of District Arts Coordinator.

2. When you are done writing, be sure to proofread, check the spelling and grammar, and revise the document as necessary. Apply formatting and text enhancements (bold, italic, and underline) as appropriate. Save and print the document as directed by your instructor.

For detailed information on this event, go to www.fbla-pbl.org.

## Think Critically

1. Why are word processing skills important to just about any career you choose?
2. How are the tone and structure of a business letter different from those of a personal letter?
3. What activities can you participate in now that will strengthen your word processing skills?

## School and Community

Have you ever gone to a public park, hiked through a forest, or canoed down a river and been troubled by the amount of litter you see? Despite the efforts of law enforcement agencies, trash collectors, and recyclers to halt littering and polluting, many people still drop their trash wherever they please. That's why more and more volunteers are needed for community cleanups. A community cleanup brings volunteers together to clean, repair, or improve public spaces, such as parks, riverbanks, and biking/hiking trails.

1. Identify a public space in your area that would benefit from a community cleanup.

2. Contact a community council member or civic leader to find out the requirements to prepare and carry out the cleanup.

3. In a word processing document, create a table of family, friends, and other potential volunteers to contact to help with the cleanup.

4. Create another table that lists additional sites to target for cleanup.

5. Using the information you have gathered, organize and lead the cleanup.

**Feeding the World**

Lack of adequate nutrition has been and continues to be one of the most critical issues for countries around the world. Most countries with a significant population of hungry citizens are among the least developed nations, but hunger is not limited to what used to be called Third World countries. Even the most developed countries in the world have citizens who are chronically hungry.

The most important cause of hunger is poverty. In areas where hunger is a persistent problem, people do not have the resources to provide themselves with food: They do not have enough land, or land that is productive enough, to grow food, and they do not have enough money to buy food.

Other issues contribute to widespread hunger in some countries.

- Conflicts such as war disrupt agriculture and may result in people having to flee their land to take up residence in another country; as refugees, they have few options for acquiring land to farm or money to buy food.
- Rising food prices in the past decade mean that even if a family has money to spend, they may not be able to afford the amount of food they need for adequate nutrition.
- Overuse of natural resources such as fresh water and farmland can result in decreasing production.

**Figure 22-3** Choosing the right crops for a region can increase food production

Chronic hunger can have devastating impacts on a population's children and adults. People are more susceptible to diseases and infections. Children may die in infancy or fail to thrive because they have not had essential nutrients.

A hungry population is not a productive population, which means the country in which hungry people live also suffers an impact. Children who are malnourished may not be able to go to school, or stay in school long enough to receive an education that would enable them to get good jobs, another impact on the country's economic development.

Providing relief to the world's hungry citizens can be accomplished in a number of ways. Food can be shipped directly to a country for distribution to citizens. Financial aid can be supplied so that people can purchase food, either from sources abroad or from local sources. If purchases can be made locally, both the buyer and the seller of food benefit.

 **TIP** A GHI score between 10.0 and 19.9 suggests a country has a serious hunger problem. A score between 20.0 and 29.9 is considered alarming. A score equal to or greater than 30.0 indicates an extremely alarming situation.

Training in modern agriculture methods can often result in higher crop yields (Figure 22-3). Education in the areas of health, nutrition, and money management can help to improve people's lives. World governments have also concentrated on programs to introduce other sources of income where traditional agriculture is not providing adequate earnings. **Microcredit loans** have been made available to villages or individual families to enable them to run small businesses and cooperatives.

Organizations track the incidence of world hunger using metrics such as the **Global Hunger Index (GHI)**, developed by the International Food Policy Research Institute. The higher the index number, the more people are in need. A review of Global Hunger Index scores over the past several decades indicate that efforts to combat world hunger have been paying off, as the score for the world as a whole has dropped from 19.7 in 1990 to 14.6 in 2011. There are still, however, plenty of hungry regions in the world.

# Assessing Basic Spreadsheet Skills

| **SS: Assessment 1** | In order to complete the spreadsheet unit (Unit 4, Using Spreadsheets to Make Economic Choices), you should have the skills and knowledge required to complete this spreadsheet assessment. |
|---|---|

Worksheet Window
Move Around in a
Worksheet

1. Open a new worksheet and maximize the screen.
2. Answer the following questions:
   a. Are rows identified with numbers or letters?  Key the answer in cells A1 and A2.
   b. Are columns identified with numbers or letters?  Key the answer in cells B1 and B2.
   c. How many worksheets are in the workbook you have open?  Key the number in cells C1 and C2 as a label.

Select a Range of Cells
Cut, Copy, and Move

3. Select the range of cells A1:C1, and move the contents to cells G6:I6.
4. Select the range of cells G6:I6, and copy the contents to cell range C3:E3.

Select and Edit Cell
Content

5. Change the font in cell C3 to dark red Times New Roman 12 point.
6. Bold and italicize content in cells D3 and E3.
7. Underline the first three letters in cell G6 contents with a single underline.
8. Underline the first three letters in cell H6 contents with a double underline.

Clear and Delete Cell
Content and Format

9. Delete the cell I6 contents.
10. Clear the bold and italic in cell D3.

View and Print Gridlines
and Column and Row
Headings

11. Set the page to print without gridlines, but with row and column headings.
12. Print the worksheet.
13. **Save as:  *ss assess 1*.**  Close the file.

| **SS: Assessment 2** | In order to complete the spreadsheet unit (Unit 4, Using Spreadsheets to Make Economic Choices), you should complete this spreadsheet assessment. |
|---|---|

1. Open *df ss assess 2*.

Insert and Delete Rows
and Columns

2. Delete column B.
3. Delete row 4.
4. Insert a row at the top.
5. Insert a column after column A, and key the following in the cells:  **102** in cell B2 and B3; **110** in cell B4; and **114** in cell B5.
6. Key **Student Name** in cell A1; **Homeroom** in cell B1; **Week 1** in cell C1; **Week 2** in cell D1; **Total** in cell E1; and % **Change** in F1.

Adjust Column Width

7. Adjust the width of each column to fit the longest item in the column.

**Figure 22-2** Global concern over dwindling resources is helping to preserve rain forests

- Caring for the world's disadvantaged is a global concern. Relief organizations from many countries cooperate to provide necessary nutritional and educational resources, foster entrepreneurship that can bring families out of poverty, and fund medical programs that fight health threats such as malaria.

- When natural disasters strike, people all over the world are able to see immediately the scope of the devastation and can contribute to relief funds by donating online.

- Global expertise can provide solutions to disasters that might not have been possible for one nation, as when a consortium of multinational companies and organizations brought trapped Chilean miners safely to the surface.

- Wildlife and habitat conservation has become more important to people around the world. Global and local organizations are focusing on protecting endangered species and conserving irreplaceable habitats such as South American rain forests (Figure 22-2).

Global interconnectedness has had other positive effects. Moving manufacturing and other jobs to countries where wages are lower means that companies in more developed nations can reduce expenses. Increased employment in **developing** or **transitional countries** has raised the standard of living in those countries.

Global interconnectedness can have downsides as well. When a situation such as an economic downturn affects one country, it often affects many others that have invested in that country or rely on that country for resources. A tsunami in Japan can mean layoffs in a U.S. auto plant that relies on getting parts from Japan, for example. Also, moving jobs to a developing country can mean a loss of employment opportunities in the country of the company that is doing the **offshoring**.

As citizens of the world, we all need to become more aware of global issues. By reading or reviewing reputable news stories, analyzing information we receive from other people and the media, interacting with persons who represent diverse cultures and nations, and using 21st-century skills such as critical thinking and communication, we can prepare ourselves to meet global challenges.

 QUICK ✔

1. Why do you think it might be important to raise the standard of living in a developing country?

2. What experience have you had with offshoring? Do you think this is a good business practice or a questionable one?

| Enter Formulas | 8. Write a formula in cell E2 to add the numbers in cells C2 and D2. Copy this formula to cells E3:E5. |
| | 9. Write a formula in cell F2 to compute the percent of change between Week 1 and Week 2 sales. Copy this formula to cells F3:F5. |

| Format Numbers | 10. Format numbers in columns C, D, and E as dollars with no cents. |
| | 11. Format the numbers in column F as a % with two decimal places. |
| | 12. Key **Total** in cell A6, right-aligned. |

| Functions | 13. In cells C6, D6, and E6, use the AutoSum function to add the numbers in column C, D, and E. |
| | 14. Key **Average** in cell A7, right-aligned. |
| | 15. In cells C7, D7, and E7, use the Average function to calculate the average for the Week 1 sales, Week 2 sales, and Total sales. |
| | 16. Adjust column widths as needed to fit the longest item. |
| | 17. Save as: *ss assess 2a*. Print but do not close the file. |

| Show Formulas | 18. Display the formulas in the worksheet. |
| | 19. Save as: *ss assess 2b*. Print and close the file. |

## SS: Assessment 3

In order to complete the spreadsheet unit (Unit 4, Using Spreadsheets to Make Economic Choices) you should complete this spreadsheet assessment.

1. Open *df ss assess chart*.

| Charts | 2. Create an embedded 3-D Column chart. Title the chart "Sales Report." |
| | 3. Save as: *ss assess chart 1* but do not close the file. |

| Change Chart Type | 4. Change the column chart to a 3-D Bar chart. |
| | 5. Save as: *ss assess chart 2* but do not close the file. |

| Change Chart Layout and Styles | 6. Change the Bar chart layout to Layout 8. |
| | 7. Key **Sales and Returns** for the X-axis title; and **Salesperson** for the Y-axis title. |
| | 8. Change the style of the chart to Style 8. |
| | 9. Save as: *ss assess chart 3*. Close the file |

# UNIT 22 Understanding Our World

Lesson **121** Thinking Globally
Lesson **122** Acting Locally
Lesson **123** Protecting Your Environment

Lesson **124** Exploring Today's Legal and Ethical Issues
Lesson **125** Evaluating Media Messages

---

## LESSON 121  Thinking Globally

**OUTCOMES**

- Identify global issues.
- Understand the impact of hunger throughout the world.
- Work with database objects.
- Learn about increasing global literacy.
- Format a report, create and format line charts, and paste charts in a report.

### Business Documents
### 121A–125A

- Database with Table, Form, Query, and Report
- Word Processed Report with Embedded Charts

**Warmup**

Key each line twice at the beginning of each lesson; first for control, then for speed.

alphabet 1 Myra's expensive black racquet is just a wrong size for children.

figures 2 Order 97-341 for 20 Series 568 storm windows was faxed on May 25.

speed 3 Claudia saw my hand signal to go right when she got to the field.

| gwam 1' | 1 | 2 | 3 | 4 | 5 | 6 | 7 | 8 | 9 | 10 | 11 | 12 | 13 |

---

### 121B

**Identifying Global Issues**

The first years of the 21st century have been a tumultuous time, marked by challenges such as wars and economic difficulties but also by dazzling technological achievements in medicine, communications, and social responsibility. Both challenges and achievements are happening all over the world at a pace that would have been inconceivable only two or three decades ago.

© ARENA Creative/Shutterstock.com

**Figure 22-1** Digital devices make it easy to get world news

**Global awareness** is easier than it ever has been. Social media allow you to connect with friends all over the world as well as visit the pages of organizations, media, and retail establishments. Mobile devices such as smartphones enable you to stay up to date with the latest news and connect at the touch of a button with friends, colleagues, and information sources (Figure 22-1). Web cams, Internet pictures, and blogs allow you to visit and experience places and events on a personal level that could be reached previously only by extensive traveling.

The ability to view the world in real time using a variety of technological tools has made it possible for people to understand and act to resolve complex issues. For example:

# UNIT 4

## Using Spreadsheets to Make Economic Choices

### Reference Guide

Spreadsheet software is used to organize information on worksheets so the information is easy to read and understand and looks attractive. Worksheets are like the word processing tables prepared in Unit 3 in that information is arranged in rows and columns. Two big advantages that spreadsheet software has over word processing tables are that calculations are more robust and easier to perform and a variety of charts can be constructed using the data in a worksheet.

Worksheets are used to report business and personal information in meaningful ways so it can be used to make important decisions. Many of the decisions enable business persons to make economic choices based on the information reported in the worksheet or chart (see Figures 4-1 and 4-2 on page 105). For example, the information about the common stock fund reported in Lesson 20H may assist the owner of the stock fund to reallocate the stock holdings in the various categories to achieve a better balance of risk and reward. Likewise, the payroll information presented in Lesson 21B may alert an employer to explore ways to reduce overtime hours worked in order to reduce payroll costs. Also, the chart in Lesson 25B provides information about the sales performance of individuals.

© iStockphoto.com/EdStock

In this unit you will learn and apply many spreadsheet features that can be used to format worksheets to make them attractive and easy to read by business persons and others. Many of the features are similar to the word processing features you use to make tables attractive and easy to understand. For example, you will learn the following spreadsheet features that can be used to format worksheets for business, educational, or personal use.

- Merge cells so worksheet titles and column headings can span more than one column or row.
- Align text horizontally and vertically within a cell.
- Wrap text within a cell so it is displayed on two or more lines.
- Shrink text so it fits within a cell.
- Increase and decrease indentations within a cell.
- Use portrait and landscape orientations to display the worksheet.
- Scale worksheets to fit on a desired number of pages.

© Corepics VOF/Shutterstock.com

### Planning a Career in Law, Public Safety, Corrections, and Security

The people who work in this field include the security officer at your school, the patrolman who directs traffic, and the paramedic who provides care in a medical emergency. They provide the services that make us all feel a little safer in our home, school, and community.

### What's It Like?

Those who work in this career cluster are responsible for planning, managing, and providing legal, public safety, and protective services, including professional and technical support services. For example:

- They pursue and apprehend individuals who break the law, issue citations or give warnings, investigate suspicious activity, gather facts and collect evidence, and respond to calls from individuals.
- They protect property against fire, theft, vandalism, terrorism, and other illegal activity.
- They help protect the public against fires and assist in a variety of other emergencies, such as traffic accidents, natural disasters, and medical emergencies.
- They represent the parties involved in criminal and civil trials by presenting evidence and arguing in court to support their client, and counsel their clients about their legal rights and obligations.
- They work with and monitor criminal offenders to prevent them from committing new crimes.

Employees in this field work in various types of environments. Some work 40-hour workweeks in offices for many different types of organizations, including government agencies as well as private companies. Other jobs are more demanding, requiring employees to work under stressful and sometimes hazardous or violent conditions.

### Employment Outlook

Generally, employment in this career cluster is expected to grow faster than the average for all other occupations. Opportunities are excellent, although in many careers, workers will face keen competition for jobs.

Education requirements for workers in this cluster vary. Most jobs require an associate's or bachelor's degree. Others require a high school diploma and extensive on-the-job training.

### What About You?

This career cluster is covered in box 12 of the Interest Survey Activity you completed in Unit 1 of this text. If this box had one of the three highest scores on your survey, you should further explore the cluster's pathways and related occupations.

1. Why do you think a career in this field could be a good choice?
2. What skills can you develop now that would be helpful to a career in this field?
3. Why are these jobs important to our country's economy?

- Set worksheet margins and center worksheets vertically and horizontally.
- Adjust column width and row height.
- Change the angle of text within a cell.
- Print row and column titles on each page of multiple-page worksheets.
- Insert headers, footers, and page breaks.

While many activities within Unit 4 focus on extending your worksheet formatting skills, you will also learn features that will make it easier to work with worksheets. These include using different worksheet views, setting print areas, checking spelling, organizing multiple worksheets within a workbook, using Auto Fill, converting text to columns, sorting data within a worksheet, creating charts and chart sheets, and saving worksheets in a portable document format. In addition, you will have several opportunities to use formulas to perform basic calculations in a more effective and efficient manner than can be done using word processing software.

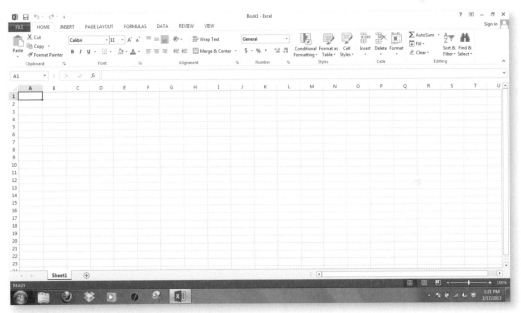

**Figure 4-1** Worksheet in *Microsoft Excel*

**Figure 4-2** Column Chart created in *Microsoft Excel*

# Academic and Career Connections

Complete the following exercises that introduce various topics that involve academic themes and careers.

## Communications: Speaking

You are going to give a presentation to your class on job interviewing skills.

1. Open the data file *df u21 communications*. The document contains an outline of tips for before, during, and after a job interview.
2. Create a new presentation from the outline and save it as *u21 communications*.
3. You may modify the tips as desired or add others of your own. Incorporate visuals such as SmartArt, pictures, animations, and transitions to enhance the presentation as desired.
4. Add speaker notes to each slide. With your instructor's permission, print the notes.
5. Rehearse the presentation with a classmate. Pay attention to your tone of voice, facial expressions, posture, and body language. Your goal is to deliver the presentation without having to read directly from your printed notes.
6. As directed by your instructor, deliver your presentation to the class.

## Art

Symbols and icons have been used as a means of communication for thousands of years. From an early age, we learn to associate symbols with certain things and emotions. As we grow older, we identify companies and institutions through their logos and trademarks. In fact, these symbols and icons are capable of creating a powerful connection between the consumer and the company.

1. Select a product you buy regularly or a company from which you purchase products, and research its logo or trademark.
2. Create a new presentation on the logo and save it as *u21 art*. You should include a visual of the logo or trademark, a brief description of the company or product it represents, a description of the logo or trademark itself, and a brief summary of the logo's effectiveness in communicating what the company or institution is all about. Your presentation should include at least five slides.
3. Add visual effects, including animations and transitions, as necessary.
4. Share the presentation with your class.

## School and Community

Conserving energy and other natural resources is as important at school as it is at home or at work. That's why it is essential for you and the rest of your school community to find ways to conserve resources and have a positive impact on the environment.

1. In teams of three to five, use the Internet to research conservation programs and tips designed specifically for schools. You might also set up an interview with your school's maintenance or facilities supervisor to discuss steps you can take to conserve resources.
2. Using what you have learned in this unit, create a presentation with at least 10 slides on how to conserve energy and water resources in your school. Incorporate pictures and graphics as desired. Add animations and transitions.
3. Share your presentation with the class. With your instructor's permission, broadcast the presentation to your school's website or share it with other classes.

# LESSON 20 — Format Cells and Columns

**OUTCOMES**

- Merge cells.
- Align text vertically.
- Wrap text.
- Shrink text to fit in a cell.
- Indent text in a cell.

## Business Documents

- Enrollment Report
- Recycling Materials
- Shareholder Distribution
- Common Stock Fund Report

### 20A-26A

**Warmup**

Key each line twice at the beginning of each lesson; first for control, then speed.

alphabet 1 Zebb likely will be top judge for the exclusive quarter-mile run.

figures 2 This association has 16,873 members in 290 chapters in 45 states.

speed 3 Jamel is proficient when he roams right field with vigor and pep.

gwam 1' | 1 | 2 | 3 | 4 | 5 | 6 | 7 | 8 | 9 | 10 | 11 |

### 20B

**Learn: Merge Cells**

Home/Alignment/Merge & Center, Merge Across, Merge Cells, or Unmerge Cells

**★TIP** When merging several cells that contain information, some of the information may be lost during the merge. If any information is lost, use the Undo feature to retrieve the information and decide on an alternate method for merging the cells.

1. Read the following information about merging and unmerging cells.

As with cells in a word processing table, cells within a worksheet can be merged with adjacent cells. As shown in Figure 4-3, the Merge Cell feature has four options: **Merge & Center** (joins the selected cells into one larger cell and centers the contents within the new cell), **Merge Across** (merges the selected cells in selected rows into a larger cell within each row), **Merge Cells** (merges selected cells into one cell without changing horizontal alignment), and **Unmerge Cells** (splits the selected cells into multiple new cells).

**Figure 4-3** Merge Cell options

2. Open a new worksheet. In cell A1, key **This text will be centered across columns A:G**.
3. Use the Merge & Center feature to merge the cells and center the text horizontally. Verify that the text is centered across columns A:G.
4. In cell B3, key **This text will be aligned at the left in the larger cell.**
5. Use Merge Cells to merge cells B3:G3. Verify that the text is aligned at the left in the merged cell.
6. In cell B6, key **Align at the right**, and then right-align the text in the cell.
7. Use Merge Cells to merge cells B6:F6. Verify that the text is aligned at the right in the merged cell.
8. Select cells B8:F12 and use Merge Cells to merge cells B8:F12. Verify that the cells have been merged into one large cell across rows 8:12 and columns B:F.
9. Use Unmerge Cells to unmerge cells B8:F12. Verify that cells B8:F12 are no longer merged.
10. Select cells C8:G12 and use Merge Across to merge the cells in each row. Verify that the selected cells in each row have been merged into one large cell.
11. **Save as:** *20b merge cells*.

3. Open *df 120d*.
4. Click the picture you want to copy (Eiffel Tower).
5. Copy the picture (Ctrl + C).
6. Return to slide 37 of *120c cade* and click the piece of the pie where you want to insert the picture.
7. Paste the picture (Ctrl + V).
8. Repeat the procedure to insert the remaining four pictures in the pie on slide 37.
9. Click slide 40 and convert the bullet points to SmartArt using the Basic Venn layout. Delete the text since the pictures you will insert include the names of the universities.
10. Copy and paste the pictures of the universities into the three circles.
11. **Save as:** *120d cade.*

## Enrichment

Pictures of the University of Wyoming, the University of Minnesota, and the University of South Dakota are available in data files *df120 u of wyo, df120 u of min,* and *df120 u of sd*. Choose one of these universities or select another university or college. Use the Internet to learn more about the school you select. Prepare a five-minute presentation for your classmates. Be sure to include the following information in your presentation.

- Estimated cost of attending
- Admission requirements
- Admission process
- How to set up a campus visit
- Other points of interest

## Learn: Vertical Cell Alignment

Home/Alignment/Select
Desired Vertical Alignment

1. Read the following information about aligning text vertically in a cell.

In addition to aligning text horizontally within a cell by using **Align Text Left, Center,** or **Align Text Right; Top Align, Middle Align,** or **Bottom Align** can be used for vertical alignment. Figure 4-4 shows that Middle Align has been selected for vertical alignment and Center has been selected for horizontal alignment.

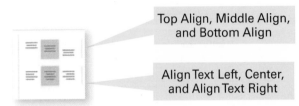

Top Align, Middle Align, and Bottom Align

Align Text Left, Center, and Align Text Right

Figure 4-4  Alignment options

2. Open a new worksheet.
3. Use Merge Cells to merge cells A1:G2. Key **Middle Align and Center were used to format this text.** Use Middle Align and Center alignment options to format the text.
4. Use Merge Cells to merge cells C4: I7. Key **Bottom Align and Align Text Right were used to format this text.** Use Bottom Align and Align Text Right alignment options to format the text.
5. Use Merge Cells to merge cells A9:H11. Key **Middle Align and Align Text Left were used to format this text.** Use Middle Align and Align Text Left alignment options to format the text.
6. **Save as:** *20c alignment.*

## Learn: Wrap Text

Home/Alignment/Wrap
Text

1. Read the following information about wrapping text in a cell.

Text that is too long for a cell will extend into the adjacent cell if the cell to the right is empty. If the cell to the right is not empty, the text that does not fit will not display. You can choose to have the text wrap within the cell's width in the same way sentences are wrapped in a word processing document. The row height will adjust as needed (see the height of row 3 in Figure 4-5).

| Fall 2010 Term | Fall 2011 Term | Fall 2012 Term | Fall 2010 Term | Fall 2011 Term | Fall 2012 Term |
|---|---|---|---|---|---|

Figure 4-5  Wrap Text

2. Open a new worksheet.
3. Key **UNION HIGH SCHOOL ENROLLMENT REPORT** in cells A1:G1 using Merge & Center.
4. Center **Females** in cells B2:D2 and **Males** in cells E2:G2.
5. Merge cells A2:A3. Key **Grade** using Center and Middle Align.
6. Using Wrap Text, center-align **Fall 2010 Term** in cell B3 and again in cell E3; **Fall 2011 Term** in cell C3 and again in F3; and **Fall 2012 Term** in D3 and again in G3.
7. **Save as:** *20d wrap text.*

Open **120b cade** and apply these animations on the slides listed.  **Save as:**  **120c cade.**

| Slide No. | Animations | Effect Options | Effect Options: Sequence | Duration |
|-----------|------------|----------------|--------------------------|----------|
| Slide 3, 12, & 17 | Fly In | From Bottom-Left | One by One | 00.50 |
| Slide 4, 11, & 14 | Wheel | 8 Spokes | One by One | 01.00 |
| Slide 15 | Wheel | 1 Spoke | As One Object | 02.00 |
| Slide 21 | Shape | In | By Paragraph | 01.00 |
| Slides 27 & 29 | Appear | By Paragraph | | Auto |
| Slide 35 | Shape | Out | One by One | 00.50 |
| Slide 37 | Wheel | 2 Spokes | One by One | 02.00 |
| Slide 39 | Zoom | Slide Center | One by One | 00.50 |
| Slide 40 | Wheel | 3 Spokes | By Paragraph | 00.50 |

## 120D

**Add Pictures to SmartArt**

Adding pictures to SmartArt can further enhance visuals to help presenters communicate the message more effectively.  Notice the impact on the visuals below when pictures were added.  To add pictures, complete the following steps.

1. Open **120c cade.**
2. Click slide 37.

## 20E

### Learn: Shrink Text to Fit

Home/Alignment Dialog Box launcher/Alignment tab/Shrink to Fit

★TIP The Increase Font Size and Decrease Font Size features in the Font group on the Home tab can also be used to change the font size as they are used with word processing software.

1. Read the following information about shrinking text to fit in a cell.

Cell contents can be shrunk to fit within the available space, as shown in Figure 4-6, so the column width and row height do not need to be changed to achieve an attractive appearance.

2. Open a new worksheet.
3. Merge & Center **GREENE COUNTY RECYCLING MATERIALS** in cells A1:D1.
4. Using the default cell width and height, key **Newspaper** in cell A2; **Clear Glass** in B2; **Aluminum** in C2; and **Electronics** in D2.
5. Shrink to fit the contents of cells A2, B2, C2, and D2.
6. Print the worksheet with gridlines and row and column headings.
7. **Save as:** *20e shrink text*.

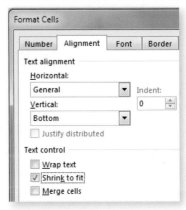

**Figure 4-6** Shrink text to fit

## 20F

### Learn: Increase & Decrease Cell Indents

Home/Alignment/Increase Indent or Decrease Indent

1. Read the following information about changing cell indents.

Use the **Increase Indent** and **Decrease Indent** features shown in Figure 4-7 to help distinguish categories or set text apart within cells. The amount of the indent can be increased or decreased by clicking the proper Indent button or changing the indent setting in the Format Cells dialog box.

**Figure 4-7** Decrease & Increase Indents

Figure 4-8 shows text that has had indents increased and decreased.

|   | A |
|---|---|
| 1 | This text is not indented from the left. |
| 2 | This text is indented once from the left. |
| 3 | This text is indented three times from the left. |
| 4 | This text was indented three times and then the indent was decreased once. |
| 5 | This text was indented four times and then the indent was decreased once. |

**Figure 4-8** Increase Indents and Decrease Indents Examples

2. Open a new worksheet, and key the text from the following worksheet using these indents:
   a. Increase indent of cells A2, A5, and A8 once.
   b. Increase indent of cells A3, A4, A6, A7, A9, and A10 twice.
   c. Increase indent of cell A11 three times.

|   | A | B |
|---|---|---|
| 1 | **Distributions to shareholders** | **Amount** |
| 2 | From net investment income | |
| 3 | Class A | $ 43,523 |
| 4 | Class B | $ 10,325 |
| 5 | In excess of net investment income | |
| 6 | Class A | $ 2,354 |
| 7 | Class B | $ 574 |
| 8 | From return on capital | |
| 9 | Class A | $ 2,765 |
| 10 | Class B | $ 750 |
| 11 | **Total distributions** | **$ 60,291** |

| Slide No. | Transition | Effect Options | Duration |
|---|---|---|---|
| Slides 7, 8, 10, 18, & 19 | Rotate | From Right | 01.50 |
| Slides 23, 26, & 28 | Vortex | From Left | 01.25 |
| Slides 24 & 25 | Conveyor | From Right | 01.60 |
| Slides 32, 34, 36, & 38 | Blinds | Horizontal | 01.50 |
| Slide 33 | Doors | Vertical | 01.40 |

## 120C

### Animations—Effect Options

Changes to basic animations can be made with the Effect Options feature. This feature allows you to change the sequence, direction, shapes, spokes, and/or the vanishing point of the various animations. For example, if the *Wheel* animation is selected, the Effect Options can be used to select the number of spokes in the animation as well as the sequence of the animation. The sequence options are:

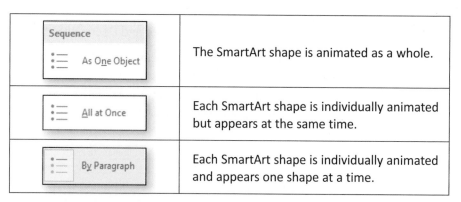

| Sequence | |
|---|---|
| As One Object | The SmartArt shape is animated as a whole. |
| All at Once | Each SmartArt shape is individually animated but appears at the same time. |
| By Paragraph | Each SmartArt shape is individually animated and appears one shape at a time. |

Figure 21-23 Animation Sequences

3. Format numbers as Accounting with dollar signs and no cents.
4. Bold text in rows 1 and 11.
5. Use AutoFit to set column widths to widest entry.
6. Print the worksheet with gridlines and row and column headings.
7. Save as: **20f indent**.

## 20G

### Apply: Shrink to Fit

1. Open a new worksheet, and key **States** in cell A1 and **Capitals** in cell B1.
2. In cells A2:A11, list the 10 states that have two words in their name.
3. In cells B2:B11, list the capital of each state named in column A.
4. Shrink to fit the contents of each cell.
5. Save as: **20g states**.

## 20H

### Apply: Format and Calculate

1. Open a new worksheet, and key the following worksheet as shown.

| MXP COMMON STOCK FUND | | | |
|---|---|---|---|
| December 31, 20— | | | |
| **Industry and Company** | **Percent of Portfolio** | **Shares** | **Present Value** |
| **Aerospace** | | | |
| Fleet Company | | 4627 | 205601 |
| Textran | | 748 | 37607 |
| Kite Technologies | | 1312 | 69459 |
| **Total Aerospace** | | | |
| **Energy** | | | |
| HPNGCO Electric | | 1701 | 103855 |
| Gertin Corp | | 7362 | 395719 |
| SH Oil | | 6333 | 348722 |
| **Total Energy** | | | |
| **Real Estate** | | | |
| The Troyer Company | | 2151 | 45324 |
| Suburban Malls, Inc | | 6446 | 164791 |
| **Total Real Estate** | | | |
| **Total Portfolio Value** | | | |

2. Calculate the sum in cells D8, D13, D17, and D18.
3. Format numbers in column B as percentages with two decimal places, column C with a thousands separator, and column D as currency with no cents.
4. Using the Present Value for each industry and the Total Portfolio Value as the base, calculate the percent in cells B8, B13, and B17.
5. Right-align all numbers and apply shading to make the worksheet attractive and easy to read.
6. Save as: **20h stock fund**.

# Enhance Visuals with Advanced Transition and Animation Features

OUTCOMES

- Use Transition and Animation Effect Options feature to enhance slides.
- Change slide transition and animation duration.
- Add pictures to SmartArt.

## Business Document

120B

- Slide Show Presentation

### Transitions—Effect Options and Duration

Transitions/Transition to This Slide/Effect Options

★TIP You must select a transition before the Effect Option is available.

Changes to basic transitions can be made with the Effect Options feature. This feature allows you to change the direction and color of the transition. For example, if the Blinds transition is used, the blinds can be changed from vertical to horizontal.

With some transitions, you can also choose the color (white or black). For example, the Reveal transition has the options shown in Figure 21-22—the first two are white, the second two use black in the transition.

Each transition has a default time setting, which varies depending on the transition, for the amount of time it takes the transition to run. For example, the Reveal transition takes 3.40 seconds. If you want, the Duration feature can be used to increase or decrease the default time setting for transitions.

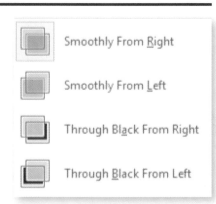

**Figure 21-22** Reveal Transition Options

Mr. Sanchez would like the presentation to include transitions not only to enhance the presentation, but to divide it into sections that will make it easier for the audience to follow. The three section dividers (slides 5, 22, & 30) will use the same transition. The slides within a section will also use the same transitions.

Open **119g cade** and add the transitions below. **Save as: 120b cade.**

| Slide No. | Transition | Effect Options | Duration |
|---|---|---|---|
| Slide 2 | Split | Vertical In | 01.75 |
| Slides 5, 22, & 30 | Random Bars | Vertical | 01.00 |
| Slides 6, 9, 13, 16, & 20 | Glitter | Diamonds from Left | 02.00 |

# LESSON 21 Worksheet Views, Page Setup, and Print

**OUTCOMES**

- Use landscape orientation.
- Change page margins and center and scale worksheets.
- Use Print Preview.
- Change worksheet views.
- Insert headers and footers.
- Adjust column width and row height.

## Business Documents

- Payroll Calculations
- Appointment Schedule
- Sales Report

### 21B

**Learn: Landscape Orientation**

Page Layout/Page Setup/ Orientation

1. Read the following information about changing page orientation.

Most documents, including letters, memos, reports, tables, and forms, are printed in portrait orientation across the width of the paper (see Figure 4-9). Many worksheets are wider than 8.5"; these can be printed in landscape orientation, which turns the page sideways so that more text will fit on a line.

2. Open *df 21b landscape* and print the worksheet in landscape orientation.

3. **Save as:** *21b landscape*.

**Figure 4-9** Landscape orientation

### 21C

**Learn: Adjust Page Margins and Center and Scale Worksheets**

Page Layout/Page Setup/ Margins

★TIP The Last Custom Setting option enables you to quickly reuse the customized margins most recently used.

1. Read the following information about changing page margins.

To arrange worksheets attractively on a page, you can change margin settings, center the worksheet horizontally and/or vertically, and/or scale the worksheet to fit specific page widths and lengths.

To change the top, bottom, and side margins, use one of the preset options (**Normal**, **Wide**, or **Narrow**) shown in Figure 4-10 or Page Layout/Page Setup/Margins/Custom Margins/Margins tab to set other margin sizes.

Use Page Layout/Page Setup/Margins/Custom Margins/Margins tab to center the worksheet horizontally and/or vertically on the paper as shown in Figure 4-11.

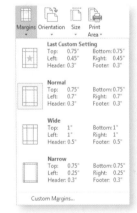

**Figure 4-10** Preset Margins

**Figure 4-11** Center worksheet

Use Page Layout/Page Setup/Margins/Custom Margins/Page tab to set the scaling settings to fit on the number of pages desired as shown in Figure 4-12.

2. Open *df 21c worksheet*; change the side margins to Narrow. Print the worksheet in landscape orientation without gridlines or headings.

3. **Save as:** *21c narrow*.

**Figure 4-12** Scale settings

| Slide to Be Enhanced | Specifications | Feature to Use | Outcome |
|---|---|---|---|
|  | **Slides 1 & 41**<br><br>Use the Insert Shapes feature and the Insert Text Box feature to enhance slide 1 as shown at the right. The text in the rectangle is:<br><br>CADE<br>Center for Advising, Development, and Enrichment<br><br>Position the date as shown on the slide at the right.<br>After you complete the slide, copy and paste it at the end of the presentation. |   Shapes<br><br> Text Box |  |
| 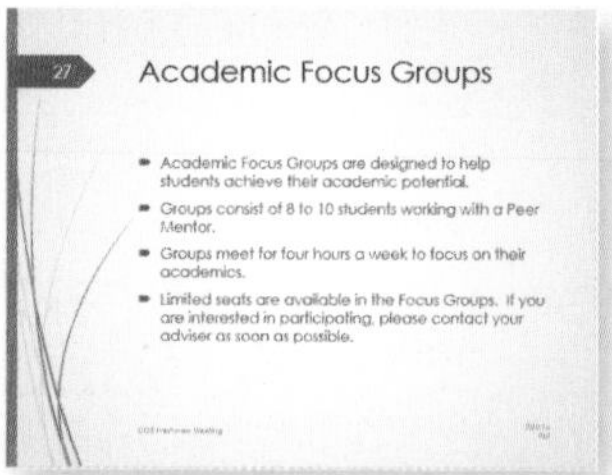 | **Slides 27, 29, & 33**<br><br>Copy and paste the graphic from slide 1 to the bottom of slides 27, 29, & 33 as shown at the right. The text may need to be moved up on the slide and the graphic resized to fit the space. | |  |
| 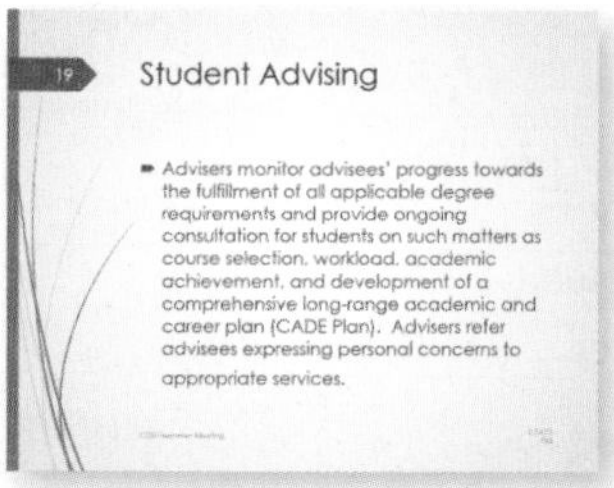 | **Slide 10**<br><br>Use the Online Pictures feature to search for a graphic similar to the one at the right using the word *adviser*.<br>**Change picture color:** Right Mouse Click/Picture/Recolor/ Brown, Accent color 3 Dark<br><br>**Change picture format:** Format Tab/Picture Styles/Rotated, White |   Online Pictures | 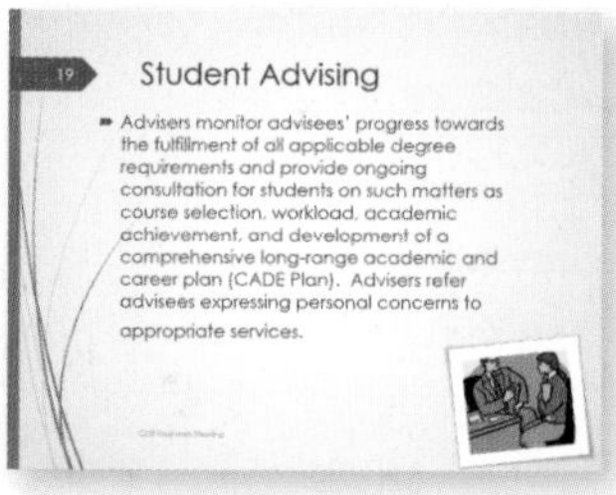 |

4. Open *df 21c worksheet* again; center the worksheet vertically and horizontally. Print in landscape orientation with gridlines and headings.

5. **Save as:** *21c landscape.*

6. Open *df 21c worksheet* again, scale the worksheet to fit on one page in portrait orientation, center it vertically and horizontally, and print it without gridlines or headings.

7. **Save as:** *21c portrait.*

---

## 21D

### Learn: Print Preview

File/Print
or
Page Layout/Page Setup/
Page Setup dialog box

1. Read the following information about using Print Preview.

Use Print Preview to see the worksheet before it is printed to make sure it is arranged on the page as desired as shown at the right in Figure 4-13. If it is not, adjustments can be made to the worksheet before it is printed by changing the Settings in the Print screen as shown on the left in Figure 4-13. These adjustments include changing the orientation of the worksheet, size of paper, and margin settings and scaling the worksheet to the desired size. If additional changes are needed, access the Page Setup dialog box from the link below the Settings on the Print Preview screen.

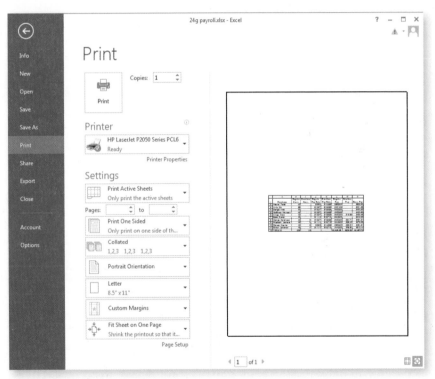

**Figure 4-13** Print screen

2. Open *df 21d preview.*

3. Review the worksheet to see the numbers of columns it has, paying particular attention to the names of the columns near the right.

4. Select Print Preview. If the worksheet doesn't fit on one page in landscape orientation, scale it to one page, and then center it horizontally and vertically.

5. Continue to use Print Preview and Page Setup as needed to ensure the entire worksheet is arranged correctly, and then print it with gridlines and column and row headings.

6. **Save as:** *21d preview.*

**★TIP** Gridlines and column and row headings can be selected to print on the Sheet tab in the Page Setup dialog box.

| Slide to Be Enhanced | Design and Color Specifications | SmartArt to Be Used | Outcome |
|---|---|---|---|
| 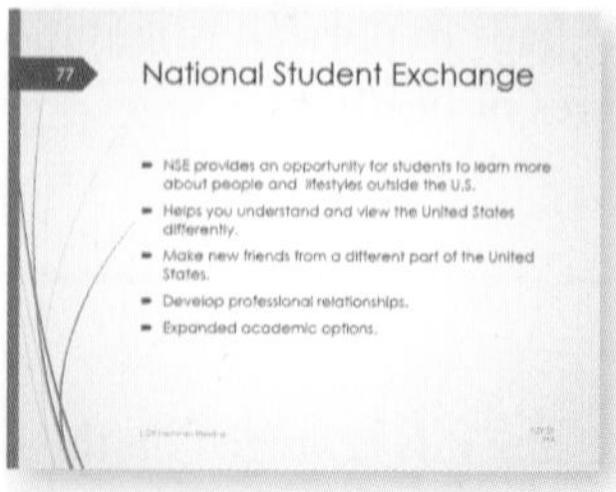 National Student Exchange | **Slide 39**<br><br>**Design Layout:**<br>Process: Circle Process<br>**Change Colors:**<br>Colorful Range – Accent Colors 4 to 5 | 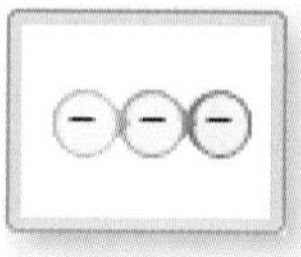 Process: Circle | 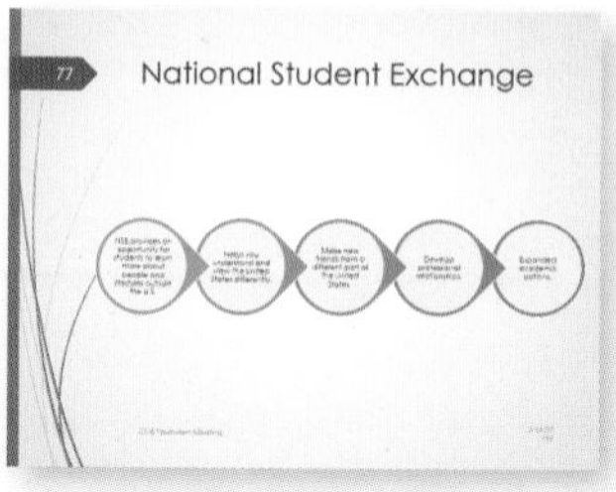 National Student Exchange |

**119F**

**Enhance Slides with Picture Styles and Position**

The position of a graphic on a page can enhance a slide. Notice how different slide 7 looks by using the Rotated, White Picture style and positioning it as shown below. Mr. Sanchez would like you to use the Format Picture Styles feature to change the way information is presented on a page. **Save as:** *119f cade*.

| Slide to Be Enhanced | Specifications | Feature to Use | Outcome |
|---|---|---|---|
| 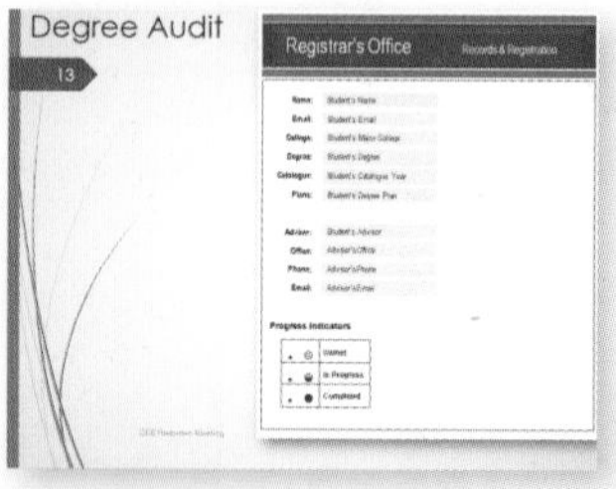 Degree Audit | **Slides 7, 8, 18, & 19**<br><br>**Format Picture Styles:** Rotated, White |  Picture Styles: Rotated White | 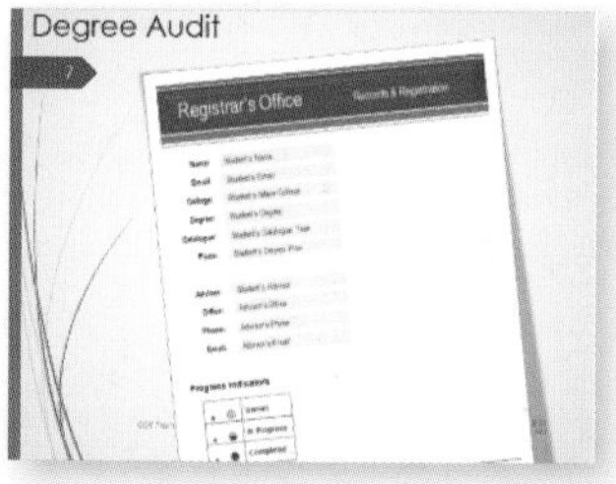 Degree Audit |

**119G**

**Enhance Slides with Clip Art and Shapes**

Shapes and Online Pictures (clip art) can also be used to enhance slides. Mr. Sanchez would like you to add shapes and clip art to the following slides in the presentation. **Save as:** *119g cade*.

| Slide to Be Enhanced | Specifications | Feature to Use | Outcome |
|---|---|---|---|
|  SPDP Workshops | **Slide 25**<br><br>Include clip art similar to the slide shown at the right. Size the graphic and then copy and paste four times. Space so there is approximately equal distance between the illustrations. |   Online Pictures | 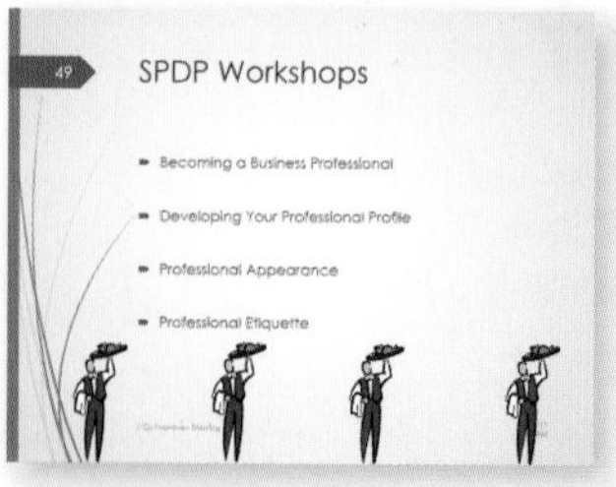 SPDP Workshops |

**Learn: Change Worksheet Views**

View/Workbook Views

1. Read the following information about changing the way a worksheet is displayed.

When a new worksheet is opened, it is displayed in **Normal view** with the formula bar, gridlines, and row and column headings displayed. Normal view is used mostly when entering and formatting data. Other views are available: **Page Layout view** lets you focus on how your worksheet will look when it is printed and is used to see headers and footers; **Page Break Preview** lets you see how data appears on pages and is used to insert page breaks. These three views can be accessed from the **status bar** (shown in Figure 4-14) or from the **View tab** (shown in Figure 4-15). A **Full Screen option** is available from the View tab. This view displays your worksheet without the Ribbon, tabs, or status bar. To return to Normal view from Full Screen view, right click and select Close Full Screen.

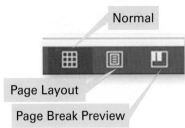

Figure 4-14 Status bar views

Figure 4-15 View tab views

2. Open *df 21c worksheet* again.
3. Using the icons on the status bar, change from Normal view to Page Layout view, to Page Break Preview view, and then back to Normal view.
4. Using the commands in the Workbook Views group in the View tab, change views from Normal to Page Layout, to Page Break Preview, to Full Screen. Close the Full Screen view and select Normal.
5. Close *df 21c worksheet* without saving the changes.

**Learn: Insert Headers and Footers**

Insert/Header & Footer

**TIP** The header/footer font does not change automatically when font changes are made in the worksheet.

1. Read the following information about inserting headers and footers.

Worksheets can contain headers and footers in much the same way as word processing documents can (see Figure 4-16). You can select predefined headers/footers from the spreadsheet software, or you can create custom headers/footers. The font, font style, and font size can also be specified. In addition, the header/footer may be left-, center-, or right-aligned.

Figure 4-16 Header & Footer

Special elements, identified in Figure 4-17, can be entered in the header/footer to print the date, time, page number, filename, etc.

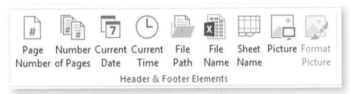

Figure 4-17 Header & Footer Elements

| Slide to Be Enhanced | Design and Color Specifications | SmartArt to Be Used | Outcome |
|---|---|---|---|
| General Education Requirements<br>GE I – Communication and Analytical Skills<br>GE II – Natural Sciences<br>GE III – Social Sciences<br>GE IV – Humanities | **Slide 15**<br><br>**Design Layout**<br>Matrix: Basic Matrix<br>**Change Colors:**<br>Colorful – Accent Colors | Matrix: Basic | General Education Requirements |
| Steps for Successful Registration:<br>Meet with your CADE adviser to discuss classes.<br>Put the classes discussed with your adviser in your shopping cart.<br>Obtain your PAC from your adviser<br>Complete the student Payment Plan Agreement<br>Clear all holds you may have.<br>Pay a $100 Deposit<br>Register on your assigned date and time. | **Slide 17**<br><br>**Design Layout:**<br>Process: Basic Timeline<br>**Change Colors:** Accent 3- Gradient Loop<br><br>Numbers can be placed in the circles by inserting text boxes in the circles and keying the numbers. | Process: Basic Timeline | Steps for Successful Registration: |
| COB Admission Requirements<br>Course Requirements<br>Complete the following five courses with at least a 2.30 GPA: Accounting I & II, Economics I & II, and Information Systems I<br>Credit Requirement<br>Complete 54 credits<br>Grade Point Requirement<br>GPA of 2.6 on all coursework completed. | **Slide 21**<br><br>**Design Layout:**<br>Matrix: Cycle Matrix<br>**Change Colors:** Colorful<br>Range – Accent Colors 4 to 5 | Cycle: Matrix | COB Admission Requirements |
| Student Professional Development Program<br>SPDP Coordinator<br>Cynthia Chen SSS 448 | **Slide 24**<br><br>Adjust the text to fit the new design theme as shown at the right. | | Student Professional Development Program<br>SPDP Coordinator<br>Cynthia Chen SSS 448 |
| Student Organizations<br>Make new friends who have similar interests.<br>Work as a member of a team.<br>Learn new skills and abilities.<br>Learn more about your major.<br>Network with professionals.<br>Personal & professional development. | **Slide 35**<br><br>**Design Layout:**<br>Cycle: Blocked Cycle<br>**Change Colors:** Colorful<br>Range – Accent Colors 4 to 5 | Cycle: Block | Student Organizations |
| International Study<br>International study provides an opportunity for students to learn more about cultures outside their home country.<br>Business continues to expand globally; employers are looking for people with international experiences.<br>Helps you understand and view the world differently.<br>Make new friends; become a global citizen.<br>Develop professional relationships. | **Slide 37**<br><br>**Design Layout:**<br>Cycle: Segmented Cycle<br>**Change Colors:**<br>Colorful Range – Accent Colors 4 to 5 | Cycle: Segmented Cycle | International Study |

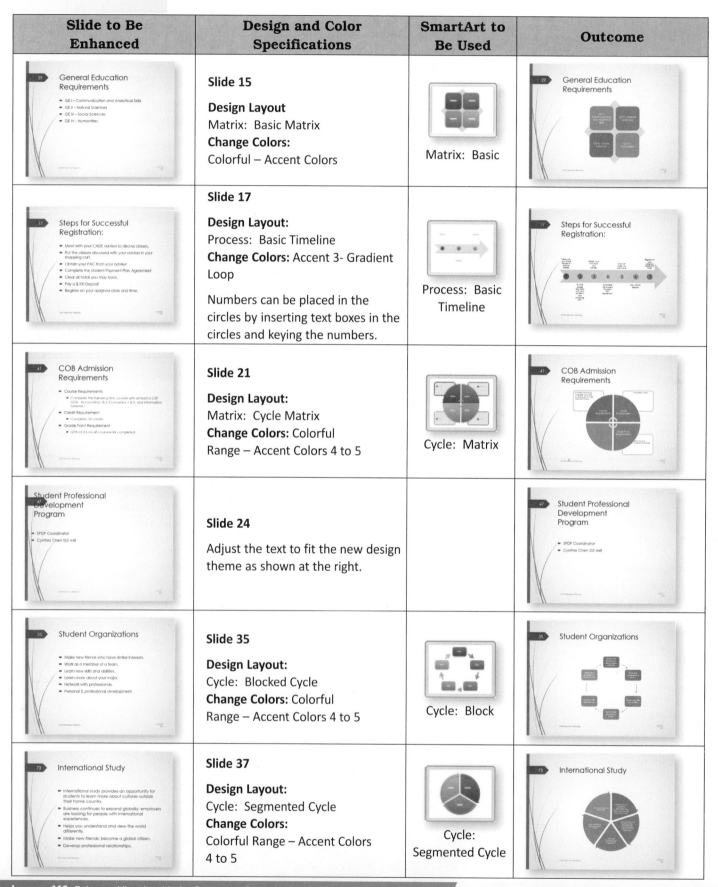

Features in the Options group (see Figure 4-18) can be selected so the footer does not appear on the first page of a worksheet or is different on odd and even pages

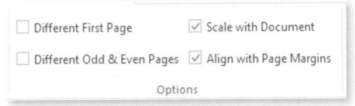

Figure 4-18 Header & Footer Options

2. Open **df 21d preview** again.
3. Using Arial 14-pt. bold font, insert the **filename** as a right-aligned header and **your name and date** as a centered custom footer.
4. Set left and right margins at 1.25". Preview the worksheet. Print the worksheet in landscape orientation without gridlines or column/row headings when it is arranged attractively on one page.
5. **Save as:  21f header.**

 **21G**

## Learn:  Adjust Column Width and Row Height

Home/Cells/Format

1. Read the following information about adjusting columns and rows.

You can increase or decrease column and row height to accommodate the contents of your worksheet cells. The column width and row height can be changed by using the mouse, specifying the desired width/height in a dialog box that appears when one of the **Cell Size** options shown in Figure 4-19 is selected, or using AutoFit. Row height will change automatically as the font size is increased for one or more cells in that row.

Figure 4-19 Column Width & Row Height

2. Open **df 21g worksheet 1** and edit cell D1 so *Wednesday* is spelled out.
3. Change the size of the text in row 1 to 18 pt.
4. Resize the columns so each is as wide as its longest entry.
5. Change height of rows 2–10 to exactly 18 pt.
6. **Save as:  21g worksheet 1.**
7. Open **df 21g worksheet 2** and designate that gridlines and column and row headings should print.
8. Adjust the width of each column so it is as wide as the longest entry in the column.
9. Change height of rows 1, 2, 4, 5, 7, and 8 to 26 pt.
10. **Save as:  21g worksheet 2.**

 **TIP** Row height is measured by points in Normal view and by inches in Page Layout view. Change the view as needed to set the specified row height.

**Enhance Slides to Communicate Effectively**

Mr. Sanchez believes there are too many slides with bulleted lists. The audience may become bored. Open *119d cade* and use SmartArt to further enhance the following slides. Follow these steps to make the changes.

1. Look at the slide to be enhanced in column 1.
2. Read the design and color specifications in column 2 and locate the slide to be enhanced.
3. Determine the SmartArt to be used to enhance the slide. Column 3 first shows a picture of the SmartArt to be used. Underneath the picture the design layout group is shown followed by the name of the SmartArt to be used.
4. Change the slide using the Convert to SmartArt feature.
5. Verify that your slide looks like the illustration in column 4.
6. **Save as:** *119e cade*.

| Slide to Be Enhanced | Design and Color Specifications | SmartArt to Be Used | Outcome |
|---|---|---|---|
| CADE Staff | **Slide 3**<br><br>**Design Layout:**<br>List: Pyramid List<br>**Change Color:**<br>Primary Theme Colors, Dark 2 Fill | List: Pyramid | CADE Staff |
| Contact Your Adviser: | **Slide 11**<br><br>**Design Layout:**<br>Relationship: Basic Venn<br>**Change Colors:**<br>Colorful – Accent Colors | Relationship: Basic Venn | Contact Your Adviser: |
| Each student shall be responsible for: | **Slide 12**<br><br>**Design Layout:**<br>Picture: Vertical Picture Accent List<br>**Change Colors:**<br>Colorful Range – Accent Colors 4 to 5 | List: Vertical Picture Accent | Each student shall be responsible for: |
| Planning Your BBA Degree | **Slide 14**<br><br>**Design Layout:**<br>List: Trapezoid List<br>**Change Colors:**<br>Colorful Range – Accent Colors 4 to 5 for first trapezoid; Accent Colors 3 to 4 for second trapezoid. | List: Trapezoid | Planning Your BBA Degree |

**Apply: Worksheet Formatting**

1. Open a new worksheet, and key the following worksheet. Specify all column widths at 12 pt. Merge cells as needed, and align cell contents in the center at the bottom of the cells.

| JENNCO MONTHLY SALES REPORT | | | | | | |
|---|---|---|---|---|---|---|
| | Northern Division | | Office | Southern Division | | |
| Office | This Month | Same Month Last Year | | This Month | Same Month Last Year | |
| Boston | 1540000 | 1444975 | Atlanta | 1653450 | 1582625 | |
| Baltimore | 1562675 | 1375755 | Dallas | 1345870 | 1467050 | |
| Cleveland | 2143750 | 2307450 | Mobile | 1873525 | 1852840 | |
| Chicago | 1957500 | 2010730 | Memphis | 2769200 | 2652810 | |
| Boise | 780560 | 755050 | Omaha | 2459550 | 2234800 | |
| Seattle | 2289570 | 2185525 | San Diego | 3000540 | 2750750 | |
| Totals | | | Totals | | | |

2. Format numbers as Currency with no cents.
3. Insert an 8-pt. column between C and D and a similar column at the right of the last column.
4. Use Percent Change for the new column headings (wrap the text).
5. Calculate totals and percent of change (use Percentage to one decimal place).
6. Format the worksheet attractively.
7. Place a border around all cells that have the percent change calculations.
8. Print in landscape orientation, centered on page with **your name** as a right-aligned header and **today's date** as a left-aligned footer, both in 18-pt. font.
9. Compare the results of the calculations in your worksheet to those shown in the following Quick Check. **Save as: 21h worksheet**.

Your calculations should be the same as those in this worksheet:

| | JENNCO MONTHLY SALES REPORT | | | | | | |
|---|---|---|---|---|---|---|---|
| | Northern Division | | | | Southern Division | | |
| Office | This Month | Same Month Last Year | Percent Change | Office | This Month | Same Month Last Year | Percent Change |
| Boston | $1,540,000 | $1,444,975 | 6.6% | Atlanta | $1,653,450 | $1,582,625 | 4.5% |
| Baltimore | $1,562,675 | $1,375,755 | 13.6% | Dallas | $1,345,870 | $1,467,050 | -8.3% |
| Cleveland | $2,143,750 | $2,307,450 | -7.1% | Mobile | $1,873,525 | $1,852,840 | 1.1% |
| Chicago | $1,957,500 | $2,010,730 | -2.6% | Memphis | $2,769,200 | $2,652,810 | 4.4% |
| Boise | $780,560 | $755,050 | 3.4% | Omaha | $2,459,550 | $2,234,800 | 10.1% |
| Seattle | $2,289,570 | $2,185,525 | 4.8% | San Diego | $3,000,540 | $2,750,750 | 9.1% |
| Totals | $10,274,055 | $10,079,485 | 1.9% | Totals | $13,102,135 | $12,540,875 | 4.5% |

| Slide to Be Enhanced | Slide and Explanation | SmartArt to Be Used | Outcome |
|---|---|---|---|
| | **Slides 5, 22, & 30**<br><br>There are three main parts to the presentation. The first section discusses *Advising* (slide 5); the second presents *Developmental Opportunities* (slide 22), and the third section presents *Enrichment* Opportunities (slide 30). Use the layout design shown to distinguish these main sections of the presentation; change color for each section to further distinguish the section. | <br>**Design Layout – List:** Vertical Box | |
| | **Slides 6, 9, 13, 16, & 20**<br><br>Within each section of the presentation, several subtopics are covered. Use the layout design shown for all subtopics under *Advising* (slides 6, 9, 13, 16, & 20). Size each graphic to a height of 4" and a width of 7". (Click outside of the text box when changing height and width of graphic.) Place the graphic box so that the top is lined up with upper 2" on the scale at the left of the slide pane. | <br>**Design Layout – Process:** Upward Arrow | |
| | **Slides 23, 26, & 28**<br><br>Use the layout design shown for all subtopics under *Development* (slides 23, 26, & 28). Size each graphic to a height of 3" and a width of 7". Place the graphic box so that the top is lined up with the upper 2" on the scale at the left of the slide pane. Select a color scheme and use the same scheme on all three slides. | <br>**Design Layout – Process:** Random to Result | |
| | **Slides 32, 34, 36, & 38**<br><br>Use the layout design shown for all subtopics under *Enrichment* (slides 32, 34, 36, & 38). Use the default settings for height and width. Use Colorful – Accent Colors. | <br>**Design Layout – List:** Vertical Accent | |

# LESSON 22     Proofread and Print Settings

**OUTCOMES**
- Set print area.
- Set page breaks.
- Select paper size.
- Check spelling.
- Show/hide worksheet elements.

## Business Documents
- Seating Charts
- Hours Worked Report
- Net Assets Reports
- Cash Flow Report
- Daily Planner

---

**22B**

### Learn: Set Print Area

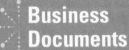
Page Layout/Page Setup/
Print Area/Set Print Area

File/Print/Settings/make
selection

1. Read the following information about printing a portion of the worksheet.

By default, most spreadsheet software prints all the information displayed in a worksheet. If you need to print only a portion, select the range of cells you want to print, select the Set Print Area command (see Figure 4-20). When the Print command is selected, only that portion of the worksheet you selected will print. Use the **Clear Print Area** to remove the selection.

Also, the **Print Selection** options (Print Active Page, Print Entire Worksheet, and Print Selection) in the Settings section of the Print screen (see Figure 4-21) can be used to set what is to be printed.

2. Open *df 22b seating chart*.
3. Set the Print Area to be Seating Chart 1 (cells A1:E12), and then print that area.
4. Clear the Print Area that was set.
5. Close *df 22b seating chart* without saving the file.

**Figure 4-20** Set & Clear Print Area

**Figure 4-21** Print Selection options on the Print screen

---

**22C**

### Learn: Set Page Breaks

Page Layout/Page Setup/
Breaks

1. Read the following information about setting page breaks.

When you are working with multiple-page worksheets, the spreadsheet software will insert automatic page breaks the same as word processing software inserts breaks in multiple-page documents. You can see the automatic page breaks (represented by dotted lines within the worksheet) in the Page Break Preview view on the status bar (see Figure 4-22). You can use the **Breaks** feature in the Page Setup group on the Page Layout tab to insert and delete page breaks (see Figure 4-23).

Alternatively, you can move page breaks to different locations by dragging them to the desired locations while using the Page Break Preview view.

**Figure 4-22** Page Break Preview

**Figure 4-23** Breaks

Your slide will look like this:

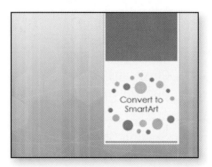

## 119D

### Define Sections of Presentation with SmartArt Graphics

**TIP** To size graphic: Right-click/Size and Position

In reviewing the slides, Mr. Sanchez believes the Convert to SmartArt feature that you just learned can be used to enhance the way the information on many of the slides is presented. He thinks SmartArt can also be used to divide a presentation into sections that will make it easier for the audience to follow. Open *119b cade* and make the changes outlined below to further enhance the presentation.

1. Look at the slide to be enhanced in column 1.
2. Read the explanation in column 2 and locate the slide to be enhanced.
3. Determine the SmartArt to be used to enhance the slide. Column 3 first shows a picture of the SmartArt to be used. Underneath the picture the design layout group is shown followed by the name of the SmartArt to be used. Change the slide using the Convert to SmartArt feature.
4. Verify that your slide looks like the illustration in column 4.
5. **Save as:** *119d cade*.

| Slide to Be Enhanced | Slide and Explanation | SmartArt to Be Used | Outcome |
|---|---|---|---|
| Introduction to CADE Staff | **Slide 2**<br><br>Use SmartArt to enhance slide 2 as shown. If necessary, review the steps outlined in 119C. | **Design Layout –**<br>**List:** Vertical Circle List | Introduction to CADE Staff |
| Today's Presentation<br>Advising<br>Development Opportunities<br>Enrichment Opportunities | **Slide 4**<br><br>Use Colorful: Colorful Range – Accent Colors 4 to 5 for the color scheme. | **Design Layout –**<br>**Relationship:** Basic Venn | Today's Presentation |

2. Open **df 22b seating chart** again, and verify that it contains three seating charts.
3. Adjust the page breaks so that one chart is printed per page.
4. Print only the second seating chart. Show gridlines, use portrait orientation, and center horizontally and vertically on the page.
5. **Save as: 22c seating chart.**

---

## 22D

### Learn: Select Paper Size

Page Layout/Page Setup/Size

1. Read the following information about selecting the paper size.

You can specify the size of paper on which the worksheet is to be printed. If you do not make a selection, it will print on 8.5" × 11" paper. The paper selection can be made by using the **Size** command on the Page Layout tab (see Figure 4-24) or selecting an option from the Letter drop down list in the Settings section of the Print screen.

2. Open **df 21d preview** again and set print area as cells A1:G12.
3. Print on Executive size paper (7.25" × 10.5") centered horizontally and vertically using portrait orientation.
4. **Save as: 22d executive.**

**Figure 4-24** Size options

---

## 22E

### Review: Check Spelling

Review/Proofing/Spelling

1. Read the following information about checking spelling.

Spreadsheet software checks spelling in much the same way as word processing software does. Words are checked for correct spelling against the words in the dictionary but not always for context. Numbers are not checked at all. It is therefore important that *you proofread* all words and numbers for accuracy and context after the checker has been used. Proper names should be checked carefully, since the dictionary may not contain many proper names.

2. Open **df 22e spelling** and use the spell checker to help proofread and correct errors in the worksheet.
3. **Save as: 22e spelling.**

---

## 22F

### Learn: Show/Hide Worksheet Elements

View/Show/ Ruler, Formula Bar, Gridlines, or Headings

1. Read the following information about showing and hiding worksheet elements.

When you open a worksheet, a standard set of elements consisting of the **Formula Bar**, **Headings** (row and column), and **Gridlines** are displayed in Normal and Page Break Preview views. If Page Layout view is selected, the **Ruler** is also displayed as an element (see Figure 4-25). One or more of these elements can be hidden if you need a little more room to see your data or if you want to see how your data looks without gridlines. To hide element(s), deselect the element(s) in the Show group; to show element(s), select the element(s).

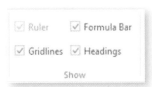

**Figure 4-25** Show/Hide elements

2. Open **22e spelling.**
3. In Normal view, hide the gridlines, formula bar, and headings.
4. Switch to Page Layout view, and hide the Ruler.
5. Show the ruler and then switch to Normal view and show all the elements.
6. Close **22e spelling** without saving any changes.

---

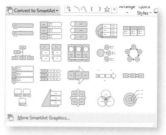

**Figure 21-18** More SmartArt graphics

5. Click Process in the left column and scroll down until you see the Random to Result Process icon appear.

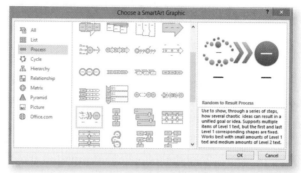

**Figure 21-19** Choose a SmartArt graphic process

6. Double-click on the Random to Result Process icon.
7. The Random to Result Process graphic appears on the slide, presenting the information in an enhanced fashion.

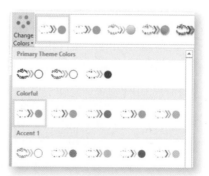

**Figure 21-20** Convert to SmartArt

8. Change the color of the graphic. On the Design tab, click the down arrow on the Change Colors button and click the first icon under *Colorful*, as shown in Figure 21-21.
9. **Save as: *119c*.**

**Figure 21-21** Change Colors

**Apply: Print Worksheet**

1. Open a new worksheet, and set font to 10-pt. Arial. Specify column A width at 7 pt; column B width at 50 pt.
2. Merge cells A1 and B1, and key **Daily Planner for** (left-aligned) in the merged cell. Increase row 1 height to 36 pt.
3. In column A, key the time in one-hour intervals in every fourth cell. Start with 8 a.m. in cell A2, and end with 7 p.m. in cell A46.
4. In column B, merge every four rows together. The first four cells to be merged are B2:B5, and the last are B46:B49.
5. Make a copy of this planner by copying the cells in the range A1:B49 to a new area beginning with cell A50.
6. Key and left-align **your name** as a header and left-align a **page number** as a footer.
7. Insert a page break so each copy of the daily planner will print on a separate page.
8. Center the worksheet on the page, and then print the second page with gridlines.
9. Save as: **22g planner**.

**Apply: Calculate Data and Print Worksheet**

1. Open a new worksheet, and key the following worksheet (wrap text and indent text as shown). Set row 2 height at 45 pt.

**PROJECTED CASH FLOW FOR 20—**

|  | January to March | April to June | July to September | October to December |
|---|---|---|---|---|
| **Cash Receipts** |  |  |  |  |
| Gross Cash Receipts | 9500 | 11000 | 19000 | 6550 |
| Returns | 445 | 555 | 935 | 305 |
| **Net Cash Receipts** | ??? | ??? | ??? | ??? |
| **Cash Disbursements** |  |  |  |  |
| **Expenses** |  |  |  |  |
| Operating Expenses | 2335 | 2357 | 2390 | 2240 |
| Other Expenses | 150 | 400 | 500 | 300 |
| **Cash Disbursements** | ??? | ??? | ??? | ??? |
| **Net Cash Flow** |  |  |  |  |
| Opening Cash Balance | 9606 | ??? | ??? | ??? |
| Net Cash Receipts | ??? | ??? | ??? | ??? |
| Cash Disbursements | ??? | ??? | ??? | ??? |
| **Ending Cash Balance** | ??? | ??? | ??? | ??? |

2. Calculate the correct dollar amount to be inserted at each set of question marks. The Ending Cash Balance becomes the Opening Cash Balance for the next quarter.
3. Key **ROARING SPRINGS GOLF CLUB** as a left-aligned header in 18-pt. bold font and **your name and date** as a left-aligned footer.
4. You decide all other formatting features to make the worksheet attractive and easy to read.
5. Check spelling, proofread, and preview before printing.
6. Save as: **22h cash flow**.

The Convert to SmartArt feature can be used to enhance slides. The feature takes text and adds SmartArt to present the information in a way that brings the information alive. Notice the difference between slide 1 and slide 2 illustrated below.

**Figure 21-15** Slide 1

**Figure 21-16** Slide 2

To convert slide 2 to SmartArt, complete the following steps.

1. Open **df 119c**.
2. Click on the text on the slide (Convert to SmartArt).
3. In the Paragraph group of the Home tab, click the down arrow of the Convert to SmartArt icon.
4. Click More SmartArt Graphics at the bottom of the drop-down menu.

Home/Paragraph/
Convert to SmartArt

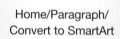

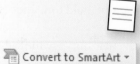

**Figure 21-17** Convert
to SmartArt

# LESSON 23

## Formatting and Worksheet Skills

**OUTCOMES**

- Use AutoFill.
- Change text orientation.
- Organize worksheets by renaming and repositioning them.
- Insert and delete worksheets.
- Convert text to columns.

## Business Documents

### 23B

- Attendance Report
- Employee Records
- Answer Sheet

### Learn: AutoFill

1. Read the following information about using AutoFill to enter data in a series.

Information can be quickly copied to adjacent cells by using the **AutoFill** feature. By using the Fill Handle, data can be entered in a series or copied to adjacent cells. The Fill Handle is the black plus sign that appears when the pointer is positioned on the lower-left corner of the selected cell. AutoFill is frequently used to enter a series of numbers, days, months, etc. and to copy text, values, or formulas to adjacent cells.

> **★TIP** If the software inserts a series when you want a copy or a copy when you want a series, select the desired action in the AutoFill Options button that appears after the cells in the fill range have been selected as shown.

2. Open a new worksheet, key **12345** in cell A1, and then use Fill Copy to copy it to cells A2:A15.
3. Use Fill Copy to copy cell A5 to B5:J5.
4. Key **Monday** in cell C7, and use Fill Series to insert Tuesday through Sunday in cells C8:C13.
5. Key **1850** in cell B1, and use Fill Series to enter the years through 1858 in the cells to the right of cell B1.
6. Key **Jan** in cell E7, and use Fill Series to enter the months through Dec below cell E7.
7. Key **1** in cell F7, and use Fill Series to enter the numbers 2–12 below cell F7.
8. Key **100** in cell H7 and 105 in cell H8, and use Fill Series to enter numbers in intervals of 5 to 150 below H8.
9. Key **January** in A19 and **March** in cell B19. Use Fill Series to enter the months for the rest of the year, skipping every other month.
10. Adjust column widths to fit contents. Print worksheet with gridlines and column and row headings on one page, using a left margin of 1.25" and top margin of 3".
11. **Save as:** *23b fill*.

AutoFill options

### 23C

### Learn: Change Text Orientation

Home/Alignment/
Orientation

1. Read about changing the orientation of text in a cell.

Text can be rotated to various diagonal or vertical angles to change the orientation (see worksheet below). The Text Orientation feature (see Figure 4-26) is used when column headings are longer than the information in the columns as shown in Figure 4-27. Rotated text is helpful when horizontal spacing needs to be reduced because it often takes less horizontal space but more vertical space.

Text Orientation

**Figure 4-26** Text orientation

**QUICK** ✔

The first slide with the footer appearing looks like this.

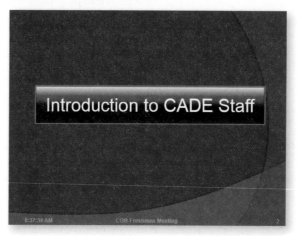

Introduction to CADE Staff

---

## LESSON 119

## Enhance Visuals with the Convert to SmartArt Feature

**OUTCOMES**

- Apply a consistent design theme to a collaborative project.
- Enhance text with the Convert to SmartArt feature.
- Use SmartArt graphics to define sections of a presentation.
- Enhance slides to communicate more effectively.

### Business Document
### 119B

**Apply a Design Theme**

- Slide Show Presentation

After seeing the combined file (*118e cade*), Mr. Sanchez felt that there should be a design theme used throughout the presentation rather than having a different design theme for each presenter's part. After reviewing several design themes, Mr. Sanchez would like you to use the *Wisp* design theme for all slides.

Open **118e cade** and apply the *Wisp* design theme. If you are not sure how to do this, see the *Reference Guide* on p. 484.

**Save as: 119b cade.**

**QUICK** ✔

Original theme

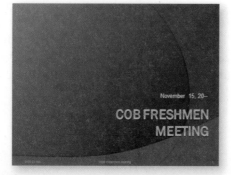

November 15, 20—

**COB FRESHMEN MEETING**

Wisp theme

November 15, 20—

COB Freshmen Meeting

---

**Figure 4-27** Rotated text

2. Open a new worksheet, and key the worksheet shown in Figure 4-27. Use Angle Counterclockwise to rotate the text in the column headings. Adjust column widths to fit the contents and hide the gridlines.

3. **Save as:** *23c orientation1*.

4. Open a new worksheet, and key the following information. Center-align the column headings and cells A2:A7.

| | A | B | C | D | E | F |
|---|---|---|---|---|---|---|
| 1 | **Month** | **Albert** | **Mary Ann** | **Roberto** | **Yin Chi** | **Zeb** |
| 2 | Sep | 1 | 0 | 0 | 0 | 1 |
| 3 | Oct | 0 | 0 | 0 | 2 | 1 |
| 4 | Nov | 1 | 1 | 0 | 1 | 1 |
| 5 | Dec | 1 | 0 | 0 | 0 | 1 |
| 6 | Jan | 1 | 0 | 0 | 0 | 1 |
| 7 | Feb | 0 | 0 | 0 | 0 | 0 |

5. Use Rotate Text Up to rotate the column heading text.

6. **Save as:** *23c orientation2*.

## 23D

**Learn: Organize Sheets**

Home/Cells/Format/ select from Organize Sheet options

1. Read the following information about organizing sheets in a workbook.

When a new Excel workbook is opened, it contains one worksheet by default. The worksheet has a **sheet tab** at the bottom left and it is named **Sheet1.** If you want to add one or more worksheets to the workbook, click the + (plus sign) to the right of the sheet tab once for each worksheet you want to add. Each sheet tab will be given a name (Sheet2, Sheet3, etc.) and you can access any of the worksheets by clicking the sheet tab.

**Figure 4-28** Organize Sheets options

Worksheet tabs can be renamed or colored, and worksheets can be moved or copied (see Figure 4-28). The Organize Sheets section of the Format feature in the Cells group is used to make these changes.

2. Open a new worksheet.

3. Add two additional worksheets to the workbook.

4. Rename Sheet1 **2015,** Sheet2 **2014,** and Sheet3 **2013.**

5. Reposition the worksheets so they are numbered low to high beginning at the left.

6. Apply a different color to each worksheet tab.

7. **Save as:** *23d sheet tabs*.

**Collaborate on Slide Presentation**

Mark Sanchez, Director of CADE (Center for Advising, Development, and Enrichment), would like you to work on a collaborative presentation project for him. Three of the staff members of CADE (Rebecca McIntyre, Robert Washington, and Kristin Southland) have developed slides that they would like to use for their part of the presentation to be made to freshmen in the college of business.

Mr. Sanchez has given you access to the three files (see below) created by the staff members. He would like you to combine the three files into one. Keep the original source formatting for each file. **Save as:** *118d cade.*

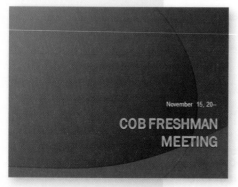

**Figure 21-10** *df mcintyre–part 1*

**Figure 21-11** *df washington–part 2*

**Figure 21-12** *df southland–part 3*

**Create Footers**

Mr. Sanchez would like to have a footer included with the slide presentation. Follow the steps below to include the footer.

1. Open **118d cade** if it is not already open.
2. On the Text section of the Insert tab, click Header & Footer to bring up the Header and Footer dialog box.
3. Click the information you want included as the footer. Mr. Sanchez would like the Date and Time (Update Automatically), Slide number, and Footer included. For the Date and Time he would like the time shown to include hours, minutes, and seconds, as illustrated in Figure 21-13.

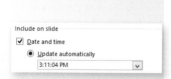

**Figure 21-13** Hours, Minutes, and Seconds

4. Key **COB Freshmen Meeting** as the text for the footer.
5. Click *Don't show on title slide* so the footer won't appear on the first slide of the presentation.
6. Click the Apply to All button as shown in Figure 21-14. The first slide with the footer appearing is shown in the Quick Check. Notice where the footer appears on the other two designs.
7. **Save as:** *118e cade.*

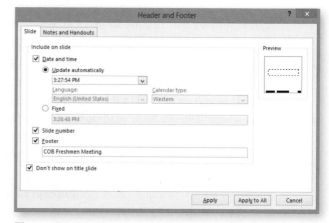

**Figure 21-14** Header and Footer

## Learn: Insert and Delete Sheets

Home/Cells/Insert or Delete/Insert Sheet or Delete Sheet

★TIP  Sheets can be inserted or deleted by right-clicking on the Sheet tab and then making the desired selection.

1. Read the following information about inserting and deleting sheets.

Additional worksheets can inserted into a workbook by using the Insert Sheet feature, or existing sheets can be deleted from a workbook by using the Delete Sheet feature. The Insert Sheet feature enables you to keep related worksheets together in one workbook. For example, you may wish to keep track of your savings on an annual basis over several years by having one worksheet for each year within the same workbook instead of creating a different file for each year. The Insert Sheet and the Delete Sheet features can be selected from the respective Insert or Delete drop-down lists in the Cells group (see Figure 4-29).

**Figure 4-29** Insert/ Delete sheets

2. Open *df 23e sheets*.
3. Delete the worksheet named *Loans*.
4. Insert a new worksheet, and name it **Contacts**.
5. Arrange the worksheets in alphabetical order from left to right.
6. Apply a color to each tab.
7. **Save as:** *23e sheets*.

## Learn: Convert Text to Columns

Data/Data Tools/ Text to Columns

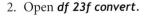

1. Read the following information about converting text into columns.

The Convert Text to Columns feature helps you separate information entered in cells in one column into cells in multiple columns. For example, if the cells in a column contain the first and last names, you can separate them so the first name appears in one column and the last name appears in a second column without rekeying the names. The **Convert Text to Columns Wizard** (see Figure 4-30) is used to make this change. The Wizard uses commas, tabs, spaces, etc. to separate the information.

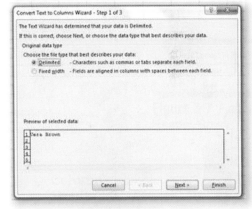

**Figure 4-30** Convert Text to Columns Wizard

2. Open *df 23f convert*.
3. Insert a new column between columns A and B.
4. Convert the text in cells A1:A10 to two columns (A and B) by using the space between the names as the delimiter.
5. Convert the text in cells C1:C10 to two columns (C and D) by using the comma between the city and state as the delimiter.
6. **Save as:** *23f convert*.

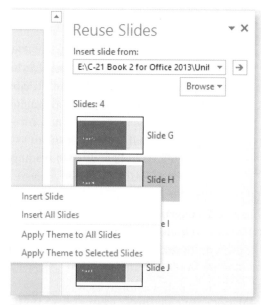

**Figure 21-9** Insert All Slides

7. Click Insert All Slides. Notice the four slides that were inserted into **118b ppt** file after slide 6 retained their design rather than being converted to the design used for the slides in **118b ppt**. This was accomplished by clicking *Keep Source Formatting*; otherwise, the four slides would have been changed to the design of the first six slides in file.

8. **Save as:** **118c ppt**.

*© iStockphoto.com/Chris Schmidt*

## 21st Century Skills: Media Literacy
At some point in your academic and professional careers, you will have to speak in front of a group or give an oral presentation. Your ability to communicate orally is one of the most important and valuable skills you will be able to apply at school, on the job, and in social situations. To deliver an effective presentation, consider the following:

- Plan your presentation by conducting research on your audience and gathering information and materials that support your topic. Prepare an attention-getting introduction, organize your main points, and develop a clear conclusion.
- Practice your presentation either in front of a mirror or with a small group of family and friends. If possible, record your presentation so you can identify areas for improvement.
- Deliver your presentation in an engaging manner. Do not read to the audience; instead, talk to them using an appropriate tone, make eye contact, and be aware of nonverbal body language, such as posture, gestures, and facial expressions.

### Think Critically

1. What are the key factors to giving an effective oral presentation?
2. Discuss an instance when you had to give an oral presentation or when you were an audience member for another individual's presentation. Was the presentation a success, or do you think it could have been improved? Explain your answer.

**Apply: Change Text and Worksheet Orientation**

1. Open *df 23g worksheet*.
2. In column B, use AutoFill to complete assigning consecutive payroll numbers (127–134).
3. Angle column heading text clockwise.
4. Make rows 2 through 9 32 pts.
5. Format column C numbers as social security numbers.
6. Display column D numbers as dates in the March 14, 2001 format.
7. Display column E numbers as telephone numbers.
8. Add a new column between columns A and B. Separate the text in column A into two columns (first name in column A; last name in column B).
9. Merge and center *Employee* in cells A1:B1. Adjust width of columns to fit contents.
10. Change orientation to landscape.
11. Rename Sheet 1 **Employee Data** and Sheet 2 **Payroll**. Color each tab.
12. Delete the Sheet 3 tab.
13. **Save as:** *23g worksheet*.

**23H**

**Apply: Format Worksheet**

1. Open a new worksheet.
2. Specify height of rows 1–27 at 18 and row 28 at 54.
3. Specify column widths as follows: A and C at 4, B and D at 10, E at 2, and F at 50.
4. Merge cells A1 to F1, and key **ANSWER SHEET**, centered in 16-pt. font.
5. Key **Item** in cells A2 and C2 and **Answer** in cells B2 and D2 using Center alignment.
6. In cell F2, key **SHORT ANSWER RESPONSES**, centered.
7. Merge the following cell ranges: F3:F10, F11:F18, F19:F27, and E2:E28.
8. Merge cells A28 to D28, and key **Student Name**, using Center and Top Align. Key **Subject and Period** in cell F28 with the same alignment.
9. Use AutoFill to enter numbers 1–25 in cell range A3:A27 and 26–50 in cell range C3:C27.
10. Key **ANSWER 1, ANSWER 2,** and **ANSWER 3** in the three large merged cell areas in column F, with ANSWER 1 being in the first merged cell. Use Center and Top Align for the text.
11. Center the worksheet on the page, and print with gridlines.
12. Compare the format of your worksheet to that shown in the Quick Check below. **Save as:** *23h worksheet*.

**QUICK** ✔

Your completed worksheet should look like this:

| ANSWER SHEET | | | | | |
|---|---|---|---|---|---|
| Item | Answer | Item | Answer | | SHORT ANSWER RESPONSES |
| 1 | | 26 | | | ANSWER 1 |
| 2 | | 27 | | | |
| 3 | | 28 | | | |
| 4 | | 29 | | | |
| 5 | | 30 | | | |
| 6 | | 31 | | | |
| 7 | | 32 | | | |
| 8 | | 33 | | | |
| 9 | | 34 | | | ANSWER 2 |
| 10 | | 35 | | | |
| 11 | | 36 | | | |
| 12 | | 37 | | | |
| 13 | | 38 | | | |
| 14 | | 39 | | | |
| 15 | | 40 | | | |
| 16 | | 41 | | | |
| 17 | | 42 | | | ANSWER 3 |
| 18 | | 43 | | | |
| 19 | | 44 | | | |
| 20 | | 45 | | | |
| 21 | | 46 | | | |
| 22 | | 47 | | | |
| 23 | | 48 | | | |
| 24 | | 49 | | | |
| 25 | | 50 | | | |
| | Student Name | | | | Subject and Period |

The Reuse Slides feature can also be used to insert slides from one file into another file. This feature allows you to insert one slide or the entire file.

1. Open *118b ppt*.
2. In the Slides group of the Home tab, click the New Slide down arrow; then click Reuse Slides.

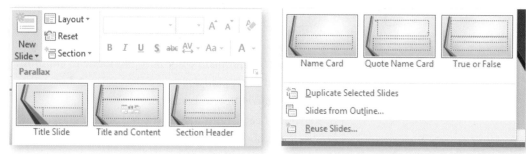

**Figure 21-6a and 6b** New Slide and Reuse Slide

3. In the Reuse Slide pane, you can click Browse and then click Browse File to access *df 118c* or you can click Open a PowerPoint File to access *df 118c*.

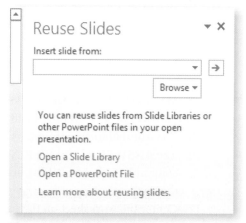

**Figure 21-7** Reuse Slides

**Figure 21-8** *df 118c*

4. Locate the cursor after slide 6 in the Slides/Outline pane.
5. Click *Keep Source Formatting* at the bottom of the Reuse Slides pane.
6. Position the arrow over any of the slides in the Reuse Slides pane and right-click to bring up the dialog box shown below.

# LESSON 24    Freeze, Hide, Zoom, Print Titles, and Sort

**OUTCOMES**

- Change the zoom level of a view.
- Freeze and unfreeze columns and rows.
- Hide columns and rows.
- Print row and column titles on each worksheet page.
- Sort worksheet information alphabetically and numerically.

## Business Documents

- Reservation Reports
- Payroll Report
- Investment Portfolios
- Sales Report

## 24B

### Learn: Zooming the View

★TIP  Additional Zoom features can be accessed in the Zoom group on the View tab.

1. Read the following information about changing the zoom level in the current view.

The Zoom feature lets you control what you see in a worksheet (see Figure 4-31). The Zoom tools are located at the bottom-right corner of the status bar. You can zoom out to see more of a large worksheet by moving the slider toward the – icon or clicking the – icon. To

**Figure 4-31** Zoom In and Zoom Out

enlarge the print, you can zoom in by moving the slider toward the + icon or clicking the + icon. As you zoom in or out, the percent informs you how much the magnification deviates from 100%, which is the normal magnification.

2. Open **df 21c worksheet** again.
3. Zoom in to about 200% to enlarge the print. Zoom out to about 50%.
4. Return to 100% magnification.
5. Close **df 21c worksheet** without saving any changes.

## 24C

### Learn: Freeze/ Unfreeze Columns and Rows

View/Window/Freeze Panes

1. Read the following information about freezing columns and rows.

Often an entire worksheet cannot be seen on the screen because when you scroll through the worksheet, the information in the column and row headings disappears from the screen. You can **freeze** the column and row headings so they remain visible as you scroll to other parts of the worksheet. Figure 4-32 describes three choices that can be selected.

Rows and columns can be unfrozen when the feature is no longer needed.

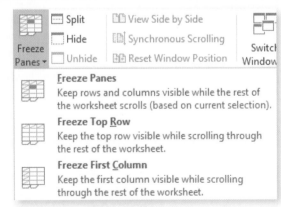

**Figure 4-32** Freeze Panes

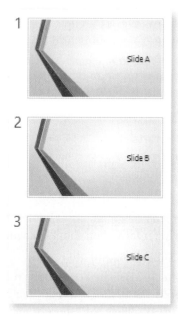

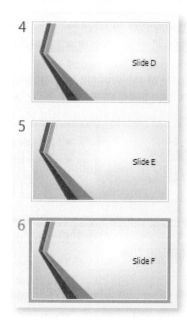

© Cheryl Savan/Shutterstock.com

## Digital Citizenship and Ethics

Online auction sites, such as eBay, uBid, and Bidz.com, enable individuals and companies to buy and sell products using an electronic bidding system. While this form of digital commerce can be convenient and economical, it is important to understand all sides of these online transactions.

- Researching online merchants and comparison shopping will help you identify the "best deal" and minimize your risk of making an unwise purchasing decision.
- Purchasing items online with a credit card can lead to the accumulation of debt. If you run up credit card debt and are unable to pay your bills, you can ruin your credit rating.
- Providing credit card numbers and other personal information to insecure sites can make you vulnerable to Internet scams and identity theft.

As a class, discuss the following:

1. How can irresponsible online purchasing practices lead to poor credit ratings?
2. How can you use an online auction site as a tool for comparison shopping?

**★TIP** Freeze Panes is not available in Page Layout view. To freeze panes, select Normal view.

2. Open *df 24c freeze*. Zoom in to 300% so the entire worksheet cannot be seen on the screen.

3. Select cell C2 and then select Freeze Panes. Verify that as you scroll down, row 1 remains visible, and that as you scroll to the right, columns A and B remain visible.

4. Select Unfreeze Panes.

5. Scroll out to 100%. Select Freeze Top Row. Verify that as you scroll down, row 1 remains visible.

6. Unfreeze the pane and then zoom in to about 300%. Select Freeze First Column. Verify that as you scroll to the right, column A remains visible.

7. Zoom back to 100%.

8. Close *df 24c freeze* without saving any changes.

---

 **24D**

## Learn: Hide Columns and Rows

Home/Cells/Format

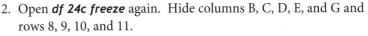

1. Read the following information about hiding columns and rows.

Rows and columns can be temporarily **hidden** to enable you to view only those parts of a worksheet that you want to see or print (see Figure 4-33). Rows and columns can be unhidden when you need to see or print them.

Figure 4-33 Hide Columns and Rows

2. Open *df 24c freeze* again. Hide columns B, C, D, E, and G and rows 8, 9, 10, and 11.

3. Unhide columns B, C, D, and E.

4. Hide columns C, D, and E.

5. Print page 1 of the worksheet.

6. **Save as:** *24d hide*.

---

**24E**

## Learn: Print Row and Column Titles on Each Page

Page Layout/Page Setup/ Print Titles/Sheet Tab

1. Read the following information about printing column and row headings.

As worksheets expand to two or more pages, it is very helpful to print the row and/or column titles (headings) on each page to make the second page and subsequent pages easier to read. To print row titles on each page, access the Sheet tab of the Page Setup dialog box (see Figure 4-34). Click the Collapse/Expand button that appears at the right of the Row to repeat at top text box. Click in the worksheet row that contains the titles you want to print at the top of each page. Click the Collapse/Expand button again, and then click OK.

Figure 4-34 Sheet tab of the Page Setup dialog box

To repeat the column titles on each page, repeat this procedure except select the Collapse/ Expand button to the right of the Column to repeat at left text box, and then click in the column you want to print on each page.

2. Open *df 24e print*.

3. Print the worksheet, repeating the headings in row 1 on each page.

4. **Save as:** *24e print*.

# LESSON 118    Reuse Slides and Combine Files

**OUTCOMES**

- Copy and paste slides between files.
- Reuse slides from previous presentation files.
- Collaborate on creating a slide presentation.
- Create footers for a slide presentation.

## Business Document

### 118A–120A

**Warmup**

Key each line twice daily.

- Slide Show Presentation

| alphabet | 1 | Giving Franklin the exact job requirements will keep Zelda happy. |
|---|---|---|
| fig/sym | 2 | Ho Chen sold the houses on Lots #3 & #6 for 487,950 and $104,200. |
| speed | 3 | Sue may work with the men on their problem with the turn signals. |

**gwam** 1' | 1 | 2 | 3 | 4 | 5 | 6 | 7 | 8 | 9 | 10 | 11 | 12 | 13 |

### 118B

**Copy and Paste Slides Between Files**

**TIP** When two files are open, press Alt + Tab to switch from one file to the other.

At times you will want to use slides from a presentation that was previously created, or you may want to combine one or more files into one file. Combining files is quite common when working on a project with other people when each person is responsible for part of the project.

Slides from previously created files or from teammates' files can be inserted into a new presentation by using the Copy and Paste feature. Simply click the slide you want to copy, press Ctrl + C, move to the file you want to copy the slide to, position the cursor where you want to place the copied slide, and press Ctrl + V.

1. Open **df 118a** (slides A, C, E) and **df 118b** (slides B, D, F).

**Figure 21-4** *df 118a*

**Figure 21-5** *df 118b*

2. Copy slide B from **df 118b** and paste it after slide A in **df 118a**. Notice how the design of a slide automatically changes to the design of the file it is being pasted to.
3. Copy slide D from **df 118b** and place it after slide C in **df 118a**.
4. Copy slide F from **df 118b** and place it after slide E in **df 118a**.
5. The titles on each slide should now appear in alphabetical order as shown in the Quick Check.
6. **Save as:** **118b ppt.**

## 24F

**Learn: Sort**

Data/Sort & Filter/Sort

1. Read the following information about sorting data.

Information in a worksheet can be **sorted**. Sorting reorganizes data to place it in an order that is more meaningful for the person interpreting it. For example, if you are a teacher, you may want to sort test scores to quickly identify the students who scored within specific ranges. You can sort the worksheet based on information in one column in different orders (A–Z, Z–A, Largest to Smallest, Oldest to Newest, etc.) as shown in Figure 4-35. You can sort information based on two or more columns by using the Custom Sort option.

**Figure 4-35** Sort options

It is always best to rename and save the worksheet before doing the sort to retain the information in its original order.

2. Open *df 24f sort*. **Save as:** *24f sort* and keep the file open.
3. Sort by Date Received (Oldest to Newest). Print the first 12 rows that include data for 9/10.
4. **Save as:** *24f sort1*.
5. Open *24f sort* again and sort the information by Last Name and then First Name, both in A–Z order. Freeze row 1 and hide columns E and G. Print rows 35–54.
6. **Save as:** *24f sort2*.
7. Open *24f sort* again and sort the list by Meal Choice (Z–A), then Last Name (A–Z), and then First Name (A–Z). Hide column G. Print the last five C and first five B meals.
8. **Save as:** *24f sort3*.
9. Open *24f sort* again and sort the information by Ticket No. (Largest to Smallest) and then Last and First Names (A–Z). Hide columns F and G. Print page 1 of the worksheet.
10. **Save as:** *24f sort4*.

## 24G

**Apply: Hide and Sort Data**

1. Open *df 21b landscape*.
2. Hide columns B–G.
3. Sort by Gross Pay in Smallest to Largest order.
4. Use your name as a right-aligned header and today's date as a right-aligned footer.
5. Print the worksheet with gridlines and row and column headings scaled to fit on one page with 2" side margins and centered vertically.
6. **Save as:** *24g payroll*.

## 24H

**Apply: Hide and Unhide Data**

1. Open *df 24h sort*.
2. Key this data into the worksheet:
   **Morris Towers, 5-story office building, $4.53, $4.86**
3. Hide column C and sort by present value (Smallest to Largest).
4. **Save as:** *24h sort1* and print the worksheet.
5. Unhide column C, hide column D, and sort by Property Cost (Largest to Smallest) and then by Property Name (A–Z).
6. **Save as:** *24h sort2* and print the worksheet.
7. Unhide column D, hide column B, and sort by Property Name (A–Z).
8. **Save as:** *24h sort3* and print the worksheet.

There is a default for the amount of time it takes to run an animation or transition. The default time can be increased or decreased by using the Duration feature. The Duration feature is part of the timing group on the Animations tab or the Transitions tab.

Headers and footers that were used in word processing documents can also be used in *PowerPoint* presentations. Headers and footers can be added to notes and handouts; however, only footers can be added to slides.

Depending on the design theme used, the information will automatically be placed at the top, bottom, or even the side of the slide. Some of the design themes place part of the information at the top and part of the information at the bottom of the slide. Information that can be placed on the slide includes date and time, slide number, and footer. In Figure 21-3, the information was placed at the right.

student organizations

**Figure 21-3** Footer on side of screen

The date and time can either be fixed or set to update automatically. When updated automatically, the current time is reflected when the presenter advances to the next slide. This allows the presenter to see how much time is left to present the remainder of the information.

The page number serves as a reference point for the presenter as well as the audience. For example, someone in the audience may have a question and ask the presenter to go back to slide 6. The presenter can also use the page number to gauge whether to go faster in order to finish the presentation within the allotted amount of time.

In addition to Online Pictures (clip art), pictures and movies can be inserted in a presentation from scanners, cameras, files, and the Internet. Care must be taken not to violate copyright laws. Inserting pictures and movies enhances a slide show and captures the audience's attention.

Graphics are used to visually communicate information. SmartArt graphic categories include List, Process, Cycle, Hierarchy, Relationship, Matrix, Pyramid, and Picture.

**Slide transition** is the term used to describe how the display changes from one slide to the next. When no transition is applied, slides go from one directly to the next. Transition effects can make it appear as though the next slide dissolves in or appears through a circle, for example. There are numerous transitions to choose from. Some are much more glitzy than others. Care should be taken to enhance the presentation with transitions rather than detract from the presentation.

Changes to basic transitions can be made with the Effect Options feature. This feature allows you to change the direction and color of the transition.

**Apply: Sort and Print Data**

1. Open **21h worksheet** again. **Save as: 24i sort**.
2. Sort the information in cells A4:D9 by Percent Change in Largest to Smallest order.
3. Sort the information in cells E4:H9 by Percent Change in Largest to Smallest order.
4. Confirm that your name is a right-aligned header and today's date is a left-aligned footer.
5. Center and print the worksheet in landscape orientation.
6. **Save as: 24i sort**.

## LESSON 25 — Charts, PDF Files, and Sparklines

**OUTCOMES**

- Create charts and chart sheets.
- Apply sparkline graphics.
- Create PDF files.
- Analyze data.

### Business Documents

- Ballplayer Statistics
- Sales Reports
- Conference Participants Reports
- Payroll Reports
- Inventory Report Analysis

**25B**

**Review: Charting**

Insert/Charts/select chart type

1. Read the following information to review charting.

Spreadsheet software provides options to create a variety of charts including **Column**, **Line**, **Pie**, **Bar**, **Area**, **Scatter**, and **Other Charts** as shown in Figure 4-36.

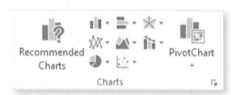

**Figure 4-36** Chart options

The chart you initially select to display your data can be changed to other chart types to help you decide which type best presents your data. Also, once a chart is created you can change the chart to display or not display such chart parts as the **title**, **data labels**, **grid-lines**, and **legend** by using features in the **Labels** and **Axes** groups on the **Layout** tab shown in Figure 4-37.

Chart Tools Layout tab/ Chart Labels or Axes/ select characteristics

Use features in the **Chart Layouts** and **Chart Styles** groups on the **Design** tab to change the overall visual appearance of your chart, including the color of the bars, lines, pie slices, etc.

**Figure 4-37** Chart label and axes options

Chart Tools Design tab/ Chart Layouts or Chart Styles/select layout or style

2. Open **df 25b bar** and create a bar chart with chart and axis titles and gridlines. Enlarge the chart as needed to make it easy to read.
3. **Save as: 25b bar**.
4. Open **df 25b column** and create a column chart with chart and axis titles, gridlines, and legend. Enlarge the chart as needed to make it easy to read.
5. **Save as: 25b column**.
6. Open **df 25b pie** and create a pie chart with chart title, legend, and data labels showing percentages. Enlarge the chart as needed to make it easy to read.
7. **Save as: 25b pie**.

Lesson 118 Reuse Slides and Combine Files
Lesson 119 Enhance Visuals with the Convert to SmartArt Feature

Lesson 120 Enhance Visuals with Advanced Transition and Animation Features

## Reference Guide

### Animations

Animations/Animation/
Select Animation Type

### Effect Options

Animations/Animation/
Effect Options

### Convert to SmartArt

### Design Theme

Design/Themes/Select
a Theme

Rather than have a slide appear in its entirety immediately in a presentation, animations can be used to make text, graphics, and other objects appear one at a time. This allows control of how the information is presented as well as adding interest to the presentation.

A variety of animations are available to choose from. For example, text and objects on a slide can be animated to fade in, spin, float, ascend, or descend. **Animation schemes** are options that are preset. They range from very subtle to very glitzy. The scheme chosen should add interest without taking away from the message. **Custom animation** allows several different animations to be included on each slide.

Changes to basic animations can be made with the Effect Options feature. This feature allows you to change the sequence, direction, shapes, spokes, and/or vanishing point of the various animations.

To communicate information more effectively, add a SmartArt graphic to existing text. A graphic can be added to existing text on a slide by using the Convert to SmartArt feature as shown in the following illustrations.

Figure 21-1 Without SmartArt

Figure 21-2 With SmartArt

*PowerPoint* comes with preset design themes. A design theme provides a consistent, attractive look. Presentations can be created by selecting the slide layout, keying the information, and inserting appropriate graphics. The fonts and font sizes, places for keying information, background design, and color schemes are preset for each design theme. Even though these themes are preset, they can be changed to better fit the needs of the user. Using design themes is a quick way to give your presentation a professional look.

## 25C

### Learn: Create a Chart Sheet

Chart Tools/Design/ Location/ Move Chart

1. Read the following information about creating chart sheets.

Charts can be created and displayed two ways—as an **Object** or as a **New sheet** (see Figure 4-38). Charts created previously have been created and displayed as embedded objects. That is, the chart is placed within the worksheet so the chart and data can be viewed at the same time. Since the chart is an object, it can be resized and moved to a different location within the worksheet.

Figure 4-38 Creat Chart sheet

In this activity, charts will be created and placed in a new chart sheet. The chart sheet is a separate sheet in the workbook. You can access the chart sheet by clicking the chart tab to the left of the worksheet tab near the bottom of the worksheet. Chart sheets are saved when the worksheet is saved. You can use the default name(s) assigned or give each chart sheet a specific name. Several charts can be prepared from a worksheet if chart sheets are used.

2. Open **25b bar** again and move the chart to a new chart sheet.
3. **Save as: 25c bar.**
4. Repeat steps 2–3 for **25b column** and **25b pie.** Save as: **25c column** and **25c pie**, respectively.

## 25D

### Learn: Sparkline Graphics

Insert/Sparklines/Line, Column, or Win/Loss

1. Read the following information about using sparklines.

A sparkline is a small graphic that can be used to show trends or variations in worksheet data. Sparklines are inserted in a single cell and are the same height and width of the cell in which they are inserted. A sparkline can be shown as a Line chart, Column chart, or Win/Loss chart. To insert a sparkline select the cells that contain the data you want to include in the graphic, click the type of sparkline chart in the Sparklines group (see Figure 4-39) to open the Create Sparklines dialog box (see Figure 4-40), click in the Location Range box, key or click the cell address that will display the chart, and then click OK.

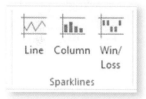

Figure 4-39 Sparklines

Figure 4-40 Create Sparklines dialog box

# Career Clusters

Transportation, Distribution & Logistics

### Planning a Career in Transportation, Distribution, and Logistics

Take a minute to think about all the people who work behind the scenes to get food to your local grocery store, or computers to your school, or fuel to the corner gas station. They are the workers who plan, manage, and execute the transport of people, produce, and products all over the world.

### What's It Like?

Those who work in the Transportation, Distribution, and Logistics career cluster are responsible for the planning, management, and movement of people, materials, and goods by road, pipeline, air, rail, and water. They are also involved in transportation infrastructure planning and management, logistics services, mobile equipment, and facility maintenance. For example:

- They are responsible for picking up and delivering freight from one place to another, whether by truck, plane, train, or ship.
- They schedule and dispatch workers, equipment, or service vehicles to carry materials or passengers, keeping records, logs, and schedules of the calls that they receive and of the transportation vehicles that they monitor and control.
- They repair and maintain the diesel engines that power trucks, locomotives, and buses.
- They develop long- and short-term plans for the use of land and the growth and revitalization of urban, suburban, and rural communities; recommend locations for roads, schools, and other infrastructure; and suggest zoning regulations for private property.

Employees in this field work in various types of environments. Some work 40-hour weeks in offices or on job sites. Other jobs are more demanding, requiring workers to travel long distances and drive or operate vehicles for long hours, or to lift and manipulate heavy equipment and engine parts.

### Employment Outlook

Generally, employment in this career cluster is expected to grow about as fast as the average for all other occupations. Opportunities are favorable for those who complete formal training in their selected occupation.

Education requirements for workers in this cluster vary. Most jobs require a high school diploma and on-the-job training, while others require a two-year, bachelor's, or master's degree. Many require a driver's license and other certification.

### What About You?

This career cluster is covered in box 16 of the Interest Survey Activity you completed in Unit 1 of this text. If this box had one of the three highest scores on your survey, you should further explore the cluster's pathways and related occupations.

1. Why do you think a career in this field could be a good choice?
2. What skills can you develop now that would be helpful to a career in this field?
3. Why are these jobs important to our country's economy?

When the cell displaying the sparkline chart is active, a Sparkline Tools Design tab is available where you can make desired changes to the sparkline chart.

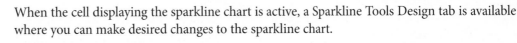

2. Open *df 25d sparkline.*
3. Using the data in cells A1:E1, insert a Sparkline Line Chart in cell F1.
4. Using the data in cells A2:E2, insert a Sparkline Column Chart in cell F2.
5. Using the data in cells A3:E3, insert a Sparkline Win/Loss Chart in cell F3.
6. Increase the height of rows A1:A3 to 25 to increase the height of the charts.
7. Change the width of Column F to 12 to widen the charts.
8. **Save as:** *25d sparkline.*

## 25E

### Learn: PDF Files

File/Save As/
Save as type list

1. Read the following information about creating a PDF.

Worksheets can be saved in a variety of file formats other than the default .xlsx format you have been using (see Figure 4-41). For example, worksheets can be saved in the .xls file format, which was used by earlier versions of *Excel*, and as a web page in .htm or .html file format. Frequently, worksheets are saved in an *Adobe Portable File* format with a .pdf file extension. Some advantages of the .pdf file format are that the worksheet will look the same on most computers; fonts, formats, and imaging are preserved; content cannot easily be changed; and free PDF viewers are available on the Web. Before saving a worksheet in another file format, be sure to save it in the regular format (.xlsx) so you have easy access to the data for any additional editing that may be needed.

**Figure 4-41** Save in PDF file format

2. Open *24g payroll* again.
3. **Save as:** *25e payroll* in PDF file format.

## 25F

### Apply: Analyze Data

1. Open *df 25f analysis.*
2. In column H, display a Sparkline Line Chart for the six-month period for each model in rows 3–8.
3. Compare your Sparkline Line Charts to those shown in the following Quick Check.
4. Using the line charts, key the answer to each question in the appropriate cell in column A.
5. **Save as:** *25f analysis* in PDF file format.

VEER.COM/STILLFX

# Academic and Career Connections

Complete the following exercises that introduce various topics that involve academic themes and careers.

## Communications: Composition

1. Open a new *Word* document. Compose a ¶ on entrepreneurship by keying the following sentences in the correct order. Correct word-choice errors as you key.

For example, they are independant and want to make their own decisoins.

Research shows that sucessful entreprenures display many of the same charicteristics.

Last, successful entreprenures are able to act quickly. Their not afraid to make a quick decision, which helps them beat there competiters.

They are self-confidant and are determined to acheive they're goals. They have a need to achieve and set hi standards for theirselves. They are creative but also technologically savy.

2. When you have finished keying, proofread, edit, and correct the document.
3. **Save as:** *u20 communications*.

## Math: Mental Math

Brian is a wildlife biologist. His main responsibilities are researching and monitoring plant and animal habitats within a 1,600-acre wildlife preserve. He uses mental math (no calculator and no figuring with pencil and paper) to make estimations.

1. In a 10-acre area, Brian spots two honeybee hives. If three-fourths of the total preserve consists of the same type of plant and animal life as in the 10-acre area, how many hives would Brian estimate to be in the preserve?
2. There is an average of five ash trees per acre. If 50 percent of the trees in the preserve have been treated for emerald ash borer, how many trees are still at risk? If these trees are dying at four per week, how many untreated trees will be alive after two years?
3. The Lakeside daisy is on the U.S. Fish & Wildlife Service's list of threatened plant species. Brian has counted 120 plants this year, which is 20 percent more than were in the preserve last year. How many plants were in the preserve last year?

## School and Community
The safety of any community depends largely on the involvement of its residents. That's why every citizen should understand general safety guidelines and be on the alert for activities and behaviors they feel are suspicious or threatening.

1. Using the Internet, library, your local law enforcement authorities, and other resources, research general safety tips for residents of a community. These might include obeying traffic and pedestrian signs, bicycling safety, preparing for weather emergencies, and paying attention to your surroundings and the people in them.
2. With the information you have gathered, develop a community safety checklist. Your checklist should include a minimum of five safety tips.
3. Prepare a creative presentation of the checklist. For example, you might design a poster, create a flyer, or develop a presentation that can be broadcast online.

Your completed worksheet should look like this:

### SIX-MONTH INVENTORY LIST

| Model | January | February | March | April | May | June | |
|-------|---------|----------|-------|-------|-----|------|---|
| CXS | 223 | 244 | 253 | 256 | 261 | 275 | |
| DGI | 341 | 301 | 315 | 352 | 334 | 362 | |
| LST | 256 | 249 | 245 | 234 | 228 | 220 | |
| OVG | 275 | 225 | 282 | 284 | 296 | 225 | |
| WST | 310 | 314 | 302 | 316 | 320 | 325 | |
| ZRX | 287 | 256 | 294 | 264 | 274 | 258 | |

## 25G

**Apply: Create Chart**

1. Open a new worksheet.
2. Key the following worksheet.

| Model | January | February | March |
|-------|---------|----------|-------|
| Sedans | 24 | 26 | 34 |
| Minivans | 36 | 30 | 42 |
| Crossovers | 28 | 34 | 38 |
| SUVs | 18 | 24 | 20 |

3. Create a column chart showing the data for the three-month period.
4. Insert **First Quarter New Vehicle Sales** as the chart title.
5. Insert **Model** as the horizontal axis title.
6. Insert **Number** as the vertical axis title.
7. **Save as:** *25g chart* in PDF file format.

## Digital Citizenship and Ethics
Bullying comes in many forms, from teasing and name-calling to pushing and hitting to excluding others from a group. Now, technology has provided new ways for people to bully each other. Cyberbullying—or using online communications technology to harass or upset someone—has become increasingly common as more and more people gain access to cell phones and the Internet.

Cell phones and email can be used to send hateful calls or messages or to share humiliating images. Threatening messages can be sent via chat rooms, message boards, and social networking sites. Name-calling and abusive remarks are thrown at players on gaming sites. What can you do about cyberbullying? As a class, discuss the following.

1. What are three things you can do so that you do not become a victim of cyberbullying?
2. If you've been the victim of cyberbullying, what course of action should you take?

7. On the *Industry Analysis* slide, add a bullet and key **See Appendix A for more details on historical and projected pet expenditures**.

8. On the *Financials* slide, add a bullet and key **See Appendix B for projected quarterly sales**.

9. Insert a bookmark and hyperlink between the *Industry Analysis* slide and *Appendix A*. Insert a hyperlink to **Return to Industry Analysis**.

10. Insert a bookmark and hyperlink between *Financials* and *Appendix B*. Insert a hyperlink to **Return to Financials**.

11. After slide 11, insert the organizational chart slide you created in Activity 10.

12. **Save as:** *112 buspres activity11.*

---

**Enrichment Activity**

The owners of A Dog's ReTreat would like you to create a customer rewards card for customers who regularly use the boarding services. The card should be the size of a regular business card.

Include the following items on the rewards card and arrange them attractively on the card:

- Company Name
- A graphic or photo, or create a logo for the company
- The words "Customer Rewards Card"
- Include the terms for the reward—"For every 10 boarding visits at *A Dog's ReTreat*, the client gets one free stay."
- An icon that can be hole punched for each boarding visit

**Save as:** *112 enrich.*

---

© iStockphoto.com/microgen

## 21st Century Skills: Entrepreneurial Literacy
Starting and running your own business requires hard work and determination, but it also involves many other skills that you might already possess. For example:

- Communication skills demonstrate your ability to speak, write, and listen well.
- Decision-making and problem-solving skills empower you to "think on your feet" and work cooperatively with others.
- Organization skills strengthen your abilities to plan and manage.
- Computer skills enable you to apply and use technology in all types of settings.
- Math skills help you understand economics and make sound financial decisions.

### Think Critically

1. Select one of the general skills listed above, or another skill that you feel you have developed to a certain degree.
2. In *Word*, write a summary that describes the skill you selected, explains how you acquired it, and provides examples of how you have applied it.
3. Think of a business you could start that utilizes your selected skill. Create a flyer or presentation that describes and advertises the business.

# LESSON 26

## Spreadsheet Applications

**OUTCOME**  Apply worksheet formatting, formula, and chart skills.

### Business Documents

- Golf Tournament Scores
- Community Service Report
- Sales Reports

### 26B

**Apply: Golf Match Information Sheet**

1. Open **df 26b worksheet**.
2. In cell I1, key **Round Score** (use Wrap Text) as a column heading, and then calculate the total score for each golfer in column I by adding the Out and In values.
3. Specify column widths as follows: columns B and F at 12; C, D, G, H, and I at 8; and E at 16.
4. Format column B as social security number and column E as phone number.
5. Insert a row at the top, and key **FOURTH ANNUAL TRI-HIGH GOLF MATCH** centered across all columns.
6. Center-align all columns except A.
7. Make all row heights 24 pts. except row 2.
8. Rotate the text in row 2 to 75°, and adjust row height to 65. Horizontally center-align all row 2 text.
9. Separate the names in column A so the first names remain in A and the last names appear in column B. Change the column headings to **First Name** and **Last Name**. Adjust width of columns A and B to fit the contents.
10. Sort by Gender (A–Z); then by Round Score (Smallest to Largest); then by Last Name (A–Z).
11. Insert a page break so the females print on page 1 and males print on page 2.
12. Set up the pages so they will print horizontally and vertically centered in landscape orientation with gridlines showing. Column headings in rows 1 and 2 (cell range A1:J2) are to be repeated on page 2.
13. Change font size as desired.
14. Add shading and color as desired.
15. Make other formatting changes as desired.
16. Insert your name as a centered header in 14-pt. font and today's date as a right-aligned footer in 14-pt. font.
17. Hide the Gender column.
18. Rename Sheet 1 tab **4th Annual.**
19. Print the worksheet.
20. Save as: **26b worksheet**.

1. Open *df 112 buspres activity11*.
2. Insert a title slide and key **A Dog's ReTreat** as the title and **Business Plan** as the subtitle. Insert a photo/graphic appropriate for this business; see Figure 20-8.
3. After slide 2, insert a slide titled **Services** and key the bulleted services from the business plan.
4. After slide 7, insert a slide titled **Marketing Plan** and key the promotional strategies listed in the business plan.
5. Copy and paste the *Pet Expenditures* chart from the business plan as **Appendix A** and key slide title as shown below (Figure 20-9).
6. Copy and paste the *Quarterly Sales Projections* chart from the business plan as **Appendix B** and key slide title as shown below (Figure 20-10).

**Figure 20-8** Title slide

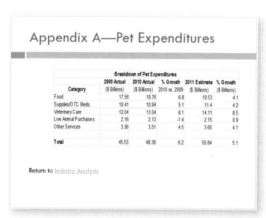

**Figure 20-9** Appendix A

**Figure 20-10** Appendix B

**Apply: Community Service Record**

1. Create a new worksheet, indenting and merging cells as shown.

| COMMUNITY SERVICE | | | | | | | | | | |
|---|---|---|---|---|---|---|---|---|---|---|
| TEAM | HOURS SERVED | | | | | | | | | |
| | SEP | OCT | NOV | DEC | JAN | FEB | MAR | APR | MAY | TOTALS |
| Givers | | | | | | | | | | |
| Young | 3 | 6 | 2 | 4 | 2 | 4 | 1 | 3 | 5 | ? |
| Yarry | 2 | 4 | 4 | 3 | 6 | 3 | 5 | 4 | 1 | ? |
| Estrada | 4 | 4 | 3 | 6 | 2 | 4 | 2 | 4 | 2 | ? |
| Johnson | 1 | 3 | 5 | 4 | 4 | 3 | 6 | 2 | 2 | ? |
| Totals | ? | ? | ? | ? | ? | ? | ? | ? | ? | ? |
| Servers | | | | | | | | | | |
| Chin | 2 | 4 | 4 | 3 | 6 | 3 | 2 | 5 | 1 | ? |
| Poole | 3 | 3 | 4 | 3 | 6 | 2 | 4 | 2 | 4 | ? |
| Everett | 2 | 3 | 5 | 1 | 2 | 4 | 4 | 3 | 6 | ? |
| Morris | 3 | 6 | 6 | 2 | 5 | 1 | 1 | 2 | 4 | ? |
| Totals | ? | ? | ? | ? | ? | ? | ? | ? | ? | ? |
| V'Teers | | | | | | | | | | |
| Quinnones | 3 | 3 | 4 | 4 | 4 | 3 | 6 | 1 | 4 | ? |
| Nester | 1 | 2 | 5 | 2 | 3 | 5 | 5 | 2 | 4 | ? |
| Veres | 2 | 4 | 4 | 3 | 5 | 2 | 2 | 4 | 4 | ? |
| Cox | 5 | 2 | 3 | 5 | 5 | 2 | 4 | 3 | 3 | ? |
| Totals | ? | ? | ? | ? | ? | ? | ? | ? | ? | ? |
| Grand Totals | ? | ? | ? | ? | ? | ? | ? | ? | ? | ? |

2. Calculate totals using the most efficient method.
3. Within each team, sort by each person's total score (descending order), and then by name (ascending order).
4. Angle the months and the Totals column headings in row 3 counterclockwise.
5. You decide all other formatting features.
6. Center the worksheet on the page using portrait orientation, and print the worksheet.
7. Save as: **26c worksheet**.

**Apply: Column Chart**

1. Open **df 26d chart**.
2. Create a bar chart with a title and legend using information in cells A2:I5.
3. Format the chart appropriately.
4. Move the chart to a chart sheet.
5. Save as: **26d chart** in PDF format.

**Apply: Sparklines**

1. Open **df 26d chart** again.
2. In column J, insert Sparkline Column Charts in rows 3–5 to chart the data for the cells in columns B:I.
3. Save as: **26e sparkline**.

6. Key **A Dog's ReTreat Business Plan** as a header on all pages except the cover page, first page of the table of contents, and first page of the report body.

7. Insert a page number using the Accent Bar 1 style as a footer on all pages except the cover page and first page of the table of contents. Check to see that the table of contents page numbers are correct.

8. If needed, make adjustments so the footnote appears on the correct page, ¶s and bullets are divided correctly, headings are kept with text, and table is not split between pages.

9. Print the complete report, unless directed otherwise.

10. Save as: *112 busplan activity9.*

**Activity 10**

1. Start a new blank presentation in your presentation software. Create a Title and Content slide with the title **Management Structure**. Add an asterisk beside *Management Structure.*

2. Insert a SmartArt hierarchy chart like the one shown in Figure 20-7.

3. In the top cell, key **A Dog's ReTreat** in bold. Increase the font size to 28 point. Adjust cell size to fit copy by using the handles of the text box.

4. In the next cell, left side, key **Benji Jackson, Partner/Employee Supervision**. Boldface the partner's name.

5. In the next cell, right side, key **Toto Jackson, Partner/Finance, Planning, Marketing**. Boldface the partner's name.

6. Add another row of cells under *Benji Jackson.*

7. In the three cells under Benji, key **Trainers (5 employees), Groomers (8 employees) and Day/Night Boarding (15 Employees)**.

8. Under Toto, key **Retail/Gift Shop (6 employees)**.

9. Center the organizational chart on the slide.

10. At the bottom of the slide, key **\*Structure when full staffing is achieved at end of Year 1**.

11. Save as: *112 buspres activity10.*

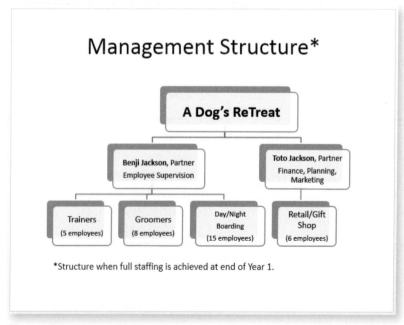

**Figure 20-7** Organization chart

Two 3' writings on two ¶s; determine *gwam*; count errors

 **all letters used**

www.cengage.com/school/
keyboarding/c21key

| | gwam | 3' |
|---|---|---|
| Each President since George Washington has had a | | 4 |
| cabinet.  The cabinet is a group of men and women selected | | 8 |
| by the President.  The senate must approve them.  It is the | | 12 |
| exception rather than the rule for the President's choice | | 15 |
| to be rejected by this branch of the government.  In | | 19 |
| keeping with tradition, most of the cabinet members belong | | 23 |
| to the same political party as the President. | | 26 |
| The purpose of the cabinet is to provide advice to the | | 30 |
| President on matters pertaining to the job of President. | | 34 |
| The person holding the office, of course, may or may not | | 38 |
| follow the advice.  Some Presidents have frequently | | 41 |
| utilized their cabinet.  Others have used it little or not | | 45 |
| at all.  For example, President Wilson held no cabinet | | 49 |
| meetings at all during World War I. | | 51 |

## 21st Century Skills:  Communicate Clearly

Spreadsheets are a powerful tool for calculating, managing, and analyzing numerical data. Businesses use spreadsheets to record market research, measure performance, and create financial documents.  Another valuable use of spreadsheets is creating charts and graphs to help illustrate complex numerical information and identify trends.

Assume you are the production manager for a manufacturing company.  You want to analyze the productivity of workers on first shift (6 a.m.–2 p.m.), second shift (2 p.m.–10 p.m.), and third shift (10 p.m.–6 a.m.).  To do this, you have collected the following information on the number of units produced per shift.

|  | Shift 1 | Shift 2 | Shift 3 |
|---|---|---|---|
| **Monday** | 145 | 120 | 109 |
| **Tuesday** | 147 | 119 | 112 |
| **Wednesday** | 144 | 123 | 112 |
| **Thursday** | 147 | 125 | 111 |
| **Friday** | 140 | 124 | 110 |

1.  Open a new worksheet, and key the data shown.
2.  Create a column chart to illustrate the number of units produced per shift.  Save the spreadsheet as *u04 21century*.
3.  Evaluate the chart.  What might account for the lower outputs for shifts 2 and 3?

1. Open *df 112 busplan activity8*.
2. Insert a page break after *Appendix A*.
3. On the new page, key **Appendix B—Quarterly Sales Projections** in the Heading 1 style 2" from the top.
4. Open an *Excel* spreadsheet and key the quarterly sales data shown below.
5. Key the following headings in column F:
   cell F1: **YEAR 1**
   cell F2: **9/15-9/14**
6. Calculate the yearly totals in cells F3:F15. Format all dollar amounts in Accounting format and decrease the decimal point to zero. Underline using Single and Double Accounting rules as shown.
7. Adjust the spreadsheet so only rows/columns appear in *Word*.
8. Bookmark *Appendix B* and name it **APP_B**.
9. Split the window and search for *Appendix B* in the report body. Select and hyperlink it to the bookmark named *APP_B*. Bookmark *Financials* and then insert a hyperlink to **Return to Financials Section** in 8-point italic font.
10. Print the pages on which the worksheet appears.
11. **Save as:** *112 busplan activity8*.

| | QTR 1<br>9/15-12/14 | QTR 2<br>12/15-3/14 | QTR 3<br>3/15-6/14 | QTR 4<br>6/15-9/14 |
|---|---|---|---|---|
| Revenue | $198,000 | $247,500 | $272,500 | $297,000 |
| Cost of Sales | $16,000 | $24,500 | $29,750 | $32,500 |
| Gross Profit | $182,000 | $223,000 | $242,750 | $264,500 |
| Expenses | | | | |
| Salaries and Wages | $99,582 | $99,582 | $99,582 | $99,582 |
| Employee Benefits | $25,200 | $25,200 | $25,200 | $25,200 |
| Direct Operating Expenses | $9,800 | $12,890 | $13,000 | $13,500 |
| Marketing | $7,500 | $8,000 | $8,500 | $8,000 |
| Energy & Utilities | $9,250 | $13,800 | $14,500 | $14,900 |
| Administrative and General | $7,000 | $10,260 | $10,602 | $10,500 |
| Repairs and Maintenance | $2,000 | $5,758 | $5,900 | $5,700 |
| Building Costs | $21,500 | $21,500 | $21,500 | $21,500 |
| Total Expenses | $181,832 | $196,990 | $198,784 | $198,882 |
| Net Income | $168 | $26,010 | $43,966 | $65,618 |

1. Open *df 112 busplan activity9*. Spell-check and proofread the entire document.
2. Hyphenate the document.
3. Insert a table of contents before the first page of the report using Automatic Table 2. Notice that three heading levels are included. Also included are leaders to the left of the page numbers and hyperlinks to the respective headings in the body of the report.
4. Change *Table of Contents* to a Title heading.
5. From the Insert tab, select the cover page named Semaphore. Key **A Dog's ReTreat** as the title of the report, **Business Plan** as the subtitle, **Benji and Toto Jackson** as the authors, and use the **current year** as the year. Delete any other fields on the Cover Page template.

# CORPORATE
## *View*

## An Integrated Intranet Application

As part of your internship with Corporate View you have the opportunity to work in several departments within the organization to see the overall operations. Your current assignment is with Finance & Accounting. Because you have the expertise to create attractive and informative charts using Excel, the F&A Director would like you to create two charts that show changes in income statement accounts and balance sheet accounts from last year to this year. He will use them in a presentation to the corporate officers. The Director has provided you with the following instructions. Complete each step before going on to the next step.

1. Our company website is: www.cengage.com/school/keyboarding/dim/cview
2. Find the *Corporate View Quarterly Report Summary* in the Finance & Accounting section of the website.
3. Create a worksheet and chart for the Income Statement that compares the Net Revenues, Operating Expenses, and Net Income amounts (in millions) for the current year to those of the previous year. The Director has indicated that he prefers a column or bar chart that has data labels but is willing to consider other chart types provided they are attractive and informative.
4. Save the worksheet and chart as *u04 corpview chart1*.
5. Create a worksheet and chart for the Balance Sheet that compares the Total Assets, Total Current Liabilities, and Total Stockholder's Equity amounts (in millions) for the current year to those of the previous year.
6. Save the worksheet and chart as *u04 corpview chart2*.

### Think Critically

1. Open a *Word* document and list some major points the Director may use in his presentation of the data in *u04 corpview chart1* and *u04 corpview chart2*.
2. Review your points to make sure the data supports each of them.
3. Save as: *u04 corpview analysis*.

## Activity 7

1. Open *df 112 busplan activity7*.
2. Insert a page break at the end of the business plan.
3. On the new page, key **Appendix A—Pet Expenditures** in Heading 1 style 2" from the top.
4. Open an *Excel* spreadsheet in *Word* and key the *Pet Expenditures* data shown below.
5. Increase the vertical size and decrease the horizontal size so only rows/columns appear in *Word*.
6. Key the reference line shown a double space below the table.
7. Bookmark *Appendix A* and name it **APP_A**.
8. Split the window and search for *Appendix A* in the report body. Select and hyperlink it to the bookmark named *APP_A*.
9. Bookmark *National Data* (second-level heading before the hyperlink); name it **National**.
10. Use the Appendix A hyperlink to go to Appendix A. Below Appendix A, key **Return to National Data** in 8-point italic font. Hyperlink the text to the *National Data* bookmark.
11. Print the pages on which the worksheet appears.
12. Using the *Pet Expenditures* data, create a column graph using the columns *2009 Actual*, *2010 Actual*, and *2011 Estimate* (Figure 20-6).
13. Insert and center the graph in the report body at the end of the *National Data* section.
14. **Save as:** *112 busplan activity7*.

| Breakdown of Pet Expenditures | | | | | |
|---|---|---|---|---|---|
| Category | 2009 Actual ($ Billions) | 2010 Actual ($ Billions) | % Growth 2010 vs. 2009 | 2011 Estimate ($ Billions) | % Growth ($ Billions) |
| Food | 17.56 | 18.76 | 6.8 | 19.53 | 4.1 |
| Supplies/OTC Meds. | 10.41 | 10.94 | 5.1 | 11.4 | 4.2 |
| Veterinary Care | 12.04 | 13.04 | 8.1 | 14.11 | 8.5 |
| Live Animal Purchases | 2.16 | 2.13 | -1.4 | 2.15 | 0.9 |
| Other Services | 3.36 | 3.51 | 4.5 | 3.65 | 4.1 |
| **Total** | **45.53** | **48.38** | **6.2** | **50.84** | **5.1** |

*National data used in the business plan are from the American Pet Products Association obtained at http://media.americanpetproducts.org/press.php?include=142817 in October 2011.

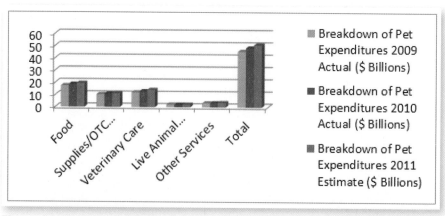

**Figure 20-6** Column graph

# Academic and Career Connections

Complete the following exercises that introduce various topics that involve academic themes and careers.

## Grammar and Writing

### Number Expression

**MicroType 6**

- References/Communication Skills/Number Expression
- CheckPro/Communication Skills 4
- CheckPro/Word Choice 4

1. Go to *MicroType 6* and use this feature path for review: References/Communication Skills/Number Expression.
2. Click *Rules* and review the rules of using numbers.
3. Under *Number Expression*, click *Posttest*.
4. Follow the instructions to complete the posttest.

***Optional Activities***

1. Go to this path: CheckPro/Communication Skills 4.
2. Complete the activities as directed.
3. Go to this path: CheckPro/Word Choice 4.
4. Complete the activities as directed.

## Communications

### Speaking

You have been selected to participate in an exchange program with students from different schools in your state. Each time you visit one of their schools or students visit your school, you must stand up in front of the group and introduce yourself. In a new word processing document, prepare your introduction by following these steps:

1. Write your name, grade, the name of your school, and the city in which it is located.
2. List the courses, activities, and organizations in which you are involved at school.
3. List your interests, hobbies, and anything else you feel is unique about you.
4. Discuss your goals for after you graduate.
5. Save the document as ***u04 communications*** and print a copy.
6. Practice your introduction by reading your document several times aloud. Add transitions as necessary. Jot additional notes on the document as needed.
7. In front of a mirror or with your friends or family, continue to practice your introduction. Pay attention to your tone of voice, facial expressions, posture, and body language.
8. As directed by your instructor, present your self-introduction to the class.

## Science

Advances in technology have had a tremendous impact on worker productivity. For example, software applications have empowered office employees to produce letters, reports, charts, graphs, and mass mailings in a matter of minutes.

1. Open a new spreadsheet file, and save it as ***u04 science***. You are going to track the time you spend on school work and work around your home every day for a week.
2. In a column, list each of your school classes followed by the chores or tasks that you are responsible for at home. Across the top of the worksheet, list each of the seven days of the week. On each day, record the amount of time you spend on homework or studying for each class as well as the time on each chore. Total the time spent on each class and chore. Which one took the most time? How could you use technology to reduce the amount of time you spend?

1. Open *df 112 busplan activity4*.
2. Use the Go To feature to find the *Jamesville Place Growth* section.  Key the text shown below after this section.
3. Apply Heading 1 style to *Market Share*.
4. **Save as:**  *112 busplan activity4*.

**Proofreading Alert**
The rough-draft copy contains two embedded errors. Proofread your work carefully, checking to make sure all errors have been corrected.

*Market Share*

A Dog's ReTreat will develop a strong presence in the Jamesville Place area and other suburbs surrounding the metropolitian area. A Dog's ReTreat will focus on dual-income, *traveling* professional families with hectic schedules. The most important *group of* customers are those who don't *sp* have as much time as they desire to invest in their pets and are willing to seek help regardless of the costs. *additional* The competitive advantage will be the eliminition of dog owner guilt in leaving their dogs because it is a safe *secure,* and fun environment.

1. Open *df112 memo activity5*.
2. Insert comment to **Format in memo style** at the beginning of the memo.
3. Insert a period after the word *shop* in the first sentence.
4. At the beginning of the second sentence, insert **Our retail/gift shop will offer**.
5. Delete the word *offering*.  Insert an **r** in the word *portaits*.
6. Insert **the** before *Jamesville Place* in ¶ 2, second sentence.
7. Insert **the greater** in front of *Milwaukee* in the same sentence.
8. Delete the **i** in the word *metropolitan*.  Insert **ing** after the word *will* in ¶ 2, last sentence.
9. Print a copy of the changes.
10. Delete the reference to email contact information.
11. **Save as:**  *112 memo activity5*.

1. Open *df 112 busplan activity6*.
2. Insert the table below after the word *assumptions* in the *Financials* section.  Center the table between the side margins.
3. Print the page on which the table appears.
4. **Save as:**  *112 busplan activity6*.

| Quarter | Customers Each Day | Revenues Per Customer | Total Revenues |
|---|---|---|---|
| September 15 to December 14 | 30 | $55 | $148,500 |
| December 15 to March 14 | 37 | $55 | $183,150 |
| March 15 to June 14 | 42 | $55 | $207,900 |
| June 15 to September 14 | 55 | $55 | $272,250 |

Chad Baker/Jason Reed/Ryan McVay/
Photodisc/Jupiter Images

### Planning a Career in Finance

The field of finance is focused on numbers and money, and, therefore, you probably immediately think of careers in banking. But the industry provides job opportunities at many different types of financial and even nonfinancial institutions. These include insurance companies, financial planners, accountant's offices, and investment banks as well as nonfinancial organizations that employ workers to handle these functions. This field is also directly tied to the stock market.

### What's It Like?

Individuals who work in this field are involved in services for financial and investment planning, banking, insurance, and business financial management. For example:

- They advise companies about taxes or offer advice in areas such as compensation, employee health-care benefits, and investing.
- They advise everyday people ("retail investors") on appropriate investments based on their needs and financial ability.
- They guide clients through the process of applying for loans.
- They process routine transactions that customers conduct at banks, such as cashing checks and making deposits, loan payments, and withdrawals.
- They investigate and manage claims, negotiate settlements, and authorize payments to insurance policyholders who make a claim.

Employees in most of these fields work a standard five-day, 40-hour week in a typical office environment. Those in investment banking and stock market jobs often work longer hours under more stressful and demanding conditions.

### Employment Outlook

Employment in the banking and insurance field is expected to grow more slowly than average, while employment in securities and investments will grow between 7 and 13 percent. Accountants and auditors should see much faster than average growth, or a 20 percent increase in employment. Employers typically require a bachelor's degree in a business or finance-related field. Many prefer a master's degree in business administration (MBA). Some jobs, such as bank tellers and loan officers, require a high school diploma, although previous banking, lending, or sales experience is highly valued.

### What About You?

The Finance career cluster is covered in box 6 of the Interest Survey Activity you completed in Unit 1 of this text. If this box had one of the three highest scores on your survey, you should further explore the cluster's pathways and related occupations.

1. Why do you think a career in this field could be a good choice?
2. What skills can you develop now that would be helpful to a career in this field?
3. Why do you think the increase or decrease in employment in these fields is tied closely to the state of the country's economy?

1. Open **df 112 busplan activity2** and key the text below after the company description.
2. Apply Heading 2 style to the side headings.
3. Print page 1.
4. **Save as:** **112 busplan activity2**.

Mission Statement

*A Dog's ReTreat's* ~~Our~~ mission is to provide *excellent* canine care and services in a pet friendly atmosphere while ensuring our customers *, both pet and owner,* receive excellent services in a playful safe environment.

Vison Statement

Within ⑤ years, A Dog's ReTreat will be recognized as one of the *five* top ~~ten~~ dog daycare and pet facilities in the *Milwaukee* area. The ownership is committed to create a service-based company whose goal is to exceed customer expectation.

1. Open **df112 track activity3**.
2. Click the Review tab and select Reviewing Pane. Select either Reviewing Pane Horizontal or Vertical to view the changes and comments to the document.
3. Review the changes and comments.
4. Accept or reject changes as directed.
   - Accept the first four changes.
   - Reject the next two changes.
   - Accept the next two changes.
   - Accept the first two changes in the last ¶.
   - Reject the next two changes.
   - Accept the change to add **even in time of recession**.
   - Accept the remaining four changes.
   - Insert footnotes 1 and 2 with citations as directed in the comments. Use the same font size as the text in the business plan.
5. Delete all comments.
6. **Save as:** **112 analysis activity3**.
7. Open **df 112 busplan activity3**.
8. Copy and insert the corrected text from **112 analysis activity3** into the business plan before the second-level heading *Jamesville Place Growth*.
9. Apply appropriate styles to the headings.
10. Print the page(s) on which *Industry Analysis* and *National Data* sections appear.
11. **Save as:** **112 busplan activity3**.

© iStockphoto.com/Izabela Habur

Complete this activity to help prepare for the **Spreadsheet Applications** event in FBLA-PBL's Finance division. You are the sales manager for a magazine publisher. You record each agent's sales on a daily basis and then prepare a summary spreadsheet at the end of each quarter. Following is the sales data for the second quarter.

| Sales Agent | April | May | June | Total | Commission |
|---|---|---|---|---|---|
| E. Juarez | $10,200 | $12,549 | $15,830 | | |
| M. Landon | $8,040 | $9,927 | $9,253 | | |
| R. Vaughn | $11,025 | $10,449 | $14,438 | | |
| S. Roos | $12,128 | $14,497 | $14,086 | | |
| B. Allison | $16,488 | $14,323 | $15,185 | | |
| Total | | | | | |

Key the data as shown in a new worksheet. Then do the following:

1. Use a formula in the Total row and Total column to sum the sales data by month and then by agent.
2. Calculate the commission on each agent's total sales. The commission rate for Juarez, Roos, and Allison is 15 percent; the rate for Landon and Vaughn is 12 percent.
3. Create an embedded pie chart that shows what percent of the whole each agent's total sales represent. Add an appropriate title to the chart, and format it as desired.
4. Create an embedded column chart that illustrates each agent's sales by month. Add an appropriate title to the chart, and format it as desired.
5. Apply cell styles and other formats as necessary.
6. Save and print the worksheet as directed by your instructor.

For detailed information on this event, go to www.fbla-pbl.org.

### Think Critically

1. Spreadsheet programs such as *Microsoft Excel* are used extensively in business. How could you use such a program at home? At school?
2. Why are visual aids, such as charts, helpful in communicating ideas and information?

## School and Community
Many nonprofit and community-based organizations connect with members and volunteers through their websites, mass emails, and blogs. A **blog** is a type of website maintained by an individual or group on which regular entries of commentary as well as a listing of events and programs are posted.

1. Think of an organization in your community for which you would like to volunteer.
2. Explore the ways in which the organization connects online with its volunteers.
3. Assume you are going to write a blog for the organization. You can use *Microsoft Word*. What topics would you discuss in your blog and why? What benefits would your blog provide to the organization?

# LESSONS 112–117    Business Plan

- Prepare a long report with a title page, table of contents, and appendices.
- Create a spreadsheet within a word processing document.
- Insert comments and tracked changes.
- Demonstrate your ability to integrate your knowledge and skills.

## Business Document

- Business Plan Report

### 112A–117A

**Warmup**

Key each line twice at the beginning of each lesson; first for speed, second for control.

alphabet 1 Sixty glazed rolls with jam were quickly baked and provided free.

numbers 2 Ted was born 1/7/42, Mel was born 3/2/86, and I was born 5/18/90.

speed 3 The auditor cut by half the giant goal of the sorority endowment.

| gwam | 1' | 1 | 2 | 3 | 4 | 5 | 6 | 7 | 8 | 9 | 10 | 11 | 12 | 13 |

### 112A–117B

**Business Plan Activity 1**

1. Open *df 112 busplan* and preview the business plan quickly to familiarize yourself with its content, organization, and length.
2. Display formatting using the Show/Hide ¶ feature and check for inconsistencies in spacing and ¶ indentations, and for spelling errors.
3. Key a list of all the errors you find.
4. **Save as:** *112 activity1*.
5. Correct the errors you found.
6. Use the *Reference Guide* to verify style set, margin settings, line spacing, etc.
7. Select and apply a character for all bulleted items found in the business plan.
8. Apply title and heading styles as follows:
   - Use Title style for the title on page 1 that is centered and keyed in bold font. If the title appears on two lines, decrease the font size to 28 point so it is on one line. Start the title at 2" from the top of the page.
   - Use Heading 1 style for headings that are centered in regular font.
   - Use Heading 2 style for all side headings except: *Public Areas, Employee Areas,* and *Outside/Grounds Areas.* These three side headings should be formatted in Heading 3 style.
9. Print pages 1 and 9 of the business plan.
10. **Save as:** *112 busplan activity1*.

# Assessing Basic Database Skills

In order to complete Unit 5, Data Mining and Analyzing Records, you will need a basic understanding of a database to include the skills and knowledge required to complete the following activities.

**Create database**

1. Open *Access* and create a new database.

**Create database table**
**Label fields**
**Select data type**
**Input field description**

2. Create a new database table (filename: ***Account Balances***) using Design view with the following fields, data types, and descriptions:

    a. Last Name       (text)        Last Name of Client
    b. First Name      (text)        First Name of Client
    c. Middle Initial  (text)        Middle Initial of Client's Name
    d. Account Balance (currency)    Account Balance of Client

**Input records in a table**

3. Input the following records:

| Acosta | Felipe | P. | $525.88 |
|--------|--------|-----|---------|
| McNair | Susan | C. | $197.56 |
| Bostwick | Paul | A. | $627.91 |

**Use Save As**

4. **Save Database As:** ***Client Account Balances***, and close the database file.

**Add new records to a database**

5. Open ***Client Account Balances***, and update the *Account Balances* table to include the following records:

| Bostwick | Rebecca | G. | $87.55 |
|----------|---------|-----|--------|
| Chen | Craig | M. | $548.22 |
| Bostwick | Rey | G. | $897.85 |

**Edit records in a database**

6. Make the following changes to the records in the *Account Balances* table.

    a. The correct spelling of Ms. McNair's first name is Suzanne.
    b. The balance of Mr. Acosta's account should be $552.88.
    c. Mr. Chen's middle initial is W.

## Go To

Home/Editing/Find/Go To

A quick way to move to a certain page or point in a long document is to use the Go To command. This command can be used to go directly to a specific page, comment, footnote, or bookmark, for example. See Figure 20-4.

Figure 20-4 Go To

## Style Set

Design/Styles/More

A style set is a predefined set of formatting options that have been named and saved so they can be used to save time and add consistency to a document. In previous activities, you have used a default style set.

When a style set is used, many formatting commands are applied at one time. Fonts, alignment, colors, and vertical spacing are all affected. The style set can be changed to one of many built-in style sets (see a list of built-in styles in Figure 20-5; yours may vary), or you can create a new one. Different color schemes can be selected, as well as different font sets.

Figure 20-5 Built-in styles

© 2014 Cengage Learning

## Digital Citizenship and Ethics

The computer has become a storage place for much of our important data, whether it's a five-page essay for English class, family and personal photos, or detailed records of bank and financial transactions. Responsible digital citizens recognize the need to protect not only their data and personal information, but also access to their computer and its resources. Following are measures you can take to ensure your digital security:

- Maintain up-to-date antivirus, anti-spyware, and firewall software.
- Limit access to your data as well as your online activity by setting strong passwords. Use different passwords for different accounts, change them frequently, and store them in a safe place away from your computer.
- Develop a schedule to conduct maintenance checks and back up your files.

As a class, discuss the following:

1. What are the characteristics of a strong password?
2. What tasks should be included in a computer maintenance check?
3. What methods for backing up your data do you use at home?

| | | |
|---|---|---|

Add new field
Input data in new field

7. Add a field for the phone number to the Account Balances table, and input the phone numbers.

| Acosta, Felipe | 608-555-1679 |
|---|---|
| McNair, Suzanne | 608-555-6009 |
| Bostwick, Paul | 608-555-8751 |
| Bostwick, Rebecca | 608-555-1405 |
| Chen, Craig | 608-555-4477 |
| Bostwick, Rey | 608-555-9075 |

Sort database field

8. Sort the table by Last Name in Ascending order.

Print table

9. Print a copy of the table.

Create and run filter

10. Create filter to show only the individuals with the last name of Bostwick. After running the filter, print a copy of the table.

11. Close the database.

## Bookmarks and Hyperlinks

Insert/Links/Bookmark or Hyperlinks

**Bookmarks** assign a name to a specific point in a document. **Hyperlinks** create a link from a point in the document to the bookmark. For example, if (*Refer to Appendix A*) appears in the body of a report and you want to make it easy for the reader to move quickly to *Appendix A* at that point, you can bookmark the title *Appendix A* in the appendices and then hyperlink the text (*Refer to Appendix A*) in the body of the report. By clicking on the hyperlink, the reader would move directly to Appendix A, the bookmarked text. See Figure 20-2.

If you want the reader to be able to quickly return to the hyperlink, you can bookmark text near the hyperlinked text in the report

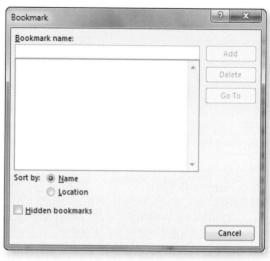

**Figure 20-2** Insert bookmark

body and add a line such as *Return to Report* at the end of *Appendix A* so readers can click it to quickly return to the point in the report body they were reading before navigating to the *Appendix A* bookmark.

## Split Window

View/Window/Split

Often it is helpful to be able to see two different sections of a document at the same time. The Split feature is used to display a document in two panes, each with its ruler bar and scroll bars to help you move around in each pane. If needed, the panes can be resized by dragging the split bar to any position. Click in a pane to make it active. (See Figure 20-3.)

This feature can be used when you copy or move text between parts of a long document or when you need to see text that is not visible in the window where you are keying.

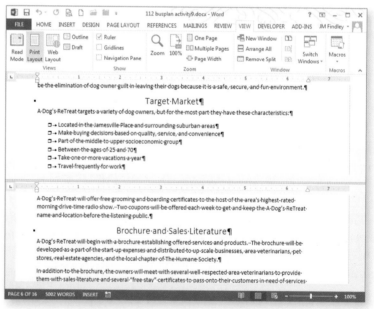

**Figure 20-3** Split window

**Lesson 27** Data Mining and Analysis Using Queries

**Lesson 28** Data Mining and Analysis Using Computed Fields

**Lesson 29** Creating Forms for Data Analysis

**Lesson 30** Creating Reports for Data Analysis

**Lesson 31** Using a Database to Create a Mail Merge

**Lesson 32** Database Applications

## Reference Guide

### Database Software

A database is an organized collection of facts and figures (information). The phone book, which includes names, addresses, and phone numbers, is an example of a database in printed form.

Databases are also stored in electronic form, as shown in Figure 5-1. Names and addresses, inventories, sales records, production records, and client information are just a few examples of information that is stored in an electronic database. Having information in an electronic database makes it easy to compile and arrange data to answer questions and make well-informed decisions.

Ribbon tabs

Ribbon

Open objects

Database objects

Navigation pane

View pane of Open objects

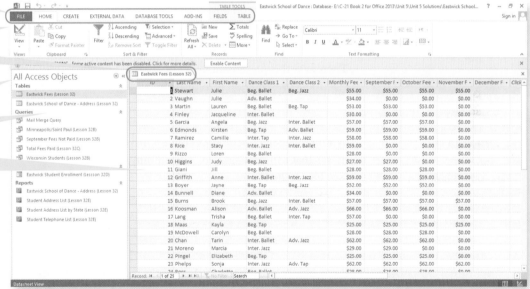

**Figure 5-1** Database stored in electronic form in *Microsoft Access*

© wavebreakmedia/Shutterstock.com

**Margins and Line Spacing.** The business plan is prepared using normal top, bottom, and side margins and 1.08 line spacing.

**Header, Footer, and Page Numbering.** A header with the company name followed by the words *Business Plan* blocked at the left margin and a footer containing a centered page number with *Page* preceding the number appear on all pages of the report body and appendices except the first page of the report body, the first page of the table of contents, and the cover (title) page. Use lowercase Roman numeral(s) for the TOC (table of contents) page(s).

**Text.** Paragraphs and single-line bulleted lists should have at least two lines (or bullets) at the bottom of the page and carry over at least two lines to the next page. Headings and at least two lines of text should be kept together. Footnotes should be the same typeface and font size as the text. Tables and worksheets should not be split between pages. The report body should be left-aligned and hyphenated.

**Style Set**

The Centered Style Set, Aspect Colors, and Office Fonts are to be used to format all parts of the report in the report body, appendices, table of contents, and cover (title) page.

**Table of Contents.** Prepare a TOC that contains hyperlinks from the TOC headings to the corresponding headings in the report and page numbers with dot leaders. Level 1, Level 2, and Level 3 headings are to be included in the TOC. Key *TABLE OF CONTENTS* in Title style at the top of the TOC page.

**Electronic Presentations**

Entrepreneurs often have to seek help from lenders or investors in order to have enough working capital to get the business started and operating until the business can become profitable. Entrepreneurs rely on a well-prepared presentation as an additional tool to convey their business plan to potential investors.

The electronic presentation in this unit will be presented to potential lenders or investors. Therefore, this presentation will be used for a formal, professional purpose. Remember, an electronic presentation is to provide talking points, not a script.

**Show/Hide ¶**

Home/Paragraph ¶

Word processing documents contain invisible formatting marks that can be displayed. Commonly used marks (see Figure 20-1) are:

>    ¶ to show the end of a paragraph,
>
>    → to show a tab,
>
>    · to show a space between words.

Being able to see the formatting marks is helpful when editing a document or solving formatting problems. The formatting marks do not print.

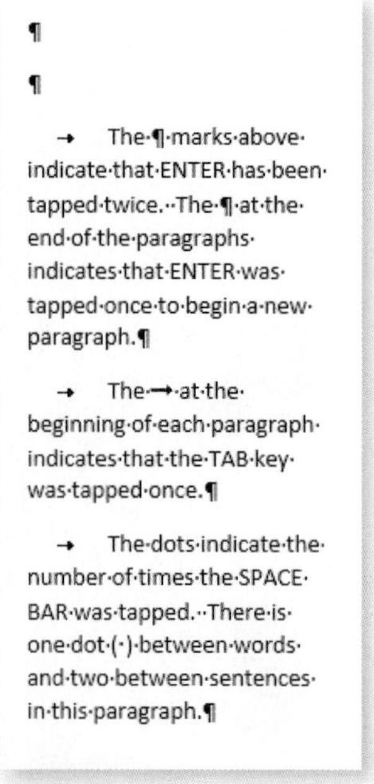

¶

¶

→    The·¶·marks·above· indicate·that·ENTER·has·been· tapped·twice.··The·¶·at·the· end·of·the·paragraphs· indicates·that·ENTER·was· tapped·once·to·begin·a·new· paragraph.¶

→    The·→·at·the· beginning·of·each·paragraph· indicates·that·the·TAB·key· was·tapped·once.¶

→    The·dots·indicate·the· number·of·times·the·SPACE· BAR·was·tapped.··There·is· one·dot·(·)·between·words· and·two·between·sentences· in·this·paragraph.¶

**Figure 20-1** Formatting marks

## Components of a Database

A database may include **tables** for entering and storing information, **forms** for entering and displaying information, **reports** for summarizing and presenting information, and **queries** for drawing information from one or more tables. Figure 5-2 shows the components that can be created in a database.

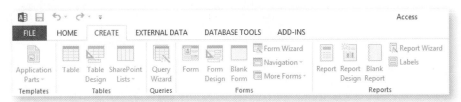

**Figure 5-2** Components that can be created in a database

## Database Table

Create/Tables/Table

Database tables are used for inputting, organizing, and storing information. The tables are set up to contain columns and rows of information. In a database table, an example of which is shown in Figure 5-3, the columns are called **fields** and the rows are called **records**. Records can contain one or more fields.

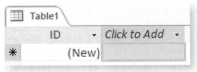

| ID | Last Name | First Name | Middle | Street Address | City | State |
|----|-----------|-----------|--------|----------------|------|-------|
| 1 | Duncan | Jerome | Z. | 117 Whispering Pines Lane | Melbourne | FL |
| 2 | DuBoisson | Gordon | J. | 8190 Markland Avenue | Fort Myers | FL |
| 3 | Fernandez | Stella | J. | 2690 Palomino Circle | Daytona Beach | FL |
| 4 | Zaida | Heidi | D. | 3718 Perkins Place, NW | Huntsville | AL |
| 5 | Holdern | Rita | W. | 605 Mendavia Aveune | Miami | FL |
| 6 | Miles | Asher | R. | 1730 Greenbay Drive | Charleston | SC |

Orlando Seminar - July 15-19

**Figure 5-3** Fields and records in a database table

## Defining and Sequencing Fields

Fields can be defined and sequenced in either **Datasheet View** (Figure 5-4) or **Design View** (Figure 5-5). In the Datasheet View, a field can be defined and sequenced by clicking on Click to Add, selecting a Data Type, and keying in the Field name.

**Figure 5-4** Defining a field in Datasheet View

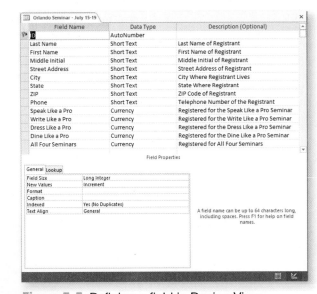

**Figure 5-5** Defining a field in Design View

**Reference Guide**

Becoming an Entrepreneur

Business Planning

Print and Electronic Reports

An **entrepreneur** is someone who starts, manages, and owns a business to earn a profit. Important factors for becoming an entrepreneur are a real desire to be your own boss, having the necessary skills and abilities, and coming up with innovative ideas. Entrepreneurs are self-starters who like to take charge of situations and work hard to meet their goals. Even when their businesses are not successful, entrepreneurs do not give up. They learn from their mistakes, start over, and eventually realize their dreams.

A successful start to a new business venture requires careful planning. The first step is creating a business plan. A **business plan** is a blueprint for a company. Developing a business plan helps entrepreneurs take an objective, critical look at their business ideas. A well-written plan communicates the company's ideas and message to lenders, investors, and employees. A business plan also is a management tool that helps measure the performance of the business. The key elements of a business plan include:

1. Description of the nature of the business, goals, and objectives
2. Competitive analysis
3. Marketing plan
4. Organizational plan
5. Financial plan

It contains strategies to help the entrepreneur put ideas into action. A well-written business plan guides the implementation of these strategies.

Business plans may be distributed in printed or electronic form. When distributed as printed copies, the document is frequently bound at the left and formatted without much color to avoid higher printing costs.

The business plan in this unit will be prepared for electronic distribution. It will, therefore, be formatted as an unbound report using color, fonts and font sizes, and ¶ spacing to make it attractive and easy to read on the computer monitor. Hyperlinks to bookmarks and headings will be inserted to make it easy for the reader to navigate from one part of the document to another.

© Hurst Photo/Shutterstock.com

| Create/Tables/ Table Design | The Data Type determines the types of values that can be displayed in the field. The most common data types are AutoNumber, Text, Number, Currency, and Date & Time. |

The Data Type determines the types of values that can be displayed in the field. The most common data types are AutoNumber, Text, Number, Currency, and Date & Time.

When defining and sequencing fields in Design View (Create/Tables/Table Design), the fields in the table are defined before entering data. The *Description* field is used to describe the content of each field. At the bottom of the Design View screen, property values for each field can be set.

When feasible, fields should be arranged in the same order as the data in the source document (paper form from which data is keyed). Doing so reduces the time needed to enter the field contents and to maintain the records.

## Database Form

Create/Forms/Form

Form

Database forms are created from database tables and queries. Forms are used for ease in entering, viewing, and editing data. Forms can be created that allow end users to access only limited amounts of data from the database. For example, a form can be designed to give one end user access to employee personal information, while another form can be designed to give another end user employee production data. Both forms use the same database table but give the two end users access only to certain fields that relate to their needs.

## Database Query

Create/Queries/ Query Design

Query Wizard  Query Design

Queries

Queries are questions. The Query feature of a database software program is used to gather specific information from tables that have been created and stored in a database. The results of a query are called a record set. A record set is displayed in a data sheet, which can be seen in Datasheet View.

There are different types of queries. A Select Query retrieves data from tables or performs simple calculations such as adding or averaging. Action queries add, change, or delete data. Queries become the basis of reports that are used for making informed decisions. Generally, queries rather than tables are used as the source for supplying the data for reports because a query limits the data to what is relevant to what is being reported.

Some of the things queries are used for include answering questions, gathering and assembling data from two or more tables, performing calculations, and even changing or deleting table data.

## Database Report

Create/Reports/ Report Wizard

Database reports are created from database tables and queries. Reports are used for organizing, summarizing, and printing information. The easiest way to generate a report is by simply clicking Report in the Reports group. This will give you a report of all the fields in the table or data sheet.

Use the Report Wizard to customize the design of the report. With the Report Wizard, specific fields can be selected to be included in the report, desired groupings can be specified, fields can be sorted in ascending or descending order, and layouts can be selected.

## Modified Table/Form

Home/View/Design View

A modified table or form is one that has been changed after it was created. Rather than creating a new database table or form each time information needs to be changed, database software allows changes to be made to existing tables and forms. Some of the most common changes that can be made include changing field properties, changing field names, adding new fields, and deleting fields no longer needed.

## Job 16

### Data Source

*I need a data source file of the students with loans who are still in college so I can send them a progress form to complete nearer the end of the year. Please create a data source file using this information. Create the file with the following fields: FirstName, LastName, AddressLine1, City, State, PostalCode.*

*After you have the data entered, sort alphabetically by last name, then first name. Save the file as 107 job16 data.*

*mh*

| | |
|---|---|
| Karley Bidwell<br>530 Simpson Howell Road<br>Elizabeth, PA 15037-1045 | Cole Wehner<br>3393 Long Hollow Road<br>Elizabeth, PA 15037-9823 |
| Kelsey Bidwell<br>530 Simpson Howell Road<br>Elizabeth, PA 15037-1045 | Juan Vasquez<br>225 Oberdick Drive<br>McKeesport, PA 15135-2956 |
| Matthew Wilkins<br>229 Firden Drive<br>Monongahela, PA 15063-4378 | Kyle Forsythe<br>188 Donna Drive<br>Elizabeth, PA 15037-3067 |
| Kate Collins<br>5724 Meade Street<br>Elizabeth, PA 15037-7601 | Justin Gozdach<br>847-15 West Newton Road<br>Elizabeth, PA 15037-4178 |
| Derek DiPerno<br>1120 E. Smithfield Street<br>McKeesport, PA 15135-8712 | Lorie Tanselli<br>922 Grant Street<br>Elizabeth, PA 15037-6390 |
| Connor DiPerno<br>1120 E. Smithfield Street<br>McKeesport, PA 15135-8712 | Harry Sutter<br>43 River Road<br>Buena Vista, PA 15018-4085 |
| Terry Steffen<br>264 Oak Lane<br>Monongahela, PA 15063-6543 | Kara Quatrini<br>670 Fallen Timber Road<br>Elizabeth, PA 15037-4680 |
| Michael Smart<br>312 Rock Run Road<br>Elizabeth, PA 15037-9876 | Ronald Reddick<br>175 Holt Road<br>Elizabeth, PA 15037-0246 |
| Louis Sredy<br>210 Grouse Drive<br>Elizabeth, PA 15037-3928 | Brandon Staley<br>207 Schaffer Avenue<br>Elizabeth, PA 15037-6713 |

New fields often need to be added to accommodate additional information. Once the field is added, the new information can be entered for each record. When information in an existing field becomes outdated or is simply no longer needed, the field can be deleted along with all the information in that field. Before deleting a field, careful consideration should be given to make sure that the information will not be needed in the future. It is simple to delete the information, but time-consuming to reenter information once deleted.

## Sort & Filter Group

Home/Sort & Filter/
Ascending or
Descending

A↓ Ascending
Z↓ Descending

Analysis of data can be done with tables, queries, and forms by using the features on the Sort & Filter group. Once data has been entered into a table or form or extracted by a query, the Sort & Filter group features can be used for data analysis.

The **Filter** feature can be used to limit which records are displayed in the table, form, or query. By using this feature, only the records that meet the specified criteria appear in the table for data analysis. For example, if a table contained employees located throughout the United States, by setting the criteria = "CA" only the employees from California would appear in the table.

The **Sort** feature can be used to sequence (order) records and forms. This feature allows sorts in ascending or descending order of words (alphabetically) or numbers (numerically). A sort can be done on one field or on multiple fields.

As the name implies, a multiple sort sorts the data more than once. The first is called the **primary sort**; the second is called the **secondary sort**. An example of this would be when it is desirable to have all records grouped by state in alphabetical order by city. The primary sort would group all the records by state. The secondary sort would arrange all the cities in the state alphabetically. See Figure 5-6.

| ID | Last Name | First Name | Middle | Street Address | State | City | ZIP |
|---|---|---|---|---|---|---|---|
| 4 | Zaida | Heidi | D. | 3718 Perkins Place, NW | AL | Huntsville | 35816 |
| 30 | Castilla | Steven | C. | 219 Syracuse Street | AL | Mobile | 36608 |
| 17 | Blackburn | Richard | M. | 5610 Cheekwood Lane | AL | Montgomery | 36116 |
| 38 | Donahue | Rochelle | L. | 1867 Montrose Avenue | FL | Daytona Beach | 32019 |
| 3 | Fernandez | Stella | J. | 2690 Palomino Circle | FL | Daytona Beach | 32019 |
| 32 | Cheney | Pierre | K. | 897 Clearlake Drive | FL | Daytona Beach | 32019 |
| 27 | Burchetta | Marcio | I. | 8912 Brickroad Court | FL | Fort Myers | 33905 |
| 12 | Stockton | William | H. | 750 Shamrock Drive | FL | Fort Myers | 33912 |

*Orlando Seminar - July 15-19*

**Figure 5-6** Primary sort by state and secondary sort by city applied to records

## Preview

In Unit 5 you will have the opportunity to work with data mining and record analysis of databases of several companies and organizations. Each database contains at least one table that will be used to complete the activities in this unit. The following table shows the companies you will be working with and the information the company has stored in its database.

| Company | Type of Information |
|---|---|
| Eastwick School of Dance | Student and billing information |
| Executive Development Seminars | Workshop registration information |
| Rockwell Technologies | Sales rep information |
| Software Professionals | Software inventory |

You, too, can participate in this worthwhile program by choosing one of the following:

- **I/we want to establish a named scholarship.** A named scholarship requires a minimum award of at least $1,000 for one or more years. Complete the form below and return this page to the address below. You will be contacted and given more information about establishing your scholarship.

- **I/we want to contribute to the CVEF General Scholarship fund.** Those contributing $100 or more will be listed as funders on a Central Valley Alumni Association scholarship. Complete the form below and return this page and your check made payable to CVEF Scholarship Program to the address below.

Name(s) of Donors: _____

Mailing Address: _____

_____

Email Address: _____ Phone: _____

*Thank you!!! Please return this page to:*

Ms. Marilyn Hardy
CVEF Assistant Director
801 Round Hill Road
Elizabeth, PA 15037-8000

*Since CVEF is a Section 501(c) organization, all contributions for scholarships are tax deductible to the extent allowed by law. Please consult with your tax attorney about your scholarship.*

3. Save the donation form in Web Page format as *107 job15 donation* and print a copy of it from your browser.
4. If needed, open *107 job15 scholarships* and insert a hyperlink from the word "link" in the second row to the *107 job15 donation* document you just completed. Save it with the same name.

# Data Mining and Analysis Using Queries

**OUTCOMES**
- Use the Query Design feature.
- Create queries to produce data sheets of record sets.
- Modify a query and analyze information extracted through queries.

## Business Documents
### 27A–32A

- Work with multiple database tables with specified information.
- Work with multiple database queries.

**Warmup**

Key each line twice daily.

| | | |
|---|---|---|
| alphabet | 1 | Jeff Pizarro saw very quickly how Jason had won the boxing match. |
| figures | 2 | Our team average went from .458 on April 17 to .296 on August 30. |
| speed | 3 | Nancy may go to the big social at the giant chapel on the island. |

**gwam** 1' | 1 | 2 | 3 | 4 | 5 | 6 | 7 | 8 | 9 | 10 | 11 | 12 | 13 |

## Digital Citizenship and Ethics

© AAresTT/ Shutterstock.com

**Digital Citizenship and Ethics** A **cyber predator** is someone who uses the Internet to hunt for victims whom they take advantage of in many ways—sexually, emotionally, psychologically, or financially. Cyber predators know how to manipulate kids. They create trust and friendship where none should exist.

Cyber predators are the dark side of social networking and other forms of online communication. They frequently log on to chat groups or game sites and pose as other kids. They try to gradually gain your trust and encourage you to talk about your problems. Even if you don't chat with strangers, personal information you post on sites such as Facebook can make you a target.

As a class, discuss the following.

**TEAMWORK**

1. Give examples of how to identify a cyber predator.
2. How can you avoid being the victim of a cyber predator?
3. What should you do if you receive a message that is suggestive, obscene, aggressive, or threatening?

## Presentation

*I prepared slides for my presentation at the upcoming financial aid meeting with CVHS parents and students. I need you to make the presentation attractive and easy to read. See the To Do List for more info. Save the file as 107 job 14 presentation.*

*mh*

### To Do List

1. Open **df 107 job 14 presentation** and insert this text on a new slide at the end:

   WHY SHOULD I TAKE A CVEF LOAN?

   - There is no interest charged while you are in college.
   - The interest rate is usually lower than student loans from other sources.

2. Apply an attractive design, appropriate transitions, and clip art (on a few slides) that is related to high school and/or loans.

## Job 15

### Web Pages

*The Board approved the Bennett scholarship, so we need to get it added to our Web site. We also need to post an updated form for those who want to establish a scholarship. See the To Do List for the copy and directions.*

*mh*

### To Do List

1. Insert the following copy into the **df 107 job 1 scholarships** file. It should be listed first in the group that targets all students. Format it as a Web page by adding an appropriate page color; font size, color, style, and so on; and borders. You may want to use colors that match or are similar to your school colors. Save the revised list as **107 job 15 scholarships** in Web Page format and preview it in your browser to make sure it will post correctly.

| The Dr. Frank R. Bennett Scholarship | $2,000 | Applicants should have a sustained record of academic excellence and participation in extra-curricular activities, community activities, and personal development and responsibility activities. |
|---|---|---|

2. Here's the copy for the donation form. Use 1.0 line spacing and 6 point after paragraphs and format it appropriately as a Web page that is similar to the scholarship Web page.

Participating in the CVEF Scholarship Program

During the first four years of CVEF's scholarship program, 502 applications were received for the 54 scholarships CVEF has administered and over $50,000 have been awarded to the recipients. We believe the number of applicants evidence the need to continue the scholarship program and increase the dollars awarded.

Create/Queries/Query
Design

## Activity 1

1. Read the following information about creating queries.

Queries are used for mining data that can be analyzed to answer questions. Queries can be used to extract (mine) information from a database table and display it in a data sheet that is a smaller table containing the record set (limited information) from the table.

2. Open the **df Rockwell Technologies** file. **Save as:** *Rockwell Technologies*.

3. Open the *Sales Reps – District 13* table of the *Rockwell Technologies* database. Study the fields in the database table. A lot of information is contained in the table such as the number of sales reps, the state where the sales reps work, how much each sales rep sold during July and August, and so on.

Questions such as "How many sales reps had sales of more than $50,000 in July?" or "How many sales reps are from Colorado?" can be answered by mining the information from this table. In order to mine or extract information and put it in a form that will quickly provide answers to questions such as these, queries are generated. A query is a question structured in a way that the software (database) can understand.

Study Figure 5-7 to see how queries can be used to extract information.

Query 1: The criteria for the *State* field was set to *=CO* to extract those reps from the state of Colorado.

Query 2: The criteria for the *ZIP* field was set to *<6* to extract only those reps with ZIP codes starting with 5.

Query 3: The criteria for the *July Sales* field was set to *>50000* to extract only those reps with sales of more than $50,000.

**Figure 5-7** Queries can be used to extract information

## Job 11

### List

*See the To Do List. Save the workbook as 107 job11 loans.*

*mh*

To Do List

Using the steps and criteria in the Delinquent Loan Payment policy you recently keyed, review each person's payment record in **107 job10 loans** to see if we need to take specific action to comply with the policy.

If you identify any needing action, record the policy step number in the Notes column for me. Also, prepare a list of the names of the individuals and the policy step that applies to them. Save the list as **107 job11 list** and email or give it to me.

## Job 12

### Letter

*Here's a draft of the letter I want to send to Ms. Simmons, who is at Step 5. Date the letter November 5, 2014. You can get her address from her account statement in one of the CVEF Loans workbooks. Send a copy of the letter to her mother, Mrs. Hazel Simmons, and her father, Mr. John Simmons. Identify them by name in the copy notation. Add Certified Mail as a mailing notation and supply all other needed letter parts. Use* **CVEF Assistant Director** *as my title. Save the file as 107 job12 letter.*

*mh*

To Do List

You have not been making payments on your Central Valley Education Foundation (CVEF) loan for an extended period of time. Please see the enclosed payment record.

It is imperative that you contact me immediately to discuss this matter. If we do not get a satisfactory resolution, CVEF will file a legal complaint in the local district court 15 days from the date of this letter. The complaint will be filed against you and your parents since they also signed the promissory notes. We will request that the court order you to pay the entire loan balance, legal fees, and court costs.

Please call me at 412-555-0337 so we can attempt to resolve this issue without needing to take legal action.

## Job 13

### Promissory Note

*Jim Howser is ready to sign for his loan. Using df 107 job13 note (a template file) and the info on the To Do List, prepare a promissory note that he and his parents can sign.*

*mh*

To Do List

Amount and Rate:  $2,000 at 5%

Date:  November 7, 2014

Student's name:  James H. Howser

Parents' names: John and Rita Howser

Expected graduation date:  December 2016

Save the note as **107 job13 note**; then add Jim and his loan info to the In College worksheet in **107 job11 loans**. Save the updated workbook as **107 job13 loans**.

The Queries feature is used to extract and display selected information from a table. The Criteria line at the bottom of the Query Design dialog box is where instructions are given to the software that tells it which information to display. The basic criteria expressions are:

A. equal to (=)

B. greater than (>)

C. less than (<)

In the following illustration, =CO was used to extract only those sales reps from Colorado. If the criteria had been =CO or AZ, the sales reps from both Colorado and Arizona would have been displayed.

## Activity 2

With the opened *Rockwell Technologies Sales Reps – District 13* table, create Query 1 by completing these steps:

1. Click the Create tab.

2. Click Query Design in the Queries group.

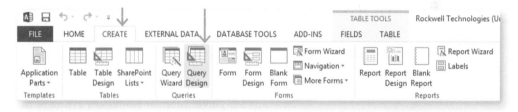

3. Highlight *Sales Reps – District 13*.

4. Click Add.

5. Close Show Table dialog box.

6. Click the down arrow in the first field.

## Job 9

### Table

We are having an unusually high number of borrowers not making payments as required. The Board of Directors approved the policy at the right at its last meeting. Please format it as a table and then print a copy, because we'll need it when we review each borrower's record. Apply an attractive style. Save the file as 107 job9 policy.

*mh*

### Policy for Handling CVEF Delinquent Loan Payments*

| Step | Situation | Initial Action | Subsequent Action |
|------|-----------|----------------|-------------------|
| 1 | At least 3 missed payments within most recent 6-month period | Send statement to borrower with note to make payments. | If not resolved, proceed to Step 2 when needed. |
| 2 | At least 6 missed payments within most recent 9-month period | Send letter to borrowers requesting they contact CVEF to seek resolution. | If not resolved, proceed to Step 3 when needed. |
| 3 | At least 10 missed payments within most recent 12-month period | Send certified letters to borrowers requesting full payment of delinquent amount to avoid legal proceedings. | If not resolved within 30 days, proceed to Step 4. |
| 4 | Satisfactory resolution at Step 3 not achieved | Send certified letter to borrowers notifying them that a legal complaint will be filed in 15 days if payment is not received within 10 days. | If not settled within 10 days, proceed to Step 5. |
| 5 | Satisfactory resolution at Step 4 not achieved | File legal complaint in appropriate court. | |

*This revised policy was approved by the CVEF Board of Directors in October 2014.

## Job 10

### Worksheet

Since we're now a few days into November, we need to bring each person's payment record up to date. I jotted down some steps on the To Do List. Save the file as 107 job10 loans.

*mh*

### To Do List

1. Using *107 job8 loans*, for each person who has not sent in his/her October payment in a timely manner, enter **0.00** as the October payment. Then update the other columns and key **No Pmt** in the Notes column.
2. Update the Remaining Balance in the Paying worksheet.
3. Print the Paying worksheet.

7. Highlight and click *Last Name.*

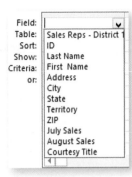

8. Click in the second field, and click the down arrow. Highlight and click *First Name.*

9. Click in the third field, and click the down arrow. Highlight and click *State.*

10. In the State column, click in the Criteria box and key **=CO**.

FILE    HO

View    Run

Results

11. On the File tab in the Results group, click Run.

12. To save the query, click the File tab, then click Save and key **CO Reps** as the name for the query; click OK. From Query 1, you quickly see that five sales reps are from Colorado.

### Activity 3

Now, using the same procedure used for Query 1, create and run Queries 2 and 3 to see if you get the same results as illustrated in the queries shown in Figure 5-7. **Save Query 2 as:** *ZIP Codes Starting with 5.* **Save Query 3 as:** *July Sales > 50,000.* If needed, review the steps in Activity 2 to complete the queries.

## 27C

### Apply: Create Queries

### Activity 1

1. Open *df Software Professionals* database. **Save as:** *Software Professionals.*

2. Open the *Software Professionals Inventory* table.

3. Use the Query Design feature to create queries to answer the questions shown in the following table.

4. Save each query using the name provided.

5. Close the database.

## Job 6

### Worksheet

*I need a worksheet showing the amount and percent of net worth increase from 2001 through 2014 using the info on the To Do List. Display the data in four columns, using the column titles shown below the numbers. Compute the **Increase** and the **% Inc**. I also need a line chart displaying the data. Use **CVEF Loan Program Net Worth** as the chart and table title. This worksheet will become part of the Financial section of the Bennett proposal that I'm drafting now. Save the file as 107 job6 net worth.*
*mh*

### To Do List

| Year | Net Worth | Year | Net Worth |
|------|-----------|------|-----------|
| 2000 | $152,339 | 2008 | $196,208 |
| 2001 | $154,306 | 2009 | $201,021 |
| 2002 | $157,512 | 2010 | $204,107 |
| 2003 | $162,060 | 2011 | $205,782 |
| 2004 | $163,409 | 2012 | $214,219 |
| 2005 | $169,818 | 2013 | $219,827 |
| 2006 | $182,261 | 2014 | $224,141 |
| 2007 | $192,773 | | |

| Year | Net Worth | Increase | % Inc |
|------|-----------|----------|-------|
| | | | |

## Job 7

### Report

*We're now ready to finish the Bennett proposal. See the To Do List. Save the file as 107 job7 bennett.*
*mh*

### To Do List

- Access the Bennett proposal you worked on earlier.
- Insert the text from **df 107 job7 insert** at the end of the report.
- Using **107 job6 net worth**, copy/paste the line chart into the Bennett proposal where indicated so it links to the chart in the worksheet.
- Copy/paste the worksheet in this same file into the Bennett proposal where indicated. Link it to the worksheet as well.
- Check the formatting of the report.
- Let me know when it is done so I can view it.

## Job 8

### Worksheet

*I was reviewing the data in the In College worksheet and noted that some students with more than one loan do not have a consolidated interest rate calculated. To do that, follow what I have on the To Do List. Save the file as 107 job8 loans.*
*mh*

### To Do List

1. Access the In College worksheet in **107 job5 loans**.
2. Bring the worksheet up to date by computing a consolidated rate (weighted average rate) for those students who have more than one loan but do not have a consolidated rate. Round all the rates to the nearest hundredths.
3. Print or email me a copy of the worksheet with the consolidated rates.

Software
Professionals

| SOFTWARE PROFESSIONALS | | | |
|---|---|---|---|
| No. | Query | Fields to Include | Criteria |
| 1 | What was the sales volume for each of the educational software packages? (Stock No. starting with E)<br><br>Save query as: *Educational Software* | Stock Number<br>Software<br>Sales | Like "E*" |
| 2 | What software sells for more than $150?<br><br>Save query as: *Sales Price > $150* | Stock Number<br>Software<br>Price | >150 |
| 3 | What software sold more than 1,500 units?<br><br>Save query as: *Sales > 1,500 Units* | Stock Number<br>Software<br>Sales | >1500 |
| 4 | What software sold less than 500 units?<br><br>Save query as: *Sales < 500 Units* | Stock Number<br>Software<br>Sales | <500 |

## Activity 2

1. Open *df Rockwell Technologies* database. **Save as:** *Rockwell Technologies*.

2. Open *Sales Reps – District 13* table.

3. Use the Query Design feature to create queries to answer the questions shown in the following table.

4. Save each query using the name provided.

5. Close the database.

| ROCKWELL TECHNOLOGIES | | | |
|---|---|---|---|
| No. | Query | Fields to Include | Criteria |
| 1 | What are the names and addresses of our sales reps working the Arizona territory?<br>Save query as: *Arizona Sales Reps* | First Name<br>Last Name<br>Address | "Arizona" |
| 2 | What are the names and addresses of our sales reps working the Montana and Wyoming territories?<br>Save query as: *Montana and Wyoming Sales Reps* | City<br>State<br>ZIP<br>Territory | "Montana" or "Wyoming" |
| 3 | Which sales reps had sales of more than $50,000 during August?<br>Save query as: *August Sales > $50,000* | First Name<br>Last Name<br>August Sales | >50000 |

**Data Analysis:** Why did Marshall Logan, who lives in Great Falls, Idaho, come up with the Montana and Wyoming Sales Reps query?

8. Verify that the Loan Balance in cell E21 is $2,730.16. If not, make the necessary corrections to the formulas.

9. Print the *Trial* worksheet and then delete it.

## Job 3

### Payment Function

*I've had an inquiry from a CVHS alumnus asking how much payments would be on a CVEF loan. Can you prepare a worksheet that answers his questions if the interest rate is 5%. Save the file as 107 job3 questions.*
*mh*

**Questions from Jack McDaniel**

What would my monthly payment be if I take out a 3-year $2,500 loan?

What would my monthly payment be if I take out a 2-year $2,000 loan?

## Job 4

### Report

*The CVEF Board of Directors is meeting in a few days. I need to prepare a proposal that money from the CVEF loan program be used to fund a scholarship. See the To Do List to find out what I need at this time. Save the file as 107 job4 bennett.*
*mh*

**To Do List**

Open **df 107 job4 bennett,** a draft I prepared. One of my colleagues proofed it and suggested changes. Please review her suggestions and then accept/reject them. Format the proposal as a report. I should have the Financial section done within a day or two and you can add it then. It will go at the end of the report.

## Job 5

### Worksheet

*I need you to record the October payments shown on the To Do List in each person's worksheet in 107 job2 loans. Print a copy of the updated Paying worksheet that shows the new balances and the Karenoski worksheet. Save the file as 107 job5 loans.*
*mh*

**To Do List**

| Borrower | Amount of Payment |
|----------|-------------------|
| Betters  | $238.83           |
| Pulman   | $146.25           |
| Karenoski | $1,409.72        |

Note: You need to know that it is CVEF's policy to charge no interest for a month in which payment in full is received. Also, add a note below the last payment noting that the loan is paid in full and then color the worksheet tab red so we will know to delete it later.

Update the Payingworksheet to show the balances after the October payments have been recorded and to show that Karenoski's loan is paid in full (see how the other paid-in-full loans are formatted).

**Learn: Modify a Query**

Home/View/
Design View

Software
Professionals

## Activity 1

1. Read the following information about modifying queries.

After running a query, additional questions may come up. Rather than create a new query, an existing query can be modified to answer additional questions. For example, Query 3 (*July Sales > 50000*) in 27B provided the number of sales reps who had more than $50,000 in sales during the month of July. However, it didn't show the sales territory where these sales reps made their sales. If that information were important to the manager of the sales reps, the query that had already been created could be modified to include the sales territory for each of these sales reps.

2. Open the *Rockwell Technologies* database.

3. Open the query *July Sales >50,000*.

4. Access Design View.

5. Click in the first empty field box to make the down arrow appear.

6. Click the down arrow and click *Territory*.

7. Click Run.

8. Save the query and close the database. The query now includes the territory of each of the seven sales reps that had sales of over $50,000.

## Activity 2

1. Read the following information about modifying queries.

When you want to keep the original query as well as the modified query, use the Copy and Paste functions. Copy a query by clicking on the query filename and using the Copy and Paste functions. After you click on the Paste function, a dialog box appears where you will name the copy.

2. Open the *Software Professionals* database.

3. Make a copy of the query named *Sales < 500 Units* by using the Copy and Paste feature. Click on the query named *Sales < 500 Units* in the left column under queries, and then click Copy, click Paste, and key **< 500 Units 0 Purchases** for the name of the copied file.

4. Click OK.

5. Open the newly created query, and go into Design View.

6. Modify the query so that it includes *Purchases*.

7. Run the query.

8. Modify the query again so that it includes only the software that sold less than 500 units and that had 0 purchases by setting the criteria at 0.

9. Save the query and close the database.

**OUTCOMES**

- Integrate your digital information management skills.
- Use creative thinking and analysis skills to solve problems, obtain information, and make correct decisions.

## Business Documents

- Scholarship Tables
- Payment Account Worksheets
- Monthly Payment Table
- Scholarship Proposal
- Account Balance Worksheets
- Net Worth Worksheet

- Line Chart
- Collection Letter
- Policy Statement
- Promissory Note
- Slide Show
- Web Page

---

## Job 1

### Table

*To learn more about the scholarship program you will be working with, follow the directions that I have used for other new employees on the To Do List. It will also give me useful information about you. Save the file as 107 job1 scholarships.*
*mh*

### To Do List

**Scholarship Program Orientation**

1. Open **df 107 job1 scholarships**.
2. Review the criteria for all the scholarships in Web Layout view and select three to five scholarships for which you could apply. Create a table that shows the name, amount, and criteria for each of them. You can copy this information from the scholarship matrix if you want.
3. Add a column at the right and include a few reasons why you believe you meet the criteria for the scholarships you selected.

---

## Job 2

### Worksheet

*To learn more about the loan program and the records we keep, follow the directions on the To Do List. Save the file as 107 job2 loans.*
*mh*

### To Do List

**Loan Program Orientation**

1. Open **df 107 job2 loans**. Let me stress that the information in this workbook and other information you will work with regarding the loan program must be kept confidential—it must not be discussed or shared with others who are not involved in administering the CVEF loan program.
2. Review the *In College* worksheet to see information about the CVHS alumni who have loans but are not yet repaying them because they have not yet been graduated from college.
3. Review the *Paying* worksheet to see summary information about the alumni who have graduated from college and are paying back their loans.
4. Review the other worksheets to see specific information on each borrower. Pay particular attention to the values and cell references used for the Payment (PMT) function in cell H5 and the formulas used to calculate the Interest in column C, the Principal Reduction in column D, and the Loan Balance in column E.
5. Insert a new worksheet and rename it **Trial**.
6. Copy the cell range A1:J21 from the *Forde* worksheet to the *Trial* worksheet.
7. Change the borrower's name to your name, the interest rate in cell H3 to **5%**, the Principal in cell C5 to **$3,000**, the Beginning Balance in cell E18 to **$3,000**, the Payment amounts in cell B19 to the value in cell H5, cell B20 to **$100**, and cell B21 to **$150**.

## Activity 3

1. Open the *Rockwell Technologies* database.
2. Make a copy of the July Sales > 50,000 query, and name it **July and August Sales > 50,000**.
3. Open *July and August Sales > 50,000*.
4. Activate Design View and add August sales with a criteria of >50000.
5. Run the query and close the database.

**Data Analysis:** What would have happened if you had keyed **5000** rather than **50000** in the criteria for August Sales?

## 27E

## Apply: Data Analysis

1. Open **df 27E Data Analysis Form** (*Word* file) to record your answers for the following activities.
2. **Save as: 27E Data Analysis Form.**
3. Complete the following activities and record the answers in the file.
4. Save and close the file.

### Activity 1

Open the *July Sales > 50000* query in the *Rockwell Technologies* database, and analyze the extracted data to answer the following questions.

1. How many sales reps had greater than $50,000 in sales during July?
2. What percentage of the sales reps in the territory had greater than $50,000 in sales during July? Round your answer to one decimal place. (Use the Calculator feature.)
3. What territory had the greatest number of sales reps with sales greater than $50,000 in July?

**★TIP** Activate the calculator by clicking the Start icon and then clicking the Calculator icon.

### Activity 2

Open the *Executive Development Seminars* database. Run queries to determine the number of registrants for each seminar to complete the *27E Data Analysis Form* tables. Those who registered for all four seminars should be included in the count of each. Use the Calculator to calculate the *Total Attending and the Percent of Registrants Attending.*

| Denver | Seminar Participants | All Four Seminars | Total Attending | Percent of Registrants Attending |
|---|---|---|---|---|
| Speak Like a Pro | | | | |
| Write Like a Pro | | | | |
| Dress Like a Pro | | | | |
| Dine Like a Pro | | | | |

After you complete the tables for Denver and Orlando, combine them into the third table to show the totals for the two locations combined. Answer the questions on the *27E Data Analysis Form* using the information from the tables you complete.

| | |
|---|---|
| **General** | Additionally, Ms. Hardy has provided the following guidelines for you. |
| | 1. You are to follow all directions that are given. |
| | 2. If a formatting guide or direction is not given, use what you have learned in your digital information management course at CVHS to prepare the documents. |
| | 3. Always be alert to and correct errors in punctuation, capitalization, spelling, and word usage. |
| **Correspondence** | Prepare all letters in modified block format with mixed punctuation and no ¶ indentations. Supply an appropriate salutation and complimentary close and use your reference initials and other letter parts as needed. |
| **Reports** | Use the unbound report format with footnotes to prepare reports. Unless directed otherwise, apply an appropriate style set. Number all pages except page 1. |
| **Tables and Charts** | Unless directed otherwise, you can determine whether spreadsheet or word processing software should be used to prepare tables. Be sure to format and identify the various parts of these documents so the reader can easily read and interpret the data you present. Print the loan worksheets on one sheet of paper unless directed otherwise. |
| **Data Source Files** | Ms. Hardy will determine the fields that are to be included in the data source file. |
| **Other Documents** | You should apply what you have learned and use your creativity to prepare other documents if specific instructions are not provided. |
| **Filenames** | Since Ms. Hardy will need to access the files you create, she will provide filenames for you to use; however, you should add your initials at the end of each filename. The filenames (including worksheet and workbook names) will be referenced in her notes to you. |

OUTCOMES

- Create computed fields using the Expression Builder.
- Create computed fields and analyze information extracted through queries with computed fields.

**Business Document**

**28B**

- Multiple database tables with computed fields.

**Learn: Expression Builder**

Design View/Query Setup/ Builder

1. Read the following information about the Expression Builder.

The **Expression Builder** in the Query feature can be used to perform calculations on existing fields in a database. In Figure 5-8, *Total Sales* were calculated for each Rockwell Technologies sales representative.

| Last Name ▾ | First Name ▾ | July Sales ▾ | August Sale: ▾ | Total Sales ▾ |
|---|---|---|---|---|
| Carter-Bond | Mary | $45,351.00 | $37,951.00 | $83,302.00 |
| Hull | Dale | $53,739.00 | $49,762.00 | $103,501.00 |
| McRae | Jessica | $33,371.00 | $38,978.00 | $72,349.00 |

**Figure 5-8** Calculated field in a query

2. Open the *Rockwell Technologies* database that was used in Lesson 27.
3. Create a query from the *Sales Reps – District 13* table of the *Rockwell Technologies* database using Query Design to include the following fields:

- Last Name
- First Name
- July Sales
- August Sales

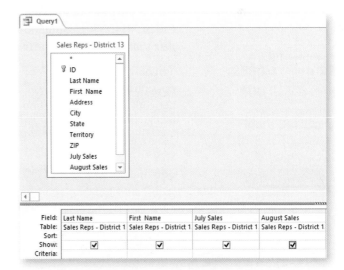

4. While still in Query Design, place the cursor in the column to the right of *August Sales* and click Builder in the Query Setup group on the File tab. This opens the Expression Builder and places the cursor in the Expression Builder dialog box.

**Work Assignment
at Central Valley
Education Foundation**

Read the following information to familiarize yourself with your work assignment with the Central Valley Education Foundation.

This unit is designed to give you experiences you likely would have working in an administrative assistant position.

Assume you are a student at Central Valley High School (CVHS) who is completing the first half of a 20-hour service learning requirement. You have been assigned to the Central Valley Education Foundation (CVEF), a group that strives to ensure that all children in Central Valley School District start school ready to learn and graduate from high school prepared for lifelong learning, careers, and citizenship.

CVEF is led by a director and several full-time staff members. You will be working with Marilyn Hardy, Assistant Director, who is responsible for administering a scholarship program and a student loan program for CVHS graduates.

Ms. Hardy, a graduate of CVHS, has been with CVEF since its inception in 2005 and has been directing the scholarship program since it was started in 2010 and the student loan program since it was transferred from the Central Valley Student Aid Fund, a separate association, to CVEF in 2007.

For the purposes of this simulation, assume you are completing your service learning during the Fall of 2014. This assumption is necessary because many of the documents and transactions are date specific, requiring the use of past, current, and future dates.

You have met with the CVEF director and your supervisor, Ms. Hardy, to learn about CVEF's mission and activities as well as such things as your work hours, work station, access to the network and communication devices, and so on. To orient you further, your first assignments will be to review a few existing documents to learn more about the scholarship and student loan programs.

5. With the cursor in the Expression Builder dialog box, key **Total Sales: [July Sales] +
[August Sales]**. Click OK.

View  Run

Results

6. Click Run on the Results group. Notice that the resulting table now includes a column
labeled *Total Sales*.
7. **Save query as: *Total Sales*.**

**Apply: Creating
Computed Fields**

### Activity 1

1. Open the *Software Professionals* database.
2. Create a query with the five fields shown in the following table.
3. Use the Expression Builder to create a formula to calculate the Ending Inventory.
4. **Save query as: *Ending Inventory*.**

Software
Professionals

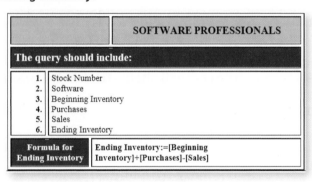

| | SOFTWARE PROFESSIONALS |
|---|---|
| **The query should include:** | |
| 1. | Stock Number |
| 2. | Software |
| 3. | Beginning Inventory |
| 4. | Purchases |
| 5. | Sales |
| 6. | Ending Inventory |
| **Formula for Ending Inventory** | Ending Inventory:=[Beginning Inventory]+[Purchases]-[Sales] |

## 21st Century Skills: Use and Manage Information

As discussed in this unit, databases are an effective tool for organizing and managing large
amounts of information. Businesses use databases to store information about customers,
employees, sales, inventories, and more. But how is all this information obtained? Most
of it is provided voluntarily. For example, individuals provide information when they file
a tax return, apply for a credit card, enroll at a school or college, apply for a driver's license,
fill out a job application, or answer a survey.

### Think Critically

1. Most organizations obtain and use database information for legitimate business
reasons. Provide examples of how a business might use customer purchasing
information to increase sales.
2. What dangers or risks are involved with supplying information about yourself that
will be stored in an electronic database?
3. If you created a database of friends, family, and other contacts, what type of
information would you store on each person? Is there any information you
think would be inappropriate to share with others?

Key two 3' or 5' writings on the three ¶s; determine *gwam*; count errors.

 all letters used

| | gwam | 3' | 5' |
|---|---|---|---|

By definition, your image is how you are perceived by other    4   2

people.  Therefore, if you never came in contact with others, you    8   5

would not have to be concerned with your image.  There is little    13   8

doubt that the positive image you express is crucial in helping    17   10

to reach wanted goals.  By the same token, the better your image    21   13

is, the more willing others will be to cooperate favorably with    26   15

you.  There are many factors that help you to develop your image.    30   18

Two of them are verbal and nonverbal communication.    33   20

You are building your image every time you speak or write    37   22

to other people.  Your ability to talk with fellow workers and    42   25

others will help to further your career.  Also, being able to    46   27

write well can move you from a retail clerk to a position as a    50   30

retail manager.  Your writing and your speaking will be analyzed    54   33

regularly by many superiors.  Your nonverbal body language, too,    59   35

must be consistent with how you speak, write, and look.  All these    63   38

things help determine how your message is received.    66   40

The initial step in building a successful image is to deter-    70   42

mine what your current image is.  You must develop an accurate    75   45

portrait of yourself as others see you.  This is not an easy task    79   47

since even a few people may not concur on precisely what your    83   50

image is.  It is important to request and accept feedback from    87   52

close friends and others as to their perceptions of you.  Also,    92   55

be consistent in your actions and be yourself; phonies can be    96   57

spotted.  Your goal is to project a winning business image.    100   60

gwam 3'    1    2    3    4
5'    1    2    3

**Creating Forms for Data Analysis**

- Create forms using the Form feature, the More Forms feature, and the Form Wizard feature.
- Summarize, format, view, and print data in forms.

## Business Document
### 29B

- Multiple database forms created with Forms group features.

**Learn: Creating Forms**

Create/Forms/

The Forms group on the Create tab can be used to quickly create forms. Forms are another method used for entering and viewing information in a database. When using the Form feature, several options are available. The easiest forms to create are those created by using the Form tool, the Form Wizard, and the More Forms tool.

### Form Feature

Create/Forms/Form

The Form feature can be used to automatically create a form that includes all the fields that have been created for a database table, as shown in Figure 5-9. Information for one record at a time can be entered or edited in a form that was created by using the Form feature.

**Figure 5-9** A form enables users to view or enter information

# SKILL BUILDER 3

- Improve keying techniques.
- Improve keying speed and accuracy.

## Warmup

Key each line twice, first for control and then for speed.

alphabet   1   Both weary girls were just amazed by the five quick extra points.

fig/sym   2   JR & Sons used P.O. #7082-B35 to order 154 chairs (Style LE-196).

speed   3   The antique bowl she saw at the downtown mall is authentic ivory.

**gwam** 1' | 1 | 2 | 3 | 4 | 5 | 6 | 7 | 8 | 9 | 10 | 11 | 12 | 13 |

## Technique: Letter Keys

**Technique Cue**
Limit keystroking action to the fingers; keep hands and arms motionless.

Key each line twice. Emphasize continuity and rhythm with curved, upright fingers.

R   1   Raindrops bore down upon three robbers during the February storm.

S   2   The Mets, Astros, Reds, Twins, Jays, and Cubs sold season passes.

T   3   Trent bought the teal teakettle on the stove in downtown Seattle.

U   4   Ursula usually rushes to the music museum on Tuesday, not Sunday.

V   5   Vivacious Eve viewed seven vivid violets in the vases in the van.

W   6   We swore we would work with the two wonderful kids for two weeks.

X   7   Rex Baxter explained the extra excise tax to excited expatriates.

Y   8   Yes, Ky is very busy trying to justify buying the yellow bicycle.

Z   9   Dazed, Zelda zigzagged to a plaza by the zoo to see a lazy zebra.

**gwam** 1' | 1 | 2 | 3 | 4 | 5 | 6 | 7 | 8 | 9 | 10 | 11 | 12 | 13 |

## Technique: Number Keys/Tab

**Technique Cue**
Eyes on copy.

1. Set tabs at 2" and 4".
2. Key the following copy. Concentrate on the location of the number keys; quick tab spacing; eyes on copy.

| | | |
|---|---|---|
| 703 Sandburg Trl. | 65 Yates Ave. | 656 Winter Dr. |
| 5214 Chopin St. | 423 Clement St. | 187 Ocean Ave. |
| 3769 Orchard Rd. | 641 Boone Ct. | 410 Choctaw St. |
| 158 Hartford St. | 901 Cassia Dr. | 792 Fairview Dr. |

## More Forms Feature

The More Forms feature can be used to create variations of the form created by the Form feature. Two commonly used forms included in this feature are the Multiple Items form and the Split form.

Create/Forms/More
Forms/Multiple Items

**Multiple Items.** As illustrated in Figure 5-10, the Multiple Items form displays multiple records at once. Notice how the records in the form are formatted and spaced in a way that makes it much easier to focus on one record than it is to focus on one record when the record is displayed in a database table.

**Figure 5-10** The Multiple Items form displays several records at the same time

**Split Form.** The Split form, shown in Figure 5-11, includes both the form and the data sheet. The form appears at the top of the screen, the data sheet at the bottom. Notice how the record selected from the data sheet appears in the form at the top of the screen. This makes it easy to select a record from the data sheet to view and edit.

**Figure 5-11** The Split form displays the form and the data sheet at the same time

## Form Wizard

Using the Wizard makes it easy to create well-designed forms. The Wizard, unlike the form features that have already been presented, allows only selected fields to appear in the form or all the fields in a database table to be included in the form.

The following forms were created using the Form Wizard. The first form includes all the fields in the *Software Professionals Inventory* table formatted in Columnar layout. Notice that this form allows viewing of one record at a time on the screen.

The second form was created from the *Ending Inventory* query created in Lesson 28C; it includes only the *Stock Number, Software*, and *Ending Inventory* fields. This form is also formatted in Columnar layout and allows the viewing of one record at a time.

The third form shows the same fields as the second, but is formatted in Tabular layout, which allows multiple records to be viewed on the screen at the same time.

# The Winning Edge

© littleny/Shutterstock.com

Complete this activity to help prepare for the **Integrated Office Applications** event in BPA's Administrative Support division. Participants in this event demonstrate advanced skills in the use and integration of word processing, spreadsheet, database, and presentation software.

You have volunteered to organize a rummage sale in your community, with the proceeds going to a local charity. You will use different software applications to develop and create the documents needed to organize the event.

1. In a new word processing document, create an outline of the tasks you will need to complete in order to hold the event. This should include contacting community officials and potential participants; securing a site for the sale along with tables, chairs, and signage; publicity; and logistics, such as parking, rest room facilities, security, and trash pickup.

2. Create a new database file that contains a table with the names, addresses, phone numbers, and email addresses of at least 30 people you will contact to participate in the event. This should include those who will sell items in the event as well as people who will help you organize, such as a community official, the police department, and the owner or manager of the location where you will hold the event. Make sure your table includes a field to distinguish between participants and organizers. Create a form to enter the records.

3. In a new spreadsheet, create a list of expenses for the event. You will need to estimate costs for renting a site, printing and postage for flyers, trash pickup, and so on. Create a pie chart that shows the estimated cost of each expense category.

4. Create a new presentation file based on the outline you created in step 1. Create a slide on which to insert the expenses pie chart from the worksheet you created in step 3. Position the slide at a logical point in the slideshow. You will show the presentation to those whose approval you need to hold the event.

5. In a new word processing document, create a one-page flyer announcing the sale. Use the database table you created in step 2 to generate mailing labels for the flyer. For detailed information on this event, go to www.bpa.org.

**Think Critically**

1. The ability to integrate files that originated in different software applications has many benefits. Describe at least two examples.

2. What types of files do you generate in school or at home that integrate various software applications?

## School and Community
Does your school district or community have an outside space that could use a green thumb's touch? Planting a community garden has many benefits:

- It beautifies the environment and raises awareness about our natural resources.
- It provides plant samples and produce that can be used to educate as well as to provide nutrition.
- It brings people of all ages and backgrounds together to work cooperatively and make improvements to the community.

Develop a plan to plant a community garden:

1. Discuss the idea with community or school district leaders and get the necessary approvals.
2. Ask local businesses to donate gardening supplies.
3. Design the garden layout.
4. Plant and maintain the garden.

## Activity 1

1. Open the *Software Professionals* database; open the *Software Professionals Inventory* table.
2. Create the following form using the Form Wizard.
3. Use Columnar layout.
4. Title: **Software Professionals Inventory**.
5. **Save form as:** *Software Professionals Inventory*.

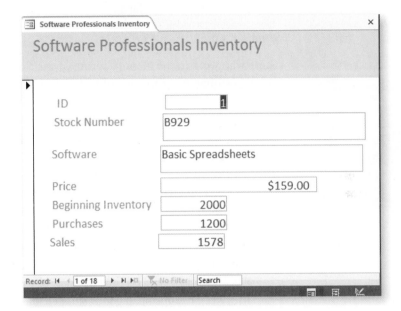

## Activity 2

1. Open the *Software Professionals* database; open the *Ending Inventory* query.
2. Create the following form using the Form Wizard.
3. Use Columnar layout.
4. Title: **Ending Inventory**.
5. **Save form as:** *Ending Inventory*.

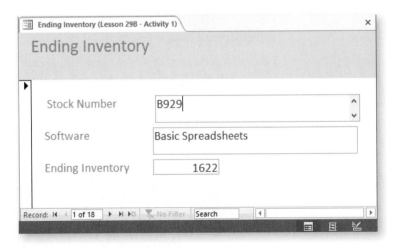

# Career Clusters

## Planning a Career in Manufacturing

Take a quick look around at the many products you use, the foods you eat, and the clothes you wear. Chances are that most, if not all, of them were developed, built, processed, or shipped through a manufacturing facility.

### What's It Like?

Those who work in the Manufacturing career cluster are responsible for planning, managing, and performing the processing of materials into intermediate or final products. They also work in related professional and technical support activities such as production planning and control, maintenance and manufacturing/process engineering. For example:

- They prepare and operate the machines that produce parts for most of the consumer products in use today.
- They use the principles and theories of science, engineering, and mathematics to solve technical problems, conduct tests, and collect data.
- They monitor or audit quality standards for virtually all manufactured products, including foods, textiles, glassware, motor vehicles, electronic components, computers, and structural steel.
- They manage the entire life cycle of a product, including acquisition, distribution, internal allocation, delivery, and final disposal of resources.
- They keep records of all goods shipped and received.
- They develop programs and policies to help prevent harm to workers, property, the environment, and the general public.

Employees in this field work in various types of environments. Some work 40-hour weeks in offices or labs. Others spend much of their workday on their feet and may do bending and lifting. Shift work is also common in this cluster.

### Employment Outlook

Generally, employment in this career cluster is expected to decline as manufacturers implement labor-saving machinery and technologies. Some sectors, such as logistics and safety assurance, will experience moderate growth.

Education requirements for workers in this cluster vary. Some production and maintenance jobs require a high school diploma and on-the-job training, while others require a two-year or bachelor's degree.

### What About You?

This career cluster is covered in box 13 of the Interest Survey Activity you completed in Unit 1 of this text. If this box had one of the three highest scores on your survey, you should further explore the cluster's pathways and related occupations.

1. Why do you think a career in this field could be a good choice?
2. What skills can you develop now that would be helpful to a career in this field?
3. Why are these jobs important to our country's economy?

## Activity 3

1. Open the *Software Professionals* database; open the *Ending Inventory* query.
2. Create the following form using the Form Wizard.
3. Use Tabular layout.
4. Title: **Ending Inventory 1**.
5. Print a copy of the form.
6. **Save form as:** *Ending Inventory 1*.

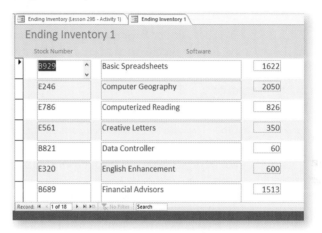

## Activity 4

1. Open the *Rockwell Technologies* database.
2. Using the *Sales Reps – District 13* table, create a form using the Form Wizard with the information requested in the Form Specifications.

> **★TIP** To expand column width, click View/ Layout View. Click the column where you want to change the width. Then click and drag the right side of the box to the desired width.

| Rockwell Technologies | Form Specifications | |
|---|---|---|
| | **Format** | **Fields** |
| | **Layout:** Tabular<br>**Title:  Rockwell Sales for July and August**<br>**Sort:**  Ascending by Last Name<br>Save form as:  *Rockwell Sales for July and August* | Last Name<br>First Name<br>July Sales<br>August Sales |

## Activity 5

1. Open the *Rockwell Technologies* database.
2. Using the *Total Sales* query, create a Split Form using the More Forms feature with the information requested in the Form Specifications.

| Rockwell Technologies | Form Specifications | |
|---|---|---|
| | **Format** | **Fields** |
| | **Title:  Total Sales**<br>**Sort:**  Ascending by Last Name<br>Save form as:  *Rockwell Total Sales* | Last Name<br>First Name<br>July Sales<br>August Sales<br>Total Sales |

# Academic and Career Connections

Complete the following exercises that introduce various topics that involve academic themes and careers.

## Grammar and Writing: Pronoun Case

**MicroType 6**

• References/Communication Skills/Pronoun Case

1. Go to *MicroType 6* and use this feature path: References/Communication Pronoun Case.
2. Click *Rules* and review the rules for pronoun case.
3. Then, under *Proofreading*, click *Posttest*.
4. Follow the instructions to complete the posttest.

## Communications: Reading

Open the ***df u18 communications*** file. Carefully read the article on Lynn Industries. When you have finished reading, close the file. Open a new word processing document and key answers in complete sentences to the following questions. Save the document as ***u18 communications***.

1. How much money did Lynn Industries award this year?
2. How much of an increase did this represent over the previous year?
3. How much has Lynn Industries donated to local nonprofits since 2004?
4. To what type of charitable organizations does Lynn Industries donate the funds it raises?
5. How does Lynn Industries raise the money it donates?
6. What is the "Chip In" campaign that Lynn Industries started this year?
7. Name and describe one of the nonprofit organizations that received a donation from Lynn Industries.
8. In one sentence, describe Lynn Industries and its line of business.

## Science

Lauren is an engineer for a newly started technology company. The president of the firm has asked her to gather information on product patents. A **patent** for an invention grants the inventor the right to exclude others from making, using, offering for sale, or selling the invention in the United States or importing the invention into the United States. A patent is issued by the United States Patent and Trademark Office (USPTO).

1. Use the Internet, library, and other sources to research the issuance of patents in the United States. Gather information on what can be patented, the conditions for obtaining a patent, the requirements to apply for a patent, how patents are enforced, and how long a patent lasts.
2. In a new word processing document, prepare a report of at least one page that summarizes your findings.
3. In a new database file, create a table that lists information about the top organizations receiving U.S. patents. Search the Web for information. List the name and location of the organization and one to two of their patented inventions. Your table should include the names of at least five organizations.

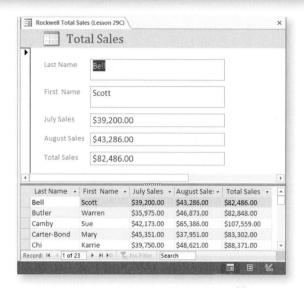

# LESSON 30

## Creating Reports for Data Analysis

**OUTCOMES**

- Summarize, format, and print data in reports for analysis using the Report feature.
- Create business reports using the *Report Wizard* feature.

**Business Document**

- Multiple database reports created with Reports group features.

**30B**

**Learn: Creating Reports**

Create/Reports/
Report Wizard

The Report features of the database are used for summarizing, formatting, and printing selected data from the database.

**Summarizing:** Generally, only a portion of the data contained in a database is needed for a particular application. The Summarizing feature allows selection of specific data for inclusion in the report.

**Formatting:** Formatting can be accomplished automatically using the Report feature in the Forms group on the Create tab; customized reports can be created using the Form Wizard feature and the Form Design feature.

**Printing:** Once the data has been specified and formatted, professional-looking hard copies can be printed and distributed for information and decision-making purposes. Today, electronic distribution of reports is also quite common.

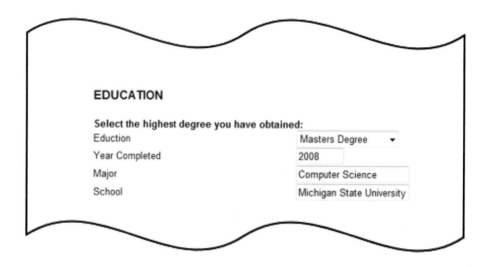

**EDUCATION**

**Select the highest degree you have obtained:**

| Eduction | Masters Degree ▾ |
| Year Completed | 2008 |
| Major | Computer Science |
| School | Michigan State University |

6. Save the database as *Corporate View*.
7. Mr. McMillan has now moved to Corporate View headquarters in Boulder and started work last week. Send him an email (gwmcmill@corporateview.com) requesting the rest of the information you will need to complete his database record.
8. Print a copy of the email to give to your instructor.

© Monkey Business Images/
Shutterstock.com

## Digital Citizenship and Ethics
An addiction is a physiological or psychological dependence on something that is harmful. You have likely heard of serious addictions, and perhaps even heard others joke about being addicted to something not so serious, like chocolate or car racing.

But Internet addiction, or psychological dependence on the online experience, is on the rise, and health experts are warning users about the long-lasting physical and psychological problems it can cause. Signs of Internet addiction include the following:

- Preoccupation with the Internet; for example, thinking about previous online activity or being anxious for the next online activity.
- Feeling the need to use the Internet more and more frequently.
- Staying online longer than intended.
- Trying to conceal use of the Internet.
- Feeling agitated, restless, and irritable when trying to cut back on Internet usage.

As a class, discuss the following:

1. What physical and psychological problems can Internet addiction lead to?
2. What can you do to avoid becoming an Internet addict?

*Software Professionals*

## Report Illustration 1

Report Illustration 1, shown in Figure 5-12, was created with the Report Wizard using the *Ending Inventory* query of the *Software Professionals* database. The report was formatted in Tabular layout with Portrait orientation and sorted in Ascending order by Ending Inventory. Column headings and columns were adjusted by using the Layout View in the Views group.

### Ending Inventory (Report Illustration 1)

| Ending Inventory | Stock Number | Software |
|---|---|---|
| 60 | B821 | Data Controller |
| 325 | B833 | Office Layout |
| 350 | E561 | Creative Letters |
| 463 | B586 | Graphic Designer |
| 600 | E320 | English Enhancement |
| 826 | E786 | Computerized Reading |
| 827 | B839 | Art Gallery |
| 1241 | B615 | Language Skills |
| 1513 | B689 | Financial Advisors |
| 1622 | B929 | Basic Spreadsheets |
| 1700 | E641 | Spelling Mastery |
| 1961 | E910 | Math Tutor |
| 2050 | E246 | Computer Geography |
| 2121 | B794 | Your Time Manager |
| 2122 | B731 | Quick Key WP |
| 2247 | E758 | Keyboard Composition |
| 4020 | B952 | Tax Assistant |
| 4127 | B658 | Telephone Directory |

**Figure 5-12** Report Illustration 1 was created with the Report Wizard

## Report Illustration 2

Report Illustration 2, shown in Figure 5-13, was also created using the Report Wizard feature. The report is in Portrait orientation with Justified layout. The report is sorted in Descending order by Ending Inventory. Only the first two entries of the report are shown.

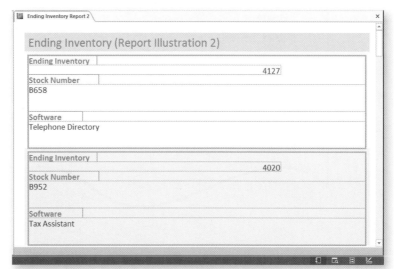

**Figure 5-13**
Report Illustration 2 has a different format, but it was also created with the Report Wizard

# CORPORATE *View*

## An Integrated Intranet Application

As part of your internship with Corporate View, you have the opportunity to work in several departments within the organization to see the overall operations. Your current assignment is with Human Resources and Management. Because of your expertise with *Access*, the HR Director would like you to create a database containing most of the information from the Employment Application Form. If an applicant is hired, the information from the application will be input into the Corporate View employee database. Of course the employee will need to provide current address and phone information once they relocate to Boulder. The Director has provided you with the following instructions. Complete each step before going on to the next step.

1. Go to our company website at www.cengage.com/school/keyboarding/dim/cview.
2. Find the Employment Application Form for Corporate View. Create a *Corporate View* database with a table called *Current Employees*. Include all of the fields shown on the application form in the table except for *Address Cont.* and *Web Page URL*.
3. Replace the field labeled *Email* with *Company Email*.
4. At this time only include information about the highest degree in the database. Information about the second degree can be added at a later date if needed.
5. After creating the database, enter the information from the partial Application Form shown below.

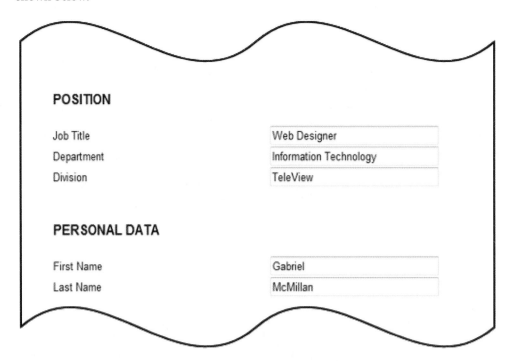

## Report Illustration 3

The report shown in Figure 5-14 is in Portrait orientation with Columnar layout. The report is sorted in Ascending order by Ending Inventory. Only the first four entries of the report are shown.

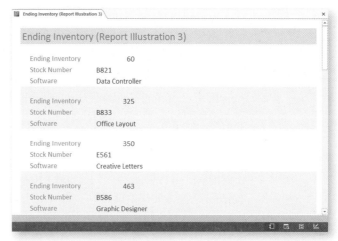

**Figure 5-14** Report Illustration 3 presents the same information in a different format

## Activity 1

1. Open the *Ending Inventory* query of the *Software Professionals* database.
2. Click the Create tab; click the Report Wizard in the Reports group.

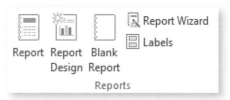

3. Highlight *Stock Number* by clicking it; move it from the box on the left to the box on the right by clicking the > button.

*Software Professionals*

## 106F

**Use Total Feature**

Use the ∑ Totals feature to calculate the following for District 14 sales reps; record your answers on the *df 106F Form:*

- Average District Sales for July.
- Average District Sales for August.
- Average District Sales for September.
- Average District Total Sales for Quarter.

*Save as:* **106F Analysis Form.**

## 106G

**Create Mailing Labels**

Prepare a set of mailing labels similar to the ones shown below for District 14 sales reps. Use Avery 5160 labels. Print the labels.

*Save as:* **106G Labels.**

| | | |
|---|---|---|
| Mr. Justin Hughes | Ms. Rose Winters | Mr. Chad Chambers |
| 313 Glenwood Drive | 1472 Prescott Street | 2317 Silver Dollar Avenue |
| Vancouver, WA 98662-1148 | Portland, OR 97217-8755 | Las Vegas, NV 89102-9964 |
| | | |
| Mrs. Harriet Hanson | Mrs. Mai Yang | Mr. Albert Zimmer |
| 1890 Rancho Verde Drive | 2187 Klamath Street | 330 Van Ness Avenue |
| Reno, NV 89511-2221 | Salem, OR 97306-9031 | Los Angeles, CA 90020-3341 |

## 106H

**Create a Form Letter**

Prepare a mail merge letter from the information below for *Rockwell Technologies – District 14* sales reps with September sales greater than $70,000. Use Courier New 12-point font and a 2½" top margin for the merge letter. You will need to create a query to determine those sales reps with sales greater than $70,000. Be sure to include all the fields in the query that you will need to complete the mail merge. Print a copy of the letter to Greg Stockton.

Date the letter **September 16, 20--**

The letter is from **Leslie R. Fenwick, President**

*Save as:* **106H Form Letter.**

«Title»«First_Name»«Last_Name»
«Address»
«City», «State»«ZIP»

Dear «Title»«Last_Name»:

Congratulations! The sales report I received from your district manager lists your name as one of the six sales representatives in District 14 with sales over $70,000 for the month of September.

September was a very good month for District 14 sales representatives. They averaged just over $60,800 of sales during September. This was an increase of approximately 8.38 percent over August sales. This increase is due in large part to your efforts during the month.

We appreciate your hard work to make this the best year ever at Rockwell Technologies.

Sincerely,

4. Highlight *Software* and move it to the box on the left by clicking the > button.
5. Highlight *Ending Inventory* and move it to the box on the left by clicking the > button.
6. Click Next.
7. Click Next again since you do not want to add any grouping levels.
8. Click the down arrow next to *Ascending*; highlight and click *Ending Inventory*.

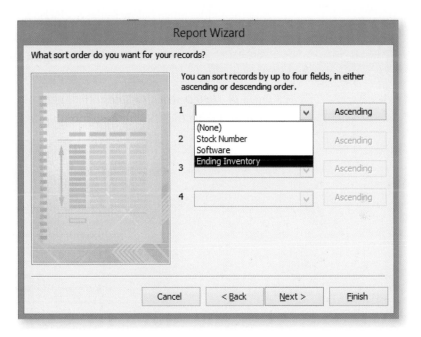

9. Click Next.
10. Select Tabular Layout and Landscape Orientation; click Next.
11. Key **Ending Inventory** in the dialog box for the report name if needed; click Finish.
12. Click Close Print Preview.

*Note:* The placement of the column headings can be adjusted by clicking Layout View in the Views group on the Home tab and then clicking one of the column headings. A gold box appears around the column heading when you click on it. Move the box to the right or left by pressing the right or left arrow keys on the keyboard.

If the box is too small for all the lettering of the heading to appear, click the heading and move the cursor to the right or left edge of the box to make the double arrow appear. When the double arrow appears, click and drag the edge of the box to expand or decrease the size of the box. The columns can be moved by clicking on one of the entries in the column to make gold boxes appear around all column entries. Once the gold boxes appear, use the arrow keys or click and drag the edges of the box to move the column entries.

**Editing Records**

Make the following changes to the records in the *Rockwell Technologies – District 14* table.

1. Change *Winters'* address to **1472 Prescott Street**.
2. Change the ZIP Code for *Culver* to **97301-8824**.
3. Change *Phillips'* address to **387 Ferguson Avenue, Modesto, 95354-3210**.

**106D**

**Add Fields to Existing Database Table**

1. Add the fields shown below to the *Rockwell Technologies – District 14* table.

**July Sales**
**August Sales**
**September Sales**

2. Open *df 106D District 14 Sales*.
3. Copy and paste the sales for each month into the District 14 table.

| ROCKWELL TECHNOLOGIES SALES REPRESENTATIVES – District 14 | | | |
|---|---|---|---|
| **Last Name** | **July Sales** | **August Sales** | **September Sales** |
| Hughes | $55,671 | $63,339 | $60,113 |
| Winters | 65,882 | 73,563 | 71,287 |
| Chambers | 43,812 | 54,650 | 56,720 |
| Hanson | 50,092 | 39,751 | 51,697 |
| Yang | 27,389 | 48,762 | 50,388 |
| Zimmer | 63,982 | 58,332 | 56,256 |
| Aguilera | 60,010 | 69,756 | 70,185 |
| Winfield | 44,396 | 58,675 | 60,805 |
| Gonzalez | 39,792 | 57,381 | 61,900 |
| Keller | 74,981 | 47,343 | 69,726 |
| Wilkins | 49,201 | 59,752 | 67,440 |
| Bushlack | 70,500 | 75,306 | 72,906 |
| Lopez | 65,730 | 62,385 | 64,820 |
| Weiss | 54,750 | 34,780 | 52,608 |
| Culver | 47,980 | 58,656 | 65,300 |
| Miller | 29,760 | 39,716 | 48,615 |
| Sherman | 80,754 | 54,354 | 75,385 |
| Bailey | 49,753 | 50,330 | 51,320 |
| Stockton | 75,880 | 82,791 | 80,408 |
| Pizarro | 54,900 | 60,230 | 56,805 |
| Davis I. | 39,763 | 48,655 | 51,402 |
| Rice | 65,830 | 66,385 | 69,720 |
| Gilmore | 40,340 | 37,381 | 41,308 |
| Chi | 52,379 | 59,659 | 64,906 |
| Phillips | 38,751 | 49,763 | 45,200 |
| Taylor | 57,925 | 50,845 | 58,301 |
| Ryan | 42,700 | 49,655 | 51,703 |
| Beckwith | 68,524 | 62,566 | 66,750 |
| Davis B. | 57,247 | 62,318 | 72,983 |
| Bolling | 42,700 | 47,930 | 59,205 |
| Montessa | 59,650 | 55,428 | 60,120 |
| McGraw | 49,831 | 54,900 | 59,590 |

**106E**

**Run a Query**

1. Run a query called *Total Sales for Quarter* on the table you completed for 106D. Include Last Name, First Name, Territory, July Sales, August Sales, and September Sales.
2. Add a new column for **Total Sales for Quarter**. Use the Expression Builder to compute the total sales.
3. Sort the query by *Total Sales* in descending order. Print a copy of the query.

**Apply: Practice Creating Reports**

### Activity 1

1. Open the *Software Professionals* database.
2. Using the *Software Professionals Inventory* table, create the reports with the information requested in the Report Specifications.

| SOFTWARE PROFESSIONALS | | |
|---|---|---|
| Report Specifications | | |
| **Report** | **Format** | **Fields** |
| 1 | **Layout:** Columnar<br>**Orientation:** Portrait<br>**Title: Software Price List**<br>**Sort:** Ascending by Software<br>**Save report as:** *Software Price List* | Stock Number<br>Software<br>Price |
| 2 | **Layout:** Justified<br>**Orientation:** Portrait<br>**Title: Software Sales**<br>**Sort:** Descending by Sales<br>**Save report as:** *Software Sales* | Stock Number<br>Software<br>Sales |

### Activity 2

1. Open the *Rockwell Technologies* database.
2. Open and modify the *Total Sales* query to include *Territory*.
3. Create reports with the information requested in the Report Specifications.
4. Using Layout View, adjust the columns and column headings to arrange text attractively on the page.

| ROCKWELL TECHNOLOGIES | | |
|---|---|---|
| Report Specifications | | |
| **Report** | **Format** | **Fields** |
| 1 | **Layout:** Tabular<br>**Orientation:** Landscape<br>**Title: July/August Sales**<br>**Sort:** Descending by Total Sales<br>**Save report as: July/August** *Sales* | Last Name<br>First Name<br>Territory<br>July Sales<br>August Sales<br>Total Sales |
| 2 | Prepare a sales report with the same information used in Report 1. Group the sales by territory. Use Block Layout. Use **July/August Sales by Territory** for the report title. Arrange the columns attractively on the page.<br>**Save report as:** *July/August Sales by Territory* | |

# LESSON 106

## Apply What You Have Learned

- Apply what has been learned about using a database to create information to analyze efficiently and effectively.

### Business Documents

- Tables
- Queries
- Forms
- Reports
- Labels
- Form Letter

**106B**

**Input Data into Form**

Open the *Rockwell Technologies – District 14 (Unit 18)* database. Enter the information shown below into the *Sales Reps – District 14* form for the two new sales reps.

| | |
|---|---|
| **Title** | Mr. |
| **Last Name** | Montessa |
| **First Name** | Carlos |
| **Address** | 852 Lake Grove Court |
| **City** | San Diego |
| **State** | CA |
| **ZIP** | 92131-3321 |
| **Territory** | California |

| | |
|---|---|
| **Title** | Ms. |
| **Last Name** | McGraw |
| **First Name** | Katherine |
| **Address** | 673 Union Street |
| **City** | San Francisco |
| **State** | CA |
| **ZIP** | 94133-8634 |
| **Territory** | California |

| July/August Sales by Territory | | | | | |
| --- | --- | --- | --- | --- | --- |
| Territory | Total Sales | Last Name | First Name | July Sales | August Sales |
| Arizona | $113,670.00 | Reese | Jay | $67,890.00 | $45,780.00 |
| | $103,450.00 | Hulett | Sandra | $56,730.00 | $46,720.00 |
| | $88,371.00 | Chi | Karrie | $39,750.00 | $48,621.00 |
| | $82,848.00 | Butler | Warren | $35,975.00 | $46,873.00 |
| | $55,530.00 | Finley | Ann | $19,765.00 | $35,765.00 |
| Colorado | $103,533.00 | LeClair | Justin | $63,212.00 | $40,321.00 |
| | $103,501.00 | Hull | Dale | $53,739.00 | $49,762.00 |
| | $93,151.00 | Rivera | Jose | $55,400.00 | $37,751.00 |
| | $83,063.00 | Donovan | Kellee | $37,198.00 | $45,865.00 |

## LESSON 31

## Using a Database to Create a Mail Merge

**OUTCOMES**
- Modify database to include additional fields for merge document.
- Create a mail merge using form letter and fields from database.

**Business Document**

**31B**

- Mail merge letter to Rockwell Technology sales reps.

**Learn: Merge Feature**

The Merge feature is used to combine information from two sources into one document. It is often used for mail merge, which merges a word processing file (form letter) with a database file. For example, if you wanted to send a letter to all Rockwell Technologies sales representatives, it would be easy to create a form letter that would be merged with the database file containing their addresses. The Merge feature allows you to personalize each letter without having to key a separate letter to each person, thus saving a lot of time and effort.

The database file contains a record for each recipient. Each record contains field(s) of information about the person such as first name, last name, address, city, state, ZIP, etc.

The word processing file contains the text of the document (constant information) plus the merge field names (variable information), as shown in Figure 5-15. The merge field names are positioned in the document where the variable information from the database is to appear. A personalized letter to each recipient is the result of merging the two files. Review the following information to see how the data file was merged with the word processing file to produce the mail merge letter.

Mailings/Start Mail Merge/Start Mail Merge

Start Mail Merge ▾

**Start Mail Merge:** Use Start Mail Merge to create a mail merge (often referred to as a form letter) to be sent to multiple recipients. Fields can be inserted in the form letter that will be replaced automatically with information from the database when the mail merge letter file and the database file are merged.

Queries and tables for each of the remaining categories have been completed. The results of those queries are shown in the table below. Open *df 105G* and enter the information for *Gender* and *Degree* to complete the Statistical Data table for Mr. Parker.
Save as: **105G Statistical Data for Parker & Sons.**

## Statistical Data for Employees Hired from 1993 to 2013

| Category | Queries | Years with Company | No. of Promotions | No. of Years Per Promotion |
|---|---|---|---|---|
| **Age When Hired** | Age When Hired: 24 or older | 212 | 14 | 15.14 |
| | Age When Hired: 23 or younger | 319 | 86 | 3.71 |
| **Gender** | Males | | | |
| | Females | | | |
| **Percent of College Expenses Earned** | 0 to 20 percent | 211 | 8 | 26.38 |
| | 21 to 40 percent | 20 | 4 | 5 |
| | 41 to 60 percent | 117 | 24 | 4.88 |
| | 61 to 80 percent | 75 | 29 | 2.59 |
| | 81 to 100 percent | 108 | 35 | 3.09 |
| **Degree** | Business Administration | | | |
| | Business Education | | | |
| | Finance | | | |
| | Management | | | |
| | Psychology | | | |
| | Sociology | | | |
| **Employment Status** (Reason for Leaving Company) | Left Company - Better Pay | 44 | 26 | 1.69 |
| | Left Company - Better Position | 10 | 5 | 2 |
| | Left Company - Married | 15 | 8 | 1.88 |
| | Still at Parker | 462 | 61 | 7.57 |

After you complete the table, Mr. Parker would like you to analyze it and provide the Human Resources Department with your conclusions as to what characteristics individuals possess that appear to be most promotable. For example, individuals who are hired at a younger age (23 or younger) averaged a promotion every 3.71 years, while those who were hired at an older age (24 or older) averaged a promotion every 15.14 years. Therefore, the conclusion would be:

**Age When Hired:** Those individuals who were 23 years of age or younger when hired were much more promotable than those hired at the age of 24 or older.

1. Open *df 105H* and record your conclusions for the remaining categories.

**Gender:**
**Percent of College Expenses Earned:**
**Degree:**
**Employment Status:**

2. Save as: **105H Conclusions.**

| Mailings/Start Mail Merge/Select Recipients |  Select Recipients ▾ | **Select Recipients:** Use Select Recipients to select the file containing the fields with the information that will be placed in the form letter. |

| Mailings/Start Mail Merge/Edit Recipient List |  Edit Recipient List | **Edit Recipient List:** If you don't want to send the merged document to all the individuals included in the data file, the Edit Recipient List feature can be used to select the individuals that you do want it sent to. This feature can also be used to modify the information contained in the data file. |

| Mailings/Write & Insert Fields/Insert Merge Field |  Insert Merge Field ▾ | **Insert Merge Field:** After selecting the file to be used in the merge using the Select Recipients feature, merge field names can be placed in the form letter. The merge field names are placed at the location in the form letter where you want the variable information from the database to appear when the mail merge letter and database file are merged. |

| Mailings/Write & Insert Fields/Greeting Line |  Greeting Line | **Greeting Line:** The Greeting Line feature can be used to automatically insert the greeting in the letter. Use the down arrows to modify the greeting from the default. For example, if you want a colon following the greeting rather than a comma, click the down arrow, click the colon, and click OK. |

| Mailings/Preview Results/ Preview Results |  Preview Results | **Preview Results:** After the mail merge letter has been completed, use the Preview Results feature to replace the merge fields in the letter with the information from the database. This allows for viewing the documents before printing. |

| Mailings/Preview Results/ Find Recipient |  | **Find Recipient:** The Find Recipient feature can be used to view an individual record in the recipient list. |

| Mailings/Finish/Finish & Merge |  Finish & Merge ▾ | **Finish & Merge:** The Finish & Merge feature is used to create separate documents for each individual included in the database. Once completed, the letters can be printed for mailing, or they can be sent via email. |

## Add a Formula to a Cell to Calculate

*fx* Formula

Data

Formulas can be added in cells of a table to perform simple calculations. For example, in the table that was created for 105D, a formula can be placed in the last cell of each degree line to calculate the Average Years Per Promotion by following these steps.

1. Place cursor in the Average Years Per Promotion for the Bus. Admin. Degree.
2. In the Data group of the Layout tab, click fx Formula.
3. The Average Years Per Promotion = the Years with Company divided by the Number of Promotions. Enter the formula:=**162/53**, as shown in Figure 18-8.

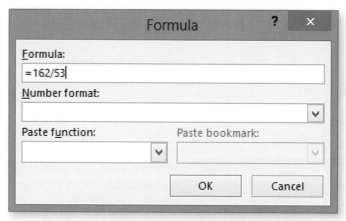

**Figure 18-8** Formula in Data group of Layout tab

4. Click OK.

| Average No. of Promotion by Degree | | | |
|---|---|---|---|
| Degree | Years with Company | Number of Promotions | Average Years Per Promotion |
| Bus. Administration | 162 | 53 | 3.06 |
| Bus. Ed. | 64 | 9 | |

5. Repeat steps 1–4 to calculate the Average Years Per Promotion for each degree.
6. Enter **No Promotions** for the degrees that received zero promotions.
7. Save as: *105E Promotions by Degree.*

## Create Queries for Variables

Next, complete a table for Average No. of Promotions by Gender using *Females* and *Males* for the category variables.

1. Follow the same procedure as was used for creating the Average No. of Promotion by Degree table. Refer to 105B-E as needed.
2. Save as: *105F Promotions by Gender.*

| Average No. of Promotions by Gender | | | |
|---|---|---|---|
| Gender | Years with Company | Number of Promotions | Average Years Per Promotion |
| Females | | | |
| Males | | | |

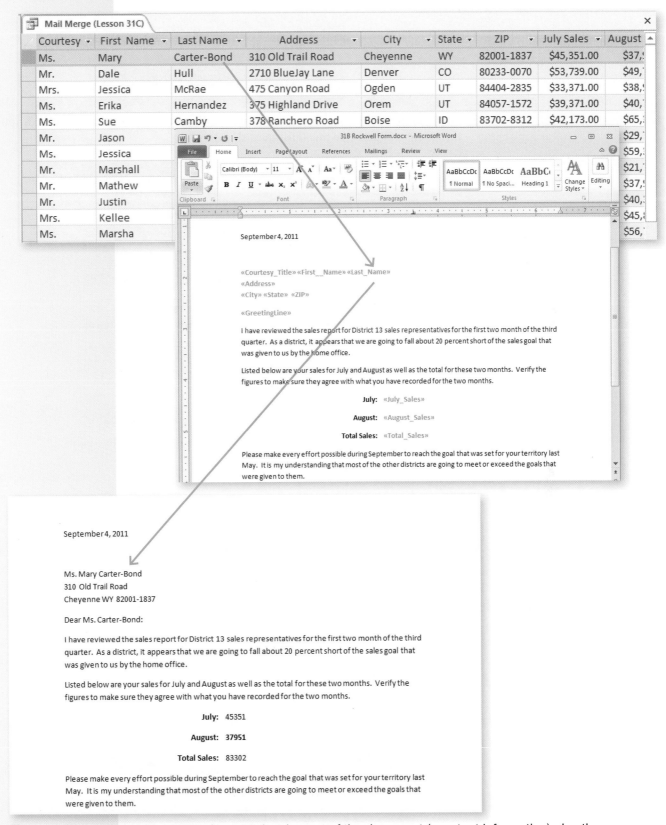

**Figure 5-15** The word processing file contains the text of the document (constant information) plus the merge field names (variable information)

| Degree: Bus Admin | | | |
|---|---|---|---|
| Last Name | Years with Company | Number of Promotions | Degree |
| | 162 | 53 | |
| Degree: Bus Ed | | | |
| Last Name | Years with Company | Number of Promotions | Degree |
| | 64 | 9 | |

7. Copy and paste the *Total* line for each of the remaining majors. When finished, your *Word* document will look like the illustration shown below.

| Degree: Bus Admin | | | |
|---|---|---|---|
| Last Name | Years with Company | Number of Promotions | Degree |
| | 162 | 53 | |
| Degree: Bus Ed | | | |
| Last Name | Years with Company | Number of Promotions | Degree |
| | 64 | 9 | |
| Degree: Finance | | | |
| Last Name | Years with Company | Number of Promotions | Degree |
| | 120 | 18 | |
| Degree: Management | | | |
| Last Name | Years with Company | Number of Promotions | Degree |
| | 75 | 20 | |
| Degree: Psychology | | | |
| Last Name | Years with Company | Number of Promotions | Degree |
| | 94 | 0 | |
| Degree: Sociology | | | |
| Last Name | Years with Company | Number of Promotions | Degree |
| | 16 | 0 | |

8. **Save as:** *105C Promotions by Degree.*

## 105D

**Modify Table Created from Access**

Tables created from *Access* can be modified to fit the user's needs. Make the following modifications to the table created for 105C.

1. Change the main heading from *Degree: Bus Admin* to **Average No. of Promotion by Degree.**
2. Change the column heading *Last Name* to **Degree**.
3. Key in the name of each degree in the *Degree* column.
4. Change the column heading *Degree* to **Average Years Per Promotion**.
5. Delete the main heading and column headings from the table for the rest of the degrees so that your table looks like the illustration shown below. You will also need to adjust the column widths, as well as left-justify the entries in the *Degree* column.
6. **Save as:** *105D Promotions by Degree.*

QUICK ✔

| Average No. of Promotion by Degree | | | |
|---|---|---|---|
| Degree | Years with Company | Number of Promotions | Average Years Per Promotion |
| Bus. Administration | 162 | 53 | |
| Bus. Ed. | 64 | 9 | |
| Finance | 120 | 18 | |
| Management | 75 | 20 | |
| Psychology | 94 | 0 | |
| Sociology | 16 | 0 | |

**Apply: Mail Merge**

★TIP  Fields to be inserted are shown in color. To get the address spaced correctly, use Insert Merge Field to insert each field for the address rather than using Address block.

★TIP  In the Mail Merge recipient's list, click the √ to the right of the Data Source. Then click in the box under the √ next to the names of the individuals to receive the letter.

### Activity 1: Merging Sources

1. Open the *Sales Reps — District 13* table in the *Rockwell Technologies* database. Create a query with all of the variable fields contained in the following form letter. **Save query as:** *Mail Merge*.

2. Use the Mail Merge feature in *Microsoft Word* to create the following form letter to send to the sales reps in the *Rockwell Technologies – District 13* database.

   a. Start Mail Merge. Click Select Recipients. (Select Use Existing List feature, and select the mail merge file created in step 1.)
   b. Key the merge letter (form letter), inserting merge fields as shown in the following form letter.
   c. Use the Edit Recipient List tool to select Hernandez, Tapani, and Butler.
   d. Preview results and make corrections/changes if needed.
   e. Use the Edit Individual Documents of the Finish & Merge feature in the Finish group to create a file of the three letters.

3. **Save as:** *31C Rockwell Merge Letter*. Print the letters.

September 4, 20--

«Courtesy_Title» «First_Name» «Last_Name»
«Address»
«City», «State» «ZIP»

«GreetingLine»

I have reviewed the sales report for District 13 sales representatives for the first two months of the third quarter. As a district, it appears that we are going to fall about 20 percent short of the sales goal that was given to us by the home office.

Listed below are your sales for July and August as well as the total for these two months. Verify the figures to make sure they agree with what you have recorded for the two months.

|  |  |
|---:|:---|
| **July:** | $«July_Sales» |
| **August:** | $«August_Sales» |
| **Total Sales:** | $«Total_Sales» |

Please make every effort possible during September to reach the goal that was set for your territory last May. It is my understanding that most of the other districts are going to meet or exceed the goals that were given to them.

If I can provide additional assistance to you to help you meet your goal, please contact me.

Sincerely,

Paul M. Vermillion
District Sales Manager

xx

Two of the queries should look like these:

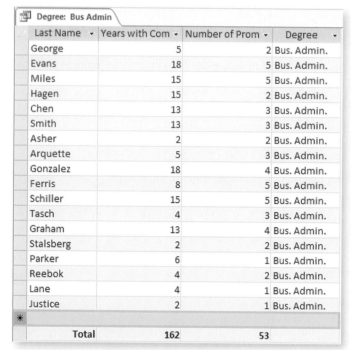

**Degree: Bus Admin**

| Last Name ▾ | Years with Com ▾ | Number of Prom ▾ | Degree ▾ |
|---|---|---|---|
| George | 5 | 2 | Bus. Admin. |
| Evans | 18 | 5 | Bus. Admin. |
| Miles | 15 | 5 | Bus. Admin. |
| Hagen | 15 | 2 | Bus. Admin. |
| Chen | 13 | 3 | Bus. Admin. |
| Smith | 13 | 3 | Bus. Admin. |
| Asher | 2 | 2 | Bus. Admin. |
| Arquette | 5 | 3 | Bus. Admin. |
| Gonzalez | 18 | 4 | Bus. Admin. |
| Ferris | 8 | 5 | Bus. Admin. |
| Schiller | 15 | 5 | Bus. Admin. |
| Tasch | 4 | 3 | Bus. Admin. |
| Graham | 13 | 4 | Bus. Admin. |
| Stalsberg | 2 | 2 | Bus. Admin. |
| Parker | 6 | 1 | Bus. Admin. |
| Reebok | 4 | 2 | Bus. Admin. |
| Lane | 4 | 1 | Bus. Admin. |
| Justice | 2 | 1 | Bus. Admin. |
| * | | | |
| **Total** | **162** | **53** | |

**Business Administration**

**Degree: Finance**

| Last Name ▾ | Years with Com ▾ | Number of Prom ▾ | Degree ▾ |
|---|---|---|---|
| Collingrood | 20 | 0 | Finance |
| Costley | 19 | 0 | Finance |
| Sprague | 18 | 5 | Finance |
| Etheridge | 1 | 0 | Finance |
| Montana | 4 | 2 | Finance |
| Garcia | 8 | 2 | Finance |
| Brown | 8 | 0 | Finance |
| Mattiacci | 8 | 0 | Finance |
| Theiler | 18 | 4 | Finance |
| Effertz | 2 | 1 | Finance |
| Kiedinger | 4 | 2 | Finance |
| Cane | 6 | 2 | Finance |
| Fisher | 4 | 0 | Finance |
| * | | | |
| **Total** | **120** | **18** | |

**Finance**

## 105C

### Create Word Table from Access Total Lines

*Word* tables can be created from *Access* tables and queries by copying and pasting rows from *Access* to *Word*. Use the six degree queries created for 105B to create a *Word* table showing the Average No. of Promotions by Degree. Follow the steps outlined below to create the table.

1. Open the *Degree: Bus Admin* query.
2. Copy the *Total* line by clicking in the cell beneath the asterisk. After you click in the cell, copy the line (Ctrl+c).

| Lane | 4 | 1 | Bus. Admin. |
|---|---|---|---|
| Justice | 2 | 1 | Bus. Admin. |
| * | | | |
| **Total** | **162** | **53** | |

3. Open a new *Word* document and use the Paste feature (Ctrl+v) to paste the line in the *Word* document.

| Degree: Bus Admin | | | |
|---|---|---|---|
| Last Name | Years with Company | Number of Promotions | Degree |
| | 162 | 53 | |

4. Open the *Degree: Bus Ed* query.
5. Copy the *Total* line.
6. Paste the Bus Ed *Total* line in the *Word* document. You shouldn't have to move the cursor; it should already be on the line beneath the Bus Admin *Total* line. The *Word* document should look like the illustration shown on the next page.

# LESSON 32    Database Applications

OUTCOME
- To apply previously-learned database skills including creating queries, forms, reports, and mail merge documents.

## Business Documents

- Database Query
- Database Query with Computed Fields
- Database Form
- Database Report
- Database Mail Merge

## 32B

**Apply: Create Queries**

1. Open the Eastwick School of Dance database, **df Eastwick School of Dance**.
2. Using the appropriate table, create queries to answer the questions shown in the following table.
3. Save each query using the name provided.

| Eastwick School of Dance | | | |
|---|---|---|---|
| **No.** | **Query** | **Fields to Include** | **Criteria** |
| Query 1 | How many of the students are from Minneapolis/St. Paul? What is the mailing information for each of those students?<br><br>Save query as: **Minneapolis/Saint Paul Students** | First Name Last Name Address City State ZIP | "Minneapolis" Or "St. Paul" |
| Query 2 | How many of the students are from Wisconsin? What is the mailing information for each of those students?<br><br>Save query as: **Wisconsin Students** | | "WI" |
| Query 3 | How many students have not paid their September fees? Who are they?<br><br>Save query as: **September Fees Not Paid** | Last Name First Name September Fees | =0 |

# LESSON 105

## Creating Documents to Analyze Information Efficiently and Effectively

**OUTCOMES**

- Compile information from database tables and queries in *Word* tables.
- Modify tables created from *Access* tables and queries.
- Add formulas to *Word* table cells.
- Compile information from multiple queries in a *Word* table for efficient analysis.
- Draw conclusions from database information.

## Business Documents

### 105B

- Queries
- Word Tables with Formulas

**Apply What You Have Learned**

Keaton Parker of Parker & Sons is expanding his business and will be hiring 25 new employees within the next six months. The Human Resources Department tracked new hires for a 20-year period (1993 to 2013) to provide data to make hiring decisions. Their database (*df Parker & Sons*) includes a table (*Employee Data*) with the following information:

- Last Name
- First Name
- Middle Initial
- Year Hired
- Age When Hired
- Gender
- Percent of College Expenses Earned
- College Degree
- Reasons for Leaving the Company
- Years with the Company
- Number of Promotions

Mr. Parker wants to know the impact each of the above categories had on the number of promotions each person received while working at Parker & Sons. In order to answer the question, queries will have to be crated for each of the variables in each category. For example, the College Degree category has six variables:

- Bus. Admin.
- Bus. Ed.
- Finance
- Management
- Psychology
- Sociology

Two of the queries created for College Degree (*Degree: Bus Admin* and *Degree: Finance*) are illustrated in the Quick Check. Create queries containing the same information for the four remaining degrees (Use *Degree: Name of Degree* for query name as was done for the *Bus Admin* and *Finance* queries). Be sure to include the *Total* line for each query. After creating the queries, you will:

- Create a *Word* table from the *Total* lines of each of the six degrees (105C).
- Modify the table to better display the information (105D).
- Add a formula to the table to calculate Average Years Per Promotion for each college degree to compare how promotable individuals were that had each of the degrees (105E).
- Repeat the process to complete a table for gender (105F).
- Enter the information for Degree and Gender in the comprehensive table for data analysis (105G).

**Apply: Create Query with Computed Fields**

1. Open the *Eastwick School of Dance* database.
2. Using the *Eastwick Fees* table, create a query with the five fields shown in the following table.
3. Use the Expression Builder to create a formula to calculate the Total Fees Paid.
4. Print the query.

| Eastwick School of Dance | |
|---|---|
| **The query should include:** | |
| 1.<br>2.<br>3.<br>4.<br>5.<br>6. | First Name<br>Last Name<br>September Fees<br>October Fees<br>November Fees<br>Total Fees Paid |
| **Formula for Total Fees Paid** | **Total Fees Paid:=[September Fees]+[October Fees]+[November Fees]** |
| **Save query as:** | ***Total Fees Paid*** |

**Apply: Create a Form**

1. Open the *Eastwick School of Dance* database.
2. Using the *Eastwick Fees* table, create a form in the database with the information requested in the following table.

| Eastwick School of Dance | | |
|---|---|---|
| **Form Specifications** | | |
| **Form 1** | **Layout:** Tabular<br>**Title: Eastwick Student Enrollment**<br>**Sort:** Ascending Order by Last Name | Last Name<br>First Name<br>Dance Class 1<br>Dance Class 2 |
| **Save form as:** | ***Eastwick Student Enrollment*** | |

The first three tables should look like this:

## Arizona Third Quarter Sales

| Last Name | Territory | July Sales | August Sales | September Sales | Total Sales for Quarter | Average Monthly Sales |
|---|---|---|---|---|---|---|
| Chi | Arizona | $39,750.00 | $48,621.00 | $50,805.00 | $139,176.00 | $46,392.00 |
| Finley | Arizona | $19,765.00 | $35,765.00 | $23,800.00 | $79,330.00 | $26,443.33 |
| Reese | Arizona | $67,890.00 | $45,780.00 | $50,775.00 | $164,445.00 | $54,815.00 |
| Butler | Arizona | $35,975.00 | $46,873.00 | $50,980.00 | $133,828.00 | $44,609.33 |
| Hulett | Arizona | $56,730.00 | $46,720.00 | $54,560.00 | $158,010.00 | $52,670.00 |
| Sanchez | Arizona | $0.00 | $0.00 | $23,891.00 | $23,891.00 | $7,963.67 |
| Totals | | $220,110.00 | $223,759.00 | $254,811.00 | $698,680.00 | $232,893.33 |

## Colorado Third Quarter Sales

| Last Name | Territory | July Sales | August Sales | September Sales | Total Sales for Quarter | Average Monthly Sales |
|---|---|---|---|---|---|---|
| Hull | Colorado | $53,739.00 | $49,762.00 | $54,829.00 | $158,330.00 | $52,776.67 |
| LeClair | Colorado | $63,212.00 | $40,321.00 | $50,705.00 | $154,238.00 | $51,412.67 |
| Donovan | Colorado | $37,198.00 | $45,865.00 | $49,814.00 | $132,877.00 | $44,292.33 |
| Rivera | Colorado | $55,400.00 | $37,751.00 | $50,880.00 | $144,031.00 | $48,010.33 |
| Bell | Colorado | $39,200.00 | $43,286.00 | $47,804.00 | $130,290.00 | $43,430.00 |
| Hayes | Colorado | $0.00 | $0.00 | $19,799.00 | $19,799.00 | $6,599.67 |
| Totals | | $248,749.00 | $216,985.00 | $273,831.00 | $739,565.00 | $246,521.67 |

## Idaho Third Quarter Sales

| Last Name | Territory | July Sales | August Sales | September Sales | Total Sales for Quarter | Average Monthly Sales |
|---|---|---|---|---|---|---|
| Camby | Idaho | $42,173.00 | $65,386.00 | $55,142.00 | $162,701.00 | $54,233.67 |
| Cirillo | Idaho | $29,731.00 | $37,956.00 | $39,885.00 | $107,572.00 | $35,857.33 |
| Walker | Idaho | $43,900.00 | $44,750.00 | $44,440.00 | $133,090.00 | $44,363.33 |
| Totals | | $115,804.00 | $148,092.00 | $139,467.00 | $403,363.00 | $134,454.33 |

## 104D

### Create Table from Query Totals Lines

The last table Mr. Vermillion would like to see is one showing the Totals for Third Quarter by Territory as illustrated below.

1. Use the tables created in 104C to create this table. Before you begin, think about the most efficient and effective way to create the table. Use the skills you have learned previously; you should have very little to key. *Hint:* Copy and paste lines.
2. **Save as:** *104D Total Sales for Third Quarter by Territory.*

## Total Sales for Third Quarter by Territory

| Territory | July Sales | August Sales | September Sales | Total Sales for Quarter | Average Monthly Sales |
|---|---|---|---|---|---|
| Arizona | $220,110.00 | $223,759.00 | $254,811.00 | $698,680.00 | $232,893.33 |
| Colorado | $248,749.00 | $216,985.00 | $273,831.00 | $739,565.00 | $246,521.67 |
| Idaho | 115,804.00 | $148,092.00 | $139,467.00 | $403,363.00 | $134,454.33 |
| Montana | $100,581.00 | $92,292.00 | $131,921.00 | $324,794.00 | $108,264.67 |
| South Dakota | $114,035.00 | $76,747.00 | $99,212.00 | $289,994.00 | $96,664.67 |
| Utah | $117,618.00 | $136,559.00 | $173,569.00 | $427,746.00 | $142,582.00 |
| Wyoming | $99,142.00 | $97,300.00 | $105,824.00 | $302,266.00 | $100,755.33 |

**Apply: Create Reports**

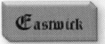

1. Open the *Eastwick School of Dance* database.
2. Using the *Eastwick School of Dance – Address* table, create reports with the information requested in the Report Specifications.

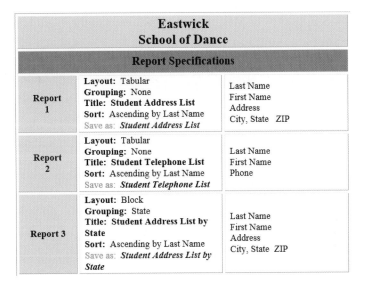

| Eastwick School of Dance | | |
|---|---|---|
| **Report Specifications** | | |
| **Report 1** | **Layout:** Tabular <br> **Grouping:** None <br> **Title: Student Address List** <br> **Sort:** Ascending by Last Name <br> Save as: *Student Address List* | Last Name <br> First Name <br> Address <br> City, State  ZIP |
| **Report 2** | **Layout:** Tabular <br> **Grouping:** None <br> **Title: Student Telephone List** <br> **Sort:** Ascending by Last Name <br> Save as: *Student Telephone List* | Last Name <br> First Name <br> Phone |
| **Report 3** | **Layout:** Block <br> **Grouping:** State <br> **Title: Student Address List by State** <br> **Sort:** Ascending by Last Name <br> Save as: *Student Address List by State* | Last Name <br> First Name <br> Address <br> City, State  ZIP |

**Apply: Create a Mail Merge**

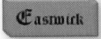

1. Create the following form letter to send to the parents of students who have not paid their September dance fees.
2. Use Mail Merge Query for the field names to be inserted in the form letter.
3. Merge the letters.  Print the letters to Finley and Dye.
4. **Save as:  *32F Eastwick Form Letter***

   **Save as:  *32F Eastwick Merge Letter***

October 15, 20--

«Title» «First_Name_Guardian» «Last_Name_Guardian»
«Address»
«City», «State» «Zip»

Dear «Title» «Last_Name_Guardian»:

Please check your records to see if you have paid for «First_Name»'s September dance fees.  Our records show that we have not received the fees in the amount of $«Monthly_Fees».  Let us know if our records are incorrect or send the fees with «First_Name» to her next dance class.

I have enjoyed working with «First_Name» this fall.  Observing the students' progress from one skill level to the next is always very satisfying to me. The students are looking forward to performing for you at the December recital.

Sincerely,

Ashley Eastwick
Dance Instructor

**Modify Table**

Once the table has been pasted in *Word*, it can be modified. The table shown below in the Quick Check has had the title deleted, the shading changed, the *First Name* column deleted, field widths adjusted to display the text more attractively, and a *Totals* cell created by merging two cells.

1. Make these modifications to the *Word* table:

| Delete Main Title | Layout/ Rows and Columns/Delete/Delete Rows |
|---|---|
| Change Shading | Table Tools/Design/Table Styles/Shading/Select Color |
| Delete *First Name* Column | Layout/Rows and Columns/ Delete/Delete Column |
| Adjust Column Width | Layout/Cell Size/Distribute Columns |
| Merge Cells | Layout/Merge/Merge Cells |

2. **Save as:** *104B Arizona*.

The table should look like this:

| Last Name | Territory | July Sales | August Sales | September Sales | Total Sales for Quarter | Average Monthly Sales |
|---|---|---|---|---|---|---|
| Chi | Arizona | $39,750.00 | $48,621.00 | $50,805.00 | $139,176.00 | $46,392.00 |
| Finley | Arizona | $19,765.00 | $35,765.00 | $23,800.00 | $79,330.00 | $26,443.33 |
| Reese | Arizona | $67,890.00 | $45,780.00 | $50,775.00 | $164,445.00 | $54,815.00 |
| Butler | Arizona | $35,975.00 | $46,873.00 | $50,980.00 | $133,828.00 | $44,609.33 |
| Hulett | Arizona | $56,730.00 | $46,720.00 | $54,560.00 | $158,010.00 | $52,670.00 |
| Sanchez | Arizona | $0.00 | $0.00 | $23,891.00 | $23,891.00 | $7,963.67 |
| **Totals** | | $36,685.00 | $37,293.17 | $42,468.50 | $116,446.67 | $38,815.56 |

## 104C

**Create a Word Document from Access Tables and Queries**

Mr. Vermillion would like to see the tables with the averages for each territory without having to flip between queries.

1. He wants to see the tables placed in a *Word* document as shown in the illustration below.
2. Use the *Title* Styles (Home/Styles/Title) and change the Font size to 20 for the headings.
3. Include in alphabetical order tables for each of the seven territories in District 13. Use a different color for the column headings of each territory.
4. If a table is split between two pages, insert lines to push it to the next page. See what the first three tables will look like in the Quick Check below.
5. **Save as:** *104C Third Quarter Sales by Territory*.

Key a 1' timing on each ¶; determine *gwam*.

Key a 2' timing on ¶s 1–3 combined; determine *gwam*.

Key a 3' timing on ¶s 1–3 combined; determine *gwam*.

**A** all letters used                                    gwam  2' | 3'

|   | 2   | 4   | 6   | 8   | 10  |   |
In deciding upon a career, learn as much as possible about        5 | 4

12  | 14  | 16  | 18  | 20  | 22  | 24  |
what individuals in that career do.  For each job class, there are  11 | 7

26  | 28  | 30  | 32  | 34  | 36  |
job requirements and qualifications that must be met.  Analyze     17 | 11

38  | 40  | 42  | 44  | 46  | 48  | 50  |
these tasks very critically in terms of your personality and what  23 | 15

52  | 54  |
you like to do.                                                   28 | 19

|   | 2   | 4   | 6   | 8   | 10  | 12  |
A high percentage of jobs in major careers demand education or    34 | 23

|   | 14  | 16  | 18  | 20  | 22  | 24  | 26  |
training after high school.  The training may be very specialized, 40 | 26

|   | 28  | 30  | 32  | 34  | 36  | 38  |
requiring intensive study or interning for two or more years.  You 42 | 28

40  | 42  | 44  | 46  | 48  | 50  | 52  |
must decide if you are willing to expend so much time and effort.  47 | 31

|   | 2   | 4   | 6   | 8   | 10  | 12  |
After you have decided upon a career to pursue, discuss the       53 | 35

|   | 14  | 16  | 18  | 20  | 22  | 24  |
choice with parents, teachers, and others.  Such people can help  59 | 39

26  | 28  | 30  | 32  | 34  | 36  | 38  |
you design a plan to guide you along the series of steps required  65 | 43

|   | 40  | 42  | 44  | 46  | 48  | 50  |
in pursuing your goal.  Keep the plan flexible and change it when-  71 | 48

52  | 54  |
ever necessary.                                                   77 | 51

### Quarter-Minute Checkpoints

| gwam | 1/4' | 1/2' | 3/4' | 1' |
|------|------|------|------|-----|
| 24 | 6 | 12 | 18 | 24 |
| 28 | 7 | 14 | 21 | 28 |
| 32 | 8 | 16 | 24 | 32 |
| 36 | 9 | 18 | 27 | 36 |
| 40 | 10 | 20 | 30 | 40 |
| 44 | 11 | 22 | 33 | 44 |
| 48 | 12 | 24 | 36 | 48 |
| 52 | 13 | 26 | 39 | 52 |
| 56 | 14 | 28 | 42 | 56 |

www.cengage.com/school/
keyboarding/c21key

gwam  2' |    1    |    2    |    3    |    4    |    5    |    6    |
      3' |      1       |      2       |      3       |      4       |

The merged labels should look like this:

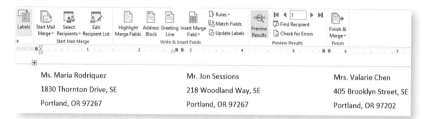

| Ms. Maria Rodriquez | Mr. Jon Sessions | Mrs. Valarie Chen |
|---|---|---|
| 1830 Thornton Drive, SE | 218 Woodland Way, SE | 405 Brooklyn Street, SE |
| Portland, OR 97267 | Portland, OR 97267 | Portland, OR 97202 |

# LESSON 104

## Creating Word Documents from Database Tables and Queries

**OUTCOMES**

- Create a *Word* table from a database table.
- Create a *Word* table from a database query.
- Create a *Word* table from query total lines.

**Business Document**

**104B**

- Tables

**Copy Access Table to Word Document**

Tables and queries created in Access can be copied and pasted in a Word document. Create a table of quarterly sales for the Arizona reps of Rockwell Technologies by following these steps.

**Copy Table from *Access* to *Word***

1. Open the Unit 18 database for Rockwell Technologies.
2. Right-click on the filename **Total Sales for Quarter - Arizona.**
3. Copy the file. (You don't have to open the file; you just click and copy the filename.)
4. Open a new *Word* document.
5. Paste the file in the *Word* document.

| Total Sales for Quarter - Arizona | | | | | | | |
|---|---|---|---|---|---|---|---|
| Last Name | First Name | Territory | July Sales | August Sales | September Sales | Total Sales for Quarter | Average Monthly Sales |
| Chi | Karrie | Arizona | $39,750.00 | $48,621.00 | $50,805.00 | $139,176.00 | $46,392.00 |
| Finley | Ann | Arizona | $19,765.00 | $35,765.00 | $23,800.00 | $79,330.00 | $26,443.33 |
| Reese | Jay | Arizona | $67,890.00 | $45,780.00 | $50,775.00 | $164,445.00 | $54,815.00 |
| Butler | Warren | Arizona | $35,975.00 | $46,873.00 | $50,980.00 | $133,828.00 | $44,609.33 |
| Hulett | Sandra | Arizona | $56,730.00 | $46,720.00 | $54,560.00 | $158,010.00 | $52,670.00 |
| Sanchez | Rey | Arizona | $0.00 | $0.00 | $23,891.00 | $23,891.00 | $7,963.67 |
| | | | $36,685.00 | $37,293.17 | $42,468.50 | $116,446.67 | $38,815.56 |
| | | | | | | | |

# Academic and Career Connections

Complete the following exercises that introduce various topics that involve academic themes and careers.

## Grammar/Writing: Quotation Marks and Italics

1. Go to *MicroType* 6 and use this feature path for review: References/Communication Skills/ Quotation Marks and Italics.
2. Click Rules and review the rules of using quotation marks and italic.
3. Then, under Quotation Marks and Italics, click Posttest.
4. Follow the instructions to complete the posttest.

*Optional Activities:*

1. Go to this path: CheckPro/Communication Skills 5.
2. Complete the activities as directed.
3. Go to this path: CheckPro/Word Choice 5.
4. Complete the activities as directed.

**MicroType 6**

- References/Communication Skills/Quotation Marks and Italics
- CheckPro/Communication Skills 6
- CheckPro/Word Choice 6

## Communications: Composition

1. Open a new word processing document and key the ¶ below, correcting word-choice errors.
2. Key a second ¶ in which you identify the kinds of behavior that help earn your respect and those that cause you to lose respect for someone else. Describe the consequences of disrespectful behavior.

That all individuals want others to respect them is not surprising. What is surprising is that sum people think their due respect even when there own behavior has been unacceptable or even illegal. Key to the issue is that we respect others because of certain behavior, rather then in spite of it. Its vital, than, to no that what people do and say determines the level of respect there given buy others. Respect has to be earned; its not our unquestioned right to demand it. You should choose behaviors that will led others to respect you.

3. Proofread, check spelling and grammar, and revise your ¶s as necessary.
4. Save the document as *u05 communications*.

## Math Skills

Thomas is in the process of starting up his own business for making personalized stationary and note cards. He has sent a letter to a potential investor in which he provided the details below. In a new word processing document, key the ¶, filling in the blanks with the correct percentages (rounded to the nearest whole number). Save the document as *u05 math*.

I estimate that I will spend $8,000 on the start-up and operation of my business for the first year. I have raised $4,600 so far. This represents ____% of the total $8,000. In the first year of operation, I am projecting that my sales revenue will be $10,000. Of that, I expect $7,000, or ____%, to be generated by online sales. My variable and fixed costs will total about $4,400, which is ____% of my sales revenue.

4. In the Label Options dialog box as shown in Figure 18-5:
   Select Continuous-feed printers for the Printer information.
   Select Avery A4/A5 for the Label information.
   Select 4423/3 for the Product No.
   Click OK.

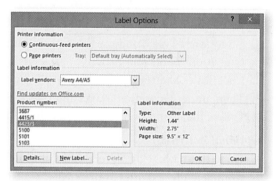

**Figure 18-5** Label Options

5. Click Select Recipients; click Use existing list.
6. Locate and select *Member's Address* table from the *df Baxter International* database.
7. Use the Insert Merge Field feature to insert the fields, as shown in Figure 18-6.

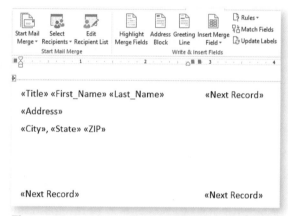

**Figure 18-6** Insert Merged Fields

8. Click Update Labels to place the fields in each label, as shown in Figure 18-7.

**Figure 18-7** Update Labels

9. Click Preview Results to see merged labels. This will replace the merged fields with data from the recipient list.
10. Print a copy of the labels.
11. **Save as:** *103D Baxter Mailing Labels.*

## Planning a Career in Science, Technology, Engineering, and Mathematics

Businesses rely on workers in the fields of science, technology, engineering, and mathematics to plan, manage, and provide scientific research as well as other services such as product testing and development, systems design and analysis, and mathematical modeling. These jobs are critical because competitive pressures and ever-changing technology force many companies and government organizations to constantly improve and update product and system designs and to optimize their manufacturing and building processes.

### What's It Like?

Individuals who work in this field invent new products, do research and development, and often serve as the link between scientific discoveries and the commercial applications that meet consumer needs. For example:

- They set up, operate, and maintain laboratory instruments, monitor experiments, make observations, and formulate results.
- They perform laboratory and field tests to monitor environmental resources and determine the contaminants and sources of pollution in the environment.
- They supervise production in factories, determine the causes of a component's failure, and test manufactured products to maintain quality.
- They apply mathematical modeling and computational methods to formulate and solve practical problems such as the most efficient way to schedule airline routes between cities, the effects and safety of new drugs, or the cost-effectiveness of alternative manufacturing processes.

These professionals work in a variety of settings, from comfortable offices and high-tech laboratories to the factory floor and outdoor labs in remote locations. They are employed in all types of industries, including pharmaceuticals, agriculture, education, aeronautics, oil and gas, chemicals, and manufacturing.

### Employment Outlook

Given the need for companies and governments to be on the cutting edge of technology, demand for workers is high and job possibilities abound, even during economic downturns. Employment is expected to increase much faster for these occupations than for others. Employers seek well-trained individuals with highly developed technical skills. Most require a bachelor's or master's degree while many in mathematics and science require a doctorate. In addition, many positions also require state licensure.

### What About You?

The Science, Technology, Engineering, and Mathematics career cluster is covered in box 15 of the Interest Survey Activity you completed in Unit 1 of this text. If this box had one of the three highest scores on your survey, you should further explore the cluster's pathways and related occupations.

1. Why do you think a career in one of these fields could be a good choice?
2. What skills can you develop now that would be helpful to a career in one of these fields?
3. Why are these jobs important to a business and to our economy?

6.  Key the return address starting where the cursor is located.

Baxter International
8076 Majestic Lane, SW
Portland, OR 97224

7.  Select the recipients by clicking Select Recipients and then clicking Use an Existing List. See Figure 18-4.

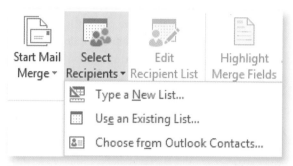

**Figure 18-4** Select Recipients

8.  Locate and double-click the *Baxter* database; then click the file (**February Fees Past Due**) containing the list of the recipients and click OK.
9.  Click at the bottom/middle of the envelope to bring up the blue box and use the Insert Merge Field feature to insert the fields as illustrated below.

10. Click Preview Results.
11. Use Find Recipient to locate and then print an envelope for Felipe Gonzalez.
12. Close and save the file.
13. **Save as:** *103C Baxter Envelopes*.

## 103D

### Mailing Labels

The Mailings feature can also be used to create and print labels. Create mailing labels for all of Baxter International's members using the *Member's Address* table by following the steps below.

1.  Open and create a new document.
2.  Click Start Mail Merge in the Start Mail Merge group of the Mailings tab.
3.  Click Labels.

Complete this activity to help prepare for the Database Design & Applications event in FBLA-PBL's Information Technology division. Participants in this event demonstrate their understanding of database usage in business and their skills in developing database objects. The owner of the Sweet Stop ice cream and dessert shop would like you to develop a database for the business. She has given you the following information:

| First Name | Last Name | Position | Address | City | State | ZIP | Phone | Hourly Rate |
|---|---|---|---|---|---|---|---|---|
| Jen | Maddox | Manager | 448 Sawyer Court | Mason | OH | 45040 | 513-555-6599 | $12.00 |
| Grant | Powers | Server | 110 Concord Drive | Lebanon | OH | 45036 | 513-555-3102 | $8.00 |
| Leah | Valdez | Server | 45 Maple St. | Lebanon | OH | 45036 | 513-555-7475 | $8.00 |
| Jackson | Volz | Server | 310 East St. | Cincinnati | OH | 45224 | 513-555-4720 | $8.00 |
| Ben | Nguyen | Server | 7636 Bethel Road | Mason | OH | 45040 | 513-555-3382 | $8.00 |
| Haley | Ashe | Server | 309 Wright Ave. | Lebanon | OH | 45036 | 513-555-0387 | $8.00 |
| Eric | Rose | Assistant Manager | 2209 Miller Road | Lebanon | OH | 45036 | 513-555-6219 | $10.00 |
| Claire | Ghent | Assistant Manager | 155 Pleasant View, Apt. 8 | Monroe | OH | 45050 | 513-555-2886 | $10.00 |

1. Start a new database and name it **Sweet Stop**.
2. Create a table named **Employees**. Use the information above to set up the table's fields. Apply appropriate data types and field descriptions.
3. Create a form based on the *Employees* table, and enter the records shown above.
4. Create a query that shows only those employees who live in Lebanon. Include the *First Name, Last Name*, and *Phone* fields in the query. Save it as **Lebanon Employees**.
5. Create a report based on the *Employees* table that includes only the *First Name, Last Name, Position*, and *Hourly Rate* fields. Name the report **Hourly Rate**.

### Think Critically

1. What other tables might the Sweet Stop owner want in her business database?
2. How can a database help a business operate more efficiently?
3. How might you use a database to organize information related to school?

## School and Community
Whether it's vehicle emissions, landfills and dumping, or endangered wildlife, all of us are affected by issues concerning the natural world.

Volunteering for an organization that promotes awareness, conservation, and preservation is one way for you to learn about environmental problems and help find solutions.

1. Research to identify an environmental issue that affects your community. You can check resources such as local newspapers or a community bulletin board.
2. Develop a list of organizations that focus on the environmental issue you identified. Find volunteering opportunities with each of the organizations.
3. Select one of the organizations and write a one-page summary about it. You should introduce the environmental issue and describe the types of activities in which the organization is involved to educate people about the issue. Then explain what you can do as a volunteer in the organization to promote its cause.

# LESSON 103

## Using a Database to Create Form Letters, Envelopes, and Labels

**OUTCOMES**
- Create a form letter.
- Create envelopes.
- Create labels.

### Business Documents
- Form Letter
- Envelopes
- Labels

### 103B
#### Create a Mail Merge

1. Use the Mail Merge feature to create the form letter shown below to send to the individuals who have not paid their February fees at Baxter International.
2. Use the query (*February Fees Past Due*) for the database file in the merge. Print a copy of the form letter.
3. **Save as:** *103B Baxter International Merge Letter.*
4. Use the Find Recipient feature to find the letter being sent to Felipe Gonzalez; print a copy of the letter.
5. **Save as:** *103B Felipe Gonzalez.*

March 15, 20—

«Title»«First_Name»«Last_Name»
«Address»
«City», «State»«ZIP»

Dear «First_Name»,

I hope you are enjoying your subscription with Baxter International. As of today, March 15, we have not received your February or March subscription fees. Please send us a check today for $50 to cover the fees for these two months.

If you have questions about your fees, please call me at 503.829.1590.

Sincerely,

Jane R. Delgado
Subscription Manager

xx

### 103C
#### Create Envelopes

Mailings/Start Mail
Merge/Start Mail Merge/
Envelopes

Use the Mailings feature to create envelopes for the letters created in 103B by following these steps.
1. Open and create a new document.
2. Click Start Mail Merge in the Start Mail Merge group on the Mailings tab.
3. Click Envelopes.
4. In the Envelope Options dialog box, select Size 10 for the Envelope size. If Size 10 doesn't appear automatically, click the down arrow beneath Envelope size and click Size 10.
5. Click OK.

# Assessing Basic Presentation Skills

| | |
|---|---|
| Open *PowerPoint* | 1. Start a new presentation. |
| Select a design theme | 2. Select the Apothecary design theme. |
| Select slide layout | 3. Select the Title Slide layout. |
| Create title slide | 4. Create the following title slide. |

| | |
|---|---|
| Change font size | 5. Change the font size of the title of the presentation to 36 point and the date to 28 point. |
| Insert new slide<br>Create table slide<br>Align text | 6. Insert a new slide with Title and Content layout; insert a table with the information shown. Increase the font size of the main heading to 40 point; increase the font size of the text in the body of the table to 28 point. Align the text as shown in the following illustration. |

**STUDENTS**

| Class | No. of Students |
|---|---|
| Freshmen | 498 |
| Sophomores | 506 |
| Juniors | 480 |
| Seniors | 475 |

3. Establish the relationship between the two tables by clicking on Last Name in the Fees table and dragging it on top of *First Name* in the *Member's Address* table. This should connect the Last Name in the Fees table to the Last Name in the *Member's Address* table. Even though it seems you should be clicking on *Last Name* in the *Fees* table and dragging it to *Last Name* in the *Member's Address* table, doing so connects *Last Name* to *ID*.

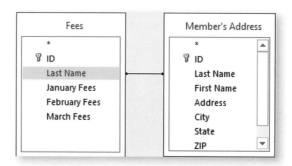

If by chance you connect the wrong fields, click on the line, tap the Delete key, and click and drag again.

4. Include the following fields in the query:
   - Last Name
   - First Name
   - Address
   - City
   - State
   - ZIP
   - February Fees

5. For the criteria in the *February Fees* field, key *Is Null*.

| Field: | Last Name | First Name | Address | City | State | ZIP | February Fees |
|---|---|---|---|---|---|---|---|
| Table: | Fees | Member's Address | Member's Address | Member's Address | Member's Address | Member's Address | Fees |
| Sort: | | | | | | | |
| Show: | ☑ | ☑ | ☑ | ☑ | ☑ | ☑ | ☑ |
| Criteria: | | | | | | | Is Null |
| or: | | | | | | | |

6. Run the query.
7. **Save as: February Fees Past Due**.
8. Edit the query to include *Title* field.

 QUICK ✔

The query should look like this:

**102D: February Fees Past Due**

| Last Name | First Name | Address | City | State | ZIP | February Fees | Title |
|---|---|---|---|---|---|---|---|
| Sessions | Jon | 218 Woodland Way, SE | Portland | OR | 97267 | | Mr. |
| Murphy | Shawn | 488 Everett Street, NE | Portland | OR | 97232 | | Mr. |
| Sabo | Kent | 77 Hampton Street, SW | Portland | OR | 97223 | | Mr. |
| Gonzalez | Felipe | 8800 Hancock Court, NE | Portland | OR | 97220 | | Mr. |
| Van Pelt | Jordan | 1440 Duke Street, SE | Portland | OR | 97202 | | Mr. |

**Create pie chart slide**
**Select data label display**

7. Insert a new slide with Title and Content layout; insert a pie chart (pie in 3-D) with the information from the previous table to create the slide shown in the following illustration. Use center for the label display layout.

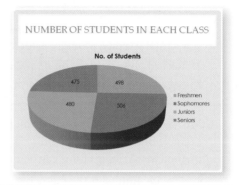

**Create slide with SmartArt**

**Copy and paste SmartArt element**

**Insert clip art**

**Change SmartArt colors**

8. Insert a new slide with Title and Content layout; insert SmartArt (trapezoid list) as illustrated below. Use the copy and paste feature to insert the fourth trapezoid. Input the information shown, insert clip art (circular sunburst design), and change colors to Colorful – Accent Colors.

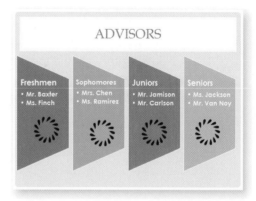

**Create slide with picture**

9. Insert a new slide with Picture with Caption layout. Open the ***df picture*** file; copy the picture and paste it in the picture area of slide 5. Input and format the title and text as shown.

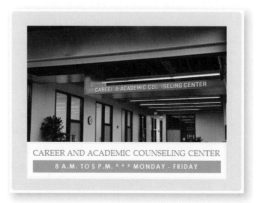

10. **Save as: *pp assessment*.**

1. Provide him with the following information for each territory:
   - Total Sales for July for each Territory.
   - Total Sales for August for each Territory.
   - Total Sales for September for each Territory.
   - Total Sales for the third Quarter for each Territory.
   - Total Average Monthly Sales for the third Quarter for each Territory.
2. Record your answers on *df 102B&C Analysis Form*.
3. **Save as:** *102B&C Analysis Form*.

## 102C

**Analyze Average Sales Information by Territory**

Mr. Vermillion would also like you to calculate the Average Sales for each territory. See the example of the Arizona territory shown below in the Quick Check. Use the most efficient method for arriving at this calculation. Record your answers on *df 102B&C Analysis Form*.

1. Provide him with the following information for each territory:
   - Average Sales for July for each Territory.
   - Average Sales for August for each Territory.
   - Average Sales for September for each Territory.
   - Average Sales for the third Quarter for each Territory.
   - Average Monthly Sales for the third Quarter for each Territory.
2. **Save as:** *102B&C Analysis Form*.

**QUICK ✓**

The Arizona territory should look like this.

| Last Name ▾ | First Name ▾ | Territory ▾ | July Sales ▾ | August Sales ▾ | September ▾ | Total Sales for Quarter ▾ | Average Monthly Sale ▾ |
|---|---|---|---|---|---|---|---|
| Chi | Karrie | Arizona | $39,750.00 | $48,621.00 | $50,805.00 | $139,176.00 | $46,392.00 |
| Finley | Ann | Arizona | $19,765.00 | $35,765.00 | $23,800.00 | $79,330.00 | $26,443.33 |
| Reese | Jay | Arizona | $67,890.00 | $45,780.00 | $50,775.00 | $164,445.00 | $54,815.00 |
| Butler | Warren | Arizona | $35,975.C | $46,873.00 | $50,980.00 | $133,828.00 | $44,609.33 |
| Hulett | Sandra | Arizona | $56,730.00 | $46,720.00 | $54,560.00 | $158,010.00 | $52,670.00 |
| Sanchez | Rey | Arizona | $0.00 | $0.00 | $23,891.00 | $23,891.00 | $7,963.67 |
| Total | | | $36,685.00 | $37,293.17 | $42,468.50 | $116,446.67 | $38,815.56 |

*Average Sales for Quarter - Arizona*

## 102D

**Create Query from Two Tables**

At times it is important to be able to merge data from two different tables in a query. In order to be able to merge data from two tables, the tables have to have a common field (a field that exists in both tables that is exactly the same). The common field allows the program to match records from one table with records in another table.

Baxter International has two tables in their database—one for address information and the other for recording subscription fees. Each month they send out a reminder to customers who are behind in paying their subscription fee. The reminder is sent on the 15th of the following month when fees were not paid. For example, if no fees were paid in February, a reminder would be sent on March 15. In order to send out such a reminder, information from both tables is required. Create a query to determine who is behind with their payments to use for mailing reminders. The following steps are required to complete the query.

1. Open *df Baxter International* database.
2. Use the Query Design feature to create a query. Add both tables to the Query dialog box.

# UNIT 6
## Building Effective Presentations

## Reference Guide

### Animations

Animations/Animation/ Select Animation Type

Rather than have a slide appear in its entirety, animations can be used to make text, graphics, and other objects appear one at a time. After text, graphics, or an object appears, animations can be used to change the size and color of the item as well as to move the item on the slide. This allows control of how the information is presented as well as adding interest to the presentation.

A variety of animations are available to choose from. A few examples include fade, spin, float, swivel, and bounce. **Animation schemes** are options that are preset. They range from very subtle to very glitzy. The scheme chosen should add interest without taking away from the message. **Custom animation** allows several different animations to be included on each slide.

Use the Animations tab to access the Animation group to select an animation. Use the down arrow to see additional *Entrance*, *Emphasis*, and *Exit* animations. See Figure 6-1.

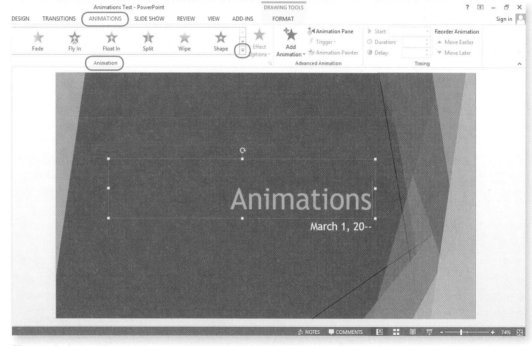

**Figure 6-1** Animation tab in *Microsoft PowerPoint*

# Data Mining and Analysis Using Queries Created From Multiple Tables

**OUTCOMES**
- Analyze sales information by territory.
- Create a query from two tables.

**Business Documents**
- Database Tables
- Database Queries
- Forms

## 102B

### Analyze Total Sales Information by Territory

Mr. Vermillion has reviewed the query you created for him on Total Monthly Sales and Average Monthly Sales for each sales rep as well as the information you provided on Total District 13 Sales and Average District 13 Sales. As he analyzed the information you provided, he felt that there was one piece missing.

He would like to have the data broken down further by territory to see if significant differences exist between the territories within District 13. Create queries (use *Total Sales for Quarter* query) showing the totals for each of the seven territories. Include the following fields with each query and save them with the query names shown below:

- Last Name
- First Name
- Territory
- July Sales
- August Sales
- September Sales
- Total Sales for Quarter
- Average Monthly Sales

- *Total Sales for Quarter - Arizona*
- *Total Sales for Quarter - Colorado*
- *Total Sales for Quarter - Idaho*
- *Total Sales for Quarter - Montana*
- *Total Sales for Quarter - South Dakota*
- *Total Sales for Quarter - Utah*
- *Total Sales for Quarter - Wyoming*

**QUICK ✔**

Include new Sales Reps in all calculations; see Lesson 101B. When completed, the Arizona and Colorado territory queries should look like the illustrations below.

**Total Sales for Quarter - Arizona**

| Last Name | First Name | Territory | July Sales | August Sales | September | Total Sales for Quarter | Average Monthly Sale |
|---|---|---|---|---|---|---|---|
| Chi | Karrie | Arizona | $39,750.00 | $48,621.00 | $50,805.00 | $139,176.00 | $46,392.00 |
| Finley | Ann | Arizona | $19,765.00 | $35,765.00 | $23,800.00 | $79,330.00 | $26,443.33 |
| Reese | Jay | Arizona | $67,890.00 | $45,780.00 | $50,775.00 | $164,445.00 | $54,815.00 |
| Butler | Warren | Arizona | $35,975.00 | $46,873.00 | $50,980.00 | $133,828.00 | $44,609.33 |
| Hulett | Sandra | Arizona | $56,730.00 | $46,720.00 | $54,560.00 | $158,010.00 | $52,670.00 |
| Sanchez | Rey | Arizona | $0.00 | $0.00 | $23,891.00 | $23,891.00 | $7,963.67 |
| Total | | | $220,110.00 | $223,759.00 | $254,811.00 | $698,680.00 | $232,893.33 |

**Total Sales for Quarter - Colorado**

| Last Name | First Name | Territory | July Sales | August Sales | September | Total Sales for Quarter | Average Monthly Sale |
|---|---|---|---|---|---|---|---|
| Hull | Dale | Colorado | $53,739.00 | $49,762.00 | $54,829.00 | $158,330.00 | $52,776.67 |
| LeClair | Justin | Colorado | $63,212.00 | $40,321.00 | $50,705.00 | $154,238.00 | $51,412.67 |
| Donovan | Kellee | Colorado | $37,198.00 | $45,865.00 | $49,814.00 | $132,877.00 | $44,292.33 |
| Rivera | Jose | Colorado | $55,400.00 | $37,751.00 | $50,880.00 | $144,031.00 | $48,010.33 |
| Bell | Scott | Colorado | $39,200.00 | $43,286.00 | $47,804.00 | $130,290.00 | $43,430.00 |
| Hayes | Jackson | Colorado | $0.00 | $0.00 | $19,799.00 | $19,799.00 | $6,599.67 |
| Total | | | $248,749.00 | $216,985.00 | $273,831.00 | $739,565.00 | $246,521.67 |

## Design Theme

Design/Themes/
Select a Theme

*PowerPoint* comes with files containing design themes (see examples in Figures 6-2 and 6-3). A design theme provides a consistent, attractive look. All the person creating the presentation has to do is select the slide layout, key the information, and insert appropriate graphics. The fonts and font sizes, places for keying information, background design, and color schemes are preset for each design theme. Even though these themes are preset, they can be changed to better fit your needs. Using design themes gives your presentations a professional appearance.

Figure 6-2 Dividend design theme    Figure 6-3 Parallax design theme

## Design Tips

As you create a slide show, consider the following design Do's and Don'ts:

- Do use bulleted lists to present concepts one at a time.
- Do use keywords and phrases rather than complete sentences.
- Do use contrasting background colors that make text stand out. Use light text against a dark background or dark text against a light background.
- Do choose a font size that the audience can read—even in the back of the room.
- Do use sound and animation to make a point, but not to distract from your message.
- Don't overcrowd slides. Two slides might be better than one.
- Don't overuse clip art. Photos have more impact.
- Don't overuse animations and transitions.

## Hyperlinks

Insert/Links/Hyperlink

A hyperlink is text that is colored and underlined that you click to take you from the current location in the electronic file to another location. See the example in Figure 6-4.

President's Cabinet

http://www.whitehouse.gov/government/cabinet.html

Figure 6-4 Slide with hyperlink

This means that a presenter can create hyperlinks to move from the current slide in a presentation to an Internet site that relates to the topic.

Use the information gathered for the *101C&D Analysis Form* to answer the following questions. Record your answers on *df 101E Analyze Information Form*. After you complete the form, print a copy of it.

1. Which month generated the greatest sales revenue?
2. Which month generated the least sales revenue?
3. What impact did the new employees have on *Total Sales for the Quarter*?
4. What impact did the new employees have on *Average Monthly Sales* when they were included in the calculation?
5. How many sales reps had average monthly sales that were 20 percent higher than the average of all sales reps? To answer this question, create and run a query using the *Total Sales for Quarter* query with the Last Name, First Name, and Average Monthly Sales. Using the calculator feature on your computer, calculate what 120% of the Average Monthly sales is and use that amount for the Criteria for the Average Monthly Sales column in Design View of the query.
6. Save the query as: *Sales 20% Higher than Average for Quarter*.
7. How many sales reps had average monthly sales that were 20 percent lower than the average of all sales reps? Run a query using the *Total Sales for Quarter* query that includes the *Last Name, First Name*, and *Average Monthly Sales* fields. Calculate what 80% of the Average Monthly Sales is and use that amount as the Criteria for the Average Monthly Sales column.
8. Save the query as: *Sales 20% Lower than Average for Quarter*.

---

## 21st Century Skills: Civic Literacy

All of us are members of a community, whether it's a small town, suburban neighborhood, or large municipality. Being a member of any type of community comes with certain rights and responsibilities.

As a U.S. citizen, you have basic constitutional rights, such as freedom to practice any religion you choose or freedom to assemble and protest government policies. But you also have responsibilities as a citizen. These include obeying laws, paying taxes, and participating in elections. Even if you are not subject to paying taxes or old enough to vote or drive, you can show your civic-mindedness in other ways. For example, you can:

- Perform community service, such as picking up trash or planting trees.
- Support political candidates and issues for which you feel strongly.
- Identify ways to stay informed and understand governmental processes.

### Think Critically

1. In groups, brainstorm issues that affect your community. This could be a local issue, such as downsizing the police force or restricting the use of skateboards in public parks, or a national issue, such as changing the federal income tax rate.
2. As a group, select the issue that you think is most important. Then create a plan of action for how you would support the issue or bring about change. Would you organize a rally or protest? Send letters to your congressional representatives? Hand out flyers? Present your plan to the class.

During a slide show presentation, you can use the shortcut menu (illustrated in Figure 6-5) to display any slide in the presentation at any time. The shortcut menu is displayed by right clicking while in Slide Show View.

The first slide, the last slide, or any slide in a slide show can also be displayed by using keyboard shortcuts.

Knowing shortcuts is particularly helpful when your audience has a question relating to what has previously been discussed or when the presenter wants to show a slide that is placed after the one currently being shown to address a question from the audience or to make changes.

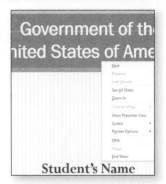

**Figure 6-5** Shortcut menu available during a presentation

## Pictures

Insert/Images

★TIP  Care must be taken not to violate copyright laws.

In addition to clip art, pictures can be inserted in an electronic presentation from a number of different sources such as scanners, cameras, files, and the Internet. Movies can also be inserted into a presentation. Inserting pictures and movies, as shown in Figure 6-6, enhances a slide show and captures and keeps the audience's attention.

**Figure 6-6** Example of slide with picture

## Slide Layout

Home/Slides/Layout/
Select a Layout

Layout refers to the way text and graphics are arranged on the slide. Presentation software allows the user to select a slide layout for each slide from a menu, as shown in Figure 6-7. Some of the more common layouts include:

- Title Slide layout
- Title and Content layout
- Section Header layout
- Two Content layout
- Comparison layout
- Title Only layout
- Blank layout
- Content with Caption layout
- Picture with Caption layout

**Figure 6-7** Slide layouts

## 101D

**Calculate Average District Sales**

Next, Mr. Vermillion would like you to calculate the following District Averages and record your answers on the *101C&D Analysis Form:*

- Average District Sales for July.
- Average District Sales for August.
- Average District Sales for September.
- Average District Sales for Quarter.

Use the procedure shown below to do the calculations to get the averages.

1. Open the *Total Sales for Quarter* query, if it isn't still open.
2. Click the Total cell for Average District Sales for July.

3. Click the down arrow that appears when you click in the cell.

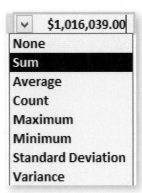

4. The figure that currently appears is the sum of the column. To calculate the Average of the column, click on Average. Note that the $1,016039.00 has changed to $39,078.42, which represents the average for the column.

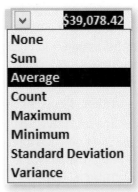

5. Follow the same procedure for the remaining columns that you want to calculate the Average for and record your answers on the form.
6. **Save as:** *101C&D Analysis Form.*

# Build Slide Show Presentations with Screen Clippings

**OUTCOMES**

- Insert a screen clipping using the screenshot feature.
- Create a slide show with graphics.
- Insert slides in an existing slide show.

**Business Documents**

**33A–38A**

**Warmup**

- Slide Show Presentation

Key each line twice daily.

| | | |
|---|---|---|
| alphabet | 1 | Zelda Jamestown backed up and forged down the exquisite driveway. |
| fig/sym | 2 | Jay's home phone number is 836.1877; his cell number is 379.2005. |
| speed | 3 | The neighbor may fix the problem with the turn signal on the bus. |

**gwam** 1' | 1 | 2 | 3 | 4 | 5 | 6 | 7 | 8 | 9 | 10 | 11 | 12 | 13 |

**33B**

**Learn: Insert a Screen Clipping**

Insert/Images/Screenshot/
Screen Clipping

1. Read the following information about images in a slide presentation.

Images enhance slide shows. Images can be pictures that you have taken, scanned pictures from books, pictures from files, or images from the Internet. As you use work created by others, you have to consider and obey copyright laws. The following image is a picture you would like to use for the first slide in the slide show that you are creating. This can be done by following these steps.

2. Open **df 33b picture**. Use the scroll bar to position the second picture from the data file so that the entire picture appears on your screen as shown in Figure 6-11.

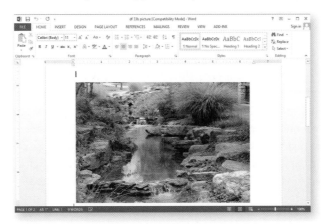

**Figure 6-11** Entire picture displayed in the word processing window

3. Open *PowerPoint* to create a new slide show.
4. Change the layout of the first slide to *Blank*.
5. Click the Insert tab and click Screenshot as shown in Figure 6-12.

**Figure 6-12** Select Screenshot

# Data Mining and Analysis Using Computed Fields and Column Totals

**OUTCOMES**

- Create queries with computed fields.
- Calculate column totals.
- Analyze information extracted through queries.

## Business Documents

- Database Tables
- Database Queries
- Forms

**101A–106A**

**Warmup**

Key each line twice daily.

Key each line twice at the beginning of each lesson; first for control; then for speed.

alphabet   1  Jack very quickly called them before swimming a dozen extra laps.

fig/sym   2  Tim's order (#37–96) is for 40 caps, 25 baseballs, and 18 shirts.

speed   3  Pamela is to pay the six auto firms for all the bodywork they do.

gwam  1'| 1 | 2 | 3 | 4 | 5 | 6 | 7 | 8 | 9 | 10 | 11 | 12 | 13 |

**Unit Preview**

In Unit 18, you will have the opportunity to analyze information compiled from the databases of three companies. The databases of these companies are available on the instructor *IRCD* and website as data files; check with your instructor. Each database contains at least one table that will be used to complete the activities in this unit. The table below shows the companies for which you will be analyzing data.

| Company | Type of Information |
|---|---|
| Baxter International | Subscription Information |
| Parker & Sons | Employee Information |
| Rockwell Technologies | Sales Rep Information |

**101B**

**Create Queries with Computed Fields**

Paul M. Vermillion, District 13 sales manager for Rockwell Technologies, would like you to create a query that shows Total Sales for Quarter (July–September) and Average Monthly Sales for the quarter for each of the sales reps in District 13. Use *df Rockwell Technologies (Unit 18)* for the database to create the query. Use the illustration below for the fields to include in the query and to verify the accuracy of the query when completed.

**QUICK ✓**

101B Total Sales for Quarter

| Last Name | First Name | Territory | July Sales | August Sales | September S | Total Sales for Quarter | Average Monthly Sales |
|---|---|---|---|---|---|---|---|
| Carter-Bond | Mary | Wyoming | $45,351.00 | $37,951.00 | $42,819.00 | $126,121.00 | $42,040.33 |
| Hull | Dale | Colorado | $53,739.00 | $49,762.00 | $54,829.00 | $158,330.00 | $52,776.67 |
| McRae | Jessica | Utah | $33,371.00 | $38,978.00 | $42,561.00 | $114,910.00 | $38,303.33 |
| Hernandez | Erika | Utah | $39,371.00 | $40,790.00 | $50,096.00 | $130,257.00 | $43,419.00 |
| Camby | Sue | Idaho | $42,173.00 | $65,386.00 | $55,142.00 | $162,701.00 | $54,233.67 |
| Henneman | Jason | Montana | $17,219.00 | $29,737.00 | $33,890.00 | $80,846.00 | $26,948.67 |

6. Click Screen Clipping at the bottom of the dialog box (Figure 6-13).

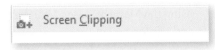

Figure 6-13 Select Screen Clipping

7. Left-click and drag over the portion of image that you want to capture as shown in Figure 6-14.

Figure 6-14 Select the portion of the image to capture

8. Release the left-click. The picture will appear on your *PowerPoint* slide.
9. **Save as:** *33b ppt*.

**QUICK ✔**

Your completed slide should look like this:

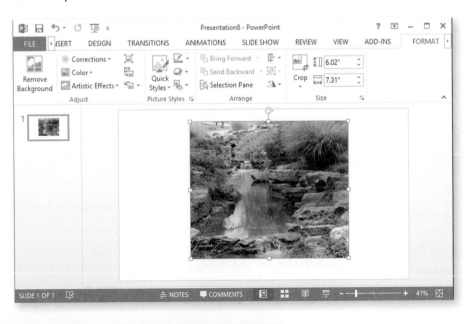

## Mail Merge

The Mail Merge feature can be used to create customized documents. Customized letters, emails, labels, directories, and envelopes are a few of the documents that are commonly created using the Merge feature. Mail merge was introduced in Unit 5; this discussion is for application and reinforcement.

The Mail Merge feature merges two files: a word processing file (form letter, envelope, or labels) and a data file. The word processing file contains the text of the document (constant information) plus the merge field names (variable information). The merge field names are positioned in the document where the variable information from the database is to appear.

The data file contains a record for each recipient. Each record contains field(s) of information about the person such as first name, last name, address, city, state, ZIP, and so on.

**Mailings/Start Mail Merge/ Start Mail Merge**

**Start Mail Merge:** Use Start Mail Merge to create a word processing document file (letter, email message, envelope, label, or other *Word* document). Fields can be inserted in the document that will be replaced automatically with information from the database when the word processing file and the database file are merged.

**Mailings/Start Mail Merge/ Select Recipients**

**Select Recipients:** Use Select Recipients to select the database file containing the fields with the information that will be placed in the word processing document.

**Mailings/Start Mail Merge/ Edit Recipient List**

**Edit Recipient List:** If you don't want to send the merged document to all the individuals included in the data file, the Edit Recipient List feature can be used to select the individuals that you do want it sent to. This feature can also be used to modify the information contained in the data file.

**Mailings/Write & Insert Fields/Insert Merge Field**

**Insert Merge Field:** After selecting the file to be used in the merge using the Select Recipients feature, merge field names can be placed in the word processing form file. The merge field names are placed at the location in the word processing form file where you want the variable information from the database to appear when the form file and database file are merged.

**Mailings/Write & Insert Fields/Greeting Line**

**Greeting Line:** The Greeting Line feature can be used to automatically insert the greeting in a form file. Use the down arrows to modify the greeting from the default. For example, if you want a colon following the greeting rather than a comma, click the down arrow and click the colon; then click OK.

**Mailings/Preview Results/ Preview Results**

**Preview Results:** After the merge form file has been completed, use the Preview Results feature to replace the merge fields in the form with the information from the database. This allows for viewing the form documents before printing.

**Mailings/Preview Results/ Find Recipient**

**Find Recipient:** The Find Recipient feature can be used to view an individual record in the recipient list.

**Mailings/Finish/Finish & Merge**

**Finish & Merge:** The Finish & Merge feature is used to create separate documents for each individual included in the database. Once completed, documents can be printed for mailing or they can be sent via email.

## Apply: Create a Slide Show with Graphics

Design/Themes/Equity

Design/Variants (down arrow)/Colors/Office

★**TIP** To move the location of the Student's Name placeholder, click the top line of the placeholder and drag to the desired location.

Insert/Online Pictures/ Office.com Clip Art

1. Open **df 33c ppt**; change variant colors of the *Equity* design theme to *Office*. Create the following 12 slides. The slides will be used again in Lessons 34–37.

   The 15 departments of the Executive Branch are listed on the Cabinet website (www. whitehouse.gov/administration/cabinet/). After accessing the website, a specific department's home page can be accessed by scrolling down to find the department and then clicking the link beneath the department listing.

2. Note in Slide 6 that an Online Picture was inserted for the Department of Agriculture. Find and insert appropriate pictures to represent each department.

3. **Save as:  33c ppt**.

**Government of the United State of America**

Student's Name
Current Date

**Slide 1**

Branches of U.S. Government

- Executive Branch
- Judicial Branch
- Legislative Branch

**Slide 2**

Executive Branch

- The power of the executive branch is vested in the President, who also serves as Commander in Chief of the Armed Forces.

**Slide 3**

George Washington

- First President of the U.S.
- 1789-1797

**Slide 4**

**Slide 5**

**Slide 6**

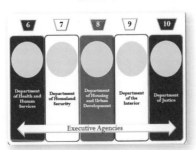

**Slide 7**

Legislative Branch

- The legislative branch of the federal government consists of the Congress, which is divided into two chambers— the Senate and the House of Representatives.

**Slide 8**

# UNIT 18 — Analyzing Information Efficiently and Effectively

## Reference Guide

**Database Query**

Create/Queries/Query Design

**Database Report**

Create/Reports/Report Wizard

The Query feature of a database software program is used to gather specific information from tables containing records with fields of information. The results of a query are called a record set. A record set is displayed in a datasheet.

Queries become the basis of reports that are used for making informed decisions. Generally, queries rather than tables are used as the source for the report data because the query limits the data to what is relevant to the report.

Queries are used for answering questions, gathering and assembling data from two or more tables, performing calculations, and even changing or deleting table data. Queries were first discussed in Unit 5.

Database reports are created from database tables and queries. Reports are used for organizing, summarizing, and printing information. The easiest way to generate a report is by simply clicking on Report in the Reports group. This will give you a report of all the fields in the table or datasheet.

Use the Report Wizard to customize the design of a report. With the Report Wizard, specific fields can be selected to be included in the report, desired groupings can be specified, fields can be sorted in ascending or descending order, and layouts can be selected.

© Xtremest/Shutterstock.com

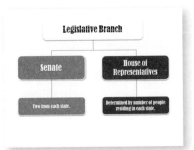

**Slide 9**

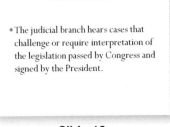

**Slide 10**

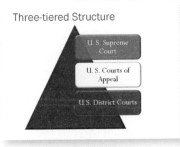

**Slide 11**

**Slide 12**

33D

**Learn: Insert Slides in a Slide Show**

1. Use Help for your presentation software to learn how to insert new slides.
2. Create the two following slides, and insert them into the presentation as instructed.
3. Create a similar one for the Legislative Branch (insert it before the Legislative Branch description) and one for the Judicial Branch (insert it before the Judicial Branch description).
4. **Save as:** *33d ppt*.

**Insert between slides 2 and 3**

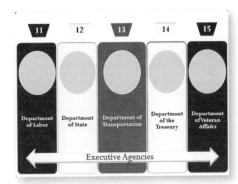

**Insert between slides 7 and 8**

**Lesson 33** Build Slide Show Presentations with Screen Clippings

UNIT 6 181

# The Winning Edge

Kheng Guan Toh/Shutterstock.com

Complete this activity to help prepare for the **Desktop Publishing** event in FBLA-PBL's Information Technology division. Participants in this event demonstrate skills in the areas of desktop publishing, creativity, and decision making.

A new ice cream and dessert parlor has just opened in your neighborhood. The owner asks you to develop and design her business documents. Following is information about the business:

**Name:** Sweet Stop
**Address:** 4032 Broadway, Lebanon, OH 45036
**Phone:** (513) 555-8787
**Hours:** Monday–Saturday 11 a.m.–8 p.m.; Sunday noon–6 p.m.
**Menu:** hand-dipped ice cream, sundaes, shakes, and floats; homemade pies, cookies, cupcakes, and other desserts; beverages, including various coffees, teas, and hand-squeezed lemonades

1. In a new word processing document, use clip art or ready-made shapes to create a logo for the business that incorporates its name and the tagline, "Your sweet tooth's dream come true!" Save the document as directed by your instructor.
2. Using the information above, create a menu for the business. If necessary, research the costs of similar menu items, and use your decision-making skills to set the price for each. Be sure to use the logo you already created. Save the document as directed by your instructor.
3. Use a template to create a business card. Save and print the document as directed.
4. Use a template to create a flyer. It should include the logo, address, phone, and hours of operation, and highlight items from the menu. Save and print the flyer as directed.

For detailed information on this event, go to www.fbla-pbl.org.

## Think Critically

1. You have learned about a number of special business documents you can create using wp software. What special documents might you create for school activities? For social or family activities?
2. How does the design of a document or publication affect its message?

## School and Community
Health fairs are an ideal way to educate people on healthy diet and nutrition, fitness, preventive health care, and how to access the medical and health care services they need. The format of a health fair can range from simply distributing and sharing information to providing full-fledged health screenings and services. Organize a health fair at your school:

1. Determine the type of fair you want to have. Will participants offer information and screenings, or just information? Will you have booths? Will there be entertainment?
2. Contact health professionals at school (school nurse, dietician, physical education instructor, and so on) and in the community (doctors, nurses, fitness trainers, nutritionists, and health-focused organizations, such as the American Heart Association or the American Lung Association).
3. Form a committee to handle logistics, such as location, booth setup, signage, parking, cleanup, and so on.
4. Publicize the fair using posters, flyers, social media, etc.

# Build Slide Show Presentations with Graphics, Animations, and Transitions

**OUTCOMES**

- Add animations to a slide show.
- Add transitions to a slide show.
- Add graphics to enhance a slide show.
- Add notes to a slide show.

## Business Documents

### 34B

- Slide Show Presentation

**Add Animations to a Slide Show**

Animations/Animation/
Select Animation

1. Read the following information about animations, and complete the activity.

Animations are special effects that can be included to enhance a presentation. For example, a bulleted list will appear all at once without animations. By using animations, each bulleted item can be made to appear one at a time. This allows the presenter to control not only what the audience sees but when they see it. The presenter can discuss the first point before the next point appears, thus keeping the audience focused on the point that is being discussed. When the speaker is ready to discuss the next point, the second point in the bulleted list can be made to appear.

In addition to the entrance animation effect, animation can be used for emphasis, to exit, and for motion paths. An example of the exit animation effect would be removing each of five possible answers from a slide at a time (exit), leaving only the correct answer. A motion path is the direction an object follows across the slide. Paths can be the standard paths available or customized by the person creating the presentation.

2. Open **df 34b ppt**.
3. In Normal View bring up slide 2.
4. Click one of the names to display the placeholder containing the bulleted items as shown in Figure 6-15.

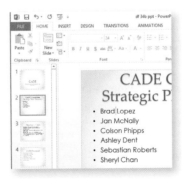

**Figure 6-15**
Bulleted items

5. Click the down arrow in the Animation group of the Animations tab as shown in Figure 6-16.

**Figure 6-16** Display the types of animations.

# Career Clusters

© Blend Images/Shutterstock.com

## Planning a Career in Human Services

Those who work in the Human Services career cluster are focused on providing care to others and helping them improve their lives. They interact with people from all walks of life, whether it's teaching a preschooler how to read or counseling a married couple or coordinating activities at a retirement community.

## What's It Like?

Workers employed in this field are involved in jobs that relate to families and human needs such as counseling and mental health services, family and community services, personal care, and consumer services. For example:

- They nurture, teach, and care for young children through daycare and preschool programs, and supervise older children.
- They provide a variety of counseling, rehabilitation, and support services to children, adolescents, adults, and families that have multiple issues, such as mental health disorders and addiction, disability and employment needs, school problems or career counseling needs, and trauma.
- They plan food and nutrition programs, supervise meal preparation, and prevent and treat illnesses by promoting healthy eating habits and recommending dietary modifications.
- They respond to customer inquiries, providing a valuable link between those customers and the companies that produce the products they buy and the services they use.
- They lead, instruct, and motivate individuals or groups in exercise activities, including cardiovascular exercise, strength training, and stretching.

Employees in this field may work in classrooms, hospitals, private medical offices, fitness facilities, corporate offices, and community clinics. They typically work regular 40-hour weeks, although those in education and health care may work varying schedules.

## Employment Outlook

Employment in this career cluster is expected to grow at an average or faster than average pace, with job openings expected to exceed the number of graduates in many areas.

Education requirements for workers in this cluster vary. Some jobs require a high school diploma, while others require a bachelor's or master's degree. Most require some form of certification or state licensure.

## What About You?

This career cluster is covered in box 10 of the Interest Survey Activity you completed in Unit 1 of this text. If this box had one of the three highest scores on your survey, you should further explore the cluster's pathways and related occupations.

1. Why do you think a career in this field could be a good choice?
2. What skills can you develop now that would be helpful to a career in this field?
3. Why are these jobs important to a community?

6. Click the *Grow and Turn* animation as shown in Figure 6-17.

**Figure 6-17** Select an animation

7. Click on Slide Show View.
8. Tap Enter to make the members appear.
9. Tap Esc to return to Normal View. Note the animation icon that now appears before slide 2 and the numbers that appear before the bulleted items in the placeholder box as shown in Figure 6-18.

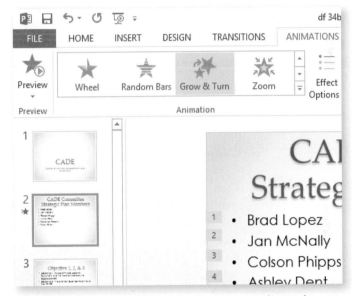

**Figure 6-18** Icons indicate that items are animated

10. Include these entrance animations on the following slides.
    a. Slide 3: Fly In
    b. Slide 4: Split
    c. Slide 5: Zoom
    d. Slide 6: Bounce
    e. Slide 7: Wipe
11. Click Slide 1; click on Slide Show View to view the animation effects.
12. Save as: *34b ppt*.

VEER.COM/STILLFX

# Academic and Career Connections

Complete the following exercises that introduce various topics that involve academic themes and careers.

## Grammar and Writing: Proofreading

**MicroType 6**

- References/Communication Skills/Proofreading

1. Go to *MicroType 6* and use this feature path: References/Communication Skills/Proofreading.
2. Click Rules and review the rules for proofreading.
3. Then, under *Proofreading*, click *Posttest*.
4. Follow the instructions to complete the posttest.

## Communications: Speaking

You have been selected to give a speech on health and wellness. Use the outline in the **df u17 communications** file to help you prepare your speech. Your presentation is to be about two minutes long. The audience is your classmates.

1. Review the outline and decide which points you will include in your speech. You may add other topics if desired.
2. Open a new word processing document and key your own outline or write summary points of your speech. Save the document as **u17 communications**, and with your instructor's permission, print a copy.
3. Practice your speech by reading your document several times aloud. Add transitions as necessary. Jot notes on the document to elaborate and embellish as needed.
4. Then, either in front of a mirror or with your friends or family, continue to practice your speech. Pay attention to your tone of voice, facial expressions, posture, and body language. Your goal is to present your speech without having to read directly from your printed document.
5. As directed by your instructor, present your speech to the class.

## History

Justin works in marketing and communications for a regional bank. In an effort to educate students on the importance of saving money and making wise financial decisions, he is visiting area schools and presenting information on saving and investing. Part of his presentation is on the history of money and how we came to use the currency system now in place.

1. Use the Internet, library, and other resources to research the history of money. You should look for information on the many material forms that money has taken and how it has evolved over the centuries. Your research should include the barter system, the use of livestock and vegetable products, the first metal money, and introduction of paper currency.
2. In a new word processing document, write a one-page summary of your findings. Be sure to note significant dates and eras in the development of modern-day currency.
3. Create a poster or large-format flyer to illustrate the information you have gathered on the history of money. Use information from your summary and incorporate hand-drawn or computer-generated graphics as necessary.
4. Share your summary and poster with the class.

## Learn: Add Transitions to a Slide Show

Transitions/Transition to This Slide/Select Transition

1. Read the following information about transitions, and complete the activity.

Animation is the special effects that occur with the graphics and text of each slide. Transitions are special effects placed between slides to enhance a slide show. A few of these special effects are illustrated in Figure 6-19.

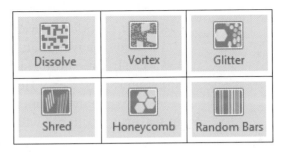

**Figure 6-19** Transitions are displayed between slides

Including transitions adds excitement to your visuals. Transitions also capture and help maintain your audience's attention. The process of adding transitions to a presentation is very similar to adding animations.

2. Open **34b ppt**.
3. Click on slide 1.
4. Click on the Transition tab.
5. Click the down arrow located on the Transition to This Slide group.
6. Click on the Random Bars transition icon.
7. Include these transitions to the following slides.
   a. Slide 2: Blinds
   b. Slide 3: Honeycomb
   c. Slide 4: Shred
   d. Slide 5: Glitter
   e. Slide 6: Vortex
   f. Slide 7: Box
8. View the slide show.
9. **Save as: 34c ppt**.

★TIP The amount of glitz added to this presentation was just to illustrate the various animations and transitions that are available. If this were a real presentation, it would be too much. Don't overuse animations and transitions; it will make your audience focus on the slide show rather than on what is being presented.

1. Open a new document. Design a flyer to present the information provided. Insert an appropriate page border. You decide the use of WordArt, SmartArt, shapes, clip art, pictures, and/or text boxes and all other formatting features.
2. **Save as:** *100b flyer*.

|  |  |
|---:|:---|
| Event: | The Dangers of Drinking and Driving |
| Sponsored by: | Students Against DUI |
| When: | Friday, November 14, at 3:30 p.m. |
| Where: | Weaver High School Auditorium |
| Cost: | Free admission with school ID card |
| Presenter: | Sgt. Terry Hollinsworth |
|  | State Trooper and Weaver Alumnus |
| Main feature: | Students will use a simulator to observe the effects of DUI |

## 100C

### Timed Writings

Key 2 5' writings on all ¶s combined; find *gwam* and errors.

**A** all letters used

gwam 3' | 5'

Something that you can never escape is your attitude. It    4 | 2 | 44
will be with you forever. However, you decide whether your    8 | 5 | 47
attitude is an asset or a liability for you. Your attitude    12 | 7 | 49
reflects the way you feel about the world you abide in and    16 | 9 | 52
everything that is a part of that world. It reflects the way you    20 | 12 | 54
feel about yourself, about your environment, and about other peo-    25 | 15 | 57
ple who are a part of your environment. Oftentimes, people with    29 | 17 | 59
a positive attitude are people who are extremely successful.    33 | 20 | 62

At times we all have experiences that cause us to be    36 | 22 | 64
negative. The difference between a positive and negative per-    41 | 24 | 66
son is that the positive person rebounds very quickly from a bad    45 | 27 | 69
experience; the negative person does not. The positive person is    49 | 30 | 72
a person who usually looks to the bright side of things and    53 | 32 | 74
recognizes the world as a place of promise, hope, joy, excite-    58 | 35 | 77
ment, and purpose. A negative person generally has just the    62 | 37 | 79
opposite view of the world. Remember, others want to be around    66 | 40 | 82
those who are positive but tend to avoid those who are negative.    70 | 42 | 84

3' | 1 | 2 | 3 | 4
5' | 1 | 2 | 3

**Apply: Add Graphics to Enhance a Slide Show**

Enhance the *Government of the United States of America* slide show that you modified for 33D by completing the following steps.

1. Open **33d ppt**.
2. Make the following changes.

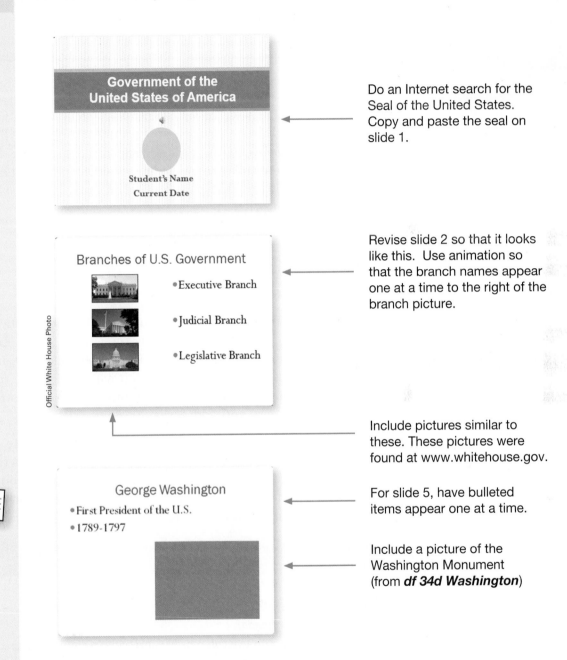

Do an Internet search for the Seal of the United States. Copy and paste the seal on slide 1.

Revise slide 2 so that it looks like this. Use animation so that the branch names appear one at a time to the right of the branch picture.

Include pictures similar to these. These pictures were found at www.whitehouse.gov.

For slide 5, have bulleted items appear one at a time.

Include a picture of the Washington Monument (from **df 34d Washington**)

**OUTCOME**

- Design documents using columns and various graphics.

## Business Documents

- Equal 2-Column Newsletter
- Calendar of Events
- Flyer

**100B**

**Design Applications**

### Newsletter

1. Open a new document. Key the text below as a newsletter that has two columns of equal width, separated by a vertical line. The newsletter title and publication information should span both columns.
2. Open **df 100b newsletter** and add the articles in the file after the shaded paragraph.
3. You decide all formatting features for the newsletter and make it fit on two pages using portrait or landscape orientation. Position the Health Tip text box wherever you prefer.
4. Save as: **100b newsletter**.

ENVIRONMENTAL ALERT!

Volume 12, No. 9      November 20--

Where to Get Help

Have you ever wondered where to turn for answers to environmental problems? One good place to start is the United States Environmental Protection Agency's (EPA) website. The home page contains numerous links to general and specific information that will be of help. You can link to sections for concerned citizens, small businesses, industry, and even get EPA telephone numbers and addresses.

Protection of the environment is a big job. Federal, state, and local agencies across the nation are all involved, employing thousands of citizens who care about their health and natural resources. Every city, county, and state networks with federal groups to share and provide information. If the first person you contact can't answer a question, he or she will know who can.

No longer can we say, "I'm too busy to be concerned with the environment— someone else can take care of it."

### Calendar of Events

1. Open **df 100b calendar**.
2. Format the text into two columns of equal width using 1.0 line spacing.
3. Insert appropriate clip art near the top of the page.
4. Use the Drop Cap feature as desired, and place a *Draft* watermark behind the text.
5. You decide all other formatting features to make the document attractive, easy to read, and fit on one page.
6. Save as: **100b calendar**.

Animations/Animation/
Wedge Effect Options/
One by One

Insert/Links/Hyperlink

3. Insert a slide following slide 9 (the third Executive Agencies slide). Select Section Header layout. Use **President's Cabinet** for the main heading.

4. In Slide Sorter view, add the following transitions:
   a. Slide 1: Glitter
   b. Slide 2: Honeycomb
   c. Slide 3, 11, 14: Vortex
   d. Slides 4–10: Flip
   e. Slides 12–13: Box
   f. Slides 15–17: Doors

5. Animate the bulleted items so they appear one at a time for slides 2 and 17.

6. Use the Wedge animation effect for the illustration for slide 16. Use the Effects option to group graphics one by one.

7. Use Help for your presentation software to learn how to insert a hyperlink. On the newly inserted slide, include a hyperlink to www.whitehouse.gov/government/cabinet.html.

8. Copy the first slide and insert it at the end of your presentation as slide 18.

9. Use *Glitter* transition for slide 18.

10. **Save as:** *34d ppt*.

© wavebreakmedia/Shutterstock.com

## 21st Century Skills: Information, Communications, and Technology (ICT) Literacy

Today's technology has drastically changed the way we present and exchange information. Through word processing and other types of software applications, we can quickly and easily prepare professional-looking correspondence, reports, tables, and other types of documents.

Being a proficient user of software applications, including word processing, spreadsheet, presentation, and database programs, is an important skill both in the classroom and on the job. Further, knowing how to use these tools to effectively communicate information and ideas will help you succeed in all areas of your life.

### Think Critically

Open a new presentation file, and create slides for each of the following software applications. Key the information as shown for each application, and then list at least two types of files you could create with each type of application. Insert graphics and apply formats as desired to enhance the presentation.

- **Word Processing**: Use to create text documents.
- **Spreadsheet**: Use to create worksheets for recording and calculating data.
- **Presentation**: Use to create multimedia slide shows.
- **Database**: Use to organize and manage data.

Save the presentation as directed by your instructor.

## Outside Front Cover

1. Arrange the following information attractively: **High School Honor Society, Induction Ceremony, Laurel High School, December 15, 20--, 6:30 p.m.**

2. Insert the following text in a shaded text box or shape.

   The High School Honor Society inducts students who have achieved academic excellence, displayed good character, demonstrated leadership qualities, and served the school and community.

## Inside Left Page

After keying the title **PROGRAM**, insert this information, including dot leaders:

Welcome.................................................Rob Jansante, President

Opening Remarks.....................................Dr. Paul Henry, Principal

Speaker..................................................Dr. Helen Rapp, Laurel Community College

Induction Ceremony

    Scholarship...................................Matt Roman, Vice President

    Character.....................................Jessica Roman, Treasurer

    Leadership...................................Stephanie Davis, Secretary

    Service........................................Meghan Johnson, Historian

    Pledge.........................................Rob Jansante

    Presentation of Certificates.................Rob Jansante and Dr. Paul Henry

    Closing........................................Rob Jansante

*All members and guests are invited to a reception in the Library immediately following the Induction Ceremony.*

(*Note:* Add decorative clip art if desired.)

## Inside Right Page

1. Key **INDUCTEES** as a title that spans both columns.

2. Insert the names of the inductees from the file *df 99b names*. Balance the names in two columns. If needed, change to 1.15 line spacing with 0 points spacing before and after.

**QUICK** ✔

Your four pages in the two files should look similar to this:

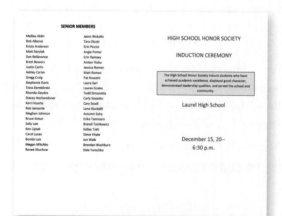

## Apply: Add Notes to a Slide Show

**Figure 6-20** Notes pane below each slide

You will be giving the slide show you just created to foreign exchange students at your school. In Normal View, notes for each slide can be placed beneath the slide by clicking in the Notes pane and keying the note as shown in Figure 6-20.

1. Open **34d ppt**. Key the following notes for each specified slide.

   Slide 1: The government of the United States as we know it today has evolved over time. Its beginnings date back prior to the U.S. gaining its independence from England.

   Slide 2: Today we have three branches of government. They include:
   the Executive Branch
   the Legislative Branch, and
   the Judicial Branch

   Slide 3: Let's start by talking about the Executive Branch.

   Slide 4: As you can see, the President of the United States is in charge of the Executive Branch. He serves as Commander in Chief of the Armed Forces, appoints cabinet members, and oversees various executive (government) agencies that we will be discussing later on in the presentation.

   Slide 5: The first Commander in Chief of the Armed Forces was our first President, George Washington. Interestingly enough, he was named the army's Commander in Chief by the Second Continental Congress before he was ever elected president.

   Slide 6: This slide shows a diagram of the 15 Executive Agencies.

   Slide 7: The Executive Agencies include: the Department of Agriculture, the Department of Commerce, the Department of Defense, the Department of Education, the Department of Energy,

   Slide 8: the Department of Health and Human Services, the Department of Homeland Security, the Department of Housing and Urban Development, the Department of the Interior, the Department of Justice,

   Slide 9: the Department of Labor, the Department of State, the Department of Transportation, the Department of the Treasury, and the Department of Veterans Affairs.

   Slide 10: Let's take a look at the President's Cabinet.

   Slide 11: Now that we know a little about the Executive Branch, let's talk briefly about the Legislative Branch of government.

   Slide 12: The Legislative Branch consists of Congress. Congress has two parts—the Senate and the House of Representatives.

   Slide 13: As shown on this slide, there are two senators elected from each state. They are elected for a term of six years. The terms of the senators are staggered so that one-third of the Senate seats are up for election every two years. With each state having two senators, each state is given equal representation regardless of size or population.
   The House of Representatives, on the other hand, is based on the population of each state. As the population changes within states, the number of representatives allocated to that state may also change.

2. Review slides 14–18. Create a note appropriate for each of these slides.

3. Print copies of your notes pages to have available for Lesson 37.

4. **Save as: 34e ppt**.

# LESSON 99 — Using Design to Create Booklets

**OUTCOME**
- Design a 4-page program booklet.

## Business Document
### 99B

**Program Booklet**

- 4-page Program Booklet

1. Open a new document. Prepare a program booklet for the High School Honor Society Induction Ceremony.
2. The brochure will be formatted on *two pages*, using 8.5" × 11" paper in landscape orientation (see Figure 17-18 below):

    **Page 1** will have the text for the outside back and front covers.

    **Page 2** will have the text for the inside left page and the inside right page.

### Page 1

| Outside Back Cover (5.5" × 8.5") | Outside Front Cover (5.5" × 8.5") |

One 8.5" × 11" paper in landscape orientation

### Page 2

| Inside Left Page (5.5" × 8.5") | Inside Right Page (5.5" × 8.5") |

One 8.5" × 11" paper in landscape orientation

**Figure 17-18** Program booklet layout

3. Set top, bottom, and side margins on both pages at 0.5".
4. Select landscape orientation and two pages per sheet. (Page Layout/Page Setup dialog box/Margins tab/Orientation: Landscape and Pages: 2 pages per sheet)
5. Set columns as follows:

    a. **Outside Back Cover:** two columns, each 2" wide, with 0.5" between them.

    b. **Outside Front Cover:** one 4.5" column.

    c. **Inside Left Page:** one 4.5" column.

    d. **Inside Right Page:** two columns, each 2" wide with 0.5" between them.

6. Key the information that is given below for the outside covers and inside pages. You decide all other formatting features and graphics that will be inserted.
7. Save page 1 as **99b booklet1** and page 2 as **99b booklet2**.

### Outside Back Cover

1. Key **SENIOR MEMBERS** so that it spans both columns.
2. Insert the senior members' names from the file **df 99b names**. Balance the names in two columns. If needed, change to 1.15 line spacing with 0 points spacing before and after.

# LESSON 35    Build Slide Show Presentations with Sound

OUTCOMES

- Learn about various types of sound that can be inserted in a slide show.
- Create a slide show with recorded sound, sound from a CD, and automatic slide timing for playback.

## Business Documents

**35B**

**Learn: Insert Sound in a Slide Show**

Insert/Media/Audio

- Slide Show Presentation

There are several different types of sounds that can be added to your presentation. These include:

- Sounds from *Online Audio*
- Sounds from a file
- Sounds from a CD audio track
- Sounds that you record—recorded sounds

**Sounds from *Online Audio*—**Prerecorded sounds available with the software.

**Sounds from a file—**Sounds that you have recorded and saved as a file that can be linked to the presentation.

**Sounds from a CD audio track—**Music that is played directly from a CD. Particular parts of the CD can be specified for playing.

**Recorded sounds—**With recording capability, words (using your voice or someone else's), sounds, or music can be recorded to specific slides.

**35C**

**Learn: Create a Slide Show with Recorded Sound, Sound from a CD, and Automatic Slide Timing**

1. Open *df 35c ppt* and create the following slides. Use *df 35c photo* for a picture of the Lincoln Monument.
2. Enhance the slide presentation with appropriate animation and transitions.
3. Use the Help for your presentation software to learn how to use the Record Sound feature of your software.
4. The script for slides 2 through 9 is on p. 190. Read through the script and practice it several times. Using the script, record the narration for the slide show.
5. Use Help for your presentation software to learn how to play a CD audio track during a slide show presentation.
6. Select music that would be appropriate to play during the slide presentation. Specify where you want the music to start and where you want it to stop. Consider whether you will need to have the music loop.
7. Use Help for your presentation software to learn how to program the Slide Timing feature.
8. Set the Slide Timing feature so that the slide show will run automatically.
9. **Save as: *35c ppt*.**

## Letterhead

1. Open a new document. Using the information below, create a letterhead for this company. Use a 0.5" top margin. Use WordArt within a text box to display the company name. Insert a horizontal *Draft* watermark. You decide all other design features.

2. **Save as:** *98d letterhead.*

## Flyer 1

1. Open a new document. Design a poster to present the information below. Use SmartArt as directed and place a border around the page. You decide the use of WordArt, shapes, clip art, pictures, and/or text boxes and all other design features.

2. **Save as:** *98d flyer1.*

|  |  |
|---|---|
| Sponsoring instructor: | Mrs. Porterfield |
| When: | Wednesday, October 3, Periods 1, 2, 5, 6, and 7 |
| Where: | Classroom 222 |
| Guest speaker: | Dr. Ida Meinert<br>Nutritionist, Blair Hospital |
| Topic: | Recognizing Eating Disorders |
| Excuse form: | Use the Vertical Chevron list in SmartArt for the form. Key **Student's name** in the first chevron, **Course and period missed** in the second chevron, and **Teacher's signature** in the third chevron. Do not key any text to the right of the chevrons. |

## Flyer 2

1. Open a new document. Design a flyer to present much of the information below that your instructor can use to inform others of the value of the course in which you are using this textbook.

- Include the name of the course.
- Identify some course activities you enjoy.
- Describe the important things you have learned.
- Specify reasons why others should take this course.
- Identify the hardware and software used in the course.
- Explain how this course helps you in other classes or at work.

2. You decide all formatting features but try to include several of the word processing features you learned in this unit.

3. **Save as:** *98d flyer2.*

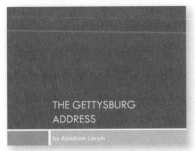

**Slide 1**

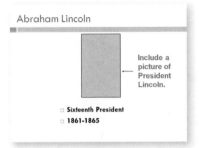

**Slide 2**

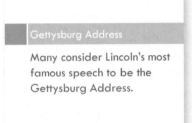

**Slide 3**

**Slide 4**

**Slide 5**

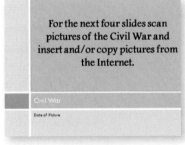

**Slides 6–9**

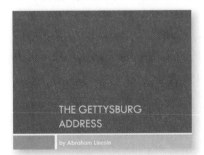

**Slide 10**

## Watermarks

Design/Page Background/
Watermark

*Note:* If using a version of *Word* earlier than *Word 2013*, follow this path: Page Layout/Page.Background/ Watermark

A watermark is any text or graphic that, when printed, appears behind the document's text (see Figure 17-16). The watermark gallery (see Figure 17-17) has several preset watermarks that are commonly used.

A watermark stating *draft* is often added to a document to indicate that it is not in final form. *Confidential* is often added to documents to make readers aware that the information is not to be shared with others.

If you want a different watermark, choose **Custom Watermark** and then use the options in **Printed Watermark** dialog box to create the watermark you want.

For example, your school's mascot may appear as a watermark on the school newspaper or stationery. If a picture is used as a watermark, you can lighten it, or wash it out, so it doesn't interfere with the document text.

### CAREER FAIR

The Annual Career Fair will be held May 15 from 9 a.m. to 12:30 p.m. in Gymnasium A. A list of the 20 employers who will attend will be published next week. The employers represent many different areas that hire scientists, technicians, and engineers within the environmental field. Therefore, there will be a variety of career opportunities for our students to explore.

All junior and senior students are urged to attend and speak to as many of the employers as possible. To ensure that students speak to many employers, they will need to obtain signatures of the employers they visit and give the signatures to the Career Fair Coordinator when they leave the gymnasium.

It is important that students dress and act

appropriately during the Career Fair. Standard or casual business dress is suggested. Students should have up-to-date resumes to distribute. Also, students should use correct grammar and speak clearly without using slang to improve their chances of making a favorable first impression.

**Figure 17-16** Watermark

**Figure 17-17**
Watermark options

Watermarks are visible only in Print Layout and Full Screen Read Mode and on the printed page. Watermarks can be changed, removed, or made to appear only on selected pages of a document.

1. Open **98b border2**.
2. Insert a diagonal *Confidential* watermark.
3. Adjust border as needed.
4. **Save as: 98c watermark1**.
5. Open **98b border1**.
6. Adjust border as needed.
7. Insert a horizontal *Urgent* watermark.
8. **Save as: 98c watermark2**.

## Applications

### Certificate

1. Open a new document. Design a certificate using the information below. You decide the font attributes, color, layout, and so on. Insert an appropriate page border.
2. Insert a diagonal Sample watermark.
3. **Save as: 98d certificate**.

Certificate of Recognition
the Harrison Rotary Club
is pleased to recognize
Matthew S. Biddle
as the Harrison Senior High School
Student of the Month
November 20--

Nancy G. Hollister, President

**Script for the Gettysburg Address by Abraham Lincoln slide presentation**

Slide 2: Abraham Lincoln is one of the best-known presidents of the United States. He was our sixteenth president and held office from 1861 until 1865, when he was assassinated.

Slide 3: The Gettysburg Address is a speech delivered by President Lincoln at the dedication of the Gettysburg National Cemetery to honor those who died in the Battle of Gettysburg during the Civil War.

Slide 4: Four score and seven years ago our fathers brought forth on this continent, a new nation, conceived in Liberty, and dedicated to the proposition that all men are created equal.

Slide 5: Now we are engaged in a great civil war, testing whether that nation, or any nation so conceived and so dedicated, can long endure. We are met on a great battlefield of that war.

Slide 6: We have come to dedicate a portion of that field, as a final resting place for those who here gave their lives that that nation might live. It is altogether fitting and proper that we should do this.

Slide 7: But, in a larger sense, we cannot dedicate—we cannot consecrate—we cannot hallow—this ground. The brave men, living and dead, who struggled here, have consecrated it, far above our poor power to add or detract.

Slide 8: The world will little note, nor long remember what we say here, but it can never forget what they did here. It is for us the living, rather, to be dedicated here to the unfinished work which they who fought here have thus far so nobly advanced.

Slide 9: It is rather for us to be here dedicated to the great task remaining before us—that from these honored dead we take increased devotion to that cause for which they gave the last full measure of devotion—that we here highly resolve that these dead shall not have died in vain—that this nation, under God, shall have a new birth of freedom—and that government of the people, by the people, for the people, shall not perish from the earth.

© wavebreakmedia/Shutterstock.com

## Digital Citizenship and Ethics

The Internet makes it easy to copy someone else's work and pass it off as your own. But this is unethical—and sometimes illegal. **Copyright** is a form of protection given to the authors or creators of original works, including literary, dramatic, musical, artistic, and other intellectual works. That means that only the author has the right to make or distribute copies of the work, perform the work publicly (such as songs or plays), or change it in any way. If you want to use copyrighted material, you have to get the author's permission first.

**Plagiarism** occurs when you copy another person's ideas, text, or other creative work and present it as your own, without getting permission or crediting the source. All schools take plagiarism very seriously. If you are caught plagiarizing, you will certainly receive a failing grade, and you might even be suspended.

As a class, discuss the following:

1. How could you legally use a copyrighted photo of a penguin in a school report on Antarctica?

2. Provide an example of plagiarism, and suggest how it could be avoided.

**TEAMWORK**

**OUTCOMES**
- Use page borders to design documents.
- Use watermarks in documents.
- Design certificates, letterhead stationery, and flyers.

## Business Documents

- Certificate of Recognition
- Certificate of Scholarship
- Letterhead Stationery
- Flyers

### 98B

### Page Borders

Home/Paragraph/Borders and Shading drop-down list/Borders and Shading

★TIP If the border does not print completely, choose the Text option instead of the Edge of Page option in the Borders and Shading Options dialog box. Increase the space between the border and the text by increasing the values in the Margin area.

**Borders** can be placed around one or more pages of text by selecting desired options in the **Borders and Shading** dialog box shown in Figure 17-15. Choose one of the styles at the left and then choose the line style, color, and width. Apply the border to the pages you want by selecting the appropriate option from the **Apply to** drop-down list.

If desired, you can use one of the borders in the Art drop-down list. Additional selections can be applied to the page border by clicking the Options button to open the Borders and Shading Options dialog box.

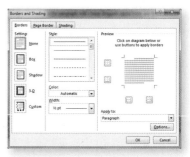

**Figure 17-15** Page Border dialog box

1. Open *df 98b border1*.
2. Insert a page border using the Shadow setting, a multiline style, a red color, and 2¼ width. Apply the border to This section-First page only.
3. **Save as:** *98b border1*.
4. Open *df 98b border2*. Choose one of the star borders from the Art drop-down list and increase the width of the art by 3 points. Apply the border to This section-First page only. Click the Options button and select the Text option. Increase the space between the text and the border by increasing the values in the Margin area to 20.
3. **Save as:** *98b border2*.

**QUICK ✔**

Your certificate should look similar to this:

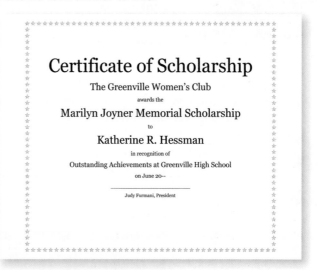

## LESSON 36

# Use Pen, Highlighter, and Shortcuts to Deliver an Effective Presentation

**OUTCOMES**

- Learn shortcuts to navigate a slide show.
- Learn to use a pen during a slide show presentation.
- Learn to use the highlighter during a slide show presentation.
- Learn pointer shortcuts.
- Create and annotate a slide.

## Business Documents

**36B**

- Slide Show Presentation

**Learn: Shortcuts to Navigate a Slide Show**

1. When you are creating a slide show and when you are delivering a presentation, you will find it helpful to know the shortcut keys for navigating your slide show. Open *34b ppt* in Slide Show View, and try each of the shortcut keys described in the following table.
2. Close *34b ppt* without saving any changes.

| Slide Show Shortcuts | |
|---|---|
| **How to:** | **Shortcut** |
| Advance to the next slide (or next animation) | Mouse click Enter, Page Down, Right or Down Arrow, Space Bar, *n* |
| Return to the previous slide (or previous animation) | Page Up, Left or Up Arrow, Backspace, *p* |
| Display a blank *black* slide | *b* or . (period) |
| Return to the presentation from a blank *black* slide | |
| Display a blank *white* slide | *w* or , (comma) |
| Return to the presentation from a blank *white* slide | |
| Stop an automatic presentation | *s* |
| Restart an automatic presentation | |
| End a presentation | Esc |
| Go to first slide | Home |
| Go to last slide | End |
| Go to a specific slide | Enter slide number; tap Enter |
| View All Slides dialog box | Ctrl + s |
| View computer task bar | Ctrl + t |

**Chart 2**

1. Open a new document. Using the Vertical Chevron List in the Process group in SmartArt, prepare a list similar to the one below. Use Title style for the list name and colors that are similar to your school colors.
2. **Save as:** *97e chart2.*

**The Writing Process**

- Step 1 • Prepare draft
- Step 2 • Proofread and edit draft
- Step 3 • Repeat Steps 1 & 2 as needed
- Step 4 • Prepare final draft
- Step 5 • Print & distribute final draft

## 97F

**Graphics Applications**

1. Open a new document. Using the information below, design a one-page ad using appropriate colors and font attributes. Use WordArt, text boxes, and clip art in the ad. You decide the placement of the information and clip art (you may use different clip art).
2. **Save as:** *97 fad.*

Stop by Our Newly Remodeled
Jackson Township
Supremo Pizza
Plus
10% Student Discount
when you show your student ID!
5043 Green City Road, Jackson Township
New
Pick-up
Window
Call Ahead:
724-555-0336

Check us out on Facebook.com/supremo for special offers and details

## Digital Citizenship and Ethics
Whether it's buying music and movies or shoes and shirts, the Internet has become a popular and convenient way to shop. But shopping online comes with its own set of risks and responsibilities. For example:

- You must pay attention to the purchases you charge on a credit card, including taxes and shipping and handling charges, and be aware of how much debt you are accumulating. The inability to pay off debt can severely damage your credit rating, which will prohibit you from taking out a loan or even renting an apartment.
- You must be able to discern credible and legitimate websites; otherwise, you may become the victim of a scam. As a class, discuss the following:

1. Share a recent example of when you used the Internet to research a product or service. What type of information did you find? How did it influence your purchasing decision?
2. How would you determine if a website is hosted by a reputable company?

For some slide show presentations, it is helpful to use pointer options other than the arrow (default option). The arrow can be changed to a:

- Pen
- Highlighter
- Laser pointer

Changing the pointer to a pen allows you to mark on the slide. For example, the person presenting the slide shown in Figure 6–21 wants to emphasize that she will be talking about *Age when Hired*. So as she says, "Today we will be looking at several categories of data relating to our employees hired between 1993 and 2013. The first category we will look at is *Age when Hired*," she places a check mark above *Age when Hired*.

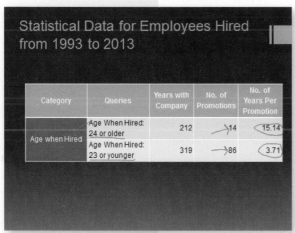

Next, she wants to explain to her audience that the *Age when Hired* category was broken down into two groups. One group was *24 years or older*, and the other group was *23 or younger*. As she explained this, she underlined the age groups.

To emphasize the point that the younger group received 86 promotions while the older group received only 14 promotions during this time period, she drew arrows by 14 and 86 as she said, "Note the difference in the number of promotions received by the 24 and older age group and the 23 and younger age group. While the older age group received only 14 promotions, the younger age group had 86 promotions."

Finally, to drill the point home, she further illustrated by presenting the difference in the No. of Years Per Promotion and circled these numbers as she explained to the audience how she arrived at them.

**Figure 6-21** Pen marks added during a presentation

Right Click/Pointer Options/Pen

Right Click/Pointer Options/Eraser

★TIP  A mark can be erased by changing the pen to an eraser and clicking and dragging the eraser on the mark.

### Activity

1. Open *df 36c ppt*.
2. Select Slide Show View.
3. Right-click, click on Pointer Options, and click Pen as shown in Figure 6-22.

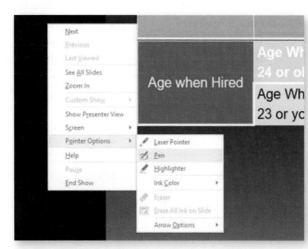

**Figure 6-22** Pointer options

4. Mark the slide as illustrated in Figure 6-21 by moving the pen to the desired locations and clicking and dragging.
5. **Save as:** *36c ppt*.

3. Change the SmartArt color to red.
4. Arrange the VP titles in alphabetic order, left to right.
5. Change width of the SmartArt to 6.5" and center-align all the titles if needed.
6. **Save as:** *97c chart1*.
7. If needed, open **97c chart1** and change the layout to a Half Circle organization chart. Change the shape fill to a light orange.
8. **Save as:** *97c chart2*.

---

## 97D

### Wrap Text Around Graphics

Page Layout or Format/ Arrange/Wrap Text or Position

You can choose how text is to appear near a graphic. Text near a graphic object can be **wrapped** (positioned) so it is above and below the object only, surrounds the object, or appears to be keyed behind or in front of the object. You can also position the graphic so it "moves along" with the text. In this example, the word processing operator selected the **Tight** option in the Wrap Text feature shown in Figure 17-14. This option places the text around the object. Options from the Position feature may also be used to position text and graphics.

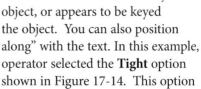

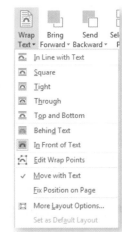

**Figure 17-14** Wrap text options

1. Open **df 97d wrap text**.
2. Choose an appropriate shape or clip art image (approximately 0.5" high) to insert in each paragraph. In paragraph 1, position the object near the center and place it behind the text. In paragraph 2, position the object at the right margin and wrap the text squarely around it. In paragraph 3, position the object at the left margin and wrap the text squarely around it.
3. **Save as:** *97d wrap text*.

---

## 97E

### SmartArt Applications

#### Chart 1

1. Open a new document. Using SmartArt, prepare an organization chart that is similar to the one below. Your chart should show that the Clerk, Treasurer, City Manager, and Attorney report directly to the Mayor and that the supervisors report to the City Manager.
2. **Save as:** *97e chart1*.

**Learn: Presentation Highlighter**

1. Read the information about highlighting, and complete the activity.

Another feature that can be used to draw your audience's attention to the slide you are presenting is the highlighter. The highlighter, as illustrated in Figure 6-23, colors over selected text or graphics.

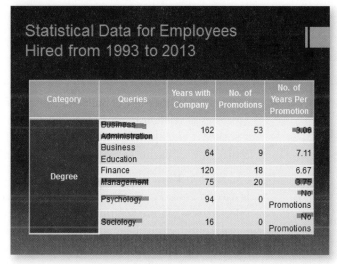

★TIP The highlight can be removed with the eraser. To remove all the markings on the slide, go into pointer options and click on Erase All Ink on Slide.

**Figure 6-23** Highlighter focuses a viewer's attention

2. Open *df 36c ppt*.
3. Select Slide Show View.
4. Go to slide 2.
5. Right-click, click Pointer Options, and click Highlighter.
6. Highlight the slide as illustrated in Figure 6-23 by moving the highlighter to the desired location and clicking and dragging over the text.
7. **Save as:** *36d ppt*.

**36E**

**Learn: Pointer Shortcuts**

1. When delivering a presentation, it is helpful to know the shortcut keys for various pointer options. Open *34b ppt* in Slide Show View, and try each of the pointer shortcut keys described in the following table as you use the pointer to annotate your presentation.
2. Close *34b ppt* without saving any changes.

| Pointer Option Shortcuts | |
|---|---|
| **Annotation Tools** | **Shortcut** |
| Show or hide arrow pointer | *a* or = |
| Change pointer to laser pointer | Ctrl + Left Mouse |
| Change pointer to a pen | Ctrl + p |
| Change pointer to an arrow | Ctrl + a |
| Show or hide ink markups | Ctrl + m |
| Change pointer to an eraser | Ctrl + e |
| Erase on-screen annotation | *e* |

# Using Design to Create Charts and Advertisements

**OUTCOMES**

- Use SmartArt to design documents.
- Wrap text around a graphic.
- Design charts and advertisements.

## Business Documents

- Organization Chart
- Process Chart
- Advertisement

### 97B

**SmartArt**

Insert/Illustrations/
SmartArt

*Office* provides a variety of built-in diagrams that convey processes or relationships in a **SmartArt** gallery. Using a SmartArt graphic makes it easy to create and modify charts without having to create them from scratch.

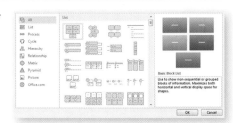

**Figure 17-13** SmartArt gallery

SmartArt in *Word* is used in much the same way as it is used in *PowerPoint*. Once a graphic is added and selected, you can use features on the SmartArt Tools Format and Design ribbons to insert text; add or delete portions of the graphic; change the shape style, WordArt style, format, layout, and orientation of the flow; and specify the position and size of the graphic.

1. Open a new document and insert the Continuous Block Process SmartArt from the Process category.
2. Key the following text in the SmartArt: **Warm up   Work out   Cool down**
3. **Save as:** *97b smartart*.

### QUICK ✔

Your SmartArt should look similar to this:

### 97C

**SmartArt Organization Chart**

Insert/Illustrations/
SmartArt/Hierarchy

You can use SmartArt to create an organization chart to show the relationship between individuals in an organization. Boxes can be added, deleted, promoted, or demoted as needed.

1. Open a new document.
2. Use the Organization Chart SmartArt in the Hierarchy category to create the following organization chart by adding/deleting and positioning the boxes as needed.

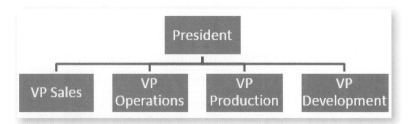

1. Create the slide shown in Figure 6-24 using the *Adjacency* design.
2. Make the annotations shown on the slide using the pen and the highlighter.
3. **Save as:** *36f ppt*.

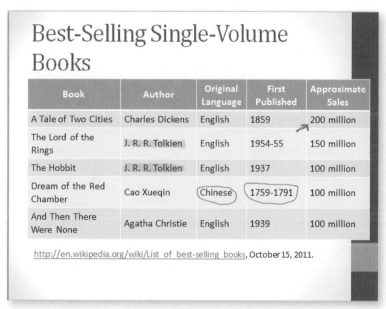

**Figure 6-24** Pen and highlighter used on the same slide

1. Open a *Word* document and key your responses to the following questions.

1. Why would a presenter highlight *J. R. R. Tolkien*?

2. Why would a presenter circle *Chinese*?

3. Why would a presenter circle *1759–1791*?

4. Why would a presenter draw an arrow by 200 million?

5. Why do you think there are no books published after 1955 that sold 100 million or more copies?

2. **Save as:** *36f*.

**STRATEGIES FOR SUCCESS**

Vol. 6, No. 3 Spring, 20--

**Reputation and Choice**

Reputation is the image people have of your standards of conduct--your ethical and moral principals. Most people think that a good reputation is needed to succeed in any job; and it is, therefore, one of the most important personal assetts you can acquire in your life.

> A bad reputation can result from one misdeed.

A good reputation is a valued asset that requires time, effort, and discipline to develop and project. A bad reputation can be a longterm liability established in a short time. It can be a result from just one misdeed and can be a heavy burden to carry throughout life.

It is important to realize, therefore, that most of you have an opportunity to develope and protect the reputation you want. You have many choices to make that will destroy or enhance the image you want to extned. The choices are hard; and honestly, loyalty, and dedicatoin are most often involved.

> Choices you make destroy or enhance your reputation.

**Learnig About People**

Many aspects of a job present challenges to those who strive to do their best in all they do. The most critical challenge all workers face is being able to relate will to the many individuals with whom they have to work. It is common for workers to have daily dealings with bosses, peers, and subordinates. Also, most workers will interact with telephone callers and visitors from outside and inside the company.

> Relating well to others is a critical challenge.

While it is critical to learn all you can about your job and company, it is often just as critical to learn about the people with whom you will work and interact. Frequently, you can rely upon experienced workers for information that will help you analyze the formal and informal structures of the organization. What you learn may help you determine what an employer expects, and likes, or dislikes, and will help you make a good adjustment to your workplace.

> Learn from experienced workers.

# LESSON 37

## Deliver an Effective Presentation

**OUTCOMES**
- Learn the keys for delivering an effective presentation.
- Practice the keys for delivering an effective presentation.
- Deliver an effective presentation with a slide show.

## Business Documents
### 37B

**Learn: Keys for Delivering an Effective Presentation**

- Slide Show Presentation

### Speaker Notes

The notes that you created for the *Government of the United States of America* presentation (34E) should only be used as an aid when you are practicing your presentation. They should remind you of what you want to say during your practice sessions.

You will know when you have practiced the presentation enough, because you will be able to give the presentation by quickly looking at the slides (and then right back at the audience) as they appear on the screen. The words on the slides will act as an outline to remind you of the key points you want to make.

Don't be concerned about giving the presentation word for word as it appears in the notes. If you do, it sounds memorized. Memorized speeches come across as unnatural; the speaker is not able to develop a rapport with the audience.

However, there is one part of the speech that you should consider memorizing. Experts generally advise speakers to memorize the first sentence. This allows you to have a strong opening and come across as knowledgeable and confident. If you memorize the first sentence, practice it so that it seems natural. This can be done by pausing in appropriate places and using vocal variety—speed, volume.

Definitely don't make the mistake that is often made by beginning presenters—bringing the speaker notes to the podium and then reading to, rather than presenting to, the audience. Speakers who read to their audience are not as credible as those who speak to their audience.

By being well prepared and only glancing at the screen as the next slide comes up, you come across as natural. This also allows you to focus on the audience rather than on your notes.

### Keys for Effective Delivery

Planning and preparing a presentation is only half the task of giving a good presentation. The other half is the delivery. Positive thinking is a must for a good presenter. Prepare and practice before the presentation. This will help you be confident that you can do a good job. Don't worry that the presentation will not be perfect. Set a goal of being a better speaker each time you present, not of being a perfect speaker each time. Use the following suggestions to improve your presentation skills.

- **Know your message.** Knowing the message well allows you to talk with the audience rather than read to them.
- **Look at the audience.** Make eye contact with one person briefly (for two to three seconds). Then move on to another person.
- **Look confident.** Stand up straight and show that you want to communicate with the audience. Avoid unnecessary movement.

WordArt should be used sparingly for a word or short phrase and should be surrounded by white space so it appears uncluttered.

**Figure 17-11** Drawing tools Format ribbon

1. Open a new document and use WordArt to insert your first and last name across the top of the page. Center-align your name; size, shape, and format it as you like.
2. In the same document, use WordArt to insert the name of your school as a footer. Center the text in the text box; size, shape, and format it as you want, using one or more of your school colors.
3. **Save as:** *96c wordart.*

**96D**

## Change Column Widths and Space Between Columns

Page Layout/Page Setup/Columns/Columns Dialog Box

Use the **Width and spacing settings** in the Columns dialog box shown in Figure 17-12 to change the widths of columns and the spacing between columns.

1. Open *df 94d columns.* Change the number of columns from 2 to 3.
2. Change the settings in the Columns dialog box so the columns will not be equal in width.
3. Set column 1 width to 1.5" and the spacing between columns 1 and 2 to 0.6". Set column 2 width to 2.0" and the space between columns 2 and 3 to 0.7". Do not change the 1.7" width for column 3.
3. **Save as:** *96d columns.*

**Figure 17-12** Column width and spacing

**96E**

## Newsletter Applications

### Newsletter 1

1. Open a new document. Format the two articles shown on the next page as a newsletter with three columns of equal width and nearly equal length with vertical lines between the columns. Correct all errors as you key.
2. The title and publication information should span the columns. Use WordArt to format the title and a 2-line dropped cap for the first word in each paragraph.
3. Hyphenate and justify the columns.
4 You decide other formatting features.
5 **Save as:** *96e newslwtter1.*

### Newsletter 2

1. Open *96e newsletter1.*
2. Make these formatting changes:
   a. Display articles as 2 unequal columns. Set column 1 width to 2.5" and column 2 width to 3.4" and the space between columns to 0.6".
   b. Drop the caps 3 lines.
   c. Remove the vertical lines.
   d. Adjust the position and width of the text boxes as needed.
   e. Make any other needed formatting changes.
3. **Save as:** *96e newsletter2.*

- **Let your personality come through.** Be natural; let the audience know who you are. Show your enthusiasm for the topic you are presenting.
- **Vary the volume and rate at which you speak.** Slow down to emphasize points. Speed up on points that you are sure your audience is familiar with. Don't be afraid to pause. It gives greater impact to your message and allows your audience time to think about what you have said.
- **Use gestures and facial expressions.** A smile, frown, or puzzled look, when appropriate, can help communicate your message. Make sure your gestures are natural.
- **Know how to use the visuals.** Practice using the visual aids you have chosen for the presentation. Glance briefly at each visual as you display it; then focus back on the audience.

## 37C

**Apply: Practice Giving a Presentation**

Using the suggestions in the previous section for delivering a presentation, practice giving the *Government of the United States of America* presentation that you created in Lessons 33 and 34.

## 37D

**Apply: Deliver an Effective Presentation**

1. Open **df 37d eval form** and review the form that will be used to evaluate your presentations in this unit.
2. Break up into groups of three. Each student in your group will give the presentation that was developed in Lessons 33–34. While one student is giving the presentation, the other two will evaluate it using the evaluation form.

## LESSON 38 — Apply What You Have Learned

**OUTCOMES**
- Develop a script for a presentation.
- Review design tips for creating an effective slide show.
- Create a slide show for the script.
- Deliver a presentation using the script and slide show.

**Business Documents**
- Professional Presentation

## 38B

**Apply: Develop a Script for a Presentation**

Prepare a two-to-three-minute presentation on the sites of Washington, D.C., by following these steps:

1. Open **df 38b wdc** and print the report on Washington, D.C., the nation's capital.
2. Read the report you printed. Highlight the parts of the report that you want to include in your presentation. Make notations as appropriate.
3. Conduct an Internet search to learn more about the nation's capital.
4. Based on the material that you have reviewed, create a script or outline of what you plan to include in the presentation.

# Using Design to Enhance Newsletter Publications

**OUTCOMES**
- Use Drop Cap and WordArt.
- Design columns of unequal widths.
- Change spacing between columns.
- Design newsletters.

## Business Documents

- Unequal 2-Column Newsletter
- Equal 3-Column Newsletter

### 96B

**Drop Cap**

Insert/Text/Drop Cap

You can format paragraphs to begin with a large initial capital letter that takes up one or more vertical lines of regular text. **Drop caps** are objects that can be formatted and sized.

Two drop cap options are usually available. As shown in Figure 17-8, the Dropped option capitalizes the first letter of the first word in the paragraph with a large dropped capital letter and then wraps the text around the drop cap.

The In margin option creates a dropped capital letter, but places it in the margin beginning at the first line. The Drop Cap dialog box can be used to change the font, the number of lines that the cap drops, and the distance the dropped cap is from the text.

Figure 17-8 Drop cap options

1. Open **df 96b drop cap**.
2. Format paragraph 1 with a drop cap with text wrapped around it.
3. Format paragraph 2 with a drop cap that is placed in the left margin.
4. Format paragraph 3 the same as paragraph 1, but drop the cap only two lines, change it to Times New Roman font, and increase the distance from text to 0.1.
5. **Save as:** **96b drop cap**.

**QUICK** ✔

Your drop caps should look similar to this:

### 96C

**Create WordArt**

Insert/Text/WordArt

**KEYBOARDING**

is for

Everyone

Figure 17-9 WordArt

You can change text into a graphic by using the **WordArt** feature (see Figure 17-9 at the left). When you use WordArt, you can choose from a variety of styles in the WordArt menu shown in Figure 17-10. After you choose a style from the menu, you can change the font, font size, and font style while keying before or after replacing the placeholder text.

Once your text has been converted to the chosen WordArt style, you can edit it by using features on the Drawing tools Format ribbon that appears when the WordArt is selected.

You can use the features within the groups on this ribbon (see Figure 17-11) to change the shape styles, WordArt styles, text direction, position, and so on.

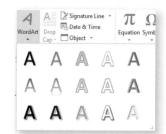

Figure 17-10 WordArt menu

1. Open *df 38c photos*. Review the file photos and illustrations.
2. Review the Design Tips in the *Reference* section.
3. Plan and create the slides to be included in the presentation. (Review the following ideas for slides.)
4. Practice the presentation on your own.
5. Give the presentation to two or three of your classmates.
6. **Save as:** *38c Washington DC*.

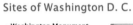

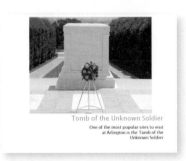

www.cengage.com/school/
keyboarding/c21key

**Newsletter 2**

1. Open **df 95e newsletter2**. Set side margins to 0.5".
2. Format *What's Up!* In Title style and then italicize it. Format the volume, number, and date in Intense Emphasis style. Right-align the date.
3. Format the four articles in two equal columns separated by a vertical line. Indent first lines of paragraphs in articles 0.25". Format the article headings using Subtitle style and apply a light blue shading to the headings.
4. Key the following three articles after the last article formatted as two equal columns. Format them to match the previous articles.

Investment Performance

If you participate in the Upton Retirement Program or Supplemental Retirement Annuity plans, daily balances of your accounts can be obtained via the Internet. All you need to do is visit www.hiaa.com and establish a PIN. With your social security number and your PIN, you can obtain end-of-day balances at any time. You no longer need to wait for the quarterly reports to see how your money is growing.

Farewell, Rudy

A retirement tea will be held for Rudy Beissel, Environmental Support Services, on Thursday, June 24, from 1:30 p.m. to 3 p.m. in the Jones Conference Center. Rudy is retiring after 35 years with Upton.

Career Track

Lorretta Slobodnick recently was named as an administrative assistant, Medical Records. She reports to Erika Cooper, head, Medical Records. Lorretta earned her associate degree from Upton County Community College and specialized in medical technology. Please welcome her at Extension 1505 or slobodni@upton.com.

5. Insert the following text as a text box at the end of the newsletter. Size the text box to fit within the column margins. Format the title within the text box in Intense Emphasis style.

> Patient Praises
> To Susan Getty, nurse: "Thank you for the compassionate and knowl-edgeable care ."--a stroke patient
> "Thanks to all who helped nurse me back to health!"--a Unit 15D pa-tient
> To Jill Holt, nurse: "Thanks, thanks, thanks! Your skill is appreciated." --a new mom

6. Justify and hyphenate the text. Adjust for any spacing inconsistencies.
7. If desired, apply an appropriate style, color combination, and/or font combination.
8. Balance the columns as needed.
9. **Save as: 95e newsletter2**.

# CORPORATE *View*

## An Integrated Intranet Application

As part of your internship with Corporate View, you have the opportunity to work in several departments within the organization to see the overall operations. Your current assignment is with Human Resources and Management. Because of your expertise with PowerPoint, the HR Director would like you to create materials for recruiting at the University of Wyoming. You will be creating two handouts and a *PowerPoint* presentation for him to use during his recruitment trip. You will need to get the information for the handouts from the company intranet site: www.cengage.com/school/keyboarding/dim/cview. Partially completed samples of what the HR Director wants the handouts and *PowerPoint* slides to look like are shown below.

Page Layout/Page Background/Page Borders

Page Layout/Page Background/Page Color

### Handouts

1. Format the first handout as a table in *Landscape* orientation with the name and a description of the seven departments that make up Corporate View. Include a *page border (box)*, and make the background color of the handout *Tan, Background 2*. **Save Handout 1 as:** *u6 corpview proj1*.

2. Format the second handout as a table in *Landscape* orientation with the name, location, division, and division description of the six divisions of Corporate View. Include a *page border* (box) around the handout. **Save Handout 2 as:** *u6 corpview proj2*.

### Corporate View Departments

| Department | Department Description |
|---|---|
| **Corporate Communications** | Corporate Communications is the guardian of the corporate message. |
| **Human Resources & Management** | The Human Resources Department manages employee services and benefits. |
| **Research and Development** | |

**Handout 1**

2. Near the horizontal and vertical center of the page, draw a text box that is about 1"
   high × 3" wide. Using center alignment and bold 12-point Arial font, key the following
   copy in the text box. Shade the text box with a dark color and remove the shape outline.
   Change the text color to white. Resize the text box to fit the text on one line.

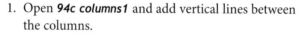

3. Near the bottom right corner of the page, insert the built-in Grid Quote text box and key
   your first and last name, your school name, and the current date inside the box on three
   lines. Change the font color of the text to black, the shape fill to green, and the shape
   outline to black. If needed, position the text box near the bottom right corner.
4. **Save as:** *95c text boxes.*

QUICK ✔

Your text boxes should look similar to this:

## 95D

**Vertical Lines
Between Columns**

Page Layout/Page Setup/
Columns/More Columns/
Line Between

If desired, vertical lines can be placed between columns to
enhance the appearance of the document by checking the
Line between option as shown in Figure 17-7. The lines
can be inserted before or after keying the document.

**Figure 17-7** Line between option

1. Open **94c columns1** and add vertical lines between
   the columns.
2. **Save as:** *95d columns1.*
3. Reformat **95d columns1** into two columns of unequal width by using
   the Left Preset. Insert a vertical line between the columns.
4. **Save as:** *95d columns2.*

## 95E

**Newsletter
Applications**

### Newsletter 1

1. Open **94e columns**.
2. Shade the second paragraph in the first article, using light blue.
3. Insert the tip below in a text box between the articles. Use
   1.0 line spacing and 9-point font for the text. Format the
   title using Emphasis style. Fill the text box with the same
   color used to shade paragraph 2. Format the text box with a
   border. Adjust spacing after text box as needed.
4. **Save as:** *95e newsletter1.*

> **This Issue's Tip**
> If you've asked for a
> doggie bag to take home
> from a restaurant, you
> should refrigerate it
> within two hours.
> Reheat leftovers to 165
> degrees Fahrenheit until
> warmed throughout.

## Corporate View Divisions

| Name | Location | Division | Division Description |
|------|----------|----------|---------------------|
| **TeleView** | Boulder, Colorado | Telephony and Electronics Division | Telephony is electronically assisted, two-way communication between people and places. |
| **RetailView** | | | |

**Handout 2**

### PowerPoint Slides

1. Use the information on the handouts you created to complete slides 3, 4, and 6.
2. Use the *Executive* design theme with the *Composite* color scheme for the slides.
3. Use the following transitions:
   - Slide 1: *random bars*
   - Slide 2: *ripple*
   - Slide 3: *honeycomb*
   - Slide 4: *gallery*
   - Slide 5: *doors*
   - Slide 6: *rotate*
4. For slides 3 and 4, use *fade* Animation with *one by one* Effects Options.
5. For slide 5, use screenshots from the department pages on the intranet for the graphics on the slide.
6. For slide 6, use *Wheel* Animation with Effects Options of Spokes:  *8 Spokes* and Sequence: *All at Once*
7. **Save as:  *u6 corpview proj3*.**

**Slide 1**

**Slide 2**

# Using Design to Improve Newsletter Publications

**OUTCOMES**

- Shade paragraphs.
- Insert text boxes.
- Insert vertical lines between columns of text.
- Design newsletters.

## Business Documents

- Unequal 2-Column Newsletter
- Equal 2-Column Newsletters
- Equal 3-Column Newsletter

## 95B

### Shaded Paragraphs

Home/Paragraph/
Shading

Paragraphs can be shaded in various colors to focus the reader's attention to their contents. The illustration below shows a shaded paragraph. Figure 17-4 shows various colors that can be applied.

> This is an example of a paragraph that has been shaded. Readers are more apt to pay attention to its contents. Various colors can be selected for the shading.

1. Open **df 95b shading**.
2. Using light colors, shade each paragraph differently.
3. Save as: **95b shading**.

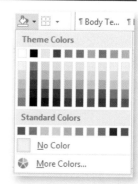

**Figure 17-4** Shading options

## 95C

### Text Boxes

Insert/Text/Text Box

**Text boxes** (see Figure 17-5) are frequently used for labels or callouts in a document. You can use a built-in text box that has predesigned information and formats, or you can draw a blank text box to hold your information and format as desired (see Figure 17-5).

> This is a shaded text box without a border that illustrates reverse type (white letters on green background) using Calibri 9-pt. bold font. The text is center-aligned.

**Figure 17-5** Text box

Once a text box is inserted in your document, you can edit it by using available features on the Text Box Tools Format ribbon that appears when a text box is selected.

You can use the features within the groups on this ribbon to change the text or text box style, change shadow or 3-D effects, and specify the position and size of your text box.

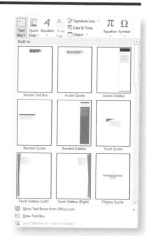

**Figure 17-6** Text box options

1. Open a new document. Draw a text box that is 1" high × 2" wide and is near the horizontal center and the top margin of the page. Key the following information in the text box, using a 12-point Arial italic font. Change the shape outline to a 3-point solid, red line, and then resize the text box to fit the text on two lines, using center alignment.

   *This text box uses Arial 12-point italic font for the letters.*

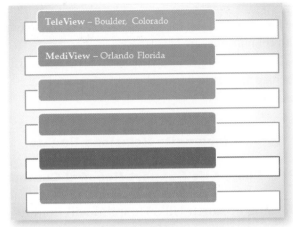

**Slide 3**

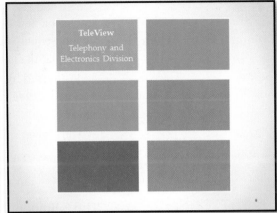

**Slide 4**

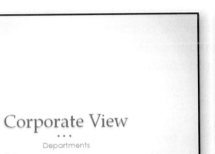

**Slide 5**

**Slide 6**

**Think Critically**

1. How can a strong understanding of presentations help you in your career pursuits?
2. Why do you think presentation skills are important to an employer?
3. What activities can you participate in now that will strengthen your presentation skills and knowledge?

1. Open a new document and format the newsletter title as one column and the two articles as three equal-width columns that are balanced.
2. Format the newsletter title using Title style and the article titles using Subtitle style.
3. Justify and hyphenate the text in the articles.
4. **Save as:** *94e columns*.

## Community Relations Update

### Basic Life Support Renewal Courses

The School of Nursing at North Hills Hospital will hold its annual basic life support (BLS) renewal courses in March. The courses are open to all staff.

Staff members whose jobs require them to hold a valid BLS completion card must attend a renewal course every two years, according to American Heart Association guidelines. Heart Saver Plus (adult) and Health Care Provider (adult, infant, and child) BLS renewal courses will be offered.

Renewal courses will be held Monday through Friday, March 15 through March 19, and March 22 through March 26, from 7 a.m. to 8 p.m. Renewal courses also will be held Saturday, March 20, from 7 a.m. to 2 p.m. All courses will be held in Wilkins Hall, Room 135.

Staff should allow 60 to 90 minutes to complete the renewal course. To receive a BLS renewal, staff will be required to complete a written test and demonstrate their BLS skills. The renewal course is open to anyone who is due to take a renewal course, even if it is not required for his or her job.

### Science Judges Sought

An additional 25 judges with expertise in science and an interest in children are needed for the 61st annual North Hills Science and Engineering Fair. The competition will be held from 8 a.m. to 1 p.m. March 31 at the North Hills Science Center.

Jeffrey Sidora, science fair coordinator, said 60 judges are needed to examine exhibits created by 150 students from 6 area schools. The judges should have technical backgrounds, such as master's degrees in biology, chemistry, physics, computer science, mathematics, engineering, robotics, medicine, microbiology, earth science, or environment.

The judges have to be willing to make a time commitment from 8 a.m. to 1 p.m. Lunch will be provided. At the fair, students in grades 6 through 12 compete for the best science and engineering projects in their age brackets.

# Academic and Career Connections

Complete the following exercises that introduce various topics that involve academic themes and careers.

## Grammar and Writing: Other Internal Punctuation

**MicroType 6**

- References/Communication Skills/Other Internal Punctuation
- CheckPro/Communication Skills 6
- CheckPro/Word Choice 6

1. Go to *MicroType 6* and use this feature path for review:  References/Communication Skills/ Other Internal Punctuation.
2. Click *Rules* and review the rules of using apostrophes, colons, hyphens, dashes, and parentheses.
3. Under *Other Internal Punctuation,* click *Posttest.*
4. Follow the instructions to complete the posttest.

*Optional Activities:*

1. Go to this path:  CheckPro/Communication Skills 6.
2. Complete the activities as directed.
3. Go to this path:  CheckPro/Word Choice 6.
4. Complete the activities as directed.

## Communications: Listening

1. You answered a telephone call from Chelsea Steward, your father's business associate. Mrs. Steward asked you to take a message for your father.
2. Open the sound file *df u06 communications.*  Take notes as you listen.
3. Key the message—in complete sentences—for your father.  **Save as:  *u06 communications*.**
4. Create a new presentation on the following office renovations that your father and Mrs. Steward are supervising. Create a slide for each renovation using the location as the slide title and inserting the specified image from the data files.  Apply an appropriate design.

| Location | Architect | HVAC | Designer | Data File |
|---|---|---|---|---|
| 105 W. Fourth Street | Lopez Brothers, Inc. | All Weather | Lauren Design Associates | df 105 W Fourth Street.jpg |
| 1220 Sycamore | To be determined | Thomas Heating & Cooling | Today's Office Environs | df 1220 Sycamore.jpg |
| 306 Clifton Avenue | To be determined | Office Comfort Systems | Grafton Design | df 306 Clifton Avenue.jpg |

5. **Save as:  *u06 communications slides*.**
6. With your instructor's permission, print the slides as handouts with one per page.

## Math Skills

Katelyn and Meredith run a successful dog boarding and grooming business.  Katelyn does the accounting for the business.  At the end of the year, she wants to determine the following:

1. The business had 43 customers who used both the boarding and grooming services.  If this represents 40 percent of their customers, how many total customers did they have? (Round to the nearest whole number.)
2. The dog boarding service generated $73,800 in sales for the year.  If this was 60 percent of total sales, what were the total sales?
3. The business's biggest expenditure is the mortgage, which totaled $19,200 for the year.  If this was 48 percent of all expenses, what were the total expenses?

**Changing the Number and Width of Columns**

Page Layout/Page Setup/
Columns/More Columns

The number and width of columns can be changed using the Columns feature. The changes can be made before or after keying the text, and both the number and width of columns can vary on a page. Typically, you can select from several preset formats, or you can design a specific format you need using the options in the Columns dialog box shown in Figure 17-2.

1. Open **94b columns** and reformat the text into two columns of equal width.
2. Save as: **94c columns1**.
3. Open **94b columns** and reformat, changing the top margin to 3.0"; formatting the title, *Career Fair*, in a single column in Title style. Center the title. Format the text into three columns of nearly equal width below the title.
4. Save as: **94c columns2**.

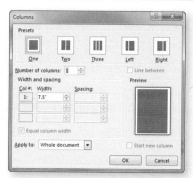

**Figure 17-2** Columns dialog box

**QUICK** ✔

Your formatted columns should look similar to this:

**Balanced Column Lengths**

Page Layout/Page Setup/
Breaks/Column

Oftentimes, columns need to be balanced (equal or nearly equal in length). The desired balance can be achieved by inserting Column breaks as needed.

Adjustments may need to be made so there are no widow/orphan lines at the end or beginning of the columns.

1. Open **df 94d columns** and balance the columns.
2. Save as: **94d columns1**.
3. Reformat **94d columns1** into two balanced columns using the Right Preset format.
4. Save as: **94d columns2**.
5. Reformat **94d columns2** into a 3-column document with balanced lengths.
6. Save as: **94d columns3**.

**★TIP** In *Word*, insert a Continuous section break at the end of the last column to automatically balance the columns if a prior break has not been inserted. If balance needs to be improved, insert Column break(s) as needed.

**Figure 17-3** Page and Section Break options

### Planning a Career in Hospitality and Tourism

Most of us interact on a regular basis with workers in the hospitality and tourism fields, whether it's ordering food at a restaurant, going to a movie, or visiting a local zoo or museum. Travel and tourism is one of the largest and fastest-growing industries in the world, with hospitality-related businesses located in communities around the globe. Employees in this field are involved in the management, marketing, and operations of restaurants and food/beverage services; lodging facilities; travel-related services; and recreation, amusements, and attractions.

### What's It Like?

Individuals who work in this field are busy, energetic, and have excellent people skills. Their responsibilities often focus on catering to the needs of others. For example:

- They advise travelers about their destinations and make arrangements for transportation, hotel accommodations, car rentals, and sites to see.
- They bring people together at meetings and conventions by identifying suitable meeting sites, securing speakers, organizing lodging and meals, and arranging for support services such as audiovisual equipment, forms of electronic communication, and transportation.
- They greet diners in restaurants, take food and drink orders, and serve food and beverages. They also answer questions, explain menu items and specials, and keep tables and dining areas clean and set for new diners.
- They lead groups in activities such as arts and crafts, sports, performing arts, camping, and other special interests. Or they might manage recreation programs in parks, playgrounds, and other settings.

Employees in the hospitality and tourism fields work in a variety of settings, from offices to restaurants and movie theaters, to parks and campgrounds. They are employed by hotels, restaurants, travel agencies, cruise ships, amusement parks, museums, and other attractions and recreation facilities.

### Employment Outlook

The job outlook is good for workers in the hospitality and tourism industry, with the recreation, amusements, and attractions sector experiencing the fastest growth. Most employers prefer workers with formal training in their field. Completion of post-secondary training is becoming increasingly important for advancement.

### What About You?

The Hospitality and Tourism career cluster is covered in box 9 of the Interest Survey Activity you completed in Unit 1 of this text. If this box had one of the three highest scores on your survey, you should further explore the cluster's pathways and related occupations.

1. Why do you think a career in this field could be a good choice?
2. What skills can you develop now that would be helpful to a career in this field?
3. Why are these jobs important to a community and to our economy?

# LESSON 94 · Using Design to Create Newsletter Publications

**OUTCOMES**
- Insert columns.
- Change number and width of columns.
- Balance columns.
- Design a 3-column newsletter.

## Business Documents
- Equal 3-Column Newsletters
- Equal 2-Column Newsletters
- Unequal 2-Column Newsletter

### 94A–100A

**Warmup**

Key each line twice at the beginning of each lesson; first for control; then for speed.

alphabet 1 Mack and Jebb expect high scores on every law quiz if they study.

figures 2 I wanted to have 557-4280 or 557-3196 as my new telephone number.

speed 3 The man with the rifle saw six turkeys by the dock at Lake Tibor.

gwam 1' | 1 | 2 | 3 | 4 | 5 | 6 | 7 | 8 | 9 | 10 | 11 | 12 | 13 |

### 94B

**Columns**

Page Layout/Page Setup/
Columns

Except for a few documents like tables, invoices, and purchase orders, the documents you have created in *Word* have had a single column of text that extended from the left margin to the right margin.

Multiple-column documents, such as pamphlets, brochures, and newsletters, use the Columns feature (see Figure 17-1) to divide a document into two or more vertical columns that are placed side by side on a page.  The columns may be of equal or unequal width.

As you key, text fills the length of a column before moving to the next column to the right.

1. Open a new document and key the text below, using a 3.5" top margin, 4" bottom margin, and three columns of equal width.
2. **Save as:  *94b columns*.**

**Figure 17-1**
Column options

CAREER FAIR

The Annual Career Fair will be held May 15 from 9 a.m. to 12:30 p.m. in Gymnasium A.  A list of the 20 employers who will attend will be published next week.  The employers represent many different areas that hire scientists, technicians, and engineers within the environmental field.  Therefore, there will be a variety of career opportunities for our students to explore.

All junior and senior students are urged to attend and speak to as many of the employers as possible.  To ensure that students speak to many employers, they will need to obtain signatures of the employers they visit and give the signatures to the Career Fair Coordinator when they leave the gymnasium.

It is important that students dress and act appropriately during the Career Fair.  Standard or casual business dress is suggested.  Students should have up-to-date resumes to distribute.  Also, students should use correct grammar and speak clearly without using slang to improve their chances of making a favorable first impression.

Complete this activity to help prepare for the **Business Presentation** event in FBLA-PBL's Marketing division. Participants in this event demonstrate their ability to deliver an effective business presentation while using presentation technology.

You will prepare a presentation of five to seven minutes on how businesses use social media to communicate with customers. The presentation should cover the following:

- Information on social media tools, such as social networks, blogs, and video sharing sites.
  - Listing of specific social media sites. The listing should include the name and type of site, a brief description of the site and its users, the costs (if any) for using it, and the advantages and disadvantages of using the site.
  - Issues regarding privacy of the business's financial and other sensitive information.
  - Ways a business can use social media to communicate with customers.
  - Basics on how to implement a social media plan.

Gather information on the topics above. Start a new word processing document, and prepare a report on your findings. Note that one-and-a-half to two pages of single-spaced, 12-pt. type translates into about four minutes of speaking.

After you have written your report, create a slide show highlighting the main points. You should have at least three slides to support each of the topics in your report. Apply a design theme and other formatting. Add graphics, tables, and charts to enhance the slide information. Using the information you learned in this unit, practice the delivery of your presentation. As directed by your instructor, share the presentation with your class.

For detailed information on this event, go to www.fbla-pbl.org.

## Think Critically

1. Why is thorough research so important to a successful presentation?
2. How can strong verbal communications and public speaking skills contribute to your academic as well as your career success?
3. What can you do while you are in school to develop your public speaking skills?

## School and Community
Under federal law, every U.S. citizen 18 years of age or older has the right to vote. But in the last presidential election, only about 55 percent of the voting age population exercised that right. What can you do to convince the voting-age population to vote?

1. Identify a group(s) in your community that focuses on voter registration and assistance. Find out how you can contribute to the group's mission.
2. Research the laws on voter registration and alternative means of voting.
3. Gather information on polling stations and resources for assisting those who may have problems getting to the polls.
4. Create a handout that provides information to potential voters on how they can exercise their right to vote. Distribute the handout in your neighborhood.

| | |
|---|---|
| **Fonts** | Use only a few fonts (Calibri, Arial, Times New Roman, Comic Sans MS, etc.) in a document. The variety of sizes and the available variations (styles and effects) within the font provide for sufficient emphasis and contrast, and lessen the need to use many different fonts. |
| **Underlining and ALL CAPS** | Use **bold,** *italic,* and variations in font size rather than underlining and ALL CAPS to emphasize text. Underlining and ALL CAPS, especially in large blocks of text, can make words harder to read. |
| **Typographic elements** | Use boxes, borders, bullets, special characters, and so on in consistent styles and sizes throughout a document to improve overall appearance. |
| **Lists** | Use numbers and/or letters in outlines to show different levels and when sequencing, cross-referencing, and quantity are important. If listing alone is the goal, bullets (or appropriate special characters) are sufficient. |
| **Line length** | Long lines tend to tire the eye quickly, and short lines cause the eye to jump back and forth too often. The use of a few long or short lines in a document is not likely to cause readers problems, however. For most documents, 1" side margins are acceptable. For newsletters, programs, and other documents that have a shorter line length, 0.5" top, bottom, and/or side margins may be used. |
| **Justification** | With normal-length lines, use a ragged-right margin. Varying the line endings of normal-length lines is easier to read than justified text, where the lines end evenly and there is inconsistent spacing between words. Justified text is permissible in documents like newsletters that use shorter lines in narrow columns. |
| **Whitespace** | Use white space in the margins to keep a document from looking crowded. Use white space between document parts to inform the reader where one part ends and another part begins. |
| **Emphasis** | Use **bold,** *italic,* and effects (<u>underlining</u>, shadow, outline, emboss, engrave, SMALL CAPS, etc.) in small amounts to call attention to some parts of a document. Avoid overusing one technique or using too many different techniques in a document. When too many parts of a document are emphasized, no one part will seem especially important. When too many different techniques are used, the document will appear cluttered. |
| **Color** | Use color to enhance the message or appearance of the document. Generally, use dark shades of color for fonts and lighter shades of color for highlights, fills, and page color. Select contrasting font colors to improve readability when different colors are used near each other. Built-in Themes provide acceptable color combinations, fonts, and effects. |
| **Graphics** | Place graphics (clip art, pictures, charts, shapes, text boxes, etc.) near the text they enhance or as close as possible to their references in the text. Keep the size of the graphic in proportion to the text, column width, and space available. |

# SKILL BUILDER 1

- Improve keying techniques.
- Improve keying speed and accuracy.

## Warmup

Key each line twice, first for control and then for speed.

alphabet 1 Hazel fixed the two pairs of jumper cables very quickly for Gwen.

fig/sym 2 Expenses increased $82,965 (5%) and net profit fell $31,470 (6%).

speed 3 Did eighty firms bid on six authentic maps of the ancient island?

gwam 1' | 1 | 2 | 3 | 4 | 5 | 6 | 7 | 8 | 9 | 10 | 11 | 12 | 13 |

## Technique: Keying

1. Key each line twice.
2. Key two 15" writings on each even-numbered line.

**Alphabet**

1 zebra extra vicious dozen happen just quick forgot way limp exact

2 Everyone except Meg and Joe passed the final weekly biology quiz.

**Figure/Symbol**

3 Account #2849 | 10% down | for $6,435.70 | Lots #8 & #9 | $250 deductible

4 The fax machine (#387-291) is on sale for $364.50 until March 21.

**Bottom row**

5 modern zebra extinct moving backbone moon vacate exam computerize

6 Zeno's vaccine injection for smallpox can be given in six months.

**Third row**

7 you tip rip terror yet peer quit were pet tire terrier pepper out

8 Our two terrier puppies were too little to take to your pet show.

**Double letters**

9 footnote scanner less process letters office cell suppress footer

10 Jill, my office assistant, will process the four letters by noon.

**Balanced hands**

11 wish then turn us auto big eight down city busy end firm it goals

12 If the firm pays for the social, the eight officials may also go.

**Shift keys**

13 The New York Times | Gone with the Wind | Chicago Tribune | WordPerfect

14 Alan L. Mari finished writing "Planning for Changing Technology."

**Adjacent keys**

15 were open top ask rest twenty point tree master merge option asks

16 The sort option was well received by all three new group members.

**Space bar**

17 it is fix and fox go key do by box men pen six so the to when big

18 Did they use the right audit form to check the new city bus line?

gwam 1' | 1 | 2 | 3 | 4 | 5 | 6 | 7 | 8 | 9 | 10 | 11 | 12 | 13 |

# UNIT 17 — Using Design to Create Effective Business Documents

## Reference Guide

### Document Design

In previous units, when you used word processing software to create documents such as letters, memos, and reports, you used specific formatting guides that follow accept document design principles to prepare documents that are attractive and easy to read and understand.

For example, when creating letters and memos, you formatted the various parts of the letter with appropriate vertical space between and within the various letter parts; arranged the letter vertically and horizontally on the page so there was ample white space in the top, bottom, and side margins; used bold, italic, and underline to emphasize small portions of text, and so on. When creating reports, you used appropriate margins, styles, bulleted and numbered lists, and indentations to make titles, side headings, quotations, and lists attractive and easy to read and understand.

In this unit, you will design documents that do not have specific formatting or design guides. Therefore, it is important that you use the following basic document design principles when creating newsletters, flyers, programs, advertisements, announcements, charts, and so on to give your documents a professional appearance and make them easy to read and understand.

### Font size

Headlines, headings, and titles in flyers, posters, announcements, brochures, advertisements, newsletters, and so on may be in a large font to capture the reader's attention. Use an 11- or 12-point font size for most of the text in a document since it is a notably readable size, preferred by most readers. A font that is too small strains the reader's eye and makes the document look crammed and difficult to read. A font that is too large uses more space than is necessary and causes readers to read slowly (letter by letter rather than whole words and phrases).

© iStockphoto.com/Yuri_Arcurs

## Technique: Letter Keys

**Technique Cue**
Limit keystroking action to the fingers; keep hands and arms motionless.

Key each line twice. Emphasize continuity and rhythm with curved, upright fingers.

A 1 Katrina baked Marsha a loaf of bread to take to the Alameda fair.

B 2 Barbara and Bob Babbitt both saw the two blackbirds in the lobby.

C 3 Carl, the eccentric character with a classic crew cut, may catch.

D 4 David and Eddie dodged the duck as it waddled down the dark road.

E 5 Ellen needed Steven to help her complete the spreadsheet on time.

F 6 Before I left, Faye found forty to fifty feet of flowered fabric.

G 7 George and Greg thought the good-looking neighbor was gregarious.

H 8 John, Hank, and Sarah helped her haul the huge bush to the trash.

gwam 1' | 1 | 2 | 3 | 4 | 5 | 6 | 7 | 8 | 9 | 10 | 11 | 12 | 13 |

## Timed Writings

Key two 3' writings on the two ¶s; determine *gwam*; count errors.

 **all letters used**                              gwam 3'

   "I left my heart in San Francisco." This expression   4
becomes much easier to understand after an individual has   7
visited the city near the bay. San Francisco is one of   11
the most interesting areas to visit throughout the entire   15
world. The history of this city is unique. Even though   19
people inhabited the area prior to the gold rush, it was   23
the prospect of getting rich that brought about the fast   26
growth of the city.   28

   It is difficult to write about just one thing that this   31
exquisite city is known for. Spectacular views, cable cars,   35
the Golden Gate Bridge, and Fisherman's Wharf are only a   39
few of the many things that are associated with this amazing   43
city. The city is also known for the diversity of its people.   48
In fact, there are three separate cities within the city,   51
Chinatown being the best known.   54

gwam 3' | 1 | 2 | 3 | 4 |

Complete this activity to help prepare for the **Personal Finance** event in FBLA-PBL's Business Management and Administration division. Participants in this event demonstrate that they possess essential knowledge and skills related to financial issues.

You are a recent college graduate and have just been hired for a full-time job. Your annual salary is $32,400, and you will receive a paycheck twice a month. You want to set up a budget for yourself.

1. In a new spreadsheet file, enter a formula to determine the amount you will be paid during each pay period before taxes. Remember, there are 24 pay periods in the year.

2. Determine the following tax deductions that will be made on each paycheck: 15 percent for federal income tax; 7 percent for FICA (includes Social Security and Medicare); 6 percent for state income tax; and 2 percent for municipal income tax.

   Enter a formula to determine the amount of each paycheck after taxes. Then, in a separate cell, determine how much you will take home in a month.

© Pressmaster/Shutterstock.com

3. Prepare a personal budget for yourself. List the monthly take-home amount as the source of income, and then list the categories of your regular expenses. Assume you pay $525 per month in rent, $125 for utilities and cable, and $150 in gas and transportation costs. You should insert your own estimates for other expenses such as phone, food, clothes, entertainment, and savings. Add your total income and your total expenses, and then subtract your expenses from the income. Did you end up with a surplus or a deficit?

4. Insert a title for the spreadsheet and apply formatting and text enhancements to the data as appropriate.

5. Save the file and print as directed by your instructor.

For detailed information on this event, go to www.fbla-pbl.org.

### Think Critically

1. Why is it useful to set up a personal budget?
2. Why would the ability to manage your personal finances be considered a transferable skill that can be used on almost any job?

## School and Community
According to constitutional law, all U.S. citizens have the right to assemble peaceably. This means that law enforcement officials cannot stop citizens from gathering in peaceful demonstrations to protest or air their grievances.

Peaceful protests have been instrumental in bringing positive attention to important issues in our country's history. For example, women in the early 20th century protested about being denied the right to vote. Martin Luther King Jr. led many peaceful demonstrations on the issue of segregation of blacks and whites.

1. Research an issue or cause that you feel strongly about. It could be a school issue, such as healthier food selections in the cafeteria, or a community issue, such as destroying the natural habitat for wildlife to develop homes or commercial property.

2. Identify at least three reasons why you would participate in a protest over the issue.

## Work Assignment at "Hoops"

Read the following information to familiarize yourself with your work assignment with "Hoops." "Hoops" is a real-world simulated business whose specialty is recreational basketball tournaments. As an employee of "Hoops," you will prepare professional-looking business documents for Mr. Todd McLemore, the owner of "Hoops," and for Ms. Julia Kingsley, his administrative assistant. You will be expected to apply the information and skills you learned in previous units.

 **TIP** Retain all document files created for Unit 7 "Hoops I"; you will need them to complete Unit 13 "Hoops II."

"Hoops" plans, organizes, and manages 3-on-3 basketball tournaments in Fort Collins, Colorado, throughout the summer. Your job requires knowledge of the following skills and software:

- Word processing
- Database
- Spreadsheet
- Electronic presentations
- Interpersonal
- Telephone
- Calendaring
- Contacts

McLemore, Todd

**Todd McLemore**
"Hoops" Tournaments
Tournament Director

(970) 555-1100 Work
tmclemore@hoops.cengage.com

618 Center Street
Fort Collins, CO 80526-1392

You will be assisting Ms. Kingsley in processing all information dealing with the tournaments. The work includes:

- Processing letters and email messages to advertisers, coaches, refs, and players.
- Creating a database for advertisers, coaches, refs, and players.
- Updating a database as registrations and advertising fees are received.
- Formatting tournament forms.
- Preparing tournament information.
- Creating a spreadsheet to keep track of tournament registrations.
- Updating spreadsheets for registration fees and refs' schedules.
  - Formatting and keying tournament brackets.
  - Preparing a slide show for an electronic presentation.
  - Preparing tournament calendars.
  - Creating a database to determine award recipients.
  - Calculating refs' pay.
  - Creating and updating contact lists.

Fuse/Jupiter Images

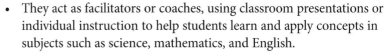

### Planning a Career in Education & Training

Workers in the field of Education & Training play an important role in fostering the intellectual, social, and professional development of people of all ages. They create the environment and provide the tools that help learners develop and strengthen their skills, talents, and knowledge.

### What's It Like?

This field is for those individuals who are interested in planning, managing, and providing education and training services and related learning support services. For example:

- They act as facilitators or coaches, using classroom presentations or individual instruction to help students learn and apply concepts in subjects such as science, mathematics, and English.
- They provide instructional leadership and manage the day-to-day activities in schools, preschools, day care centers, and colleges and universities.
- They assist people by helping them cope with and solve issues in their everyday lives, such as family and personal problems and dealing with relationships.
- They help their companies effectively use employee skills, provide training and development opportunities to improve those skills, and increase employees' satisfaction with their jobs and working conditions.

Jobs in this field can be very rewarding as workers are able to observe others acquiring new skills and knowledge and applying it in positive ways. But they can also be stressful at times. Those who work in schools typically work a traditional 10-month school year. Trainers, instructors, and others who work in professional settings usually work a 40-hour week.

### Employment Outlook

Employment in this cluster is projected to grow as fast as the average or faster than average for all occupations. Job prospects are best for teachers in high-demand fields, such as mathematics, science, and bilingual education. The growing elderly population will create greater demand for health and social services workers. Ongoing revisions to standards governing employment in general and employee benefits will create growing employment opportunities for those in human resources.

Most workers in this cluster are required to have at least a bachelor's degree, and many must obtain a license to work in certain fields and institutions. Those in administrative education positions are usually required to have a master's degree.

### What About You?

This career cluster is covered in box 5 of the Interest Survey Activity you completed in Unit 1 of this text. If this box had one of the three highest scores on your survey, you should further explore the cluster's pathways and related occupations.

1. Why do you think a career in this field could be a good choice?
2. What skills can you develop now that would be helpful to a career in this field?

## Processing Instructions

Ms. Kingsley will attach general processing instructions to each task you are given.  If a date is not provided on the document, use the date included on the instructions.  If the instructions given with the document are not sufficiently detailed, use your decision-making skills to process the document.  Since "Hoops" has based its office manual on the Century 21 textbook, you can also use the text as a reference.

Documents should be attractively formatted.  You are expected to produce error-free documents, so proofread and correct your work carefully before presenting it for approval.

## Calendar, Notes, and Tasks

Some processing instructions include notes like "Remember that we are meeting with the printer on April 19 at 3:30.  Be sure to put that on your calendar." And "Make a reminder note to check with the graphic artist on Thursday to see if the letterhead is ready."  Use the calendar, notes, and tasks features of your software to remind you to take care of pending meetings and tasks to be completed at a later date.

## Filenames

Use hoops + job no. for the filename for each document (*hoops job 1, hoops job 2,* etc.).  Include the name of the document when a job has more than one document to file.  For example, *hoops job 3 flyer* and *hoops job 3 rules.*

## Letter Format

Mr. McLemore likes his letters formatted in block format with mixed punctuation.  Use the following for the closing lines of his letters:

Sincerely,


Todd McLemore
Tournament Director

## Tournament Dates

"Hoops" Tournament Schedule
20-- Tournament Dates

June
- June 15-16
- June 22-23
- June 29-30

July
- July 6-7
- July 13-14
- July 20-21
- July 27-28

August
- August 3-4

For additional information, contact:
Todd McLemore, Tournament Director
"Hoops" Tournaments
618 Center Street
Fort Collins, CO 80526-1392

Phone:  970.555.1100
Email:  tmclemore@hoops.cengage.com

VEER.COM/STILLFX

# Academic and Career Connections

Complete the following exercises that introduce various topics that involve academic themes and careers.

## Grammar and Writing: Word Usage

**MicroType 6**

- **References/Communication Skills/Word Usage**

1. Go to *MicroType* 6 and use this feature path: References/Communication Skills/Word Usage.
2. Click *Rules* and review the rules for word usage.
3. Then, under *Word Usage*, click *Posttest*.
4. Follow the instructions to complete the posttest.

## Communications: Listening

1. Open the sound file *df u16 communications*. It contains three math problems that are presented to you verbally.
2. Each problem starts with a number, followed by several addition and subtraction steps.
3. Handwrite the first number followed by each step for all three problems.
4. After the third problem, close the sound file.
5. Open a new spreadsheet file. In cell A1, key **Problem 1**. In cell A2, enter the problem from your handwritten notes as a formula. Repeat in cells B1:B2 and C1:C2 for the second and third problems.
6. **Save as: *u16 communications*.**

## Personal Finance

Lucy and Roberto were recently married. They received more than $5,000 in cash as wedding gifts and have decided that now is a good time to explore saving and investing options.

1. Open a new spreadsheet and save it as *u16 finance*. Lucy and Roberto want to determine how much their $5,000 will be worth if they invest it for a few years. In cell A1, key **Future Value**. In cell B1, use the future value (FV) function to determine what the $5,000 investment earning 6 percent interest a year will be worth in five years if no additional investments are made.
2. Lucy and Roberto are thinking they might want to buy a home. They want to determine how much they would need to invest now in order to have $10,000 for a down payment in five years. In cell A3, key **Present Value**. In cell B3, use the present value (PV) function to determine what amount needs to be invested today at 6 percent annual interest to have $10,000 in five years. Will the $5,000 in wedding money earn them enough over the next five years to cover the down payment?
3. Lucy and Roberto know that they will probably need to buy a new car soon. If they put $2,000 of their wedding money toward the purchase of a new car and then take out a loan for $19,000 to pay the balance, how much will their monthly payments be if the interest rate on the loan is 5 percent and the term is three years? In cell A5, key **Car Payment**. In cell B5, use the payment (PMT) function to determine how much the monthly payments will need to be to pay off the loan at 5 percent interest for three years. The payments are made at the beginning of the month.

OUTCOME

• Use decision-making, creative-thinking, and document-processing skills to complete real-world application jobs for a simulated business.

**Business Documents**

• Tournament Application
• Mail Merge Letter
• Tournament Flyer
• Tournament Rules Handout
• Hotel Information Table
• Coach and Player Databases
• Confirmation Letters and Reminders
• Spreadsheet of Tournament Income
• Email with Attachment
• Contact File for Referees

## Job 1

**Application
April 17**

From the desk of:

**Julia Kingsley**

*Here is a copy of last year's tournament application. Using df hoops I application, prepare one for this year with the changes marked on the application.*

*Merge the Birth Date (Month, Day, and Year) cell with the Age cell and change the name of the merged cell to Age as of First Day of Tournament for each of the five player listings.*

*Remember that we are meeting with the printer on April 19 at 3:30. Be sure to put that on your calendar.*

*JK*

### "Hoops" Tournament Application

| Division: | Tournament Date: | Age Level of Players: |
|---|---|---|
| ☐ Males | | ☐ 11-12 year age bracket |
| ☐ Females | | ☐ 13-14 year age bracket |
| Name of Your Team: | | ☐ 15-16 year age bracket |
| | | ☐ 17-18 year age bracket |
| | | ☐ 19 and over age bracket |

**Coach or Contact Person** (Must be 21 years of age or older):

| Last Name | First | Middle Initial | E-mail Address |
|---|---|---|---|
| Street Address | City | State | ZIP | Phone |

**Player 1:**

| Last Name | First | Middle Initial | Birth Date (Month, Day, Year) | Age |
|---|---|---|---|---|
| Street Address | City | State | ZIP | Phone |

**Player 2:**

| Last Name | First | Middle Initial | Birth Date (Month, Day, Year) | Age |
|---|---|---|---|---|
| Street Address | City | State | ZIP | Phone |

**Player 3:**

| Last Name | First | Middle Initial | Birth Date (Month, Day, Year) | Age |
|---|---|---|---|---|
| Street Address | City | State | ZIP | Phone |

**Player 4:**

| Last Name | First | Middle Initial | Birth Date (Month, Day, Year) | Age |
|---|---|---|---|---|
| Street Address | City | State | ZIP | Phone |

**Player 5:**

| Last Name | First | Middle Initial | Birth Date (Month, Day, Year) | Age |
|---|---|---|---|---|
| Street Address | City | State | ZIP | Phone |

**Verification by Coach:** To the best of my knowledge the information presented on this form is correct. Please sign below.

| Signature: | | Date: |
|---|---|---|
| *shade in gold* | | *shade in gold* |

10. Embed the following text as a *Word* file using 9-pt. font below row 6 in *OVT RPT*:

This worksheet shows the total overtime hours worked by each employee.

11. Print the *OVT RPT* worksheet.
12. **Save as: *93g worksheet*.**

1. Open a new worksheet. In cell A1, use the future value function to determine what a current $8,000 investment earning 6 percent interest will be worth in 10 years if no additional investments are made.
2. In cell A3, use the present value function to determine what amount needs to be invested today at 6 percent interest to have $13,000 in five years.
3. In cell A5, use the payment function to determine how much the monthly payments will need to be to pay off a $10,000 loan at 6 percent interest for eight years. The payments are made at the beginning of the month.
4. **Save as: *93h functions*.**

 **A**    all letters used     **gwam**   3'

| | gwam 3' |
|---|---|
| Attitude is the way people communicate their feelings or | 3 \| 72 |
| moods to others.  A person is said to have a positive attitude | 8 \| 77 |
| when he or she anticipates successful experiences.  A person | 12 \| 81 |
| such as this is said to be an optimist.  The best possible | 16 \| 85 |
| outcomes are expected.  The world is viewed as a great place. | 20 \| 89 |
| Good is found in even the worst situation. | 23 \| 92 |
| Individuals are said to have negative attitudes when they | 26 \| 95 |
| expect failure.  A pessimist is the name given to an individual | 31 \| 100 |
| with a bad view of life.  Pessimists emphasize the adverse | 35 \| 104 |
| aspects of life and expect the worst possible outcome.  They | 39 \| 108 |
| expect to fail even before they start the day.  You can plan on | 43 \| 112 |
| them to find gloom even in the best situation. | 46 \| 115 |
| Only you can ascertain when you are going to have a good or | 50 \| 119 |
| bad attitude.  Keep in mind that people are attracted to a | 54 \| 123 |
| person with a good attitude and tend to shy away from one with a | 58 \| 127 |
| bad attitude.  Your attitude quietly determines just how | 62 \| 131 |
| successful you are in all your personal relationships as well as | 66 \| 135 |
| in your professional relationships. | 69 \| 138 |

gwam   3'  |     1     |     2     |     3     |     4     |

**Mail Merge**
**April 17**

From the desk of:
**Julia Kingsley**
Please format and key the attached as a mail merge letter to last year's advertisers. Use the Advertisers' database file, df hoops I advertisers. Print a copy of the form letter to Mona Lisa's Cuisine and Park Place Plaza.

When our letterhead design is final, you should begin using it. Make a reminder note to check with the graphic artist on Thursday to see if the letterhead is ready.

JK

April 17, 20--

<Courtesy Title> <First Name> <Last Name>
<Business>
<Address>
<City>, <State> <ZIP>

Dear <Courtesy Title> <Last Name>:

"Hoops" will again be sponsoring 3-on-3 basketball tournaments each weekend from June 15-August 4. Over 600 basketball players plus their families and relatives will travel to Fort Collins for each of the nine weekends. This will have a huge impact on the economy of the Fort Collins area.

We are starting to work on the program that will be distributed at the tournaments to players, coaches, and spectators. Last year you purchased advertising space in the program for <Business>. The advertisement appeared in each of the five tournament programs. This year we have increased the number of tournaments from five to eight.

As you know, we have three different sizes of advertisements. The costs for the different advertisement sizes are as follows:

| | |
|---|---|
| Quarter-page advertisement | $200 |
| Half-page advertisement | $400 |
| Full-page advertisement | $750 |

If you are interested in placing an advertisement in this year's tournament programs, please complete the enclosed form and return it by May 15.

Sincerely,

Todd McLemore
Tournament Director

xx

Enclosure

1. Open a new worksheet and key the worksheet below, formatting it as desired.

| FRAMES BY yourframes.com | | | | |
|---|---|---|---|---|
| **Size** | **Quantity** | | | |
| | **1–6** | **7–12** | **13–24** | **24+** |
| 4" X 6" | $ 17.98 | $ 16.18 | $ 14.56 | $ 13.11 |
| 5" X 7" | $ 19.98 | $ 17.98 | $ 16.18 | $ 14.57 |
| 8" X10" | $ 21.98 | $ 19.78 | $ 17.80 | $ 16.02 |

2. **Save as: *93e source*** but do not close it.
3. Open **df 93e destination** (*Word* file) and copy the worksheet, with a link, into the document between the first two ¶s.
4. Save the *Word* file as **93e destination** and close both files.

1. Open worksheet **93e source** and increase each amount by $2.00. Save as **93e source** and close the file.
2. Open *Word* file **93e destination**, which will update the letter with the new amounts. Use today's date and address it to:

   Dr. Patricia Kurtz
   1246 Warren Drive
   Denver, CO 80221-7463

4. **Save as: *93f destination*.**

1. Open **df 93g worksheet** and make Sheet 1 active, if needed.
2. Write an IF function in cell H4 to calculate the number of hours in excess of 40 during each week.
3. Copy this formula to cell H4 in each of the worksheets 2, 3, 4, and 5 and then to H5:H14 in each of the five worksheets.
4. Calculate the total overtime hours in cell H15 in worksheet 1, and then copy the formula to H15 in the other four worksheets.
5. Rename each of the worksheets using the last name of the employee, and then arrange them in alphabetical order starting at the left.
6. Insert a new worksheet. Position it so it is the first worksheet.
7. Rename the new worksheet **OVT RPT** and key the information shown below.

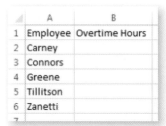

8. In cell B2 of the *OVT RPT* worksheet, insert a 3-D reference to cell H15 in the *Carney* worksheet.
9. In a similar manner, enter a 3-D cell reference in cells B3, B4, B5, and B6 in the *OVT RPT* worksheet to cell H15 in each of the employee's worksheets.

From the desk of:
**Julia Kingsley**

*A tournament packet will be sent to last year's participants and to new inquiries. We will include "Hoops" Tournament Rules (copy shown at right) and a flyer ("Hoops" Tournament Schedule Flyer) in the packet. Use your creativity and decision-making skills to create these two documents.*

*Format and key the copy at the right with the changes shown on the copy. Center the document on the page; DS before and after each of the main bullets.*

*The tournament flyer should contain relevant tournament information along with the tournament dates (given on p. 207) and appropriate graphics. The Internet has some great basketball graphics that could be imported.*

*Include an entry on your Task list to have tournament packets ready to mail by May 1.*

*JK*

*"Hoops" Tournament Rules*

- Each team may consist of up to five players; three players will play at one time. *There will be a male division and a female division.*

- Teams will be grouped by age level. *∧*Copies of participants' birth certificates must accompany registration materials. Participants may be required to verify their age at the tournament if another team requests verification. *∧*

- The age-level groupings are as follows: *Age is based on first day of tournament.*
  - 11–12 years old
  - 13–14 years old
  - 15–16 years old
  - 17–18 years old
  - ~~19 and over~~

  *Players can play up one age level. For example, an 11-year-old can play on a team of 13- and 14-year-olds. However, players cannot play down; a 17-year-old player cannot play on a team of 15- and 16-year-olds.*

- A team is guaranteed at least three games each tournament and may have as many as five games if they advance to the championship game. Each grade level will have a maximum of 16 teams competing. The 16 teams will be divided into two brackets. The first-place winners in each bracket will play each other for the championship of the age level.

- Games will be played on half court and will have a 25-minute time limit.

- Game scoring is as follows:
  - One point for baskets under 20 feet
  - Two points for baskets over 20 feet

# LESSON 93

## Spreadsheet Applications

**OUTCOME**

- Apply the spreadsheet features learned in this and the previous spreadsheet units.

### Business Documents

- Correspondence Report
- Payroll Journal
- Payroll Analyses
- Cost Chart
- Employee Time Card Report
- Future Value of Money
- Present Value of Money
- Loan Payment Amount

---

## 93B

### Integrate Word and Excel and Charting

1. Open a new *Word* document and key the table below.

| CORRESPONDENCE REPORT | | | | | |
|---|---|---|---|---|---|
| **TYPE** | **MON** | **TUE** | **WED** | **THU** | **FRI** |
| **U.S. Postal Service** | 10 | 12 | 11 | 10 | 9 |
| **Interoffice** | 14 | 12 | 10 | 8 | 11 |
| **Email** | 24 | 18 | 15 | 14 | 12 |
| **Facsimile** | 8 | 7 | 10 | 11 | 6 |
| **Private carrier** | 9 | 11 | 10 | 13 | 8 |

2. Save as **93b source** but do not close it.
3. Open a new worksheet file and copy the table into a blank worksheet; make formatting adjustments as desired.
4. Create a column chart with title, legend, and other features you choose.
5. Move the chart to a chart sheet.
6. Save the worksheet as **93b destination** and close both files.

---

## 93C

### Worksheet with Calculations and Conditional Formatting

1. Open **df 93c worksheet**.
2. Calculate the hours worked by each employee in column G.
3. Write an IF function for calculations in column H so that all hours worked up to and including 40 are paid at the hourly rate in cell D17.
4. Write an IF function for column I to calculate overtime pay that is paid at 1.5 times the hourly rate in D17 for all hours worked over 40.
5. In column J, calculate each employee's gross pay and apply conditional formatting to highlight those who earned more than $425.
6. Calculate totals for cells G15–J15.
7. Calculate the average pay in cell D18, the minimum pay in D19, and the maximum pay in D20.
8. Use two decimal places for currency.
9. Use data bars in column I (cell I4:I14) to show different levels of overtime pay.
10. Save as: **93c worksheet**.

---

## 93D

### What If

1. If needed, open **93c worksheet** and answer this question: What is the total payroll if the hourly rate is increased to $10.75?
2. Clear the conditional formatting in column J, and then reapply to highlight those who would earn more than $430.
3. Save as: **93d worksheet**.

---

## Update Database
## April 19

From the desk of:

**Julia Kingsley**

One of the businesses that advertised in last year's program was missing from the letters I signed yesterday. Send a letter to:

Ms. Glenna McCormack
21st Century Sports
749 Center Avenue
Fort Collins, CO
80526-1394

Update the database to include 21st Century Sports. Also make the change noted on the attached letter to the database and print a copy of the letter.

JK

Todd McLemore, Tournament Director
**"Hoops" Tournaments**
618 Center Street
Fort Collins, CO 80526-1392

April 17, 20—

*Mr. Justin Kummerfeld bought the Pizza Palace. Redo the letter, addressing it to Mr. Kummerfeld. Update the database.*

~~Mr. Jason Dixon~~
Pizza Palace
608 Main Street
Fort Collins, CO 80524-1444

Dear Mr. ~~Dixon~~:

"Hoops" will again be sponsoring 3-on-3 basketball tournaments each weekend from June 15-August 4. Over 600 basketball players plus their families will travel to Fort Collins for each of the nine weekends. This will have a huge impact on the economy of the Fort Collins area.

5. Make cell B3 active. Use the PMT function to enter the quarterly investment required to have $5,000 at the end of six years. The annual interest rate is 5.5 percent. Accept the default value for Type.

6. In column C, calculate the total amount of the investments over the six-year period for each plan.

7. In column D, calculate the amount of interest each investment plan earned. *Note:* Since column C has negative values, you will need to add 5,000 to cell C2 and to cell C3 to find the interest. Therefore, the formula in cell D2 will be =5,000+C2.

8. Shade cell D2 or cell D3 to identify the plan that earned the most interest.

9. Save as: **92c pmt**, check your answers, and close the file.

## 92D

**Application**

1. Open *df 92d apply* and make these calculations:
   a. In row 8, calculate the total number of payments for each loan.
   b. In row 9, use the PMT function to calculate the payment amount for each loan.
      *Note:* If desired, you can insert cell references for the arguments from the worksheet in the Function Arguments dialog box for this and other financial functions rather than keying the values in the Function Arguments dialog box.
   c. In row 10, calculate the total amount for all payments for each loan.
   d. In row 11, calculate the total interest charge for each loan.
      *Note:* The values in rows 9,10, and 11 will be negative values.
2. Format the worksheet to make it attractive and easy to read.
3. Save as: **92d pmt**, check your answers, and close the file.

## 92E

**Application**

1. Open *df 92e apply* and make these calculations:
   a. In row 8, calculate the total number of investments for each plan.
   b. In row 9, use the PMT function to calculate the amount of each investment for each plan.
   c. In row 10, calculate the total of all investments for each plan.
   d. In row 11, calculate the total interest earned for each investment plan.
      *Note:* The values in rows 9 and 10 will be negative values.
2. Format the worksheet to make it attractive and easy to read.
3. Save as: **92e apply**, check your answers, and close the file.

**QUICK ✔**

Your answers for Plan 1 should agree with the answers below.

| | A | B |
|---|---|---|
| 1 | Investment Plans | |
| 2 | | |
| 3 | Plan Information | Plan 1 |
| 4 | Investment Goal | $500 |
| 5 | Annual Interest Rate | 4.00% |
| 6 | No. of Years | 1 |
| 7 | Investments Per Year | 12 |
| 8 | Total No. of Investments | 12 |
| 9 | Amount of Each Investmen | ($40.91) |
| 10 | Amount of All Investments | ($490.90) |
| 11 | Total Interest Earned | $9.10 |
| 12 | | |

**Table**

**April 24**

From the desk of:

**Julia Kingsley**

*Create a Hotel Information sheet with the information shown on the attached sheet. Center the information on the page. Note the price changes since last summer for the following hotels:*

*Country Inn: $50–$98*

*Cozy Cottage: $50–$75*

*The Inn: $69–$129*

*Red Cedar Inn: $50–$65*

*Also, include the following email address for The Inn: theinn@fortcollins.com.*

*Mark your calendar for April 26 at 2 p.m. to go over the final copy with me.*

*JK*

# Hotel Information

| Hotel and Address | Price Range | Features |
|---|---|---|
| **Country Inn**<br>2208 Main street<br>Fort Collins, CO 80524-1733<br><br>Phone: 970-555-6553<br>Email: countryinn@fortcollins.com | $50-$98 | Nonsmoking rooms, onsite restaurant, free full breakfast, kitchenettes, whirlpool, indoor pool, fitness center |
| **Cozy Cottage Inn**<br>689 Center Avenue<br>Fort Collins, CO 80526-2210<br><br>Phone: 970-555-7752 | $50-$75 | Cable, pets allowed, nonsmoking rooms, complimentary coffee |
| **Four Season Suites**<br>4817 Main Street<br>Fort Collins, CO 80524-2056<br><br>Phone: 970-555-9805 | $59-79 | Suites, nonsmoking rooms, onsite restaurant, free continental breakfast, cable, in-room Jacuzzi, indoor pool, courtesy van, free local calls |
| **The Inn**<br>310 Main Street<br>Fort Collins, CO 80524-1403<br><br>Phone: 970-348-7382<br>Email: theinn@fortcollins.com | $69-$129 | Suites, nonsmoking rooms, onsite restaurant, free continental breakfast, kitchenettes, indoor pool, fitness center |
| **Park Place Plaza**<br>320 Park Place Court<br>Fort Collins, CO 80525-1621<br><br>Phone: 970-348-1239<br>Email: mail@parkplaceplaza.com | $60-140 | Nonsmoking rooms, free continental breakfast, kitchenettes, cable, in-room whirlpools, indoor and outdoor pool, sauna, fitness center, Internet connections in rooms |
| **Red Cedar Inn**<br>453 Cedar Street<br>Fort Collins, CO 80524-1237<br><br>Phone: 970-555-5610 | $50-$65 | Budget motel, nonsmoking rooms, waterbeds, kitchenettes, cable, pets allowed |

*Insert a row in the table before the Red Cedar Inn for the information given below.*

*Park Place Plaza*
*320 Park Place Court*
*Fort Collins, CO 80525-1621*
*Phone: 970-348-1239*
*Email: mail@parkplaceplaza.com*

*$60-$140*

*Nonsmoking rooms, free continental breakfast, kitchenettes, cable, in-room whirlpools, indoor and outdoor pool, sauna, fitness center, Internet connections in rooms*

1. Open a blank worksheet, key **Plan A Monthly Payment** in cell A1, and adjust the width of column A to fit the contents.
2. Make cell B1 active. Use the PMT function to enter the monthly payment for the following loan in cell B1: A three-year $15,000 loan at 5.5 percent that will be repaid in full by making equal monthly payments. Accept the default values for Fv and Type.
3. Key **Plan B Monthly Payment** in cell A2.
4. Make cell B2 active. Use the PMT function to enter the monthly payment for the following loan in cell B2: A two-year $15,000 loan at 4.75 percent that will be repaid in full by making equal monthly payments. Accept the default values for Fv and Type.
5. **Save as:** *92b pmt*, check your answers, and close the file.

**92C**

**Payment (PMT) Function for an Investment**

Formulas/Function Library/
Insert Function/PMT

The PMT function can also be used to calculate how much you need to invest (save) regularly to have a specified amount of money at the end of a specified time. For example, how much do you need to invest each month to have $8,000 after four years if the investment will earn 3.5 percent interest annually?

When you use the payment function for this purpose, the Rate is the interest rate for each investment period, Nper is the total number of investments, and Pv is zero since you are starting out with no investment. Fv is $8,000, the amount you want to have after four years. Type is 0 or 1. If investments are made at the end of each period, accept the default value of 0. If investments are made at the beginning of each period, key 1 for Type.

Figure 16-13 shows the Function Arguments dialog box and entries for the investment plan that will be worth $8,000 in four years.

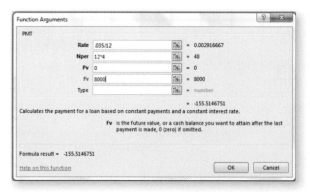

**Figure 16-13** Payment function for an investment

The Rate is 3.5%/12 (or .035/12) to convert the annual interest rate to a monthly rate, since investments are made monthly. Nper is 12*4 since there are 12 investments during each of four years. The Pv is 0 since there is no investment before the first monthly deposit is made. FV is 8,000 to specify the amount desired in four years. Since investments are made at the beginning of the investment period, the default value of 0 for Type is accepted and nothing is keyed. The formula result is displayed as a negative number since it represents money spent.

1. Open a blank worksheet and add the following information: Key **Plan** in cell A1, **Investment** in cell B1, **Total Investments** in cell C1, and **Interest Earned** in cell D1. Key **Plan A** in cell A2.
2. Adjust the width of the columns to fit the contents.
3. Make cell B2 active. Use the PMT function to enter the monthly investment required to have $5,000 at the end of six years. The annual interest rate is 5.5 percent. Accept the default value for Type.
4. Key **Plan B** in cell A3.

## Job 6

**Letter**
**April 24**

From the desk of:

**Julia Kingsley**

Ms. Radeski, manager of the Sub Shoppe, returned the advertisement form to place a half-page ad in the tournament program. She did not include payment for the advertisement. Format and key the letter I've drafted on the attached sheet.

Make a note to contact Ms. Radeski by phone if you haven't heard from her by May 15.

JK

April 24, 20--

Ms. Karin Radeski
The Sub Shoppe
88 Manchester Circle
Fort Collins, CO 80526-1118

Dear Ms. Radeski:

Thank you for returning your form for placing an advertisement in the "Hoops" Tournament Program. In order for your advertisement to appear in the program, we will need to receive your check for $400 for the half-page advertisement before we have the programs printed. Our deadline for submitting the program to the printer is May 28.

If you have any questions or would like to preview your advertisement, you can call or stop by the office between 10:30 a.m. and 3:30 p.m. Monday through Friday.

Sincerely,

Todd McLemore
Tournament Director

xx

## Job 7

**Database**
**April 30**

From the desk of:

**Julia Kingsley**

The first "Hoops" Tournament applications for the June 15–16 tournament arrived today. Please create a database for the tournament. Set the database up so there will be two separate tables—one for coaches and one for players. I've listed the fields to be included in each table on the attached sheet. After you create the database, enter the information from the two applications on the next page. Print a copy of the Players table in landscape orientation.

JK

**Table for Coaches**
- ✓ Division
- ✓ Age Level
- ✓ Team
- ✓ Last Name
- ✓ First Name
- ✓ Initial
- ✓ Email
- ✓ Street Address
- ✓ City
- ✓ State
- ✓ ZIP
- ✓ Phone

**Table for Players**
- ✓ Division
- ✓ Age Level
- ✓ Team
- ✓ Last Name
- ✓ First Name
- ✓ Initial
- ✓ Age
- ✓ Street Address
- ✓ City
- ✓ State
- ✓ ZIP
- ✓ Phone

1. Open **df 91d apply** and calculate the future value or present value for each scenario. Record your answers in column B.
2. Check your answers. Save the worksheet as **91d apply** and close the file.

## LESSON 92 — Payment Function

**OUTCOMES**

- Use the payment function (PMT) to calculate loan payments.
- Use the payment function (PMT) to calculate investments.

**Business Documents**

- Loan Payments Amounts
- Investment Amounts

**92B**

**Payment (PMT) Function for Loans**

Formulas/Function Library/ Insert Function/PMT

The payment function is a financial function that can be used to calculate the payments for a loan that has constant and equal payments and a fixed interest rate. To use this function, the interest rate, the number of payments, and the amount of the loan must be known. The function is abbreviated **PMT** and its syntax is **PMT(Rate, Nper, Pv, Fv, Type)**. The Rate, Nper, and Type mean the same as they do when used in FV and PV functions that were previously learned.

In this activity, Pv is the amount (present value) of the loan and Fv is an option argument. If a value is not entered for Fv, a value of 0 is assigned to indicate that the entire loan will be paid off when the last payment is made. When the payment is calculated, it is displayed as a negative value to show that the value represents money spent. Figure 16-12 shows the Function Arguments dialog box for the PMT function for $1,000 loan at 6 percent. The borrower is required to make equal monthly payments at the end of the payment period for two years. The Rate is 6%/12 (or .06/12) to convert the annual interest rate to a monthly rate since payments are made monthly.

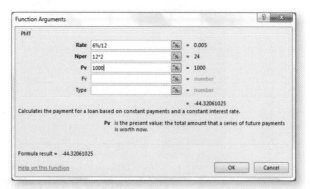

**Figure 16-12** Payment function for a loan

The Nper is 12*2 to indicate the loan has 12 payments in each of the two years. The Pv is 1000—the amount of the loan. Since the loan will be paid off in full at the end of two years, the default value of 0 is accepted and nothing is keyed for Fv.

Since payments are made at the end of each payment period, the default value of 0 for Type is accepted and nothing is keyed. The monthly payment (PMT) is indicated as a negative number beneath the last argument.

# "Hoops" Tournament Application

| Division: | Tournament Date: | Age Level of Players: |
|---|---|---|
| ■ Males<br>☐ Females | June 15–16 | ☐ 11–12 year age bracket<br>☐ 13–14 year age bracket<br>■ 15–16 year age bracket<br>☐ 17–18 year age bracket |

**Name of Your Team:**
Frontiersmen

**Coach or Contact Person** (Must be 21 years of age or older):

| Last Name | First | Middle Initial | E-mail Address |
|---|---|---|---|
| Trussoni | Matthew | P. | mtrussoni@home.com |

| Street Address | City | State | ZIP | Phone |
|---|---|---|---|---|
| 732 Bozeman Trail | Cheyenne | WY | 82009 | 307-376-8756 |

**Player 1:**

| Last Name | First | Middle Initial | Age as of First Day of Tournament |
|---|---|---|---|
| Sinclair | Mark | A. | 16 |

| Street Address | City | State | ZIP | Phone |
|---|---|---|---|---|
| 615 Clark Street | Cheyenne | WY | 82009 | 307-376-7652 |

**Player 2:**

| Last Name | First | Middle Initial | Age as of First Day of Tournament |
|---|---|---|---|
| Finch | Jeff | R. | 15 |

| Street Address | City | State | ZIP | Phone |
|---|---|---|---|---|
| 879 Columbus Drive | Cheyenne | WY | 82007 | 307-345-7733 |

**Player 3:**

| Last Name | First | Middle Initial | Age as of First Day of Tournament |
|---|---|---|---|
| Remmington | Jay | M. | 16 |

| Street Address | City | State | ZIP | Phone |
|---|---|---|---|---|
| 33 Sagebrush Avenue | Cheyenne | WY | 82009 | 307-376-1090 |

**Player 4:**

| Last Name | First | Middle Initial | Age as of First Day of Tournament |
|---|---|---|---|
| Martinez | Felipe | J. | 16 |

| Street Address | City | State | ZIP | Phone |
|---|---|---|---|---|
| 458 Yellowstone Road | Cheyenne | WY | 82009 | 307-345-5648 |

**Player 5:**

| Last Name | First | Middle Initial | Age as of First Day of Tournament |
|---|---|---|---|
| Roberts | Reece | R. | 16 |

| Street Address | City | State | ZIP | Phone |
|---|---|---|---|---|
| 730 Piute Drive | Cheyenne | WY | 82001 | 307-376-9023 |

**Verification by Coach:** To the best of my knowledge the information presented on this form is correct. Please sign below.

| Signature: | Matthew P. Trussoni | Date: | April 15, 20-- |
|---|---|---|---|

---

# "Hoops" Tournament Application

| Division: | Tournament Date: | Age Level of Players: |
|---|---|---|
| ☐ Males<br>■ Females | June 15–16 | ☐ 11–12 year age bracket<br>☐ ■3–14 year age bracket<br>☐ 15–16 year age bracket<br>☐ 17–18 year age bracket |

**Name of Your Team:**
Boulder "Dashers"

**Coach or Contact Person** (Must be 21 years of age or older):

| Last Name | First | Middle Initial | E-mail Address |
|---|---|---|---|
| Perkins | Brett | P. | bpperkins@cs.com |

| Street Address | City | State | ZIP | Phone |
|---|---|---|---|---|
| 837 Roundtree Court | Boulder | CO | 80302 | 303-347-3728 |

**Player 1:**

| Last Name | First | Middle Initial | Age as of First Day of Tournament |
|---|---|---|---|
| Baxter | Barbara | A. | 14 |

| Street Address | City | State | ZIP | Phone |
|---|---|---|---|---|
| 830 Dennison Lane | Boulder | CO | 80303 | 303-368-2839 |

**Player 2:**

| Last Name | First | Middle Initial | Age as of First Day of Tournament |
|---|---|---|---|
| Washington | Natasha | K. | 13 |

| Street Address | City | State | ZIP | Phone |
|---|---|---|---|---|
| 892 Hazelwood Court | Boulder | CO | 80302 | 303-368-1427 |

**Player 3:**

| Last Name | First | Middle Initial | Age as of First Day of Tournament |
|---|---|---|---|
| Thurston | Jane | M. | 14 |

| Street Address | City | State | ZIP | Phone |
|---|---|---|---|---|
| 890 Driftwood Place | Boulder | CO | 80301 | 303-347-2225 |

**Player 4:**

| Last Name | First | Middle Initial | Age as of First Day of Tournament |
|---|---|---|---|
| Santiago | Maria | A. | 13 |

| Street Address | City | State | ZIP | Phone |
|---|---|---|---|---|
| 834 Dennison Lane | Boulder | CO | 80303 | 303-368-7877 |

**Player 5:**

| Last Name | First | Middle Initial | Age as of First Day of Tournament |
|---|---|---|---|
| Kelley | Rebecca | C. | 14 |

| Street Address | City | State | ZIP | Phone |
|---|---|---|---|---|
| 1711 Rockmont Circle | Boulder | CO | 80303 | 303-368-5678 |

**Verification by Coach:** To the best of my knowledge the information presented on this form is correct. Please sign below.

| Signature: | Brett P. Perkins | Date: | April 16, 20-- |
|---|---|---|---|

---

## Job 8

**Email**
**April 30**

**From the desk of:**
**Julia Kingsley**

Send the attached email message to Matthew Trussoni (Tournaments 1, 2, and 3) and Brett Perkins (Tournament 1) confirming that we have received their tournament applications. If the coach didn't list an email address, send a letter. Include Tournament Confirmation for the subject line.

JK

Your "Hoops" Tournament application for the June 15-16, June 22-23, and June 29-30 tournaments has been received. We are looking forward to having the Frontiersmen participate in these tournaments.

As soon as your bracket has been filled and the schedule completed, we will mail the schedule to you. If you have any questions before then, please email me or call the office. Our office hours are 10:30 a.m. to 3:30 p.m. Monday through Friday.

Note: Please adjust the message to fit the situation. If someone registers for only one tournament, you will have to modify the message slightly.

## Present Value (PV) Function

Formulas/Function
Library/Insert Function/PV

The **present value** function can be used to determine the amount you need to invest to accumulate a desired amount at a future date. For example, if you need to have $40,000 for college in five years, what single amount (present value) must you invest now if your investment is likely to earn 8 percent interest each year?

This function is abbreviated **PV** and its syntax is =**PV(Rate,Nper,Pmt,Fv,Type)**. The terms represent the same values used in calculating FV.

- **PV** is today's value (the present value) of the amount that is desired at a future date.
- Rate is the interest rate for each investment period.
- Nper is the total number of investment periods.
- Pmt is omitted in this example since additional are not made during the life of the investment.
- Fv is the future value—the amount that is desired in the future.
- Type is the value 0 or 1, depending on when investments are made. The default value of 0 is used when the investment is made at the end of the period. A Type value of 1 is used when the investment is made at the beginning of the period.

Figure 16-11 shows the Function Arguments dialog box for the PV function for the following scenario: What amount do I need to invest today to have $1,000 in two years if the investment is likely to earn 7 percent interest each year? Accept the default value of zero for Type.

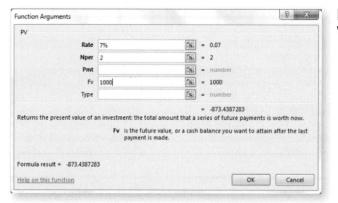

**Figure 16-11** Present Value

The Rate is keyed as 7%. Nper is 2 to indicate the length of the investment. Pmt is left blank since no additional investments are to be made. Fv is 1000 since that is the desired amount at the end of two years. Since the default value of zero is accepted, nothing is keyed for Type. The Pv displayed in the dialog box is shown as a negative number since it represents the amount of money that needs to be invested (spent).

1. Open a blank worksheet, key **Present Values** in cell A1, and adjust the column width to fit the contents.
2. Make cell A2 active. Use the PV function to calculate the amount of money to be invested today so $25,000 will be available in 10 years. The investment is likely to earn 10 percent interest annually. No additional investments will be made during the 10 years. Accept the default value for Type.
3. Make cell A3 active. Use the PV function to determine how much must be invested now to have $1 million at the end of 20 years if the investment is likely to earn 9 percent annually during the life of the investment. Accept the default value for Type.
4. Check your answers. Save the worksheet as *91cpv* and close it.

**Spreadsheet**
**May 1**

From the desk of:

**Julia Kingsley**

From the desk of:

**Julia Kingsley**

*I have roughed out what I would like the spreadsheet for the tournament registration revenues to look like. Several other tournament registrations have come in since I did the rough. Prepare a spreadsheet that contains the information shown at the right plus the information shown below.*

*JK*

| | A | B | C | D | E | F |
|---|---|---|---|---|---|---|
| 1 | | | | | | Registration Rev |
| 2 | | | Tournament 1 | Tournament 2 | Tournament 3 | Tourna |
| 3 | Team Name | Coach | June 15-16 | June 22-23 | June 29-30 | July |
| 4 | Frontiersmen | Trussoni M. | $100 | $100 | $100 | $ |
| 5 | Boulder "Dashers" | Perkins B. | 100 | | | |
| 6 | Rockies | De Los Santos L. | 100 | | 100 | |
| 7 | Jazzettes | Woodward D. | 100 | 100 | 100 | |
| 8 | Gold Nuggets | McKinney K. | 100 | | | |
| 9 | Cavaliers | Quaid M. | 100 | 100 | 100 | |
| 10 | Mustangs | Brady S. | 100 | | | |
| 11 | Huskers | Reed S. | 100 | | 100 | |
| 12 | | | | | | |
| 13 | | Totals | | | | |
| 14 | | | | | | |
| 15 | | | | | | |

*Team:* **Cowgirls**
*Amount Paid:* **$400**
*For Tournaments:* **1, 2, 3, 4**
*Coach:* **Steve Chi**

*Team:* **Aggies**
*Amount Paid:* **$300**
*For Tournaments:* **1, 3, 8**
*Coach:* **Tanya Hanrath**

*Team:* **3-Pointers**
*Amount Paid:* **$100**
*For Tournaments:* **1**
*Coach:* **Marge Jenkins**

**Email**
**May 1**

From the desk of:

**Julia Kingsley**

*Mr. McLemore is out of the office today. In order for him to stay apprised of the Fort Collins tournament revenues, he would like you to email him a copy of the registration revenues spreadsheets. Compose a message to accompany the spreadsheet. His email address is tmclemore@ hoops.cengage.com.*

*JK*

| | E | F | G | H | I | J | k |
|---|---|---|---|---|---|---|---|
| | ...istration Revenues | | | | | | |
| | ...ament 3 | Tournament 4 | Tournament 5 | Tournament 6 | Tournament 7 | Tournament 8 | |
| | ...e 29-30 | July 6-7 | July 13-14 | July 20-21 | July 27-28 | August 3-4 | |
| | $100 | $ | $ | $ | $ | $ | |
| | | | | | | | |
| | 100 | | 100 | | 100 | | |
| | 100 | 100 | 100 | 100 | 100 | 100 | |
| | | | | | | | |
| | 100 | | | | | | |
| | | 100 | | | 100 | | |
| | 100 | 100 | | | | | |
| | | | | | | | |
| | | | | | | | |

- **Pv** is the present value—the amount the investment is worth today. This argument can be omitted if there is not an amount invested before the constant, regular investments are made.
- Type is the value 0 or 1. It indicates when the investments are made. The default value of 0 means that the investment amounts are made at the end of an investment period(s). Key a 1 for Type if the investment amounts are made at the beginning of the investment period(s).

*Note:* Investment amounts such as *Pmt* and *Pv* are entered in the formula as negative numbers since they represent money paid. *FV* is represented by a positive number since it is money received.

Figure 16-10 shows the Function Arguments dialog box for the *FV* function for the following investments: $1,000 is invested initially and $50 will be added monthly for the next three years. The investments are projected to earn 6 percent interest. The *Type* default value of 0 is used since the money will be invested at the end of each month.

The *Rate* is keyed as 6%/12 to convert the annual interest rate to a monthly rate to agree with the monthly investment amounts that are planned. The *Nper* is 12*3 to indicate that 12 monthly payments will be made during each of the 3 years. The *Pmt* is −50 to indicate the constant, regular investment amount; the minus sign indicates that it is money paid. The *Pv* is −1000 since that is the beginning investment amount. It too represents money paid and is therefore entered as a negative number. Since the default value of 0 for *Type* is accepted, nothing is keyed. The formula result is given near the bottom of the Function Arguments dialog box.

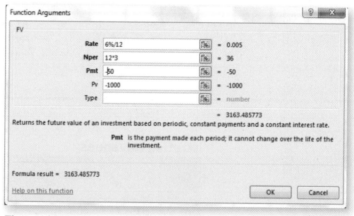

**Figure 16-10** Future Value

1. Open a blank worksheet and key **Future Value** in cell A1. Adjust the column width to fit the contents.
2. Make cell A2 active. Use the FV function to calculate the future value of the investment described in the section above; that is, an initial investment of $1,000 to which $50 monthly investments will be added during the next three years. It is projected that 6 percent interest will be earned. Accept the default value for Type.
3. Verify that your Formula result is the same as that shown in Figure 16-10.
4. Make cell 3A active. Use the FV function to calculate a future value for $30,000 that is invested today and expected to earn 8 percent interest each year for the next 10 years. No additional investments are planned. Accept the default value for type.
5. Check your answer. Save the worksheet as **91b fv** and close it.

## Job 11

**Contacts File**

**May 3**

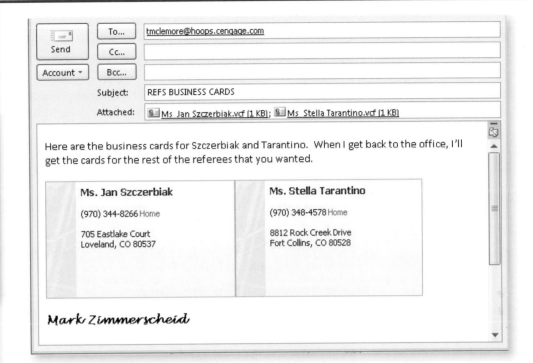

To... tmclemore@hoops.cengage.com

Cc...

Bcc...

Subject: REFS BUSINESS CARDS

Attached: Ms_Jan Szczerbiak.vcf (1 KB); Ms_Stella Tarantino.vcf (1 KB)

Here are the business cards for Szczerbiak and Tarantino. When I get back to the office, I'll get the cards for the rest of the referees that you wanted.

**Ms. Jan Szczerbiak**

(970) 344-8266 Home

705 Eastlake Court
Loveland, CO 80537

**Ms. Stella Tarantino**

(970) 348-4578 Home

8812 Rock Creek Drive
Fort Collins, CO 80528

*Mark Zimmerscheid*

## Job 12

**Letter**

**May 3**

1. Open **df 90f loan** and select cell B32.
2. Create a new *Word* document at this place. Notice that a small screen opens near that cell and *Word* ribbons and tabs replace the *Excel* ribbons and tabs. *Word* features can be used to format the text that is keyed within this *Word* screen.
3. Format and key the text below in the *Word* screen. When the text has been keyed, click outside the *Word* screen to return to the worksheet. The text will appear in the worksheet. The screen can be moved and sized as you have done with other objects like shapes, text boxes, etc.

Joshua, on behalf of the JHSAF Board of Directors, I want to thank you for paying off the $3,000 loan you received from JHSAF. We appreciate greatly that you were able to pay the entire principal in less than one year after your graduation. Your promptness will enable us to support another worthy graduate of JH who will begin college this fall.

Please retain this and the enclosed note marked paid as your evidence that your loan was paid in full on May 9, 20--.

Marian Thaxton, JHSAF Treasurer.

4. **Save as: 90f loan.**

# LESSON 91 — Future Value and Present Value Functions

**OUTCOMES**

- Use the future value function (FV) to calculate the future value of an investment.
- Use the present value function (PV) to calculate the present value of a desired future amount.

## Business Documents

**91B**

- Future Values of Money
- Present Values of Money

### Future Value (FV) Function

Formulas/Function Library/Insert Function/FV

The **future value function** is a financial function that is used to calculate the amount that an investment or a series of constant, regular investments will be worth at a future date.

The future value function is based on projecting that the investment(s) will grow at a constant interest rate. For example, the future value function will answer this question: What will the $5,000 I have invested be worth in 20 years if it earns 6 percent interest during the 20 years? Likewise, the future value function will answer the same question if $100 were added monthly to the $5,000 during the 20-year period.

This function is abbreviated **FV** and its syntax is =**FV(Rate,Nper,Pmt,Pv,Type)**.

- **FV** is the amount the investment will be worth at a future date.
- **Rate** is the interest rate for each investment period.
- **Nper** is the total number of investment periods.
- **Pmt** is the amount of the investment made in each period; the amount cannot change over the life of the investment, and the amounts must be invested at regular periods. Pmt can be omitted if investments are not added to the original investment. If Pmt is omitted, a Pv argument must be included.

**Update Database and Letter**
May 8

From the desk of:
**Julia Kingsley**

*Ms. De Los Santos registered the Rockies for the June 15–16, June 29–30, July 13–14, and July 27–28 tournaments. Please input the information in the database tables for coaches and players.*

*Check to see if I've already updated the spreadsheet with this information.*

*After you enter the information in the database, send a letter to Ms. De Los Santos confirming receipt of her registration fees and the tournaments that the Rockies are registered for. See Job 8.*

*JK*

# "Hoops" Tournament Application

| Division: | Tournament Date: | Age Level of Players: |
|---|---|---|
| ☐ Males  ■ Females | June 15–16 | ☐ 11–12 year age bracket  ☐ 13–14 year age bracket  ■ 15–16 year age bracket  ☐ 17–18 year age bracket |

**Name of Your Team:** Rockies

**Coach or Contact Person** (Must be 21 years of age or older):

| Last Name | First | Middle Initial | E-mail Address |
|---|---|---|---|
| De Los Santos | Loretta | L. | – – – – |

| Street Address | City | State | ZIP | Phone |
|---|---|---|---|---|
| 2115 Gaylord Drive | Loveland | CO | 80537 | 303-776-1375 |

**Player 1:**

| Last Name | First | Middle Initial | Age as of First Day of Tournament |
|---|---|---|---|
| De Los Santos | Maria | A. | 15 |

| Street Address | City | State | ZIP | Phone |
|---|---|---|---|---|
| 2115 Gaylord Drive | Loveland | CO | 80537 | 303-776-1375 |

**Player 2:**

| Last Name | First | Middle Initial | Age as of First Day of Tournament |
|---|---|---|---|
| Erstad | Janet | K. | 16 |

| Street Address | City | State | ZIP | Phone |
|---|---|---|---|---|
| 3157 Sierra Vista Drive | Loveland | CO | 80537 | 303-776-2909 |

**Player 3:**

| Last Name | First | Middle Initial | Age as of First Day of Tournament |
|---|---|---|---|
| Radke | Tabetha | J. | 16 |

| Street Address | City | State | ZIP | Phone |
|---|---|---|---|---|
| 80 Mulberry Drive | Loveland | CO | 80538 | 303-629-4439 |

**Player 4:**

| Last Name | First | Middle Initial | Age as of First Day of Tournament |
|---|---|---|---|
| Edmonds | Cynthia | S. | 16 |

| Street Address | City | State | ZIP | Phone |
|---|---|---|---|---|
| 8880 Snowberry Place | Loveland | CO | 80537 | 303-776-1529 |

**Player 5:**

| Last Name | First | Middle Initial | Age as of First Day of Tournament |
|---|---|---|---|
| Poquette | Paula | B. | 15 |

| Street Address | City | State | ZIP | Phone |
|---|---|---|---|---|
| 672 Mustang Drive | Loveland | CO | 80537 | 303-629-6110 |

Verification by Coach: To the best of my knowledge the information presented on this form is correct. Please sign below.

| Signature: | Loretta L. De Los Santos | Date: | May 5, 20-- |
|---|---|---|---|

6. Change the contents of cell B2 to **158**, C2 to **162**, B3 to **164**, and cell C3 to **166**.
7. Save as: *90d source*.
8. Open *90d destination* and update the data in the table.
9. Save as: *90d destination*.

QUICK ✔

The data in your chart should be the same as shown in the chart below.

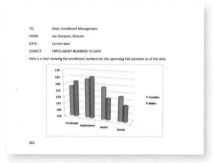

## 90E

### Application

1. Open *df 90e source* and save it as *90e source*.
2. Open *df 90e destination* and save it as *90e destination*.
3. Copy and paste the chart in *90e source* into *90e destination* as a *Microsoft Office Excel* Chart Object with a link.
4. Save and close *90e destination*.
5. If needed, open *90e source*.
6. Change the contents of cell B2 to **1450**, C2 to **360**, B3 to **1600**, cell C3 to **425**, B4 to **1250**, and C4 to **275**.
7. Save as: *90e source*.
8. Open *90e destination* and update the data in the table.
9. Save as: *90e source*.

## 90F

### Embed a New Word Document in an Excel Worksheet

Insert/Text/Object/Create New tab/Microsoft Word Document

You can embed a new or existing *Word* document (as well as documents in other file formats) into an *Excel* worksheet. See Figure 16-9. You have embedded *Excel* worksheets into *Word* documents.

In this activity, you will embed a new *Word* document in an *Excel* file. Once inserted, the embedded file can be edited with the commands and toolbar buttons used to create the source file.

Any changes you make in the embedded file appear only in the destination file and not the source file since they are not linked. Figure 16-9 shows the Create New tab with *Word* selected as the type of object to be created in the worksheet.

**Figure 16-9** Embed a *Word* document in an *Excel* worksheet

# UNIT 8

## Creating Effective Reports

Lesson 44    Report with Textual Citations
Lesson 45–46   Report with Footnotes
Lesson 47–48   Collaborative Report with Footnotes

Lesson 49 Two-Column Reports with Pictures
Lesson 50 Report Applications

---

### Reference Guide

**Bound Report**

Reports are written to provide the reader with information. Reports may be formatted as unbound reports or as bound reports. Unbound reports are formatted with a 1" left margin for all pages, while bound reports are formatted with a 1.5" left margin on all pages to accommodate the binding. The other margins are the same for bound and unbound reports.

---

**Standard Margins— Bound Report**

|  | First Page | Second page and subsequent pages |
|---|---|---|
| **Left Margin (LM)** | 1.5" | 1.5" |
| **Right Margin (RM)** | 1" | 1" |
| **Top Margin (TM)** | 2" | 1" |
| **Bottom Margin (BM)** | Approximately 1" | Approximately 1" |
| **Page number** | Optional, bottom at center if used | Top; right-aligned |

---

**Internal Spacing**

All parts of the report are SS using the 1.08 default line spacing.

**Long quotes.** Quoted material of four or more lines should be indented 0.5" from the left margin.

**Enumerated items.** To format numbers and bullets, the default 0.25" indentation should be used.

---

**Titles and Headings**

**Title.** The title of the report is formatted using the Title style, 28-point Calibri Light font (Headings). Add a hard return after the title.

© Pressmaster/Shutterstock.com

**Side headings.** Side headings are keyed at the left margin and formatted using Heading 1 style, 16-point Calibri font (Calibri Light Headings, Blue, Accent 1, Darker 25%). Capitalize the first letters of all words except prepositions in titles and side headings.

**Paragraph headings.** Paragraph headings are keyed at the left margin using Heading 3 style (12-point Calibri Light Headings, Blue, Accent 1, Darker 50% font). Capitalize only the first letter of the first word and any proper nouns. Place a period after the heading.

1. Open a new *Word* document and key the table below.
2. **Save as:** *90c source* but do not close it.
3. Open a new worksheet and copy the table into the worksheet. Close *90c source*.

| APRIL PAY SCHEDULE | | | |
|---|---|---|---|
| **Salesperson** | **Sales** | **Commission** | **Salary** |
| Frederick Adams | $1,856 | $464 | $600 |
| Janice Brown | $2,235 | $558 | $625 |
| Carlos Cruz | $1,975 | $493 | $600 |
| Enrico Duarte | $1,857 | $464 | $575 |
| Lisa Ford | $1,785 | $446 | $600 |
| Marian Mosley | $2,145 | $536 | $650 |
| Jerry Roberts | $2,098 | $524 | $600 |
| Leona Williams | $1,674 | $418 | $575 |

4. Add **Bonus** and **Total** columns at the right of the worksheet.
5. Calculate bonuses: Bonuses are 25 percent of the salary if the sales are more than $1,900. If not, no bonus is earned.
6. Total each salesperson's pay for April.
7. Add an indented **Totals** row at the bottom, and calculate a total for each column.
8. Format the worksheet to make it attractive.
9. **Save as:** *90c destination*.

Like worksheets, worksheet charts can be copied into a word processing document by using Copy and Paste (or Paste Special) commands to avoid recreating the chart. See Figure 16-8.

The chart can be pasted in a variety of ways: with or without a link to the source document, with source file or destination file formatting, or as a chart that can be edited in *Word* or *Excel*, etc.

In this activity, paste the chart so it is linked to the worksheet, can be edited as an *Excel* document, and retains the formatting of the source document.

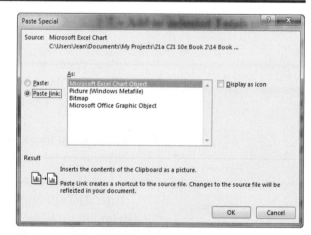

**Figure 16-8** Link worksheet chart to word processing document

1. Open **df 90d source** (an *Excel* file) and save it as **90d source**.
2. Open **df 90d destination** (a *Word* file) and save it as **90d destination**. Close **df 90d destination**.
3. Copy and paste the chart in **90d source** into **90d destination** as a *Microsoft Office Excel* Chart Object with a link.
4. Save and close **90d destination**.
5. If needed, open **90d source**.

## Page Numbering

Insert/Header & Footer/ Page Number

The first page of a report is usually not numbered. However, if a page number is used on the first page, center it at the bottom of the page. On the second and subsequent pages, position the page number at the top of the page using right alignment.

## Documentation

Documentation is used to give credit for published material (electronic as well as printed) that is quoted or provides information or an idea that is not common knowledge. Two types of documentation will be used in this unit: textual citation and footnotes.

**Textual citation.** The textual citation method of documentation includes the name(s) of the author(s), the date of the referenced publication, and the page numbers(s) of the material cited. For example, **(McWilliams, 2009, 138)** would be inserted in the text following the citation, as shown in Figure 8-1.

When a textual citation appears at the end of a sentence, the end-of-sentence punctuation follows the textual citation. However, if a textual citation follows a long quote that is indented from the margin, the end-of-sentence punctuation precedes the textual citation.

When the author's name is used in the text introducing the quotation, only the year of publication and the page number(s) appear in parentheses. For example, *McWilliams (2009, 138) said that . . .* would be keyed for the citation. For electronic references, include the author's name and the year. When there are two articles by the same author, the title of the article will also be included.

**Footnotes.** The footnotes method of documentation identifies the reference cited by a superscript number . . . .[1] The complete documentation for the reference is placed at the bottom of the same page and is identified with the same superscript number, as shown in Figure 8-2. Footnotes should be numbered consecutively throughout the report. Each footnote is indented 0.5" and SS, with a DS between footnotes. Following is an example of a footnote for a journal article.

[1]**Richard G. Harris, "Globalization, Trade, and Income,"** *Canadian Journal of Economics,* **November 1993, p. 755.**

**★TIP** If software is used to create the footnotes, minor reformatting may need to be done in order to have the footnote indented 0.5" and SS with a DS between footnotes.

**Figure 8-1** Bound report with textual citations

**Figure 8-2** Bound report with footnotes

1. Open word processing file *df 89e destination* and save it as *89e destination*. Do not close it.
2. Open a new worksheet and create a worksheet from the data given below; save it as *89e source* but do not close it.

| Business | Address | Points | Amount |
|---|---|---|---|
| Avenue Deli | 309 Franklin Avenue | 92 | $15,000 |
| Ford's Newsstand | 302 Franklin Avenue | 88 | $15,000 |
| Hannon Shoes | 415 Shefield Avenue | 86 | $10,000 |
| Unger Appliances | 525 Station Street | 83 | $10,000 |
| Best Food Market | 311 Franklin Avenue | 76 | $ 5,000 |
| Avenue Restaurant | 376 Franklin Avenue | 76 | $ 5,000 |

3. Paste *89e source* into *89e destination* as a *Word* table (without a link) between the ¶s.
4. Format the destination file as needed, save it as *89e destination*, and close both files.

In this activity you will revise a worksheet that has been linked to a *Word* file and then open the *Word* file, update it, and save it.

1. Open the worksheet *df 89f source* and save it as *89f source*.
2. Delete values in the worksheet file *89f source* for Last Year; move the values for This Year to Last Year; and move the values for Next Year to This Year.
3. Key these new numbers for Next Year from left to right, formatting as necessary:

   6     $68,217     104     $47,24815     $49,017

4. Save changes to *89f source* and close it.
5. Open *df 89f destination*, update it, and save it as *89f destination*.

# LESSON 90 — Integrating Worksheet and Word Processing Documents

**OUTCOME**

- Convert a word processing table to a worksheet, copy a worksheet chart to a word processing document, and embed a *Word* file in an *Excel* file

## Business Documents

- Hitter Statistics
- Monthly Pay Schedule
- Enrollment Reports
- Sales Report
- Payment Record

**Convert a Word Processing Table to a Worksheet**

Home/Clipboard/Copy/
Paste

Data from a word processing table can be converted (copied) to a worksheet, and then calculations can be performed on the data. If the word processing document is a table or data separated by tabs, it will be copied to separate cells in the worksheet; otherwise, the information will be copied into the highlighted cell of the worksheet.

1. Open the *Word* document *df 90b source* and copy it into a blank worksheet. Close *df 90b source*.
2. Add a column at the right of the worksheet with **TotalHits** as the heading; add a row at the bottom with *Totals* as a row heading.
3. Perform the calculations in the added column and row.
4. Adjust font size, row height, and column width as needed to improve the appearance.
5. **Save as:** *90b destination*.

An ellipsis (. . .) is used to indicate material omitted from a quotation. An ellipsis is three periods, each preceded and followed by a space. If the omitted material occurs at the end of a sentence, include the period or other punctuation before the ellipsis, as shown in the following example.

> In ancient Greece, plays were performed only a few times a year. . . . The festivals were held to honor Dionysius in the hope that he would bless the Greeks. . . . (Prince and Jackson, 1997, 35)

## References, Bibliography, or Works Cited Page

Home/Paragraph/Line and Paragraph Spacing

**TIP** Move the hanging indent to 0.5", and verify that the Line and Paragraph Spacing defaults are set correctly before keying the references page.

Long reports generally include a references page, which is a listing of all the works cited in the report. The references page may also be called a bibliography or works cited page.

All references used in a report are listed alphabetically by author's last name at the end of the report on a separate page using the title *References* (or *Bibliography* or *Works Cited*). Use the same margins as for the first page of the report and include a page number. SS each reference. Use the default line (1.08) and paragraph spacing settings, as shown in Figure 8-3. Begin the first line of each reference at the left margin; use the Hanging Indent feature to indent other lines 0.5", as shown in Figure 8-4.

The title of the page (*References, Bibliography,* or *Works Cited*) is formatted with the same style that was used for the report title.

**Figure 8-3** Line and Paragraph Spacing settings for the references page

**Figure 8-4** Hanging indent

## Table of Contents

A table of contents lists the headings of a report and the page numbers where those headings can be found in the report. A table of contents makes it easy for a reader to see what is included in the report and to locate a specific section of the report. The table of contents, as shown in Figure 8-5, can be created manually or electronically using the Table of Contents feature of the software.

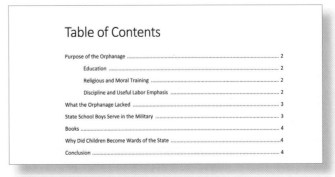

**Figure 8-5** Sample table of contents

In this activity, you will use Copy/Paste Special to paste a worksheet (source file) into a Word document (destination file) and establish a link between them. In the next activity, you will update the source file and then the destination file.

1. Open the word processing document *df 89c destination* and save it as *89c destination* but do not close it.
2. Open the worksheet *df 89c source* and save it as *89c source* but do not close it.
3. Use Paste Special to paste the worksheet into the document as an *Excel* Worksheet Object, and choose Paste Link to establish a link between the *Word* and *Excel* documents.
4. Place the worksheet below the last line of the memo body. Leave about one blank line before and after the worksheet and then key your initials.
5. Center the worksheet between the left and right margins with gridlines. You decide other formatting features.
6. **Save as:** *89c destination* and *89c source*.

## 89D

**Update a Worksheet and Linked Word Processing Document**

After you change a source file (*89c source*), the destination file (*89c destination*) can be updated when you open it by clicking Yes in the dialog box that will appear when the destination file is opened (see Figure 16-7).

**Figure 16-7** Updating *Word* file linked to *Excel* file

1. Open **89c source** and change the numbers to those given below:

| Increase in net assets | |
|---|---|
| Operations | |
| Net investment income | $ 415,676 |
| Net realized gain | $ 3,297,811 |
| Change in net unrealized appreciation (depreciation) | $ 2,877,590 |
| Net increase in net assets resulting from operations | $ 6,591,077 |
| Distributions to shareholders | |
| From net investment income | $ (399,456) |
| From net realized gain | $ (2,195,315) |
| Total distributions | $ (2,594,771) |
| Share transactions | |
| Net proceeds from sales of shares | $ 897,120 |
| Reinvestment of distributions | $ 2,987,407 |
| Cost of shares redeemed | $ 10,976,866 |
| Net increase in net assets resulting from share transactions | $ 897,120 |
| Total increase in net assets | $ 10,082,968 |
| Net assets | |
| Beginning of period | $ 48,595,195 |
| End of period | $ 58,678,163 |

2. Save the changes to **89c source** and close the file.
3. Open **89c destination**, click Yes in the *Word* dialog box, and note that the numbers in the financial report have been updated automatically when the destination file opens.
4. **Save as:** *89d destination* and close the file.

### Manual Table of Contents

The side and top margins for the table of contents are the same as those used for the first page of the report. Key *Table of Contents* (using the Title style, 2" from top). Then list side and paragraph headings (if included). Side headings are started at left margin; paragraph headings are indented 0.5". Page numbers for each entry are keyed at the right margin; use a right dot leader tab to insert page numbers. Space once before and once after inserting the dot leader to leave a space after the heading and before the page number.

References/Table of Contents/Table of Contents/Automatic Table 2

Page Layout/Page Setup/Breaks/Section Breaks

### Electronic Table of Contents

After keying and formatting a report, creating a table of contents is a relatively easy task when using the software features. Place the cursor where you want the table of contents to appear. Next, click the *Table of Contents* button, located in the Table of Contents group on the References tab. Then select the table of contents style you would like to use. Insert a **section break** to place the table of contents on a separate page and to allow you to use the Roman numeral format (i, ii, iii, and iv) on the table of contents page and then change to Arabic numbers (1, 2, 3, and 4) on the report pages.

### Cover Page

Insert/Pages/Cover Page

A cover or title page is prepared for most bound reports (see Figure 8-6). To format a cover page, center the title (Title, Calibri Light Heading, 28 point) in ALL CAPS approximately 2" from the top. Center the writer's name in capital and lowercase letters (Heading 1, Calibri Light Heading, 16 point) approximately 5" from the top. The date (Heading 2, Calibri Light Heading, 13 point) should be centered approximately 9" from the top. The font color should be the same for all text, normally black or blue. To further emphasize the title page, the text on the page may be bolded. Margin settings are the same as the report body.

The Cover Page feature of the software can also be used (see Figure 8-7) to format professional-looking cover pages. Fonts, font sizes, and colors are preset.

**TIP** The title on the cover page in Figure 8-7 was not keyed in all caps because the preset font size was 48 point. Keying the title in ALL CAPS would have overwhelmed the rest of the text on the page.

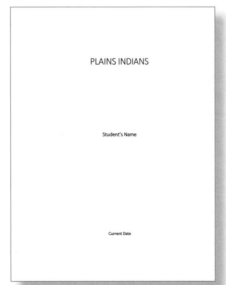

**Figure 8-6** Manually formatted cover page

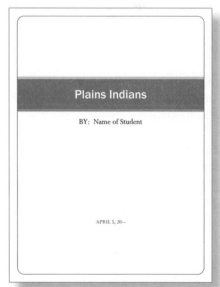

**Figure 8-7** Software-formatted cover page

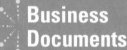

OUTCOME
- Copy and link a worksheet to a word processing document.

**Business Documents**

- Golf Match Scores
- Change in Assets Report
- Incentive Program Recipients
- Average Salary Report

## 89B

### Copy a Worksheet into a Word Processing Document

Home/Clipboard/Copy/ Paste

*Note:* The *Excel* file that is to become a source copy for an activity will be saved with a filename that ends in "source." For example, the source file for this activity is named ***89b source.*** The *Word* file into which the worksheet will be pasted ends in "destination."

Frequently, worksheets are copied into a word processing document by using Copy and Paste (or Paste Special) commands to avoid rekeying the information. The worksheet can be pasted in a variety of ways: with or without a link to the source document; with source file or destination file formatting; as a *Word* table, *Excel* worksheet, text, hyperlink, etc.

In this activity, the worksheet will be pasted as a *Word* table by using Copy/Paste. It can be formatted using *Word* table formatting features but is not linked to the source file.

1. Open the word processing document ***df 89b destination.***
2. Open the worksheet ***df 89b source*** and save it as ***89b source.***
3. Copy the worksheet into the word processing document (use Copy/Paste), placing it about a DS below the last line of the memo body. Leave about one blank line after the table, and then key your initials.
4. Center the table between the left and right margins with gridlines. Format the table in Calibri 10 point to keep the memo to one page. You decide other formatting features.
5. **Save as:** ***89b destination.***

## 89C

### Link a Worksheet to a Word Processing Document

Home/Clipboard/Copy/ Paste Special/Microsoft Excel Worksheet Object/ Paste or Paste Link

Worksheets can be copied and pasted (using Copy/Paste Special) into a *Word* document as an Excel Worksheet Object with or without a link between the two files (see Figure 16-6).

If the data in the worksheet is likely to change, establishing a link between the *Word* document and the *Excel* worksheet will eliminate the need to rekey the changes in the *Word* document each time the worksheet data changes.

If the worksheet data is not likely to change, the worksheet can be pasted without a link.

**Figure 16-6** Paste Special dialog box

Worksheets that are pasted into a *Word* document as *Excel* worksheets can be formatted within the *Word* document by using *Excel* commands and features.

# Report with Textual Citations

**OUTCOMES**
- Format a bound report.
- Insert text files into a report.

## Business Documents
### 44A–50A

**Warmup**

- Bound Report with Textual Citation
- Reference Page

Key each line twice daily.

alphabet 1 Zach and our equipment manager will exchange jobs for seven days.

fig/sym 2 If you call after 12:30 on Friday, you can reach him at 297-6854.

speed 3 The eight men in the shanty paid for a big bus to go to the city.

**gwam** 1' | 1 | 2 | 3 | 4 | 5 | 6 | 7 | 8 | 9 | 10 | 11 | 12 | 13 |

### 44B

**Learn: Bound Report**

1. Review the reference guide on pp. 218–221 for bound reports.
2. Format the following text as a bound report with textual citations.

### PLAINS INDIANS

The *American* Plains Indians are among the *best* ~~most~~ known of all Native Americans. *These* Indians played a *significant* role in shaping the history of the West. Some of the more noteworthy Plains Indians were big Foot, *Black Kettle,* Crazy Horse, Red Cloud Sitting Bull, and Spotted Tail.

### Big Foot

Big Foot (?1825-1890) was also known as Spotted Elk. Born in the northern Great Plains, he eventually became a Minneconjou Teton Sioux chief. He was part of a *tribal* delegation that traveled to Wash ington, D.C., and worke*d* to establish schools throughout the Sioux territory. He was one of those massacred at Wounded Knee in December 1890 (Bowman, 1995, 63).

### Black Kettle

Black Kettle (?1803-1868) was born near the Black Hills in present-day South Dakota. He was recognized as a *Southern* Cheyenne peace chief for his efforts to bring peace to the region. However, his attempts at accommodation ~~failed~~ *were not successful* and his band was massacred at sand creek in 1864. Even though he continued to seek peace, he was killed with the remainder of his tribe in *the Washita Valley of* Oklahoma in 1868 (Bowman, 1995, 67).

The settings for each of these specialized conditional formats can be changed by selecting the More Rules options in each list.

1. Open **df 88h formatting**.
2. Apply a Data Bar conditional format to values in column B.
3. Apply a Color Scale conditional format to values in column C.
4. Apply an Icon Set conditional format to values in column D.
5. Save as: **88h formatting**.

Your formatted worksheet should look similar to this:

| | A | B | C | D |
|---|---|---|---|---|
| 1 | CANDY BAR SALES | | | |
| 2 | ROOM | MON | TUE | WED |
| 3 | 101 | 23 | 45 | 32 |
| 4 | 103 | 45 | 65 | 82 |
| 5 | 105 | 45 | 23 | 10 |
| 6 | 107 | 34 | 23 | 15 |
| 7 | 109 | 23 | 35 | 46 |
| 8 | 111 | 22 | 33 | 55 |
| 9 | 113 | 24 | 57 | 80 |
| 10 | 115 | 23 | 56 | 80 |
| 11 | 117 | 78 | 67 | 56 |
| 12 | 119 | 35 | 65 | 73 |
| 13 | 121 | 44 | 56 | 71 |
| 14 | 123 | 35 | 58 | 56 |
| 15 | | | | |

## 21st Century Skills: Financial Literacy

Managing your money and making smart economic choices are critical to your financial success. Credit cards are a tool you can use to help manage your finances.

A credit card is like a loan—you make a purchase using the card and agree to pay for it at a later date. By law, you must be 18 years of age to apply for a credit card and you must have a steady source of income in order to qualify. Credit cards are convenient in that you do not need to have enough money to pay at the time of the purchase.

But if you do not have the funds to pay in full when your credit card bill is due, you will have to repay the full amount plus interest, which is a percentage of the amount you owe. Interest can accrue quickly and significantly increase the balance due on your credit card. It is best to pay off your bill completely every month.

### Think Critically

Cameron is a full-time college student and also works part-time at a local restaurant. He makes about $350 a week. He was recently approved for a credit card and just activated it for use. In the first few weeks, Cameron uses the card to buy some new clothes, a flat-screen TV, and gas for his car. He also charges several meals at restaurants to the card. When the first bill arrives, Cameron owes more than $1,500! What should he do? In a *Word* document, write an ending to the story in which you advise Cameron on how he should handle the first bill and how to be a more responsible user of his credit card.

**Crazy Horse**

Crazy Horse *(?1842–1877)* was also born near the Black Hills.  His father was a medicine man; his mother was the sister of Spotted Tail.  He was recognized as a skilled hunter and fighter.  Crazy Horse believed he was immune from battle injury and took part in all the major Sioux battles to protect the Black Hills.  He was named supreme war chief *against white intrusion* and peace chief of the Oglalas in 1876 and led the Sioux and Cheyenne to victory at the battle of Rosebud in January that year.  Perhaps he is remembered most for leading the Sioux and Cheyenne in the battle of the Little Bighorn where his warriors defeated Custer's forces.  Crazy Horse is regarded as the greatest leader of the Sioux and a symbol of their heroic resistance *(Bowman, 1995, 160–161)*.

3.  Insert the **df 44b red cloud** text file.  Make the corrections shown.

**Red Cloud**

Red Cloud (1822-1909) was born near the Platte River in present-day Nebraska.  Because of his intelligence, strength, and bravery, he became the chief of the Oglala Sioux.  "Red Cloud's War" took place between 1865 and 1868.  These battles forced the closing of the Bozeman trail and the signing of the Fort Laramie Treaty in 1868.  In exchange for peace, the U.S. government accepted the territorial claims of the Sioux (Bowman, 1995, 601).

*Sitting Bull*

Sitting Bull (?1831-1890), a leader of the Sioux, was born in the region of the Grand River in South Dakota (Encarta, 2004).  He was known among the Sioux as a warrior even during his youth.  He was bitterly opposed to white encroachment, but made peace in 1868 when the U.S. government guaranteed him a large reservation free of white settlers.  When gold was discovered *in the Black Hills*, he joined the Arapaho *and Cheyenne* to fight the invaders (Bowman, 1995, 673).  According to fellow tribesmen, the name Sitting Bull suggested an animal possessed of great endurance that planted immovably on its haunches to fight on to the death (Utley, 1993, 15).

Insert/Text/Object/Text from file/filename

In this activity, you will use conditional formatting within the **Highlight Cells Rules** options (see Figure 16-3) and the **Top/Bottom Rules** (see Figure 16-4).

1. Open **df 88f test scores**.
2. Apply conditional formatting so that all test scores above 93 are highlighted with green fill and dark green text.
3. Save as: **88f test scores 1**.
4. Clear the rules. Apply conditional formatting to display the Top 10 percent of the scores in column G with dark red outline.
5. Save as: **88f test scores 2**.
6. Clear the rules. Apply conditional formatting to display scores in column G that are below the average score with formatting you choose.
7. Save as: **88f test scores 3**.
8. Clear the rules. Apply conditional formatting to highlight all scores of 100 with formatting you choose.
9. Save as: **88f test scores 4**.
10. Clear the rules. Apply conditional formatting to highlight all duplicate test scores in column D with formatting you choose.
11. Save as: **88f test scores 5**.

## 88G

### Application

1. Open **df 88g swim**. Apply conditional formatting using the following criteria. You choose the format to apply and clear the rules as needed.
   a. Highlight all boys and girls whose club is Seneca.
   b. Save as: **88g swim 1**.
   c. Highlight the scores of all boys who earned between 350 and 400 points.
   d. Save as: **88g swim 2**.
   e. Highlight the times of the girls whose time was below 101.
   f. Save as: **88g swim 3**.
   g. Format the points of the boys who earned more than the average points.
   h. Save as: **88g swim 4**.

## 88H

### Apply Specialized Conditional Formatting

Home/Styles/Conditional Formatting

You can use data bars, color scales, and icon sets as specialized conditional formats as shown in Figure 16-5. A **data bar** shows the value of a cell relative to other cells—larger values have a longer data bar.

A **color scale** uses a two- or three-color gradient to show how values vary—the shade of the color represents the value in the cell.

An **icon set** can classify data into three to five categories—each icon represents a value in the cell.

| | A | B | C | D | E |
|---|---|---|---|---|---|
| 1 | SPECIALIZED CONDITIONAL FORMATTING | | | | |
| 2 | Data Bar | | Color Scale | | Icon Set |
| 3 | 10 | | 10 | | 10 |
| 4 | 20 | | 20 | | 20 |
| 5 | 30 | | 30 | | 30 |
| 6 | 40 | | 40 | | 40 |
| 7 | 50 | | 50 | | 50 |
| 8 | 60 | | 60 | | 60 |
| 9 | 70 | | 70 | | 70 |
| 10 | 80 | | 80 | | 80 |
| 11 | 90 | | 90 | | 90 |
| 12 | | | | | |

**Figure 16-5** Specialized conditional formatting examples

4. Insert *df 44b spotted tail* text file. Make the corrections shown.

**Spotted Tail**

Spotted Tail (?1833-1881) was born along the White River *either* in present-day South Dakota or near present-day Laramie, Wyoming. He be came the leader of the Brulé Sioux and was one of the signers of the Fort Laramie Treaty of 1868. Eventually, he became the government appointed chief of the agency Sioux and made frequent trips to Washington, D.C. in that capacity (Bowman, 1995, 688). Starting in 1870 spotted Tail became the statesman that made him the greatest chief the Brulés ever new (Fielder, 1975, p. 29).

5. Proofread your copy and correct any errors.
6. **Save as:** *44b report*.

**Learn: Reference Page**

1. Review the *Reference Guide*, p. 219, for preparing a references page.

2. Use the following information to prepare a reference for the report.

3. Proofread; correct errors.

4. **Save as:** *44c reference page*.

★TIP  Move the hanging indent to 0.5".

Bowman, John S. (ed). *The Cambridge Dictionary of American Biography*. Cambridge: Cambridge University Press, 1995.

Encarta, http://encarta.msn.com/encyclopedia_761578750/sittingbull.html (5 February 2004).

Fielder, Mildred. *Sioux Indian Leaders*. Seattle: Superior Publishing Company, 1975.

Utley, Robert M. *The Lance and the Shield: The Life and Times of Sitting Bull*. New York: Henry Holt and Company, 1993.

**QUICK ✔**

Your completed references page should look like this:

## Application

1. Key the worksheet below.
2. In column F, calculate the average score to the nearest whole number.
3. In column G, key an IF function that compares the scores in column F to a score of 75. If the score is less than 75, print **TUTORING** in column G. If the column F score is 75 or more, print nothing.
4. You decide all formatting features.
5. **Save as:** *88e grade book*.

|   | A | B | C | D | E | F | G |
|---|---|---|---|---|---|---|---|
| 1 | GRADE BOOK | | | | | | |
| 2 | NAME | TEST 1 | TEST 2 | TEST 3 | TEST 4 | AVG | NEEDS TUTORING |
| 3 | ABEL | 78 | 85 | 72 | 78 | | |
| 4 | BOGGS | 64 | 66 | 71 | 73 | | |
| 5 | CARR | 78 | 82 | 86 | 75 | | |
| 6 | FRYZ | 90 | 93 | 88 | 86 | | |
| 7 | GOOD | 95 | 82 | 86 | 92 | | |
| 8 | MILLS | 71 | 75 | 73 | 76 | | |
| 9 | POPE | 62 | 71 | 73 | 66 | | |
| 10 | SIA | 75 | 76 | 81 | 71 | | |
| 11 | TODD | 66 | 65 | 50 | 61 | | |
| 12 | WILLS | 75 | 64 | 75 | 70 | | |
| 13 | ZEON | 81 | 74 | 65 | 60 | | |

## 88F

### Apply Conditional Formatting

Home/Styles/Conditional Formatting

Conditional formatting enables you to quickly apply formatting features in a cell when the data in the cell meet specified conditions. For example, your teacher can apply conditional formatting to change the font color and cell fill color to quickly identify students who have (1) scores above, below, or equal to a specific value; (2) the top and bottom score(s); and (3) scores above or below the average score on a test.

Conditional formats remain until they are cleared. Also, revisions that cause cell data to meet the specified condition will display the conditional formats, and revisions that cause cell data to not meet the specified condition will not display the conditional formats.

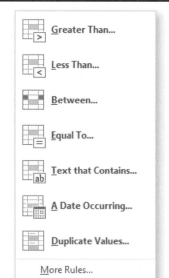

Greater Than...

Less Than...

Between...

Equal To...

Text that Contains...

A Date Occurring...

Duplicate Values...

More Rules...

**Figure 16-3** Highlight Cells Rules options

Top 10 Items...

Top 10 %...

Bottom 10 Items...

Bottom 10 %...

Above Average...

Below Average...

More Rules...

**Figure 16-4** Top/Bottom Rules

**OUTCOME**
- Format a bound report with footnotes.

### Business Documents

- Bound Report with Footnotes
- Reference Page
- Cover Page
- Table of Contents

**45–46B**

**Learn: Bound Report with Footnotes**

1. Review the report reference guide on pp. 218–221 for bound reports; study the model report on p. 226. Note the format of the footnotes.
2. Key the first page of *The Faces of Mt. Rushmore* report from the model on p. 226; continue keying the report from the rough-draft copy that follows the model.
3. The information for footnotes 2–5 is provided in the left column of the rough-draft copy.
4. Proofread your copy and correct errors.
5. **Save as: *45-46b report*.**

---

@ iStockphoto.com/Sean Locke

**Digital Citizenship and Ethics** The rules governing appropriate and courteous behavior while you are online are called **netiquette**. Think of netiquette as online manners—the way you should behave as you surf the Web or correspond via email, text messaging, and chats.

You might already know some netiquette rules. For example, you should not send emails or text messages in all caps because it implies shouting. Long and wordy postings on discussion groups and forums are another no-no. Sarcasm should be avoided because readers may not pick up on it without the benefit of hearing the tone of your voice or seeing your facial expressions. Don't flood your friends' mailboxes with "funny" messages or cute pictures you've found online. And don't start **flame wars**—hostile, insulting arguments meant to cause trouble rather than discuss issues.

You can find out more about netiquette rules online. Go to your favorite search engine and key *netiquette*.

As a class, discuss the following.

1. People commonly use online slang as well as emoticons in personal messages they exchange with friends. Do you think it is appropriate to use slang and emoticons in professional correspondence? Why or why not?
2. Why is it important to avoid using sarcasm, cynicism, or a joking, flippant tone in electronic messages?

## Answer "What If" Questions

An advantage of spreadsheet software is its ability to show the effects on all cells of a change in one cell. For example, in the worksheet you created in the above activity, you determined next year's quota for each salesperson if the company were to make next year's quota 1.05 (105 percent) of this year's quota. By changing the 1.05 in cell A2 to other numbers representing other possible changes, the effect of the change on the quotas for all salespersons can be computed at the same time.

1. Using the **88b quotas** worksheet, answer the following three "what if" questions. Unless directed otherwise, print the worksheet after each question is answered.
   a. What is each salesperson's quota if the goal is decreased to 95 percent of this year's quota?
   b. What is each salesperson's quota if the goal is increased to 105.5 percent of this year's quota?
   c. What is each salesperson's quota if the goal is decreased to 110 percent of this year's quota?
2. **Save as:** **88c what if.**

## Use the IF Function

Formulas/Function
Library/Logical

The **IF function** compares the contents of two cells. Conditions that contain logical operators (listed below at the left) provide the basis for the comparison. For example, an instructor could use an IF function (see formula in Figure 16-2) to determine whether a student passed or failed a course.

The IF function involves three arguments. The first is the comparison of the scores in column B to the criteria (a score that is greater [>] than 60 in the formula entered in cell E2 in the example). The second argument is the text or value ("Pass" in the formula entered in cell E2) that is to be displayed in cell E2 if the comparison is true. The third argument is the text of value ("Fail") that is to be displayed in cell E2 if the comparison is false.

**Figure 16-2** IF function

As shown in the formula for cell E2, the arguments of the IF function are keyed inside parentheses and are separated from each other with commas. If text is to be displayed for argument 2 or 3, the text should be keyed inside quotation marks. Quotes are not keyed if values are to be displayed.

The text box at the left shows the logical operators that are used in IF functions.

### Logical Operators
= (value of two cells are *equal*)
< (value of one cell is *less than* the other)
> (value of one cell is *greater than* the other)
<= (value of one cell is *less than* or *equal* to the other)
>= (value of one cell is *greater than* or *equal* to the other)
<> (values are *unequal*)

1. Open a new worksheet.
2. Key **25** in cell A1 and **35** in cell B1. In cell C1, key an IF function that prints **EQUAL** if cell A1= cell B1 or **UNEQUAL** if cell A1 and cell B1 are unequal.
3. In cell D1, key an IF function that prints **HELP** if the sum of cell A1+B1 is less than 75 and **NOHELP** if the sum is 75 or greater.
4. In cell A5, key **11; 22** in cell B5; **33** in cell C5; **44** in cell D5. In cell E5, key an IF function that prints **1-149** if the sum of cells A5:D5 is less than 150 and **150+** if the sum of cells A5:D5 is greater than 150.
5. **Save as:** **88d if function.**

Title

# The Faces of Mt. Rushmore

1.5" LM

The Black Hills of South Dakota and Wyoming is the home to two national forests (Black Hills National Forest and Custer National Forest), three national grasslands (Buffalo Gap National Grassland, Grand River National Grassland, and Fort Pierre National Grassland), and several national treasures (Badlands, Devils Tower, Jewel Cave, Minuteman Missile National Historic Site, and Wind Cave National Park). This area of the United States was also home to many historical legendary figures. Among the more famous legends of the Black Hills were Native Americans Crazy Horse, Sitting Bull, and Red Cloud. General Custer, Wild Bill Hickok, Calamity Jane, and Jim Bridger are other legendary figures that are part of the colorful history of this region. The main attraction in the Black Hills, however, is Mt. Rushmore. Mt. Rushmore draws close to three million visitors to this part of the country each year.

1.0" RM

Side Heading

## Mt. Rushmore

Mt. Rushmore honors four presidents whose contributions to the United States of America during their lifetime are historic in nature. George Washington, Thomas Jefferson, Abraham Lincoln, and Theodore Roosevelt are the *Faces of Mt. Rushmore*. These four granite faces sculptured by Gutzon Borglum tower 5,500 feet above sea level and are scaled to men who would stand 465 feet tall. Each head is as tall as a six-story building.[1]

Footnote Superscript

Paragraph Heading

George Washington. George Washington is often referred to as the father of this country because of the central role he played in its formation. After serving in the French and Indian War, Washington became a lasting part of history from his service as the commander of the Continental Army and later as the first President of the United States of America. Some individuals seek such leadership positions for the recognition and fame. Others serve and continue to serve because of their civic responsibility.

Long Quote

> Several times in his life, George Washington set aside his hopes for a quiet life to serve his country. After winning the battle of Yorktown in 1781, Washington ached to return home. Still, he led the army until a peace treaty was signed two years later. In 1787, though ill, he yielded to friends who urged him to attend the Constitutional Convention.

Footnote

---

[1]Black Hills Badlands and Lake Association, http://blackhillsbadlands.com/home/thingstodo/parksmonuments/mtrushmore (December 29, 2011).

**Bound Report with Footnotes**

**Application**

1. Open *df 87f loans*.
2. In the Loans worksheet, enter a 3-D reference in cell C3 that refers to the value in cell G3 in the Bates worksheet.
3. Insert the same 3-D reference in cells C4, C5, and C6 for Evans, Martinez, and Pope, respectively.
4. Save as: *87f loans*.

**Digital Citizenship and Ethics**   Through the Internet, people are now able to conduct many of their banking and financial transactions without ever having to leave their homes. Using **electronic fund transfers (EFTs)**, you can move money from one account to another, make deposits, and pay bills quickly and easily from your home computer.  EFTs require that you have electronic access to your bank account and have the authority to conduct transactions.  Most people find EFTs to be convenient and effective, but there are some considerations:

© Andrey_Popov/Shutterstock.com

- Errors can occur even in an automated system. You should check your account statements diligently.
- Funds are usually released quicker from your accounts than when using a paper system, so you must be sure there is enough money in the account to cover the transaction.
- When paying bills, there is often a two- to four-day processing period, so you must initiate the payment early enough to avoid a late payment and a late fee.

As a class, discuss the following:

1. Provide examples of how you already use EFTs or could use them to manage your personal finances.
2. What security risks should you consider when using EFTs?

# LESSON 88   "What If" Questions, IF Function, and Formatting

**OUTCOME**

- Answer "what if" questions and use the IF function, apply conditional formats, and apply specialized conditional formats.

**Business Documents**

- Sales Quota Calculations
- Grade Book Analysis
- Test Scores
- Swim Meet Result Analyses
- Sales Report Analyses

**Prepare to Learn**

1. Open *df 88b quotas*.
2. Calculate Next Year's Quota by multiplying column B values by cell A2.  Enter A2 as an absolute reference address in the formula.
3. You decide all formatting features.
4. Save as: *88b quotas*.

After his first term as president, Washington sought to retire. Once again, Washington was persuaded to stay on to keep the young republic stable.[2]

*Thomas Jefferson* ⊙

A patriot, an author, a President, and a land purchaser are but a few of *the* things Thomas Jefferson was known for that landed his face on Mt. Rushmore *and his imprint* on the history of the United States. As a patriot he was steadfast in his commit*ment* to this country. As the primary author of the Declaration of Independence he created a document that moved *was the beginning of moving* this country from a colony of the English to an independent country. *During his presidency,* The United States almost doubled in size with the Louisiana Purchase in 1803 for approximately $15 *million*.

*Abraham Lincoln* ⊙

The most controversial of the *four* Presidents of Mt. Rushmore was Abraham Lincoln. Even before he was elect*ed* there were discussions in the South about leaving the the Union if he should be elected. Within a few weeks of when he took the Oath of Office, Fort Sumter was taken over by the Confederate troops. This marked the beginning of the civil war.[3]

Lincoln is remembered for many things; however, he may best be remembered for the Gettysburg Address *, a speech* that is a profound statement *of American ideals*. The Gettysburg Address was only ten sentences long and took about three minutes to deliver. [4]

*Theodore Roosevelt* ⊙

Of the *four* Presidents, Theodore Roosevelt was the most colorful. Active in New York Politics *lc* at an early age, he arrived on the national *scene* stage with the notoriety achieved as a member of the Rough Riders, a volunteer cavalry brigade noted for the battle *at San Juan Hill* in Cuba. While the "other Roosevelt," Franklin, was noted for the New Deal (providing relief and reform during

## Use 3-D Cell References

A **3-D cell reference** refers to a cell or range of cells on another worksheet. A 3-D cell reference contains the cell or range name preceded by the worksheet name and the exclamation (!) mark. As shown in Figure 16-1, a 3-D reference in cell D1 in Sheet 2 to cell A1 in Sheet 1 would appear as =Sheet2!A1 in the formula bar when cell D1 in Sheet 2 is selected.

**Figure 16-1** 3-D Cell reference

To insert a 3-D reference:

1. Click the cell that is to contain the reference.
2. Key an = sign.
3. Click the tab for the worksheet that has the cell or range of cells you want to reference.
4. Select the cell or range of cells to be referenced. Tap Enter.

To confirm the 3-D cell reference:

1. Activate the worksheet and then the cell where the reference was entered.
2. Read the information in the formula bar to verify it has been referenced correctly.

1. Open *df 87d references*. Verify that cell B2 in Sheet 2 contains a 3-D cell reference to cell B6 in Sheet 1.
2. Enter a 3-D cell reference so cell B3 in Sheet 2 references the value in cell C6 in Sheet 1.
3. Enter a 3-D cell reference so cell B4 in Sheet 2 references the value in cell D6 in Sheet 1.
4. **Save as:** *87d references*.

## Application

1. Key the worksheet below as shown.
2. Calculate the % of Net Revenues for each item (use two decimal places).
3. Format the worksheet appropriately.
4. Print centered on the page.
5. **Save as:** *87e revenues*.

★TIP % of Net Revenue = Each value in column B/Net Revenues.

### Jones Electric

| | 12/31/20-- | % of Net Revenues |
|---|---|---|
| Revenues | $2,257,650 | |
| Returns and Allowances | $ 1,568 | |
| Net Revenues | $2,256,082 | |
| Cost of Goods Sold | | |
| Beginning Inventory | $ 125,612 | |
| Purchases | $ 834,972 | |
| Cost of Goods Available for Sale | $ 960,584 | |
| Ending Inventory | $ 126,829 | |
| Cost of Goods Sold | $ 833,755 | |
| Gross Profit | $1,422,327 | |
| Expenses | $1,165,750 | |
| Net Profit | $ 256,577 | |

**Footnotes 2-5**

[2]James W. Davidson and Michael B. Stoff, *The American Nation* (Upper Saddle River, NJ: Prentice Hall, 2003), p. 266.

[3]Davidson, pp. 478–481.

[4]Davidson, p. 508.

[5]Gerald A. Danzer, et al., *The Americans, Reconstruction to the 21st Century* (Evanston, IL: McDougal Littell Inc., 2003), pp. 318–319.

the Great Depression), Theodore was noted for the Square Deal—progressive reforms to protect the common people against big business.[5]

## Summary

As one stands and gazes up at the faces of these four Presidents, it is easy to imagine how the face of our nation would be dramatically changed without the contributions of these four men. It is altogether fitting that their faces are chiseled into the granite of this nation.

## 45–46C

**Learn: Reference Page**

1. Review the *Reference Guide*, p. 220, for preparing a references page.
2. Use the information from the footnotes to prepare a references page for the report. Proofread; correct errors.
3. **Save as:** *45-46c reference page*.

## 45–46D

**Learn: Cover Page**

1. Review the Cover Page section of the *Reference Guide*, p. 221.
2. First, manually create a cover page for the *Faces of Mount Rushmore* report. Then open *df 45-46d* to prepare a cover page based on a template for the report.
3. **Save as:** *45-46d cover page*.

## 45–46E

**Table of Contents**

1. Review the *Reference Guide*, p. 220, for preparing a table of contents.
2. Prepare a table of contents for the report.
3. **Save as:** *45-46e table of contents*.

QUICK ✔

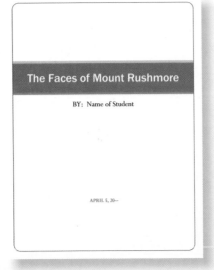

The Faces of Mount Rushmore

BY: Name of Student

APRIL 5, 20—

Table of Contents

1. Key this worksheet.
2. In cell D3, key =**A3+B3+C3** and then copy to cells D4:D7. Notice that the formula added the numbers in columns A–C across each row since relative cell referencing was used.
3. In cell E3, key =**$A$3+$B$3+$C$3** and then copy to cells E4:E7. Notice that the formula added the numbers in columns A, B, and C across the same row (row 3) since absolute cell referencing was used for the row.
4. In cell F3, key =**A$3+B$3+C3** and then copy to cells F4:F7. Notice that the formula always added the numbers in columns A and B, row 3, to each value in column C as the formula was copied to each row.
5. Copy cell F3 to cell G3 and then copy cell G3 to cells G4:G7. In cells G3:G7, notice that the A changed to B and B changed to C in each cell reference in column G since the A and B are relative references. The $3 remained the same in each row in column G since it is an absolute reference. Since C3 is a relative reference, it changed to D3 when copied to cell G3, and then the number changed each time it was copied to a new row in column G.
6. **Save as:** *87b references*.

|   | A | B | C | D | E | F | G |
|---|---|---|---|---|---|---|---|
| 1 | | | | Cell Referencing | | | |
| 2 | Numbers | | | Relative | Absolute | Mixed | Mixed |
| 3 | 1 | 2 | 3 | | | | |
| 4 | 4 | 5 | 6 | | | | |
| 5 | 7 | 8 | 9 | | | | |
| 6 | 10 | 11 | 12 | | | | |
| 7 | 13 | 14 | 15 | | | | |

## 87C

**Application**

1. Key the worksheet as shown, supplying the totals (*TOT*) in column I and row 15.
2. Specify column A width at 6, B–I at 5, and J at 9.
3. Make all row heights 18.
4. Calculate the total revenue (*$REV*) in column J by multiplying column I values by cell A17. Format column J as Currency with two decimal places.
5. Add a column at the right with the heading **% of REV**. Set its width to 9.
6. Calculate each room's percent of the total revenue (cell J15), and display it in the *% of REV* column. Format it as Percent with two decimal places.
7. **Save as:** *87c candy sales*.

|   | A | B | C | D | E | F | G | H | I | J |
|---|---|---|---|---|---|---|---|---|---|---|
| 1 | CANDY BAR SALES BY HOMEROOM | | | | | | | | | |
| 2 | ROOM | MON | TUE | WED | THU | FRI | SAT | SUN | TOT | $ REV |
| 3 | 101 | 23 | 45 | 32 | 66 | 66 | 72 | 23 | | |
| 4 | 103 | 45 | 65 | 82 | 45 | 45 | 56 | 33 | | |
| 5 | 105 | 45 | 23 | 10 | 75 | 75 | 63 | 77 | | |
| 6 | 107 | 34 | 23 | 15 | 34 | 56 | 45 | 23 | | |
| 7 | 109 | 23 | 35 | 46 | 53 | 53 | 49 | 66 | | |
| 8 | 111 | 22 | 33 | 55 | 88 | 88 | 46 | 23 | | |
| 9 | 113 | 24 | 57 | 80 | 76 | 76 | 62 | 54 | | |
| 10 | 115 | 23 | 56 | 80 | 55 | 55 | 65 | 29 | | |
| 11 | 117 | 78 | 67 | 56 | 46 | 61 | 33 | 60 | | |
| 12 | 119 | 35 | 65 | 73 | 59 | 92 | 47 | 59 | | |
| 13 | 121 | 44 | 56 | 71 | 48 | 98 | 32 | 45 | | |
| 14 | 123 | 35 | 58 | 56 | 59 | 84 | 15 | 38 | | |
| 15 | TOT | | | | | | | | | |
| 16 | CANDY BAR PRICE | | | | | | | | | |
| 17 | $1.25 | | | | | | | | | |

# LESSON 47–48 — Collaborative Report with Footnotes

**OUTCOMES**
- Format a collaborative report.
- Format footnotes provided by group members.
- Insert text files that need reformatting to match the destination file.

## Business Documents
- Bound Report with Footnotes
- Reference Page
- Cover Page
- Table of Contents

### 47–48B

**Apply: Bound Report**

You are working on a report project on the Minnesota State Public School for Dependent and Neglected Children with fellow students Rebecca Caden, Steven Fong, Maria Gonzalez, and Josh Parker. As part of your contribution to the project, you agreed to key and format the final report.

Some of the copy for the report was given to you as hard copy (see below). The rest of the report was given to you as electronic files. You will need to reformat some of the files so all parts of the report are in the same font and font size. For this report, all side headings should be in Heading 2 style.

The guidelines for the report state that the report is to be keyed as a bound report with footnotes. When completed, the report should look like one report completed by five people, not five separate reports put into one report.

**Save as:** *47-48b report.*

[1]"Minnesota State Public School for Dependent and Neglected Children," Museum Brochure, February 14, 2009.

*Remember the Orphans*

If you take exit 42B off of 135 south of Minneapolis/St. Paul you will soon find yourself in

Owatonna, Minnesota, driving past a large stately structure with an imposing turret

*located*
~~positioned~~ up on a hill. Stopping and looking at the structure, you can't help but feel that
                                        *to be told                 and entering the main building,*
there is a story. By driving up to the parking lot you will learn that there are stories. Some
                *many          left*
have been told; more have been un~~told.

In 1885 the Minnesota State Public School for dependent and neglected children was
                                                                                    *dependent,*
created by the state legislature. The doors of this structure were opened to orphaned and
        *starting in 1886*
neglected children. The campus grew to thirteen buildings, and the school would become
*third*                                          *10,635*
the 3rd largest orphanage in the U.S. in the 1920's with (get number for here) wards
        *, some of whom never left*
passing through its doors. During the Great Depression, the orphanage was the home to as

many as 500 wards of the state. If you listen carefully as you read the signboards (signage)

and wander the halls, you can still hear the sounds of the children's voices that once

inhabited the halls even though the doors were closed to the orphanage for the last time in

1945.'
        *Insert 1: df 47-48b gonzalez*

# LESSON 87

## Cell References

### OUTCOME

- Use relative, absolute, mixed, and 3-D cell references.

- Sales Report
- Loan Balance Report
- Income Statement

**Warmup**

Key each line twice at the beginning of each lesson; first for control, then speed.

alphabet 1 Zebb likely will be top judge for the exclusive quarter-mile run.

figures 2 This association has 16,873 members in 290 chapters in 45 states.

speed 3 Jamel is proficient when he roams right field with vigor and pep.

gwam 1' | 1 | 2 | 3 | 4 | 5 | 6 | 7 | 8 | 9 | 10 | 11 | 12 | 13 |

## 87B

**Learn Relative, Absolute, and Mixed Cell References**

You have learned that spreadsheet software copies a formula across a row or up or down a column. As the formula is copied into new cells, its contents are automatically adjusted to reflect the new address and the addresses of other cells in the formula.

When formulas are copied in this manner, the software is using **relative cell referencing**. That is, the copy of the cell is related to its new address. For example, if cell D1 contains the formula =B1+C1, when this formula is copied to cell E2, it changes automatically to =C2+D2. Since cell E2 is down one row and one column over, the cells in the formula are also one row and one column over from the cells in the original formula.

Sometimes you will not want the software to change a formula to reflect its new address when copying it to other cells. In these instances, you will use **absolute cell referencing**. Absolute cell referencing is used by keying a $ sign before the column and row reference in the cell address that is not to change. For example, if you want to divide all the numbers in column B by a number that is in cell A1, you would use absolute cell referencing in cell A1 by keying a $ before the A and a $ before the 1 ($A$1).

A **mixed cell reference** is one that maintains a reference to a specific row or column but not to both. For example, D$1 is a mixed cell address. The reference to column D is relative, and the reference to row 1 is absolute. When copied to other cells, the reference to column D will change, but the reference to row 1 will remain the same.

The chart below further summarizes the three different types of cell references.

> ★TIP To quickly change a cell reference from one type to another, select the cell you want to change and then repeatedly tap the F4 key until the desired relative, absolute, or mixed cell reference is displayed.

| Cell Reference | Example | Explanation |
| --- | --- | --- |
| Relative | A1 | Column A and row 1 *will change* when copied to a new cell. |
| Absolute | $A$1 | Column A and row 1 *will not change* when copied to a new cell. |
| Mixed | $A1 | Column A *will not change* when copied to a new cell (absolute), but row 1 *will change* when copied (relative). |
| Mixed | A$1 | Column A *will change* when copied to a new cell (relative), but row 1 will not change when copied (relative). |

## Purpose of the Orphanage

The primary purpose of the orphanage was to provide a place to live *on a short-term basis* for children whose parents were unable *or unwilling* to provide a home for them. In many instances, but not all, children were provided with resources and opportunities that they would not have had otherwise. As you peruse the displays in the museum it quickly becomes evident that this orphanage was established to serve several purposes in addition to providing a roof over their head.

## Education.

*Insert 2a : df 47-48b Parker*

## Religious and Moral Training.

*Insert 2b : df 47-48b Parker*

*Discipline and Useful Labor Emphasis. There was a steadfast belief in the value of work at the school. Students either worked at the school or were signed to indentured contracts. "It is believed labor, no matter how dreary the task, or how paltry the remuneration, is good for the children. Each child, no matter the age, should be a part of some 'worth-while, demanding activity' each day."[1] Many of the children were required to be up doing chores by 5 a.m., others by 6 a.m. Wards of the state were signed to indentured contracts with local farmers. Some of the outcomes were less than desirable. Erwin Varns, Ward of the State from 1932-1944, shares his experience with indenture contracts.*

*Insert 3 : df 47-48b Caden*

## What the Orphanage Lacked

*Insert 4 : df 47-48b Fong*

## State School Boys Serve in the Military

*Insert 5 : df 47-48b Gonzalez 2*

[1] Minnesota State Public School for Dependent and Neglected Children, "History," www.orphanagemuseum.com /history.php (January 10, 2012).

# UNIT 16

## Preparing and Analyzing Financial Documents

### Reference Guide

In this unit, you will use cell referencing, formulas, and built-in financial functions to perform worksheet calculations that provide information needed to analyze various financial documents so proper business and personal decisions can be made.

You will learn how to use mixed and absolute cell referencing to perform calculations efficiently. Absolute cell referencing is especially important when you want to answer "What If" questions. For example, "What If" questions can help you see how your profits will be affected if your sales go up 5 percent and your costs go up 7 percent.

Marnie Burkhart/Corbis

In addition, you will use basic built-in financial functions to determine matters relating to saving, investing, and borrowing money and advanced formatting features that identify and format worksheet information that meets a criterion you specify.

While this unit focuses primarily on extending your ability to use spreadsheet software to perform calculations, you will also learn how you can copy worksheets into word processing documents and create word processing documents in a worksheet. Knowing how to integrate the two software packages will enable you to become more efficient in creating and presenting information.

**Books**

Other wards of the state (or their children) wrote books that provide additional insight into what it was like being a ward of the state and living at the State School during their childhood. Some of the publications include:

*alphabetize*

- ***Boy from C-11 Case #9164, A Memoir*** *(Harvey Ronglien)*
- ***While the Locust Slept*** (Peter Razor)
- ***My Light at the End of the Tunnel*** (Helen Bowers)
- ***Iris Blossom and Boxing Gloves*** (Iris Wright)
- ***No Tears Allowed*** (Eva Carlson Jensen)
- ***Patty's Journey*** (Donna Scott Norling)
- ***Crackers and Milk*** *(Arlene Nelson)*

**Why Did Children Become Wards of the State**

*Insert 6 : df 47-48b Caden 2*

*Conclusion*

*Many of the orphanages that once dotted the landscape of the United States have closed their doors. They have been replaced by foster care and adoption programs. However, in many less developed nations, orphanages are still common place and continue to be the home to many of the world's children.*

---

## 47–48C

### Apply: Table of Contents

1. Prepare a table of contents for the report.
2. Save as: **47-48c table of contents**.

---

## 47–48D

### Apply: Reference Page

1. Use the information from the footnotes to prepare a references page for the report. Proofread; correct errors.
2. Save as: **47-48d reference page**.

---

## 47–48E

### Apply: Cover Page

1. Prepare a cover page for the *Remember the Orphans* report. Use an appropriate template to create the cover page. Insert a picture of the orphanage (**df 47-48e picture**) on the cover page.
2. Save as: **47-48e cover page**.

# The Winning Edge

Chris Hermann/F1online digitale
Bildagentur GmbH/Alamy

Complete this activity to help prepare for the **Word Processing II** event in FBLA-PBL's Business Management and Administration division. Participants in this event demonstrate that they have acquired word processing proficiency beyond entry level.

1. You work for your community's travel and tourism office. You have been asked to write a business letter to travel agents in neighboring states inviting them to visit your community and experience its attractions. Your goal is to motivate them to share their experience with their clients. Use the following guidelines to write your letter.

   • Locate the names and addresses of at least three travel agencies in neighboring states. In a new word processing document, use the Table feature to create a data source and type the names and addresses of the agencies. Save the document with an appropriate name.

   • Use the Mail Merge Wizard to create the main letter. Insert the current date and the *Address Block* and *Greeting Line* merge fields where appropriate.

   • Create the body of the letter. It should consist of three ¶s. In the first ¶, introduce your community and state the purpose for writing the letter. In the second ¶, provide a basic description of your community, including its general location, climate, and major attractions. In the third ¶, state why your community would be a good place to visit and why the travel agent should recommend it to his or her clients. For the complimentary close, use your name and the title of **Communications Assistant**.

2. Proofread and revise the document as necessary. Apply formatting and text enhancements (bold, italics, and underline) as appropriate.

3. When you have completed the letter, merge it with the data source. Save the merged letters with an appropriate name.

For detailed information on this event, go to www.fbla-pbl.org.

## Think Critically

1. How can strong word processing skills help you be a more productive employee?
2. How can you use written communications as a tool for persuading others?

---

## School and Community

You have probably seen many posters and advertisements for charitable runs, walks, and races that are organized to raise money for a good cause. This type of community service activity is a great way to motivate people to help others and do something good for themselves at the same time.

1. Identify a charity or cause for which you would like to raise money and determine who you should contact to discuss fund-raising activities.

2. Determine the type of run, walk, or race you would like to organize. Establish the date, time, location, estimated number of participants, and entry fee for the event.

3. Using what you have learned in this unit, write a letter to the contact you have identified and explain the event you would like to organize. Include as many details as possible and, if necessary, ask for advice on planning and managing the event.

# Two-Column Reports with Pictures

**OUTCOMES**

- Format a two-column report.
- Set margins for a two-column report.
- Insert pictures in a report.
- Format pictures in a report.
- Size and position pictures in a report.

## Business Document

- Two-Column Report with Pictures

### 49B

**Learn: Format Report in Two Columns**

Page Layout/Page Setup/Columns/Two

Page Layout/Page Setup/Margins/Custom Margins

Your teacher thought your group report was excellent and would like you to submit it to the local magazine for possible publication. You will need to reformat the report into two columns to follow the magazine's submission requirements, as shown in Figure 8-8.

This can be done by using the Columns feature of the Page Setup group found on the Page Layout tab.

The magazine wants the margins set at 0.5" for all margins. Change the font color for all headings in the report to Orange, Accent 2, Darker 50%. Remove the page numbers.

Open **47-48b report** and make the changes required for submitting the report for possible publication. Keep the report open to complete 49c.

**Figure 8-8** Two-column report

### 49C

**Learn: Insert Pictures in the Report**

The magazine also encourages that pictures be included with submissions. Your teacher provided you with a file of pictures (*df 49c pictures*) with captions to include and suggested that you use software features to make the pictures appear as though they were taken during the period the school was open. Change the picture style to soft edges, and change the pictures to sepia, as follows.

1. Open the file *df 49c pictures*.
2. Click on the first picture.
3. Click Format on the Picture Tools tab.
4. Click Soft Edge Rectangle for the picture style.
5. Click on each picture and press Ctrl+Y to change the picture style to Soft Edge Rectangle.

© iStockphoto.com/Steve Debenport

### Planning a Career in Architecture & Construction

From the roof over your head to the floor under your feet, every structure in which you live, learn, work, and socialize came about through workers in the Architecture & Construction career cluster. This field is for those individuals who are interested in planning, designing, building, and maintaining the built environment.

### What's It Like?

Workers employed in this field are involved in planning, designing, and building the homes, office buildings, schools, shopping malls, hospitals, roads, and parks you see and use. They also take care of and maintain those structures. For example:

- They design the overall look of built structures and facilities and ensure they are functional, safe, and suit the needs of the people who use them.
- They create functional outdoor areas, and upgrade and maintain existing landscapes.
- They frame walls and build doors, window frames, and stairwells out of wood; install and maintain pipe, electrical, and power systems; and apply paint and other finishes to the interiors and exteriors of structures.
- They prepare technical drawings and plans, which are used by production and construction workers to build everything from microchips to skyscrapers.
- They design and supervise the construction of roads, buildings, airports, tunnels, dams, bridges, and water supply and sewage systems.

Many jobs in this field, such as construction work, carpentry, painting, and landscaping, can be strenuous and require working under harsh weather conditions. Many may also require long working hours in order to meet deadlines and budgets. Workers in other jobs, including architecture, engineering, and computer-aided design, typically work in offices with a regular 40-hour workweek.

### Employment Outlook

The ever-growing population requires more space in which to live, work, learn, and play and, thus, will drive growth in the building and construction industries. Employment opportunities are expected to grow at an average or faster-than-average pace.

Education requirements for workers in this cluster vary. Employers in fields such as architecture and engineering almost always require a college degree plus licensure for some professions. Craftsmen and workers in other fields are typically expected to have vocational training or on-the-job training.

### What About You?

This career cluster is covered in box 2 of the Interest Survey Activity you completed in Unit 1 of this text. If this box had one of the three highest scores on your survey, you should further explore the cluster's pathways and related occupations.

1. Why do you think a career in this field could be a good choice?
2. What skills can you develop now that would be helpful to a career in this field?
3. Why are these jobs important to our country's prosperity and well-being?

6. Right-click on the first picture.
7. Click Format Picture to bring up Format Picture dialog box.
8. Click the Picture Icon under Format Picture.

9. If the options are not showing under PICTURE COLOR, click PICTURE COLOR.
10. Click the Recolor icon under PICTURE COLOR.

11. Click on the Preset color Sepia.

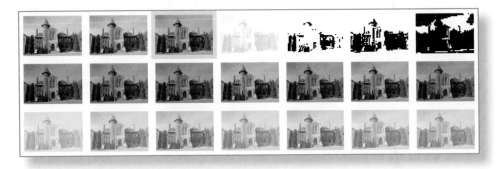

12. Click the X to close the Format Picture Options.
13. Click on each picture and press Ctrl + Y to change the picture color to Sepia.

The Ctrl + Y shortcut can only apply one formatting change at a time.

14. Insert the pictures and captions into the report at appropriate places; see Figure 8-8.
15. The size of some of the pictures may need adjustments to make the copy a better fit.
16. With the two-column format, the footnotes will look better on the page by changing the indention to 0.25" rather than 0.5". Make this change.
17. **Save as:** *49c report.*

Compare the first page of your report to Figure 8-8.

# Academic and Career Connections

Complete the following exercises that introduce various topics that involve academic themes and careers.

## Grammar and Writing: Semicolons

**MicroType 6**

- References/Communication Skills/Semicolons

1. Go to *MicroType 6* and use this feature path: References/Communication Skills/Semicolons.
2. Click *Rules* and review the rules of using semicolons.
3. Then, under *Semicolons*, click *Posttest*.
4. Follow the instructions to complete the posttest.

## Communications: Composition

You are going to write a letter to three employers in your area inviting them to speak to the class about employment opportunities.

1. Open a new *Word* document and save it as **u15 communications source**.
2. Use the Table feature to create a data source with three records, each with the fields shown below. Enter the appropriate information for three employers in your area. Select businesses for which you might be interested in working.

| First Name | Last Name | Title | Company Name | Address | City | State | ZIP Code |
|---|---|---|---|---|---|---|---|
| | | | | | | | |

3. Open another new *Word* document and save it as **u15 communications main letter**.
4. Start the Mail Merge Wizard and use the current document to write a letter in block format that invites the employer to visit your class. The letter should be at least three ¶s long. Use the **u15 communications source** file as the data source. Insert the *Address Block* and *Greeting Line* merge fields where appropriate.
5. When you have completed the letter, merge it with the data source. Save the merged letters as **u15 communications merged letter**.
6. With your instructor's permission, print the letters and send to the employers.

## Math Skills: Measures of Central Tendency

The measures of central tendency are mean, median, and mode. The **mean**, or average, is a value that is intermediate between other values; the **median** is the middle number in a data set when the data are arranged in numerical order; the **mode** is the value in the data set that occurs most often. Courtney has pulled this information from her company's database.

1. During the month of December, the company recorded these transactions:

   **East**: 814 transactions, $76/transaction     **West**: 637 transactions, $46/transaction
   
   **North**: 870 transactions, $53/transaction     **South**: 749 transactions, $67/transaction
   
   Find the mean number of transactions for the four stores during the month (rounded to the nearest whole number). What was the average amount spent per transaction?

2. The best-selling items are priced as follows. What is the median-priced item?

   New game: $36     Used game: $16     New handheld device: $169
   
   Used handheld device: $80     New game console: $299     Used game console: $199
   
   Accessory starter kit: $34     Car adapter kit: $12     Carrying case: $19

# LESSON 50

**OUTCOME**

- Work independently to format a bound report, references page, table of contents page, and cover page.

## Business Documents

- Bound Report
- Reference Page
- Table of Contents Page
- Cover Page

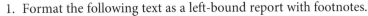

**50B**

**Apply: Bound Report**

1. Format the following text as a left-bound report with footnotes.
2. Proofread your copy and correct any errors.
3. **Save as:** *50b report.*

### Seven Wonders of the World

Key **"Seven Wonders of the World"** into any Internet search engine, and you will be given numerous sites to visit. The original Seven Wonders of the World (also referred to as Seven Wonders of the Ancient World) included:[1]

- Great Pyramid of Giza
- Hanging Gardens of Babylon
- Temple of Artemis
- Statue of Zeus at Olympia
- Mausoleum of Maussollos at Halicarnassus
- Colossus of Rhodes
- Lighthouse of Alexandria

The only remaining one of these ancient structures is the Great Pyramid of Giza located near Cairo, Egypt. Today, many other lists exist proclaiming their "Wonders of the World." *USA Today's* list even includes the Internet as one of their seven. An interesting historical list is the "Seven Wonders of the Industrial World."

### Seven Wonders of the Industrial World

Another list, Seven Wonders of the Industrial World,[2] includes wonders made by man that made the world a different place, improving the lives of those who inhabit it. Three of the wonders included on this list are engineering endeavors undertaken in the United States–the Brooklyn Bridge, the First Transcontinental Railroad, and Hoover Dam.

**Brooklyn Bridge.** Today, the Brooklyn Bridge is a landmark of New York. In early 1870, the year construction on the Brooklyn Bridge started, the East River separated Manhattan from Brooklyn. Thirteen years later, the almost 6,000-foot bridge connected the two cities, making it much easier for the horse-drawn carriages and pedestrians to reach their destinations. Over 140 years later, the legendary bridge has been modernized to accommodate six lanes of automobile traffic.

As with all great engineering feats, the cost of creating the structure (slightly over $15 million) was almost as breathtaking as the structure itself. "If you don't believe that, I have a bridge in Brooklyn to sell you."

# CORPORATE
## *View*

**An Integrated
Intranet
Application**

## Corporate Communications

You are beginning the second half of your internship with Corporate View by completing an orientation program within the Corporate Communications department. As part of the orientation, your supervisor requests that you write a letter so she can assess your writing skills and how well you can follow established letter-writing practices.

Since you are learning so much from this internship, you decide to write a letter to Melissa Kim to formally thank her for selecting you as an intern and arranging for you to work in departments related to your career objectives. Also, you want the letter to create a favorable impression of you because you may want to be considered for full-time employment at Corporate View upon your graduation.

1. To show that you can follow established practices, use the Corporate View guidelines for *Writing Letters* that can be found in the *Corporate Communications* section of the company website at: www.cengage.com/school/keyboarding/dim/cview

2. Next, you want to make sure you use an appropriate personal title and correct position title in the letter for Melissa Kim. Research this by using the Employee Contacts link in the *Regular Features* section of the website. Use the street, city, and state address on the letterhead (*df u15 Corp View letterhead*) as needed in the letter address.

3. Draft the body of the letter. Be sure to identify yourself, describe briefly what you have learned via the internship, and thank her for selecting you. You may want to review the Corporate View activities you completed in Units 4, 6, and 10 so you can include specific examples of what you have learned from carrying out the duties and responsibilities of your various assignments. Include other information you believe may help her recall you and your performance if you apply for full-time employment in the future.

4. Save the letter as: *u15Corp View letter 1*.

### Think Critically

1. Form a team of four students and have each one review the letter drafted by the others. Use Track Changes and Comments to suggest changes that you believe will improve the message of the letter.

2. Review the suggested comments and changes and then make the changes you believe are warranted.

3. Save as: *u15Corp View letter 2*. Print and sign the letter.

**Footnotes**

[1]"Seven Wonders of the World," www.newworld encyclopedia.org/entry/Seven_ Wonders_of_the _World (December 30, 2011).

[2]Deborah Cadbury, "Seven Wonders of the Industrial World," www.bbc.co.uk/history/ british /victorians/seven_wonders_01 .shtml (December 30, 2011).

[3]"First Transcontinental Railroad," http://schools-wikipedia. org/wp/f/First_Transcontinental _ Railroad.htm (December 30, 2011).

[4]James W. Davidson and Michael B. Stoff, *The American Nation* (Upper Saddle River, NJ: Prentice Hall, 2003), p. 6.

[5]"Hoover Dam," http:// en.wikipedia.org/wiki/Hoover_Dam (January 2, 2012).

[6]"Hoover Dam Visitors Guide," www.arizona-leisure.com /hoover-dam.html (December 30, 2011).

**First Transcontinental Railroad.** "Making the world a smaller place" could be used in conjunction with several of the industrial world wonders. It is most true with the first transcontinental railroad. The railroad joined the nation with 1,776 miles of track, making it possible to travel from coast to coast in approximately a week. Today, we travel from coast to coast in a matter of hours, but in 1869 the primary means of travel were the stagecoach lines, a much slower and more dangerous means of travel.

The railroad system transported not only people but goods, making what was produced on one coast much more available to those living on the opposite coast or anywhere in between.

The railroad took approximately six years to complete, with the final spike being driven on May 10, 1869, at Promontory Summit in Utah.

Completing the 1,776 miles of track was a huge undertaking for the Union Pacific and the Central Pacific. Much of the track laid by the Union Pacific was done by a workforce comprised of Irish laborers and veterans of both the Union and Confederate armies, with much of the track laid in the Utah territory being done by Mormons. The portion of the track completed by Central Pacific was completed mainly by Chinese immigrants. The men were paid between one and three dollars a day, with the Chinese immigrants receiving less, which resulted in their going on strike.[3]

**Hoover Dam.** Hoover Dam is a breathtaking structure well worth visiting. It is considered one of the greatest engineering projects ever undertaken by man. "The presence of the dam makes it possible for people to live in an area that is largely desert. Surrounding farmland is irrigated, and there is a ready supply of water and electric power."[4]

Hoover Dam, named after President Herbert Hoover, is located between the borders of Nevada and Arizona approximately 30 miles southeast of Las Vegas. Originally called Boulder Dam, the dam was not only the largest concrete structure in the world but also the largest hydroelectric power–generating station in the world when it was completed in 1936. Since that time, larger hydroelectric generating stations have been built as well as larger concrete structures.[5] Hoover Dam stands over 726 feet tall and is 1,244 feet wide. By comparison the Empire State Building is approximately 1,450 feet tall.

The engineering marvel, which was believed by many to be impossible to build, took the collaboration efforts of over 200 engineers and approximately 7,000 dam workers to build. The dam was completed in five years, almost two years ahead of schedule despite the harsh conditions and extreme dangers that the dam workers endured during the construction.[6]

The popularity of the dam is established by the seven million visitors from around the world who visit the site each year. By comparison Mt. Rushmore attracts about three million visitors annually.

Almost as impressive as Hoover Dam itself is the Hoover Dam bypass bridge that was completed in 2010. The cost of the bypass project is estimated at around $240 million; the cost of Hoover Dam is estimated at $50 million. The bridge arches majestically over the Colorado River, connecting Nevada and Arizona.

### Conclusion

Even though these industrial wonders were constructed many years ago, they still have a huge impact on the lives of Americans. Whether it is connecting two cities, two states, or the entire United States, the social and economic impact of these wonders is as great today as it was when they were constructed years ago.

## Mail Merge: Labels

1. Open a new *Word* document and then open the Mail Merge Wizard.
2. Using **86c data**, create a mailing label for every alumnus who has an entry in the Career Field column. Unless directed otherwise, select 5160 Easy Peel Address Labels from the Avery US Letter vendor list. Save the labels as **86e labels**. Print the labels.
3. Using the Mail Merge Wizard and **86c data**, create an attractive name badge for every alumnus who has an entry in the Career Field column. The badges should show each person's name and city. Unless directed otherwise, select 5095 Self Adhesive Name Badges from the Avery US Letter vendor list. Save the labels as **86e badges**. Print the name badges.

## Timed Writings

Key 2 5' writings on all ¶s combined; find *gwam* and errors.

 all letters used

| | gwam | 3' | 5' |
|---|---|---|---|
| Many people support the notion that a worker with a healthy | 4 | 2 | 43 |
| body and mind is a valued worker. Healthy employees often have a | 8 | 5 | 46 |
| greater chance for professional growth, produce more on the job, | 13 | 8 | 48 |
| are happier with their lives, and are likely to be more success- | 17 | 10 | 51 |
| ful than those who are in poor physical health or are not men- | 21 | 13 | 54 |
| tally alert. | 22 | 13 | 54 |
| If you want to have a healthy body, you should try to | 26 | 15 | 56 |
| perform appropriate activities during your leisure time or try to | 30 | 18 | 59 |
| find ways to enhance the level of your physical activity during | 34 | 21 | 61 |
| your regular school day or workday. Brisk walking is a great way | 39 | 23 | 64 |
| to bring exercise into daily activities with amazing ease and | 43 | 26 | 67 |
| quick results. | 44 | 26 | 67 |
| Fast walks from your home to the bus stop, from the bus stop | 48 | 29 | 70 |
| to your class, or from one class to another are very good ways to | 52 | 31 | 72 |
| reap the benefits of exercise while you carry out your daily | 56 | 34 | 75 |
| routine. Doing isometric exercises as you study, read, or watch | 61 | 36 | 77 |
| television will produce excellent results. You should, of | 64 | 39 | 80 |
| course, do only exercises that will not disrupt others. | 68 | 41 | 82 |

gwam 3' | 1 | 2 | 3 | 4 |
5' | 1 | 2 | 3 |

## 50C

### Apply: Reference Page

1. Use the information from the footnotes to prepare a references page for the report. Proofread; correct errors.
2. **Save as:** *50c reference page.*

## 50D

### Apply: Table of Contents

1. Prepare a table of contents for the report.
2. **Save as:** *50d table of contents.*

## 50E

### Apply: Cover Page

1. Prepare a cover page for the report. Use an appropriate template to create the cover page. Insert a picture of Hoover Dam *(df 50c pictures)* on the cover page.
2. **Save as:** *50e cover page.*

## 50F

### Timed Writing

Key a 1' timing on each ¶; determine *gwam*. Key a 2' timing on ¶s 1-3 combined; determine *gwam*. Key a 3' timing on ¶s 1-3 combined; determine *gwam*.

**A**  all letters used | gwam | 2' | 3'

| | 2' | 3' |
|---|---|---|
| Atlanta, the capital of Georgia, is a gem of the South. | 6 | 4 |
| It is the largest city in the state and exists because of | 12 | 8 |
| railroads. The original site was selected as the end of the | 18 | 12 |
| line for the railroad to be built northward. Eight years | 23 | 16 |
| later, the area became known as Atlanta. Because of the | 29 | 19 |
| railroad, Atlanta was the key supply center for the Confederacy | 36 | 24 |
| and was virtually destroyed during the Civil War. | 40 | 27 |
| One of the more famous Atlanta citizens was Margaret | 46 | 30 |
| Mitchell. The book she wrote exquisitely portrays the area | 52 | 34 |
| during the Civil War period. During the war, much of the city | 58 | 39 |
| was destroyed. However, a few of the elegant southern homes | 64 | 43 |
| of this time period have been restored and are open for the | 70 | 47 |
| public to see. Today, Atlanta is recognized as a modern city | 76 | 51 |
| that gives those who visit as well as the residents of the city | 83 | 55 |
| a variety of cultural and sporting events for their enjoyment. | 89 | 59 |

gwam 2' | 1 | 2 | 3 | 4 | 5 | 6
     3' | 1 | 2 | 3 | 4

www.cengage.com/school/keyboarding/c21key

**Create a Main Document; Set Up and Perform a Mail Merge**

1. Open a new *Word* document and then open the Mail Merge Wizard.
2. Using the data source file **86c data** and the information below, create a main document in block letter format with mixed punctuation for every alumnus who has an entry in the *Career Field* column in the data source file. Adjust spacing as needed. Save the main document as **86d main** and the merged letters as **86d merge**.
3. Print the first two letters.

September 15, 20—

<<AddressBlock>>

<<GreetingLine>>

Thank you for agreeing to participate in the Hamilton College Career Fair on October 7 at the Charles Center for Leadership. It is important that current students have an opportunity to meet and discuss career objectives with Hamilton College alumni who have expertise in the students' chosen fields of study.

Plan to arrive at the CCL by 9:30 a.m. and report to the registration area in the lobby area inside the main entrance. From 10:15 a.m. to 12 noon, students pursuing a career in <<Career Field>> will be able to meet with you in one of the conference rooms.

<<First Name>>, I look forward to having you on campus for this popular event. I hope you will be able to join the faculty, academic administrators, student leaders, and me for lunch. The lunch should end by 1:30 p.m.

If you need any other information, don't hesitate to call me at 800-555-9470 or email me at fjburns@hamilton.edu.

Sincerely

Fred J. Burns, Director
Career Planning and Placement

Enclosure

xx

<<FirstName>>, I've enclosed a parking pass that permits you to park in any campus parking lot.

# Academic and Career Connections

Complete the following exercises that introduce various topics that involve academic themes and careers.

## Grammar and Writing: Abbreviations

**MicroType 6**

- References/Communication Skills/Abbreviations
- CheckPro/Communication Skills 7
- CheckPro/Word Choice 7

1. Go to *MicroType 6* and use this feature path for review: References/Communication Skills/Abbreviations.
2. Click *Rules* and review the rules of using abbreviations.
3. Then, under *Abbreviations*, click *Posttest*.
4. Follow the instructions to complete the posttest.

*Optional Activities:*

1. Go to this path: CheckPro/Communication Skills 7.
2. Complete the activities as directed.
3. Go to this path: CheckPro/Word Choice 7.
4. Complete the activities as directed.

## Communications: Reading

Open the document **df u08 communications**. Read the document carefully, and then close the file.

In a new document, key your answers in complete sentences to the following questions.

1. Who founded the organization Habitat for Humanity International?
2. What motivated the founder to start the organization?
3. What is the basic mission of Habitat for Humanity?
4. Habitat is not a giveaway program. When Habitat works on a home, what are the partner family's financial obligations? What other obligation does the family have?
5. Habitat for Humanity operates at the grassroots level. What does this mean?
6. **Save as:** **u08 communications**.

## Math Skills: Markups and Discounts

1. Will is a pharmacist who operates a small drugstore. In order to achieve a targeted level of gross profits (sales revenue minus product costs) to cover his fixed expenses—such as rent, utilities, and payroll—he needs to determine how much he should mark up his products. For example, if he expects to sell $2.5 million of products (based on cost) and he needs to produce gross profits of $500,000 to cover fixed expenses, how much does he have to mark up his products, on average, to achieve that target?
2. Will's drugstore has just signed up to participate in a health-care discount program. Although he does not know yet exactly how many customers will sign up to be club members, he expects that purchases on average will earn a 4 percent discount. How much will that reduce the store's projected sales revenue?
3. If he wanted to make up for the discounts, how much would Will now have to mark up his products to achieve his target of $500,000 in gross profits?
4. **Save as:** **u08 math**.

# LESSON 86 Mail Merge Applications

OUTCOME

- To apply previously learned Mail Merge features.

## Business Documents

- Data Source Files
- Block Business Letters from Mail Merge
- Address Labels from Mail Merge
- Name Badges from Mail Merge

### 86B

**Create a Data Source File**

1. Using the Table feature in *Word*, key the following data source. Make the rows 0.2" high and use AutoFit Contents to set column widths.
2. **Save as:** *86b data*.

| Title | First Name | Last Name | Address 1 | City | State | ZIP |
|-------|-----------|-----------|-----------|------|-------|-----|
| Ms. | Gaynell | Boucher | 88 Strophmore Road | Haines City | FL | 33844 |
| Mr. | Kenneth | Chomas | 2912 John Morris Street | Sebring | FL | 33872 |
| Mr. | Roy | Crawford | 9180 Springfield Drive | Jacksonville | FL | 32256 |
| Mrs. | Teresa | George | 962 SW 114th Way | Ft Lauderdale | FL | 33325 |
| Mr. | Fred | Graham | 1634 SE 28th Street | Cape Coral | FL | 33904 |
| Mrs. | Lorraine | Hommell | 603 Shorewood Drive | Cape Canaveral | FL | 32920 |
| Mrs. | Alberta | Lasch | 102 Pinehurst Lane | Boca Raton | FL | 33431 |
| Ms. | Kay | Matthews | 3606 Landings Way, Apt 103 | Tampa | FL | 33624 |
| Ms. | Barbara | McKeever | 14961 Egan Lane | Miami Lakes | FL | 33014 |
| Mrs. | Sandra | Preuss | 5814 Silver Moon Avenue | Tampa | FL | 33625 |
| Mr. | Kenneth | Provins | 10019 Colonade Drive | Tampa | FL | 33667 |
| Mr. | Robert | Stevenson | 331 Garfield Avenue | Lake Placid | FL | 33852 |
| Mrs. | Betty | Wawrin | 8950 Park Boulevard | Seminole | FL | 33777 |
| Mr. | James | Westwood | 6207 Riverwalk Lane | Juniper | FL | 33458 |
| Mr. | Robert | Young | 12526 Terrence Road | Summerfield | FL | 34491 |

### 86C

**Edit a Data Source File**

1. If needed, open **86b data**. Change the orientation to Landscape.
2. Change Ms. Kay Matthews to **Mrs. Kay Collins**.
3. Add a column at the right, key **Career Field** as the column heading, and insert the following in that column for the persons named below:

| Last Name | Career Field |
|-----------|-------------|
| Chomas | Education |
| George | Accounting |
| Collins | Engineering |
| Preuss | Marketing |
| Provins | Political Science |
| Wawrin | Psychology |
| Young | Finance |

4. Sort the table by ZIP Code in ascending order.
5. **Save as:** *86c data*.

# Career Clusters

© iStockphoto.com/Neustockimages

### Planning a Career in Health Science

When you hear about a career in "health science," you probably think of doctors, dentists, and nurses. But this field provides opportunities in many other occupations that focus on health, wellness, diagnosis, treatment, and research and development. In fact, health care is now the largest and fastest-growing industry in the United States.

### What's It Like?

Individuals who work in this field are involved in planning, managing, and providing therapeutic services, diagnostic services, health information, support services, and biotechnology research and development. They might work directly with people, or they might be in a lab researching disease or collecting and analyzing data. In addition:

- They work with patients to rehabilitate muscle or bone injuries or educate them on how to reduce their risk for injuries.
- They examine and analyze body fluids and cells to help detect, diagnose, and treat diseases.
- They organize and manage patients' health information including medical history, symptoms, examination results, diagnostic tests, treatment methods, and all other health-care provider services.
- They combine their knowledge of biology and medicine with engineering principles and practices to design and develop devices, procedures, and systems that solve medical and health-related problems.
- They dispense prescription medicines, advise physicians about medication therapy, and counsel patients on the use of medications as well as general health topics such as diet, exercise, and stress management.

Employees in the health science field work in a variety of settings, from hospitals and doctor's offices to schools and research labs to sports arenas and cruise ships.

### Employment Outlook

Employment in the health-care industry is projected to grow by almost 20 percent by 2014. And, according to the Bureau of Labor Statistics' *Occupational Outlook Handbook*, more than half of the top fastest-growing occupations will be in the health science area. Most employers prefer a four-year or advanced degree, although in some occupations, a two-year degree is acceptable. Many occupations have state and/or national licensure requirements.

### What About You?

The Health Science career cluster is covered in box 8 of the Interest Survey Activity you completed in Unit 1 of this text. If this box had one of the three highest scores on your survey, you should further explore the cluster's pathways and related occupations.

Why do you think a career in this field could be a good choice? What skills can you develop now that would be helpful to a career in this field? Why do you think employment in this career cluster is growing so quickly?

**Mail Merge Applications: Labels and Directory**

Use data source *82c data 2* to prepare the address labels, name badges, and directory as directed below. Unless directed otherwise, use the same address label and name badge that were used in 85B.

### Address Labels

Prepare a standard mailing label for each record that has *Garland* or *Mesquite* in the *City* field. Save the merged file as *85c labels*. Print the labels.

### Name Badges

Prepare a name badge for each record that has *Plano* or *Irving* in the *City* field. Horizontally center the *First Name* and *Last Name* fields on one line. Center the *City* field on the next line. Use an appropriate-sized font. Save the name badges as *85c badges*. Print the badges.

### Directory

Prepare a directory listing all records in alphabetical order by City and then by Last Name within City. Left-align last and first names (insert a comma and space between the last and first names) and set a dot leader right tab at the 6.5" position for the city. Include a heading **CITY DIRECTORY**, center-aligned before the directory entries. Save the directory as *85c directory*. Print the directory.

© iStockphoto.com/philsajonesen

## 21st Century Skills: Collaborate with Others

The ability to work well with others is one of the most important skills an employer looks for in job candidates. When you work with others to achieve a common goal, you demonstrate your willingness to share ideas and produce results that will benefit you, your team, and your company. Technology has facilitated teamwork in the workplace.

- Through videoconferencing, employees at virtually any location around the world can see and speak to each other.
- Collaborative software enables multiple users in different locations to work on an electronic file at the same time.
- Blogs allow Web users to post commentary on selected topics and issues and respond to those comments posted by others.
- Wikis are websites that allow multiple users to add and edit content in real time.

### Think Critically

1. In teams of three or four, brainstorm ideas for a wiki on a current school topic. Some possibilities include school recycling programs, bullying, and Internet acceptable-use policies.
2. Create a list of tasks to be completed to create the wiki, such as writing articles and gathering photos or artwork. Assign at least one task to each team member.
3. In a *Word* document, prepare the wiki content. Save as: *u15 21century*.

# The Winning Edge

Complete this activity to help prepare for the **Advanced Word Processing Skills** event in BPA's Administrative Support division. Participants in this event demonstrate advanced skills in word processing and document production.

The Internet is a necessary and invaluable tool for just about every type of business in operation today. Although it provides quick and easy access to a vast array of resources, it can also have negative effects in the workplace. Many employers attribute a decline in worker productivity to Internet use on the job. They also are concerned about privacy and the security of confidential company information.

Your manager wants to establish an Internet usage policy for your company. He has asked you to research Internet usage policies for the workplace and prepare a report on your findings. Your report should cover the following:

- Ways in which employees misuse the Internet, such as sending personal email, reading news or sports articles, shopping, accessing and sharing explicit or offensive websites, and entering contests and sweepstakes
- Negative effects of Internet misuse on the company and other employees; for example, decline in productivity, loss of data security and confidentiality, and the use of offensive material to harass others
- How to design an Internet usage policy and the issues it should address
- Consequences for violating the policy

Use the Internet and other resources to gather information. Prepare a report of at least two pages on your findings. Apply what you have learned in this unit to the format and design of the report. In addition, your report should include a cover page, footnotes (as needed), and a references page.

For detailed information on this event, go to www.bpa.org.

## Think Critically

1. How can the Internet help businesses operate more efficiently?
2. List examples of Web content that might be considered offensive to some people.
3. How is your school's acceptable-use policy similar to an Internet usage policy put in place for a business?

## School and Community
Homelessness in America continues to be an issue of deep concern for many people. Some estimates indicate that there are more than 3 million people who do not have a place to call home, and close to half of them are children.

Many government agencies and nonprofit groups are working to address the issues of inadequate housing, poverty, and unemployment, which are the major causes of homelessness.

1. Research homelessness in your community. What is the estimated homeless population?
2. Identify the government offices and other organizations that exist to address the problem of homelessness.
3. Contact a homeless shelter or organization for helping the homeless in your community, and learn about the opportunities for volunteers in your age group.

6. In step 5, preview the labels and make any necessary changes.

7. In step 6, save the merged file as **85b badges** and then print the first page of badges. Compare your name badges to those shown in the Quick Check below.

8. Close the file.

### Directory

1. Open a new *Word* document and the Mail Merge Wizard.

2. In step 1, select Directory.

3. In step 2, select Use the current document.

4. In step 3, browse to find **df 85b data** that will be used as the data source.

5. In step 4, Using the More items option, insert the *Last Name* field, *First Name* field, and *Email* field. Insert a comma and space between the *Last Name* and *First Name* fields; align the names at the left margin. Align the email addresses at the right margin using a right dot leader tab. Tap Enter once at the *Email* field.

6. In step 5, preview the directory entry and make any necessary changes.

7. In step 6, select To new document. Insert Email Directory center-aligned above the first directory entry, print the directory, and save the merged file as **85b directory**. Compare your directory to the one shown in the Quick Check below.

8. Close the file.

Your completed address labels, name badges, and directory should look like these:

Address labels          Name badges          Directory

# UNIT 9

# Using Design to Enhance Communication

Lesson 51 Agendas and Meeting Minutes
Lesson 52 News Releases
Lesson 53 Itineraries and Invitations

Lesson 54 Purchase Orders, Invoices, Thank You Cards, and Certificates
Lesson 55 Business Documents Applications

## Reference Guide

### Business Documents

Business documents in this unit include a variety of documents other than letters, tables, and reports that are created using word processing software. In this unit, you will create agendas, meeting minutes, news releases, itineraries, invitations, thank you cards, certificates, purchase orders, and invoices. Each document can be formatted from "scratch" using appropriate design principles as you did with memos, letters, tables, and reports; however, templates are often used for these documents to save formatting and keying time. A **template** is a master copy of a set of predefined styles for a particular type of document. The template may contain text placeholders and formatting for margins, line spacing, colors, borders, styles, themes, etc. Using a template saves time because you use it as a starting point rather than designing every document from scratch.

### Agenda

An agenda is a list of tasks to be done or actions to be taken, usually at a meeting. When an agenda is formatted from scratch, use margins and page numbering for an unbound report and default line spacing. If desired, an agenda may be centered vertically.

Key the name of the group holding the meeting in Title style as the first line (see model in Figure 9-1). In Subtitle style, key the word *Agenda*, the meeting date, and the time and location on three separate lines at the left margin beneath the name of the group.

In Normal style, key the information about the type of meeting, the meeting facilitator, the invitees, etc., on separate lines, each beginning at the left margin.

Use the Numbered List feature to format items in the agenda.

Figure 9-1 Agenda

### Meeting Minutes

**TIP** An agenda is written *before* a meeting to tell attendees what is expected to happen during a meeting. Minutes are written *after* a meeting to record what actually happened at the meeting.

Meeting minutes are a record of important details that occurred at a meeting; including when the meeting was held, who attended, and the actions taken during the meeting. When formatting meeting minutes from scratch, use margins and page numbering for an unbound report and default line spacing.

Key the name of the group that met in Title style on the first line (see model in Figure 9-2). Key the words *Meeting Minutes* and the meeting date on separate lines in Subtitle style, each beginning at the left margin.

Use the Numbered List feature to format the items in the minutes.

After the last item, indicate the name of the person who submitted the minutes, blocked at the left margin.

Figure 9-2 Meeting minutes

## LESSON 85 — Mail Merge and Envelopes, Labels, and Directories

**OUTCOME**

- To use mail merge to prepare labels (address labels and name badges), directories, and envelopes.

### Business Documents

- Data Source Files
- Address Labels from Mail Merge
- Name Badges from Mail Merge
- Directories from Mail Merge

### 85B

**Mail Merge: Labels and Directory**

Mailings/Start Mail Merge/ Start Mail Merge/Step by Step Mail Merge Wizard

Mail Merge can be used for many other tasks. Frequently, labels (address labels, name badges, etc.), directories, and envelopes are prepared by using the Mail Merge Wizard to create the document in the same manner it was used to create personalized letters. In this lesson, you will create address labels, name badges, and a directory.

#### Address Labels

1. Open a new *Word* document and the Mail Merge Wizard.
2. In step 1, select Labels.
3. In step 2, select Change document layout and then click Label options and select your address labels. Unless directed otherwise, select 5160 Easy Peel Address Labels from the A very US Letter vendor list.
4. In step 3, browse to find **df 85b data** that will be used as the data source.
5. In step 4, select Address Block to insert the merge fields and then click Update all labels. See Figure 15-4.
6. In step 5, preview the labels and make any necessary changes.
7. In step 6, save the merged file as **85b labels** and then print the labels. Compare your labels to those shown in the Quick Check on the next page.
8. Close the file.

**Mail Merge** ▾ ✕

**Arrange your labels**

If you have not already done so, lay out your label using the first label on the sheet.

To add recipient information to your label, click a location in the first label, and then click one of the items below.

- 📄 Address block...
- 📄 Greeting line...
- 🖃 Electronic postage...
- 🖽 More items...

When you have finished arranging your label, click Next. Then you can preview each recipient's label and make any individual changes.

**Replicate labels**

You can copy the layout of the first label to the other labels on the page by clicking the button below.

[ Update all labels ]

**Figure 15-4** Insert Merge Fields and Update All Labels in step 4

#### Name Badges

1. Open a new *Word* document and the Mail Merge Wizard.
2. In step 1, select Labels.
3. In step 2, select Change document layout and then click Label options and select your address labels. Unless directed otherwise, select 5095 Self Adhesive Name Badges from the A very US Letter vendor list.
4. In step 3, browse to find **df 85b data** that will be used as the data source.
5. In step 4, Using the More items option, insert the *First Name* field and *Last Name* field on line 1 of the name badge and the *City* field on line 2. Format all three fields in Calibri 18-point font and center-align them. Update all labels.

## News Release

A news release is a document prepared by a business and sent to desired media outlets (newspapers, radio stations, television stations, etc.) to announce something that the business considers newsworthy. When formatting a news release from scratch, use margins and page numbering for an unbound report and default line spacing.

Key the words *News Release* on the first line in Title style (see model in Figure 9-3). On the next line at the left margin, key the words *For Release: . . .* in Subtitle style. On the next line, key *Contact: . . .* in Subtitle style at the left margin. Tap Enter once; begin the news release body. Key the body using default line spacing and indented ¶s. Center the symbols ### below the last line of the news release.

**Figure 9-3** News release

## Itinerary

An itinerary is an outline of a person's travel plans. The itinerary typically contains information about flights, transportation at the destination site, hotel lodging, and the travel agency used. Itineraries may also include information about specific activities (meetings, presentations, conferences, etc.) while at the destination.

An itinerary can be prepared as an attractively formatted table with or without gridlines (see model in Figure 9-4).

## Purchase Order, Invoice, and Other Business Documents

When a business makes a purchase from a **vendor** (seller), a buyer typically prepares and sends a purchase order to the vendor. It lists the items to be purchased and their prices, delivery terms, and other information relating to the purchase.

When a seller sells goods or services to a buyer on credit, the seller typically prepares an invoice and gives it to the buyer. It lists the items that were purchased, their prices, and delivery and payment information. These two documents as well as invitations, thank you cards, and certificates (see Figure 9-5) are generally prepared by using a template rather than creating them from scratch.

**Figure 9-4** Itinerary

**Figure 9-5** Certificate

## 84C

**Apply Mail Merge: Letters to Selected Recipients**

1. Open a new *Word* document, and then open the Mail Merge Wizard.
2. Create a main document file using modified block letter format with ¶ indentations and mixed punctuation that will be linked to the data source file **82d data 2**. Center the letter vertically on the page. Save the main document file as **84c main**.
3. Edit the recipient list so letters are sent to all except those with Inglewood in the *City* field. Complete the merge and save the merged file as **84c merge**.
4. Print the Barichal letter.

May 25, 20—

<<AddressBlock>>

<<GreetingLine>>

We know what a burden it is for small businesses like <<Company>> to offer excellent health insurance benefits to employees. That is why First Health is holding an informational session at the Hartley Hotel on Wednesday, June 10, from 4:30 p.m. to 6 p.m.

<<Title>><<Last Name>>, we invite you and another representative from <<Company>> to join us. You will learn about the major features of our medical, dental, and long-term disability coverage so that you can compare them to your present plan's features. We are convinced that you will be pleasantly surprised by what we can offer at affordable premiums.

Please use the enclosed card to reserve your places at the informational session. Refreshments will be served, and you will have ample time to discuss your specific needs with one of our staff members who will be attending.

Sincerely, | Robyn L. Young-Masters | Regional Marketing Manager |

xx | Enclosure | <<First Name>>, Tom Durkin has told me a great deal about the success of <<Company>>, and I am looking forward to meeting you to find what you are doing to be so successful in such a competitive field.

# LESSON 51    Agendas and Meeting Minutes

**OUTCOMES**
- Use a *Word* template.
- Format and key agendas and meeting minutes from scratch and templates.

## Business Documents 51A–55A

- Facsimile Transmittal Form
- Agendas
- Meeting Minutes

### Warmup

Key each line twice at the beginning of each lesson; first for control, then for speed.

alphabet 1 Beth Vegas excluded quick jaunts to the town zoo from many plans.

fig/sym 2 Kaitlin renewed Policies #23-4598 (truck) and #65-9107-44 (auto).

speed 3 The man is to visit the widow when he works by the mall downtown.

**gwam** 1' | 1 | 2 | 3 | 4 | 5 | 6 | 7 | 8 | 9 | 10 | 11 | 12 | 13 |

## 51B

### Learn: Templates

File/New/Select template or Search for online templates

Figure 9-6 Agenda template

1. Read the following information about templates and complete the activity.

Many business and personal documents are keyed using a template. In this unit, you will use templates to create a variety of documents including agendas, meeting minutes, news releases, itineraries, invitations, thank you cards, certificates, purchase orders, and invoices.

A template is a master copy of a set of predefined styles for a particular type of document (see Figure 9-6). The template may contain text placeholders and formatting for margins, line spacing, colors, borders, styles, themes, etc. A template saves time because you use it as a starting point rather than creating every document from scratch. For example, if you have weekly meetings and have to create a similar agenda for each meeting, starting out with a template that is formatted and has a lot of the repetitive information already in place will save time, because you will need to change only the details that differ from week to week.

Normally, you select templates from the sample templates that are installed on your computer (see Figure 9-7), from those you search for, or from templates you have created. In this unit, you will mostly use *Word* templates that use appropriate design principles and have been saved to your data files. However, when selecting from templates installed on your computer or those you find by searching, be sure to select ones that use good design principles to convey your information clearly. This includes using boldface, italic, shading, underlining, text boxes, all caps, etc. sparingly for emphasis rather than in large blocks of text. Also, select templates that include an appropriate amount of white space between words, lines, and paragraphs to organize the text and guide the reader's eyes.

Figure 9-7 Available templates

<<Title>><<Last Name>>, now that you know more about the Association, we ask you to schedule a 20-minute consultation with one of our staff members to discuss your health concerns. This consultation is free and carries no obligation to use our services. Just call me at 972-555-0119 to schedule a mutually convenient time.

Sincerely, | Margarita L. Jiminez | Director of Services | xx

---

## LESSON 84    Mail Merge Management Skills

**OUTCOMES**

- To edit mail merge documents.
- To select recipients for a mail merge.

### Business Documents

- Data Source Files
- Main Document Files
- Block Business Letters for Selected Recipients from Mail Merge
- Modified Block Business Letters for Selected Recipients from Mail Merge

### 84B

**Mail Merge: Letters to Selected Recipients**

Mailings/Start Mail Merge/ Start Mail Merge/Step by Step Mail Merge Wizard

When linking the data source file to the main document, you can edit the recipient list in a variety of ways. One frequent edit is to specify those in the data source who are not to receive the merged document. When the merge is performed, a letter will not be created for the records not selected. The checks to the left of the names in Figure 15-3 indicate the individuals who will receive the document. Those with no check will not receive the document.

You can also refine your recipient list by sorting the records on one or more of the fields in the record and

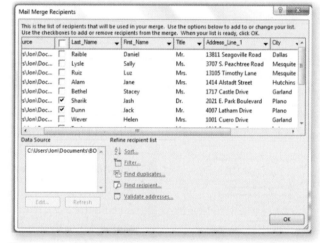

**Figure 15-3** Selecting recipients in the Mail Merge Recipients dialog box

by filtering your list to include only the records you want to include in the merge by using the options in the lower part of the Mail Merge Recipients dialog box.

1. Open a new *Word* document, and then open the Mail Merge Wizard.
2. Using *83c main* and *82c data 2*, use the Mail Merge Wizard to refine your recipient list and create a letter for each record with Plano in the City field.
3. Print the letters.
4. **Save as:** *84b plano*.

When you open a template, a new document opens that is based on the template you selected. That is, you're really opening a copy of the template, not the template itself. You work in that new document, using what was built into the template and adding or deleting text as necessary. Because the new document is not the template itself, your changes are saved to the copy of the template, and the template is left in its original state. Therefore, one template can be the basis for an unlimited number of documents.

2. Open the fax template, **df fax**, from your data files (or the Equity Fax template that is installed on your computer).

3. Replace the text in the template with that shown in the following fax transmittal sheet by clicking the text in the template that is to be replaced and then keying the desired text. Replace the text in the From section with your name. To pick a date for the Date section, click the [Pick the date] text, click the down arrow at the right, and then select the current date from the calendar.

4. Key the following text in the Comments section.

**I'll call you on Thursday to set up an appointment to discuss the proposal.**

5. Save as: **51b fax.**

| To: | Mr. Harold Robelen | From: | Student's name |
|-----|---------------------|-------|----------------|
| Fax: | 213-555-0181 | Pages: | Six |
| Phone: | 213-555-0810 | Date: | Current date |
| Re: | Newtown Project Proposal | CC: | None |

| Urgent | x For Review | Please Comment | Please Reply | Please Recycle |

## 51C

**Learn: Agendas**

**Agenda 1**

1. Read the guides for formatting agendas on p. 240.
2. Key the following agenda.
3. Save as: **51c agenda1.**

AITKEN HIGH SCHOOL SERVICE CLUB
Agenda
April 2, 20--
2:45 p.m. in Room 108
Type of Meeting:  Monthly meeting
Meeting Facilitator:  Kyle Johns, President
Invitees:  All members and faculty sponsor
    1) Call to order
    2) Roll call
    3) Approval of March meeting minutes
    4) Unfinished business

January 15, 20—

<<AddressBlock>>Tap Enter Once

<<GreetingLine>>Tap Enter Once

It was a pleasure to meet you last week to discuss your long-term health-care needs.  As you requested, I have charted the various policy features from three leading insurance providers.

The chart will show the various options each provider extends and the cost for each option.  You can select those that meet your needs the best.

I will call you in a week to arrange an appointment so we can discuss this matter thoroughly.

Sincerely

Katherine Porter
Agent

xx

Enclosure

## 83C

### Mail Merge Application

1. Open a new *Word* document, and then open the Mail Merge Wizard.
2. Use the information below to create the main document in block letter format with mixed punctuation.  The data source file is the updated **82c data 2** from Lesson 82D.
3. Save the main document as **83c main**, and then merge the main document and data source files using the Mail Merge Wizard.  Make sure the third ¶ has the *Title* and *Last Name* fields merged.  Adjust spacing as needed.
4. Print the Raible and White letters. Save merged letters as **83c merge**.

October 5, 20--

<<AddressBlock>>Tap Enter Once

<<GreetingLine>>Tap Enter Once

Thank you for attending the recent open house reception sponsored by the Dallas Area Environmental Health Association.  We hope that you enjoyed meeting our expert staff of scientists, physicians, nutritionists, technicians, and others who work on your behalf to improve your quality of life.

Headaches, sinusitis, fatigue, joint aches, and asthma are some of the common ailments that are often caused by our environment.  The Dallas Area Environmental Health Association is dedicated to conducting the research that documents the link between the common ailments and the environment so effective treatments can be offered.

      a. Finalize team assignments for flower sale that begins May 1

      b. Plan approved community service project to care for one mile of Morrison City Park

      c. Discuss recommendation that the Club help support an international student attending Aitken High School

5) New business

      a. Appoint nominating committee

      b. Discuss plans for regional leadership conference on May 25

      c. Discuss annual give-back gift to Aitken High

6) Adjournment

### Agenda 2 (Using Template)

1. Open **df agenda** (a template file).
2. Key the previous agenda using the template settings for font, font size, font style, line spacing, etc. Add to and delete from the template content as needed.
3. Compare the format of your agenda to that shown in the following Quick Check.
4. **Save as:** *51c agenda2.*

**QUICK** ✔

Your completed agenda should look like this:

## 51D

**Learn: Meeting Minutes**

### Meeting Minutes 1

1. Read the guides for formatting meeting minutes on p. 240.
2. Key the following meeting minutes.
3. **Save as:** *51d minutes1.*

AITKEN HIGH SCHOOL SERVICE CLUB

MEETING MINUTES

April 2, 20--

1. Call to order: President Kyle Johns called the Service Club meeting to order at 2:45 p.m. on April 2, 20-- in Room 108.
2. Attendance: Melanie Janes, Secretary, recorded the attendance. All officers, 23 members, and the faculty sponsor were present.
3. Approval of minutes: The minutes were approved as read by Melanie Janes.

# LESSON 83    Main Document Files and Mail Merge

**OUTCOMES**
- To create main document files.
- To merge main document files and data source files.

## Business Documents
- Data Source Files
- Main Document Files
- Block Business Letters from Mail Merge

### 83B

**Create a Main Document Setup and Perform a Mail Merge**

The main document file contains the generic text and format of the document that remains constant in each letter, plus the merge fields. After the data source has been selected, the merge fields are inserted into the main document file where the variable information from the data source is to appear. For example, the <<AddressBlock>> and <<GreetingLine>> in Figure 15-2 are examples of merge fields inserted into a main document as it is written. The letter address lines will replace the <<AddressBlock>> merge field and a salutation will replace the <<GreetingLine>> merge field when the data source file and main file are merged.

The merge process will create the merged file, which consists of a document for each record included in the merge. Each document will contain the personalized information for each individual in the data source.

1. Open a new *Word* document, and then open the Mail Merge Wizard.
2. In step 1, select Letters.
3. In step 2, select Use the current document.
4. In step 3, browse for the data source file *82d data 1*.
5. In step 4, key the letter shown on the next page in block format with open punctuation, inserting the *Address Block* and *Greeting Line* merge fields. Save the letter as *83b main*.
6. In step 5, preview your letters. If necessary, remove the space between the lines of the letter address and make any other formatting changes.
7. In step 6, print the Popelas letter and save the merged file as *83b merge*.

**Figure 15-2** Mail Merge Wizard step 4

© Wavebreakmedia/Shutterstock.com

4. This unfinished business was acted upon:

   a. There will be five teams of four members each for the flower sale that begins on May 1. Team captains are Bruce Holstein, Anita Jones, Roberto Nuez, Ty Billops, and Gracie Walton. Each captain will select three members for his/her team.

   b. Bill Eaton will organize a team of volunteers for the Morrison City Park project. He will try to get at least 15 members to clean up the litter on May 15. The Chamber of Commerce will provide adult supervision, safety vests and gloves, and collection bags. The volunteers will begin at 9:15 a.m. and work until about 11:30 a.m. They are to meet at the Carriage Inn parking lot at 8:45 a.m.

   c. The officers recommended that the Club not provide financial support for an international student this coming year since all members who attend the Fall Regional Leadership Conference will need financial assistance for travel, food, and lodging. The officers' recommendation was approved.

5. This new business was discussed and acted upon:

   a. President Johns appointed the Nominating Committee (Connor Anthony, Roberta Shaw, and Jim Vance), and they are to present a slate of officers at the April meeting.

   b. The membership approved officers to attend the Spring Regional Leadership Conference at Great Valley Resort and Conference Center on May 25. Their expenses for travel and meals will be reimbursed.

   c. Three suggestions for a give-back gift were discussed. The possibilities include planting a tree near the student parking lot, donating one or more biology reference books to the school library, and purchasing a banner that can be used to welcome students back to school each fall. The Give-Back Committee, chaired by Katherine Henzel, will study all three options and report back at the April meeting.

6. The next meeting is May 3 at 2:45 p.m. The meeting was adjourned at 3:35 p.m. by Kyle Johns.

Minutes submitted by Melanie Janes, Secretary

### Meeting Minutes 2 (Using Template)

1. Open *df minutes* (a template file).
2. Using the same information that you used to prepare *51d minutes1* and the template file, prepare another set of meeting minutes. Use the template settings for font, font size, font style, line spacing, etc. Add to and delete from the template content as needed.
3. Save as: *51d minutes2*.

### Data Source 2

1. Open **df 82d data2**.
2. Add the records in the table below to **df 82d data2**.

| Field Name | Record 1 | Record 2 | Record 3 |
|---|---|---|---|
| Title | Mrs. | Dr. | Ms. |
| First name | LaJunta | Vjay | Rita |
| Last name | Greene | Awan | Martz |
| Address Line 1 | 8606 Wiley Post Avenue | 1148 Hyde Park Boulevard | 601 Centinela Avenue |
| City | Los Angeles | Inglewood | Inglewood |
| State | CA | CA | CA |
| ZIP Code | 90045-8600 | 90302-2640 | 90302-5519 |

3. Add a **Company** field and a **Plan** field to **df 82d data 2**, the data source table.

| Records 1–4 | | | Records 5–8 | | |
|---|---|---|---|---|---|
| Last Name | Company | Plan | Last Name | Company | Plan |
| Perez | P & B Auto Trim | Family | Barichal | Ace Auto Parts | Husband/Wife |
| Brletich | Security Auto Service | Family | Greene | Greene Auction House | Husband/Wife |
| Kamerer | Bank and Trust | Individual | Awan | Inglewood Orthopedics | Individual |
| Neumann | Lawndale Bakery | Individual | Martz | Hercules.com | Parent/Child |

4. Key the additional information for the 8 records above into **df 82d data 2**.
5. **Save as:** **82d data2**.

# LESSON 52

**News Releases**

OUTCOMES
- Format and key news releases from scratch and from templates.
- Create a Quick Part.
- Use a Quick Part.

## Business Document
### 52B

Learn: News Releases

- News Releases

**News Release 1**

1. Read the guides for formatting news releases on p. 241.
2. Format and key the following text as a news release.
3. Compare the format of your news release to that shown in the Quick Check.
4. **Save as:** *52b news release1.*

News Release

For Release:  Immediate

Contact:  Heidi Zemack

CLEVELAND, OH, May 25, 20--.  Science teachers from school districts in six counties are eligible for this year's Teacher Excellence awards funded by The Society for Environmental Engineers.

Nominations can be submitted through Friday, July 31, by students, parents, residents, and other educators.  Nomination forms are available from the participating school districts or on the Society's website at www.tsee.webhost.com.

An anonymous committee reviews the nominations and selects ten finalists.  From that group, seven "teachers of distinction" and three award winners are selected.  The top award winner receives $5,000, the second receives $2,500, and the third receives $1,500.  Each teacher of distinction receives $500.  The teachers of distinction and the award winners will be announced on September 5 at a dinner at the Cleveland Inn.

School districts participating in the program include those in these counties:  Cuyahoga, Lorain, Medina, Summit, Lake, and Geauga.

###

## QUICK ✔

Your completed news release should look like this:

**Edit Data Sources**

You can edit both records and fields in a data source. For example, you can add records to, delete records from, revise records in, or sort records in an existing data source file.

Also, you can add, delete, or revise fields in an existing data source file. Data source files can be word processing, spreadsheet, database, or email files.

### Data Source 1

1. Open **82c data1** and make the following changes:
   a. In Record 3, change Elizabeth's title to **Mrs.** and last name to **Popelas**.
   b. Delete the record for Harold Dominicus, and add these two records:

   **Dr. Eugene Whitman, 531 Kiefer Road, Ballwin, MO 63025-0531**
   **Ms. Joyce Royal, 417 Weidman Road, Ballwin, MO 63011-0321**

   c. Change the orientation of the file to Landscape.
   d. Add two fields (**Company** and **EMail**), and then insert the company name and email address in each record as indicated below:

   Mueller—**Allmor Corporation;** mueller@AC.com
   Popelas—**Kurtz Consumer Discount;** epopelas@kurtz.com
   Whitman—**Whitman Family Practice;** whitman@wfc.com
   Royal—**Better Delivery, Inc.;** jroyal2@betdel.com

2. **Save as: 82d data1** and compare your data source file to the one shown in the Quick Check below.

**QUICK** ✔

Your completed data source file should look like this:

| Title | First Name | Last Name | Address Line 1 | City | State | ZIP Code | Company | EMail |
|-------|-----------|-----------|----------------|------|-------|----------|---------|-------|
| Mrs. | Noreen | Mueller | 15037 Clayton Road | Chesterfield | MO | 63017-8734 | Allmor Corporation | mueller@AC.com |
| Mrs. | Elizabeth | Popelas | 1843 Ross Avenue | St. Louis | MO | 63146-5577 | Kurtz Consumer Discount | epopelas@kurtz.com |
| Dr. | Eugene | Whitman | 531 Kiefer Road | Ballwin | MO | 63205-0531 | Whitman Family Practice | whitman@wfc.com |
| Ms. | Joyce | Royal | 417 Weidman Road | Ballwin | MO | 63011-0321 | Better Delivery, Inc. | jroyal@betdel.com |

### News Release 2 (Using Template)

1. Open *df news release* (a template file).
2. Use the text from News Release 1 and format a news release using the template. Use the template settings for font, font size, font style, line spacing, etc. Add to and delete from the template content as needed.
3. **Save as:** *52b news release2.*

### News Release 3

1. Format the following text as a news release. If desired, you may use the template, *df news release.*
2. **Save as:** *52b news release3.*

News Release

For Release: Upon Receipt

Contact: Guy Madison

LORAIN, OH, March 24, 20--. Three East Lorain County High School students, members of the ELCHS Science Club, have been invited to exhibit their projects at the Eastern Ohio Academy for Science Fair on April 21–24. The fair will be held in the Stern Exhibit Hall at the Erie Civic Center.

Susan Marks, Juanita Perez, and John Lavic earned this honor by placing first in their respective categories at the Lorain County Academy for Science Fair on March 15. Marks competed in microbiology, Perez in chemistry, and Lavic in physical science. Ms. Kelly Wyatt, ELCHS physics teacher, is the club's sponsor.

###

## 52C

### Learn: Quick Parts

Insert/Text/Quick Parts/
Save Selection to Quick
Part Gallery

1. Read the following information about Quick Parts and complete the activity.

Use the **Quick Part** tool to save reusable pieces of content. The content is saved as a **building block template** in the **Quick Part Gallery**. The content can include text, images, and special formats. Whatever you save in the Quick Part Gallery can be placed in the new document, thereby saving you time because the content does not need to be rekeyed and formatted. A building block template can be used as is, edited, or deleted using the Building Blocks Organizer in the Quick Parts drop-down list shown in Figure 9-8.

To save content in the Quick Part Gallery, select the text to be saved, click the Quick Parts drop-down list in the Text group on the Insert tab, select Save Selection to Quick Part Gallery, name the Quick Part in the Create New Building Block dialog box (shown in Figure 9-9), and click OK.

To insert the Quick Part in a document, click the Quick Parts drop-down list and select the desired Quick Part from the gallery that is displayed.

**Figure 9-8** Quick Parts drop-down list

**Figure 9-9** Name a Quick Part

## Data Source 2

1. Create a data source using the 15 records shown below.
2. Use the column headings as field names.
3. Save as: *82c data2.*

| Title | First Name | Last Name | Address Line 1 | City | State | ZIP Code |
|-------|-----------|-----------|----------------|------|-------|----------|
| Mr. | Daniel | Raible | 13811 Seagoville Road | Dallas | TX | 75253-1380 |
| Ms. | Sally | Lysle | 3707 S. Peachtree Road | Mesquite | TX | 75180-3707 |
| Mrs. | Luz | Ruiz | 13105 Timothy Lane | Mesquite | TX | 75180-1310 |
| Mrs. | Jane | Alam | 1414 Alstadt Street | Hutchins | TX | 75141-3792 |
| Ms. | Stacey | Bethel | 1717 Castle Drive | Garland | TX | 75040-1717 |
| Dr. | Jash | Sharik | 2021 E. Park Boulevard | Plano | TX | 75074-2021 |
| Mr. | Jack | Dunn | 4007 Latham Drive | Plano | TX | 75023-4000 |
| Mrs. | Helen | Wever | 1001 Cuero Drive | Garland | TX | 75040-1001 |
| Ms. | Ann | Buck | 1919 Senter Road | Irving | TX | 75060-1919 |
| Mr. | Peter | Como | 701 W. State Street | Garland | TX | 75040-0701 |
| Ms. | Karen | Rolle | 1026 F Avenue | Plano | TX | 75074-3591 |
| Mr. | Dale | Zeman | 4412 Legacy Drive | Plano | TX | 75024-4412 |
| Mr. | Yu | Wei | 12726 Audelia Road | Dallas | TX | 75243-7789 |
| Ms. | Anne | Sige | 532 N. Story Road | Irving | TX | 75061-0506 |
| Mr. | David | White | 3700 Chaha Road | Rowlett | TX | 75088-3700 |

2. Use the following information to create a heading for meeting minutes as a building block. You choose the format.
3. Save the information as a building block to the Quick Parts Gallery, using **BCIT Advisory Committee** as the name.

Central Morris School District
Business, Computer, and Information Technology Studies
Advisory Committee Meeting Minutes
Month Day, Year

## 52D

**Learn: Use a Quick Part**

1. Open a blank document and insert the *BCIT Advisory Committee* Quick Part.
2. Replace the date placeholder with the current date.
3. Key the following text.
4. **Save as:** *52d quick part*.

Committee members present:  Robert Dry-Kenich, Deborah Edington, Amy Lovetro, Ray Meucci, Kenneth Ryave, and Leo Yazzani

District employees present:  Mary Araral, Drew Bowen, Larry Kauffman, Fed Niklas, and Carla Nilson

Recorder of minutes:  Joseph Gloss

## 52E

**Apply: Quick Part**

Using the following information, create a Quick Part saved as **perotta** for later use.  Use an 11-point font.

TRAVEL ITINERARY FOR LISA PEROTTA

222 Pine View Drive

Coraopolis, PA 15108

(412) 555-0120

perotta@fastnet.com

---

Digital Vision/Photodisc/Jupiter Images

## 21st Century Skills:  Make Judgments and Decisions

Caroline is the manager of a customer service center for a large online retailer.  She has just been told by upper management that starting next week, the service representatives will be responsible for selling additional products to customers who call to place orders. Caroline informs the reps of the change during a weekly department meeting.  She immediately hears groans and complaints from several of the workers.  Sales, they claim, is not in their job description.

### Think Critically
1. Evaluate the manner in which Caroline announced the added responsibility to her department.  Do you think her approach was appropriate?
2. With a partner, brainstorm ideas for how Caroline could have more successfully promoted this new responsibility to the service reps.  Write a report that summarizes your strategy.  Save as instructed.

## Create Data Sources

Insert/Tables/Insert or Draw Table

The data source file contains unique information for each individual or item. Each individual or item is called a **record**, and each record contains **fields**. Fields are the information about the item or individual, such as her or his title, first name, last name, street address, city, state, and ZIP Code. The column headings in the data source table are the names of the fields.

When you create a main document, you will insert the fields (called **placeholders** or **merge fields**) into the document at the desired locations.

Once you have created your data source and inserted the merge fields into the main document, you can perform the merge.

### Data Source 1

1. Open a new *Word* file.
2. Use the Table feature to create a data source with three records, each with seven fields, as shown below.
3. Save as: **82c data1.**

| Title | First Name | Last Name | Address Line 1 | City | State | ZIP Code |
|-------|------------|-----------|----------------|------|-------|----------|
| Mr. | Harold | Dominicus | 14820 Conway Road | Chesterfield | MO | 63025-1003 |
| Mrs. | Noreen | Mueller | 15037 Clayton Road | Chesterfield | MO | 63017-8734 |
| Ms. | Elizabeth | Theilet | 1843 Ross Avenue | St. Louis | MO | 63146-5577 |

© StockLite/Shutterstock.com

## Digital Citizenship and Ethics

Blogs are a common way for Web users to share their opinions, ideas, products, and services. A **blog**, which is derived from the words *Web log*, is an online personal journal typically written and maintained by an individual (referred to as a *blogger*). A blog consists of regular commentary on issues that are important to the blogger.

Blogs are easy to set up and enable just about anyone to bring their opinions to the forefront for all to read. A feature of many blogs is the ability for readers to respond with their own comments, thus providing a forum that promotes dialogue among people with a common interest. All blogs allow postings to be linked to other blogs, creating a network of blogs called the *blogosphere*. As a class, discuss the following:

1. What opportunities do blogs provide for education and collaboration?
2. What are some drawbacks of blogs?

OUTCOMES
- Format and key itineraries from scratch and from templates.
- Format and key invitations from templates.

## Business Documents

**53B**

- Itineraries
- Invitations

**Learn: Itineraries**

### Itinerary 1

1. Read the guides for formatting itineraries on p. 241.
2. Format the itinerary as a table. You decide format.
3. Insert the *perotta* Quick Part where indicated.
4. Center the itinerary on the page.
5. **Save as:** *53b itinerary1*.

<table>
<tr><td colspan="4" align="center">**TRAVEL ITINERARY FOR LISA PEROTTA**<br>**222 Pine View Drive**<br>**Coraopolis, PA 15108**<br>**(412) 555–0120**<br>perotta@fastnet.com<br>**Pittsburgh, PA to Santa Ana, CA—April 18-22, 20--**</td></tr>
<tr><td>**Date**</td><td>**Time**</td><td>**Activity**</td><td>**Comments**</td></tr>
<tr><td>Tuesday<br>April 18</td><td>3:30 p.m. (ET)</td><td>Depart **Pittsburgh International Airport** (PIT) for Santa Ana, CA Airport (SNA) on **USEast Flight 146**. *Arrival time is 5:01 p.m. (PT)*</td><td>The flight is nonstop on an Airbus A319, and you are assigned seat 22E.</td></tr>
<tr><td></td><td>5:30 p.m. (PT)</td><td>Reservation with **Star Car Rental** (714-555-0190) at a rate of $45 per day. Return by 12 noon (PT) on April 22.</td><td>Confirmation No.: 33-345. Telephone: (714) 555-0190.</td></tr>
<tr><td></td><td>6:00 p.m. (PT)</td><td>Reservations at the Hannah Hotel, 421 Race Avenue, Santa Ana for April 18 to April 22 for a single, nonsmoking room at $145 plus tax. Telephone: (714)-555-0100.</td><td>Confirmation No.: 632A-04/18. Check-in after 6 p.m. is guaranteed. Check out by 11 a.m.</td></tr>
<tr><td>Saturday<br>April 22</td><td>1:25 p.m. (PT)</td><td>Depart **Santa Ana Airport** (SNA) for Pittsburgh International Airport (PIT) on **USEast Flight 148**. *Arrival time is 8:52 p.m. (ET).*</td><td>The flight is nonstop on an Airbus A319, and you are assigned seat 16A.</td></tr>
<tr><td colspan="4">Travel Agency Contact Information—Agent is Mary Grecco; 444 Grant Street, Pittsburgh, PA 15219; Telephone: (412) 555-0187; Fax: (412) 555-0188; Email: greccom@netway.com</td></tr>
</table>

# Mail Merge and Data Source Files

**OUTCOMES**

- To perform a mail merge.
- To create and edit data source files.

## Business Documents

**82B**

- Block Business Letters from Mail Merge
- Data Source Files

### Perform a Mail Merge

Mailings/Start Mail Merge/
Start Mail Merge/Step by
Step Mail Merge Wizard

**★TIP** To save a copy of all the letters, click Edit Individual Letters in the task pane in step 6 of the Mail Merge Wizard. Choose All in the Merge New Document dialog box. Click OK and then save the letters as **83B letters**. The letters may be saved before or after one or more of them are printed.

The Mail Merge feature is often used to merge a letter file (main document) with a name and address file (data source) to create a personalized letter (merged file) to each person in the data source file.

Data sources can be word processing, spreadsheet, database, or email files. In this unit, you will use data sources created in *Word*.

You can use the Mail Merge Wizard task panes to lead you through the process of setting up and performing a mail merge. Or you can use the commands on the Mailings tab. In this unit, you will use the Mail Merge Wizard to set up and perform mail merges. As Figure 15-1 below shows, the Select document type options in step 1 of 6 in the Mail Merge Wizard can be used to create letters, email messages, envelopes, labels, and a directory.

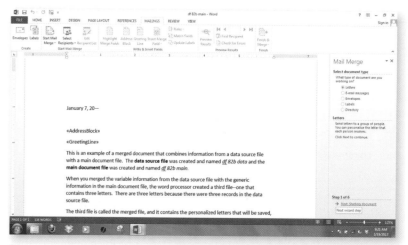

**Figure 15-1** Step 1 of 6 in the Mail Merge Wizard

1. Open the main document file (**df 82b main**) and the Mail Merge Wizard.
2. In step 1, choose Letters as the type of document.
3. In step 2, choose Use the current document as the starting document.
4. In step 3, choose Use an existing list and then browse for **df 82b data**, the data file that contains the recipient's information.
5. In step 4, the letter is keyed and the merge fields are inserted. Since the letter is already keyed and contains the needed merge fields, step 4 is completed; proceed to step 5.
6. In step 5, preview the three letters by using the forward or backward chevrons in the task pane.
7. In step 6, select the Print option in the task pane and choose to print the Current record.
8. **Save as:** **82b letters** and close the file.

### Itinerary 2

1. Open *df itinerary* (a template file).
2. Use the information from Itinerary 1 to format an itinerary using the template. Use the template settings for font, font size, font style, line spacing, etc. Add to and delete from the template content as needed.
3. **Save as:** *53b itinerary2.*

## 53C

### Learn: Invitations

1. Open *df invitation* (a template file).
2. Use the following information to prepare a party invitation.
3. **Save as:** *53c invitation.*

★TIP  "FUN & GAMES" is upside down because the paper will be folded to create a card.

Date: September 15
Time: 7:30 p.m.
Location: 527 Longview Drive
RSVP: (724) 555-0129
Your hosts: Don and Sharon

### QUICK ✔

Your completed invitation should look like this:

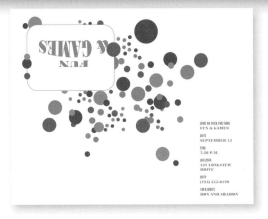

## Digital Citizenship and Ethics

**Digital Citizenship and Ethics** File-sharing technology lets you search for and copy files from someone else's computer. (This is called "peer-to-peer" or P2P technology.) File sharing is most often used to trade MP3s, but movies, games, and software programs can also be shared. BitTorrent, uTorrent, Kazaa, FrostWire, and Shareaza are popular file-sharing programs. File-sharing programs are a convenient way to share public domain files (material that isn't owned by anybody). But file sharing can quickly turn into piracy. **Piracy** is sharing or downloading copyrighted material without paying for it. It is another form of stealing, and it is illegal.

As a class, discuss the following.

1. "Borrowing" someone's copy of the latest computer game and installing it on your own PC is piracy. Why do you think this is considered stealing?
2. How could illegal file sharing cause harm to the holders of copyrighted materials?

TEAMWORK

© iStockphoto.com/eyecrave

**TIP** When a company name is used in the closing lines, tap Enter once after the complimentary close and key the name in ALL CAPS; then tap Enter twice and key the writer's name.

Letter 3 (Business Letter)

1. If needed, open **81c letter 2** and format it using modified block with no ¶ indentations, mixed punctuation, and Times New Roman 12 point.
2. Add the subject line: **EMPLOYEE TRIAL MEMBERSHIP.**
3. Bold the name of the fitness center in the body of the letter.
4. Add the center's name as a company name in the closing lines (see Tip at the left).
5. **Save as: 81c letter 3.**

Letter 4 (Two-Page Business Letter)

1. Open **df 81c letter 4.**
2. Format it as a modified block style letter with open punctuation and no ¶ indentations. Use 14-point Calibri font.
3. Add **CERTIFIED** as a mailing notation.
4. Add **YOUR REQUEST FOR ADDITIONAL INFORMATION** as a subject line.
5. Format the fourth through eighth ¶s as a bulleted list using bullets of your choice.
6. Add a copy notation for Mr. Josh Greenberg.
7. Add the following as a postscript: **Carol, thank you for giving Protect III the opportunity to provide your company's health-care benefits. We're looking forward to serving you and your employees.**
8. Add a second-page heading, using Calibri 14-point font.
9. Correct any page ending and beginning problems, and compare your letter to the one shown in the Quick Check below.
10. **Save as: 81c letter 4.**

Your completed letter should look like this:

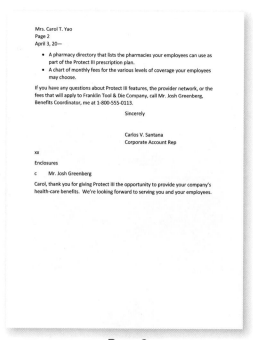

Page 1                                    Page 2

## LESSON 54    Purchase Orders, Invoices, Thank You Cards, and Certificates

**OUTCOME**

- Format and key purchase orders, invoices, thank you cards, and certificates from templates.

**Business Documents**

- Purchase Orders
- Invoice
- Thank You Card
- Certificate

**54B**

**Learn: Purchase Order**

1. Open *df purchase order* (a template file).
2. Use the following information to prepare a purchase order.
3. Save as: *54b purchase order*.

<table>
<tr><td colspan="2">Your Company Info:</td><td colspan="2">Vendor Info:</td></tr>
<tr><td colspan="2">Name: Alpha Mortgage, Inc.</td><td colspan="2">Name: Janet McDougal, Manager</td></tr>
<tr><td colspan="2">Street: 1590 Clifton Avenue</td><td colspan="2">Company name: Webster's Office Supply</td></tr>
<tr><td colspan="2">City, State, ZIP: Columbus, OH 43202-1704</td><td colspan="2">Street: 4646 West Broad Street</td></tr>
<tr><td colspan="2">Phone: (614) 555-0001</td><td colspan="2">City, State, ZIP: Columbus, OH 43228-1687</td></tr>
<tr><td colspan="2">Fax: (614) 555-0002</td><td colspan="2">Phone: (614) 555-0149</td></tr>
<tr><td colspan="2">Email: purdir@alpha.com</td><td colspan="2">Customer ID: W-1567</td></tr>
<tr><td colspan="2">P.O. #: AQ-4931</td><td colspan="2"></td></tr>
<tr><td colspan="2">Date: July 25, 20--</td><td colspan="2"></td></tr>
<tr><td colspan="4">Ship To Info:</td></tr>
<tr><td colspan="2">Name: Ned Thomas</td><td colspan="2">City, State, ZIP: Columbus, OH 43202-1704</td></tr>
<tr><td colspan="2">Company name: Alpha Mortgage, Inc.</td><td colspan="2">Phone: (614) 555-0112</td></tr>
<tr><td colspan="2">Street Address: 1590 Clifton Avenue</td><td colspan="2">Customer ID: A-2612</td></tr>
</table>

| Qty | Item # | Description | Unit Price | Line Total |
|-----|--------|-------------|------------|------------|
| 6 | F5-16 | Computer Printers | 119.95 | 719.70 |
| 24 | E4-501 | 8" Book Display Stands | 3.95 | 94.80 |
| 24 | B5-12 | Three-ring binders (3" burgundy) | 3.45 | 82.80 |
| | | | Subtotal | 897.30 |
| | | | Sales Tax | 53.84 |
| | | | Total | 951.14 |

Letter 1 (Personal-Business Letter)

1. Format the text below as a modified block style personal-business letter with mixed punctuation, using Arial 14-point font and hyphenation.
2. **Save as:** *81c letter 1*.

1331 Penn Ridge Court | Coraopolis, PA 15108-6001 | May 20, 20-- | Mrs. Helena Lopez| Community Healthcare | 911 Center Avenue | Sewickley, PA 15143-0900 | Dear Mrs. Lopez

My father will be retiring from full-time employment at the end of this coming July. He and my mother will lose their health insurance that is provided by their employer as of July 31.

I am trying to assist them in securing insurance to supplement the coverage provided by Medicare. Will you please send me information explaining the plans available through Community Healthcare. At the moment, they seem to be primarily interested in electing the traditional Medicare coverage and want to purchase a Part B supplemental policy and Part D for prescription drug coverage.

Once we have had time to review the information, we will contact you to set up an appointment. Thank you.

Sincerely | Richard Courtney

Letter 2 (Business Letter)

1. Format the letter below as a block style business letter with open punctuation, using Calibri 12-point font and hyphenation.
2. **Save as:** *81c letter 2*.

March 5, 20-- | Attention Human Resources Department | Central Life Assurance, Inc. | 1520 W. Ohio Street | Indianapolis, IN 46222-1578 |Ladies and Gentlemen

The Action Fitness Center is offering an introductory membership to employees of area corporations. This membership is for 90 days and costs only $50, the regular monthly membership fee.

During this 90-day trial period, your employees can use the indoor running track, weight-lifting stations, and exercise equipment (including treadmills, stair climbers, and rowing machines).

Your employees can also enroll in any of the aerobics, weight-control, and healthy-eating classes that are offered on a regular basis.

To take advantage of this offer, distribute the enclosed cards to interested employees. These cards can be presented on the first visit.

Sincerely | Ned V. Mowry | President | xx | Enclosures | c Mary Parker, Club Membership Coordinator

**Learn: Invoice**

### Invoice

1. Open *df invoice* (a template file).
2. Use the following information to prepare an invoice.
3. Save as: *54c invoice*.

| | |
|---|---|
| **Your company name:** Park's Office Depot | **To Info:** |
| **Street:** 5704 Hollis Street | **Name:** Margaret Stiddard |
| **City, State, ZIP:** Oakland, CA 94608-2514 | **Company name:** Century Publishing, Inc. |
| **Phone:** (415) 555-0101 | **Street:** 1661 East 32nd Street |
| **Fax:** (415) 555-0102 | **City, State, ZIP:** Long Beach, CA 90807-5291 |
| **Email:** acctpay@parks.com | **Phone:** (462) 555-0150 |
| **Invoice #:** AP-1659-T | **Customer ID:** C-12-98 |
| **Date:** October 21, 20-- | |

★TIP  If an Item # or Part # column is not included in a Purchase Order or Invoice, key the value at the beginning of the *Description* field.

| Qty | Item # | Description | Unit Price | Line Total |
|---|---|---|---|---|
| 1 | PS2PR | Electronic Postage Scale | 179.95 | 179.95 |
| 2 | KP33-BG | Electronic Sharpener | 24.95 | 49.90 |
| 5 | N1-502 | Double Pen Desk Set | 57.00 | 285.00 |
| 10 | P2-S52 | Box of #10 Envelopes | 7.05 | 70.50 |
| | | | Subtotal | 585.35 |
| | | | Tax | 40.98 |
| | | | Shipping | 10.45 |
| | | | Total | 636.78 |

**Learn: Thank You Cards and Certificates**

### Thank You Card

1. Open *df thanks* (a template file).
2. Revise the message on the inside of the card, using the following information to prepare a thank you card. Key the president's name and title on a separate line(s) in the box.
3. Save as: *54d thanks*.

. . . with your generous support,  the Aitken High School Service Club was able to raise $1,515 to help pay for the medical costs of our member, Jane Wilhelm.  Kyle Johns, President

### Certificate

1. Open *df certificate1* (a template file).
2. Prepare the certificate using **Wilson High School** for the school name and **Mary Killiany** for the student name.
3. Save as: *54d certificate*.

# LESSON 81    Business and Personal-Business Letters and Memos

**OUTCOMES**

- To review memo format.
- To review personal-business and business letters in block format and modified block format.
- To review multiple-page letter format.

## Business Documents

- Memorandum
- Modified Block Personal-Business Letter
- Block Business Letter
- Modified Block Business Letter
- Two-Page Modified Block Business Letter

---

### 81A–86A
### Warmup

Key each line twice at the beginning of each lesson, first for control, then speed.

alphabet   1   Jimmy wants seven pens and extra clips in a kit for the big quiz.

figures   2   I sold 56 advertisements for $6,738 between 9/12/04 and 12/19/05.

speed   3   A goal of the proficient tutor is to quantify the right problems.

gwam   1' | 1 | 2 | 3 | 4 | 5 | 6 | 7 | 8 | 9 | 10 | 11 | 12 | 13 |

---

### 81B
### Memo

Memo

1. Format as a memo, adding any parts that may be missing.
2. Use hyphenation and correct the marked errors and the five embedded errors.
3. **Save as:** *81b memo*.

TO: Olu T. Sangoeyhi, Physical Therapy

FROM: William M. Glause, Administrative Services

DATE: May 14, 20--

SUBJECT: PHYSICAL THERAPY BROCHURE

*Change this and all other occurrences of "brochure" to "pamphlet."*

Here is the first draft of the physical theraphy brochure that has been ~~okayed~~ *authorized* for publication in this years budget. Please *proofread* ~~check~~ the copy ~~very~~ carefully, *and make sure the pictures are correct.*

The public relations staff is in the process of getting permission to use each persons picture in the brochure. All permission forms should be completed within the next ⑩ days. *sp* If there are ~~any~~ changes in the pictures ~~we are using~~, I will see that you get to review ~~all the~~ changes ~~before we go to printing~~ *new pictures.*

Please ~~make the necessary~~ *mark your suggested* changes ~~in the copy~~ and retrun the brochure to me by next Monday.

Enclosure

---

# Business Documents Applications

- Format and key business documents from scratch and from templates.

## Business Documents

- Board of Directors Meeting Minutes
- Itinerary
- Invoice
- News Release
- Certificate

**55B**

**Apply: Business Documents**

Bora Ucak/Dreamstime.com

### Meeting Minutes

1. Key the following meeting minutes; do not use a template.
2. Save as: **55b minutes.**

Johnsonville Service Club

Meeting Minutes

December 10, 20—

1. Call to order:  President Aurelia Rios called the annual reorganization meeting of the Board of Directors to order at 6:30 p.m. in the River Room at the Red Carpet Conference Center.

2. Attendance:  Aurelia Rios (President), Masu Hori (Vice President), Beth Gola (Treasurer), Charles Salas (Secretary), David Laird, Don Parkinson, Jenna Young, LaShona Jackson, and Paul Lissinger were present.

3. Approval of minutes:  The minutes from last year's reorganization meeting were approved as read by Secretary Salas.

4. Nomination and election of board of directors:  President Rios announced that Ida Kite resigned due to her relocation out of state. The following persons were nominated and upon motion by C. Salas, second by J. Young, were unanimously elected to serve three-year terms beginning on this date.

    a. Masu Hori

    b. Henrietta Means

    c. David Laird

5. Nomination and election of officers:  The following persons were nominated and upon motion by J. Young, second by D. Parkinson, were unanimously elected to serve until the next reorganization meeting.

    a. President:  Masu Hori

    b. Vice President:  David Laird

    c. Treasurer:  Beth Gola

    d. Secretary:  Charles Salas

## Reference Guide

### Understanding Mail Merge

Many businesses and other types of organizations communicate with their existing or prospective customers, clients, or members by means of letters, newsletters, promotional pieces, etc.  For example, banks send out credit card offers, cable and other utility companies send out special offers, corporations must send out privacy notices on a regular basis, and restaurants send out advertisements, etc.  One effective way to manage documents that are the same for everyone except for things like name, address, account balance, etc. is to use the Mail Merge feature.

When using **Mail Merge**, you combine one file that has the information that is the same for all recipients with a second file that contains the information that is different for each recipient. When combined, a personalized document for each recipient is prepared.

The file that contains the information that is the same for everyone is called the **main document**. The file that contains the information that is different for everyone is called the **data source**. When combined, a **merged file** is generated.

Frequently, main document and data source files are used repeatedly after they have been updated.  The capability to reuse these files with the Mail Merge feature increases the effectiveness of managing written communications.

Beginning with Lesson 82 in this unit, you will prepare main document files and data source files and then merge them using the **Mail Merge Wizard**.  The merged files you will create are letters, labels, and directories.

© Pablo Calvog/Shutterstock.com

6. Other business: None was brought before the board.

7. Next meeting: The next meeting will be held next year on the 2nd Tuesday of December.

8. Adjournment: The meeting was adjourned at 7:05 p.m.

Minutes prepared by Charles Salas, Secretary

**Itinerary**

1. Use the following information to format and key an itinerary from scratch using these features:
   a. Horizontally center all lines.
   b. Use a 2" top margin.
2. Insert the *perotta* Quick Part as directed.
3. You decide other formatting features.
4. Save as: **55b itinerary**.

| | | | |
|---|---|---|---|
| **TRAVEL ITINERARY FOR LISA PEROTTA** | | | |
| **222 Pine View Drive** | | | |
| **Coraopolis, PA 15108** | | | |
| **(412) 555–0120** | | | |
| perotta@fastnet.com | | | |
| **Roundtrip Between Indianapolis, IN, and Shreveport, LA** | | | |
| **August 18 and August 20, 20--** | | | |
| **Flight** | **Departure** | **Arrival** | **Equipment** |
| Segment One--August 18--Indianapolis to Shreveport | | | |
| Amerifast #1233 | 8:38 a.m. Indianapolis | 11:04 a.m. Houston, TX | Boeing 737–300 |
| Amerifast #3482 | 1:10 p.m. Houston, TX | 2:15 p.m. Shreveport | Aerospatiale ATR |
| Segment Two--August 20--Shreveport to Indianapolis | | | |
| Southern #3416 | 5:55 p.m. Shreveport | 7:20 p.m. Memphis, TN | Saab-Fairchild 340 |
| Southern #1706 | 8:30 p.m. Memphis, TN | 9:48 p.m. Indianapolis | Boeing 737–300 |

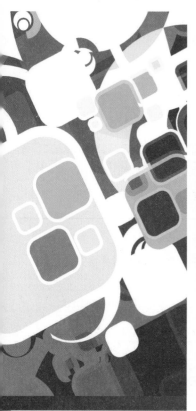

# Cycle 2

## Advanced Personal, Academic, and Business Information Management Skills

© iStockphoto.com/Henk Badenhorst

In this cycle, you will apply intermediate skills to help you with your future career and education.

You will apply these skills to manage written communication, prepare financial documents, analyze information, learn about entrepreneurship, use visuals for presentation, prepare for the workplace, and become an effective employee.

As before, you will apply these skills in real-world scenarios that give you hands-on experience selecting and using software as a tool to clearly communicate your ideas.

### Invoice

1. Open *df invoice* (a template file).
2. Use the following information to prepare an invoice.
3. Save as: *55b invoice*.

© Baloncici/Shutterstock.com

| | |
|---|---|
| **Your company name:** The Apparel Store | **To Info:** |
| **Street:** 2365 Beaver Grade Road | **Name:** Robert Knight |
| **City, State, ZIP:** Moon Township, PA 15108-2638 | **Company name:** Century Publishing, Inc. |
| **Phone:** (412) 555-0101 | **Street:** 4235 Beverly Drive |
| **Fax:** (412) 555-0102 | **City, State, ZIP:** Aliquippa, PA 15001-6932 |
| **Email:** aps@parks.com | **Phone:** (724) 555-0150 |
| **Invoice #:** 45-6789-A | **Customer ID:** CPI-1210 |
| **Date:** June 6, 20-- | |

| Qty | Item # | Description | Unit Price | Line Total |
|-----|--------|-------------|------------|------------|
| 5 | 456–396 | Pkg of 3 White Athletic Socks, Regular Size | 9.49 | 47.45 |
| 8 | 305–624 | Blue Polo Shirts, Medium Size | 18.99 | 151.92 |
| 6 | 201–781 | Athletic Shorts, Medium Size | 15.79 | 94.74 |
| | | | Subtotal | 294.11 |
| | | | Shipping | 10.45 |
| | | | Total | 304.56 |

**Lesson 55** Business Documents Applications

UNIT 9

**255**

## 80H

**Create Contact Group**

You have been assigned to work on a history project with three other classmates at George Washington High School that are not currently listed with your contacts. You will need to use the New Email Contact feature to add these classmates to your contact group. Use **History Project** for the name of the contact group.

**Group Members:**

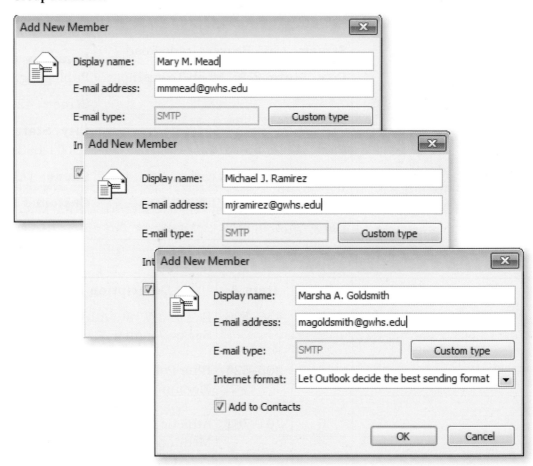

## 80I

**Delay Delivery**

Send an email to your instructor with the following message:

You asked me to remind you that I am having my tonsils out and will not be in class for the next two days.

I have completed the assignments for these two days. They are attached.

Attach *df February 20-21 class assignment* to the email, and delay the delivery of the email until Monday at 8:00 a.m. of the following week.

## 80J

**Schedule Meeting**

Schedule a meeting with your instructor for Friday from 3:00 p.m. to 3:30 p.m. to discuss your history project. Schedule the meeting for your instructor's office.

## News Release

1. Format the following text as a news release. If desired, you may use the **df news release** template.
2. Save as: **55b news release**.

News Release

For Release:  Upon Receipt

Contact:  James Dawson

Indian Land, SC, July 24, 20--.  The Indian Land Eagles are the champions of the South Carolina Legion Baseball District 7.

The Eagles advanced to the championship game by winning their first three tournament games.  To win the championship, they defeated Fort Mill 4-3 behind a stellar defense and timely hitting.

Juan Perez, Ken Hutton, and Larry Morris were named to the Region 7 All-Star Team and will compete for a spot on the South Carolina All-Stars, who will participate in a national baseball tournament from August 10-14 in Mobile, AL.

###

## Certificate

1. Open **df certificate2** (a template file).
2. Use the following information to prepare a certificate.
3. Save as: **55b certificate**.

Name:  SHANETA DAVIS

Subject:  INFORMATION TECHNOLOGY

School:  WARREN HIGH SCHOOL

## Web Page

1. Open *df 80d web page*.
2. Change the font, font colors, and font sizes to make the text attractive and easy to read.
3. Add an appropriate page background.
4. Remove the borders from the 1 × 8 table.
5. Insert *df 80d basketball*, a picture file, in the first column of the four-column table. Size it to about 1" square.
6. Insert *df 80d soccer*, a picture file, in the third column of the four-column table. Size it so it appears to be the same size as the basketball.
7. Shade the table white and remove all the borders.
8. Bookmark the text *Morris* at the top of the web page, and insert a hyperlink from the *back to top* text to it.
9. Preview the web page in your browser, and make any needed design changes to make the web page easy to read and attractive.
10. **Save as:** *80d web page* in Web Page format with **Morris Family Sports Center** as the page title.

## 80E

### Create Contact

*Note:* Use *Outlook* to complete 80E-80J.

Open *Outlook* and create a contact that includes the following information:

| | |
|---|---|
| **Contact Name:** | Paul M. Vermillion, CEO |
| **Company:** | Rockwell Technologies |
| **Address:** | 1623 Dartmouth Avenue E<br>Denver, CO 80210 |
| **Email:** | pmvermillion @rockwell.tech |
| **Business Phone:** | (303) 339-8100 |

## 80F

### Insert Contact Attachments

1. Insert (add) the following file as an attachment to the contact you created for 80E: *df district 13 sales reps.docx*.
2. Insert a table with the following information.

| Date of Meeting | Note(s) on Meeting |
|---|---|
| January 23, 20-- | Met with Mr. Vermillion to introduce our company and products. |
| February 15, 20-- | Sales call: Order #12-342 in the amount of $1,397.48. |

## 80G

### Edit Contact

Make the following changes to Paul Vermillion's contact information:

| | |
|---|---|
| **Phone:** | (303) 665-1090 |
| **Address:** | 225 Roanoke Place W<br>Denver, CO 80236 |

Key two 3' or 5' timings, as directed.  Compute *gwam* and count errors.

 **all letters used**    | gwam | 3' | 5' |

| | 3' | 5' |
|---|---|---|
| Character is often described as a person's combined moral | 4 | 2 | 43 |
| and ethical strength.  Most people think it is like integrity, | 8 | 5 | 46 |
| which is thought to be a person's ability to adhere to a code or | 12 | 7 | 48 |
| a set standard of values.  If an individual's values are accepted | 17 | 10 | 51 |
| by society, others are likely to view her or him as having a some- | 21 | 13 | 53 |
| what high degree of integrity. | 23 | 14 | 55 |
| You need to know that character is a trait that everyone | 27 | 16 | 57 |
| possesses and that it is formed over time.  A person's character | 31 | 19 | 59 |
| reflects his or her definition of what is good or just.  Most | 35 | 21 | 62 |
| children and teenagers model their character after the words and | 40 | 24 | 65 |
| deeds of parents, teachers, and other adults with whom they have | 44 | 26 | 67 |
| regular contact. | 45 | 27 | 68 |
| Existing character helps mold future character.  It is impor- | 49 | 29 | 70 |
| tant to realize that today's actions can have a lasting effect. | 53 | 32 | 73 |
| For that reason, there is no better time than now to make all your | 58 | 32 | 73 |
| words and deeds speak favorably.  You want them to portray the | 62 | 37 | 78 |
| things others require of people who are thought to possess a high | 67 | 40 | 80 |
| degree of character. | 68 | 41 | 81 |

| gwam | 3' | 1 | | 2 | | 3 | | 4 | |
|---|---|---|---|---|---|---|---|---|---|
| | 5' | | 1 | | 2 | | 3 | | |

Greenwood High School Science Club

Meeting Minutes

February 15, 20--

1. Call to order:  President Dee McClinton called the meeting of the Greenwood High School Science Club to order at 2:15 p.m. on February 15, 20-- in Room 107.
2. Attendance:  Sue Smedley recorded the attendance.  Fifteen members and Terry L. Gronbacher, Sponsor were present.
3. Secretary Sue Smedley read the minutes, which were accepted.
4. Unfinished business
   a. President McClinton reported that the school science fair date has been set for April 23–25.
   b. The Science Club's request for a table to display promotional materials was approved by Principal Huerta.
   c. Awards have been decided.  They will be given to first-, second-, and third-place winners by grade level in 12 different categories.
   d. Engineers from Greenwood Laboratories will serve as judges and assist in presenting the awards.
5. New business
   a. The Club approved the purchase of a microscope as the Science Club's gift to the Greenwood High School Science Department.
   b. The club officers will present the microscope to Principal Huerta at the march meeting of the Greenwood Board of Education.
6. Adjournment

Dee McClinton adjourned the meeting at 3:10 p.m.

## 80C

### Invoice

1. Open the *df 80c invoice* template file.
2. Key the information shown below, and then apply a 6 percent sales tax and compute the total.  There are no shipping charges.
3. **Save as:** *80c invoice*.

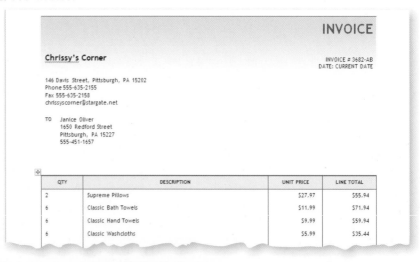

# Academic and Career Connections

Complete the following exercises that introduce various topics that involve academic themes and careers.

## Grammar and Writing: Sentence Types

**MicroType 6**

- References/Communication Skills/Sentence Types
- CheckPro/Communication Skills 8
- CheckPro/Word Choice 8

1. Go to *MicroType 6* and use this feature path for review: References/Communication Skills/Sentence Types.
2. Click Rules and review the rules of using simple, compound, and complex sentences.
3. Then, under *Sentence Types*, click *Posttest*.
4. Follow the instructions to complete the posttest.

***Optional Activities:***
1. Go to this path: CheckPro/Communication Skills 8.
2. Complete the activities as directed.
3. Go to this path: CheckPro/Word Choice 8.
4. Complete the activities as directed.

## Communications: Speaking

You have been selected to introduce a speaker, Douglas H. Ruckert, to your class. You can find his resume in the data file ***df u09 communications***. The introduction is to be 30 seconds to 1 minute long. The audience is your classmates.

1. Review the résumé and decide which points you will include in your introduction.
2. Open a new word processing document, and key an outline of these points. Save the document as ***u09 communications***, and with permission, print a copy.
3. Practice your introduction by reading aloud. Add transitions as necessary. Pay attention to your tone of voice, facial expressions, posture, and body language. Your goal is to introduce the speaker without having to read directly from your printed document.
4. As directed by your instructor, present your introduction to the class.

## Math Skills: Probability

Matt is an actor who has just moved to New York City and is trying to find work. He is 6'2" tall, has blond hair, plays the piano, and has worked as a stand-up comedian.

1. Matt auditions for the role of a piano teacher. He learns that he is one of eight actors in contention for the role. What is the probability that Matt will get the role? Express the probability as a fraction, ratio, and percent (rounded to the nearest whole percent).
2. Matt goes to an audition for a television commercial for which the advertiser is seeking four males with blond hair who are at least 6' tall. If Matt is one of 20 males who meet these qualifications, what is the probability that he will get the part? Express the probability as a fraction, ratio, and percent (rounded to the nearest whole percent).
3. Matt finds a job working as a comedian in a nightclub. Every Saturday, the club holds a competition in which the audience votes for the best comedian. The winner receives $250. If Matt is one of 12 comedy acts, what is the probability that he will win? Express the probability as a fraction, ratio, and percent (rounded to the nearest whole percent).

Interestingly enough, most of Edison's learning ^took^ place at home under the guidance of his mother. "Nancy Edison's secret: she was more dedicated than any teacher was likely to be, and she had the flexibility to experiment with various ways of nurturing her son's live for learning."[2]

## Benjamin Franklin

Benjamin Franklin was a man of many talents. He was an inventor, printer, diplomat, philosopher, author, postmaster, and leader. A few of his more noteworthy accomplishments included serving on the committee that created the Declaration of Independence; ~publishing~ Poor Richard's Almanac; and ~inventing~ the lightning rod, ~the~ Franklin stove, ~the~ odometer, and bifocal glasses.

## Abraham Lincoln

For many Americans the impact of Abraham Lincoln is as great today as it was during his lifetime.

Abraham Lincoln is remembered for his vital role as the leader in preserving the Union and beginning the process that led to the end of slavery in the United States. He is also remembered for his character, his speeches and letters, and as a man of humble origins whose determination and perseverance led him to the nation's highest office.[3]

DS Lincoln is a great example of one who dealt positively with adversity in his personal and professional life. His contributions towards the shaping of America will be long remembered.

---

## LESSON 80

# Special Document Formatting Skills, Personal Information Management, and Web Page Design Skills

**OUTCOMES**
- Assess special documents formatting skills.
- Assess Personal Information Management and web page design skills.

**Business Documents**
- Meeting Minutes
- Invoice from Template
- Web Page with Graphics and Hyperlinks
- Contact with Attachments
- Contact Group
- Email with Delay Delivery
- Schedule a Meeting

**80B**

**Meeting Minutes**

1. Format the meeting minutes on the next page without using a template.
2. Save as: **80b minutes**.

# Career Clusters

## Planning a Career in Arts, Audio/Video Technology, & Communications

Have you ever dreamed of becoming a famous actor? Maybe you'd like to write the next Great American Novel. Perhaps you'd rather be an anchor for the evening news. Then again, maybe your goal is to operate a graphics and printing shop or manage audio/video operations for a local television station. If you're interested in the arts, communications, or entertainment, then this cluster field is for you.

### What's It Like?

Individuals who work in this field are involved in designing, producing, exhibiting, performing, writing, and publishing multimedia content including visual and performing arts and design, journalism, and entertainment services. For example:

- They set up and operate audio and video equipment, including microphones, projectors, and recording equipment for concerts, sports, and news conferences.
- They create animated images or special effects seen in movies, television programs, and computer games.
- They serve as curators for museums and galleries, directing the acquisition, storage, and exhibition of art collections.
- They write content for radio and television broadcasts, movies, and the Web.
- They set up and maintain the sophisticated equipment used to transmit communications signals around the world and enable billions of users to connect to the Internet.

Employees in these fields work in a variety of settings, from indoor broadcast booths to concert halls to outdoor sports stadiums. They might work from home or on the road, in computer labs or in offices. They are often required to travel, and many work under strict deadlines.

### Employment Outlook

Most observers expect the job growth rate within this cluster to be at about 14 percent for the foreseeable future, although in just the AV technology field, growth is expected to be closer to 20 percent. Many people are drawn to these creative fields, so the competition for jobs is tough. Employers are looking for experienced workers, preferring those with a college degree or comparable on-the-job training.

### What About You?

The Arts, AV Technology & Communications career cluster is covered in box 3 of the Interest Survey Activity you completed in Unit 1 of this text. If this box had one of the three highest scores on your survey, you should further explore the cluster's pathways and related occupations.

1. Why do you think a career in this field could be a good choice?
2. What skills can you develop now that would be helpful to a career in this field?
3. Why do you think so many people are attracted to these types of occupations?

© Sheftsoff/Shutterstock.com

### Bound Report

**Report**

Format the text at the right as a bound report with footnotes. Use **Four Outstanding Americans** for the title.

**Footnotes**

[1]**Susan Clinton,** The Story of Susan B. Anthony **(Chicago: Children's Press, 1986), p. 5.**

[2]**Jim Powell, "The Education of Thomas Edison,"** http://www.self-gov.org/ freeman/9502powe.htm**, April 25, 2000.**

[3]**"An Overview of Abraham Lincoln's Life,"** http://home .att.net/~rjnorton/ Lincoln77.html**, March 30, 2004.**

1. Open a new *Word* document and format the text below as a bound report with footnotes. Use **Four Outstanding Americans** for the title. Information for the footnotes is shown in the left column.
2. **Save as:** *79c report*.

Many outstanding Americans have influenced the past, and many more will impact the future. Choosing the "Four Greatest Americans" does injustice to the hundreds of others who left their mark on our country and diminishes their contributions. This report simply recognizes four great Americans who helped make America what it is today.

Without these four individuals, America perhaps would be quite different from the country we know. The four individuals included in this report are: Susan B. Anthony, Thomas A. Edison, Benjamin Franklin, and Abraham Lincoln.

*Susan B. Anthony*

Susan B. Anthony is noted for her advancement of women's rights. She and Elizabeth Cady Stanton organized the national woman suffrage association. The following quotation shows her commitment to the cause.

> At 7 a.m. on November 5, 1872, Susan B. Anthony broke the law by doing something she had never done before. After twenty years of working to win the vote for women, she marched to the polls in Rochester, New York, and voted. Her vote—for Ulysses S. Grant for president—was illegal. In New York state, only men were allowed to vote.[1]

Anthony continued to fight for women's rights, however, for the next 33 years of her life. Even though she died in 1906 and the amendment granting women the right to vote (nineteenth amendment) was not passed until 1920, that amendment is often called the Susan B. Anthony Amendment in honor of Anthony's efforts to advance women's rights.

*Thomas Alva Edison*

Imagine life without the incandescent light bulb, phonograph, kinetoscope (a small box for viewing moving films), or any of the other 1,090 inventions patented by Edison. Life certainly would be different without these inventions or later inventions that came as a result of Edison's work.

Complete this activity to help prepare for the Basic Office Systems & Procedures event in BPA's Administrative Support division. Participants in this event demonstrate knowledge of basic office procedures and document production.

You are in charge of fund-raising for a midsize college and are preparing to kick off a new campaign to raise money for capital improvements. You have recruited a number of alumni and student volunteers to make calls soliciting donations. You now want to provide them with an outline of proper telephone etiquette.

1. Using the Internet, research telephone etiquette. Search for tips on answering the phone, transferring calls, and placing callers on hold.
2. In a new *Word* document, prepare an outline or tip sheet based on the telephone etiquette information you gathered. Format it appropriately.
3. Now that you have your telephone etiquette document ready, you will schedule a meeting with the volunteers. Use a *Word* template to prepare an agenda for the meeting. You should cover the following:
   a. Goal of the fund-raising campaign (to raise money for capital improvements)
   b. Date the campaign begins (one week from today's date)
   c. Telephone etiquette tips
4. Format the agenda appropriately.
5. The fund-raising campaign has ended and was a great success. Use a *Word* template to create a thank you card to send to all the volunteers.

For detailed information on this event, go to www.bpa.org.

## Think Critically

1. How can understanding basic office procedures benefit you regardless of the type of job you hold?
2. Besides telephone etiquette, what other skills would help you in an office environment?
3. What can you do while you are in school to further develop your basic office procedures skills?

## School and Community
The growth of the older population (65+) in the United States is increasing at an unprecedented rate. The aging of baby boomers, better health care, and healthier lifestyles have all contributed. But even though people are living longer, the quality of life for many is dependent on the help of volunteers and non-family members. There are many ways you can volunteer to help the elderly:

- Be a friendly visitor
- Run errands
- Read a book or newspaper

- Deliver meals
- Perform seasonal yardwork
- Clean and do other basic housework

1. Contact a retirement community or organization for the elderly in your town and learn about the volunteer opportunities for people in your age group.
2. Prepare a one-page report on the organization that describes its focus, summarizes the activities for which it uses volunteers, and encourages readers to take action and volunteer their time. Share the report with your class.

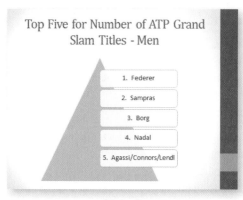

Slide 3

Slide 4

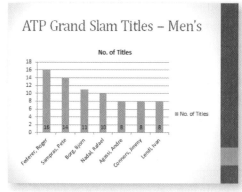

Slide 5

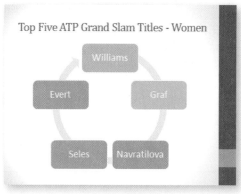

Slide 6

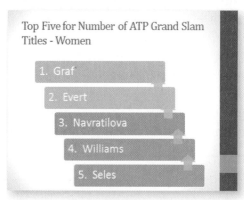

Slide 7

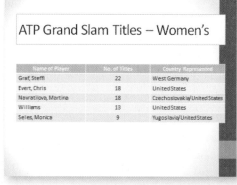

Slide 8

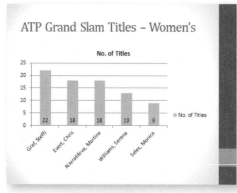

Slide 9

Slide 10

# Assessing Basic Personal Information Management (PIM) Skills

In order to complete the personal information management unit in Part 1 (Unit 10, Managing Communications and Schedules), you should have the skills and knowledge required to complete this assessment.

Create Email Subject Line

Send cc of Email

Create Body of Email

Include Bullets in Email

1. Format and key the text below as an email to your instructor. Be sure to proofread and correct all errors before sending. Use **PROFESSIONAL DEVELOPMENT OPPORTUNITIES** for the subject line. Send a copy of the email to yourself.

As you are aware, our company has implemented a new program for professional development this year. Every employee will be given time off with pay to participate in an approved seminar. Executive Development Seminars will be presenting four seminars in San Francisco August 13–17 that have been approved. These seminars include:

- Speak Like a Pro
- Write Like a Pro
- Dress Like a Pro
- Dine Like a Pro

I have placed brochures in the break room. If you are interested in attending one of the seminars, let me know, and I'll complete your registration forms.

2. Print a copy of the email.

Create Contact Folder

Enter Contacts

Print Contacts in Business Card View

3. Open *Outlook*. Create a new contact folder called **My Contacts**. Enter the information from the three business cards below into the contacts file. Print a copy of the file in Business Card view.

Technology Specialists

Erik N. Howard
310 Garrison St.
Portland, ME 04102
207.512.2846 ph
207.512.2800 fax
www.howarden@g-mail.com

**78G**

**Create Database Computed Fields**

1. Using the updated database from 78E, create a query with the three fields shown below.
2. Use the Expression Builder to create a formula to calculate the Amount Due for each registrant.
3. **Save as:** *Amount Due — New York Seminars.*

| Executive Development Seminars | |
|---|---|
| **The query should include:** | |
| 1.<br>2.<br>3. | Last Name<br>First Name<br>Amount Due |
| **Formula for Amount Due** | *To be determined by student.* |

## LESSON 79 — Presentation Skills and Report Formatting Skills

**OUTCOME**
- Assess presentation and report formatting skills.

**Business Documents**
- Presentation
- Bound Report

**79B**

**Presentation**

1. Open the *PowerPoint* file **df 79b presentation** and create the slides shown below and on the next page, using the Adjacency design theme.
2. Apply the following transitions:
   Slides 2 and 6: *Honeycomb*
   Slides 3 and 7: *Vortex*
   Slides 4 and 8: *Shred*
   Slides 5 and 9: *Rotate*
   Slide 10: *Switch*
3. Apply the following animations:
   Slide 3 and 7: *Wheel*
   Special Effects: 8 spokes, one-by-one sequence
4. **Save as:** *79b presentation.*

Slide 1

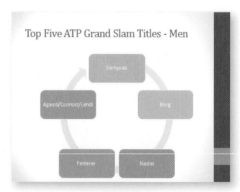
Slide 2

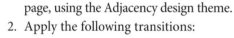

Brandon J. Phelps

General Contractor

216 Robinhood Road
Portland, ME 04107

(307) 626-2300
(307) 626-2301 fax
www.bjphelps@yahoo.com

Rebecca A. Kent
Local Sales Agent

Rodriguez
REAL ESTATE
COMPANY

207-383-1599
rakent@yahoo.com

10 Knickerbocker Rd.
Portland, ME 04108

---

Enter Appointments in
*Outlook* Calendar

Change Calendar View
to Work Week

Print Calendar

4.  Record the appointments shown below.
5.  Change the calendar view to Work Week.
6.  Print a copy of the calendar for the week.

- Board Meeting on June 18, 2014, from 8 to 11:30 a.m. in the Lincoln Conference Room.
- Board Luncheon on June 18, 2014, from 12:00 to 1:30 at Bartorolli's.
- Jamison Russell, Vice President of Riley Manufacturing, on June 17, 2014, from 1:30 to 3:00.
- Vivian Bloomfield, Manager of Garnett Enterprises, on June 19, 2014, from 8:30 to 9:30.
- Chamber of Commerce meeting on June 17, 2014, from 5:30 to 7:30 p.m. at Carter's Restaurant.

---

Create Notes Folder

Input Notes

Categorize Notes as
*High Importance*

7.  Create a new notes folder labeled **email Assessment.**
8.  Input the notes shown below using the Notes feature.

- Get the agenda ready for the June 23 opening meeting with branch managers.  Tag as *High Importance*.
- Call Brookstone Travel Agency to discuss discounts for volume travel.
- Check with Paul to discuss his role at the branch managers meeting.
- Schedule meeting with Ms. St. Claire to finalize board luncheon.  Tag as *High Importance*.
- Call Jamal Carter to get report on the Gender Communication seminar.

---

1. Open the *Access* file **df 78e database**.
2. Update the database table (*New York Seminar – September 8–11*) to include the last two registrants for the New York seminars.
3. After entering the two registrants, continue on with 78F.

| Field | Registrant | Registrant |
|---|---|---|
| Last Name: | Sanchez | Canfield |
| First Name: | Maria | Gerald |
| Middle Initial: | S. | W. |
| Street Address: | 318 Harbor View Avenue | 508 Park Place |
| City: | Boston | New York City |
| State: | MA | NY |
| ZIP: | 02191 | 14301 |
| Phone: | (837) 212-0929 | (646) 380-0055 |
| Speak Like a Pro: | | $259.00 |
| Write Like a Pro: | | $319.00 |
| Dress Like a Pro: | | |
| Dine Like a Pro: | | |
| All Four Seminars: | $750.00 | |

1. Using the updated database from 78E, create the following three queries. Save each query using the name provided.

| | Executive Development Seminars | | |
|---|---|---|---|
| **No.** | **Query** | **Fields to Include** | **Criteria** |
| 1 | *Who registered for all four of the* New York *seminars?*<br><br>Save as: **All Four New York Seminar Registrants** | *First Name*<br>*Last Name*<br>*All Four Seminars* | *To be determined by student.* |
| 2 | *How many of those attending the New York seminar are coming from out of state?*<br><br>Save as: **New York Out of State Registrants** | *First Name*<br>*Last Name*<br>*State* | *To be determined by student.* |
| 3 | *How many of those attending the New York seminar are from Brooklyn?*<br><br>Save as: **New York City Registrants** | *First Name*<br>*Last Name*<br>*City* | *To be determined by student.* |

# Managing Communications and Schedules

**Lesson 56** Manage Contact List
**Lesson 57** Create and Edit Contact Groups
**Lesson 58** Organize and Manage Emails

**Lesson 59** Manage Emails by Rules
**Lesson 60** Schedule Meetings with Calendars
**Lesson 61** Share and Print Calendars

## Reference Guide

**Managing Messages, Contacts, and Calendars**

To keep track of your personal friends and business associates, your email contact list can be used to create Contact Groups connected to you. For example, you can have study groups, sports teams, church groups, and other associations. You can add or remove members of these groups as necessary. These groups allow you to send email messages to the group rather than having to send messages individually.

Smartphones, tablets, and other mobile devices have made email and messaging more accessible than ever. The vast amounts of email being sent and received have made managing and classifying messages more difficult. How do you separate the "junk" from the "good stuff"? How do you set up a system to help you organize your messages so you can find them later? Junk filters and rules help you automatically sort through your email messages and more efficiently address those of importance.

Managing your time is difficult. Whether you are a student or a business professional, it is sometimes hard to keep track of all the responsibilities and tasks you need to remember. You can use your calendar program to keep track of your class schedule and appointments, schedule meetings, and share your schedule with others. Managing your schedule using a calendar can increase productivity while maximizing the time you spend with friends and family. Software such as *Microsoft Outlook* (Figure 10-1) combines these functions in one location.

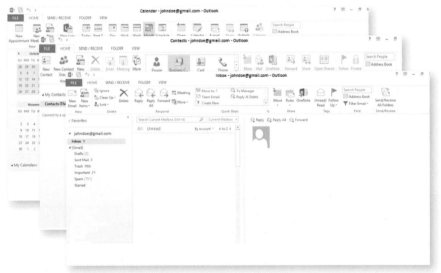

**Figure 10-1** *Microsoft Outlook* manages messages, contacts, and schedules

8. Separate the names in column A so the first names remain in A and the last names appear in column B. Change the column headings to **First Name** and **Last Name**. Adjust width of columns A to D to fit the contents.

9. Sort by Class (A–Z); then by Homeroom (Smallest to Largest); then by Last Name (A–Z).

10. Insert a page break so the Juniors print on page 1 and Seniors print on page 2.

11. Set up the pages so they will print horizontally and vertically centered in landscape orientation with gridlines showing. Column headings in rows 1 and 2 (cell range A1:H2) are to be repeated on page 2.

12. Add shading and color as desired.

13. Change font size as desired.

14. Make other formatting changes as desired.

15. Insert your name as a centered header in 14-point font and today's date as a right-aligned footer in 14-point font.

16. Hide the *Class* column.

17. Rename Sheet 1 tab **1st Quarter**.

18. Print the worksheet.

19. **Save as:** *78b worksheet*.

## 78C

### Column Chart

1. Key the worksheet below.

| Student | GPA |
|---|---|
| **Sally** | |
| Freshman | 3.24 |
| Sophomore | 3.56 |
| Junior | 3.42 |
| Senior | 3.78 |
| **Carlos** | |
| Freshman | 3.18 |
| Sophomore | 3.71 |
| Junior | 3.54 |
| Senior | 3.55 |

2. Create a Column chart for Sally. Move it to a New sheet. Rename Chart1 worksheet tab **Sally's GPA**.

3. Insert **Sally's Grade Point Average** as the chart title; remove the legend; display the GPA value outside the end of each column; insert **Year in School** as a horizontal axis title; insert **Grade Point Average** as vertical text beside the vertical axis.

4. Print the chart.

5. **Save as:** *78c worksheet*.

## 78D

### Sparkline Graphics

1. If needed, open *78c worksheet*.

2. Insert a row before Carlos.

3. In cell B7, insert a Line Sparkline graphic.

4. In cell B13, insert a Column Sparkline graphic.

5. **Save as:** *78d worksheet* as a PDF file.

## Editing Contacts

People/Double-click contact

When you create a business or personal contact, you store information about that person such as address, phone number, and job title. You can also record notes such as the name of a project you worked on together. It is important to keep your contact information current and accurate. You can edit existing contact information quickly and easily.

## Adding Attachments to Contacts

People/Double-click contact/Insert/Include/ Attach File

You can add attachments to your contact information. Items such as pictures, tables, graphs, or any item associated with the contact can be added to your contact information. Any files you attach to a contact are displayed in the Notes section of the Contact window. You can also attach an Outlook Item, an additional Business Card, or Signature.

## Viewing Contacts

People/Home/Current View

The People view is an easy way to quickly view a person's contact information (from all different sources) in the Preview Pane. The People view combines duplicate contacts and information from multiple email accounts, instant messaging, calendar, and updates from social networks including Facebook and LinkedIn.

Business Card view displays contact information as business cards. Phone view arranges your contact information by name, company, and phone number. List view provides all the contact's information in a list format. Card view is similar to Business Card, but contact information and any attached documents are listed in boxes.

## Sorting Contacts

People/View/Arrangement

Depending on the view you select, you can sort your contact list in a variety of methods. In the Business Card view, you can reverse the alphabetic listing of your contacts. In the Phone or List view, you can sort alphabetically, by categories, by location, or by company. Consider the information you are trying to find to determine the appropriate view and sort method. For example, if you are looking for all contacts by company, you would select the List view and Company sort. You can also change the view of your contact list from the View tab.

## Contact Groups

People/Home/New/New Contact Group

When you frequently email several contacts as a group for personal or work purposes, you can create a **Contact Group** and name it. A Contact Group allows you to work more efficiently when emailing because you can send a message to the group rather than to each contact individually. For example, you could create a group named Friends and add your friends to the group. Whenever you want to send the same email message to all your friends, you enter the Contact Group, Friends, as the recipient, and every group member will receive the email message.

## Add/Remove Name to Contact Group

People/Home/My Contacts (on Navigation menu)/Double-click Group/Add Members or Remove Member

As the group changes, you can add or remove its members. When you add a member, you can choose the source of the contact information you want to add to your Contact Group. Removing a contact from a Contact Group does not delete the contact from your contact list or address book.

| Central Administration Support Services Staffing Chart | | | |
|---|---|---|---|
| Current Position Title | Proposed Position Title | Immediate Supervisor | Administrators and Staff Supported |
| Secretary | Confidential Senior Administrative Assistant, Superintendent | D. Griffiths, Superintendent | • D. Griffiths, Superintendent<br>• C. Nezzo, Director of Student Achievement<br>• B. Zestawniak, Public Relations Director |
| Clerk | Administrative Assistant, General and Business Operations | J. Zanone, Business Manager | • J. Zanone, Business Manager<br>• C. Nezzo, Director of Student Achievement<br>• B. Zestawniak, Public Relations Director |
| Payroll Officer | Administrative Assistant, Payroll and Personnel | | • J. Zanone, Business Manager |
| Bookkeeper | Administrative Assistant, Financial Operations | | • J. Zanone, Business Manager |

## 77H

**Table**

1. Open the *Word* document *df 77h table*.
2. Convert the text to a table.
3. Format the table so it is easy to read and attractive.
4. **Save as:** *77h table*.

## LESSON 78 — Spreadsheet and Database Skills

**OUTCOME**
- Assess spreadsheet and database skills.

**Business Documents**
- Multiple-Page Worksheet
- Column Chart
- Worksheet with Sparkline Graphics
- Database Table
- Database Queries

## 78B

**Worksheet**

1. Open the *Excel* file *df 78b worksheet*.
2. In cell G1, key **Total 1st Quarter Hours** (use Wrap Text) as a column heading, and then calculate the total hours for each student in column G.
3. Specify column widths as follows: columns E, F, and G at 12.
4. Insert a row at the top, and key **FIRST QUARTER COMMUNITY SERVICE HOMEROOM LEADERS** centered across all columns.
5. Center-align all cells except A3:A24.
6. Make all row heights 24 pts. except row 2.
7. Rotate the text in row 2 to 75°, and adjust row height to 90. Horizontally center-align all row 2 text, if needed.

## Printing a Contact List

People/File/Print/Settings/
Print

You can print one or all of your contacts in several different views or print styles—see Table 10-1. Having a printout of all contacts can serve as reference material if your storage medium is lost or becomes corrupted and you need to recreate your contact list.

| Table 10-1 Print Styles for Contacts | |
|---|---|
| Card | List contacts separated by alphabet dividers with space for adding contacts. |
| Small Booklet | List contacts similar to Card style, but designed to be folded into a small booklet. |
| Medium Booklet | List contacts similar to Card style, but designed to be folded into a medium-sized booklet. |
| Memo | Each contact is printed on a page formatted like a memo. |
| Phone Directory | List only contacts and phone numbers. |

## New Email Folders

Mail/Folder/New/New
Folder

A cluttered and unorganized mailbox can make it difficult to find the email you need. By creating new mail folders, you can group messages related to each other. For example, you can group messages by project, topic, contact, or other categories that make sense to you. You can even create a folder for all the messages from your friends or family.

© iStockphoto.com/Squaredpixels

1. Open *Word* and create a 7 × 6 table grid.
2. Set column 1 width at 0.7"; set columns 2–7 width at 0.6"; set row 1 height at 1".
3. Bottom center-align cells in row 1.
4. Center-align cells A2:A6.
5. Set a decimal tab at or near the center of cells B2:G6.
6. Key the table below.

| Zone | Time | Gal per Min | Monday | Wednesday | Friday | Sunday |
|------|------|-------------|--------|-----------|--------|--------|
| 1 | 6.7 | 15.8 | | | 0 | |
| 2 | 10 | 14 | 0 | | 0 | |
| 3 | 8.15 | 12.25 | | | | |
| 4 | 9.33 | 1.3 | 0 | 0 | | 0 |
| Totals | | | | | | |

7. Merge cells A6:C6 and right-align the cell contents.
8. Insert a row at the top. Set its height to 0.17". Merge cells A1:A2; merge cells B1:B2; merge cells C1:C2.
9. Merge cells D1:G1; key **Irrigation Days** in the merged cells; center-align the text.
10. Insert a row at the top; merge the cells; key **IRRIGATION SYSTEM WATER USAGE** in the merged cells; center-align the text.
11. Key a formula in each empty cell in range D2:G5 that calculates the gallons used each day to two decimal places.
12. Key a formula in cells D6:G6 that calculates the total for each day.
13. Center the table on the page.
14. Bold rows 1, 2, 3, and 8.
15. Increase top and bottom cell margins to 0.03".
16. Save as: *77f table*.

1. Open a blank *Word* document.
2. Key the table on the next page using the following formatting guides:
   a. Set row height so each row is at least 0.5".
   b. Set column A width to 1.25", columns B and D to 2.5", and column C to 1.5".
   c. Use Align Center in cells in rows 1 and 2; use Align Center Left in cells in rows 3–5.
   d. Center the table on the page in landscape orientation.
   e. Apply shading as shown.
3. Save as: *77g table*.

## Junk Email Folder

**Mail/Home/Junk Email Folder**

A message suspected of being junk is moved to the Junk Email folder. You should periodically check messages in the Junk Email folder to verify that legitimate messages were not classified as junk. See Figure 10-2.

**Figure 10-2** Junk email folder

## Junk Email Filter

**Mail/Home/Delete/Junk/ Junk Email Options**

The Junk Email filter helps reduce unwanted messages in your Inbox. Junk mail, also known as **spam**, is moved by the filter to the Junk Email folder. The filter evaluates each incoming message to assess whether or not it might be spam, based on several factors such as the message content and the time the message was sent. By default, the Junk Email filter is turned on and the protection level is Low. This protection level catches only the most obvious spam. You can make the Junk Email filter more aggressive by changing the level of protection. See Figure 10-3.

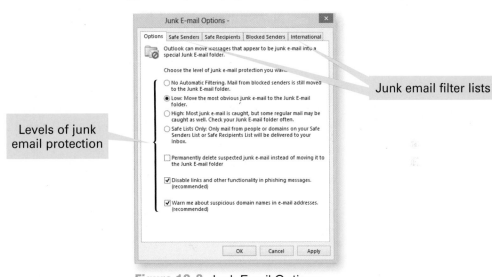

**Figure 10-3** Junk Email Options

## Junk Email Filter Lists

**Mail/Home/Delete/Junk/ Junk Email Options/ (see tabs)**

While the Junk Email filter checks all incoming messages automatically, the Junk Email filter lists give you more control over what is considered spam. You can add names, email addresses, and domains to these lists so the filter allows for messages from sources you do trust, or block messages that arrive from specific email addresses and domains that you do not know or trust. See Figure 10-3 for the filter lists available to you. Each filter tab focuses on a characteristic of the message:

**Safe Senders**—email from addresses or domain names on your Safe Senders List will never be treated as junk email.

**Safe Recipients**—email sent to addresses or domain names on your Safe Recipients List will never be treated as junk mail.

**Block Senders**—email from addresses or domain names on your Block Senders List will always be treated as junk email.

**International**—Block messages that come from another country/region or that appear in another character or alphabet.

**Two-Page Memo**

1. Open the *Word* file *df 77c memo*.
2. Read and follow the directions in the comments and then delete the comments.
3. Accept or reject the tracked changes.
4. Proofread the document carefully. Use Track Changes to mark additional changes that you believe should be made.
5. Print the final copy of the memo with your markups showing.
6. **Save as:** *77c memo*.

**77D**

**Business Letter**

1. Key the following letter in modified block format using mixed punctuation and no ¶ indentations.
2. **Save as:** *77d letter*; do not close the file.

June 9, 20-- | Mrs. Vera L. Bowden | 3491 Rose Street | Minneapolis, MN 55441-5781 | Dear Mrs. Bowden | SUBJECT: YOUR DONATION

What a pleasant surprise it was to find your $50 donation to Beta Xi in my mail this morning. I think it is great that you thought of Beta Xi and decided to help members of your local chapter serve those who are less fortunate.

Your contribution will be used to purchase food and clothing for young children in our community as part of Community Day. As you know, Beta Xi, Minnesota Epsilon Chapter, conducts a fall drive to support this event.

I have heard about the success you are having in microbiology. Perhaps you would return to speak to our Beta Xi members? Please let me know if you can.

Yours truly | Miss Amelia R. Carter | Beta Xi Sponsor |xx | Enclosure | c Thomas Turnball, Treasurer |A receipt is enclosed since your contribution is tax deductible.

**77E**

**Business Letter**

1. Open *77d letter*, if needed.
2. Format the letter in block style with open punctuation; delete the enclosure notation and postscript; add **Facsimile** as a mailing notation; make the necessary changes on the original to change the copy notation to a blind copy notation.
3. Change side margins to 1.25" and font to 12-point Times New Roman.
4. **Save as:** *77e letter*.

## Managing Email by Rules

Another method in managing your email messages is the creation of rules for your email account. A **rule** is an action you create to automatically handle particular emails in a certain way. Rules fall into two categories—organization and notification. Rules do not operate on messages that have been read, only on those that are unread. The Rules Wizard includes templates for the most frequently used rules, which include:

**Staying Organized**—Helps you file and follow up on messages. For example, email from addresses or domain names on your Safe Senders List will never be treated as junk email.

**Stay Up to Date**—Notifies you in some way when you receive a particular message. For example, you can create a rule that automatically alerts your mobile device when you receive an email message from a friend.

## Delaying Delivery

Mail/Home/New/New
Email/Options/More
Options/Delay Delivery

If you want an email to be delivered to a contact on a particular future date and time, use the Delay Delivery feature. To send the message as specified, the software must be running and connected to the email server at the selected time. If the software is not running or connected at the specified time, the message will be sent when the software is launched and connected to the email server.

## Voting

Mail/Home/New/New
Email/Options/Tracking/
Use Voting Buttons

The Voting Buttons allow contacts reading the message to vote for any options you specify in the email if their email software supports this feature. As recipients vote, the votes are sent to you as special email messages.

## Auto Replying to Emails

If you are on vacation or a business trip, you might want to notify people who contact you that you are "Out of the Office" and provide an alternative method to contact you or someone else for assistance. Auto Reply gives you that option. You will need to create a template and a rule in order to make this function work for you.

## Creating Meetings

Calendar/Home/New/New
Meeting

In a business, you will likely have to schedule meetings with colleagues or reply to a meeting invitation. A **meeting** is an appointment that includes others to whom you send an invitation. The person who creates the meeting and sends the invitation is the **meeting organizer**. The meeting organizer schedules a meeting by creating an email meeting request or invitation to a meeting that is sent to each attendee.

## Replying to a Meeting Request

In many cases, the meeting organizer would like the attendees to respond whether or not they can attend the meeting. If the meeting organizer requests a response and the attendee's software supports this feature, the attendee can choose from four response options: Accept, Tentative, Decline, or Propose New Time.

If the attendee accepts or tentatively accepts a meeting request, the invitation is deleted from the Inbox, and the meeting is added to his or her calendar. A meeting response is sent to the meeting organizer. The meeting response can be found in the Sent Items folder.

If the attendee declines the meeting request, it is deleted from his or her Inbox and the meeting is not added to the calendar. A reply response is sent to the meeting organizer and can be found in the Sent Items folder.

Key 2 5' writings on all ¶s combined; find *gwam* and errors.

 all letters used                                    gwam  3' | 5'

Being able to communicate well is one of the leading keys      4 | 2 | 42

to the success of any business.  Information must move outside a    8 | 5 | 45

business and up, down, and sideways within a business so people   12 | 8 | 48

can use acquired facts to make good decisions.  The report is one   17 | 10 | 50

medium that a business can use to relay information in internal   21 | 13 | 53

and external directions.                                          23 | 14 | 54

A business report is generally thought to be a written mes-    27 | 16 | 56

sage that is used to make business decisions.  To be of value,   31 | 19 | 59

the message must be based on factual information rather than   35 | 21 | 61

fancy and should be presented in a format that is easy to read,   39 | 24 | 64

consistent in style, neat, and free of keying and language skills   44 | 26 | 66

errors.                                                           44 | 26 | 67

Business reports can be done in many formats.  Informal ones   48 | 29 | 69

can utilize a letter or memo style.  Progress, proposal, annual,   52 | 32 | 72

or other major reports are often done in a formal style.  These   57 | 34 | 74

formal reports have a required style for margins, spacing, and   61 | 37 | 77

headings and often have parts such as a title page, a table of   65 | 39 | 79

contents, and an abstract.                                        67 | 40 | 80

 gwam 3' | ___1___|___2___|___3___|___4___|
            5' | _____1_____|_____2_____|_____3_____|

## Proposing a New Meeting Time

If the attendee has a conflict with the meeting request, he or she can propose a new time for the meeting. A proposal is sent to the meeting organizer via email indicating that the attendee tentatively accepts the request, but proposes the meeting be held at a different time or date.

## Creating Additional Calendars

Calendar/Folder/New/New Calendar

In addition to your main calendar, you can create other calendars. For example, you can create a calendar for personal appointments.

## Printing Calendars

Calendar/File/Print/ Settings

You can print a daily, weekly, or monthly view of your calendar for posting or sharing with friends or colleagues. Table 10-2 lists the print styles available for printing your calendar from Calendar View.

| Table 10-2 Print Styles for Calendar | |
|---|---|
| Daily | Prints a daily appointment schedule for a specific date including one day per page, a daily task list, an area for notes, and a two-month calendar. |
| Weekly Agenda | Prints a seven-day calendar with one week per page and a two-month calendar. |
| Weekly Calendar | Prints a seven-day calendar with one week per page, an hourly schedule, and a two-month calendar. |
| Monthly | Prints five weeks per page of a particular month or date range and a two-month calendar. |
| Tri-fold | Prints each day, including a daily task list and a weekly schedule. |
| Calendar Details | Prints calendar items and supporting details. |

© iStockphoto.com/Johnnyscriv

# UNIT 14 — Assessing Intermediate Information Management Skills

**Lesson 77** Input Skills, Correspondence, and Table Formatting Skills

**Lesson 78** Spreadsheet and Database Skills

**Lesson 79** Presentation Skills and Report Formatting Skills

**Lesson 80** Special Document Formatting Skills, Personal information Management, and Web Page Design Skills

---

## LESSON 77 — Input Skills, Correspondence, and Table Formatting Skills

### OUTCOMES
- Assess input speed and accuracy skills.
- Assess memo and letter formatting skills.

### Business Documents
- Two-Page Memo with Table
- Business Letter in Modified Block Format
- Business Letter in Block Format
- Table with Merged Cells and Rotated Text
- Table with shading in Landscape Orientation
- Table from Text

### 77A–80A

**Warmup**

Key each line twice at the beginning of each lesson; first for control, then speed.

| | | |
|---|---|---|
| alphabet | 1 | Mrs. Gaznox was quite favorably pleased with the market projects. |
| fig/sym | 2 | Book prices increased 17% from 05/09/06 to 08/03/06 in 42 stores. |
| speed | 3 | The widow may visit the city to see the robot shape an auto body. |

gwam 1' | 1 | 2 | 3 | 4 | 5 | 6 | 7 | 8 | 9 | 10 | 11 | 12 | 13 |

# LESSON 56

## Manage Contact List

**OUTCOMES**

- Edit contacts.
- Add attachments to contacts.
- View and sort contact list.

### Business Documents

**56A–61A**

- Email Contacts
- Resume

### Conditioning Practice

Key each line twice daily.

| | | |
|---|---|---|
| alphabet | 1 | Jewel had Zeb quickly give him five or six points on the test. |
| fig/sym | 2 | I did receive checks #456 & #869, which total $12,790, on 03/18/12. |
| speed | 3 | He paid the man eight bucks for the big antique ornament and map. |

**gwam** 1' | 1 | 2 | 3 | 4 | 5 | 6 | 7 | 8 | 9 | 10 | 11 | 12 | 13 |

### 56B

**Learn: Create New Contacts**

1. Open *df 56b contacts*.
2. Key the six contacts into your contact list.
3. Select five friends or family members, and add them to your contact list. For their Job Title, key **Friend** or **Family**.

### 56C

**Learn: Edit Contacts**

1. Read the following information about editing contacts, and complete the activity.

After contacts have been keyed into your contact list, they can be easily edited.

> People/Double-click contact

- Double-click the contact file.
- Key the new or additional information.
- Click Save & Close. See Figure 10-4.

Add missing data or key updated contact information

**Figure 10-4**
Editing Contact information

2. For Mike Sweety, add the phone number **919-449-8767** and change his title to **Owner**.
3. For Kathryn Zinna, add the email address kzina@fullertown.net.
4. For Mark Cummings, add the web page address www.FullertownBakerySupply.com.
5. For Misty Walker, add the fax number **919-888-4949**.
6. For Pat Smith, change the Job Title to **CFO**.

Key two 3' or 5' writings on the three ¶s; determine *gwam*; count errors.

 **A**   all letters used

gwam | 3' | 5'

Have you ever stopped to ponder how important science is in    4  | 2

your daily life?  Science is important to everyone.  It has played    8  | 5

a part in many amazing advances that make our homes, schools, and    13 | 8

work activities easier and more pleasant.  Science has improved how    17 | 10

we produce goods, provide services, get from one place to another,    21 | 13

and speak to each other.  Science has even made it possible for    26 | 15

us to live longer.    27 | 16

Your science education began in elementary school in the    31 | 19

early grades where you learned to describe, to measure, and to    35 | 21

draw conclusions.  You got simple explanations of what makes it    40 | 24

rain, what keeps airplanes in the sky, and how sound moves so    44 | 26

quickly from one place in the world to another through or without    48 | 29

wires.  From these general ideas about the world, you began to    52 | 31

build an understanding of science.    55 | 33

In subsequent grades, science learning was more formal when    59 | 35

it became a separate subject.  In high school you are likely to    63 | 38

take a science course each year so that you can learn more about    67 | 40

the specific fields of science.  In addition, you are apt to take    72 | 43

other courses and complete projects that enable you to apply the    76 | 46

science concepts learned in your specific science courses.    80 | 48

gwam | 3' | 1 | 2 | 3 | 4
      | 5' | 1 | 2 | 3

## Learn: Add Attachments to Contacts

People/Double-click contact/Insert/Include/ Attach File

1. Read the following information about attachments, and complete the activity.

In your contact information, you may want to add a photo, resume, or other documents.

- Select the contact and click the Insert tab. Click Attach File in the Include group.
- Navigate to the file location using the Insert File dialog box.
- Click Insert. The file is attached and can be found in the Notes section of your contact information. See Figure 10-5.

Insert tab

Include/ Attach file

Notes section

**Figure 10-5** Contact attachments

2. Open the contact Janice Coats. Attach *df 56d resume* to her contact.
3. In the Notes section, key **Janice Coats Resume**.
4. Return to the Contact tab, and click Save & Close.

## Learn: View and Sort Contacts

People/Home/Current View and People/View/ Arrangement

**Figure 10-6** View contacts

1. Read the following information, and complete the activity.

To change the contact view, select the icon for the view arrangement you want. See Figure 10-6. The view you choose will depend on the task and the information from your contacts you need to access. You can also change the view of your contacts from Change View. See Figure 10-7.

To sort contacts, select the view you want, and tap the View tab if necessary. The sort options available are displayed in the Arrangement group. Notice that you can only access the Categories, Location, and Company sorts in the Phone and List views. See Figure 10-7.

Change View

Sort Arrangements

**Figure 10-7** Sort contacts

2. Select the Business Card view. Notice the contacts appear as regular business cards.
3. Select the People view. Notice that you can link to your contacts' Facebook accounts, add alternate email addresses, etc.
4. Select the Phone view. The contacts change so the phone number is easier to read.
5. From the Phone view, select Company. The contacts are arranged by company.
6. Change the view and arrangement to the settings you find most useful.

# SKILL BUILDER 2

**OUTCOMES**
- Improve keying techniques.
- Improve keying speed and accuracy.

## Warmup

Key each line twice, first for control and then for speed.

alphabet 1 If Marjorie has extra help, jigsaw puzzles can be solved quickly.

fig/sym 2 Tom mailed checks #398 & #401 to show he paid for Model #325-769.

speed 3 The busy maid is to rush the clay to the eight girls in the dorm.

gwam 1' | 1 | 2 | 3 | 4 | 5 | 6 | 7 | 8 | 9 | 10 | 11 | 12 | 13 |

## Technique: Letter Keys

Key each line twice. Emphasize continuity and rhythm with curved, upright fingers.

**Technique Cue**
Keep fingers curved and upright.

I 1 Michigan, Illinois, Indiana, and Missouri are all in the Midwest.

J 2 Jeff juggled jobs to join Jane for juice with the judge and jury.

K 3 Katie knocked the knickknacks off the kiosk with her knobby knee.

L 4 Please allow me to be a little late with all legal illustrations.

M 5 Mary is immensely immature; her mannerisms make me extremely mad.

N 6 Nancy knew she would win the nomination at their next convention.

O 7 Roberto opposed opening the store on Monday mornings before noon.

P 8 Pam wrapped the peppermints in purple paper for the photographer.

Q 9 Qwin quietly queried Quincy on the quantity and quality of quail.

gwam 1' | 1 | 2 | 3 | 4 | 5 | 6 | 7 | 8 | 9 | 10 | 11 | 12 | 13 |

## Technique: Keystroking Patterns

Key each line twice.

**Technique Cue**
Key at a continuous pace; eliminate pauses

**Adjacent key**
1 are ire err her cash said riot lion soil join went wean news
2 pew art sort try tree post upon copy opera three maker waste
3 sat riot coil were renew forth trade power grope score owner

**One hand**
4 ad bar car deed ever feed hill jump look null noon poll upon
5 him joy age kiln noun loop moon bear casts deter edges facet
6 get are save taste versa wedge hilly imply phony union yummy

**Balanced hand**
7 go aid bid dish elan fury glen half idle jamb lend make name
8 oak pay hen quay rush such urus vial works yamen amble blame
9 cot duty goal envy focus handy ivory lapel oriel prowl queue

gwam 1' | 1 | 2 | 3 | 4 | 5 | 6 | 7 | 8 | 9 | 10 | 11 | 12 |

## Learn: Printing A Contact List

People/File/Print/Settings/ Print

1. Read the following information, and complete the activity.

For various reasons, you may wish to have a hard copy of your contact list—for example, if your storage medium is lost or becomes corrupted. However, before you print, you need to specify how you want the contacts to be printed. You can choose from Card, Small Booklet, Medium Booklet, Memo, and Phone Directory. See Table 10-1 for an explanation of the various print settings. You can print one, all, or a selection of contacts in your list. Follow the steps below. See Figure 10-8.

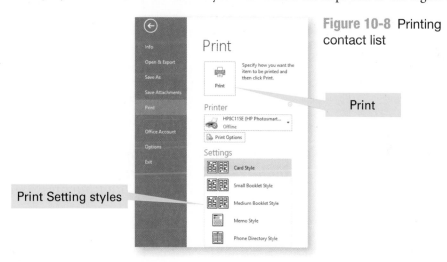

**Figure 10-8** Printing contact list

**To print one contact in your list:**

- From Contacts, double-click the contact you wish to print.
- Then click File, click Print, select a style, and click Print.

**To print all contacts in your list:**

- From Contacts, click File, click Print, select a Setting, and click Print.

People/View/Current View/ View Settings

**To print a subset of your contacts:**

- Click Filter and key a descriptor such as business names or last names separated by a comma in the Search box. Select name fields only to describe which fields should be filtered. Click OK and OK once more to close both dialog boxes. See Figure 10-9.
- Your selected contact will be shown; click File, Print, select Setting, and Print. To reset contacts, click Reset View and click "yes" when prompted.

People/View/Current View/ Reset View

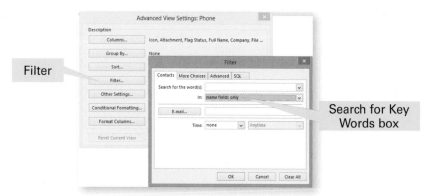

**Figure 10-9** Filtering contact list

2. From your contact list, print all your *Friends and Family* contacts in Phone Book style.

**Mail Merge**
**June 19**

From the desk of:
**Julia Kingsley**
*Prepare a mail merge letter from the information shown at the right so we will be ready to send checks to the refs tomorrow. Since the letter is relatively short, leave a 2.8" top margin for better balance. Save the form letter, and print the letter to Ms. Tarantino.*
*JK*

June 20, 20—


«Title»«First_Name»«Last_Name»
«Address»
«City», «State»«Zip»

Dear «Title»«Last_Name»:

Enclosed is your check for $«Amount» for the work you did at the "Hoops" tournament this week. Based on the feedback we received, the refereeing was outstanding. Thank you for helping make this week's tournament so successful.

As always, we are looking for ways to improve our tournaments. If you have any suggestions, please let us know. Our contact information is on the enclosed business card.

We look forward to seeing and working with you at future "Hoops" tournaments.

Warmest regards,


Todd McLemore
Tournament Director

# LESSON 57    Create and Edit Contact Groups

**OUTCOMES**

- Create a Contact Group.
- Add/remove contacts from group.
- Print contacts.

## Business Document

**57B**

- Contact Groups

**Learn: Create Contact Groups**

People/Home/New/New Contact Group

1. Read the following information about Contact Groups, and complete the activity.

Often, you will want to send the same information to several contacts in your contact list. Creating a Contact Group will allow you to send emails more efficiently. An email message addressed to a Contact Group is sent to every member of the group. Rather than sending multiple individual messages, you send only one message. For example, you can send a message to the 25 members of the drama club by placing the members in a Contact Group and sending a single message to the group.

- When you click New Contact Group, an Untitled—Contact Group window is displayed. See Figure 10-10.
- Key the name of the new group; then click Save & Close.

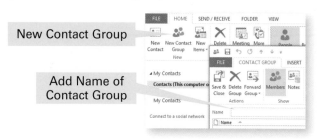

**Figure 10-10** New Contact Group

2. Create a Contact Group and name it **Bakery Businesses**. Click Save & Close.

**57C**

**Learn: Add Members to a Contact Group**

People/Home/ Double-click the Contact Group/Members/ Add Members

1. Read the following information, and complete the activity.

A Contact Group is not useful until you add members to it. You will add members immediately after creating the Contact Group, and you may add members later if the group grows. It is important to keep your contact list, including your Contact Groups, up to date.

- Double-click the Contact Group.
- Click Add Members. A drop-down menu appears for you to select the source of the new group member.
- Select the source. If the source is your Address Book, double-click the contact. The selected contact appears in the Members box at the bottom of the dialog box. If there are other contacts from the Address Book you want to add, keep double-clicking until all members are selected.
- Click OK and the members are added to your Contact Group. See Figure 10-11.

**Figure 10-11** Add member to Contact Group

**Spreadsheet**

**June 18**

From the desk of:

**Julia Kingsley**

*Create a table similar to the one shown at the right for the Ref Fees for the June 15–16 Tournament. Use the spreadsheet from Job 19 to calculate the Ref Fees. Add a column for Amount Owed to the spreadsheet, and enter formulas to calculate how much each ref is owed. Include a total at the bottom of the column.*

*JK*

# Ref Fees for *June 15-16* Tournament

| Name of Ref | Amount Owed |
|---|---|
| Carlisle, Jamal | $ 00 |
| Chen, Trenton | 00 |
| Ginobli, Michael | 00 |
| Goldfarb, Farrel | 00 |
| Jackson, Tamika | 00 |
| Martinez, Travis | 00 |
| Szczerbiak, Jan | 00 |
| Tarantino, Stella | 00 |
| Totals | $ 00 |

**Job 24**

**Database**

**June 18**

From the desk of:

**Julia Kingsley**

*Create a database with the name and address for each ref who worked the June 15–16 tournament. The address information should be in the Referee folder in the Contacts file. Use the table created in Job 23 for the amount owed. Be sure to include a courtesy title for each ref. Give the database table an appropriate name.*

*JK*

2. Double-click the *Bakery Businesses* group.
3. From your Address Book, add all the contacts related to bakery businesses. You should have six contacts in the group.
4. Click Save & Close.

57D

**Learn: Remove Members from a Contact Group**

Contacts/Home/Contacts (on Navigation menu)/ Double-click the Contact Group/Select the member/ Remove Member

1. Read the following information, and complete the activity.

Over time, groups change—for example, when an employee leaves a business or a company's sales representative has changed. When members leave a group, they should be removed from the Contact Group as well.

- Double-click the Contract Group.
- Select the member you wish to remove.
- Click Remove Member; then Save & Close. See Figure 10-12.

**Figure 10-12** Remove a member from Contact Group

2. In the *Bakery Business* group, remove Misty Walker from the group.
3. Click Save & Close.

57E

**Apply: Create and Modify a Contact Group**

1. Create another Contact Group, and name it **Friends and Family**. Click Save & Close.
2. Double-click the *Friends and Family* group.
3. From your Address Book, add all of the friends and family contacts to this group. You should have five contacts in the group.
4. Remove a member from the Contact Group. Add the member to the group again, or add a different member to the group.
5. Click Save & Close.

TEAMWORK

## Digital Citizenship and Ethics
According to recent research, 60 percent of students aged 10–14 own a cell phone, as do close to 85 percent of teens between the ages of 15 and 18. While cell phones and smartphones provide a convenient and quick way to communicate and can be invaluable in emergency situations, they are also frequently misused or used irresponsibly in social and public situations. Following are some cell phone etiquette tips:

- Turn your phone off in school, theaters, libraries, and doctor's offices.
- Do not use your cell phone while you are doing something else, such as driving, riding a bike, or simply having a conversation with others.
- Do not shout or speak loudly to compensate for a bad connection.

As a class, discuss the following.

1. How is a cell phone useful for school?
2. What are some of the health risks associated with extensive cell phone usage?

| Males 15-16 Year Age Bracket Total Points | | | | | | |
|---|---|---|---|---|---|---|
| Team Name | Last Name | Initial of First Name | Game 1 Total Points | Game 2 Total Points | Game 3 Total Points | Game 4 Total Points |
| Tetons | Mathews | S. | 2 | 6 | 3 | 10 |
| Tetons | Lin | Q. | 12 | 28 | 16 | 12 |
| Tetons | Sanchez | Z. | 24 | 20 | 15 | 18 |
| Tetons | Washington | D. | 7 | 9 | 8 | 16 |
| Tetons | Smyth | I. | 5 | 9 | 6 | 15 |

| Males 15-16 Year Age Bracket Total Points | | | | | | |
|---|---|---|---|---|---|---|
| Team Name | Last Name | Initial of First Name | Game 1 Total Points | Game 2 Total Points | Game 3 Total Points | Game 4 Total Points |
| Wolves | Jeffreys | R. | 22 | 12 | 16 | 20 |
| Wolves | Kappus | G. | 13 | 16 | 8 | 9 |
| Wolves | Jennings | T. | 8 | 15 | 17 | 9 |
| Wolves | Teague | P. | 10 | 11 | 7 | 12 |
| Wolves | Fleming | C. | 2 | 0 | 15 | 12 |

## Job 22

**Form**

**June 17**

From the desk of:

**Julia Kingsley**

*After you have entered the points for the last four teams, please determine the winners of the awards and prepare a form similar to the one at the right. Use the Sort feature to determine the top five scorers in each category.*

*Record the winners based on the information in the database. The awards will be presented at the tournament next week.*

*JK*

Games of:  **June 15 - 16**

Bracket:  **Males 15 - 16**

Most Points Scored in a Single Game:

| Name | Team | Points Scored |
|---|---|---|
| Clarke, T | Pikers | 29 |
| Filippo, K. | Railroaders | 29 |
| Gonzalez, K. | Cavilers | 28 |
| Lin, Q. | Tetons | 28 |
| Montana, T. | Miner | 28 |

Most Points Scored for Tournament:

| Name | Team | Points Scored |
|---|---|---|
| Gonzalez, K. | Cavilers | 95 |
| Vermillion, A. | Shooters | 92 |
| Filippo, K. | Railroaders | 90 |
| Montana, T. | Miners | 90 |
| Nowak, S. | Pioneers | 89 |

# LESSON 58 — Organize and Manage Emails

**OUTCOMES**
- Create folders to organize/manage emails.
- Learn about the Junk Email folder.
- Use the Junk filter to remove unwanted emails.

## Business Document

### 58B

- Junk email

**Learn: Create New Folder**

Mail/Folder/New/New Folder

1. Read the following information, and complete the activity.

A cluttered and unorganized mailbox can make it difficult to find the email you need. Creating new mail folders can be used to reduce the clutter.

- From the Create New Folder dialog box, key the name of the new folder. See Figure 10-13. Click OK. Your new folder appears in the Navigation pane on the left. To further organize your files, you can create folders within folders. For example, within a folder named School Activities, you may have other folders to separate school projects, sports teams, and FBLA activities.
- In the Navigation pane, right-click the folder you want to organize.
- Click New Folder and key the name in the dialog box.
- Your new folder appears beneath the original folder in the Navigation pane.

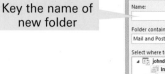
Key the name of new folder

**Figure 10-13** Create New Folder dialog box

2. Create the following email folders: **Friends, Family, School Activities,** and **Act Now.**

### 58C

**Learn: Junk Email Folder**

Mail/Home/Junk Email Folder/Delete/Junk/Junk pull-down

1. Read the following information, and complete the activity.

A message suspected of being junk is automatically moved to the Junk Email folder. You should periodically check messages in the Junk Email folder to ensure that legitimate messages were not classified as junk. Reclassifying messages that are erroneously moved into the Junk Email folder can improve the accuracy of automated classification.

- From the Junk pull-down menu, you can reclassify messages sent to the Junk Email folder in error.
- If a message is not junk, select the message and click Not Junk. This sends the message back to your Inbox.
- From this menu, you can Block Sender, Never Block Sender, Never Block Sender's Domain, and Never Block this Group or Mailing List. These options tell the software how to handle emails from the identified sources. See Figure 10-14.

| Team | Last Name | Initial of First Name | Game 2 | Game 3 | Game 4 |
|---|---|---|---|---|---|
| Frontiersmen | Sinclair | M. | 15 | 9 | 12 |
| Frontiersmen | Martinez | R. | 12 | 15 | 21 |
| Frontiersmen | Finch | J. | 24 | 18 | 21 |
| Frontiersmen | Remmington | J. | 9 | 8 | 22 |
| Frontiersmen | Roberts | R. | 10 | 12 | 7 |
| Railroaders | Johnson | M. | 25 | 17 | 22 |
| Railroaders | Baxter | M. | 13 | 9 | 7 |
| Railroaders | Filippo | K. | 24 | 29 | 18 |
| Railroaders | Jackson | J. | 15 | 18 | 16 |
| Railroaders | Martinez | J. | 8 | 4 | 7 |

## Job 21

**Database**

**June 17**

From the desk of:
**Julia Kingsley**

*I input the point totals for most of the teams after you left work yesterday and saved the file as df hoops II job 21 db. The points for the four teams shown at the right still need to be entered into the database.*

*JK*

| Males 15-16 Year Age Bracket Total Points | | | | | | |
|---|---|---|---|---|---|---|
| Team Name | Last Name | Initial of First Name | Game 1 Total Points | Game 2 Total Points | Game 3 Total Points | Game 4 Total Points |
| Rainmakers | Kaufmann | M. | 4 | 18 | 3 | 17 |
| Rainmakers | Heckendorf | F. | 17 | 9 | 19 | 18 |
| Rainmakers | Polk | N. | 20 | 15 | 18 | 22 |
| Rainmakers | Fechter | D. | 12 | 14 | 15 | 7 |
| Rainmakers | Lincoln | F. | 3 | 8 | 6 | 9 |

| Males 15-16 Year Age Bracket Total Points | | | | | | |
|---|---|---|---|---|---|---|
| Team Name | Last Name | Initial of First Name | Game 1 Total Points | Game 2 Total Points | Game 3 Total Points | Game 4 Total Points |
| Shooters | Smith | R. | 18 | 20 | 21 | 25 |
| Shooters | Mead | S. | 9 | 11 | 8 | 20 |
| Shooters | Pondexter | S. | 27 | 20 | 22 | 18 |
| Shooters | Vermillion | A. | 22 | 21 | 26 | 23 |
| Shooters | Kennedy | L. | 10 | 9 | 11 | 8 |

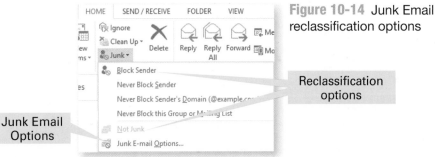

**Figure 10-14** Junk Email reclassification options

2. Check your Junk Email folder. Use one of the reclassification options to move any messages that are not junk back to your Inbox.

3. For other messages, consider using the other reclassification options from the Junk pull-down menu.

## 58D

### Learn: Junk Email Filter

Mail/Home/Junk Email folder/Delete/Junk/Junk Email Options

1. Read the following information, and complete the activity.

From the Junk pull-down menu, you selected settings that automatically move messages that appear to be junk into a special Junk Email folder. See Figure 10-14. You can use Junk Email Options at the bottom of the pull-down menu to choose the level of junk email protection you want, specify safe senders and recipients, block senders, and block email from international email addresses or in foreign languages.

2. Select Junk Email Options from the Junk pull-down menu. The Junk Email Options dialog box is displayed.

3. Under the Options tab, increase your level of junk email protection to either Low or High. Verify that the "Disable Links" and "Warn me" boxes are checked. These options protect you from **phishing** messages (scams that ask you for personal or confidential information) and warn you about suspicious domain names. Click Apply after making changes.

4. Explore the other tabs to see how you can increase your level of protection from junk email.

© michaeljung/Shutterstock.com

## 21st Century Skills: Productivity and Accountability

Email has become one of the most common ways for computer users to communicate, both personally and for business purposes. Although email is considered less formal than other business communications, it is still important to articulate your thoughts and ideas effectively in an email message. You should:

- Write in complete, active sentences.
- Organize using paragraphs and bulleted or numbered lists.
- Proofread and check your spelling.

Most importantly, you should always know your audience and understand that your message could be shared either intentionally or by mistake with someone else.

Open a new word processing document, and answer the following questions.

1. What perception might you form of a person who sends an email that has spelling and grammatical errors?
2. When might email not be the best form of communication?
3. **Save as:** *u10 21century*.

## Database
## June 16

**From the desk of:**
**Julia Kingsley**

Create a database that will provide the information we need to present an award to the five players in each bracket who scored the most points during the tournament and to the five players who scored the most points in a single game. Include the following fields:

Team
Last Name
Initial of First Name
Game 1 Total Points
Game 2 Total Points
Game 3 Total Points
Game 4 Total Points

Enter the total points for each team member. Game 1 points for the Frontiersmen and the Railroaders are shown at the right. The points for games 2–4 are shown on the next page. I'll try to enter the rest of the information as the final results are available. Use Males: 15-16 Year Age Bracket for the table you create.

Once you have the database set up, use the Expression Builder to create a query with computed fields to calculate the "Total Points for Tournament."

Save the Query as Total Points – Males 15-16 Year Age Bracket.

*JK*

**Game 1 Score Sheets**

TEAM: Frontiersmen / Railroaders

| TIME OUTS | | | | | QUARTER SCORES | | | | OVERTIME | | PLAYED AT Fort Collins |
|---|---|---|---|---|---|---|---|---|---|---|---|
| 1st Q. | 2nd Q. | 3rd Q. | 4th Q. | 20 Sec. | First | Second | Third | Fourth | First | Second | FINAL SCORE 72 |
| / | | | // | 1 2 3 4 | 19 | 18 | 18 | 17 | | | |

| Pos. | No. | NAME | QUARTERS PLAYED 1 2 3 4 | 1st Q. | 2nd Q. | Fouls | 3rd Q. | 4th Q. | Fouls | OVER TIME | TOTALS 2 3 ft f pts |
|---|---|---|---|---|---|---|---|---|---|---|---|
| F | 12 | M. Sinclair | ✓✓✓ | 223 | 22 | F₁ | 20 | 20 | F₅ | | 6 1 2 2 17 |
| F | 10 | F. Martinez | ✓✓✓ | 00 | 22 | F₁ | 003 | 02 | F₂ | | 3 1 4 2 13 |
| C | 38 | J. Finch | ✓✓✓ | 022 | 2000 | F₅F₆ | 2202 | 202 | F₅F₄ | | 8 0 5 4 21 |
| G | 8 | J. Remmington | ✓✓✓ | 2 | 220 | F₁ | 0020 | 20 | F₂ | | 5 0 3 2 13 |
| G | 3 | R. Roberts | ✓ ✓ | 22 | | F₅F₅0 | 30 | | F₃ | | 2 1 1 3 8 |

| REFEREE E. Hayes | FREETHROWS ATTEMPTED 20 | SUMMARY OF TOTALS 24 3 15 13 72 |
|---|---|---|
| UMPIRE C. Logan | FREETHROWS MADE 15 | PERCENT 75% |

| TIME OUTS | | | | | QUARTER SCORES | | | | OVERTIME | | DATE June 15 |
|---|---|---|---|---|---|---|---|---|---|---|---|
| 1st Q. | 2nd Q. | 3rd Q. | 4th Q. | 20 Sec. | First | Second | Third | Fourth | First | Second | FINAL SCORE 73 |
| // | | | // | 1 2 3 4 | 19 | 17 | 24 | 13 | | | |

| Pos. | No. | NAME | QUARTERS PLAYED 1 2 3 4 | 1st Q. | 2nd Q. | Fouls | 3rd Q. | 4th Q. | Fouls | OVER TIME | TOTALS 2 3 ft f pts |
|---|---|---|---|---|---|---|---|---|---|---|---|
| F | 15 | M. Johnson | ✓✓✓ | 223 | 22 | F₁ | 20 | 22 | F₅ | | 7 1 1 2 18 |
| F | 18 | M. Baxter | ✓✓✓ | 00 | 22 | F₁ | 0023 | 00 | F₅ | | 3 1 4 2 13 |
| C | 58 | K. Filippo | ✓✓✓ | 022 | 2000 | F₅F₆ | 2202 | 20 | F₅F₄ | | 7 0 5 4 19 |
| G | 23 | J. Jackson | ✓✓✓ | 2 | 22 | F₁ | 0020 | 23 | | | 5 1 1 1 14 |
| G | 27 | J. Martinez | ✓✓ | 22 | 00 | F₅F₂ | 2200 | | | | 4 0 1 2 9 |

| SCORER A. Phipps | FREETHROWS ATTEMPTED 19 | SUMMARY OF TOTALS 26 3 12 11 73 |
|---|---|---|
| TIMER L. Cody | FREETHROWS MADE 12 | PERCENT 63% |

# LESSON 59  Manage Emails by Rules

**OUTCOMES**

- Delay the delivery of a message.
- Send a message that enables recipients to vote.
- Respond to emails using Auto Reply.

## Business Document 59B

- Auto Reply Email Messages

**Learn: Delay Delivery**

Mail/Home/New/New Email/Options/Delay Delivery

★TIP  The software must be running and have access to the email server to send the message at the specified time. If not, the message will be sent after the specified time when the software is running and has access to the server.

**Proofreading Alert**
The data file copy contains two embedded errors; correct before sending the email.

1. Read the following information, and complete the activity.

There are times you create a message and you want it to be sent sometime in the future. For example, you may create a birthday or an anniversary email you want delivered on the date of the occasion. Delay Delivery gives you this option. In the Properties dialog box, key the date and time for the delivery. See Figure 10-15.

Key the date and time you want the email to be delivered

**Figure 10-15**  Delay delivery

2. Open **df 59b email**.
3. Cut and paste the contents into an email.
4. Proofread the email and correct any errors you find.
5. Select an email address from your *Friends and Family* Contact Group to send this email to. The subject will be the title of the copy.
6. Delay delivery of the email until one week from today at 2:00 p.m.

## 59C

**Learn: Voting**

Mail/Home/New/New Email/Options/Tracking/ Use Voting Buttons

1. Read the following information, and complete the activity.

The Voting Buttons allow contacts reading your message to provide feedback on questions/options you specify in your message. You can select Approve/Reject, Yes/No, Yes/No/ Maybe, or customize your vote. The voting method you choose will depend on the question you propose. See Figure 10-16.

**Figure 10-16**  Voting options

2. Choose two contacts from your *Friends and Family* Contact Group to send your email vote.
3. Include a question in your email that they can answer by Yes/No/Maybe.
4. Send the email.

**Spreadsheet**
**June 11**

From the desk of:
**Julia Kingsley**
*Mr. McLemore would like the spreadsheet (df hoops II job 19 ss) for the June 15–16 tournament completed with the attached information.*
*JK*

June 15 Refs:
Stella Tarantino (All June 15 games on Court A-1)
Michael Ginobli (All June 15 games on Court A-2)
Trenton Chen (All June 15 games on Court B-1)
Travis Martinez (All June 15 games on Court B-2)


June 16 Refs:
Tamika Jackson (All June 16 games on Court A-1 plus the 3rd place game on Court A, 1st place game on Court A, and the Championship game on Court A)

Jamaal Carlisle (All June 16 games on Court A-2 plus 3rd place game on Court B and the 1st place game on Court B)

Farrel Goldfarb (All June 16 games on Court B-1)
Jan Szczerbiak (All June 16 games on Court B-2)


Please add a Ref Fees column to the spreadsheet. Format the cells in the column as currency cells. Refs are paid $15 for each game on June 15 and $20 for each game on June 16. The refs are paid $25 for 1st and 3rd place games. The ref fee for the championship game is $35. Input the fees and calculate the total fees for referees.


Make these formatting changes to the spreadsheet.
- Center the text in the Court column.
- Indent all left-aligned columns 1 space.
- Center information on page horizontally.
Add a note to your tasks list to pay referees for June 15–16 games on June 18.

**Learn: Auto Reply**

★TIP Use the Save as type drop-down menu to select Outlook Template (*.oft).

1. Read the following information, and complete the activity.

When you are away from the office, you want to provide people who try to contact you with an alternative method of contacting you or identify someone else in the organization to contact to answer the question. Auto Reply gives you this notification option.

2. From Home, click New Email. Compose a simple message for your Auto Reply notice.

3. **Save as: *59e outoffice.oft*.** See Figure 10-17.

Name of Auto Reply message

Outlook Template (*.oft )

**Figure 10-17** Saving Auto Reply Template message

File/Manage Rules & Alerts/Email Rules/ New Rule

4. From the File tab, click Rules and Alerts.

5. Click New Rule to display the Rules Wizard dialog box. In step 1, under Start from a blank rule, select *Apply rule on messages I receive*, and click Next.

6. For the conditions, check *sent only to me*, and click Next.

7. For the actions, check *reply using a specific template*. Click the underlined a *specific template* in step 2.

★TIP The Auto Reply message is sent when a message is received. To receive a message, the software must be running and have access to the email server.

8. The Select a Reply Template dialog box appears. Look in *User Templates in File System*. You should see the Auto Reply (Out of Office) template you just created. Double-click the template you created, and click Finish.

9. You will return to the Rules and Alerts dialog box. Now you can see the newly created rule named *sent only to me*. See Figure 10-18. Click OK to continue.

Name of rule just created

New rule description

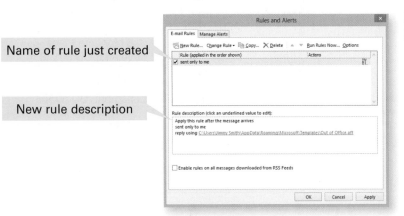

**Figure 10-18** Manage Rules and Alerts

**Apply: Create Auto Reply Message**

★TIP Remember to cancel message when completing this activity.

1. Create an Auto Reply message to be sent to contacts sending you an email message.

2. Create the template with the following message:

I am unavailable until April 15. If this is an emergency, please contact my assistant at 919-555-8888.

[Your Name]

General Manager

Sweety Pie Bakery

3. **Save template as: *59e outofoffice*.**

## Job 18

**Contact File**

**June 9**

From the desk of:

**Julia Kingsley**

*Mr. Zimmerscheid sent the attached table with contact information for other refs in the area. Please add these refs to our Referees folder in the Contacts file.*

*Add to your Tasks list that we need to request Business Telephone Numbers, Fax Numbers, and Email Addresses for those referees with incomplete information.*

*After you have keyed the information for each of the referees, please print two copies of the Referees folder, one in Business Card style and one in Phone Directory style.*

*JK*

Contact File: **Referees**

Szczerbiak, Jan

**Ms. Jan Szczerbiak**

970-344-8266 Home

705 Eastlake Court
Loveland, CO 80537

Tarantino, Stella

**Ms. Stella Tarantino**

970-348-4578 Home

8812 Rock Creek Drive
Fort Collins, CO 80528

## Potential Referee List

| Name & E-mail | Address | Phone |
|---|---|---|
| Ms. Tamika Jackson<br>jackson289@yahoo.com | 801 – 10th Street<br>Fort Collins, CO 80524 | 970.389.1128 (W)<br>970.546.1932 (H) |
| Mr. Derek Chatzky<br>chatzkydd@networld.com | 185 Kenosha Court<br>Fort Collins, CO 80525 | 970.753.2095 (W)<br>970.348.8855 (H) |
| Mr. Mitchell Grisham | 311 Glacier View road<br>Longmont, CO 80503 | 970.381.1838 (H) |
| Mr. Farrel Goldfarb<br>fgoldfa@yahoo.com | 77 Broadview<br>Fort Collins, CO 80521 | 970.753.1080 (W)<br>970.546.0357 (H) |
| Mr. Jamaal Carlisle | 3480 Ottawa Court<br>Fort Collins, CO 80526 | 970.348.2209 (H) |
| Mr. Scott Prior | 991 Gaylord Drive<br>Loveland, CO 80537 | 970.344.9011 (H) |
| Mr. Clark Layton | 888 Greenway Drive<br>Fort Collins, CO 80525 | 970.546.2890 (H) |
| Mr. Michael Ginobli | 29 Yorkshire Street<br>Fort Collins, CO 80526 | 970.344.6602 |
| Mr. Trenton Chen<br>trentocc@charter.net | 736 Montana Place<br>Loveland, CO 80538 | 970.389.8301 (W)<br>970.344.0739 (H) |
| Mr. Travis Martinez | 4173 Huntington Court<br>Longmont, CO 80503 | 970.381.4621 (H) |
| Ms. Dyan Parker<br>Parker10@comcast.net | 56 Village Park Court<br>Fort Collins, CO 80526 | 970.753.5610 (W)<br>970.490.1208 (H) |
| Mr. Boyd Knight | 8311 Yellowstone Road<br>Longmont, CO 80503 | 970.381.7834 (H) |

## Schedule Meetings with Calendars

**OUTCOMES**
- Schedule a meeting.
- Reply to a meeting request.
- Propose a new meeting time.

### Business Document
**60B**

- Meeting Invitation

**Learn: Create Meetings**

Calendar/Home/New/
New Meeting

1. Read the following information about creating meetings, and complete the activity.

In business or at school, you will have to schedule meetings with colleagues or classmates or reply to a meeting invitation. Your calendar allows you to create meetings with members of your contact list or Contact Groups.

- Click New Meeting in the Calendar window. A Meeting window appears for you to fill in the details of the meeting. See Figure 10-19.
- Select contacts to invite to the meeting. The email addresses will appear in the To text box.
- Key the title or purpose of your meeting in the Subject text box.
- Key the location of the meeting in the Location text box.
- Use the drop-down boxes to select the Start time and End time of your meeting.
- Click the Response Options drop-down menu in the Attendees group. You will notice both Request Response and Allow New Time Proposals boxes are checked. These options request the attendee to respond to the invitation or to offer a new time for the meeting. See Figure 10-20.
- Click Send and your meeting invitation will be sent to the attendee's Inbox.

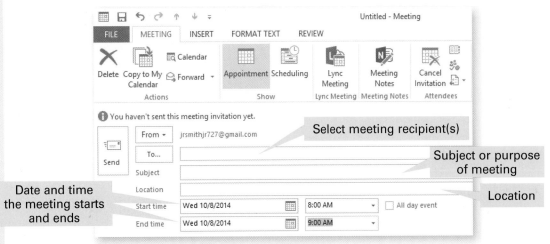

**Figure 10-19** Meeting request window

**Figure 10-20** Response Options

2. Choose four classmates to invite to a meeting. If their contact information is not in your contact list, add them now.

3. In the Meeting window, invite the four classmates to a **Project Team Meeting** one week from today from 4:00 to 5:00 p.m. The location is the school library. Request a response, and allow invitees to propose a new time for the meeting.

4. Send your meeting request.

## Fort Collins "Hoops" Sponsors

- Jay's Smokehouse
- The Sub Shoppe
- Grandma's Home Cookin'
- Mona Lisa's Cuisine
- Pizza-to-Go
- Marge's Café
- Sports Outfitters
- Country Inn
- Cozy Cottage Inn
- Four Season Suites
- The Inn
- Park Place Plaza
- Red Cedar Inn
- Royal Motel
- Pizza Palace
- 21st Century Sports

## Information Requests

**For Additional Information Contact:**

Todd McLemore, Tournament Director
"Hoops" Tournaments
618 Center Street
Fort Collins, CO 80526-1392

970-348-1500     tmclemore@hoops.cengage.com

## Learn: Reply to a Meeting Request/ Invitation

When you open a meeting request, you will notice a *Please Respond* icon. This means the meeting organizer wants you to indicate if you will be at the meeting. You will also notice the choices for your response across the top of the email request. See Figure 10-21.

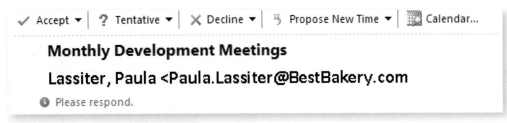

**Figure 10-21** Meeting request responses

If the attendee selects Accept or Tentative, the invitation is deleted from the Inbox and the meeting is added to the recipient's calendar. If the attendee selects Propose New Time, he or she is tentatively accepting the request but proposing that the meeting be held at a different time or date.

## Learn: Propose a New Meeting Time

1. Read the following information, and complete the activity.

If you are unable to attend the meeting or want to attend but not at the date/time proposed, you have an option to suggest a new meeting time. In Figure 10-22, you see the Propose New Time option for responding to meeting requests. This option allows you either to tentatively accept but propose a new meeting time, or decline but propose a new meeting time. Rather than just declining the meeting request, you can let the meeting organizer know you are interested in meeting but cannot attend at the time proposed in the request.

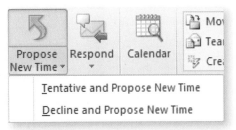

**Figure 10-22** Choices for proposing a new meeting time

2. Open the meeting request sent by a classmate.
3. Select Propose New Time, and tentatively accept and propose that the meeting be changed to 5:00 p.m. on the same date.
4. If you received more than one meeting request, decline all other requests.

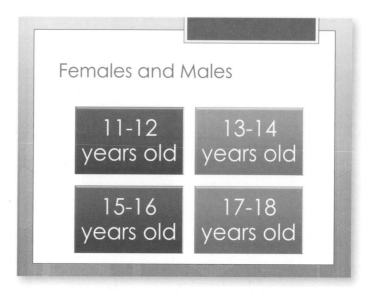

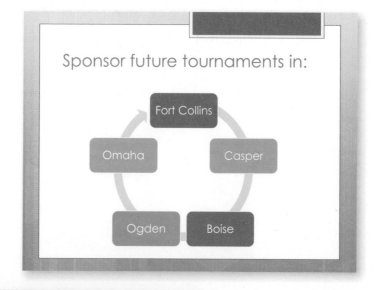

# LESSON 61

## Share and Print Calendars

**OUTCOMES**

- Create additional calendars.
- Share calendar with others.
- Print calendars in various styles.

---

**Business Document 61B**

- Calendars

---

**Learn: Create Additional Calendars**

Calendar/Folder/New/
New Calendar

1. Read the following information, and complete the activity.

In addition to your main calendar that you use to schedule important items for work or school, you can create additional calendars. For example, you can create a sporting event calendar to record your practice schedule, games, and tournaments.

- Display the Create New Folder dialog box. Key the name of your new calendar. See Figure 10-23.
- Click OK. The new calendar appears in the Calendar Navigation pane.
- To view the new calendar, select the checkbox for the calendar.

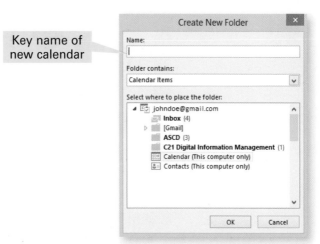

**Figure 10-23** Create New Calendar folder

2. Create a new calendar, and name it **Jackie's Personal Calendar**.
3. Create the following appointments in Jackie's Personal Calendar. Use the current month for the calendar.
   - Business Trip, date: 8th to 12th, time: 2:35 p.m., location: Boston Marriott
   - Susie's Birthday, date: 15th
   - Veterinarian's Appointment, date: 22nd, time: 2:00 to 3:00 p.m., location: 1124 Walker Street
   - Project Team Meeting, date: 31st, time: 1:00 to 3:00 p.m., location: 5th Floor Conference Room

## Slide Presentation
## June 4

From the desk of:

**Julia Kingsley**

*Mr. McLemore lost the flash drive with his slide show for next week's presentation at the Coaches' Conference. However, he does have a printed copy of the handouts for the presentation.*

*Using df hoops II job 17, please recreate slides similar to those shown on the handout. You may have to use different clip art. Use your judgment in applying transitions and animation.*

*JK*

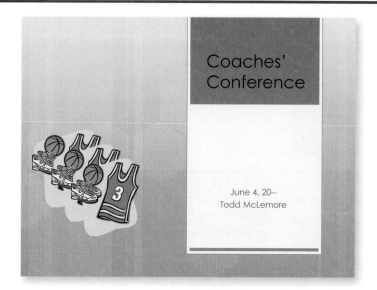

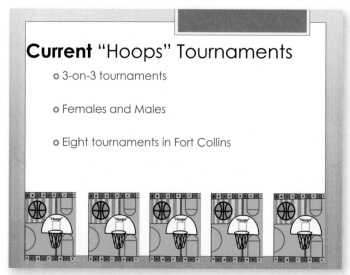

## Learn: Printing Calendars

Calendar/File/Print/ Settings

1. Read the following information, and complete the activity.

Before you print your calendar, you need to specify how you want it to appear. You can choose from Daily, Weekly Agenda, Weekly, Monthly, Tri-fold, and Calendar Details. See Table 10-2 for an explanation of the print settings.

- Select the calendar style.
- Specify Start and End dates. See Figure 10-24.
- Click Print.

**Figure 10-24** Printing calendar

2. Print Jackie's Personal Calendar, which you created in the previous activity.
3. Select the Monthly Calendar setting. Use the current month for the Start and End dates.
4. Turn in your printed calendar. Be sure to write your name on the calendar before turning it in to your teacher.
5. Delete Jackie's Personal Calendar by right-clicking *Jackie's Personal Calendar* on the Calendar Navigation menu. Select Delete Calendar. Confirm that you wish to delete the calendar when prompted.

**Table**

**June 3**

From the desk of:

**Julia Kingsley**

Please key this handwritten tournament schedule for the males in the 15–16-year-old age bracket. Use the table you created for Job 14. Change the colors of the shaded cells so we can easily see the difference between the female and male tournament schedules.

JK

## MALES 15–16 YEARS OLD
### Blue & Gold Brackets
### June 15–16

| Blue Bracket Middle School Gym—Court C | | Date and Time | Gold Bracket Middle School Gym—Court D | |
|---|---|---|---|---|
| Score | Teams | | Teams | Score |
| | Frontiersmen Railroaders | June 15 3:00 p.m. | Cavaliers Miners | |
| | Rainmakers Cowboys | | Ghost Shooters Pikers | |
| | Wolves Shooters | June 15 3:45 p.m. | Tetons Platters | |
| | 3-Pointers Free Stylers | | Pioneers Mustangs | |
| | Frontiersmen Rainmakers | June 15 6:00 p.m. | Cavaliers Ghost Shooters | |
| | Railroaders Cowboys | | Miners Pikers | |
| | Wolves 3-Pointers | June 15 6:45 p.m. | Tetons Pioneers | |
| | Shooters Free Stylers | | Platters Mustangs | |
| | Frontiersmen Cowboys | June 16 10:00 a.m. | Cavaliers Pikers | |
| | Railroaders Rainmakers | | Miners Ghost Shooters | |
| | Wolves Free Stylers | June 16 10:45 a.m. | Tetons Mustangs | |
| | Shooters 3-Pointers | | Platters Pioneers | |
| | 3rd and 4th place games | June 16 2:00 p.m. | 3rd and 4th place games | |
| | 1st and 2nd place games | June 16 2:45 p.m. | 1st and 2nd place games | |
| | Championship game | June 16 5:00 p.m. | Championship game | |

Key two 3' or 5' timings, as directed. Compute *gwam* and count errors.

 all letters used

| | gwam | 3' | 5' |
|---|---|---|---|

Appearance, which is often defined as the outward aspect of    4   2   41

someone or something, is quite important to most of us and af-    8   5   44

fects just about every day of our lives. We like to be around    12   7   46

people whom and things that we consider attractive. Because of    16   10   49

this preference, appearance is a factor in almost every decision    21   12   52

we make.    21   13   52

Appearance often affects our selection of food, the place in    25   15   54

which we live, the clothes we purchase, the car we drive, and the    30   18   57

vacations we schedule. For example, we usually do not eat foods    34   20   64

that are not visually appealing or buy clothing that we realize    38   23   65

will be unattractive to others who are important to us.    42   25   67

Appearance is important in business. People in charge of    46   27   68

hiring almost always stress the importance of good appearance.    50   30   70

Your progress in a job or career can be affected by how others    54   33   73

judge your appearance. It is not uncommon for those who see but    59   35   73

do not know you to evaluate your abilities and character on the    63   38   78

basis of your personal appearance.    65   39   70

www.cengage.com/school/
keyboarding/c21key

| gwam | 1' | 1 | 2 | 3 | 4 | 5 | 6 | 7 | 8 | 9 | 10 | 11 | 12 | 13 |
|---|---|---|---|---|---|---|---|---|---|---|---|---|---|---|
| | 3' | | 1 | | | 2 | | | 3 | | | 4 | | |
| | 5' | | | 1 | | | | 2 | | | | 3 | | |

**Calendar**
**June 2**

From the desk of:
**Julia Kingsley**

*Prepare monthly calendars for June, July, and August. Use the Help feature for your software if you don't know how to prepare a calendar. Refer to the list of tournament dates I gave you (p. 325) to get the dates for August. You can choose the colors for August. Use landscape orientation and center the calendars on the page.*

*JK*

## June 20--

| | Mon | Tue | Wed | Thu | Fri | Sat | Sun |
|---|---|---|---|---|---|---|---|
| **Hoops** Tournaments | | | | | | 1 | 2 |
| | 3 | 4 | 5 | 6 | 7 | 8 | 9 |
| | 10 | 11 | 12 | 13 | 14 | 15 | 16 |
| | | | | | | Tournament 1 | |
| | 17 | 18 | 19 | 20 | 21 | 22 | 23 |
| | | | | | | Tournament 2 | |
| | 24 | 25 | 26 | 27 | 28 | 29 | 30 |
| | | | | | | Tournament 3 | |

## July 20--

| | Mon | Tue | Wed | Thu | Fri | Sat | Sun |
|---|---|---|---|---|---|---|---|
| **Hoops** Tournaments | 1 | 2 | 3 | 4 | 5 | 6 | 7 |
| | | | | | | Tournament 4 | |
| | 8 | 9 | 10 | 11 | 12 | 13 | 14 |
| | | | | | | Tournament 5 | |
| | 15 | 16 | 17 | 18 | 19 | 20 | 21 |
| | | | | | | Tournament 6 | |
| | 22 | 23 | 24 | 25 | 26 | 27 | 28 |
| | | | | | | Tournament 7 | |
| | 29 | 30 | 31 | | | | |

# CORPORATE *View*

## An Integrated Intranet Application

As part of your internship with Corporate View, you have the opportunity to work in several departments within the organization to see the overall operations. Your current assignment is with Human Resources and Management. Melissa Kim, Intern Coordinator for Human Resources, would like you to create a My Contacts folder for CorpView.

She has provided you with copy illustrating her contact card and with the information she has gathered on the other people she would like included in the My Contacts—CorpView folder. You will need to complete the contact information by gathering the *Title* and *Email* address from the Corporate View intranet site: www.cengage.com/school/keyboarding/dim/cview

---

**Kim, Melissa**

**Melissa Kim**
Corporate View
Human Resources Intern Coordinator

(303) 487-5100 Ex 110 Work
mkim@corpview.com

Building A, L2-15
318 Canyon View Road
Boulder, CO 80302

---

| Bravo, Maria | |
|---|---|
| Full Name: | Maria Bravo |
| Company: | Corporate View |
| Business: | Building A, L2-08 |
| | 318 Canyon View Road |
| | Boulder, CO 80302 |
| Business: | (303) 487-5100 Ex. 108 |

| Cooper, Charles | |
|---|---|
| Full Name: | Charles Cooper |
| Company: | Corporate View |
| Business: | Building B, L3-15 |
| | 321 Canyon View Road |
| | Boulder, CO 80302 |
| Business: | (303) 487-5100 Ex. 243 |

| Delgado, Luis | |
|---|---|
| Full Name: | Luis Delgado |
| Company: | Corporate View |
| Business: | Building A, L1-33 |
| | 318 Canyon View Road |
| | Boulder, CO 80302 |
| Business: | (303) 487-5100 Ex. 188 |

| Jones, Casey | |
|---|---|
| Full Name: | Casey Jones |
| Company: | Corporate View |
| Business: | Building C, L5-50 |
| | 324 Canyon View Road |
| | Boulder, CO 80302 |
| Business: | (303) 487-5100 Ex. 509 |

| Spencer Malone | |
|---|---|
| Full Name: | Spencer Malone |
| Company: | Corporate View |
| Business: | Building B, L4-25 |
| | 321 Canyon View Road |
| | Boulder, CO 80302 |
| Business: | (303) 487-5100 Ex. 222 |

| Wu, David | |
|---|---|
| Full Name: | David Wu |
| Company: | Corporate View |
| Business: | Research Park |
| | 328 Canyon View Road |
| | Boulder, CO 80302 |
| Business: | (303) 487-5100 Ex. 723 |

**OUTCOME**

- To use decision making, creative thinking, and document processing skills to complete real-world application jobs for a simulated business.

**Business Documents**

- Tournament Table
- Tournament Calendar
- Coaches' Conference Slide Show
- Contact File for Referees
- Referee Spreadsheet

- Player Scoring Database
- Award Winner Table
- Table of Referee Fees
- Referee Address Database
- Mail Merge Letter

## Job 14

Table
June 2

**From the desk of:**

**Julia Kingsley**

*I found several copies of the blank tournament table we used last year. I've filled in a blank tournament form for the females in the 15–16-year-old bracket and attached it. Since I can't find the file, you will have to create the table shell again and input the information.*

*Put the heading in Cambria 26 pt.; put the subheading in Cambria 14 pt.*

*Save the table shell, as we will be doing similar tables for all age brackets.*

*JK*

**FEMALES 15–16 YEARS OLD**
*Yellow & Green Brackets*
*June 15–16*

| Yellow Bracket Middle School Gym—Court A | | Date and Time | Green Bracket Middle School Gym—Court B | |
|---|---|---|---|---|
| Score | Teams | | Teams | Score |
| | Columbines / Rockies | June 15 3:00 p.m. | Mavericks / Gold Nuggets | |
| | PikesPeakers / Bronkettes | | River Rafters / Rebounders | |
| | Cowgirls / Larks | June 15 3:45 p.m. | Flyers / Snow Shooters | |
| | Jazzettes / Aggies | | Vailers / Huskers | |
| | Columbines / PikesPeakers | June 15 6:00 p.m. | Mavericks / River Rafters | |
| | Rockies / Bronkettes | | Gold Nuggets / Rebounders | |
| | Cowgirls / Jazzettes | June 15 6:45 p.m. | Flyers / Vailers | |
| | Larks / Aggies | | Snow Shooters / Huskers | |
| | Columbines / Bronkettes | June 16 10:00 a.m. | Mavericks / Rebounders | |
| | Rockies / PikesPeakers | | Gold Nuggets / River Rafters | |
| | Cowgirls / Aggies | June 16 10:45 a.m. | Flyers / Huskers | |
| | Larks / Jazzettes | | Snow Shooters / Vailers | |
| | 3rd and 4th place games | June 16 2:00 p.m. | 3rd and 4th place games | |
| | 1st and 2nd place games | June 16 2:45 p.m. | 1st and 2nd place games | |
| | Championship game | June 16 5:00 p.m. | Championship game | |

1. After you complete the CorpView contacts folder, Ms. Kim would like you to create a Contact Group for the six individuals you have in the folder because you will be sending email to them quite frequently.
2. Next, she would like you to create two documents.

**Document 1:**

On the company intranet site, there is a section on *Regular Features*. One of the features deals with intranet FAQs. Open the *Netiquette on the Corporate View Intranet* link, and create a document similar to the one she started to remind employees about the use of the intranet.

Use the Copy and Paste feature to gather the information from the intranet to create the document and then reformat it. Use the *Title* Style feature for the heading, but change the font size to 20-pt. Cambria so that it doesn't overwhelm the page. Reformat the text so that it is 11-pt. Arial. **Save as:** *u10 corpview doc1*.

## Intranet Netiquette

1. Make sure all the information you copy from the Web is owned by Corporate View or is in the public domain. Do not copy proprietary information—that is, information owned by another corporation or individual. If you use information from others, reference it or document it properly.

2. To protect yourself,

**Document 2:**

Using information found on the same link, create another document (formatted the same as Document 1) for Email Netiquette. **Save as:** *u10 corpview doc2*.

## Email Netiquette

1. Keep e-mail messages short and to the point. Long messages should be delivered in some other format.

3. Madeline Tucker, President and CEO, who is very concerned about the Corporate View image, has requested Human Resources & Management to send the following email message on her behalf to the Contact Group you previously created. Use **MESSAGE SENT ON BEHALF OF MADELINE TUCKER** as the subject line of the email. Include the two documents on Intranet and Email Netiquette as attachments to the email. Print a copy of the email and attachments for Ms. Kim to review and approve before you send the email. (Your teacher will review the documents.)

## Work Assignment at "Hoops"

© iStockphoto.com/strickke

Unit 13 is a continuation of "Hoops I," the real-world application completed for Unit 7. Some of the jobs you will be completing in this unit for the owner of "Hoops" and his administrative assistant will require you to access information from "Hoops I" on pp. 206–217 and from the 13 jobs you have already completed. Use the information and skills you learned in previous units to complete the following:

- Processing letters to referees.
- Updating a database as registrations and advertising fees are received.
- Formatting tournament forms.
- Updating spreadsheets for registration fees and refs' schedules.
- Preparing a slide show for a presentation.
- Preparing tournament calendars.
- Creating a database to determine award recipients.
- Creating a database for referees.
- Updating the contacts folder.

McLemore, Todd

**Todd McLemore**
"Hoops" Tournaments
Tournament Director

(970) 555-1100 Work
tmclemore@hoops.cengage.com

618 Center Street
Fort Collins, CO 80526-1392

As in the previous unit, Ms. Kingsley will attach general processing instructions to each task you are given. If a date is not provided on the document, use the date included on the instructions. If the instructions given with the document are not sufficiently detailed, use your decision-making skills to process the document. Since "Hoops" has based its office manual on the *Century 21* textbook, you can also use the text as a reference.

Documents should be attractively formatted. You are expected to produce error-free documents, so proofread and correct your work carefully before presenting it for approval.

## Filenames

Use hoops + job no. for the filename for each document (***hoops job 14, hoops job 15***, etc.).

## Tournament Dates

"Hoops" Tournament Schedule
20-- Tournament Dates

June
- June 15-16
- June 22-23
- June 29-30

July
- July 6-7
- July 13-14
- July 20-21
- July 27-28

August
- August 3-4

For additional information, contact:
Todd McLemore, Tournament Director
"Hoops" Tournaments
618 Center Street
Fort Collins, CO 80526-1392

Phone: 970.555.1100
e-mail: tmclemore@hoops.cengage.com

**Email message:**

*There have been some complaints about inappropriate use of the company intranet. The complaints deal with such things as copying proprietary information, viruses, and copying software. Please review the attached documents to make sure you are in compliance with company policy regarding use of the intranet.*

*I am also attaching a document on Email Netiquette that I would like you to review as well. Remember, emails sent become part of the corporate image. A positive corporate image is key to our success.*

*After reviewing the documents, please share with the employees under your supervision.*

### Think Critically

1. Why is Corporate View concerned about the image created by emails?
2. Do you think the company has the right to monitor the emails you send using company email?
3. Do you think you should be able to send personal email on company time?
4. Do you think employees who violate company rules regarding use of the Internet and email should be fired?

© iStockphoto.com/kupicoo

# The Winning Edge

Complete this activity to help prepare for the **Cyber Security** event in FBLA-PBL's Information Technology division. Participants in this event demonstrate their understanding of security needs for technology. You will create a presentation on the things that successful digital citizens should do to protect themselves and others while using technology.

1. Identify at least ten security activities that technology users should undertake to protect their hardware, their data, and their personal safety. Activities to consider include:

   a. Installing firewalls, antivirus software, and spyware/malware detection programs.
   b. Setting user account controls that limit who has permission to make changes to your system.
   c. Setting unique, strong passwords for every instance when you need a password.
   d. Opening only those email attachments that are from a legitimate source.
   e. Avoiding the download and running of programs that come from an unknown source or whose security you cannot confirm.
   f. Never sharing personal or financial information online.
   g. Avoiding online discussions and chats with strangers.
   h. Arranging an ergonomically safe and comfortable work area.
   i. Balancing your use of technology with time away from the screen.

2. Select a format for your presentation, such as a word processing report, slide show presentation, or poster.
3. Create the presentation and save it as directed by your instructor.

For detailed information on this event, go to www.fbla-pbl.org.

## Think Critically

1. Why would an employer value a worker who is security-conscious about technology?
2. How important are the digital safeguards you put into place to protect yourself as compared to the nondigital measures?

## School and Community

Recycling has become a way of life for many people, but most associate recycling with aluminum cans, plastic bottles, and paper. With the substantial increase in the use of electronic and digital products over the last 20 years, though, many communities and organizations have launched programs to properly dispose of and recycle a variety of electronic devices and equipment. These include computers, printers, cell phones, televisions, gaming systems, and digital cameras.

In addition, many schools are involved in fund-raising programs in which they collect electronics from students, parents, and other community members, and then get paid upon delivery of them to a recycler.

1. Research the electronics recycling programs or events sponsored by your community. What are the guidelines? How often are they held?
2. Is your community or school in need of an electronics recycling program? If yes, what can you do to contribute to the start of one?

www.cengage.com/school/keyboarding/c21key

# Academic and Career Connections

Complete the following exercises that introduce various topics that involve academic themes and careers.

## Grammar and Writing: Subject-Verb Agreement

**MicroType 6**

- References/Communication Skills/Subject-Verb Agreement
- CheckPro/Communication Skills 9
- CheckPro/Word Choice 9

1. Go to *MicroType 6* and use this feature path for review: References/Communication Skills/Subject-Verb Agreement.
2. Click *Rules* and review the rules of using subjects and verbs.
3. Then, under Subject-Verb Agreement, click *Posttest.*
4. Follow the instructions to complete the *posttest.*

***Optional Activities:***

1. Go to this path: CheckPro/Communication Skills 9.
2. Complete the activities as directed.
3. Go to this path: CheckPro/Word Choice 9.
4. Complete the activities as directed.

## Communications: Composition

1. Read the ¶ below.

Narcissus, a mythical young man, saw his image reflected in a pool of water; fell in love with his image; and starved to death admiring himself. Unlike Narcissus, our self-esteem or self-image should come not from mirror reflections but by thinking about who we are—inside. Further, our self-image is affected by the opinions of people who matter to us and whether they see us as strong or weak, good or bad, positive or negative. No one is perfect, of course; but we can all improve. It's time to start.

2. Start a new word processing document, and compose a ¶ about your self-image. The ¶ should include the following information:

   - The level of your self-esteem: high, low, or in-between; and factors that make it what it is.
   - Plans you have to raise your self-esteem.

3. Proofread, revise, and correct the document.
4. Save as: *u10 communications*.

## Math Skills

1. When Jennifer arrived at work on Monday morning, she had received 136 email messages over the weekend. She skimmed through the list and deleted 42 that she knew were junk email or advertisements. What percentage of the emails did she delete? (Round to the nearest whole number.)
2. Of the remaining emails, Jennifer determined that she should reply to half of them before the end of the day. How many replies would she have to send?
3. Jennifer organizes the emails that she wants to keep into three different folders: Customers, Suppliers, and Coworkers. She has 35 messages in her Customers folder, 17 in her Suppliers folder, and 42 in her Coworkers folder. What percentage of the total does each represent? (Round to the nearest whole number.)

Government & Public Administration

Creatas/Jupiterimages

## Planning a Career in Government and Public Administration

The highest-ranking job in the U.S. government and one of the most powerful positions in the world—that of President of the United States—falls within this career cluster. This field is for those individuals who are interested in setting and implementing public policy, protecting citizen's rights, and helping to shape the future of their city, their state, and their country.

## What's It Like?

Workers in this field are involved in planning and performing government functions at the local, state, and federal levels. This includes governance, national security, foreign service, planning, revenue and taxation, and regulations. For example:

- They oversee budgets, ensure that resources are used properly, nominate citizens to boards and commissions, encourage business investment, and promote economic development.
- They carry out and supervise the fundamental operations of the military in combat, administration, construction, engineering, health care, human services, and other areas.
- They develop laws and statutes.
- They review filed tax returns for accuracy and determine whether tax credits and deductions are allowed by law.

Jobs in this field often require long hours, including evenings and weekends. Individuals in public administration typically work in offices, while those in security and regulations often work in the field in different locations around the country and around the world.

## Employment Outlook

Employment opportunities in the various pathways of this cluster range significantly. Little to no change is expected in the area of governance; those in the military and other national security areas can expect excellent job growth; those in planning, taxation, and regulations can expect job growth to be about as fast as average, or 7 to 13 percent.

Education requirements range widely, too. Some positions require on-the-job training in an administrative role or as a member of the armed forces; others may require a two-year college degree in public administration, health-care administration, human services management, or political science; and still others may require a four-year college degree or higher in political science, public administration, national security, or law.

## What About You?

This career cluster is covered in box 7 of the Interest Survey Activity you completed in Unit 1 of this text. If this box had one of the three highest scores on your survey, you should further explore the cluster's pathways and related occupations.

1. Why do you think a career in this field could be a good choice?
2. What skills can you develop now that would be helpful to a career in this field?
3. Why are these jobs important to our country's prosperity and well-being?

# Career Clusters

## Planning a Career in Marketing

Virtually every business in operation has to use marketing in some shape or form. Marketing is the process by which a company determines what products or services it can sell to others, and the strategy to use in sales, communications, and business development. The marketing function is closely tied to the organization's goals and objectives.

Marketing is a career area that provides a multitude of diverse and exciting job opportunities. For example, marketing professionals might conduct focus group interviews to determine consumers' wants and needs. Or they might travel the world to introduce a new product. Or they might organize a community event that is sponsored in part by their company.

## What's It Like?

Individuals who work in marketing are responsible for planning, managing, and performing the marketing activities that meet the organization's objectives. For example:

© Golden Pixels LLC/Alamy

- They formulate business's policies and manage its operations.
- They conduct sales and ensure the timely delivery of products and services to the customer.
- They develop merchandising strategies aimed at promoting and sustaining sales of the company's products or services.
- They plan, coordinate, and implement advertising, promotion, and public relations activities.
- They collect and analyze data to develop comprehensive profiles of customers and their wants and needs.

Marketing professionals work in a variety of settings in all types of industries, including entertainment, technology, health care, and manufacturing. Businesses can be any size, ranging from a small start-up to a multinational corporation with thousands of employees. Positions are available at all levels, from CEOs and vice presidents to creative directors and account managers to sales clerks and public relations associates.

## Employment Outlook

Employment in marketing careers is projected to grow between 7 and 13 percent over the 2008–2018 decade, with sales and marketing managers expected to experience the most growth. Most employers require marketing personnel to have a bachelor's or master's degree in business administration with an emphasis on marketing.

## What About You?

The Marketing career cluster is covered in box 14 of the Interest Survey Activity you completed in Unit 1 of this text. If this box had one of the three highest scores on your survey, you should further explore the cluster's pathways and related occupations.

1. Why do you think a career in marketing could be a good choice?
2. What skills can you develop now that would be helpful to a career in marketing?
3. Why are these jobs important to a business?

# Academic and Career Connections

Complete the following exercises that introduce various topics that involve academic themes and careers.

## Grammar and Writing: Spelling and Modifiers

**MicroType 6**

- References/Communication Skills/Spelling
- References/Communication Skills/Modifiers
- CheckPro/Communication Skills 11
- CheckPro/Word Choice 11

1. Go to *MicroType* 6 and use this feature path for review: References/Communication Skills/Spelling.
2. Click Rules and review the rules of spelling.
3. Then, under *Spelling*, click *Posttest.*
4. Follow the instructions to complete the posttest.
5. Repeat this process for *Modifiers.*

***Optional Activities:***

1. Go to this path: CheckPro/Communication Skills 11.
2. Complete the activities as directed.
3. Go to this path: CheckPro/Word Choice 11.
4. Complete the activities as directed.

As desired, complete Word Choice 12–18.

## Communications: Reading

Open the data file ***df u12 communications***. Carefully read and then close the file. Start a new word processing document, and key answers to the following questions, using complete sentences.

1. What was the final score of yesterday's soccer match?
2. Was the winning goal scored in the first or second half?
3. Will last year's City League champion be playing in this year's championship match?
4. Will the top-ranked team in the state be playing in this year's championship match?
5. Will the top-ranked team in the city be playing in the championship match?
6. Is the championship game to be played during the day or the evening?
7. Has either of the teams in the match won a City League championship before?
8. **Save as:** ***u12 communications***.

## Math Skills: Simple Interest

*Interest* is the fee paid to a lender for the use of borrowed money. Interest is always expressed as a percent. The *principal* is the amount of money borrowed. Simple interest (I) is calculated by multiplying the principal (P) by the annual interest rate (R) by the length of time in years (T). The formula is written as: $I = P \times R \times T$.

1. Emily wants to buy a car in two years, so she's starting to save for it now. She expects to pay about $20,000. She figures her part-time job working at the mall will allow her to save $250 a month toward a down payment. After two years, how much will she have saved?
2. Emily figures if she takes her first year of savings and buys a one-year certificate of deposit (CD), she can earn even more. If the CD pays a 2 percent annual interest rate, how much more money will she earn on one year of savings? How much after two years?

# The Winning Edge

© Image Point Fr/Shutterstock.com

Complete this activity to help prepare for the **Business Communication** event in FBLA-PBL's Business Management and Administration division. Participants in this event demonstrate their business communication skills in writing, speaking, and listening.

1. In a new word processing document, use the information you learned in this unit to write a one-page report on how to write an effective email message. Use the following guidelines to write your report.

   • **Introduction:** Define email and discuss how it is used to communicate in business and professional settings.
   • **Body:** List and explain tips on writing an effective email. Concepts to cover include subject line, audience/recipients, organization, spelling and grammar, format, tone, and length.
   • **Conclusion:** Discuss the importance of preparing well-written email messages and how their quality and format reflect on both the writer and the organization for which he or she works.

   You may use references to assist in preparing the ¶s (e.g., help screens, spell check, thesaurus, user's manual, and dictionary). When you are finished, be sure to proofread and revise the document as necessary. Apply formatting and text enhancements (bold, italic, and underline) as appropriate. Save the document as directed by your instructor.

2. With your instructor's permission, send the document as an email attachment to a classmate. You should write a brief email message explaining the document you have attached and asking your classmate to edit it as necessary.

3. When your classmate returns the document, make revisions as necessary. Submit the document as directed by your instructor.

For detailed information on this event, go to www.fbla-pbl.org.

## Think Critically

1. Why is writing considered an essential skill in just about any career you choose?
2. The writing process involves planning, composing, editing, proofreading, and revising. Why is each stage important to effective written communications?
3. What activities can you participate in now that will strengthen your writing skills?

**School and Community** Do you have a younger sibling who likes to tag along with you and your friends? Maybe you know a young neighborhood kid who's always checking in to see what you're up to. While this might be annoying at times, you should realize that young kids look up to teenagers and often view them as role models. There are many ways you can mentor young children. For example, you can volunteer for an after-school tutoring program or with your local library's reading program. You might volunteer at a daycare center or with a community program for children.

1. Research the need for youth mentors in your school district or community. You might contact elementary schools, preschools, daycare centers, and the library.
2. Create a spreadsheet that lists the following information: name of the organization, address, volunteer opportunities for youth mentors, and a contact name and number. Print the spreadsheet and make copies to post in your school.

**Figure 12-10** Thoroughly research online retailers before you purchase a product from them.

When you shop online, though, you're basically limited to what you see, and what you see is not always what you get. Online purchasing requires you to be a discerning consumer and to think carefully about the consequences of these types of transactions before you complete them. Consider the following tips when engaging in digital commerce:

- Learn to identify reputable and legitimate online retailers. A reliable website clearly lists contact details, including the retailer's address, phone number, and a name or department to contact with questions or complaints. By directly contacting the organization, you can verify that the products or services advertised are indeed legitimate and the information is accurate.

- Research the business or organization before making a purchase. You can conduct a general search of the Web to find information on the company, search a specific site such as the Better Business Bureau to verify the organization, or read reviews and feedback from other consumers.

- Make sure the retailer's website is secure. A secure Web address begins with "https," where the "s" indicates the site is secure. Also look for a padlock or key icon at the bottom of the site's window or on the "Checkout" button. This indicates that any information you provide is scrambled into code, or encrypted, before it is transmitted over the Internet. Note that the "https" and/or key icon may appear only on the checkout or payment processing page of the website.

- Carefully monitor and track your online credit card purchases and account statements. Responsible consumers pay close attention to the purchases they charge, whether online or in-person. These include the sometimes hidden "extras," such as taxes and shipping and handling. Accumulating debt and failing to pay off your credit balances can damage your credit rating, and a poor credit rating can follow you throughout your life.

- Be aware of buying and selling intellectual property and copyrighted materials. As discussed in Lesson 69C, buying and selling copyrighted materials without the owner's permission is illegal. This includes music, movies, software downloads, and "virtual merchandise," such as accounts, characters, and other items, for online games.

## 71D

### Creating a Product Comparison Database

You will gather information on flat-screen TVs and record it in a database.

1. Start a new database, and save it as **71d TVs**.
2. Create a table with the following fields and field types: Manufacturer & Model (Text), Size (Text), Price (Currency), Features (Memo), Website (Text), and Free Shipping (Yes/No). Enter a field description, and set field properties as desired. Name the table **tblFlatScreenTVs**. Create a form named **frmFlatScreenTVs**.
3. Gather information on at least ten different brands of TVs from at least five different websites. For example, you can use information on two different brands from one website, such as Amazon.com. You should search for LCD TVs that are between 30 and 39 inches in size. Enter the information in the form.
4. Create a query based on the table that shows only those records that have free shipping. **Save as: qryFreeShipping**. Create another query that sorts the records from lowest to highest price and displays all fields. Name the query **qryTVsByPrice**.
5. Create a report based on the *qryTVsByPrice* query that groups the records by the Free Shipping field and sorts in ascending order by Price. Name it **rptTVsByPrice**. Rearrange fields and format as desired. With your instructor's permission, print the report. Then close the database.
6. Which TV do you think represents the best deal? Discuss your choice in class.

# UNIT 11 — Creating Websites

**Lesson 62** Word and Excel Web Pages
**Lesson 63** Web Page Tables, Graphics, and Pictures

**Lesson 64** Web Page Hyperlinks and Bookmarks
**Lessons 65–66** Web Construction

## Reference Guide

### Creating Web Pages

There are many different ways to create web pages. Often, large companies employ expert programmers who write time-consuming code to create and maintain complicated websites. Other businesses contract with web page design companies or consultants to create their web pages. Some businesses create and maintain their websites by using web page design software that does not require knowledge of HTML (HyperText Markup Language)—a computer language that specifies the codes that browsers use to format and display the content.

Many smaller companies, and individuals creating personal websites, use word processing and spreadsheet software to create web pages. Pages created with these two application packages can be very effective. They are likely, however, to lack the "bells and whistles" that specialized software and expert programmers can provide.

### Microsoft Word and Excel Web Pages

Some *Microsoft Office* programs, including *Word* and *Excel*, provide tools you need to create and save your documents as web pages in HTML format without needing to learn HTML. Once saved in HTML format, a document can be previewed in the *Office* program in which it was created or in a browser such as *Internet Explorer*. When the web page is previewed in a browser, you are able to see the *Office* document as if it were already on the Web.

When you preview your web page, its format may look a little different than it does when viewed within the *Office* program because browsers do not support all *Office* software features. For example:

- Character formatting such as shadow, emboss, and engrave is not supported by all browsers.
- Tab settings may not appear when the browser is used.
- Spacing after the punctuation ending a sentence may change from two spaces to one space.
- The alignment of pictures and graphs and the placement of wrapped text may change.
- Headers and footers and page numbers may not appear.
- Row height in tables may change.

# LESSON 71     Digital Commerce

OUTCOMES
- Define digital commerce activities.
- Understand how to be a responsible online consumer.

## Business Document
### 71B

**Defining Digital Commerce**

- Database with Table, Form, Query, and Report

**Digital commerce**, or making purchases over the Internet, is considered by many to be an easy and convenient way to shop and make comparisons. You can do it from the comfort of your home any time of the day or night, and all you need is a computer or smartphone and an Internet connection.

Digital commerce includes the following activities:

- Buying products or services online. Users shop for products or services they wish to buy, typically through a commercial website or auction site. Once they identify the goods to purchase, they supply a credit card number and submit an electronic order form.
- Selling products or services online. With this type of commercial activity, sellers do not need a physical store in order to sell their goods. They can set up their own online store or sell their wares through an existing website such as eBay, Etsy, or Craigslist.
- Subscribing to media services. Users pay a fee to receive services, such as music and movie downloads, online storage space and file backups, and memberships in shopping "clubs" that guarantee free shipping and other perks.
- Downloading **apps**, which are small software applications designed specifically to run on smartphones and other digital devices. Many apps are Web-based, meaning they are designed to be used within an Internet browser, eliminating the need to download software to your computer or digital device. There are apps for just about everything, from creating documents to playing games to finding the cheapest gas in town. Many apps can be downloaded for free, while others are available for purchase.

Source: © craigslist.org

**Figure 12-9** Craigslist is a popular website for consumers to buy and sell products and services.

In addition, digital commerce offers a convenient method for comparison shopping. All you need to do is run a search on the Web for a product or service that will return a comprehensive list of options that meet the criteria you specify. Even if you do not buy the product or service online, the research and information you gather can be helpful in the purchasing decisions you make in-store.

### QUICK ✔

What types of products do you think shoppers are more likely to purchase online? What types do you think are best suited for buying in a "brick-and-mortar" location?

### 71C

**Understanding the Digital Consumer's Responsibilities**

Leaving your home to go shopping may be more time-consuming than shopping online, but it does have its benefits. You can physically interact with a product before buying it, whether that's seeing it, hearing it, touching it, or even tasting or smelling it. You can ask questions about it and usually get answers immediately. You can judge its quality based not only on its physical characteristics, but also on those of the environment in which it is sold and the people with whom you interact.

*Word* and *Excel* software will be used to create web pages in this unit. *Internet Explorer* will be the browser used to preview the web pages, unless you have another browser set as your default browser.

In Lesson 62, you will learn to create, edit, and save documents in Web Page format and preview web pages. The pages include a background, text box, and text in various font sizes, styles, and colors.

In Lessons 63 and 64, you will create web pages for a community service organization. (Some of the pages are shown below.) Hyperlinks connect to places within the same web page, to other web pages within the same website, to different websites, and to email addresses. Bookmarks will be used to move quickly from one place to another within a web page. Pictures, graphics, and tables are used.

In Lessons 65–66, you have an opportunity to create a website of your choice. It can be web pages for yourself, your family, your school, a business, an organization, etc. You should, therefore, think about the purpose of your website and identify the web pages you will include in your site as you complete the activities in Lessons 62–64.

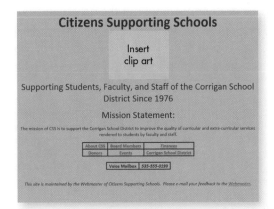

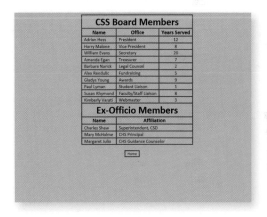

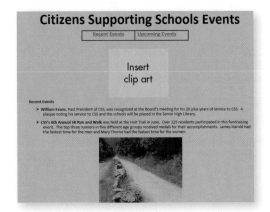

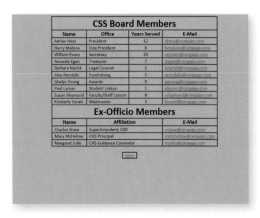

- Avoid gossip and contributing to the rumor mill. This is a form of cyberbullying and can have serious consequences for all parties involved.
- Respect the privacy of others. Sharing information about friends and acquaintances or tagging photos can be an unwelcome intrusion in their lives.
- Refrain from sharing personal photos and videos.

When in doubt about what is or is not appropriate for sharing online, consider the fact that anything you transmit digitally becomes a permanent part of cyberspace and will be around for the long term. So you have to ask yourself, "Do I want a college admissions officer or a prospective employer or even my current friends and family to see or read this about me?"

1. Open the data file **df 70e safety**. **Save as:** **70e safety**. The document contains a list of questions on online safety with point values assigned so participants can assess their safety level.
2. Reformat the questions in table format with subtotal rows and a row at the bottom for the total score. Apply other formatting that will enhance the survey's appearance and make it "user-friendly."
3. With your instructor's permission, print the survey and complete it. How did your score rank? What things could you change to make you safer in the online world?

QUICK ✔

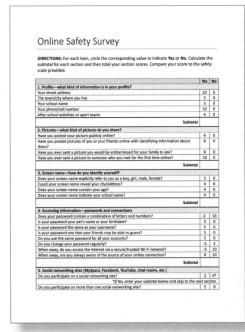
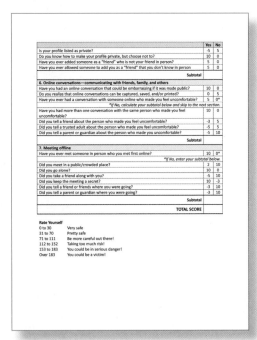

Sample safety survey

# Word and Excel Web Pages

**OUTCOMES**

- Save, open, edit, and preview *Word* and *Excel* documents as web pages.
- Create web pages with backgrounds, page titles, and text boxes.
- Determine basic *Word* features supported by a browser.

## Business Documents

- Business Documents Web Page
- Stock Fund Web Page
- Financial Report Web Page
- Course Web Page
- Formatting Web Page

### 62A–66A

**Warmup**

Key each line twice at the beginning of each lesson; first for control; then for speed.

alphabet 1 If Marge has extra help, the jigsaw puzzle can be solved quickly.

fig/sym 2 A & W Co. used P.O. #708-A to buy 125 chairs (#94-63) @ $25 each.

speed 3 The shamrock ornament is an authentic memento for the busy girls.

| gwam | 1' | 1 | 2 | 3 | 4 | 5 | 6 | 7 | 8 | 9 | 10 | 11 | 12 | 13 |
|------|----|---|---|---|---|---|---|---|---|---|----|----|----|----|

### 62B

**Learn: Save Word and Excel Documents as Web Pages**

File/Save As/Save as type/Web Page

1. Read the following information, and complete the activity.

A *Word* document can be saved as a Web Page in three formats. The desired format is selected from the Save as type list in the Save As dialog box. The formats available in *Word* are:

- Web Page
- Single File Web Page
- Web Page, Filtered

An *Excel* worksheet can be saved as a Web Page or a Single File Web Page. *Excel* does not offer the Web Page, Filtered format.

Figure 11-1 shows the Save As dialog box in *Word* with the three formats showing in the Save as type list. The Web Page format is selected, and the other two formats are listed above and below it in the illustration.

All three formats automatically insert HTML code into the document. Without the HTML code, browsers are unable to display the document on the Internet or intranet.

The **Web Page format** saves the document in one file and creates a folder to hold the graphics used in the web page.

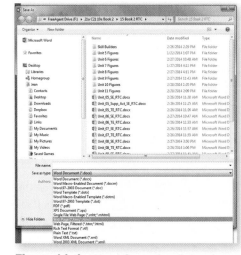

**Figure 11-1** *Word* Save As dialog box

The **Single File Web Page format** saves the document and supporting graphics in one file. This format may be used when the web page is to be viewed in an *Internet Explorer* browser, Version 4.0.1 or later, or when the web page is to be distributed via email.

## 70C

**Examining Security Tools**

Most of us go to great lengths to protect our valuables and property. We install security systems in our homes. We lock our car doors. We deposit our money in secure bank accounts. It is equally important to secure our computing equipment and devices and the data stored on them. A number of tools are available to help prevent cyber attacks. You learned about many of these in Unit 1 (see Lesson 4B on pp. 23–24), including:

- Antivirus, anti-spyware, and other malware detection programs that are designed to scan your system continuously as you work, check emails for problems, and even recommend against opening some websites that may threaten your system.
- Firewalls that check incoming data against specific rules and then either block the data or allow it to pass.
- Permissions and passwords that limit access to your system or its files.
- Maintenance plan that includes regular backups of data.

You can also take some commonsense measures to safeguard your data:

- Never respond to emails asking for personal information or requesting that you log in to a site to verify information. Always be suspicious if you get a message asking you to verify an account.
- Do not run programs if you are not sure where they came from or if they are safe.
- Do not open attachments to email if you don't know the sender, and even then use caution.

**QUICK ✔**

What types of passwords would be easy for a hacker to guess? How could you modify such a password to make it stronger and more effective?

## 70D

**Understanding Personal Digital Safety**

© Mika/Corbis/Glow Images

**Figure 12-8** You should avoid sharing the address of your employer with a stranger you have communicated with online.

You've probably seen stories like this on the news: a girl exchanges messages with someone online, thinking it's just another kid interested in the latest movies or the hottest band. However, the "friend" turns out to be an adult, who showed up one day at the girl's after-school job, followed her to the parking lot, forced her into his car, and assaulted her.

It's scary, and it's not something anyone likes to think about, but you have to know: there are bad adults out there waiting to take advantage of vulnerable kids. Law enforcement officials estimate that more than 5,000 kids every year become victims as a result of their online activity.

How can you avoid becoming a statistic? Here are some guidelines:

- Do not share your address or phone numbers or those of your employer, friends, and relatives.
- Do not become "friends" or chat with people you do not know.
- Never agree to a face-to-face meeting with a stranger you have met online.

Even the content you share online with friends and acquaintances can play a role in your personal safety and welfare. Every string of text you write and photo or video you post, referred to as your **digital footprint**, leaves a trail of information about you for millions of other digital users to read and view. Even applying privacy settings on social networking accounts does not ensure that personal information will stay private. That's why it is important to always keep private information *private*.

- Do not discuss personal issues or social plans online, even with your close friends. Make a phone call or talk face-to-face.

The **Web Page, Filtered format** is similar to the Web Page format except some of the HTML code is removed, making the file smaller than it is when saved in Web Page format. This option should only be used when you are finished editing the document as a *Word* file, because it may lose some of its HTML coding that is needed to display the document in its original format. Because of this, it is wise to save a version of the file in its original format when using the Web Page, Filtered option.

★TIP When you save the *Excel* file as a web page, click Yes if a box is displayed that says the file may contain features not compatible with Web Page format.

All web pages in this unit will be saved in the Web Page format to increase the likelihood they will be supported by most browsers.

2. Using *Word*, **open df 62b wp doc** and key your name in the bottom row, left aligned.
3. **Save in Web Page format as: 62b wp web page.**
4. Using *Excel*, open **df 62b ss wks**.
5. **Save in Web Page format as: 62b ss web page.**

## 62C

**Learn: Open a Web Page in Office**

File/Open

1. Read the following information, and complete the activity.

After saving a *Word* or *Excel* document as a web page, you can open the web page in the *Office* program in which it was created so it can be edited, if needed. For example, if you save an *Excel* workbook in Web Page format and then reopen the web page file in *Excel*, the workbook will look the same as the original worksheet you created in *Excel*. *Excel*, like *Word*, preserves the original formatting of the document. This allows you to easily switch from the file in HTML format (Web Page) to the standard *Office* program format and back again as needed when you are creating or editing web pages.

2. Using *Word*, **open 62b wp web page**.
3. Add a row at the bottom, and key your school's name, left-aligned.
4. **Save in Web Page format as: 62c wp web page.**
5. Using *Excel*, open **62b ss web page**.
6. Change the date to June 30, 20--.
7. **Save in Web Page format as: 62c ss web page.**

## 62D

**Learn: Preview Web Page in Browser**

Quick Access Toolbar/ Web Layout

★TIP When using *Word*, a document can be viewed as a Web page by using Web Layout view on the status bar.

1. Read the following information and complete the activity.

You can see how a *Word* document will look after it is posted on the Internet or intranet by previewing the web page. This enables you to see if there are any errors that need to be corrected or formatting features that need to be added, changed, or deleted. Previewing the web page is similar to using the Print Preview feature before you print a document.

To preview your web page, click the Web Layout button on the Quick Access Toolbar. This command opens a browser and displays the document as a web page in it. If the Web Layout button (see Figure 11-2) is not on your toolbar, follow the steps at the right to add it.

**Placing the Web Preview Button on the Quick Access Toolbar**

1. Display the Customize Quick Access Toolbar options by clicking the list arrow to the right of the Quick Access Toolbar.
2. Select *More Commands*.
3. Under *Choose commands from*, select *All Commands*.
4. Scroll down the All Commands list to *Web Page Preview*, select it, and then click *Add* to insert it into the existing list of commands on the Quick Access Toolbar.
5. Click OK.

**Figure 11-2** Web Layout

# LESSON 70

## Security Risks and Precautions

**OUTCOMES**
- Identify digital security risks.
- Examine security tools to protect hardware and data.
- Understand personal digital safety.

### Business Document

**70B**

- Word Processing Survey

**Identifying Digital Security Risks**

**Figure 12-7** Computer hackers can unleash viruses that destroy data and software.

© Andrey_Popov/Shutterstock.com

Digital technologies connect us to vast resources in every corner of the world, at any time of the day or night. But with that exposure and access come many risks that pose dangers to our digital equipment, our data, and our personal well-being. As a responsible digital citizen, you must be able to recognize the dangers that exist in the digital world. These include:

- Hackers, who access computers and networks without proper permission and steal personal information or unleash viruses that destroy data and software.
- Identity theft, which occurs when someone uses your personal identifying information without your permission to commit fraud or other crimes. For example, if thieves gain access to your Social Security number, they can use it to get more personal information about you or to obtain more credit. They might establish a credit card in your name, go on a spending spree, and stick you with the bill. Or they might take money out of your bank account.
- Phishing, a common Internet scam in which you get emails that appear to be from a legitimate source that asks for sensitive information, such as your Social Security number, credit card or bank account numbers, or other personal information. A variation is **smishing**, which is done with text messaging on your cell phone.
- Pharming, or spoofing, a scam where thieves redirect a real website's traffic to a bogus site. The "pharmer" secretly hijacks your computer and takes you to a copycat website that looks just like the real thing. Once there, you'll be asked to provide personal information.
- Cyber predators, or people who use the Internet to hunt for victims—usually children and teens—to take advantage of and exploit. They participate in chat groups or game sites, posing as other kids. Or they request to be your "friend" on a social networking site. They manipulate you into sharing information and talking about personal issues. They are experts at taking advantage of others—either sexually, emotionally, psychologically, or financially.
- Inappropriate content, such as pornography, violence, sexting, and cyberbullying. Viewing and participating in online activities such as these can lead to addictions, unhealthy relationships, low self-esteem, and violent or detrimental behaviors.

Connecting online and being part of the digital community come with a very real set of risks. It is your personal responsibility to identify those risks and take measures to protect yourself from influences that can harm not only you but others in the digital community as well.

**QUICK**

1. What is the purpose of an Internet scam?
2. What might you look for in an email or text message that would identify it as a scam?

2. Open **df 62b wp doc** and preview it using the Web Layout button.
3. Switch to Print Layout view, and preview it as a web page using the Web Layout view.
4. Close the file without saving.

## Learn: Page Color

Design/Page Background/
Page Color

**TIP** In *Excel*, a picture background can be added to a worksheet (Page Layout/Page Setup/ Background). The image will be displayed as the background of the web page if the *Excel* file is saved as a web page.

1. Read the following information, and complete the activity.

Page Color (background) can be used to create attractive web pages in *Word*. With Page Color, you can apply various colors and fill effects: a solid color, a color in a variety of textures or patterns, different gradients that use one or two colors, or a picture.

A good design practice is to select the background and the color of the font together so the combination is easy to read and attractive.

Figure 11-3 shows the Theme Colors, Standard Colors, No Color, More Colors, and Fill Effects options for backgrounds. Click Fill Effects to display the Fill Effects dialog box, where you can click the tabs to select gradients, textures, patterns, and pictures as backgrounds.

If you want to add a solid color background to an *Excel* worksheet, apply cell shading to all cells in the worksheet.

2. Using *Word*, open **df 62b wp doc.**
3. Explore creating backgrounds using solid colors of your choice.
4. Explore creating backgrounds using textures of your choice.
5. Explore creating backgrounds using patterns of your choice.
6. Create a background using a picture from the *u11 css events pictures* folder. Follow this path to find the pictures: Solutions folder/u11 css xxx folder/u11 css events pictures.
7. Choose a background and font color that you believe to be very easy to read and attractive. Show your instructor what you have chosen.
8. Save the file in Web Page format named **62e wp web page**, preview it, and print it. (The background won't print.)

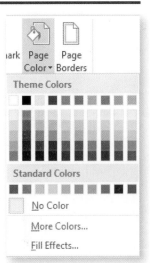

**Figure 11-3** Page Color options

© iStockphoto.com/MachineHeadz

## Digital Citizenship and Ethics
From homework help to music downloads to online shopping, the Internet has become a valuable resource that provides many benefits when it is used responsibly. But searching on the Internet can lead you to websites containing inappropriate content, such as antisocial or reckless behavior, violence, pornography, and gambling.

Many search engines provide options for controlling access to inappropriate websites, but you can also limit your exposure to offensive content by understanding what constitutes illegal or misleading content. In addition, do not take everything you read on the Internet at face value, because anyone can set up a website and use it to publish just about anything they please, including extremist views and false information.

As a class, discuss the following:

1. What would you do if you came across an offensive website?
2. What does Internet safety mean to you?

## Identifying Piracy and Illegal File Sharing

**Figure 12-6** Listening to music on a digital device can be relaxing and even motivational, but you should never download music files without the copyright holder's permission.

It is not hard to find music files, movies, and software online that you can download for free. And that's OK—as long as you download only from sites where the copyright holder has given permission. But many people download files—or make copies of software programs—without the copyright holder's permission. This is known as **piracy**, and it is another way people use the Internet to steal what doesn't belong to them. Sometimes pirates burn copies of CDs or DVDs and sell them for a couple of dollars to their friends or at flea markets. Or they "borrow" someone's copy of the latest computer game and install it on their own computer. Or they swap MP3 files with their friends. These are all forms of piracy.

File-sharing technology, too, can lead to piracy. Also referred to as "peer-to-peer" or P2P, file-sharing programs let you search for and copy files from other computers, or "peers," that participate in the network. While file sharing is a convenient way to share public-domain files or access files for which you pay a fee, it can quickly turn to piracy.

One of the most notorious P2P-based systems was Napster, a software utility that, when downloaded to individual computers, or peers, enabled users to share songs in MP3 format. The songs "lived" on each peer's machine instead of on a centralized server. As you might imagine, millions of people downloaded millions of songs for free, and the music industry was not happy about it. Napster was eventually sued by a number of recording companies and was forced to shut down.

Piracy and illegal file sharing are theft, and many software companies and the music and movie industries have successfully prosecuted digital pirates. While it is not illegal to download a P2P file-sharing program, you should take extreme care to ensure that you are not sharing copyrighted materials.

## Creating a Table in a Document

1. Open the data file *df 69d legal*. **Save as:** **69d legal**. The document contains several scenarios regarding the use of copyrighted material.
2. Insert a 2-column, 5-row table below the heading of the document, with the column headings of **Legal** and **Illegal**.
3. Read each of the scenarios, and determine if it is a legal or illegal action. Cut and paste the scenario to the correct column in the table. Format as desired. With your instructor's permission, print the document. Then save and close the file.

# 21st Century Skills: Use and Manage Information

The Internet provides many different ways for users to obtain news. Newspaper and magazine publishers provide online editions with updates to the content in their print versions. Television and radio networks stream broadcasts over the Web. While online sources are a convenient way to access news and information, there are drawbacks:

- Objectivity can be compromised. Many online news outlets have limited limited staff to gather and report the news, especially overseas. So, they purchase the rights to publish news from another organization, which means that often the same story shows up on different news websites.
- More time staring at a screen can strain the eyes and have other negative health effects.

### Think Critically

1. What are the benefits of accessing news online?
2. Why is objectivity important in reporting the news?

## Learn: Web Page Title

File/Save As/Save as type/
Web Page/Change Title

1. Read the following information and complete the activity.

Each web page has a title displayed in the browser title bar at the top of the window. If you do not specify a title for a web page, the software will create one for you. Since you want the title to accurately describe the content of the web page, you should specify a title to be displayed. In *Word* and *Excel*, go to the Save as Web Page dialog box and specify a web page title. Click the Change Title button, click in the Enter Text dialog box, and key the desired title, as shown in Figure 11-4.

**Figure 11-4** Web page title

2. Open **df 62f wp doc.**
3. Save in Web Page format as **62f wp web page,** and key Ms. Dilligan's Home Page as the web page title.
4. Preview the document in a browser, noting that the web page title is displayed in the browser's tab.
5. Open **df 62f ss wks.**
6. Save in Web Page format as **62f ss web page,** and key Bristol Student Aid Fund as the web page title.
7. Preview the document in a browser; see the title displayed in the browser's tab.

## Apply: Application

1. Open a new *Word* document.
2. Key the following text, using the directions given in the text.

Center-align this text using 36-pt. Verdana font

Left-align this text using 18-pt. Verdana font

Right-align this text using 18-pt. Verdana font

Using left alignment, 12-pt. Verdana font, and a bullet style you select, list the following lines:

- Bullet 1
- Bullet 2
- Bullet 3

Using 16-pt. Comic Sans MS font, indent the following lines as directed:

    Indent this line 0.5" from left margin

        Indent this line 1" from left margin

            Indent this line 1.5" from left margin

> Center a shaded text box with a border. Use 14-pt. Comic Sans MS font for the text. Select a font color.

★**TIP** To ensure that the text box will be centered horizontally in the browser window, click outside the text box in the *Word* document and center the line of text containing the text box.

★**TIP** Line breaks will differ based on the width of the browser window.

3. Preview the document in your browser, using Web Layout view.
4. Compare the web page text with the text you keyed and directions you followed. Does your browser support all of the word processing features used in this activity? If so, your text should look like the text in the following Quick Check.
5. Save in Web Page format as **62g wp web page**, and key Alignment and Indentations as the title of the web page.

# LESSON 69

## Digital Law

- Understand copyrights and copyright infringement.
- Define plagiarism.
- Explain illegal file sharing and piracy.

## Business Document

### 69B

**Understanding Copyrights and Plagiarism**

- Word Processing Document with Table

Digital technologies allow us to share, copy, and download information at the click of a button. The ease and speed with which we can do this is a major reason we acquire and use these technologies. But it can also be their drawback, as copying and pasting from the Web can result in the inappropriate—and sometimes illegal—use of copyrighted material.

A **copyright** is a form of protection granted by law to the creators of original works of authorship. These works, referred to as **intellectual property**, include books, articles, software, music, plays, movie scripts, and artwork. Copyrighted material may carry the © symbol, but even if you do not see the symbol, it may still be copyrighted.

Generally, when a work is copyrighted, you cannot use the material unless you have the owner's written permission. However, the "Fair Use" provision in the 1976 Copyright Act allows students and educators to use portions of copyrighted materials for educational, scholarly, or research purposes, as long as the usage does not affect the original author's profits. You should always credit the source for any copyrighted material you use—whether it is obtained through the owner's permission or under the fair use doctrine. The penalties for copyright infringement range from fines to jail time.

**Plagiarism**, like copyright infringement, is a highly unethical practice and can result in legal repercussions. When you plagiarize, you are stealing somebody else's idea, text, or other creative work and claiming it as your own. Even if you copy material that is not copyrighted or in the **public domain** (intellectual property that is not protected by copyright or belongs to the public in general, such as government publications), you could be guilty of plagiarism if you do not credit the source. Schools and educators take plagiarism seriously. In fact, many instructors use software programs specifically designed to identify material that has been copied from other sources.

The best way to avoid plagiarism and copyright infringement is to be diligent in citing the sources from which you obtain information, even if it is written material that you have paraphrased. That does not mean you must credit every fact or statistic you use. Information that is common knowledge—such as the equator is the imaginary dividing line between the Earth's northern and southern hemispheres—does not need to be cited. When you are unsure, it's best to be on the safe side and cite your sources.

## QUICK ✔

You have learned about the types of materials that can be copyrighted. What types of things are not or cannot be copyrighted? Use the Internet and other sources to research and share your findings with the class.

Your web page text should look like this if your browser supports all of the word processing features.

Center-align this text using 36-pt. Verdana font.

Left-align this text using 18-pt. Verdana font.

Right-align this text using 18-pt. Verdana font.

Using left align, 12-pt. Verdana font, and a bullet style you select, list the following lines:

➤ Bullet 1
➤ Bullet 2
➤ Bullet 3

Using 16-pt. Comic Sans MS font, indent the following lines as directed:

Indent this line 0.5" from left margin.

Indent this line 1" from left margin.

Indent this line 1.5" from left margin.

Center a shaded text box with a border. Use 14-pt. Comic Sans MS font for the text. Select a font color.

## LESSON 63

# Web Page Tables, Graphics, and Pictures

**OUTCOMES**

- Create *Word* web pages containing a page color, text, tables, pictures, clip art, and graphics.
- Create an *Excel* web page with a page color.

### Business Documents

- Service Organization Home Web Page
- Web Page with Table
- Board of Directors Web Page
- Web Page of Events

### 63B

**Apply: Website for Citizens Supporting Schools**

In this lesson and the next lesson, you will complete the first few pages of a website for Citizens Supporting Schools that supports the Corrigan School District.

1. Find the folder named *u11 css xxx* in the Solutions folder, and change its name by replacing the *xxx* with your initials.

2. Open a new *Word* document, and apply a Page Color that uses red or blue, Corrigan School District's school colors.

3. Key your name in a font and font color that are attractive and easy to read. It is a good design principle to use a sans serif (without "feet" at the end of each main stroke of the letter) font such as Arial, Calibri, Comic Sans, or Verdana that is easy to read on a computer monitor.

4. Save the background and font selections as a Web Page file named ***u11 background*** in the *u11 css xxx* folder. This file will be used for the three CSS web pages in Lessons 63 and 64.

 **★TIP** All files in Lessons 63 and 64 relating to the Citizens Supporting Schools website can be found in the *u11 css xxx* folder. Unless directed otherwise, save all files in Web Page format in the *u11 css xxx* folder so hyperlinks to your files can be easily inserted in later activities. The website then can be uploaded to the Internet or an intranet, if applicable.

Figure 12-5 Videoconferencing and other collaborative technologies can help increase worker productivity.

- Like videoconferencing, **video chatting** enables users with an Internet connection and camera or Webcam to communicate face-to-face via computer, smartphone, or other digital device. Video chatting, which can be accomplished with programs such as Skype, Windows Live Messenger, and FaceTime, can be likened to instant messaging with video capabilities. The technology has also been incorporated into social networks, including Facebook and Twitter.
- A **wiki**, which is Hawaiian for "quick," is a website that allows multiple users to add and edit content in real time. Wikis are powerful collaboration tools, both at school and on the job. While one person is developing content on a topic, others can add to it or make modifications.
- **Blogs** allow Web users to post commentary on selected topics and issues and respond to those comments posted by others. Since blog entries can be linked, blogs facilitate dialogue among users with common interests. Like wikis, blogs are effective tools for collaboration, allowing users to share information, comments, and opinions.

1. Identify a hobby, sport, pastime, or other topic that interests you.
2. Search the Internet for directories of blogs. Select a directory and search for blogs that relate to your interest. Review at least three blogs, noting the types of content they contain, the things you like about the blog, and the things you do not like.
3. Start your presentation program. Using the information you have gathered, create a presentation on a blog you would develop yourself on your interest. Include slides on the three blogs you evaluated earlier, highlighting their pros and cons. Add at least three slides that cover the topics and content you would include on your own blog. Be sure to insert a title slide for the presentation.
4. Format the presentation and enhance it with graphics, transitions, and animations as desired. **Save as: 68e blog**. Share the presentation with your class.

**Digital Citizenship and Ethics** You've probably used the Internet to gather information for a school project, or maybe you visit websites as part of your classroom learning, or perhaps you've accessed an online tutorial to learn about effective study habits or how to write better essays. **E-learning**, or online education, has become a popular and accessible way for learners at all levels to take classes and further their academic pursuits. Many colleges and universities now offer online degree programs, and businesses often use online and computer-based training for employees.

E-learning offers many advantages, including:

- Flexible scheduling, which enables learners to complete coursework when it's convenient for them.
- Self-paced learning, which allows participants to learn at their own pace as long as coursework is turned in by the due date.
- No transportation costs or hassles, as you typically work from your home computer.

As a class, discuss the following.

1. How have you used e-learning at home or in school within the last six months?
2. What are some drawbacks of taking online courses?

TEAMWORK

1. Using Word, open **u11 background**, delete the text, and save it as a Web Page named **index** in the *u11 css xxx* folder.  The filename for the home page for the CSS website is **index**.
2. Key the following text as the home page of the website.  Use 1.0 line spacing and tap Enter once after each ¶.  Key the first line in 36-pt. font; the next two lines in 24-pt. font; the first ¶ in 12-pt. font; and the last ¶ in italic 10-pt. font.

Citizens Supporting Schools

Supporting Students, Faculty, and Staff of the Corrigan School District Since 1976

Mission Statement:

The mission of CSS is to support the Corrigan School District to improve the quality of curricular and extra-curricular services rendered to students by faculty and staff.

*This site is maintained by the Webmaster of Citizens Supporting Schools. Please email your feedback to the Webmaster.*

3. View it as a web page.  **Save as: index**.

1. Read the following information, and complete the activity.

Many web pages use tables to organize information in an attractive manner.  The Table feature of your word processor can be used to create tables for your web pages. You can use features you learned in previous units to format the tables so they are attractive, easy to read, and consistent with your background and font colors.

2. Using *Word*, open **index**.
3. Insert the tables below the mission statement.  Center them horizontally, use a 12-pt. bold font, and use colored borders around the cells.  Use the same font styles used elsewhere in this web page.
4. Key **Citizens Supporting Schools** as the web page title.
5. Compare your web page to the one shown in the following Quick Check.  **Save as: index**.

| About CSS | Board Members | Finances |
|-----------|---------------|----------|
| Donors | Events | Corrigan School District |

| Voice Mailbox | 535-555-0193 |
|---------------|--------------|

Your web page should look like this.

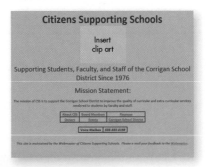

1. List and describe three rude behaviors you have noticed in other cell phone users. What methods could you employ to deal with inappropriate behaviors such as these?
2. Investigate restrictions your state or municipality has placed on cell phone use while driving. In your opinion, should individuals be allowed to use their cell phones while driving? Why or why not?

## 68D

### Evaluating Messaging Tools

While mobile phones were originally developed for voice communication, many users now rely on cell phone texting as their primary means of communication with family and friends. According to recent research, **texting**, or sending text messages via cell phones or other mobile devices, has overtaken all other forms of communication and interaction among teens. This includes talking face-to-face.

Other forms of text messaging are also popular with digital technology users. **Instant messaging** is a system for exchanging messages in real time—or instantaneously—via the Internet or a shared network. **Email**, or electronic mail, allows individuals to send messages to other users via telecommunications links between computers.

WORDS AND MEANINGS/MARK SYKES/Alamy

**Figure 12-4** Use messaging shorthand and abbreviations in personal messages to close friends and family only.

Text messages in any form are convenient in that you do not have to be physically present or available to speak in order to communicate your message. They also provide a record of the communication. But therein lies one of the drawbacks of text messaging. Users often forget that even though they delete a message, it is still stored on a server somewhere in cyberspace and can be retrieved and reviewed. Also, once you hit the send button, your message can be shared—either intentionally or by mistake—with the rest of the digital world. To avoid these pitfalls and others, consider the following:

- Do not use inappropriate language or content in text messages, such as crude jokes, sarcasm, or other comments that could be misinterpreted by readers.
- Limit the use of messaging shorthand and abbreviations to personal communication with close friends and family only. In all other cases, spell out all words and write in clear, grammatically correct sentences. Never use all caps, as that implies shouting.
- Do not rely on text messages as an alternative to face-to-face conversations or phone calls. These forms of communication are often more suitable to solving a problem and interpreting thoughts and ideas.

1. Start your spreadsheet application, and open the data file *df 68d teen usage*. Save it as *68d teen usage*.
2. Apply appropriate cell styles to the data.
3. Create a column chart based on the data. Format the chart as desired.
4. Start your word processing application, and create a new document. Save it as *68d teen usage report*. Using the information in the spreadsheet file, write a half-page report that summarizes teen use of the various communications methods during the four-year period listed. Copy the column chart from the spreadsheet to the report to illustrate your summary.
5. Format the document as desired. With your instructor's permission, print the report.

## 68E

### Understanding Videoconferencing, Blogs, and Wikis

Communal and collaborative communication technologies, such as videoconferencing, video chatting, wikis, and blogs, have enabled users to share thoughts and ideas and work together to achieve a common goal.

- **Videoconferencing** allows two parties in different locations to communicate "face-to-face" in real time using both video equipment and an Internet link. Many businesses use videoconferencing to link employees in different offices, thereby eliminating the time and money spent on traveling.

**Apply: Create Web Page Table**

1. Open *u11 background*, delete the text, and save it as a Web Page named *u11board members* in the u11 css xxx folder. Key **CSS Board Members** as the web page title.
2. Format the two following tables so they are attractive, easy to read, and consistent with the other web page of this website.
3. **Save as:** *u11 board members.*

| CSS Board Members | | |
|---|---|---|
| **Name** | **Position** | **Years Served** |
| Adrian Hess | President | 12 |
| Harry Malone | Vice President | 8 |
| William Evans | Secretary | 20 |
| Amanda Egan | Treasurer | 7 |
| Barbara Narick | Legal Counsel | 2 |
| Alex Rendulic | Fundraising | 5 |
| Gladys Young | Awards | 9 |
| Paul Lyman | Student Liaison | 1 |
| Susan Rhymond | Faculty/Staff Liaison | 8 |
| Kimberly Varati | Webmaster | 3 |

| Ex-Officio Members | |
|---|---|
| **Name** | **Affiliation** |
| Charles Shaw | Superintendent, CSD |
| Mary McHolme | CHS Principal |
| Margaret Julio | CHS Guidance Counselor |

Home

## 21st Century Skills: Creativity and Innovation

Being a creative thinker and communicating ideas with others are important skills, whether you are in the classroom, on the job, or in a social situation. When you are willing to suggest and share ideas, you demonstrate your originality and inventiveness. When you are open and responsive to the ideas and perspectives of others, you show consideration and cooperation.

In teams of three to four, develop a class newsletter to be published on your school's website. The newsletter should include a minimum of three articles and at least two graphics. Article ideas include recent projects, field trips, guest speakers, upcoming tests or assignments, study tips, teacher profiles, or student achievements. Divide duties as necessary. Save the newsletter as a web page, and publish it to your school's website as directed by your instructor.

### Think Critically

1. Creativity can mean a lot of different things. How do you define creativity?
2. What idea creation techniques do you think work best for groups? What about for you individually?
3. What positive things can you learn from an idea that "flops"?

TEAMWORK

## LESSON 68    Digital Communications

**OUTCOMES**

- Define digital communication.
- Distinguish between proper and improper use of cell phones.
- Evaluate texting, instant messaging, and email communications.
- Describe videoconferencing, video chats, blogs, and wikis.

### Business Documents

**68B**

- Formatted Spreadsheet
- Word Processing Document with Chart
- Presentation

**Defining Digital Communication**

**Figure 12-3** Do you understand the proper and acceptable use of cell phones?

Most of us use digital communications technology daily. We use our cell phones to make calls or send text messages. We use instant messaging to exchange electronic messages in real time on social networking and other websites. We transfer electronic files via email. We connect to the Internet with our computers and smartphones.

**Digital communication** is the electronic exchange of information. It provides users with quick—often instantaneous—access to each other as well as to enormous electronic databases that store volumes of information. Through digital communication, students and their parents can access homework assignments, lesson plans, and scheduling information at any time of the day or night. Doctors can retrieve a patient's medical records, issue prescriptions, and evaluate tests at the click of a button. Companies can use videoconferencing to communicate "face-to-face" with employees in remote locations, thus saving travel costs and boosting worker productivity.

Digital technology tools have transformed the way we communicate, and new and faster tools come on the market regularly. As a successful digital citizen, you should understand the various technologies and devices that are becoming mainstream methods for communication. It is equally important that you understand their proper and acceptable use.

 **QUICK** ✔

1. What digital communication technologies do you use at school? At home?
2. Assume you do not have access to the digital communication technologies that you listed for question 1 above. How would you accomplish the same things?

**68C**

**Using Cell Phones Responsibly**

A **cellular phone**, or cell phone, is a mobile telephone that uses radio waves to transmit calls. Early mobile phones date back to the 1940s, when they were used by ships at sea and in police cars. But it was not until the 1980s that the predecessor of today's cell phones appeared on the market. Today, more than two-thirds of the U.S. population is connected via mobile technology, and recent reports indicate that about eight in ten teens now own a cell phone.

While mobile phones have become a primary means of communication, many people often forget basic manners and rules of etiquette that should be followed when using them. For example:

- Always turn your phone off in theaters, libraries, places of worship, and doctor's offices.
- Set your ringer at a low volume or, better yet, consider using vibrate mode.
- Do not use your cell phone while you are doing something else, such as riding a bike, studying, or simply having a conversation with others. You should never use your phone while you are driving a vehicle. Many states and municipalities have adopted laws restricting the use of cell phones while driving.

## Learn: Insert Clip Art in Web Pages

 **TIP** If you use clip art from an Internet web page, first check the copyright policy. If necessary, obtain permission for the item's use and give proper credit to the source.

Clip art can be inserted into web pages in the same manner as it is inserted into other *Office* documents. Once inserted, it can be moved, edited, and used as a hyperlink, if desired. (Hyperlinks are presented in Lesson 64.)

### Activity 1

1. Open *index* in *Word*.
2. Using clip art, find a lion to represent Corrigan School District's mascot.
3. Insert the lion graphic in the horizontal center after the first heading. Size the image so it is about 1.5" wide. Format it appropriately.
4. **Save as:** *index*.

### Activity 2

1. Open *u11 background*. **Save as a Web Page:** *u11 events*.
2. Delete the existing text, and key the following information using a background, font, and color that are consistent with the other web pages in the website.

Citizens Supporting Schools Events

| Recent Events | Upcoming Events |
|---|---|

3. If needed, open *index*. Copy the mascot (lion) graphic. Close the file. Paste the lion centered below the table in *u11 events*. **Save as:** *u11 events*.

## Learn: Insert Pictures in a Web Page

1. Read the following information, and complete the activity.

Picture and graphic files, like clip art, can be inserted into web pages just as they are inserted into word processing documents. Once inserted, a picture can be moved, edited, and used as a hyperlink. *Note:* If you use pictures from another website, you must give proper credit to that website.

2. Open *u11 events*.
3. Insert the *Word* file named *df u11 events text* below the lion clip art. It is in your *u11 css xxx* folder. Format it as needed to maintain consistency with the other CSS web pages.
4. Insert the pictures as directed in the text, and then delete the text indicating where to insert the pictures. Follow this path to find the pictures: Solutions folder/u11 css xxx folder/u11 css events pictures.
5. Size the pictures so they are about 3" wide, but keep them in proportion and center-align them, if possible.
6. View *u11 events* as a web page, and make any needed changes.
7. Key **CSS Events** as the web page title.
8. **Save as:** *u11 events*.

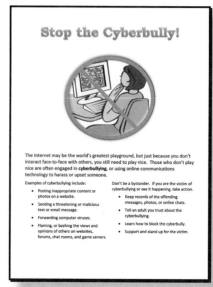

Sample flyer on cyberbullying

## 67D

**Physical and Mental Health Issues**

Figure 12-2 Working on a laptop while lying on your bed or the floor can result in poor posture.

You might find it hard to imagine that digital technologies can be dangerous to your physical and mental health. But to be a successful digital citizen, you must learn how to recognize these risks and protect your well-being. Some of the most common dangers include the following:

- Carpal tunnel syndrome (CTS), which is a condition of pain and weakness in the hand or wrist caused by repetitive motions, such as keyboarding and using a mouse. You can minimize the risk of developing CTS by arranging your space so that you can sit in a comfortable position while you do your work or digital activities.
- Eyestrain, also called computer vision syndrome, which results from staring at a digital screen for hours at a time without a break. Doctors recommend stopping every 20 minutes and looking at something 20 feet away for 20 seconds.
- Poor posture, as a result of using digital technologies on inappropriate surfaces, such as a bed or the floor. You should use a computer on a hard surface, such as a table or desk, and avoid use for extended periods of time.
- Phoning and texting while driving or biking, which is a leading cause of accidents.
- Addiction, or psychological dependence on the online experience. This can lead to a variety of other problems including a decline in social interaction, sleep disorders, obesity due to decreased physical activity, and poor performance in school and on the job.

The key to minimizing or eliminating both physical and mental health risks is to find a balance between the use of digital technologies and your time away from the screen. Limit your time in front of a screen or on your cell phone so that it does not interfere with other activities, such as doing homework, interacting with family and friends, and engaging in physical activity.

1. Open a blank presentation, and save it as *67d digital health*.
2. Create a presentation consisting of at least six slides on the health risks associated with digital technologies. You may use information presented in this lesson or do further research using the Internet and other resources. Use appropriate slide layouts and insert images and graphics as necessary.
3. Share your presentation with the class.

# LESSON 64  Web Page Hyperlinks and Bookmarks

- Create *Word* and *Excel* web pages.
- Insert hyperlinks and bookmarks in web pages.

**Business Documents**

- Informational Web Page
- Web Page with Financial Report
- Web Page with List of Donors
- Board of Directors Web Page
- Web Page of Events
- Service Organization Home Web Page

## 64B

**Apply: Create Word and Excel Web Pages**

© zippy/Shutterstock.com

### Activity 1

1. Using *Word*, open **df u11 about css** from your *u11 css xxx* folder.
2. Format it as needed to maintain consistency with the other CSS web pages.
3. **Save as:** **u11 about css.** Key **About CSS** as the title of this web page.

### Activity 2

1. Using *Excel*, open **df u11 finances** from your *u11 css xxx* folder.
2. Add a Home box in or near cell B20. Format it appropriately.
3. Format the worksheet using fill and font colors consistent with those used in this website.
4. **Save as:** **u11 finances.** Key **CSS Finances** as the title of this web page.

### Activity 3

1. Using *Word*, open **u11 background**, and delete the text. **Save as a Web Page:** **u11 donors.**
2. Key the following information. Format the tables to be consistent with other web pages in the CSS website.
3. **Save as:** **u11 donors.** Key **CSS Donors** as the web page title.

| CSS DONORS | |
|---|---|
| **Amount** | **Last Year's Donors** |
| $500 or more | Paul Adamek, Bob Rothey, Kristine Wood |
| $250-$499 | Toni Bauer, Cyd Booth, Jon Burd, Ira Mays, Dee Spahr |
| $100-$249 | Harry Held, Eugene Lytle, Dennis Marks, Wallace Rapp, Jen Sinclair, Bob Turner, Laura Weigel |
| Up to $100 | Connie Cain, Debbie Cole, Sue Cranston, Jeremy Davis, Janet Krise, Stanley Lang, Victor Ophar, Walter Suchy, Michael Wray |

Home

## Cyberbullying and Flaming

**Figure 12-1** Cyberbullying is a serious concern and an irresponsible use of digital technologies

We're all familiar with the schoolyard bully—the kid who teases others or steals their lunch or pushes and punches in order to intimidate. Bullies have been around a long time, but today's digital technologies have given them a new platform from which they can threaten, harass, or torment others. This is known as **cyberbullying**.

Cyberbullying takes many forms; for example, groups of people can decide to pick on or ignore certain individuals on social networking sites; email is used to forward harassing messages or computer viruses to unpopular kids; and threatening messages can be sent via text messaging, chat rooms, and message boards.

Another form of cyberbullying is **flaming**, or bashing, which is hostile and overly harsh arguments made via Internet forums, chat rooms, video-sharing websites, and even game servers. These arguments typically focus on heated or sensitive real-world issues, but they can also target less important, even mundane issues. They are intended to cause trouble rather than actually discuss the issue at hand.

Cyberbullying is a serious concern in the digital community, and, more and more, authorities are taking action against those who bully others online. As a responsible digital citizen, you can do your part to help stop cyberbullying. The first rule is to respect others. Always watch what you say online, and be careful about the images you send or post. You may think only a few people will see, but whatever you share online could be made public within minutes. If you are the victim of cyberbullying or see it going on, keep records of offending content, and report it to an adult you trust.

1. Open a new word processing document, and save it as *67c bullying flyer*.
2. Use the following text to create a flyer on cyberbullying. You can create the flyer from scratch or use a template. Insert photos and graphics as desired.

Stop the Cyberbully!

The Internet may be the world's greatest playground, but just because you don't interact face-to-face with others, you still need to play nice. Those who don't play nice are often engaged in cyberbullying, or using online communications technology to harass or upset someone.

Examples of cyberbullying include:

- Posting inappropriate content or photos on a website.
- Sending a threatening or malicious text or email message.
- Forwarding computer viruses.
- Flaming, or bashing the views and opinions of others on websites, forums, chat rooms, and game servers.

Don't be a bystander. If you are the victim of cyberbullying or see it happening, take action.

- Keep records of the offending messages, photos, or online chats.
- Tell an adult you trust about the cyberbullying.
- Learn how to block the cyberbully.
- Support and stand up for the victim.

3. With your instructor's permission, print the flyer and post it at your school.

## Learn: About Hyperlinks

Insert/Links/Hyperlink/
Insert Hyperlink dialog box

Web pages can be enriched through the use of **hyperlinks**. When hyperlinks are inserted into a web page, the user can click them to go to a different location. The location can be a different website, a different web page within the same website, another location within the same web page, or an email address. The appropriate Link to option in the left column of the Insert Hyperlink dialog box is used to establish hyperlinks, as shown in Figure 11-5.

**Figure 11-5** Insert Hyperlink

Both graphic and text hyperlinks can be used. Text hyperlinks usually appear in a different font color and are underlined.

In the next four activities, you will insert each of the four kinds of hyperlinks into the web pages you have created for the Citizens Supporting Schools website.

## Learn: Hyperlinks to Email Addresses

Insert/Links/Hyperlink/
Insert Hyperlink dialog
box/Email Address

1. Read the following information, and complete the activity.

When a user clicks a hyperlink to an email address, a new email message box is created with the linked email address appearing in the To line. The user then keys the subject line and email-message and clicks Send when the message is ready to be delivered.

Figures 11-6 to 11-8 show three methods of creating hyperlinks to an email address. Figure 11-6 is to an address that is represented by a graphic, the mailbox graphic in this case. When the user clicks the mailbox, the email message box will open.

Figure 11-7 shows an email address that is used as a hyperlink. It appears in a different font color and is underlined. Most often, the software will recognize the format of an email address and automatically create a hyperlink as soon as the Space Bar is tapped after the last character of the email address is keyed.

Figure 11-8 also uses text to hyperlink to an email address, but in this example, the text is the person's name rather than the person's email address.

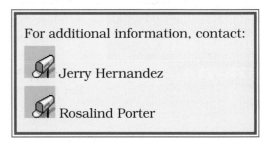

For additional information, contact:

Jerry Hernandez

Rosalind Porter

**Figure 11-6** Email hyperlink from a graphic

For additional information, contact:

Jerry Hernandez,
hernanj@webgate.com

Rosalind Porter,
porter@webgate.com

**Figure 11-7** Email hyperlink from an email address

For additional information, contact:

Jerry Hernandez

Rosalind Porter

**Figure 11-8** Email hyperlink from a name

# UNIT 12

# Becoming a Successful Digital Citizen

## LESSON 67 — Digital Etiquette and Well-Being

**OUTCOMES**

- Define digital etiquette.
- Describe responsible digital behavior.
- Understand cyberbullying and flaming.
- Explain physical and mental health issues related to digital technologies.

### Business Documents 67A–71A

- Flyer
- Presentation

**Warmup**

Key each line twice at the beginning of each lesson; first for control, then for speed.

alphabet 1 Max and Jack have the best grades for the two philosophy quizzes.

fig/sym 2 I can call Shirley at 542-3195 on Friday or 542-6807 on Saturday.

speed 3 The neighbor may fix the rifle, bugle, and cycle for the visitor.

| gwam | 1' | 1 | 2 | 3 | 4 | 5 | 6 | 7 | 8 | 9 | 10 | 11 | 12 | 13 |

### 67B

**Defining Digital Etiquette**

Have you ever been in the middle of a face-to-face conversation when the person you are talking to abruptly interrupts you to reply to a text message? Or maybe you've been annoyed by another passenger on the bus or train who is speaking loudly on his cell phone.

Hola Images/Getty Images

Digital technologies have provided us with quicker and sometimes easier ways to communicate, but they have also led to the decline in face-to-face interaction. In turn, communication has become highly impersonal, making it easy to forget the good manners and etiquette we practice in face-to-face contact.

Digital etiquette is an informal set of rules governing the proper and courteous behaviors expected of digital technology users. Successful digital citizens are honest, respectful of others, and capable of adjusting their use of digital technologies to adapt to the situation. For example, when you walk into a library, you should know to turn off your cell phone; when you participate in a chat room, you should know the rules and expectations; when you are in a classroom, you should not be texting your friends. In general, you should think of digital etiquette as an extension of the manners you practice every day in your personal, academic, and business relationships.

2. Open *index*. Select *Webmaster* (the last word in the last line of text) to create a hyperlink to this email address: kvarati@cengage.com. Use **Kimberly Varati** as the screen tip, as shown in Figure 11-9.

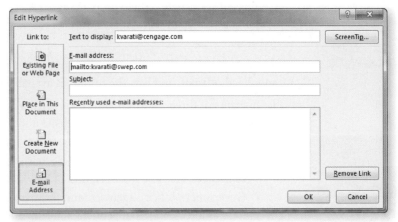

Figure 11-9 Edit Hyperlink

3. **Save as:** *index*.
4. Open *u11 board members*. Insert a column at the right; key **email** for the column heading; merge cells as needed. Key each email address in the last column so that the entire email address is the hyperlink. Key each person's email address in lowercase letters. The email address for each person is the **first initial** of his or her name plus the **last name**, followed by **@cengage.com**—for example, ahess@cengage.com and hmalone@cengage.com. Use the default screen tip.
5. **Save as:** *u11 board members2*.
6. Open *u11 events* from the *u11 css xxx* folder, and create an email hyperlink to *Alex Rendulic* (arendulic@cengage.com) by inserting the mailbox graphic file (*mailbox* in *u11 css xxx* folder) between *mailbox* and *to* in the *Golf Outing* section. Use **Alex Rendulic** as the screen tip. Key **REQUEST FOR CSS GOLF OUTING INFO** as the subject in the subject line in the Insert Hyperlink dialog box.
7. **Save as:** *u11 events*.

## 64E

### Learn: Hyperlinks to Other Websites

Insert/Links/Hyperlink/ Insert Hyperlink dialog box/Existing File or Web Page

1. Read the following information, and complete the activity.

As with email, hyperlinks to other websites can be inserted by selecting a graphic, text, or using the site's URL (the website address). When the site's URL is used as the hyperlink, the software will usually create the hyperlink as soon as the Space Bar is tapped after keying the last character of the URL. Examples of the three methods are shown in Figure 11-10.

| Using a graphic | Select the clip art graphic |
|---|---|
| Using selected text | Corrigan School District |
| Using the URL as the text | http://www.css.cengage.com |

Figure 11-10 Three kinds of hyperlinks to other websites

# The Winning Edge

Complete this activity to help prepare for the Web Site Design event in FBLA-PBL's Information Technology division. Participants in this event demonstrate skills in creating and designing websites.

You will create a website that explains your local system of government, identifies elected and appointed officials, and lists the resources available through local government agencies.

1. In teams of three, research your local form of government. You can obtain information from your municipality's official website and by interviewing local officials. You should obtain the following information:

    • Type of governing structure, such as mayor-council, council manager, commission, board of trustees, etc., and a description of how it operates.

    • Government offices, agencies, and departments that operate within your municipality, such as a recreation department, a health and safety office, an agency for the aging, a career and jobs counseling office, etc.

    • List of elected and appointed officials in local government, their areas of responsibility, and how to contact them.

2. Create a website about your local government. It should have a home page that identifies your team and explains the website's purpose. It should also include one page for each item listed in step 1, and any additional pages you deem necessary.

3. Apply color to each page, and insert tables, graphics, clip art, and pictures as desired to enhance the individual pages. Insert hyperlinks to link all the pages.

4. If possible, publish the website. Solicit feedback from other students, faculty, and community leaders about the organization and design of the site.

For detailed information on this event, go to www.fbla-pbl.org.

## Think Critically

1. Do you think publishing information on a website is as effective as posting a flyer or handing out information?
2. What activities can you participate in that will strengthen your web design skills?

---

## School and Community
Community animal shelters rely heavily—and sometimes solely—on volunteers to help run the facility, fund services, and provide care for the animals. According to the Humane Society of the United States, there are more than 3,500 animal shelters in operation, and between six and nine million cats and dogs enter these shelters every year. You can make a difference in your community by volunteering at an animal shelter.

1. Using the Internet or the yellow pages, develop a list of animal shelters in your area. The list should include the name, address, and contact information.
2. Contact each shelter and find out the opportunities for volunteers in your age group. Add this information to the list.
3. Create a flyer that includes your list and any other information or graphics that you think will motivate others to volunteer. Print the flyer and make copies to post in your school.

www.cengage.com/school/
keyboarding/c21key

2. Open *index*.
3. Create a hyperlink to *Corrigan School District* using the lion mascot. The URL is www.css.cengage.com. Use **Corrigan School District** as the screen tip.
4. Create a hyperlink to Corrigan School District using the text in the lower-right cell of the 3 x 2 table. The URL is www.css.cengage.com.
5. **Save as:** *index*.
6. Open *u11 events*.
7. Create a hyperlink from the text *Joplin's Public Golf Course* (in the *Upcoming Events* section). The URL is www.joplins.cengage.com. Use the default screen tip.
8. Create a hyperlink to Corrigan School District using the lion mascot. The URL is www.css.cengage.com. Use **Corrigan School District** as the screen tip.
9. **Save as:** *u11 events*.

---

## 64F

### Learn: Hyperlinks to Other Web Pages in the Same Website

Insert/Links/Hyperlink/ Insert Hyperlink dialog box/Existing File or Web Page

1. Read the following information and complete the activity. In this activity, hyperlinks using text will lead to other files within the CSS website.

You can hyperlink to other web pages (files) within a website by selecting the text or graphic that the user can click to access the other file. As with other hyperlinks, the hypertext link usually appears in a different font color and underlined. Once the path has been followed, the hypertext link usually changes to another color to indicate that the hyperlink has been used.

> This text represents a portion of a Web page done using a red font. This <u>first hyperlink</u> is in blue and is underlined. In this example, blue is used as the color for a hyperlink that has not been followed. This <u>second hyperlink</u> uses purple to indicate that this link has been followed.

**Figure 11-11** Hyperlink colors

In Figure 11-11, the first hyperlink (in blue) has not been followed; the second hyperlink (in purple) has been followed.

2. Open *index*. Insert the following five hyperlinks in the 3 x 2 table. **Save as:** *index*.
   a. *index* to *u11 about css* by making *About CSS* the hyperlinked text.
   b. *index* to *u11 board members2* by making *Board Members* the hyperlinked text.
   c. *index* to *u11 finances* by making *Finances* the hyperlinked text.
   d. *index* to *u11 donors* by making *Donors* the hyperlinked text.
   e. *index* to *u11 events* by making *Events* the hyperlinked text.
3. Open each of the following web pages in the appropriate *Office* program, and link *Home* at the bottom of the web page to the home page (*index* file). Verify that each hyperlink works properly. Save each file as a Web Page with the same filename.
   *Word* files: *u11 board members2*, *u11 donors*, *u11 events*, and *u11 about css*
   *Excel* file: *u11 finances*

© Monkey Business Images/
Shutterstock.com

## Planning a Career in Agriculture, Food, and Natural Resources

From the food on our table to the clothes in our closet to the fuel that runs our car, we all are dependent in many ways on agriculture, food, and natural resources. Employees in this field work on farms, in dairies, and on rangelands, but they also work in manufacturing facilities and labs to develop and produce the raw materials used for clothing, shelter, energy, and medicine. In addition, they help maintain our parks and beaches; they care for animals and livestock; and they monitor air, soil, and water quality.

## What's It Like?

Employees in this field are involved in the production, processing, marketing, distribution, financing, and development of agricultural commodities and resources including food, fiber, wood products, natural resources, horticulture, and other plant and animal products and resources. For example:

- They own or manage farms, ranches, nurseries, greenhouses, and timber tracts.
- They provide veterinary services for herds or individual animals.
- They identify, remove, and properly dispose of hazardous materials from buildings, facilities, and the environment.
- They patrol hunting and fishing areas and enforce fishing, hunting, and boating laws.
- They study plants and their interaction with other organisms and the environment.
- They design agricultural machinery, equipment, and structures, and develop ways to conserve soil and water and to improve the processing of agricultural products.

Jobs in this field often require work outdoors in all kinds of weather. Employees in some careers work long hours, with their schedules dictated by weather and environmental conditions. Others work standard 40-hour workweeks in offices and labs.

## Employment Outlook

Employment opportunities in the various pathways of this cluster differ significantly. Jobs in farming are expected to decline; those in environmental and natural resource services can expect favorable employment opportunities; and those in plant and animal systems can expect much faster than average job growth. Education requirements range widely, too. A high school diploma and on-the-job training are sufficient for some jobs, while others require an associate's or bachelor's degree, or higher.

## What About You?

This career cluster is covered in box 1 of the Interest Survey Activity you completed in Unit 1 of this text. If this box had one of the three highest scores on your survey, you should further explore the cluster's pathways and related occupations.

1. Why do you think a career in this field could be a good choice?
2. What skills can you develop now that would be helpful to a career in this field?
3. Why are these jobs important to our economy?

## Learn: Bookmarks and Hyperlinks in a Web Page

**Bookmark**

Insert/Links/Bookmark/ Bookmark dialog box

**Hyperlink**

Insert/Links/Hyperlink/ Insert Hyperlink dialog box/Place in This Document

1. Read the following information, and complete the activity. In this activity, you will link to specific places (bookmarks) in the web page titled *u11 events*.

Bookmarks assign a name to a specific point in a document. Hyperlinks create a link from a point in the document to a bookmark. Bookmarks and hyperlinks are frequently used in a web page that is longer than a window and contains multiple sections. Bookmarks are inserted into the web page to mark the different locations you want the user to be able to quickly move to within the web page.

Also, hyperlinks are frequently inserted at strategic points in a web page to allow the user to quickly return to text near the top of the web page that has been bookmarked.

See Figure 11-12 for the Insert Bookmark dialog box. See Figure 11-13 for the Insert Hyperlink dialog box with the Place in This Document option selected.

**Figure 11-12** Insert bookmark

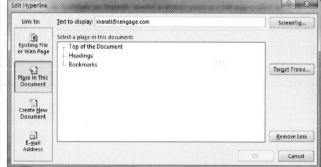

**Figure 11-13** Insert hyperlink to a bookmark

2. Open *u11 events* and preview this activity by scrolling through the web page looking for these items:
   a. Locate *Recent Events* and *Upcoming Events* in the top table that identify the two major sections within this web page. You will use these headings as your hyperlinks.
   b. Locate the heading *Recent Events* within the web page. You will bookmark this text so your hyperlink will move the user to it.
   c. Locate the heading *Upcoming Events* within the web page. You will bookmark this text so your hyperlink will move the user to it.
   d. Locate the *Return to the Top* phrase in the web page. You will hyperlink this phrase to text at the top of the web page that serves as a bookmark.
3. Select the *Recent Events* heading in the web page, and insert a bookmark.
4. Select the *Upcoming Events* heading in the web page, and insert a bookmark.
5. Select the web page title, and insert a bookmark.
6. Link *Recent Events* in the top table to the *Recent Events* bookmark.
7. Link *Upcoming Events* in the top table to the *Upcoming Events* bookmark.
8. Link *Return to the Top* to the top of the web page to the web page title bookmark.
9. Preview the web page in your browser, and verify that the hyperlinks move the user to the various bookmarks within the web page.
10. **Save as: *u11 events*.**

# Academic and Career Connections

Complete the following exercises that introduce various topics that involve academic themes and careers.

## Grammar and Writing: Pronoun Agreement

**MicroType 6**

- References/Communication Skills/Pronoun Agreement
- CheckPro/Communication Skills 10
- CheckPro/Word Choice 10

1. Go to *MicroType 6* and use this feature path for review: References/Communication Skills/Pronoun Agreement.
2. Click *Rules* and review the rules of using pronoun.
3. Then, under *Pronoun Agreement*, click *Posttest*.
4. Follow the instructions to complete the posttest.

*Optional Activities:*

1. Go to this path: CheckPro/Communication Skills 10.
2. Complete the activities as directed.
3. Go to this path: CheckPro/Word Choice 10.
4. Complete the activities as directed.

## Communications: Listening

1. You have answered a telephone call from Maria MacDonald, who serves as an officer in the alumni association of which your mother is president. She asks you to take a message.
2. Open the data file *df u11 communications*, and listen to the message, taking notes as needed.
3. Close the file.
4. Start a new word processing document. Using your notes, key a message in sentence form for your mother.
5. **Save as:** *u11 communications*.

## Geography

In this activity, you will explore the geography, economics, and politics of selected countries of the world and create a website about them.

1. Select five countries of the world that you would like to learn more about. You may focus on a group of countries within a continent—such as South Africa, Zimbabwe, Botswana, Mozambique, and Zambia in Africa—or you may select countries in all different parts of the world.
2. Using the Internet, library resources, or textbooks, research the countries you have selected. You should gather information on the following:
   - Geography: location, climate, terrain, waterways, and natural resources.
   - Economics: population size, literacy level, technology, infrastructure, and primary industry.
   - Politics: government system, political stability, and business regulations.
3. Using what you have learned in this unit, create a website on your selected countries. The website should have a page for each country that includes the following:
   - Map of each country with identifying labels such as the capital city and important waterways, mountain ranges, lakes, deserts, etc.
   - Description of each country based on the information gathered in step 2.
4. Insert a page color as well as tables, graphics, clip art, and pictures as desired to enhance the web pages. Insert hyperlinks to link all the pages.
5. Save the website in a folder named *u11 geography*.

# LESSONS 65–66  Web Page Construction

- Design web pages for a website.
- Create and improve a functional interactive website.

## Business Document
### 65–66B

**Apply: Web Page Design**

- Student-Designed Web Pages

1. You are to design web pages for a website that you choose. Include these elements:
   a. At least three web pages that have hyperlinks to each other.
   b. One or more graphics from the Internet or clip art.
   c. One or more pictures with descriptive text from the Internet or from files.
   d. One or more hyperlinks to another website.
   e. Two or more hyperlinks to different locations (bookmarks) within the same web page.
   f. Tables within each page.
   g. A background with texture, color, picture, or image.
2. Select a purpose for your website. Obtain approval of your website purpose from your instructor.
3. Read the Web Page Design Tips in the following chart.

| Web Page Design Tips | |
|---|---|
| Use a background and font color combination that is attractive but easy to read. | Do not use big blocks of text. Users tend to scan text and not read long blocks of text carefully or thoroughly. |
| Keep pictures and graphics small to avoid long download times. | Use hyperlinks and bookmarks in long web pages to reduce the need for users to scroll long distances. |
| Use hyperlinks that enable the user to move from one website to another, one web page to another, and within a web page easily. | Use descriptive titles in the title bar and headings at the beginning of each web page so the user always knows where he/she is. |

4. Using word processing software, outline the structure and content of each web page.
5. *Save as: 65-66b website plan.*

### 65–66C

**Apply: Website Construction**

1. Create a new folder called **u11 wpc xxx** (use your initials rather than *xxx*).
2. Create the web pages, including the hyperlinks, for the website you designed in 65–66B. Name each file and save each in Web Page format in your *u11 wpc xxx* folder.
3. Submit your website to your instructor.

## 65–66D

**Learn: Web Page Design Tips**

1. Review the Web Page Design Tips in 65–66B.
2. Search the Internet for additional tips on designing web pages or websites. Keep a record of Web addresses where the tips were found for later use.
3. Summarize the tips you find, and present them in a word processing document along with the Web address where the tips were located.
4. **Save as a Word document:** *65-66d my tips.*
5. Form groups as instructed by your teacher.
6. Discuss the tips that each member found, and identify the tips you want to share.
7. Design a web page to display the tips you identified in step 6, and apply them in the web page your group designs. Include the web addresses for the tips you add.
8. **Save as Web Page:** *65-66d group tips.*

## 65–66E

**Apply: Web Page Critique**

1. Using what you have learned about web page design in 65–66D, have your group members critique each other's web pages that were created in 65–66C.
2. Using the suggestions from the group, revise the web pages you constructed in 65–66C, and save them in the *u11 wpc xxx* folder.
3. Submit your revised web pages to your instructor.

## 65–66F

**Timed Writings**

Two 3' or 5' writings on the two ¶s; determine gwam; count errors.

 **A**   all letters used

| | gwam | 3' | 5' |
|---|---|---|---|
| As you move through the grades in your school, you are apt to | 4 | 2 | 42 |
| need to maintain a calendar to keep track of your major | 8 | 5 | 44 |
| activities. The calendar system you choose might be recording your | 12 | 7 | 47 |
| activities on pages in a pocket organizer, on a monthly calendar | 17 | 10 | 50 |
| posted at home, or in a personal digital organizer. Regardless of | 21 | 13 | 52 |
| the method you choose, you usually need to record such things as | 25 | 15 | 55 |
| the date, time, place, length, and purpose of each activity. Also, | 30 | 18 | 58 |
| you need to remember who is involved in the activity. | 33 | 20 | 60 |
| Using a calendar will lessen the chance that you will forget | 38 | 23 | 62 |
| or be late to a practice or club meeting in school. People have | 42 | 25 | 65 |
| the right to expect you to be where you are required to be and | 46 | 28 | 67 |
| arrive and depart appointments at the appropriate time. You will | 50 | 30 | 70 |
| be much more successful if you do not gain the reputation of being | 55 | 33 | 73 |
| forgetful and tardy. The habits you develop while attending school | 59 | 36 | 75 |
| will carry over into your professional and personal affairs after | 64 | 38 | 78 |
| you are graduated from school. | 66 | 40 | 79 |

www.cengage.com/school/
keyboarding/c21key

gwam | 3' | 1 | 2 | 3 | 4
| 5' | 1 | 2 | 3

# GLOSSARY

**3-D cell reference** refers to a cell or range of cells on another worksheet

## A

**absolute cell reference** in a spreadsheet, when a cell is copied, the copy of the cell maintains a reference to a specific row and column

**agenda** a list of tasks to be done or actions to be taken, usually at a meeting

**animation schemes** preset animation options that range from very subtle to very glitzy

**application form** applicants often fill in forms at the company, using a pen to write on a printed form or keying information into an online employment application form

**application software** a computer program designed to perform a specific task

**apps** small software programs designed specifically to run on smartphones and other digital devices; used to accomplish specific tasks such as finding directions, browsing multimedia content, sending email, or creating office documents such as presentations and spreadsheets

**attachment/enclosure notation** if another document is attached to a letter, the word *Attachment* is keyed at the left margin; if the additional document is not attached, the word *Enclosure* is used

## B

**bit** the most basic unit of data stored or processed by a computer, either a 1 or a 0, which corresponds to an On or Off state in the computer's electronic circuits

**blind copy notation** indicates that a copy of the letter is being sent to someone other than the addressee without the knowledge of the addressee

**block letter format** commonly used format in which all letter parts begin at the left margin

**blog** an online personal journal or log

**bookmarks** used to assign a name to a specific point in a document

**business letter** letter typically printed on letterhead stationery (stationery that has a preprinted return address)

**business plan** a blueprint for a company; key elements include description of the business, goals and objectives, competitive analysis, marketing plan, organizational plan, and financial plan

**byte** the primary unit of measurement used in defining computer memory

## C

**career portfolio** a place to store items and information that show off your best work abilities

**cell phone** a mobile telephone that uses radio waves to transmit calls

**central processing unit (CPU)** hardware that carries out the instructions of installed computer programs

**clock speed** the rate at which a processor can complete processing

**cloud computing** software and files are stored on remote computer servers and accessed through the Internet rather than residing on an individual user's computer

**color scale** uses a two- or three- color gradient to show how values vary—the shade of the color represents the value in the cell

**Contact Group** allows you to work more efficiently when emailing because you can send a message to a group rather than to each contact individually

**copy notation** indicates that a copy of the letter is being sent to someone other than the addressee

**copyright** a form of protection given to the authors or creators of original works, including literary, dramatic, musical, artistic, and other intellectual works

**custom animation** allows several different animations to be included on each slide

**cyberbullying** threatening, harassing, or tormenting others via digital technologies

## D

**data bar** shows the value of a cell relative to other cells—larger values have a longer data bar

**data sheet** a record set is displayed in a data sheet

**data source** file in a mail merge that contains the information that is different for everyone

**data type** determines the kinds of values that can be displayed in a database field

**database** an organized collection of facts and figures (information)

**developing or transitional countries** what used to be called Third World countries

**digital communication** the electronic exchange of information

**digital etiquette** an informal set of rules governing the proper and courteous behavior expected of digital technology users

**digital footprint** every string of text you write and photo or video you post leaves a trail of information about you for millions of other digital users to read and view

**distribution** enables the computer to share information with computers and other users, typically across a network

**distribution list** list of names of the persons who will receive a copy of the memo

**drop cap** large initial capital letter that takes up one or more vertical lines of regular text

**E**

**E-learning** a popular and accessible way for learners at all levels to take classes and further their academic pursuits; also called online education

**electronic fund transfers (EFTs)** ability to move money from one account to another, make deposits, and pay bills quickly and easily from your computer

**ellipsis (. . .)** series of three periods used to indicate material omitted from a quotation

**email** communication system that allows individuals to send messages to other users via computers

**employment application letter** letter that accompanies a resume, whether print or digital; includes three topics: the position you are applying for, the evidence that you qualify for the position, and a request for an interview

**entrepreneur** someone who starts, manages, and owns a business to earn a profit

**Expression Builder** part of the Query feature that be used to perform calculations on existing fields in a database

**F**

**fields** the columns in a database; in a database form, the blanks in which information is entered are called fields

**file-sharing** technology that lets you search for and copy files from someone else's computer (this is called "peer-to-peer," or P2P technology)

**Filter feature** database feature used to display specific records in a table instead of all the records

**firewall** a means of blocking outside users from having network access to computers within a system

**flaming** hostile and overly harsh arguments made via Internet forums, chat rooms, video-sharing websites, and game servers

**forms** used to enter and display database information

**future value function** a financial function that is used to calculate the amount that an investment or a series of constant, regular investments will be worth at a future date

**G**

**global awareness** ability to view the world in real time using a variety of technological tools, making it possible for people to understand and act to resolve complex issues

**H**

**HTML (HyperText Markup Language)** a computer language that specifies the codes that browsers use to format and display content

**hyperlink** text or graphic that links one HTML document or Web page to another

**I**

**icon set** classifies data into three to five categories—each icon represents a value in the cell

**IF function** compares the contents of two cells

**information management** the collection, management, and distribution of data, or information

**input** the raw data a user enters into the computer

**instant messaging** a system for exchanging messages in real time—or instantaneously—via the Internet or a shared network

**intellectual property** original works of authorship that include books, articles, software, music, plays, movie scripts, and artwork

**interview follow-up letter** letter sent to the person(s) interviewing you to thank them for the time given and courtesies extended to you during the job interview

**itinerary** an outline of a persons travel plans

**L**

**literacy** generally defined as an ability to read and write; in the 21st century, definitions of literacy also include the ability to think critically, to understand basic mathematics, and to use technology

**M**

**Mail Merge** used to combine information from two files, such as a letter and an address list, into a third merged file

**main document** file in a mail merge that contains the information that is the same for everyone

**meeting** an appointment that includes others to whom you send an invitation

**meeting minutes** a record of important details that occurred at a meeting, including when the meeting was held, who attended, and the actions taken during the meeting

**meeting organizer**   person who creates the meeting and sends the invitation

**memo body**   message portion of a memo

**memo heading**   portion of the memo that provides the To, From, Date, and Subject information

**mentor**   someone who is willing to share business experiences and knowledge

**microcredit loans**   loans made available to villages or individual families to enable them to run small businesses and cooperatives

**mixed cell reference**   in a spreadsheet, when a cell is copied, the copy of the cell maintains a reference to a specific row or column but not to both

**mixed punctuation**   letter format using a colon after the salutation and a comma after the complimentary close

**modified block letter format**   commonly used letter format in which some letter parts are indented

**N**

**netiquette**   the rules of email and Internet usage

**networking**   the practice of establishing and maintaining business associations with persons to support mutually beneficial relationships

**news release**   a document prepared by a business and sent to desired media outlets (newspapers, radio stations, television stations, etc.) to announce information that the business considers newsworthy

**O**

**offshoring**   moving jobs to a developing country

**open punctuation**   letter format with no punctuation after the salutation or complimentary close

**output**   results of a computer process, which may be displayed on a screen, printed on a report, played over speakers as sound, or sent via a network link to another computer

**P**

**peripherals**   the various external hardware parts and components of a computer system, such as the monitor, printer, scanner, speakers, disk drives, etc.

**personal interview**   part of the employment process that provides the employer an opportunity to assess your personal attributes, demeanor, job qualifications, etc. in a formal setting to assist them in selecting the best person for the position; it also provides you with an opportunity to demonstrate that you are the best candidate and to gather information that will help you decide if you want the position

**personal-business letter**   a letter written by an individual to deal with business of a personal nature

**phishing**   a common Internet scam in which you get emails that appear to be from a legitimate source that asks for sensitive information, such as your Social Security number, credit card or bank account numbers, or other personal information. A variation is smishing, which is done with text messaging on your cell phone.

**piracy**   sharing or downloading copyrighted material without paying for it; it is a form of stealing, and it is illegal

**plagiarism**   the unauthorized use of someone else's words, ideas, music, or writing without acknowledgment

**postscript**   note added to the end of a letter or memo, usually on a different topic

**present value function**   a financial function that can be used to determine the amount you need to invest to accumulate a desired amount at a future date

**primary key**   used to identify each record in the database table with a number

**primary sort**   the first sort

**print resumes**   resumes printed on paper and mailed to prospective employers

**private cloud**   cloud computing in which only a limited number of people have permission to access the server, usually employees in a company or members of a team

**public cloud**   cloud computing in which the server and its files are open to the public

**public domain**   intellectual property that is not protected by copyright or belongs to the public in general, such as government publications

**Q**

**queries**   questions used for drawing information from one or more database tables

**Quick Part tool**   used to save reusable pieces of content

**R**

**Random Access Memory (RAM)**   temporary memory used by a computer to store information currently being used by the computer

**Read-Only Memory (ROM)**   data on a computer that has been prerecorded and cannot change; permanent memory used by a computer in order for it to know how to function as soon as it is turned on

**records**   rows in a database

**record set**   the results of a query

**redundant system**   system in which components are duplicated so if any fail, there will be a backup

**reference initials**   if someone other than the originator of the letter keys it, his/her initials are keyed in lowercase letters at the left margin below the writer's name and/or title

relative cell referencing  in a spreadsheet, when a cell is copied, the copy of the cell is related to its new address

reports  used to summarize and present database information

resume  an honest summary of your experiences and qualifications for the position you are seeking

rule  an action you create to automatically handle particular emails in a certain way

**S**

secondary sort  the second sort

second-page header  text (such as the name and address of the sender of a letter) printed in the top margin of a page

Single File Web Page format  saves the document and supporting graphics in one file

slide transition  the term used to describe how the display changes from one slide to the next

Smart Art  a variety of built-in diagrams that convey processes or relationships

software  a general term used to describe computer programs such as applications and operating systems

Sort feature  database feature used to sequence (order) records and forms

source document  a paper form from which data is keyed

spam  junk mail; unwanted and unsolicited electronic advertising

storage device  hardware component used to store data even when the computer is turned off; examples include CD-ROM, DVD, hard disk drive, and USB flash drive

system software  programs that keeps the computer running well and perform routine tasks associated with file maintenance

**T**

table  a grid for arranging information into rows and columns

template  master copy of a set of predefined styles for a particular type of document

texting  sending text messages via cell phones or other mobile devices

**V**

video chatting  enables users with an Internet connection and camera or webcam to communicate face-to-face via computer, smartphone, or other digital device

videoconference  allows two parties in different locations to communicate "face-to-face" in real time using both video equipment and an Internet link

**W**

watermark  any text or graphic that, when printed, appears behind the document's text

Web Page format  saves the document in one file and creates a folder to hold the graphics used in the web page

Web Page, Filtered format  similar to the Web Page format except some of the HTML code is removed, making the file smaller than it is when saved in Web Page format

wiki  a website that allows multiple users to add and edit content in real time

WordArt  word processing feature that changes text into a graphic object